W9-CKF-963

Economic Development

PRINCIPLES AND PATTERNS

The Authors

HENRY G. AUBREY
RESEARCH ASSOCIATE
INSTITUTE OF WORLD AFFAIRS

FRANCIS L. K. HSU
ASSOC. PROF. OF ANTHROPOLOGY
NORTHWESTERN UNIVERSITY

YALE BROZEN
PROFESSOR OF ECONOMICS
NORTHWESTERN UNIVERSITY

HELEN B. LAMB
RESEARCH ASSOCIATE
CENTER FOR INT'L STUDIES
M.I.T.

JOHN A. BUTTRICK
ASSOC. PROFESSOR OF ECONOMICS
UNIVERSITY OF MINNESOTA

JOSEPH P. McKENNA
ASSOC. PROFESSOR OF ECONOMICS
UNIVERSITY OF MINNESOTA

HERMAN FINER
PROFESSOR OF POLITICAL SCIENCE
UNIVERSITY OF CHICAGO

JOSEPH J. SPENGLER
PROFESSOR OF ECONOMICS
DUKE UNIVERSITY

JOSEPH L. FISHER
STAFF ECONOMIST
COUNCIL OF ECONOMIC ADVISERS
U.S. OFFICE OF THE PRESIDENT

CHARLES D. STEWART
ASSISTANT COMMISSIONER
U.S. BUREAU OF LABOR STATISTICS

JOSEPH N. FROOMKIN
RESEARCH ASSOCIATE
INT'L PROGRAM IN TAXATION
HARVARD UNIVERSITY LAW SCHOOL

IRENE B. TAEUBER
RESEARCH ASSOCIATE
OFFICE OF POPULATION RESEARCH
PRINCETON UNIVERSITY

HAROLD F. WILLIAMSON
PROFESSOR OF ECONOMICS
NORTHWESTERN UNIVERSITY

Economic Development

PRINCIPLES AND PATTERNS

Edited by

HAROLD F. WILLIAMSON
Professor of Economics
Northwestern University

and

JOHN A. BUTTRICK
Associate Professor of Economics
University of Minnesota

PRENTICE-HALL, INC.
Englewood Cliffs, N. J.

Copyright, 1954, by

PRENTICE-HALL, INC.

Englewood Cliffs, N. J.

ALL RIGHTS RESERVED. NO PART OF THIS BOOK MAY BE REPRODUCED IN ANY FORM, BY MIMEOGRAPH OR ANY OTHER MEANS, WITHOUT PERMISSION IN WRITING FROM THE PUBLISHERS.

Library of Congress
Catalog Card No.: 54–9455

First printing............August, 1954
Second printing.......September, 1955
Third printing........February, 1961
Fourth printing..........April, 1962

PRINTED IN THE UNITED STATES OF AMERICA

22398–C

HD
82.
W538.
c. 4

Preface

There is abundant evidence of a widespread interest in economic development. The problem of how to achieve higher living standards, particularly in the so-called underdeveloped areas, has attracted the attention of administrators and research workers in the United Nations, in the governments of various countries, in business organizations, and in colleges and universities. The goal of improved material well being has more and more come to be accepted by all people throughout the world, regardless of their location and cultural and institutional setting. It is against this background that this book was planned, and should be read.

The volume is a venture into an area of study that is itself relatively underdeveloped, where there is no generally accepted theory of economic growth, and where information about the processes involved in particular settings remains fragmentary. Under the circumstances, it is inevitable that competent scholars of the subject differ in their evaluation of the importance that should be attached to various elements which encourage or discourage economic growth. It was for this reason that the editors, while assuming responsibility for the plan of the book, left each co-author free to present his own analysis and conclusions. No one should be astonished, therefore, to find that on occasion there are wide differences among them in their evaluation of specific points. Any such differences, however, should not obscure the substantial agreement on general principles held by the authors, each of whom accepted an assignment of a particular phase or example of economic development. If this book aids persons not trained in the field—students, administrators, and general readers—in their efforts to gain a better understanding of the complex pattern of economic growth, our objectives will be realized.

We thank the many persons who have helped us during the various stages of preparation of this volume. Our fellow authors, by their enthusiasm and cooperation, have truly made it a joint venture. We are particularly indebted to Professor Karl Deutsch, the Technology Press, and John Wiley and Sons for making available the map which appears on page x; to the editors of the *Journal of Economic History*, the *Milbank Memorial Fund Quarterly*, and the *Far Eastern Quarterly* to reproduce material contained in Chapter XI; and to Professor Richard Wohl for permission to incorporate the bibliography prepared at the Center for Cultural Change and Economic Development of the University of Chicago into our bibliography.

HAROLD F. WILLIAMSON
JOHN A. BUTTRICK

Table of Contents

:sistance of the Work Force to Economic Development. Organization of the Labor Market.

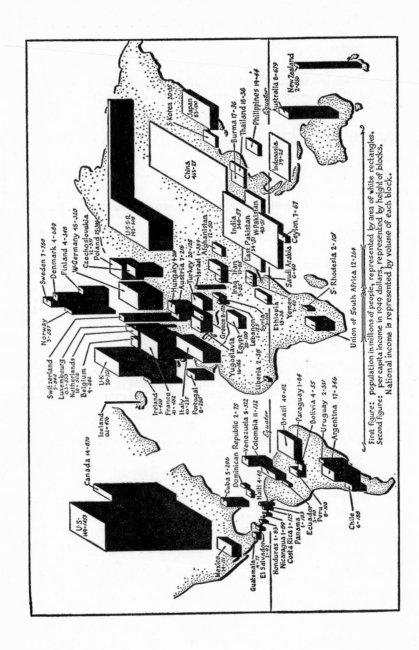

First figure: population in millions of people, represented by area of white rectangles.
Second figure: per capita income in 1949 dollars, represented by height of blocks.
National income is represented by volume of each block.

Foreword

The map * which appears on the opposite page demonstrates the magnitude of the task of economic development that faces most of the world. Only a tiny fraction of the world's people have incomes which North Americans would consider adequate, and over half receive less than $100 a year. Indeed, only 6 per cent of the world's population of 2.4 billion people receive more than $900 in goods and services per annum.†

No redistribution of incomes, even if it were possible, between the "haves" and the "have nots" can do much to improve the economic position of the vast majority of mankind. The only possible solution is to increase the production of goods and services. Even this possibility offers no immediate or easy solution. The difficulties can be visualized if we assume a goal of $900 per capita annual income for the world as a whole, which is about half as much as the average resident of the United States receives today. Given an annual increase of 5 per cent in output and of 2 per cent in population, and assuming that the entire increase in production will be devoted to raising the level of those countries below the $900 mark, it would take about 50 years to reach this objective. When it is realized that over the past

---

* Reprinted with permission from Karl W. Deutsch's *Nationalism and Social Communication* (1953), John Wiley & Sons, Inc. and the Technology Press of the Massachusetts Institute of Technology, p. 40.

† *See*, United Nations, *Statistical Papers*, Series E, Numbers 1 and 3 (1951). While the estimates made by the United Nations, from which this map was constructed, are subject to error because of problems arising from currency conversion and the fragmentary nature of national income statistics in many countries, they undoubtedly reflect the relative size of the incomes for particular countries with reasonable accuracy. The following table, adapted from the above mentioned publications, shows the distribution of the world's national populations by size of per capita income in 1949:

Per capita income	Population (in millions)	Per cent of total
Less than $100	1,342	56
Less than $200	1,626	68
Less than $600	2,132	90
Less than $900	2,221	94
Less than $1500	2,370	100

century the United States has been able to achieve no more than a 3 to 4 per cent annual increase in total income, and that the wealthy nations are not apt to relinquish all their output above that needed to maintain customary living standards, it is clear that even this estimate is optimistic. Such a conclusion, however, does not mean that economic development is impossible; it suggests only that realistic goals should be set at fairly modest levels.

PART I

FACTORS IN ECONOMIC DEVELOPMENT

CHAPTER I

Introduction

HAROLD F. WILLIAMSON *

INTEREST IN ECONOMIC DEVELOPMENT

THROUGHOUT THE WORLD THERE IS A GROWING CONVICTION THAT ECO-
nomic growth holds the key to the realization of a variety of hopes
and aspirations. This belief is not confined to those areas where economic development has made little headway. Among advanced nations, there is a strong feeling that economic development has a
definite export value, not only to the recipient, but to the exporting
country as well.

In its modern context, economic growth is to be distinguished from
the slow changes in productive factors and accretion of knowledge
that even the most nearly static societies experience. It means a rate
of expansion that can move an underdeveloped country from a near
subsistence mode of living to substantially higher levels in a comparatively short period of time, i.e., in decades rather than centuries. For
nations already advanced economically, it means a continuation or
acceleration of existing rates of growth.

Frequently this type of economic development is described as industrialization. Historically, it is true that rapid economic growth has
most commonly been associated with industrial expansion. It is more
accurate, however, to describe the process in terms of a greater commercialization of economic activities. Thus, a country whose principal
economic activity is based on a near subsistence agriculture, could,
without becoming industrialized, experience a marked economic

* Professor of Economics, Northwestern University. Coauthor (with A. H.
Cole): *The American Carpet Manufacture*; author: *Edward Atkinson: The Biog-
raphy of an American Liberal*; editor and author: *The Growth of the American
Economy*; Winchester, *The Gun That Won the West*.

3

growth through changes in productive techniques and marketing procedures which bring about greater interregional trade.

Widespread interest in this type of development is relatively new. For several centuries economic growth was largely centered in and associated with those countries bordering the North Atlantic which shared a common cultural background best described as Western European. For reasons too detailed and complex to be discussed at this point, the physical and institutional environment of these nations encouraged an emphasis upon material growth and development. For most persons in these countries economic development not only became familiar, but was identified with aspects of social and economic life that were considered highly desirable.

Outside these areas similar enthusiasm was slower to emerge. In many instances the idea that material gains were of primary importance was inconsistent with fundamental philosophies. Quite often the ruling classes saw little to be gained in changing long established economic procedures, especially when they feared changes might endanger their economic and social positions.

Yet these areas could not entirely escape the influence of Western Europe which became increasingly pervasive from the 16th century on. During the 17th and 18th centuries much of this influence was associated with colonialism, and followed a general Mercantilist philosophy. Economic development was encouraged although it was severely restricted as to the form it might take. Ideally the colonies were to be integrated into an economic system under which they served as suppliers of raw materials and as markets for the manufactured products of the mother country. Under British legislation, for example, the American colonies were prohibited (not always successfully) from engaging in certain types of manufacturing which were competitive with British home industry, and a long list of raw and semi-manufactured materials had to be shipped from the colonies directly to England. Regulations promulgated by the other European colonial powers, such as Spain and Portugal, were even more stringent.

In their roles both as suppliers of raw materials and as markets, the colonies were profoundly affected. The channeling of productive resources, sometimes ruthlessly, into supplying goods acceptable to the mother country had lasting results on work habits and occupations. Imports of Western merchandise influenced the consumption habits of at least a part of the colonial population and awakened a desire for the products of a commercialized or industrialized society.

Nor did the non-colonial areas of the world escape being pulled into the economic orbit of the Western European powers. Raw materials were increasingly drawn from the far corners of the earth and markets were vigorously promoted. This was especially the case after steam transportation cut shipping costs on land and sea. Advertising, the efforts of salesmen, the distribution of catalogues, the impact of mass media of communication, and the example of the more "Europeanized" members of the community, all stimulated the demand for products that could be obtained only through export or by changes in the structure of domestic economies.

Reactions to these influences varied considerably. In regions settled largely by Europeans the idea of economic growth was readily accepted. This was especially true of British North America, Australia, and New Zealand. Where native populations continued to predominate, the response was usually less favorable. Indeed, particularly in colonial areas, there was often a strong resentment against what was termed "exploitation" under "imperialistic" domination. Yet, when given the opportunity through revolution or the relaxation of colonial policies, such areas did not entirely reject the idea of economic development.

In practically all cases, colonial and non-colonial alike, the leadership for the promotion of economic growth has come from small elite groups. In some instances members of these groups were motivated by the possibility of personal aggrandizement in their social and economic position. In other cases they were prompted by a genuine concern for improving the material welfare of their countrymen. Even where these possibilities held no attraction, the obvious connection between economic, and especially industrial development, and military and political strength, was a powerful stimulant for the acceptance of the idea. Regardless of the value systems held, the concept of national power was universally recognized and appreciated. This did not mean that all countries could aspire to the position of being great powers, but their political bargaining position *vis-à-vis* the major nation-states, was closely correlated with economic development.

Two World Wars not only dramatized these relationships but loosened the hold of the colonial powers. Old or newly realized nationalistic ambitions were aroused, accompanied by a virtual world interest in economic development. In the period following World War II this interest was further stimulated, as aid to economically underdeveloped countries became accepted as a means of enlisting the loyalties, or at least the support, of existing or potential allies in the struggle that emerged between Russia and the West.

These events have thrown the whole subject into new perspective and stimulated a more intensive study of the processes involved. Scholars have been prompted to re-examine the historical record of economic development for the purpose of getting a more accurate analysis of its components. Individuals and groups charged with extending aid or advice on how to promote growth have sought principles or yardsticks which would make their efforts more effective. Leaders in underdeveloped areas have tried to find solutions to the problem of how to secure material advancement without losing cherished aspects of native cultures and institutions. They have looked for procedures under which outside aid might be accepted without the danger of undue or politically unacceptable foreign influence or domination.

THE MEANING OF ECONOMIC DEVELOPMENT

The basic difficulty of formulating a precise definition of economic development has been pointed out by a competent observer:

Indeed, to speak of development, or lack of it, at all, is to assume that the society to which the term is applied is proceeding, or failing to proceed, in a certain direction—towards a preconceived foreseeable goal or end, the attainment or partial attainment of which indicates a more desirable state of affairs than that now being experienced or than that which the society experienced in the past. In other words, to speak of the process of development is to assume, or imply, consciously or unconsciously, certain standards or criteria of such development.[1]

As the foregoing quotation reveals, economic development is not ordinarily thought of as an end in itself, but rather as a means to other objectives or goals. We are thus faced with the apparent dilemma of having to consider as many different definitions as there are goals. Fortunately, this dilemma is more apparent than real. Whatever may be the goals or ends under consideration, almost everyone seems to agree that a necessary (though not sufficient) requirement is an in-

---

[1] S. Herbert Frankel, "Some Conceptual Aspects of International Economic Development of Under-developed Territories," *Essays in International Finance.* (Princeton, 1952), No. 14, p. 1.

creased output of scarce goods and services. While we shall examine the validity of this assumption presently, it has been accepted as the basis for formulating a working definition. As used in this volume, therefore, economic development or growth refers to the process whereby the people of a country or region come to utilize the resources available to bring about a sustained increase in per capita production of goods and services.

Conceptually this definition of economic development views the economic organization of a society as a productive unit. It reflects or measures the capacity of the economy to increase the supply of goods and services, such as food, clothing, housing, manufacturing equipment, radio programs, and the services of government, that require scarce resources for their production and which derive their value because of their ultimate contribution to the satisfactions of consumers. It subordinates other considerations to the problem of how a greater output of scarce goods and services per capita may be obtained. Questions regarding the structure of a society, the size and composition of its population, its institutions and culture, the resource patterns, and even distribution of output among the society's members, are relevant only insofar as they bear on this main consideration.

An objection may be made to the use of per capita instead of total income as a yardstick. Certain countries, especially concerned with increasing their military strength, might be interested in supporting a larger population with no per capita increase, and indeed might be willing to accept a reduction in this standard in exchange for more people. This might also be true of a country where large families were accepted as desirable *per se*. But this problem need not detain us. It may be assumed that no country is interested in decreasing its total income and any analysis of how to increase income per capita must of necessity consider ways of expanding total income. Although, for many purposes, per capita income is the more useful standard to employ, those who prefer will have little difficulty in employing total income as a yardstick.

The Measurement of Economic Development

While our definition may be helpful in identifying the major conditions and characteristics of economic growth, its usefulness would be greatly enhanced if changes in per capita output of goods and services could be measured quantitatively. Recent improvements in national income accounting techniques do make this possible with considerable accuracy, given adequate data. Using these techniques the monetary value of income flows and their composition can be calculated on a regional or national basis. By correcting for price changes these estimates can be put into "real" terms; dividing total national income by the population gives the per capita income.

There are a number of ways of calculating national income, all of which are designed to achieve the same results, i.e., to measure the net flow of goods and services during a given time period, by taking into account the resources used up in production as well as the additions that have been made to productive capacity.[2]

Certain technical and conceptual problems faced in applying national income accounting should be briefly noted. One is how to treat the production of government. How much of the services of such agencies as the public schools, the post office, the courts, the police, highways and sanitation departments, or the military should be considered final income or services "used up" in production of other goods? It is not easy to calculate accurately the value of reductions and additions to capital equipment during a given period of time. What values should be assigned to products which do not pass through markets, such as services performed within the family and products consumed by those who produce them?

While the solution of these problems often requires rather arbitrary decisions, they do not, in themselves, pose any insurmountable difficulties. A more serious problem is encountered when national income estimates are used as a basis for comparing real income for the same economy over time, or different economies at the same time. For reasons that are outlined in detail in Appendix I, it is generally agreed that their usefulness for this purpose varies inversely with time and space. In other words, for one area over a relatively short period, during which it may be assumed that tastes and price ratios have not changed and no important new products have been introduced or important old products dropped from production, their accuracy is

[2] For a description of the methods used in national income accounting see Simon Kuznets, *National Income and Its Composition*, 1918–1938. National Bureau of Economic Research, Inc., New York, 1941, Vols. I, II. Also Simon Kuznets, "Measurement of Economic Growth," *Journal of Economic History, Supplement VII*, 1947, pp. 14–18.

high. Where these patterns have changed or where they differ substantially from one economy to another, the possibility of making accurate comparisons is correspondingly reduced.

Obviously national income accounting techniques have little, if any, application when appropriate statistical data are nonexistent or unavailable. The gathering of such information in the past has been confined to a few countries which were both interested in measurement of this kind and could afford the time and effort involved. Whereas it will no doubt be a slow process, this particular problem promises to be of diminishing significance in the future as more countries turn their attention to the gathering of pertinent statistics.

The absence of data adequate for national income measurement does not necessarily preclude the use of other techniques of measuring economic growth. For example, an increase in the average life expectancy at birth reflects a more effective use of human resources as more children live to become productive members of the labor force. Total productive capacity is often correlated with observable changes in segments of the economy under consideration, such as the size of the labor force or the growth of industry or agriculture. For historical purposes and until more adequate data are generally available, such methods as these will have to be employed to determine how incomes have changed.

Even the most carefully calculated national income estimates per capita drawn from the best of available data do not (nor are they intended to) measure certain aspects of economic development which may be important. Such estimates, for example, do not ordinarily take into account increases or decreases in leisure, or the services of housewives, or activities outside the law, which might well be considered in computing real income. Nor do average per capita estimates tell us anything about the actual distribution of incomes. Thus, as long as simple national income statistics alone are used, economic development could occur without any increase (or even a decrease) in the amount of income going to large numbers of the population.

There is no technical reason why these or other quantitative aspects of national income should not be calculated. Their inclusion or exclusion is largely a question of the purpose for which the estimates are made and the availability and cost of gathering and manipulating the data.

Economic Development and Social Goals

As has already been noted, most people look upon economic development, not as an end in itself, but as a means of achieving other objectives. A careful observation of how the people of a particular society react to various situations will ordinarily reveal the identity of the goals they value most highly. Such an analysis is quite likely to show, however, that what appear at first glance as final ends are in reality only means of achieving still other objectives. This may be especially true of the stated goals which economic development is expected to help in achieving, in contrast to the goals which the actions of the people reveal as their final objectives. No country, in modern times at least, would admit that it is planning to conquer its neighbors, however much this may appear to be the case to the prospective victims. Few politicians, in democratic or totalitarian societies alike, admit to any other interest than the general welfare or good of the people.

With these qualifications in mind let us examine the possible relationship between an increase in per capita income and a few of the more immediate objectives which it is commonly held to achieve. To what extent, for example, can economic development contribute to military strength? Will an expansion of national income per capita increase the well-being of a given population, or result in a better adjustment of the population to its physical and social environment?

That there is a correlation between economic development and military strength seems so obvious that it scarcely warrants extended discussion. Other things being equal, the higher the per capita income, the greater the amount of total energy and resources that can be devoted to military production without seriously weakening the civilian economy. While national income statistics offer a convenient "rule of thumb" measurement for this purpose, they are by no means sufficient to give definitive conclusions. Whether a particular expansion has, in fact, increased the military potential of an area presents a more complex problem. Its solution depends upon a careful analysis of the requirements for modern warfare. It is quite possible that a given country might show a marked increase in its per capita income and still be frustrated in its attempts to gain military supremacy because of a lack of, or inaccessibility to, the required kinds of resources and techniques.

What can be concluded about the relationship between the widely held objective of welfare and economic development? More explicitly, will the satisfactions experienced by the members of a society be enlarged by increasing the supply of scarce goods and services? Unfortunately, no unequivocal answer can be given to this question, largely because there are no adequate ways of identifying or measuring changes in satisfaction for the same person or comparing satisfaction between people. If we assume that the tastes of a given group remain unchanged and that the increase in income has been distributed among the members so that no one has less real income than before (and some have more), few would question the assumption that welfare had been improved, although even this cannot be demonstrated conclusively.

What conclusions can be drawn if the first assumption regarding unchanging tastes is relaxed? There are several possibilities. It is conceivable, for example, that once people become accustomed to higher incomes they derive no more satisfaction from the extra income available. It is also possible that "a taste of the better life" may even make individuals want still more and thus render them less satisfied than they were before. On the other hand, increased incomes may intensify the desire for familiar and attainable products or make it possible to cultivate tastes for new ones. In such a case total satisfactions would be increased if the satisfaction of more intense desires brought more satisfaction than less intense desires. It should also be pointed out that through a change in tastes, welfare can increase without any increase in the per capita output of goods and services. In other words, if for any reason, people derive more satisfaction from their current real income, they will be better off. In the absence of any way of testing just how changes in taste ordinarily respond to changes in income, it is not possible to move beyond the realm of speculation.

Much the same sort of problem is encountered if the second assumption regarding distribution of incomes is relaxed. If, for example, an increase in average per capita income were to be accompanied by a decrease in the incomes of a portion of the income receivers, we have no way of knowing whether there has been a net gain or loss in total satisfaction. It may be argued that if the group whose incomes are decreased are among the high income receivers and those who gain are among the low income receivers, total satisfactions have in fact been increased. However appealing this proposition may be on some sort of egalitarian principle, its proof, at present, lies beyond the scope of scientific method. Much the same sort of problem would be raised by the extent to which people valued their incomes because a particular position on the income scale enabled them to feel superior (or less inferior) to others. Indeed, it is difficult to imagine any change in the distribution of incomes that would not disturb these relationships.

These qualifications serve to indicate only some of the pitfalls that stand in the way of any easy generalizations regarding the relationship between economic development and welfare. They do not, however, suggest that national income is unrelated to welfare. Certainly there would be little debate on the point that reliable income figures are an acceptable and probably useful starting point for speculations as to what has in reality happened. Moreover, for large sections of the world these limitations may be more academic than real. It would be difficult to argue that in a country where any substantial portion of the population is at, or near, a starvation level, an increase in per capita income in which they shared to any extent would not increase welfare. Even in countries more advanced economically, there is no reason a priori to assume that economic development is any more likely to decrease welfare than increase it.

At first glance the assumption that economic development reflects an improved adjustment of humans to their physical environment seems reasonable. Increased national income per capita would ordinarily result from a more effective use of resources and techniques. While this is generally true, there are aspects of adaptation that a focus on the income yardstick may not reveal. As one prominent scholar has put it, "Our economy can expand quantitatively to the ruin of subsequent generations in a variety of ways, including soil mining and what may be more serious, the erosion of the social-moral basis which is nowadays more important than ever as a foundation for an economic system that will work." [3] Nor does any available quantitative measure give a ready clue to the extent to which social maladjustments may accompany economic growth. One observer, for example, has pointed out how the drives and impulses of the emotional life of the adult in industrial-urban societies have become

[3] J. M. Clark, *Problems in the Study of Economic Growth*, Universities National Bureau Committee on Economic Research (mimeographed), National Bureau of Economic Research, Inc., New York, 1951, p. 23.

". . . increasingly disturbed, diverted, frustrated, or distorted in response to the progressively accelerating changes of the psychosocial environment." [4] Until means of identifying these disturbances are perfected and their influence more accurately measured, it will be impossible to determine their relationship with economic efficiency. But to the extent these reactions are typical of industrial-urban society and are found in nonindustrial economies that are undergoing change, it may be concluded that economic development carries a heavy psychic cost.

ECONOMIC DEVELOPMENT AND PROGRESS

Questions regarding economic development may be raised at still another level. Is economic growth (or more accurately, the objectives to which economic growth may lead) a "good thing" from an ethical or moral point of view? What of the value of the process if it is channeled into conventional military weapons or devoted in part to the perfection of an atomic or hydrogen bomb? What are the benefits of applying the results of economic growth to the promotion of "soap operas," mystery novels, or popular music? What are the merits of the more complex and perhaps more frustrating economic and social structure that seems the inevitable concomitant of an increased national income? What can be said in defense of placing heavy influence upon the material aspects of life at the risk of neglecting spiritual and aesthetic values? What can be done to meet the dilemma posed by Professor Boulding: "Economic progress helps in getting what we want; . . . but if we want the wrong things then it will simply enable us to damn ourselves all the more easily." [5]

Answers to these questions will be conditioned by the personal philosophy and background of those who make them. In a world subject to war, many argue that national sovereignty (or the sovereignty of a group of nations with similar institutions) is of overriding importance and must be preserved at all costs. What may be viewed by some people as superficial products of economic development can be defended by others as worthwhile. It is possible that material and spiritual and aesthetic values are not incompatible; that the prob-

[4] James L. Halladay, *Psycho-Social Medicine* (New York: W. W. Norton & Company, Inc., 1948), p. 121.
[5] Kenneth Boulding, *Economic Analysis*, rev. ed. (New York: Harper & Brothers, 1948), p. 647.

lems of a more complex industrial civilization are susceptible to a satisfactory solution through the application of greater knowledge. Even more forceful is the assertion that for large portions of the world, what is at stake is the difference between near or actual starvation and standards of living that have come to be regarded as minimal, even by the peoples of such areas.

It should be clear that answers to questions of this kind involve value judgments, i.e., judgments that can be neither verified nor disproved by the application of scientific principles. To quote Boulding once more: "The critique of ends, i.e., the study of what are the right things to want—is not within the province of economic analysis; indeed, it lies within the domain of wisdom rather than knowledge, of religion rather than science." [6]

The authors of this volume disclaim any special competence which would enable them to determine what are the right things for a society to want. In general we have adopted the position that these decisions must be made by the individuals or groups of individuals concerned. In our professional capacities we have set ourselves the more modest, although still complex, task of suggesting how increases in national income per capita can be brought about in those areas where this objective is held in high esteem. Within these limitations we have tried to indicate the "opportunity" costs involved in particular policies designed to expand output; how specific results can oftentimes be obtained only by the sacrifice of alternative values; and the extent to which many programs are inherently inconsistent in the objectives they are supposed to achieve. Thus, although we subscribe to the principle of *caveat emptor*, we urge the purchaser to be sure that he wants the product, and to realize that economic growth and progress are not necessarily synonymous.

The Analysis of Economic Development

The task of prescribing how to achieve a larger income per capita would be greatly facilitated if there were a generally accepted theory of economic growth. Despite the considerable amount of attention that was given to the subject over the years by social scientists, no such theory has emerged. This has been partly because of the inherent complexity of the subject and partly for historical reasons. Among the economists, for example, the group of writers who con-

[6] *Ibid.*, p. 647.

stituted the Mercantilist School did much to stimulate interest in how the material growth of a nation might be encouraged. The narrowness of their definition of wealth and the important role they attributed to the government in the process prompted Adam Smith to write his famous *Wealth of Nations*. Smith also addressed himself to the general problem of how to create a social and political framework that would encourage sustained economic growth. This, he thought, would come primarily through the removal of restrictions, chiefly imposed by government, so as to permit a greater division of labor and specialization and the expansion of markets. These ideas formed the basic structure of his analysis, although in his discussion Smith revealed both the breadth of his scholarship and a considerable appreciation of the multiplicity of the factors that go into an explanation of the process.

Smith's work laid the basis for a laissez-faire policy on the part of the government respecting economic affairs. However useful this may have been at the time in hastening the removal of measures restrictive to economic growth, an acceptance of his position tended to underestimate the positive role that governmental authorities might take in the process.

While they generally accepted Smith's position respecting the role of government, an interest in the problems of resource allocation led Ricardo and Malthus to narrow the scope of their inquiries and to consider how, under given political and social institutions, wages, interest, and rent were determined, and to reflect on the conditions that affected the supplies of labor, capital, and land. Both John Stuart Mill and Alfred Marshall devoted their primary attention to a refinement of the findings of these earlier classical writers. As a result, less emphasis was paid to the considerations affecting long-run growth that had intrigued Smith, and more attention was given to the development of principles which could be applied with greater precision to problems that were essentially short run or static in character.

At the same time the writers from Smith through Marshall did develop what came near to being a general theory of economic growth. As pointed out by Joseph Schumpeter,

Taking institutional, political, and natural factors for granted, these economists and most others, start from the assumption that a social group —we may call it a "nation"—will, unless periodically plundered, experience a certain rate of economic growth that is accounted for by increase in numbers and by saving. This induces a "widening of market" which in turn increases division of labor and thus increases "productivity". . . . In the Smith-Mill-Marshall theory the economy grows like a tree. This process is no doubt exposed to disturbances by external factors that are not economic, or not strictly so, but in itself it proceeds steadily, continuously. Each situation grows out of the preceding one in a uniquely determined way, and the individuals whose acts combine to produce each situation count individually for no more than do the individual cells of a tree.[7]

As an explanation of economic development this near-theory left much to be desired. This was particularly true respecting the assumptions which took social and political institutions and natural factors as given.[8] Yet, with few exceptions, students of economics following Marshall continued to concentrate on problems which were essentially static in nature and largely related to a Western European framework of social and cultural institutions. To be sure, a study of business cycles and the possibility of secular stagnation contributed much to a clearer understanding of the savings and investment analysis. More important, it raised doubts about whether, even in the absence of external disturbances, the economy grew "like a tree." But it was not until attention was directed toward the problem of stimulating economic growth in non-European types of cultures that the full complexities of the subject began to be realized. It then became increasingly clear that political and social institutions could no longer be accepted as givens in the analysis, and that their role in the economic process, especially as it related to growth, needed careful consideration.

These complexities have led one authoritative source to describe our present understanding of the process of economic development in the following words: "Even a casual glance at the existing literature reveals not only the absence of a satisfactory theory but also the absence of agreement as to which of the many problems apparent to the observer are important for study. The research worker seeking path-

[7] Joseph Schumpeter, "Theoretical Problems," *Journal of Economic History, Supplement VII,* 1947, pp. 6–7.

[8] Both Mill and Marshall did in fact recognize that different social and political institutions had varied effects on economic development. Mill was primarily interested in the contemporary British scene and did not give the subject any extended consideration. Marshall was more aware of their influence but as these elements could not be brought into his models without unduly complicating the analysis, he excluded such considerations from his theoretical framework. See W. W. Rostow, *The Process of Economic Growth* (New York: John Wiley & Sons, Inc., 1952), pp. 6–9.

ways to adequate theory finds no blazed trails, but instead a veritable jungle of vicious circles, obstacles to change, and necessary (but never sufficient) preconditions for economic growth." [9]

It is quite possible that the foregoing quotation paints too gloomy a picture. There is no question of the complexity of the subject. There may be serious doubt whether it will ever be possible to formulate an acceptable general theory of economic development. At the same time it would be a mistake to minimize the potential contributions which may emerge as an increasing number of competent scholars devote their attention to the questions involved. As W. W. Rostow has put it, "The present position of our knowledge with respect to economic growth is not unlike the preliminary and formative stages of our knowledge of business cycles before the first World War. It may be predicted with some confidence that increase in knowledge will result in a narrowing of the factors which we regard as casual and an arraying of the aspects of growth along lines which distinguish fundamental forces from their possible determinants on the one hand and the consequences of their action on the other." [10]

In studying the components of economic growth, it is helpful at the outset to recognize that changes in the national income per capita are the result of many factors or determinants, all of which are more or less interdependent. For purposes of analysis, these determinants may be listed or grouped in a variety of ways, provided any such listing is comprehensive in its coverage, and is made up of elements that are analytically and operationally distinguishable.[11] In the present volume, these determinants or factors have been grouped into three broad categories of resources, institutions, and culture. These categories, however, indicate only the general orientation of individual chapters. Each author has recognized the interdependence of the subject matter and has both explicitly and implicitly indicated the more important relationships between his topic and the others.

Particular attention has been given to the question of how each of

[9] Editorial, "Economic Development and Cultural Change," The University of Chicago Research Center for Cultural Change and Economic Development, Vol. I, No. 1 (March 1952), p. 3.

[10] W. W. Rostow, *op. cit.*, p. 73.

[11] For such lists, see article by Joseph Spengler, *"Problems in the Study of Economic Growth"* (mimeographed), National Bureau of Economic Research, Inc., p. 153; W. W. Rostow, *op. cit.*, chap. 2; Pei-kang Chang, *Agriculture and Industrialization* (Cambridge: Harvard University Press, 1950), pp. 77–90.

the major factors of production may be enlarged or utilized more effectively; how, for example, natural resources can be augmented by new discoveries, by conquest of territory, or by interregional trade; capital funds by changing the spending patterns of the population or by borrowing from abroad; the labor force by an increase in population, through getting a larger percentage of a given population to enter the labor force, by immigration; a management group by effective processes of selection or training. Attention has also been given to the way the application of specific types of production techniques to a given or changing pattern of resources will bring about a larger output of goods and services.

It has been further recognized that the mere possibility of increasing resources or applying different productive techniques is not sufficient in itself to bring about economic development, because such changes do not occur in an institutional or cultural vacuum. Social institutions and customs must be organized in such a way that resources can be expanded and can be transferred freely from one use to the other. Moreover such expansion and such transfers must be regarded as normal and desirable when they lead or promise to lead to an increase in the output of relatively scarce goods and services. By way of example, if land potentially useful in agriculture or mining is immobilized in large estates devoted to game preserves through the operation of an inheritance or property system, economic growth is thereby limited. Laws affecting royalty agreements and taxation may encourage or discourage the discovery and exploitation of natural resources. If, in the absence of appropriate financial institutions, savings are hoarded in the form of jewelry or precious metals, the supply of capital funds available for development is reduced. If custom or habits dictate particular kinds of investments even in the face of higher returns elsewhere, economic growth will not be stimulated. A labor force bound to or prevented from entering certain occupations by family ties, a caste system, or trade union practices will not contribute its share to increasing output.

Finally we have attempted to point out that full utilization of resources cannot be achieved unless there is a continual and active search for opportunities to be gained by introducing new techniques and by transferring resources from one use to another. This means that there must be present in the society a sufficient number of economic innovators so that few such opportunities go unexploited.

Moreover, the managers of economic units generally must be willing and able to follow the leadership of successful innovators so that improvements once introduced will become widespread. To attract capable and qualified individuals into the innovating and imitating groups, positions of control over economic resources must be open to those having such qualities. This cannot be done effectively if such control is largely dependent upon family connections, membership in a particular social class, or through political power. Nor will it be achieved unless the society's value and prestige system recognizes and rewards their contributions.

APPENDIX TO CHAPTER I*

Income for a given period consists of all the goods and services produced during that period. It may be measured by valuing each good and service with the price which either is (or would have to be) paid for it and then adding together all these amounts of money. If these prices never changed, comparisons of this "money" income in each year would provide a way of telling whether more or less was being produced, i.e., whether "real" income was changing. Unfortunately, prices are notoriously unstable over time, so that it is not altogether easy to tell what is happening to real income.

The nature of the problem can be seen in outline if we imagine a nation which produces only two commodities, A and B. Let us suppose that in "year 1" there were produced 900 physical units of A and 1,000 of B, valued respectively at $5 and $4 per unit and totaling $8,500. During "year 2" let us assume that output consisted of 1,000 units of A priced at $6 per unit and 900 of B at $8 per unit. This total comes to $13,200. The difference, $4,700, reflects both the changes in prices and changes in physical quantities. What we need is a single, unambiguous measure of the change in quantity. At first glance it would appear that the influence of the price changes may be removed by valuing the commodities in each of the two years by the same set of prices, as follows in Table 1.1:

TABLE 1.1

	Value of goods in year 1	Value of goods in year 2	Change in value
In year 1's prices	$ 8,500	$ 8,600	+$100
In year 2's prices	$13,400	$13,200	−$200

* The editors jointly compiled this Appendix.

This example suggests, however, that the difficulties are complicated rather than simplified by removing the influence of price changes. Using the first year's prices, we find that the stock of goods has increased between the two years. Using the prices of the second year, we find a decrease; and there seems no particular reason to prefer one set of prices over the other.

This paradox does not depend on the fact that only two commodities were assumed nor is it the consequence of selecting particularly atypical quantity and price changes. It arises because price changes may reflect any or all of four things: first, the fact that the quantities of the two goods may have changed (in this case they have) which, *ceteris paribus*, would cause prices to change; second, the consumers' desires for these commodities may have undergone a change, i.e., even if the quantities available remained the same, consumers might be willing to pay more for one of the commodities in the second year than in the first; third, the distribution of spending power among the consumers may have altered, which could have the same effect as if their desires had changed; finally, there may have been a general increase or decrease in the amount of money in the economy either because of a change in its quantity or in the velocity of circulation. In the example given, it seems likely that most of these things happened at the same time.

Now, if year 2's goods are valued by the prices prevailing in year 1, what we actually obtain is an estimate of the value of year 2's goods based on the initial desires of the consumers. Under the best of circumstances, however, this will be a guess because we cannot be sure how the consumers would have reacted to the different quantities had they been available in the first year. The fact that there was more of commodity A might have made each unit less valuable while the decrease in the amount of B might have enhanced its value. Our estimate of the change in value based on the first year's prices (which will be called ED_1), then, must be greater than, or at the very least, equal to the "true" value.

Using the same reasoning, we are sure only that the estimate of the difference based on the second year's prices (ED_2) will be equal to or less than the "true" difference. In the example given, therefore, we can make no statements about whether there was actually a greater or smaller quantity of goods in year 2. As a matter of fact, in general, we can make definite statements only in those cases where ED_1 is zero or negative, or ED_2 is zero or positive. Of course, if the two measures contradict one another we are also left up in the air. In general, the most that can be indicated is the direction of change; only under particular circumstances are we able to provide an accurate measure of an income change.†

† See Tibor Scitovsky, *Welfare and Competition* (Homewood, Illinois: Richard D. Irwin Inc., 1951) pp. 51–82; P. A. Samuelson, "Evaluation of Real National Income," *Oxford Economic Papers*, New Series, Vol. II, January, 1950, pp. 1–29.

CHAPTER II

The Role of Natural Resources

JOSEPH L. FISHER*

IT IS NEITHER ACCURATE NOR ESPECIALLY HELPFUL TO SINGLE OUT A particular ingredient of economic development and attribute to it the role of first or primary cause in such development. Natural resources, skilled labor, plant and equipment, scientific and managerial resources, and economic location are all important. Regions and nations must combine these factors effectively if they are to advance in economic well-being.

Nevertheless, there is logic in beginning with a consideration of the role which basic natural resources play in economic development, although taken alone natural resources are of no economic significance. Certainly, few regions or nations have yet achieved substantial economic development without access to, or control over, relatively large and cheap supplies of raw materials. Furthermore, despite the increasing importance of "services" in the total product of economically advanced countries, a fairly large amount of "goods" appears to be a necessary prior condition. In times of war or threat of war, command over natural resources and raw materials becomes overwhelmingly important; indeed, the desire for command over these, and the enhanced security which it is supposed to bring, frequently have been a cause of war.

This chapter will deal first with the broad objectives and concepts of resource development, emphasizing particularly their role in general economic development. It will note some of the main economic characteristics of natural resources and will consider briefly the part

* Economist, Staff of the Council of Economic Advisers, Executive Office of the President; Member, United States Delegation to the United Nations Scientific Conference on the Conservation and Utilization of Resources, New York, 1949.

22

they play in the location of industry. The changing role of resources development in the whole process of economic growth will be sketched quickly, and the economic and related conditions for their development will be examined systematically in terms of both past and potential development. The relevance of these conditions to areas in different stages of economic development will be pointed out. Examples of more specific obstacles to resource development will be discussed briefly, again noting especially the resource problems of both less and more developed countries. An attempt will be made then to state certain general principles for guiding resource development. Finally, the chapter will conclude with a section presenting outlines of a resource development policy and program designed to overcome obstacles and fulfill potentialities.

OBJECTIVES

The objective of natural resource development, briefly stated, is to achieve the maximum sustained contribution to economic growth and to national security. Economic development has already been given the general definition of increasing per capita real income. In the light of present and probable future conditions, national security should be established as an equally important objective, closely related to economic development and interdependent with it, but also standing somewhat apart. The national security objective has particular importance for resource development and the augmentation of protectable supplies of essential raw materials. In the present world, national security implies international security, or at least progress toward that end.

The objective of maximum sustained contribution to economic development and to national security is stated above in general terms rather than in relation to particular resources and raw materials. While it is difficult to foresee the kinds of future technological developments and substitutions which undoubtedly will take place, some limited objectives may still be set down for the major resource clusters. Thus, for energy resources the objective, as usually stated, is to *provide amply* and as *economically* as possible for the prospective rapidly growing requirements for both primary energy and for electrical and other forms of secondary energy. Precise changes in the amount of energy which comes from coal, oil, gas, falling water, or other sources are less important than that an increasing total amount of energy with suitable characteristics be available as requirements grow, and at prices which encourage rather than block new or expanded uses.

For land, water, and forests, the so-called renewable resources, the objective of development implies conservation (enlarged and sustained yield) and *careful use* of the resources. Only in this way can regions and nations find a degree of protection against possible dangers of exhausting limited supplies—or, more realistically, against mounting costs. Of course, it is always possible that new discoveries and advances in technology, or drastic changes in the pattern of demand, will obviate the need for a particular resource at some future time. However, it would be risky policy to count on such changes as a means of solving problems of resource depletion. Conservation and stimulation to technological progress should go hand in hand, the one buttressing and protecting the other. For the minerals and other exhaustible raw materials, the objective must place greater emphasis directly upon discovery and development of new sources at home and abroad, the search for new techniques, processes and substitutes, and the avoidance of waste through careful handling and through re-use of materials.

Underlying these objectives for development of the principal resource clusters, which have been stated in conventional terms, are more precise economic concepts. Most basic is the principle of "least cost" which means that resources should be developed, conserved, or used, so that the ultimate services and satisfactions desired from them are obtained at the least possible cost, having in mind the full range of alternative resources or means for yielding final services.[1] This principle furnishes a guide to the meaning of such conventional phrases as "provide amply for," "careful use of," and "avoid waste of." The optimum economic rate of use of various resources—the rate which balances the advantages of use in the present against use in the future, as well as use of a particular resource compared to alternatives—may be defined as that rate, or rather that complex of rates of use of various resources, which maximizes the present value of expected net revenues.[2] Present value is obtained by discounting

[1] See President's Materials Policy Commission, *Resources for Freedom*, "Foundations for Growth and Security" (Washington, D.C.: Government Printing Office, 1952), Vol. I, pp. 20–21.

[2] In terms of social or welfare economics, the optimum rate is that at which the present value of net *social* revenue (however defined) is maximized. For a thor-

expected future net revenues at an appropriate rate. There is a tendency for successive units of each resource to be used to that point at which the cost of using one more unit would exceed the return ascribable to it—in the economist's language, the point at which marginal cost and marginal revenue are equal. The conditions under which this tendency will hold true in strict logic have been spelled out in economics textbooks. Some of the limitations on its usefulness in connection with natural resources are considered in following sections. On the whole, these generalized economic principles provide basic guides to an understanding of the way resources are used, but they should be supplemented by other guides, such as those relating to defense and social welfare, which are frequently more important, but which cannot easily be derived from ordinary market considerations.

Some Economic Characteristics of the Resource Base

It should be noted at the outset that natural resources have value only because people want to use them now or in the future, a characteristic that is sometimes overlooked. Thus, a study of natural resources must always emphasize the relations between people and their wants on the one hand and, on the other, how these wants may be served by resources.

With few exceptions, such as changes brought on by an earthquake, a tidal wave, or long-run weather cycles, natural resources in themselves are essentially passive in their influence on economic growth. They remain dormant and largely unknown until such time as the general culture, including technology, reveals their use-value. They acquire a dynamic character largely through changes introduced by man. Land, water, mineral, forest, and energy resources acquire new and different significance with shifts in the evolution of economic and social patterns. Coal, for example, whose physical properties change only over thousands of years, has gone through various phases in respect to its economic importance. Little used prior to the eighteenth century, coal was producing around 90 per cent of the energy used in the United States in 1900. Since that time its contribution has dropped to around 40 per cent. It may well be that the

---

ough treatment of this and other theoretical questions, see S. V. Ciriacy-Wantrup, *Resources Conservation Economics and Policies* (Berkeley, Calif.: University of California Press, 1952), chaps. 6, 17, and *passim*.

relative importance of coal will increase over the decades ahead, especially if oil and gas become more costly and technological possibilities for obtaining liquid fuels from coal are widely applied. Furthermore, with any given level of technical and cultural advancement, material resources set ceilings on economic growth. Thus, lack of coal, oil, and other sources of energy severely limits industrialization in many South American countries. Limitations on water supply imposes a rather rigid condition for the expansion of economic activities in certain parts of western United States.

Resources gain particular economic significance when they are located in such relation to other resources and to people that they may be brought into effective economic use. This juxtaposition aspect largely explains why a resource located in an accessible place develops sooner and more fully than the same resource known to exist in an inaccessible place. Indeed, making resources more accessible through the development of cheaper transportation has become a principal objective in the opening up of newer areas.

Resources also have importance in reference to time. Many, such as protected soil and minerals, are storable, and their use may be deferred; while others, such as a particular amount of water moving downstream, have to be used at once. The rate at which resources will be used in the present as compared to the future depends partly upon the amount of return which can be obtained in the present as compared to the future, and this depends on the rate at which future returns are discounted to give them present value. It depends also on public decisions regarding the timing of resource conservation programs and investments. Thus, the rate at which a fishery resource will be exploited in part depends on an estimate, however crude, of present net return compared to probable future net returns. This implies assumptions regarding future prices of the fish and future costs of catching and marketing, as well as the rate at which future net returns are discounted. Furthermore, these calculations are made within a framework of existing and foreseeable fishery technology, markets, and conservation laws and practices.

Natural resources, therefore, in their economic meaning are far from being static. They are not simply stocks or flows of materials which remain constant until used. Instead, they are dynamic and shifting, and their economic value is relative to place, time, and the particular technological and cultural setting. Natural resources have significance only in conjunction with enterprise (which sees their economic value), capital equipment (which transforms and transports them), and labor (which is trained in the necessary techniques of mining, farming, forestry, fishing, and manufacturing).

Resources and the location of industry. Some of these dynamic elements are brought out by a consideration of the role they play in determining generally the location of industries and economic activities. A complex of factors, including the present and probable future location of the resources, the transportation facilities, the other materials and services used, the labor supply, and the market, all influence industrial location. Generally speaking, an industrial process will tend to be located so that the product can be marketed at the lowest possible cost, with transport costs of both raw materials and the finished product as well as other costs being taken into account. Natural resources invariably affect the location of economic activities, sometimes in a critical and determining way.

Those making location decisions try to anticipate changes in the costs of the various input factors which may occur during the lifetime of the particular plant or other activity, so that the location selected will reflect any expected changes in optimum location. The anticipated cost of resource raw materials, such as fresh water, fuel, or mineral products, may actually dictate the selection of a plant site, an electric power unit, or an agricultural or mineral development. The selection of a site for a pulp mill, for example, is likely to be governed by the need for an adequate supply of pulpwood at a favorable price over an indefinitely long period into the future.

Transport may be regarded as an input factor, along with labor, materials, fixed capital, and enterprise, and to a degree is substitutable for these other factors. Indeed, a raw material, coal for example, is of no economic significance apart from the service of transporting it to a blast furnace, power plant, or other place of usefulness. Assuming a given plant location, the "distance input" of one material will tend to be substituted for that of another to the point at which the ratio between the two "distance inputs" equals the reciprocal of the ratio of their transport rates.[3] In this manner, transport, or "distance input,"

---

[3] A "distance input" is the movement of a unit weight over a unit distance; e.g., a ton-mile. See Walter Isard, "A General Location Principle in an Optimum Space-Economy," *Econometrica*, July 1952, p. 247. Also Isard, "Distance Inputs and Space-Economy," *Quarterly Journal of Economics*, May and August, 1951.

can be incorporated in general production theory and used to help explain industrial location.

A new blast furnace, for example, will tend to be located with respect to coal mines, iron mines, scrap sources, and markets for steel products so that transport costs of assembling the necessary coal, iron, and scrap and shipping final products to the markets will be minimized, other factors being left out of account. Should the ton-mile rate for coal transport rise, for example, the optimum location would shift toward the coal mine, although actually the character of the terrain, the existence of fixed plant, or the establishment of the labor supply in the existing community might prevent, or at least delay, any shift of location. Should technology change so that more scrap is used relative to iron ore, assuming no change in freight rates for either scrap or ore, the optimum location for the plant would shift toward the source of scrap. The pull of raw materials on industrial location will tend to be great when the ton-mile transport cost of that material is high relative to the transport cost of other materials and the finished product, and when it is high relative to labor and other non-material costs. Of course, transport rates may also be altered as the volume of shipments changes, as the market value of the products changes, as technical improvements in transportation are made, and as over-all patterns of location of population and economic activities shift.

Many industries that process materials are, like other types of industries, linked closely together. This is exemplified by placing blast furnaces and steel furnaces close together to cut the heat losses which would arise if the intermediate product, iron, were allowed to cool from the molten state it is in when it leaves the blast furnace or, to put it another way, to reduce the high transport costs of moving the molten iron any distance to the steel furnace. This, and similar tendencies, partly explain the agglomerating of industrial and other economic activities in certain favorable or nodal transport points at which economies due to linkage among the various activities are numerous.[4]

In other cases, large economies may be achieved by locating the processing facilities at the site of the natural resources. For example, in Texas an aluminum plant is being built close to large deposits of lignite which will be used to produce the electric power needed in

---

[4] Edgar M. Hoover, *The Location of Economic Activities* (New York: McGraw-Hill, 1948), pp. 117–123, and *passim*.

that industrial process. The expansion of chemical plants on the Texas Gulf Coast in large part is a result of the nearby location of such natural resources as oil and natural gas, sulphur, shells for calcium, and seawater, as well as of excellent rail, water, highway, and pipeline transportation.

RESOURCE DEVELOPMENT AND THE
PROCESS OF ECONOMIC GROWTH

The particular role natural resources play in the process of economic development depends upon a number of factors, including the level of development, the kinds of natural resources available, and the quantity and quality of capital and human resources. In the large areas of diverse climate, topography, and geology, natural resources tend to play a many-sided part in development; areas with more limited resources must depend more upon imports for economic growth. In any case some degree of dependence upon overseas markets and upon overseas sources for materials, as well as for investment funds in the case of less developed countries, is sure to be present. Some imports will be a necessary requirement for reaching more advanced stages of economic and industrial growth.

Interaction of resources and other elements in economic growth. Economic historians have traditionally depicted successive stages through which most advanced countries and regions have passed in their economic development. In the very early stage, natural resources contributed directly toward meeting requirements for food, fuel, and crude metals. As population grew and markets widened, natural resources provided a base for a more complex economic organization with increasing specialization of labor and larger accumulations of capital. These in turn made possible the establishment of manufacturing industries, first on a small, more or less handicraft scale; later on a light machine basis, for such products as textiles; and finally on a heavy machine and large-scale capital basis. Ultimately, as in the large advanced Western countries, the industrial pattern becomes highly diversified, while in the smaller advanced countries a higher degree of specialization remains, based on internal resources, labor skills, and on location with respect to world supply sources and markets. In each of these various stages, the availability of natural resources and derived raw materials exerted decisive influence.

While early industrialization of Great Britain, for example, cannot be accounted for solely in terms of domestic natural resources, it can be explained, to a significant extent, by Britain's location and transport accessibility to raw materials (such as cotton and ferro-alloy metals) and to markets.

Throughout the growth process, interchange of technological ideas tends to open up new possibilities for utilization of natural resources. For example, the interaction in the late eighteenth century between an advancing metallurgy, increased facility in the design of machinery, and the growing knowledge of the possibilities for machine-handling of fibers, along with certain cultural elements, led to a remarkable sequence of inventions in textile machinery. Each of these chains or complexes of technological advance, in turn, reacted upon the raw materials and natural resources, such as cotton and coal, to increase production. This, in turn, led to other chains of events, such as the expansion of cotton production in southeastern and southwestern United States during the nineteenth century, which was closely linked to technological advances in the textile industry in Britain.

As technological advances multiplied throughout the Western world, in particular, and as the demands for raw materials enlarged, private groups and governments increasingly have engaged in large-scale resource developments. The more advanced countries entered the stage of building multiple-purpose dams and reservoirs, engaging in large land reclamation projects, opening large new mining areas, and, in the past decade, developing atomic energy. In natural resources, as in other lines, capital investment has both widened and deepened.[5] Many of the resource developments of the future, will require even larger blocs of financial capital than in the past, since the hydroelectric power sites, potential irrigation areas, additional flood control protection, new mineral developments, and large agricultural and forestry improvement programs will take increasingly costly and massive efforts. In a sense, the cream has been skimmed off, and the easy and most profitable resources development work already done. This tendency does not hold true in every instance, however. Smaller investments in improved forestry on small holdings and in forest access roads, for example, may yield large returns.

In countries at an intermediate stage of their growth the phase of

[5] For a discussion of the role of capital formation in economic development see Chapter V.

rapid prospective cost increases for new developments has, for the most part, not yet been reached. Indeed, one of the characteristics of a country in this stage of development is that the application of existing technological knowledge and capital equipment, especially if applied in reasonably large blocs, will result in the production of raw materials and products at progressively lower unit cost. As development proceeds on the basis of the same technology, the economics of larger scale industry and more skilled labor are more fully realized. Eventually, however, it is inevitable that the historical cost curves will turn upward so that increasing amounts of raw materials will be procured only at increasing average costs.

Resource development in underdeveloped areas. Countries or areas have been defined as underdeveloped if they have a relatively low rank in per capita real income. Such areas are also characterized by low per capita production, low level of value added by manufacturing, and relatively great emphasis on agricultural and other primary industries. Natural resources are still largely in the potential stage, awaiting capital, skilled management and labor, or larger markets for their development. The potentials must be there, however, along with an awareness of them, for the area to be properly called underdeveloped.

The Congo, therefore, is an underdeveloped area because, within the context of the culture and technology which may be brought to bear in that vast basin, a large known potential of minerals, forests, grasslands, fish, water power, and other resources awaits exploitation. Indeed, the development process is already launched on a large scale, although apparently only the surface of the full potential has thus far been scratched.

On the other hand, speaking generally, such areas as Antarctica, the islands bordering the North Polar sea, and the large desert tracts in Africa and Asia should probably not be classified as underdeveloped since within the available culture and technology it is not yet possible to define with any appreciable degree of realism their economic potentials. They are, strictly speaking, undeveloped areas which may or may not ultimately follow a course of economic growth of population, industry, and income. Their development awaits further discovery and technological change, the establishment of settlements, the shifting patterns of economic location, and the rapidly changing strategy and logistics of defense. Underdeveloped in the economic sense, then, is to be understood only in relation to reasonably clearly defined potentialities.

Underdeveloped areas are of many types. Some, such as the sub-Arctic regions and much of Australia, are sparsely inhabited and have no long history of civilization. Some, such as India, are crowded with people and have venerable records of cultural achievements in many lines. Others in past times have been leaders in the world known to them (for example, Egypt and Greece) but have long since lost economic, cultural, and military leadership. Each of these types may be called economically underdeveloped, if the potentiality for such development exists. Availability of natural resources constitutes an important part of potentiality.

It would not be accurate to say that natural resources play a more significant role in the advancement of underdeveloped areas than for developed; rather, the roles are different. Perhaps the principal difference is that a developed area has more options for further growth than does a less developed place, because of such factors as a more diversified base of capital equipment and labor supply, more favorable bargaining and trading relations with other areas and countries, and the larger public revenues available. Underdeveloped areas usually have to begin with and concentrate on the development of locally available natural resources as an initial condition for lifting local levels of living and purchasing power, for obtaining foreign exchange with which to purchase capital equipment, and for setting in motion the development process.

The precise role played by resources in economic development depends on the route by which an underdeveloped area advances. They may follow the historical sequence noted above and move from hunting and fishing, herding, or simple agriculture, to more complex agriculture combined with simple machine industry, and so on. To follow this sequence, however, natural resources appropriate to the several development stages must be available at the right time for self-generating development to continue. The lack of a critically needed resource may block further advance until such time as it becomes available, or until technology finds a substitute, or figures some other way around the obstacle.

Thus, in such crowded, underdeveloped areas as India or Java, the problem of raising per capita food consumption by means of extending and improving domestic agriculture is given high priority. This, in turn, depends on an adequacy of such things as farm implements, good seed, fertilizer, and water control. More broadly, it depends on an advancing level of agricultural and general education, improved disease control and public health generally, a well-planned program of agricultural development, the provision of necessary financing, frequently imports of particular capital items, and a stable government. As will be discussed more fully in the following chapter, in such crowded countries the problems of raising per capita real income are compounded by the tendency of improvements along these lines to be followed immediately by further population increases.

Underdeveloped areas with natural resources of clear potential value may be able to speed up their development. This is notably the case when rich mineral deposits are discovered and the world demand-supply situation indicates the profitability of development. Assuming a sufficient degree of freedom and security for international investment, a strong incentive for exploitation comes into play. With appropriate policies regarding such things as the employment and training of local people, conservation standards and avoidance of waste, severance taxation for the benefit of more permanent capital improvement of the area, and the wide distribution of the gains from such development, mineral exploitation can be the engine for driving forward rapidly a whole program of desirable economic growth. Without these accompanying policies, the development may become unbalanced and impossible to sustain, or worse, it may proceed recklessly and wastefully so that nothing of permanent value remains in the area.

Examples of the powerful incentive which resources may impart to economic development include oil development in the Middle East and Venezuela, and mineral exploitation in Central Africa. The harnessing of water power on the British Columbia and Alaska coasts as a basis for aluminum production, and the establishment in that area of pulp and paper production, afford examples of resource incentive based primarily on water power and forest resources rather than minerals.

It may not be necessary for underdeveloped areas to follow the traditional historical sequence in economic growth. Advances in technology, especially as they have affected trade and transportation, have made it technically possible to skip some of the intermediate steps.

In certain parts of the world, notably Northern Canada, Alaska, and the Soviet Arctic, air transport has permitted considerable economic development without the necessity of building highways or railroads. On a somewhat broader basis, areas rich in unutilized energy resources, such as coal or hydroelectric sites, or heavy raw materials like iron ore, could conceivably move directly into an advanced industrial stage of development. Even areas less well endowed with these particular types of resources may proceed directly to an advanced agricultural level and to the extensive development of light industry.

Quite aside from the problem of securing the heavy capital investments that such programs usually require, there are serious risks involved in following such a course. Any relatively sudden change in the organization of the economy requires a corresponding change in social, political, and cultural institutions. As many observers have pointed out, the Point Four type of program may fail not because the techniques in themselves are poor, but because the institutions, laws, customs, and educational systems in less developed areas cannot be changed and adapted with sufficient speed to accommodate the new technology. Many efforts are being made to reduce the chances of this happening by such means as careful educational and demonstration programs and by the exchange of students and farm and industrial leaders between underdeveloped and advanced countries. The fact remains, however, that the pace with which economic development now can, and in some cases does, take place means that the skipping of traditional stages is inevitable. One of the great problems of the modern world is to make possible these rapid changes without destruction of political and social order.[6]

CONDITIONS FOR RESOURCE DEVELOPMENT AND OBSTACLES TO BE OVERCOME

There is little reason to expect natural resource development if people are indifferent (or antagonistic) to the products or services which such resources can contribute. The extent to which this attitude will prevail depends largely upon the general cultural background and outlook of the particular group. It would be characteristic of a society bound by tradition, where the people were content to follow the same procedures year after year, generation

---

[6] This problem is discussed in some detail in Chapter X.

after generation, and where change was unwelcome because it would disturb familiar patterns of behavior.

Resource development is not likely, either, to be carried very far in the absence of knowledge respecting the potential contributions available resources can make. Even with an awareness of potential output, development may be blocked because of lack of technical understanding of how such resources may be brought into use. Oil seepage, exposed coal veins, or even precious metals have no significance to individuals who see no way of using them. An appreciation of the potential uses to which such resources could be put has little effect on their exploitation if appropriate techniques of drilling or mining are unknown.

In other words, interest in developing natural resources comes only where there is dissatisfaction with current ways of supplying economic needs and an awareness or belief that improvements can be made. While the initiative for change may come from a relatively small percentage of the total population, it is not enough that they alone have this awareness or belief. They must be working in a social environment that accepts change and encourages the adoption of new processes and new products. The pace of discovery and exploitation will be conditioned by the level of technical knowledge and experience. Moreover, within a favorable social environment, advances in technology and experience form the most dynamic element in bringing about changes in the organization of economic life, including the utilization of natural resources. Among a few of the more dramatic historical examples, one may note the introduction of steam transportation on land and sea, the perfection of the means of generating and distributing electricity, the impact of the internal combustion engine, the development of the airplane, and the latest products of the scientists and the laboratories—the atomic and hydrogen bombs.

Given a favorable social or cultural environment and a certain level of technical knowledge and experience, it is possible to point out somewhat more explicitly how resources may be developed and some of the obstacles to be overcome.

Feasibility of resource development. Before any successful resource development can be undertaken it is necessary to have some idea of the economic feasibility of the project. This depends in turn upon the amount of scientific and engineering information that can be brought to bear. It would not occur to anyone to meet an oil shortage from coal or oil shale unless it was feasible to produce oil from these sources. The proposed multiple purpose development of the Indus or Yangtze rivers can be visualized much more readily with the example of the Tennessee Valley Authority already in operation. The potentiality of resource development on this scale depends not only upon material and engineering feasibility but also upon what may be called administration and social feasibility as well. Unless it can be planned, organized, financed, and operated in such a way as to meet the economic goals of the society, it will not be seriously considered.

Knowledge of resources. It goes almost without saying that the gathering of basic factual data is a necessary preliminary step for effective resource development. On a specific project, like a coal or iron mine, information concerning the quality of the coal or ore, the extent of the deposit, the depth below the surface, and the character of the surrounding materials is needed. A more complex project involving a whole area or region requires the kind of data that can be secured from surveys and mapping. The extent to which such information is appreciated or can be obtained will vary with the scope of the project and the expansion of knowledge. For example, a hundred years ago levees and other attempts at stream control were used on the Mississippi River without the benefit of much scientifically gathered information about stream flow, shifting channels, bank erosion, and so forth. Today no stream control measures are put into place without this kind of information plus a careful evaluation of alternative methods in terms of their effect, not only locally but also up and down the river valley.

Market and economic research. Marketing and economic surveys provide another type of basic data useful for the best development of natural resources. To the extent they reveal the costs of development, processing, transportation, and the nature of potential markets for resources, they help to indicate which projects are economically feasible. Investors and entrepreneurs can use such information to calculate the returns which may result from various scales of exploitation; they can better choose which of a number of technically feasible ways will be most economical; their attention may be directed toward the possibilities of the development of resources previously overlooked or neglected. Furthermore, surveys of this kind can give an indication of the nature of the demand for the products or services under consideration; whether it will be sufficient to warrant the proposed investment; what risks, if any, may be encountered through price uncertainties or fluctuations; the possibility of competition from substitutes. For areas or countries that are dependent for income on the sale of one or two commodities, like coffee in Brazil, tin in Malaya, possibilities for substitutes and the probable extent of price movements in both the original and the substitute commodity are especially significant.

Technological, labor, and capital requirements for resource development. Because these three topics are treated in some detail in later chapters, only their particular relevance for resource development will be touched upon here. The choice of the best technology for the exploitation of a particular resource or cluster of resources depends upon several variables. These include the size and skill of the labor force, the managerial skills available, and the abundance of capital funds. In some areas the most appropriate technology may be relatively simple—perhaps the use of better plows, or even hand agricultural implements; elsewhere, tractors with gang plows and combines would be more appropriate. Even for the same country the technological requirements may be extremely varied. In countries like India or Pakistan the technological requirements for capital equipment may run the whole gamut from simple plows to huge hydroelectric generators. Multiple-purpose river valley developments, such as that now being undertaken in the Damodar Valley in India or proposed for the Jordan Valley in Israel, will require the latest, most advanced technology. On the other hand, resource development for a mountainous province in Iran or Colombia may be met by simpler forms of capital, such as gravel roads, common types of fertilizer, slaughtering facilities, and more wells.

One of the most difficult aspects in analyzing development problems is to determine precisely what types and amounts of capital plant and equipment are, in fact, needed. It is all too easy to overshoot the mark in this respect by providing complicated types of machinery for which the area or the group of persons involved are not yet ready, with the result that development fails to take place.

Resource development will be made easier if there is a labor force that is skilled and flexible, and mobile from place to place. In part this is a matter of education and training for skills necessary to use new tools and technology, and in part a matter of shaping and adapting work patterns and habits to the requirements of the new technology. Despite strong tendencies for segments of the labor force to become rigid through seniority rules, restrictions on the number of apprentices, and the like, the labor force in advanced countries is highly trained and usually meets the requirements of a reasonably fluid labor market. In underdeveloped areas a different situation generally prevails. Most of the labor force receives little general education and lacks the skills required in machine agriculture and industry. Furthermore, the prevalence of disease and other factors may mean work habits not congenial with modern industry. In such areas the problem of breaking down unfavorable work habits and creating a situation in which labor genuinely wishes to acquire better habits and higher levels of skill may be the single most difficult obstacle to overcome.

While the contribution that capital investment can make to resource development will be conditioned by all the factors previously noted, there are few, if any, situations where additional capital could not be used to advantage. For less developed areas, financing to meet capital needs may be all important if development is to be lifted above a subsistence level.

The most difficult forms of development to finance are those which do not promise a profitable return in terms of the calculation of private business. Public health and education programs, along with more simplified programs for increasing farm or forest production, may pay off only in terms of general economic and social advance over a rather long period of time. To some extent less developed areas may be able to recapture some of the profits of the more exploitable forms of development by means of lease fees or taxes, which may then be invested in these social improvements.

The problem of the right kind of finance is not confined to the oversea, underdeveloped areas. For example, in many parts of the United States, notably in the South, new types of agricultural and forestry improvement loans are needed which will run for long periods of time with repayments made on a flexible schedule depending upon the rate at which the properties are improved.

Favorable domestic and international environment. Most national governments encourage the development of resources within their borders, and in the case of capital-exporting nations, may take an active part in promoting development in other countries. In general, a social, political, and economic environment that encourages enterprise and provides rewards meaningful to all participants is most conducive to natural resource development. The exact role of the government in the process tends to vary with time and circumstances. At one end of the spectrum would be a policy of simply providing favorable conditions for private initiative to take over the responsibility. This may be done, for example, by furnishing basic information and research, through appropriate laws affecting leases, and by equitable tax treatment. Most governments have found it necessary to go beyond this, especially if socially desired resource development which will not pay off in terms of private business calculations is to be achieved. This consideration has led to subsidies and loans to private concerns or individuals on favorable terms, or to direct investment and operation by governmental authorities. At the other extreme is the situation where the government takes the sole or primary responsibility for all resource development, and private participation is either nonexistent or exceptional.

The governments of less developed countries are faced with a special problem of attracting foreign investment in their resources. Frequently the desire for large-scale aid in the form of foreign capital comes into conflict with nationalistic tendencies, either legitimate or extreme in character. This may result in the expropriation of foreign-owned capital, or it may take a somewhat milder form of heavy taxation of returns on the capital investment, or in the exchange restrictions which prevent the foreign owners from recovering their profits in their own currencies. For the less developed capital-shortage areas particularly, an international system which encourages a large flow of trade and investment is essential for a rapid and orderly development of resources. This will permit the underdeveloped area to market its raw and partially processed materials widely over the world, thereby obtaining the foreign exchange with which to repay capital loans and with which to purchase additional capital equipment.

Approaches to understanding the role of resources in economic development. In partnership with the labor force, capital equipment, and the other major factors of production, natural resources form at once the base and an important instrument for economic development. Regions and nations cannot go far beyond the resources which they have within their own borders or over which they are able to assert economic control. Resources, therefore, set the basic material framework, especially over the long run, for economic development and for national security.

The role of resources in economic development and national security may be visualized quantitatively by attempting to look forward to the longer-range requirements which will be placed upon resources and to the resource development necessary for meeting the requirements. One way of doing this is to estimate the gross national product and its principal components at future dates in the light of the trend of past growth. For the United States, as an example, a 1975 population of approximately 190 million, including a labor force of some 70 million, would mean roughly a doubling of the total national product. This assumes an increasing over-all productivity of about 2½ per cent a year, making an allowance for a 15 per cent reduction in number of hours worked per worker. This may be translated into requirements placed upon raw materials and the basic land, water, and mineral resources. The projections, shown in Table 2.1, were made within a fairly rigid framework of assumptions, including the assumption of no price changes and no new techniques of production beyond those clearly marked for early use.

As against these indications of probable level of demand a generation hence, analyses can be made of the prospects for increasing the supplies of materials to meet anticipated demands. The important thing is not whether supplies can be increased physically to this extent, for in most cases they can, but to determine at what cost these increases can be achieved. If the cost of increase becomes excessive, attention will be turned to new materials and sources. This in turn places a check upon further price increases of the original material and upon further expansion of its use. The role of relative price changes becomes critical in determining the precise materials and resources used in meeting the anticipated requirements. It is here that the dynamic aspect of resource and economic development come into full view, since cost increases operate as a spur to technological innovation. Failing this, cost increases may eventually turn consumption into other directions altogether. This approach tacitly assumes that somehow or other the resources and other factors necessary to produce the projected national product will be forthcoming. This, of course, may not happen unless policies are directed toward that end. Furthermore, it is difficult through this approach to take proper account of technological change.

TABLE 2.1

PROJECTED PERCENTAGE INCREASE IN TOTAL DEMAND
FOR SELECTED MATERIALS, 1950–1975*

Material	Per Cent
Copper	45
Lead	61
Zinc	38
Tin	27
Aluminum	358
Iron ore	54
Nickel	100
Cobalt	340
Rubber	104
Sulphur	110
Petroleum	110
Coal	56
Natural gas	138
Electric energy	260
Food products	41
Nonfood agricultural products	25
Fresh water	90
Fertilizers	250
Lumber	10

Source: President's Materials Policy Commission, *Resources For Freedom*, Vol. II, "The Outlook for Key Commodities," p. 118, *passim.*

* For many metals the increase in demand for new material will differ from the increase in total demand because of changes in the proportion of scrap used.

It goes almost without saying that resources must play a basic and continuing part in economic development, and this is easily seen when feasible patterns of over-all economic growth are related to the required supplies of raw materials and natural resources. For most countries, even the United States, the fact that a portion of the materials will have to be imported creates additional problems of international trade and investment, but it does not alter the essential role of resources in the development of national economies.

Another useful approach to understanding the role of resources in economic development, one which is related to the requirements approach just discussed, is to begin with clear resource development objectives and standards, stated appropriately for the various resources, and then formulate the policies and programs which will result in the most efficient progress toward the goals. Thus, an objective might be to restore the Columbia River salmon fishery to a certain level of average annual catch and to maintain this level indefinitely. Building of dams and reservoirs, establishing fishing regulations, and the execution of other programs would then be directed toward this goal. Similarly, objectives and standards may be worked out for hydroelectric power, land reclamation, forestry, and other resources, with programs fashioned to reach established goals in a stipulated period of time. This approach has the advantage of clarity and permits accurate measurement of progress, but it may not allow adequately for basic shifts in demand or in technology, and in practice it frequently overlooks alternative possibilities for achieving a desired result. The economic aspect of choice among alternatives, in short, may be sacrificed to a technical or engineering feasibility approach.

A third general approach, and one commonly used especially in underdeveloped areas, may be termed the "bottleneck" approach. Here the effort is to discover the critical obstacle or problem which, once disposed of, will permit economic development to go forward until the next bottleneck is reached and, in its turn, overcome. This approach has certain advantages. It serves to direct attention to critical and strategic points of attack and does not become lost in generalities or a multiplicity of problems. Consequently, it more readily provides sharp incentive to specific action. For example, in a South American mountainous area the critical problem may be the overgrazing by goats to such an extent that soil and moisture conservation necessary for improved agriculture and a higher standard of living is impossible. A sharp definition of the problem is a spur to action along various helpful lines. This approach may throw overall development out of alignment, however, if it is not consistent with a general framework of resources requirements and potentialities.

Closely related to the bottleneck approach is the approach which strives always for "balanced" resource development. Sometimes, by balanced development is meant a diversified program which, in underscoring both human wants and technical feasibilities, attempts to move forward simultaneously on many resource fronts, including land, water, power, and other major natural resources, plus industries based upon them. The idea of what constitutes balance shifts with the resource potentialities, the individual and social objectives, and the economic complexity of the area. In a primitive area balance may be confined largely to agriculture and possibly other extractive industries, with emphasis, for example, on a balance between crops for domestic consumption and crops for export, or on a balance among grains, livestock, fruits and vegetables. In an advanced economy like that of the United States, balance is much more complex and involves the whole range of resources and related industries. In the southeastern states, for example, balance generally means more industry relative to agriculture as a way of promoting higher per capita real income. In this region, thinking only in terms of the agricultural segment, balance usually means more livestock and pasture as compared to cotton, corn, and tobacco. Both the "bottleneck" and "balanced" approaches may be thought of as pointing to the particular investment or other action which promises the highest net marginal return.

Finally there is the approach to resources development which emphasizes military security for a country or area. Here the measure is maximum effective contribution to defined security goals. Fortunately, in the case of many long-range resource programs military and civilian requirements tend to merge since, for example, more hydroelectric power, improved industrial water supplies, more fertilizer, and larger supplies of metals can serve either purpose.

These several interrelated and overlapping approaches are meant to clarify the role of resources in economic development. Different areas in different stages of economic development, faced with different problems, and endowed with different resource potentials will emphasize different approaches in understanding the role of resources in their development programs.

PRINCIPLES OF RESOURCE DEVELOPMENT

Over the years, especially during recent decades, certain principles of resource development have emerged which may guide the formulation and evaluation of projects and programs. In general, these principles are applicable to both advanced and underdeveloped areas, although precise formulation and interpretation of the principles would vary somewhat, depending on the stage of development and on legal and other political and institutional characteristics.

Multiple purpose. The first principle is that of development for a number of related purposes, such as the development of a river for flood control, navigation, irrigation, municipal and industrial water supply, recreation, and general watershed management. This principle now appears obvious, but it is only in fairly recent years that technological and cultural levels have enabled persons to see fully the advantages of developing a given resource for its multiple purposes and uses. Though by no means the originator of the idea, the Tennessee Valley Authority has become in this country and before the world a leading example of the multiple purpose development of a whole river system.

Areal integration. This principle flows directly from the previous one. It means that a resource development program must fit together in terms of the area or region in which it is located, as well as in terms of the functions it performs. Thus, a watershed management program in the upper reaches of a river valley must be geared to the development of dams and reservoirs, the enlargement of channels, and other works in the lower portion of the river. The function of watershed management (that is, the useful control of water on the land and the development of forests, pastures, and other suitable land uses to do this) must be looked at in the light of the needs and total resources of the region. The area, whether it is a watershed, an agricultural plain, or an island, should be examined and developed as a unit made up of interrelated parts. The economic relationships with other areas is a part of the picture.

Sustained use. This principle simply means that, where possible, resources should be developed in such a way that a high and technically and economically supportable level of use may be sustained indefinitely. It applies especially to the so-called inexhaustible or flow resources, such as land and water. In terms of soil conservation this means the application of soil improvement methods to the point where the soil will sustain permanently a certain level of agricultural production. In some instances this will mean a lower level of production, especially on lands which are being "over-used," such as certain of the dry wheat farming areas. For most lands, however, sustained use at the highest economic level will undoubtedly mean a larger agricultural production because of increased use of fertilizers, better soil management, and other improvements.

Minimum waste. This principle, which implies an economic rather than a physical concept of waste, though applicable to all resources, is especially relevant to the so-called exhaustible or stock resources, notably minerals. For example, a mineral or metal is wasted if it is left unmined, discarded in processing, or lost through incomplete use or failure to reclaim whenever foreseeable patterns of demand and cost indicate the wasted mineral or metal could have been put to profitable use. Waste also is a dynamic concept and is related to a number of things, including the aggressiveness with which enterprisers and workers seek to reduce it, the prevailing laws and attitudes toward conservation, and the rate and directions of technological change. The practice of minimum waste conveys an alertness to economic possibilities for reducing the proportion of materials which never find their way into use, and a desire to experiment with new methods of extraction and processing, of reclaiming used materials, of developing by-products, and of finding cheaper and more plentiful substitutes. In reducing raw material waste, care should be taken that this is not achieved only by the extravagant and wasteful use of labor, machinery, or time. Reduction of waste is partly a matter of "good business" in the sense of yielding a net marginal return; but it is also a matter of an attitude and habit of avoiding waste even when there is no clear economic advantage in terms of typical individual or business firm calculations of profit.

Wide diffusion of benefits. The wide diffusion of benefits, in many countries, has become a cardinal principle in resource development activities. In countries like the United States this is left to the workings of a predominantly private enterprise, competitive system. A progressive income tax system, such as prevails in the more advanced countries, serves indirectly to diffuse the benefits derived from large holdings of privately owned resources. Direct taxes upon resources may also serve to redistribute benefits, as may the requirement of forced sale to the government.

The wide diffusion of benefits from publically owned resources over large regions and groups of people has become a guiding principle in most countries. In the United States, for example, it has become a firm part of government policy that the power from publicly constructed hydroelectric power projects be distributed widely among various users at low developmental rates. Toward this end, the government has given a degree of preference to publicly and cooperatively owned electricity distribution companies in the purchase of power produced at government plants. Also, it has insisted upon the right to build basic transmission lines to carry the power from the government's large generating stations to the ultimate distribution facilities, so that private transmission companies, assuming they wished to, could not intervene effectively to raise power rates unduly to the ultimate consumer.

Economic in the sense of maximizing net returns or benefits. This is an obvious common-sense principle for resources development, but it has not always been applied systematically to the evaluation of resources projects and programs. This is partly due to the fact that the measurement of revenues or benefits, and costs is an exceedingly difficult and, in many respects, arbitrary matter. For example, there is the problem of deciding what particular set of price and cost estimates to use for future years in arriving at reasonable monetary estimates for benefits and costs. Furthermore, there are difficulties concerned with deciding the rate at which to discount future benefits and costs in order to arrive at comparable present values. Estimates of net benefit for public projects, such as watershed management, flood protection works, and the preservation of scenic values, include a broader range of benefits and costs. Here the government has an obligation to ascertain the public interest in long-range conservation, in the protection of human life and communities, and in other values hard to measure by normal profit and loss calculations. Part of the problem is to establish guides which will indicate not only the way in which the estimates should be made but also the weight which should be placed upon monetary estimates of net benefit as compared to factors not susceptible to monetary evaluation. Much will depend upon the accounting techniques used and upon the process used to prepare estimates of net benefits. Judgment factors have to be applied at all stages of the process, thereby making efficient organizational form and competent personnel highly desirable.

Many decisions regarding resource development, especially private decisions, should be guided by the least-cost principle. For example, changes in the relative amount of electric power produced from coal, oil, gas, falling water, or atomic fission may be determined largely by the shifting cost patterns, with the cheaper sources displacing the more costly at favorable points. The search always should be for substitutions of materials, methods, capital, and labor which will result in lower cost per unit of product. This principle, however, so useful in private decisions, must play a somewhat different role when a public project is in question since, by its nature, such a project must be modified by a consideration of political and social factors not amenable to money-cost calculations.

It may well be that the best guide to the wide selection of projects and programs, public or private, is a historical guide. This would mean that projects, after they have been built and have been in operation for a period of time, should be given a careful postaudit or postevaluation, to see whether the benefits and costs originally claimed to be associated with the project have, in fact, resulted. To the extent that there is deviation between the post-evaluation and the pre-evaluation of benefits and costs, corrections can be made for future projects. Based upon this kind of historical analysis, economic guides for the selection of future projects and programs may be worked out. Of course, the test of historical experience has long been used to guide economic development. What is suggested here is that carefully planned systematic records be kept for all projects throughout their useful lives, so that future projects may be selected more wisely.

Contributing to economic stability. Expenditures for certain resource development projects and programs may be timed so as to contribute to the moderation of excessive ups and downs of the business cycle, especially in more advanced countries and in less developed areas tied closely by trade and investment to advanced countries. There should not be a blind reliance upon any and all public works as a means of stimulating a depressed economy. However, careful rescheduling of selected projects can help to stabilize income and employment. When inflation threatens, and labor and materials are scarce, only essential projects should be continued and less essential ones should be deferred. This means a careful identification of those resource projects and programs which lend themselves to business cycle rescheduling and those which can be rescheduled only at a considerable sacrifice in efficiency and service. For example, most of the large-scale, heavy engineering projects can make little contribution to employment and income during a mild and short business recession. These require a long period for planning and land acquisition, and can be neither accelerated nor decelerated rapidly except at considerable loss. Their greatest contribution to economic stability lies in the steady year-in-year-out unfolding of carefully planned sequences of projects. In this way they provide an underpinning to investment, construction, and, to a degree, the whole economy, and a partial guarantee of attaining goals of economic growth. On the other hand, the rescheduling of a variety of smaller-scale rural improvements, such as upstream flood control work and land conservation generally, along with certain extensions and improvements in larger projects, can make significant contributions to economic stability during recessions of a mild and short character. If the prospect is clearly for a severe depression of long duration, larger public works projects may be undertaken. Anticyclical scheduling of resources and other public works is only one of a number of economic measures, some of them automatic in operation and some not, which may be employed to offset the ups and downs of business. Public works will be most helpful in this connection when conceived and utilized as one part of a broader, integrated program.

Generally speaking, less developed areas dependent on trade with advanced countries would benefit from anticyclical development programs, but frequently they do not have the fiscal capacity for such programs. Primitive areas with few foreign economic connections are not much subject to the business cycle. A large, more or less self-sufficient country with a centrally planned and controlled economy, such as that of the Soviet Union, seems able to control its economy so that it does not move through business cycles as they are known in the economically advanced countries of the free world. Undoubtedly, the Russians experience the misfortune of large-scale mistakes in the use of resources when judged in terms of intended results, but there is little evidence that these misallocations cumulate periodically as business cycles.

Sharing of costs and responsibilities. The principle of wide sharing of costs and responsibilities for resource projects is becoming more and more accepted over the world, although with considerable differences in application in different countries.

In a federal, democratic, predominantly private enterprise system, such as operates in the United States, it is generally considered desirable policy that the costs of large-scale resource development works be shared broadly by various levels of government and by various groups and individuals, and that other responsibilities connected with the works likewise be shared. This has been achieved only to a limited degree and with a good deal of inconsistency, although efforts are continually under way to improve the equity of the cost sharing. Generally speaking, a good or service, produced as a result of resource projects, which is vendible and finds a ready and competitive market, is priced so that the entire portion of the cost allocated to that particular good or service is recovered. This is the case with the sale of electric power produced at publicly owned power projects, and with the sale of water for certain beneficial consumptive uses. At the other end of the scale there are benefits produced as a result of resource projects, such as certain types of public recreation and general conservation, the cost of which cannot be easily assigned and collected. In these cases the cost is borne by the public generally and paid for out of taxes, borrowing, and the usual forms of public finance. When a number of vendible goods or services are produced as a result of the same project, it frequently happens that only the direct or variable costs are covered in the price charged.

Over a range of goods and services between these extremes the principles of cost sharing are not clearly or systematically worked out. Thus, in the United States, in the case of water made available by Federal dams and reservoirs and sold for use in irrigation, purchasers are required to pay only to a predetermined extent of their ability to pay, which is based upon calculations of net income which will result from the use of the water. Furthermore, users are not required to make any payment for interest on the portion of the investment outlay which has been allocated to irrigation. In this case, the actual collection of money from the ultimate users to this limited extent is handled by irrigation districts established under the laws of the various states through taxes levied roughly in accordance with the benefits received.

In the case of flood protection in the downstream portions of many of the major river valleys in the United States, the entire cost of construction of levees, diversion channels, channel control work, and the like, is borne by the Federal Government. Local governments, in this case levee boards authorized under state law, contribute rights of way for various stream control works and are responsible for the maintenance of the projects. In both the upstream and the down-stream case, the tendency has been for the local groups to bear less and less of the cost of the protection and development works.

Many anomalies and inconsistencies exist. For example, a dam may be built and reservoir established in the upper reaches of a stream furnishing irrigation water to farmers in nearby areas, thereby making it possible for them to increase their net income, and at the same time providing flood protection to farmers located immediately below the dam, thereby permitting them also to increase their net income. The farmer benefited by irrigation is required to pay to the extent of his ability for at least a portion of the cost of the project allocated to irrigation, while the farmer benefited by flood protection is required to pay nothing. Beyond this, the farmers located in other parts of the country, who pay in taxes a portion of the costs of such projects, receive no direct benefit from the Federal Government comparable to those received by the irrigation farmer and the farmer receiving flood protection.

In most of the other more advanced countries a good deal of attention is given to the principle of sharing costs and responsibilities among levels of government, groups, and individuals, although the problems are somewhat less complex with nonfederal types of government. Many varieties of loans and grants from the national government to local governments and to private farmers or water users have been tried, frequently with some sharing provision which calls for local government or private individual contribution, perhaps in labor. In cases of outright gift from the central government, with no contributory or matching requirement, reliance is usually placed on education, extension services, or demonstration programs to insure that beneficiaries make good use of the gift, whether it is money, seed, equipment, or something else.

Some tendency is visible, less in the United States than in many other countries, for the central government to plan and pay for the basic resource conservation and development works as a matter of national welfare and security, leaving to local government and private beneficiaries the job of paying for certain separable features, the benefits of which are localized and not essential to national purposes. In most countries, effort is made to draw all interested parties into the planning, or at least reviewing, of projects.

Consideration of nonmeasurable aspects. Perhaps the thorniest problem in the evaluation of resource projects and programs is to determine which of the variety of costs and benefits should be considered and estimated as a basis for deciding which projects and programs to pursue. Certain general aspects of benefits and costs having to do with public welfare, national defense, public health, and economic stability are difficult to estimate in precise dollar terms. Even more specific aspects, such as recreation, fish and wildlife preservation, and the enhancement of historical and archeological features, likewise defy precise quantitative measure. For example, what is the monetary value to a person of a week spent in a national park with its magnificent natural scenery? What public or other cost may be justified for this purpose? Only the roughest kind of quantitative estimate of such benefits and costs seems possible; indeed, the whole matter might better be left to general description and judgment.

Yet, these aspects which have been termed intangibles are obviously real and frequently of overriding importance. They cannot be left out of account in the final selection of projects and programs, despite the fact that they do not yield satisfactorily or completely to quantitative measurement. The best approach seems to be to identify all those benefits and costs which can be estimated in dollar terms reasonably successfully, and to make the most careful and systematic estimates possible of them. For those other aspects which cannot be estimated with reasonable satisfaction in dollars, other forms of appraisal should be used. Even for these aspects, however, monetary estimates of benefit and cost sometimes can be used as rough indicators of their value to users and of the cost which may be justified in developing them. The problem is to make decisions as to the degree of reliance in project selection and evaluations which shall be placed upon monetary evaluation as compared to other forms of evaluation. There is no clear and simple line of demarcation. History and experience seem to offer the best guides.

A special type of benefit and cost deserves mention. This is secondary benefits and costs which flow indirectly as a result of resource projects and programs. For example, water provided for irrigation generally results in an increase in the net income of the irrigation farmer. This is a direct or primary benefit. In addition, as the increased agricultural production resulting from the additional irrigation finds its way into various channels of processing and dis-tribution, there undoubtedly is an increase in net income to various processors and distributors along the line, and finally to the consumer. There is, however, serious question as to whether this is a net increase above what would accrue generally if some other form of investment rather than the particular irrigation investment had been made. Yet the historical fact remains that certain resources investments have paid off handsomely in terms of the net secondary benefits produced, while others have been failures. One need only recall the difference between the successful investment in the Panama Canal and such investment failures as the numerous connecting canals through the Midwestern portion of the United States made in the 1830's and 40's. In any event, despite the absence so far of an acceptable technique for its measurement, the effect of a resource investment upon the national income of a country needs to be considered and compared with the national income effect of alternative investments.

Promotion of national security and world peace. No one will dispute that a large and steady development of basic resources makes a major contribution to national security. During periods of war and of intense rearmament most resources development programs are given a defense and security emphasis which is different from that of peace and general economic development. For instance, during the defense build-up in the United States beginning in mid-1950, all resources development activities were reviewed with an eye to deferring those which did not make a fairly direct and important contribution to national defense and accelerating those which did. Thus programs of minerals exploration and electric power development were enlarged, while those relating to public recreation and more generalized conservation were curtailed, at least relatively to what would have happened in the absence of a defense need.

For any country the degree to which the normal unfolding of resource development programs should be modified to take account of security needs remains one of the most difficult questions of public policy. In the most basic and long-run sense, there is little opposition between security and peacetime resource development policies since the total strength of the nation for defense and for peacetime development derives from the same land, water, mineral, and energy resources. The particular pace of development, however, in the various segments is different, depending upon the urgency of defense. There is danger in conceiving national security in short-run terms as a matter of increasing quickly power output or minerals output, rather than in long-run terms in which technological advance, soil and water conservation, and generalized resources development are of equal importance.

The ways in which resource development promotes world peace are subtle, but very important. Development which increases the national security of the free-world countries may be said to contribute importantly to this end. Resource development in the United States which contributes to the expansion and stabilization of its national economy also makes a contribution to world stability and development, and hence world peace. This is obviously true when so much of the world depends upon the United States for a variety of loans and grants, used for military and economic purposes, and upon selling in a prosperous American market to obtain dollars. Indeed, the economic health and stability of the whole free world seems now to depend in large measure upon the preservation of a strong and active United States economy.

The problem of conservation and use. A special word needs to be said regarding resource conservation. This term has generally been used to mean a "wise and economic" use of resources, with a more precise definition of "wise and economic" being worked out differently for the various major resources. Conservation cannot be separated from use since neither one has meaning apart from the other. Thus, for forest resources, conservation has come to mean the management of forests in such a way as to sustain a high net yield of forest products. The precise level of sustained yield aimed at depends in part on natural or physical characteristics of forests and in part upon economic characteristics of products, costs of management and development, and patterns of demand. The problem becomes one of determining the best level and rate of use; conservation, through such measures as fire protection, insect and pest control, planting of new stock, and better cutting practices, is merely a total program for promoting wiser use.

Conservation has been depicted as an effort to change the rate of use toward the future and to diminish it relatively in the present. This has been true in many areas for such resources, for example, as forests and grazing land. Just the opposite has been the goal for such resources as falling water, certain wildlife resources which exist in numbers beyond the capacity of the habitat to support even with good management, and many arid sections which will remain unused unless water is brought to them. In these cases, the object has been to shift the use toward the present. Conservation, therefore, involves an appraisal of resource potentialities and rates of use, the aim of which, as noted previously, is to maximize net returns over a long period. Full play should be allowed for the shifting of demands, both individual and social, and for the changing structure of costs of developing the various resources to the point of usefulness.

Conservation, in the popular use of the term, represents an attitude of caution and husbandry toward resources, especially the so-called exhaustible resources, as opposed to an attitude of quick and ready exploitation which places its trust in the development of substitutes and new sources as soon as diminishing supplies drive prices into a range where both users and developers will more actively seek new discoveries and substitutes. Conservationists in the best sense cast a shrewd eye to the likelihood that scarcity will not necessarily bring in its wake lifesaving discoveries and substitutes. They propose to solve this problem not through policies of nonuse but rather through controlled use which, combined with measures to avoid waste and increase yield, will provide time for the development of alternatives in those cases where sustained yield at higher levels is impossible. In certain instances, "conservationists" have turned out to be correct in their skepticism that suitable substitutes will not be automatically forthcoming. In other instances, the "opportunists" have been proved correct in their optimistic belief that new technology will solve the problem.

Principles of resource development especially relevant for under-developed areas. Underdeveloped areas have the particular task set them of moving as rapidly as possible through certain intermediate phases of development toward a mature economy usually made up of industry, agriculture, and services. Except for a few areas which develop special lines, such as dairying and agriculture in Denmark, precision manufacturing in Switzerland, or mining in parts of interior Alaska and Canada, areas seem to require an assortment of well-developed economic activities before per capita incomes reach high levels. This means an area must itself produce or be able to import a variety of raw materials. Natural resource development is generally a prerequisite to industrial development and economic growth. Equally important, and closely related, is the fact that an underdeveloped area needs transportation facilities, electric power, and other forms of basic capital equipment. These and other conditions for development will be discussed later. It suffices here to point out that the development principle of overriding importance for many underdeveloped areas is that they broaden their base of effective resources as a means toward industrialization. Depending on the area, this may mean cotton or wool for cloth, forests for pulp and paper, minerals for smelting and refining, water for irrigation, or electric power for mineral and chemical processing. Special attention may have to be given to building export markets for raw materials as a way of purchasing or attracting transport and other capital equipment necessary for development.

OUTLINE OF A RESOURCE DEVELOPMENT POLICY AND PROGRAM

The discussion to this point can be most conveniently reviewed and summarized by outlining the major requirements of an effective resource development program. This will be done partly with the United States in mind, and partly in terms of less developed regions in other parts of the world.

Research. First emphasis in a resource development policy and program should be placed upon research in all of its varied forms. In the long run, enlargement of the resource base of land, water, minerals, and energy will be determined largely by the amount and quality of research, and its success in opening up new sources of resources and applying them to the production of needed goods and services.

The kind of over-all research program needed will, of course, vary from country to country. The more wealthy and advanced countries have a tremendous advantage. Not only can they devote large amounts of money to research, but they also have more trained research workers and equipment at their disposal.[7] The problem of research leadership and coordination is apparently critical in many countries. Partly, this is a matter of arranging for the exchange of information. Partly, it involves encouragement of private research. More and more, it is a matter of integrating the government's share of research expenditure into a well-considered plan. Since a great deal of private research in the United States particularly is done directly for government or with government aid, a coordinated program for government research would have profound effects on the total research pattern. Also, there are critical shortages of research personnel and facilities for their training.

Improved planning and programming. Much headway has been made in recent years, not only in the planning of resource development projects and programs but also in the coordination and scheduling of the variety of projects and programs which fall under the responsibility of many different public and private organizations. This tendency has been greatly accelerated in most countries by the obvious needs of war and preparation for war. In the more advanced countries of the free world, large resource requirements, combined with resource limitations, have required a careful allocation of both materials and manpower to serve critical national purposes. Among other things, it became necessary to plan and schedule resource development from a national security point of view, with the various private and public actions fitted into the total scheme.

[7] For the United States it has been suggested that at least 3 per cent of the national income might well be directed toward research through both private and government agencies. This would have required, in 1953, about 9 billion dollars, more than twice what was actually devoted to this purpose. Some of the larger and more progressive American corporations, however, have been devoting as much as 5, 10, or even a higher per cent of their total expenditures to research. In recent years, more than half of all research funds have been supplied by the Federal Government with only a trace of this going for research relating directly or fairly closely to natural resources. See The President's Scientific Research Board, *Federal Research Program* (Washington, D.C.: Government Printing Office, 1952), Vol. II, p. 3. Also Lawrence P. Lessing, "The National Science Foundation Takes Stock," *Scientific American* (March, 1954) pp. 29–33.

For example, in the United States during the defense build-up following the outbreak of war in Korea, expansion goals for more than 150 industries, covering a large part of the entire industrial structure of the nation, were established by the Defense Production Administration. In working out these goals, it was necessary to take account of both defense and civilian requirements, looking several years ahead, and to reckon closely the supplies of raw materials and other items which would be necessary to meet these requirements. In each instance a point of view as broad as the free world had to be taken, and requirements and supplies in each of the countries given consideration. In instances where supplies did not appear to be available or could not be called forth by appropriate investment and other activities, adjustments had to be made in the goals.

In many less developed areas, the problems of resource planning and programming are at once more simple and yet more critical. They are more simple in that the industrial structure in such countries is less complex, thereby diminishing the number of variables which have to be taken into account. They are more critical in that frequently such areas depend heavily upon one or a few raw materials which are exported and upon one or a few industries which process these materials, at least in the initial phases. National or area plans and programs, in such instances, obviously have to be derived from and made a definite part of broader international planning and programming. In this connection the recent work of the International Materials Conference in arranging for the voluntary allocation of certain scarce materials among participating free-world countries may be cited.

Resource plans and programs, prepared on the basis of geographic areas, such as river basins, usually take into account the relationship of the area and its resources to the larger national unit. Most such plans and programs have had as their core development of the land and water resources, with secondary emphasis on minerals and other resources. In this respect the Tennessee Valley Authority has provided a prototype for river basin planning and development which many other countries, both advanced and less-developed, are adapting to meet their special conditions.

In totalitarian countries, planning and programming of resource development are done in considerable detail, with little room for individual choice. In a country like the United States, particular business firms or other economic units, as well as government agencies, may plan and schedule carefully their own investments and other activities. Over-all national planning, however, is not attempted except as more general goals may be projected and discussed as guides to be used voluntarily, or as defense necessities may require. A wide variety of organizational forms have been tried both in the United States and elsewhere to carry out programs of development.

The standards and processes by which resource projects and programs are evaluated are especially important. Monetary estimates of benefits and costs, returns on investment, and effects on regional and national income may be used with caution as indicators of the worth of projects. As noted earlier, however, such measurements are full of pitfalls and should be accompanied by descriptive kinds of evaluation and experienced judgment. Monetary estimates appear to be more reliable in evaluating the more immediate and direct benefits and costs of a project, especially when the resulting goods or services are sold in competitive markets. Certain project effects, such as recreation or watershed management improvements, are intangible in nature, remote in time, or generalized in their incidence and seem to defy precise appraisal.

Public and private roles. In most countries a great amount of attention has been given to the question whether resource development should be carried out by public or private agencies. Historically, the degree to which public and private enterprise have been combined for this purpose has varied both within and between countries. In the United States most of the oil, gas, and mineral development has been undertaken privately, all the way from the initial exploration to the final processing and sale, although the basic geologic mapping has been largely a government undertaking. Hydroelectric power development has been undertaken by both public and private agencies on a large scale, with the Federal Government predominating in cases where power is only one element in large multiple-purpose projects. In the case of flood control, most of the work is done by government, although small-scale flood control work, for example on individual farms, is undertaken either entirely by private means or with limited government aid. Navigation improvement has been almost exclusively in the hands of the Federal Government. The development of atomic energy in the United States has been a government monopoly so far, both in its military and its civilian aspects. Where possible and within the bounds of security, however, work of the Atomic Energy Commission, whether research, development, construction, or plant operation, has been accomplished by means of contracts with private firms and agencies.

Elsewhere, and especially in underdeveloped areas, the role of government seems to have been somewhat larger. In some instances, this has been a reflection of a political and economic philosophy that favored governmental participation. In many cases it was because private interests within such areas have been unable to accumulate the funds necessary for many of the larger resource projects. It is true that foreign corporations often engage in large developmental programs in underdeveloped areas, but frequently these are carried on with some degree of financial or other support and protection from the governments in these areas.

In the free-world countries the division between public and private responsibility has been, and is, shifting and uncertain. For the most part the two roles are complementary rather than competing. Difficulties do arise at the various border zones; but by and large, in most countries, government activity tends to extend to the point of insuring that what are thought to be sound principles of resources development are being followed. This means that government generally takes care of resource developments which are of strategic importance for security purposes or economic growth, and which will not be done by anyone else.

In many fields the government may assume a more limited role and encourage private enterprise to make investments and improvements which are for the long-range benefit of the nation and which can be made to pay in private accounting terms once such aid is given. This pattern has been used in the United States, particularly in agriculture, where emphasis has been placed upon research, experiment, credit aids, and extension programs. For massive engineering works, the Federal Government has assumed a major share of responsibility, although wherever possible, reimbursement has been sought from the various beneficiaries, including private persons and groups. In most places efforts have been made to draw the private and local government interests into the planning as well as the reimbursement process so that they will feel a degree of responsibility for the operation and maintenance of the projects.

In the Soviet Union resource developments for the most part are directly planned, organized, and carried out by government agencies. In the Soviet Arctic, for example, a single government administrative agency, charged originally with developing water transportation along the Arctic Coast, was broadened to include responsibility for exploration, surveys, resource management, all forms of transportation, local administration, and general cultural advancement. Our knowledge of the operation of these programs is insufficient to permit an accurate appraisal of their success.

Resource development in economic stability. For the future, a somewhat new approach toward the use of resource expenditure programs to offset the business cycle may be needed. Most desirable would be a compromise between the heavy orientation of such programs to combat depression, which was characteristic of many countries during the depression of the 1930's, and the more recent tendency to view resource programs entirely in terms of their steady, long-run contribution to economic growth. Anticyclical resources expenditures should, therefore, be tailored to the kind of depression in prospect. Account should be taken of such things as the location of the project, the type of employment afforded and the skills required, the types and amounts of materials and equipment needed, the status of planning and other preparations, and the speed with which the programs can be accelerated and then turned off. These should be matched against the characteristics of the anticipated recession so that the contribution of public works to the combatting of the recession may be maximized, and so that fruitless "work-making" activities may be avoided. The importance of steady progress in resource development investments as a major stabilizing factor should not be overlooked.

Resource development and defense. For the foreseeable future, all resource policies and programs will have to be worked out in a context of defense needs as well as economic growth and stability. This is more than a matter of stockpiling certain critical materials, important though this is. It means that all future estimates of need for agricultural land, forest products, water, minerals, and so forth will have to recognize the possible requirements of both all-out war and of various degrees of defense, in addition to more normal economic requirements. This argues for flexible resource development policies, for providing a cushion of materials and processing facilities, and for making full use of overseas sources, especially protectable sources, of strategic raw materials.

For less developed countries it means, obviously, careful attention to alliances and connections with those larger, more advanced countries for both economic and political reasons. So long as essential security requirements are met, the less developed countries will gain by seeking their economic and political security within the framework of international organizations and arrangements, partly so as to reduce their dependence upon one or a few of the larger countries. Flexible resource development policies, especially for the more advanced countries, argue for intensified research, for cheaper and more plentiful substitutes for scarce materials. It also suggests a constant state of readiness to shift rapidly the pattern of resource use from predominantly peacetime directions to full-scale war. While laying preparations for all-out war, major attention must also be directed toward meeting the difficult requirements of a state of affairs which is neither war nor peace, but more nearly like that prevailing in the years after the outbreak of the Korean war.

In this kind of situation, the United States has chosen to emphasize the building up of a limited force capable of swift employment in case of widespread hostilities, while at the same time expanding greatly the natural resources, materials, and productive capacity necessary to meet the larger requirements of full-scale war. All of this is to be achieved while imposing a minimum of restraint and hardship upon the civilian segments of the economy. Fortunately, in the case of most natural resources the problem is somewhat simplified, since the same resources and the same emphasis on development in a general way are required, whether the objective is rapid economic growth of a more normal and peacetime character, or whether it is for a rapid transfer of the economy to the mission of war. The difference lies mainly in the timing, that is, the speed-up necessary to meet defense goals and the relative emphasis placed on various elements.

Other free-world countries, reacting variously to the Korean, Indo-Chinese, and other military actions, find their economies subjected to added burdens and restraints upon civilian activities. Many less developed economies have been pitched about by the violent movements in the price of raw materials brought on by the necessity for speedy rearmament in the larger countries. The best hope of the smaller countries, as indeed of the advanced countries also, is for peace and stability as the conditions under which their economic development can be advanced most rapidly.

Resource problems are now clearly as wide as the free world. This means that the United States, for example, must take full advantage of materials obtainable from other free-world countries at less cost than they can be produced at home. It also implies that other free-world countries which wish to provide such materials be encouraged and aided to develop and export them to this country without undue hindrance. Important for the achievement of these objectives are measures designed to broaden and solidify the countries of the free world into a single area from which raw materials may be drawn and in which finished products may be marketed. Thus, it has been found desirable among many of the free-world countries to enter into cooperative arrangements to insure that a fair distribution of certain materials is achieved, and to prevent the competitive bidding up of prices and the consequent pressure toward general inflation.

As long as the world is torn between the conflicting ideologies of communism and democracy, however, we cannot expect to achieve a maximum economic growth. The whole objective, principle, and program for resource development should be for the general welfare which includes an increase in living levels. We hope someday to be able to interpret the general welfare not only in local, regional, and national terms, but with all areas and countries of the world in mind.

CHAPTER III

Demographic Patterns

JOSEPH J. SPENGLER*

THE THREE PARTS OF THIS CHAPTER ARE CONCERNED WITH THE ROLE of population in economic growth and development. The first part examines the manner in which a population's various dimensions impinge upon the level and the movement of per capita income. The second part describes the major population types found in the world today, their evolving characteristics and prospects, the determinants of evolution, and an indication of the range of paths along which this prospective evolution will proceed. The third part considers the implications of these prospective growth paths for economic development.

Population and its movements are variously connected with per capita income and its movements. It is not easy, however, to isolate all these connections, describe them in concrete terms, and indicate their relative importance. Both difficulties of theoretical formulation and shortcomings with respect to data are encountered. Some of the connections are direct while others are indirect; and most if not all the relations between population movements are reciprocal in nature. It is inevitable, therefore, that a considerable amount of conjecture must enter into interpretations of the impact of the population factor upon the income factor.

The societal universe of which man is a part may be looked upon

* Professor of Economics and Business Administration and Director of Graduate Studies in Economics, Duke University. Author: "Evolutionism in American Economics" in *Evolutionary Thought in America* (Stow Persons, ed.); "Population Theory" in *A Survey of Contemporary Economics*, Vol. II (Bernard Haley, ed.); "Monopolistic Competition and the Use and Price of Urban Land Service," *Journal of Political Economy* (October, 1946); "The Problem of Order in Economic Affairs," *Southern Economic Journal* (July, 1948).

as a system of mutually interacting variables which include such dimensions of a population as its size and its birth rate. When the conditions external to such a system change, or when, for whatever reason, a variable undergoes qualitative modification, then other variables in the system must undergo readjustment until a stable balance has been established. This readjustment resembles what takes place in a bowl of marbles when one of them undergoes modification in size, or when the shape of the bowl itself is changed. So also with population variables: If a subdimension, such as natality or mortality, changes, then some other dimension, such as age composition, or some nondemographic variable, such as rate of capital formation, will also change until a balance compatible with the new set of conditions is established. Although it is difficult to deal adequately with the causes and the effects of population movements in terms of a complicated system of mutually interrelated variables, the concept of such a system is useful, nonetheless. It indicates that a change in a population dimension or subdimension acts, just as does a change in any other variable, both as a "cause" and as an "effect," and it illustrates why it is difficult to isolate and assess all the direct and indirect effects of a given change.

Since it is not possible to deal in so intricate a fashion with the connections obtaining between population and income, an alternative approach must be employed. For example, we may classify a population with respect to its various dimensions, specify the major determinants of per capita income, and then see how a change in any one of these population dimensions will affect one or more of the determinants of per capita income.

DIMENSIONS OF POPULATION AND THE DETERMINANTS OF PER CAPITA INCOME

The dimensions of a population are of five kinds. (1) By *size* we mean the absolute number of people occupying the territory of a country or region. (2) *Composition* refers either to a population's sex-mix (the proportion of the population which is male or female), or to its age-mix (the proportions of the population found in various age groups). (3) The *rate of growth* is either the absolute number of persons, or the percentage, by which a population is increasing or decreasing each year. Thus it represents the annual number of births, minus the annual number of deaths, plus the annual number of immigrants, minus the annual number of emigrants, or, more briefly, natural increase plus net in-migration. (4) A population's *distribution* describes the manner in which population is spread among various categories based upon specifiable indexes. In this chapter four such categories will be used: (a) genetical structure, i.e., the genotypes found in a population, together with the frequencies with which they occur;[1] (b) racial composition, i.e., the proportions of a population formed by specifiable races; only the racial differences which have social significance will be considered since genetical differences are treated under (a); (c) occupational or industrial composition, i.e., the proportions of the labor force attached to the various occupations or industries in an economy; (d) spatial distribution, i.e., the manner in which a population is divided between rural and nonrural categories, among cities of various size and situation, among regions, or among other categories of geographical space; (5) under *growth differentials* we consider the differentiating growth patterns of a population. These are encountered only when a population is heterogeneous and its diverse elements are growing at different rates.

The connections existing between the determinants of per capita income and the dimensions of population will now be examined, with the discussion organized in terms of the determinants of per capita income. Unless otherwise indicated, the treatment of any one income determinant assumes that the other determinants remain unchanged.[2]

Absolute size of the labor force.[3] "Labor force," or "working force," refers to that part of a population which is economically active, or

[1] The term "genetical" refers to that which is associated with, or affected by, genes; "genotype" refers to a kind of gene combination or pair with which a specific bodily trait or difference is associated. See Lancelot Hogben, *An Introduction to Mathematical Genetics* (New York: W. W. Norton & Company, Inc., 1946), p. 1.

[2] There probably exist important determinants of per capita income, which will not be discussed, and many more connections, reciprocal and otherwise, between income determining factors and population dimensions than will be indicated. Furthermore, our treatment is not intended to suggest that the connections between income and population changes are everywhere the same, since they necessarily vary with variations in cultural patterns.

[3] On the points discussed in this section, see A. J. Jaffe and C. D. Stewart, *Manpower Resources and Utilization* (New York: John Wiley & Sons, Inc., 1951); Wilbert E. Moore, *Industrialization and Labor* (Ithaca: Cornell University Press, 1951); G. J. Stigler, "The Division of Labor Is Limited by the Extent of the

"gainfully employed." It includes, in the United States, all individuals who are currently in the labor market, whether employed or unemployed. Because the statistical definition of the term "labor force" varies somewhat from country to country, labor-force data of countries are not strictly comparable. Furthermore, as a community progresses economically, relatively more of its output of goods and services is bought and sold and relatively more persons become engaged in the production of goods and services for sale. When an individual, who has been devoting his full time to household production and consumption, begins to produc. for sale in the market, he becomes a member of the labor force as usually defined, even though the volume of his production remains substantially unchanged. This fact must be taken into account when making certain international and intertemporal labor force comparisons.

As the labor force occupying a territory increases in size, a number of effects tend to occur. If the labor force of a relatively small community increases, a relatively smaller proportion of the able-bodied population will be required to guard its military and political security than was formerly the case. Relatively more manpower will be made available thereby for other purposes. As a country's population and labor force increase in size, the amount of communication that takes place per capita will tend to increase, with the result that there will be an increase in the exchange of ideas, in stimuli to activity, and so on.[4] Eventually, of course, a limit is reached to the amount of interpersonal communication that is economically practicable. Regardless of how well developed the facilities for communication, only a limited fraction of an individual's waking time can be devoted to communication with others.

Of much greater importance is the influence of an increase in the size of a country's labor force upon the division of labor. Within

Market," *Journal of Political Economy*, LIX, 1951, pp. 185–93; Manuel Gottlieb, "The Theory of an Optimum Population for a Closed Economy," *Journal of Political Economy*, LIII, 1945, pp. 289–316; A. A. Young, "Increasing Returns and Economic Progress," *Economic Journal*, XXXVIII, 1928, pp. 527–42; John Jewkes, "The Population Scare," *Manchester School of Economics Studies*, X, 1939, pp. 101–21; P. K. Whelpton, *et al.*, *Forecasts of the Population of the United States 1945–1975*, Washington, D.C.: U. S. Gov't Printing Office, 1947, pp. 64–66; J. J. Spengler, "Measures of Population Maladjustment," reprinted from *Proceedings* of the XIV International Congress of Sociology, III, Rome, Italy, 1950.

[4] The argument that population growth stimulates invention is examined later.

limits, increments in a labor force tend to be accompanied by increments in the division of labor.[5] The increase in the division of labor in turn makes for both internal economies (i.e., those dependent on the size of individual business and plant units) and external economies (i.e., those dependent upon the aggregate amount of production taking place in the various parts of the economy). In other words, methods of production become more indirect and roundabout; complex processes give place to simpler ones; "industries" and "firms" become more specialized;[6] productive agents become more differentiated, with the result that more satisfactory combinations of productive agents are attainable; better spatial distributions of economic activities are possible; and so on.

Increases in the size of the labor force may increase what Adam Smith called "the extent of the market," making possible enough sales to permit realization of increasing returns through extensions of the division of labor. The resulting increases in income may in time stimulate a further growth of population and so facilitate a further extension of the division of labor. At any given time, however, there is a limit to the division of labor which is economic. For reasons indicated below in our discussion of the income-optimum population, a labor force of the size permitting a maximum division of labor will usually exceed that compatible with the maximization of output per head.

There is dispute concerning how many people and hence how many workers are essential to maximize returns per head from division of labor. For example, Jewkes estimates that a population of 20 million—i.e., a labor force of about 10 million—is sufficient to permit realization of "the full economies of large-scale production." P. K. Whelpton concludes that a population of 100–135 millions is sufficient to maximize output per head in the United States. If these inferences are valid, it follows that the populations of many countries

[5] The effects of an increase and a decrease in the size of the labor force are not symmetrical. Suppose that, after a 5 per cent increase in the labor force has been accompanied by a 3 per cent increase in the division of labor, the labor force declines 5/105 to its original size. The division of labor, if it diminishes as a result, will usually decline by less than 3/103; for rarely are all the original production, distribution, and income conditions restored.

[6] The terms "industry" and "firm" are here understood to include not only units engaged in the private production of goods and services but also public units similarly engaged. For example, the firm and industry concepts refer to collections of such activities as education, policing, and the work of governmental bureaus.

of the world are in excess of the size required to extend the division of labor to the point where, under existing conditions, per capita income can be maximized. M. Gottlieb has suggested, furthermore, that technological change is no longer operating, as in the nineteenth century, to increase the size of the labor force required to maximize the economies associated with division of labor.[7]

Ratio of the labor force to the total population.[8] This ratio is important because international and intertemporal differences in per capita income may largely be attributed to international and intertemporal differences in this ratio. For example, around 1940 Denmark's per capita productive power was about 50 per cent higher than that of Cuba and Chile because at that time Denmark's labor force was 51 per cent of its population, while in Chile and Cuba the corresponding percentages were respectively only 34 and 32. Again, per capita income was considerably higher in the United States in 1940 than in 1850 because in 1940 about 41 per cent of the population were in the labor force whereas in 1850 the figure was only about 30 per cent.

The significance of this ratio is reduced somewhat, however, by the fact that the number of hours a fully employed person works varies over time and from country to country. For example, while the gainfully occupied population of the United States increased from 7.7 millions in 1850 to 54.4 in 1940, the customary number of hours worked per week fell from about 70.9 to 45.4. Presumably, a part of the increase in the number of persons in the labor force is attributable to the decline in the number of hours employees are willing and able to work under present institutional arrangements. Similar differ-

[7] Some economies which are associated with population size may be realized not through an increase in population in a given country but through the consolidation of a number of smaller countries into one that is much larger in numbers and territory. This type of argument is found among those advanced in support of European Union or Federation.

[8] On the points discussed in this section see J. F. Dewhurst, *et al., America's Needs and Resources* (New York: Twentieth Century Fund, 1947); Jaffe and Stewart, *op. cit.*; J. D. Durand, *The Labor Force in the United States* (New York: Social Science Research Council, 1948); Gregorz Frumkin, "Pre-War and Post-War Trends in Manpower of European Countries," *Population Studies*, IV, 1950, pp. 209–40; C. D. Long, *The Labor Force in War and Transition: Four Countries* (New York: National Bureau of Economic Research, 1952); New York Joint Legislative Committee on Problems of the Aging, *Birthdays Don't Count*, (Newburgh, New York, 1948).

ences are found at the international level, where hours worked per week exceed the American figure by perhaps as much as 30 per cent, and the standard work week ranges, as a rule, from 40 to 48 hours.

The circumstances which account for international and intertemporal differences in the ratio of the labor force to the population may be variously classified. Long states that "the peacetime labor force, as a proportion of population standardized for demographic composition, has been highly stable over both the long and the short run." If one restricts the term demographic to sex and age composition, then the circumstances affecting this ratio, together with their effects, may be treated as follows: First, some essentially nondemographic, socio-economic factors make for the increase of this ratio, e.g., industrialization, urbanization, the expansion of tastes and wants, while others make for its diminution, e.g., rising output per man-hour, increases in the relative number of married women; second, the sex composition of the population can affect the ratio, but it usually exercises little influence since the relative number of males does not, as a rule, vary greatly in time or space. In countries experiencing heavy in- or out-migration sex composition and the ratio vary appreciably, for the fraction of the population enrolled in the labor force usually is much smaller among females than among males. For example, the percentage of the population reported economically active in the 1930's ranged, among females, from 9 in Spain to 52 in Roumania and the Soviet Union, and among males, from 58 in Turkey to 69 in a number of countries of western Europe.

Of greater significance than the two circumstances just discussed is age composition, since the extent to which individuals are enrolled in the labor force varies greatly with their ages. For example, the percentage of the English population aged 15–64 rose by one-sixth from 59.5 in 1841 to 70 in 1939, thereby permitting an increase, on this ground alone, of about one-sixth in per capita income. United States data may be utilized to illustrate the relationship between age and enrollment in the labor force. In 1940 about 95 per cent of all males aged 26–41 were enrolled in the labor force, while the proportion of those over 40 in the labor force varied inversely with age. For example, of those aged 49 to 51, only about 92 per cent were in the labor force; of those aged 59 to 61, about 85 per cent. Only 45 per cent of those aged 70 and only 17 per cent of those aged 80 remained in the labor force. A somewhat similar pattern is found in the female population. Whereas about 45 per cent of the native white females in their early 20's were members of the labor force in 1950, only 28 per cent of those aged 55 to 64 and 10 per cent of those aged 65 and over remained in the labor force. Data reported for a number of countries indicate that whereas about 95 to 98 per cent of males aged 20 to 64 are in the labor force, the corresponding range of percentages for the age groups 15 to 19 and 65 and over, respectively, approximated 36 to 91 and 30 to 86. This relationship between age and frequency of enrollment in the labor force has a double origin: Because of health and other personal conditions which vary with age, the relative number of persons who are employable declines as age increases beyond the 30's; because of institutional conditions (e.g., compulsory retirement provisions; because of arrangements which penalize employers who take on older workers), individuals in the upper age groups frequently are denied access to employment even though they are capable and efficient.

Variation in age composition may also affect income per capita in a way that is not directly connected with the ratio of the labor force to the population. The productivity of workers employed full time tends to decline somewhat after their ages have passed the 40's or the 50's. There often is a falling off in the worker's productive powers and perhaps also an increase in his involuntary absenteeism from work. Presumably, with continuing progress in the treatment of post-middle-age illnesses, the onset of this decline will be deferred and its rate of progress slowed down. If this occurs, the comparatively stationary and older populations of advanced industrial countries will be made economically more productive.

The percentage of the labor force actually employed.[9] This percentage obviously varies with the relative amount and type of employment. Unemployment may assume one of several forms: (1) normal, which includes seasonal, frictional, and similar types; (2) cyclical, which moves with the trade cycle; (3) structural, which com-

[9] See *Papers* of the Royal Commission on Population, III, London, 1950, pp. 39 ff.; B. Higgins, "The Theory of Increasing Under-Employment," *Economic Journal*, LX, 1950, pp. 257–74; Janet Fisher, "Postwar Changes in Income and Savings among Consumers in Different Age Groups," *Econometrica*, XX, 1952, pp. 47–70; Simon Kuznets, "Proportion of Capital Formation to National Product," *American Economic Review, Proceedings* XLII (2), May, 1952, pp. 507–26; A. C. Pigou, "Over-Employment," *Economica*, XVII, 1950, pp. 211–214.

prises the labor surpluses attached to particular industries and which originates from permanent declines in the demand for particular kinds of labor; and (4) persisting, general unemployment, arising out of a continuing deficiency in the aggregate demand for goods and services relative to the capacity of the society to produce these goods and services.

Population factors and changes may affect the level of employment either in particular ways or in an over-all way. Analysis of the direct impact of population growth upon structural unemployment presupposes a distinction between a country's population and the number of households or families found therein. In general, the aggregate demand for anything is conditioned by the number of consuming units which use it, together with the amount of purchasing power available per consuming unit, but some goods and services are used by individuals while others are used by households. Thus the response of the rate of change of consumption of "household-oriented" goods to population growth or decline will differ somewhat from that of "individual-orientated" goods. Since with population growth there is typically associated an increase in the number of relevant consuming units, growth tends to cushion the impact of forces making for a shrinkage of per capita demand and hence somewhat alleviates structural unemployment. Actually, structural unemployment can be reduced several per cent a year, other conditions being given, if the recruitment of workers by industries in which such unemployment prevails is prevented. Representative statistics reveal that death, disability, and retirement will remove 2 or more per cent per year of the membership of a body of workers of representative age composition.

Variations in the rate at which new members are added to the labor force may also affect the amount of cyclical unemployment. *Ceteris paribus,* booms tend to be intensified and prolonged by the availability of labor and curbed by its nonavailability, with the probable result that, under the former condition, cyclical unemployment tends to be greater than under the latter. Actually, of course, evidence of this tendency does not stand out in indices of cyclical unemployment, presumably because so many other cycle-influencing forces are at work. Then too, it is possible, when population pressure is great, that labor may be undervalued, or that it may be more difficult for employment-increasing forces to operate as effectively as when pressure is less pronounced. The likelihood of this outcome depends not so much on population pressure itself as on complexes of conditions usually associated with population pressure: inefficient economic institutions, relatively low rate of capital formation, a pre-dominance of agricultural employment, and so on.

Finally, spatial redistributions of population consequent upon changes in transportation and in methods of production generally stimulate investment, especially in housing, public utilities, and so on, and so tend to push up the level of employment.

The impact of population movements upon the level of employ-ment usually is treated in general Keynesian rather than in specific terms. It is argued thus: (1) The level of employment depends pri-marily upon the rate at which goods and services and hence labor are purchased for the satisfaction of consumption and investment re-quirements. (2) For full employment, the rate of purchase must be sufficient to keep something like 95 per cent of the labor force em-ployed. (3) A considerable fraction of net investment—perhaps as much as half—is oriented to population growth. (4) It is not likely that a change in the rate of population-oriented investment (conse-quent upon a change in the rate of population growth) will be com-pensated by a change in other forms of private investment, or by a change in the rate of consumption. Whatever likelihood there may be will be further diminished if, as some have held, the relative rate of consumption tends to fall with an increase in average income. (5) Therefore, in the absence of collective intervention, a change in the rate of population growth will be accompanied by a similar change in the aggregate rate at which goods and services are purchased and labor hired. (6) If the economy is technologically progressive, but not enough so that net investment at full employment will absorb net savings at full employment, there will, according to Higgins, "be a growing gap between the trend of potential income and the trend of actual income and increasing under-employment."

On the basis of these propositions it follows that mature economies with slowly growing populations will tend to be beset with under-employment and deflationary pressures. Developing economies with rapidly growing populations, on the other hand, will tend to be char-acterized by overemployment and inflationary pressures, provided that population growth operates to cause relatively large govern-mental borrowings and expenditures, or to depress the price of labor, or to stimulate private investment by increasing actual and prospective consumption and profits. If this conclusion is valid—and it will hold only where suitable institutional conditions are found—it follows that, in economies marked by considerable population growth, a tendency toward overemployment, i.e., an excess of jobs over men to fill these jobs, will mitigate, when it does not eliminate, cyclical, structural, and persisting unemployment. On the other hand, in economies marked by little population growth, the tendency toward increasing underemployment will intensify cyclical and persisting general unemployment and make more difficult the provision of jobs for the surplus of workers attached to declining industries.

How empirically valid the preceding line of argument is remains to be determined. In the past, perhaps because other circumstances have intervened, the level of employment has not been highly correlated with the rate of population growth. In addition, crucial proposition (4) does not receive much support from United States' experience, perhaps again because unanticipated circumstances have intervened. Indeed, it may be inferred that a decline in investment oriented to population growth will be accompanied by an increase in investment intended for the increase of per capita income, particularly since the supply of savings appears to limit the total volume of investment.

Despite the decline in the rate of population growth, the fraction of the national income devoted to capital formation has fallen while that going into consumption has increased. This trend is a consequence, not of the decline in the rate of population growth, but of a variety of changes which have taken place *pari passu* with this decline and the associated rise in per capita income (e.g., diminution in income-inequality; increase in the urban, employee, and other elements in the population among whom the disposition to save is relatively low; a greater rise in aspirations than in income; an increase in the ratio of liquid assets held relatively to income; changes in age composition; governmental policy; and so on). Thus, while an upward or downward shift in the level of population growth may create problems, it seems probable that the economy will finally become adjusted to the new level of growth under conditions permitting something like full employment. It follows from what has been said that a decline in the rate of population growth may or may not be accompanied by an increase in unemployment, and that a relatively high or rising rate of population growth may or may not be accompanied by a tendency toward overemployment.

Distribution of the labor force among occupations and industries. This distribution has two significant aspects for the present discussion: the state of technical advancedness of the labor force as a whole and, given some state of advancedness, the manner in which workers are distributed among the available occupations and employments. The first of these depends only slightly upon demographic factors. At the time of their birth children are socially undifferentiated, but they become progressively more differentiated as they pass through the selective meshes and presses of the social structure. Most important of these are the educational system and the set of occupational choices presented to the members of a society who must eventually enter the labor force. The set of occupational choices, together with the educational system, may be technically advanced and advancing, or technically backward and lagging. In the former case the initially undifferentiated children are transformed into a highly differentiated, skilled, and productive labor force. In the latter case there is differentiation, of course, but it is limited in amount, and it is not well calculated to produce a skilled and highly productive labor force.

If population pressure is great there will be only limited time available for the training of children and the formation of that kind of personal capital known as skill. Consequently, the development of a highly differentiated and productive labor force will be retarded just as will the formation of physical capital. However, even when population pressure is great, there probably exists a considerable range of choice respecting the relative amount of effort to be devoted to the formation of a more skilled labor force. In general, therefore, population pressure, together with a high rate of natural increase, limits the rapidity with which a skilled labor force can be developed; it does not usually determine the extent to which such development will be undertaken.

Turning to the distribution of the labor force, the question is whether workers are as well distributed among existing occupations as is economically desirable and feasible from the standpoint of society as a whole. An ideal, or optimum, distribution of workers does not exist so long as some workers would be more productive in employments other than those in which they are at present—in more technical terms, so long as the marginal product of labor is higher in some occupations and industries than in others net national product may be increased by the transfer of labor from less productive to more productive situations. As long as such transfers remain possible, "hidden," or "disguised" unemployment may be said to exist.

While hidden unemployment may conceivably exist in any industry, in relatively large volume it tends to be found in employments whose relative membership is declining, and in those which are relatively easy to enter either because the job requirements are not exacting or because artificial barriers to entry have not been erected. Agriculture is typical of the former category, and distributive and service trades of the latter. In advanced economies during and before the early nineteenth century approximately four-fifths of the labor force were in agricultural employment. Today it may engage as little as one-tenth of the labor force, and possibly even less in advanced countries that import considerable raw produce. In the underdeveloped parts of the world, by contrast, the agricultural population still comprises 70 to 75 per cent of the total. If, through the introduction of better agricultural methods and the removal of excess rural population, this fraction could be reduced to something like 30 to 40, per capita real income could be increased by at least 40 per cent. The increase in per capita income that might be realized through the removal of similar concealed unemployment in nonagricultural occupations, though only roughly determinable, appears to be very much smaller.[10]

Demographic factors also immobilize labor and contribute to its maldistribution. When a population is growing slowly or not at all, the ratio of persons newly entering the labor force to the total number gainfully employed is relatively low, making it more difficult to preserve a satisfactory occupational balance through the distribution of recruits to the labor force. Since institutional conditions surrounding the employment of older workers tend to reduce their mobility, an increase in the relative number of older workers may be accompanied by an increase in labor immobility and hence in occupational maldistribution. So long as the rates of natural increase are relatively

[10] See Colin Clark, "Australian Development in a World Setting," in *Looking Ahead*, August, 1951, pp. 8–11; also, *Conditions of Economic Progress*, 2d ed. (London: Macmillan & Co., Ltd., 1951), especially chap. 9; C. A. Anderson, *et al.*, "Intelligence and Occupational Mobility," *Journal of Political Economy*, LX, 1952, pp. 218–39.

high in households whose family heads are attached to unskilled, semiskilled, and other unfavorably situated occupational groups in agriculture or elsewhere, the recruits to these groups tend to be relatively numerous. A society's labor-distributing mechanisms rarely suffice to counterbalance this occupation-crowding effect of differential natural increase. For example, a relatively high rate of natural increase in the farm population may slow down the reduction of the overcrowding of agricultural employments. Similarly, a relatively heavy in-migration of unskilled and semiskilled workers may contribute to the overcrowding of the occupations into which they move. There may, however, be a tendency on the part of social scientists to overestimate the influence of differential natural increase; for the ratio of unskilled to skilled wages has risen significantly in the present century despite the persistence of reproduction differentials and advances in technology.

The occupational distribution of the labor force may also be conditioned by its racial composition and accentuated by racial differences in natural increase. This will the the case if membership in a given racial group operates for genetical reasons or because of prejudice, to make an individual's achievement of a relatively favorable occupational situation more difficult. If natural increase is greater in a group suffering disadvantage with respect to access to superior occupations, then occupations considered inferior will tend to be relatively more overcrowded and, as a result, per capita income will be lower than it otherwise would have been.

The qualitative composition of the labor force. Under this head fall the genetical, health, and educational composition of the population. Genetical composition is important in setting outside limits to a population's capacity for development in various directions, for the capacity of any individual to acquire or develop and exercise skills is conditioned by the physical and mental characteristics which he inherits through his parents. (Of course, whether an individual's inherited capacities eventually are effectively expressed hinges on his own experiences.) A population's genetical composition is affected by differential mortality, by differential fertility, and by societal restrictions placed upon mating. The selective influence of differential fertility and mortality probably is most pronounced after gross reproduction has started to fall and the population has begun to change from one that is relatively stationary at a high-natality level into one that is relatively stationary at a low-natality level. In the transition, group differences increase for a time, then diminish, until finally a new and somewhat different pattern of small relative differences is established. If these group differences produce unfavorable changes in the population's genetical composition, not only its potential but also its actual productive power may be reduced.

Health composition is important because it conditions the number of persons capable of being enrolled in the labor force, the number of days the representative worker can work during a year, and the amount of effort put forth each work day. While ill health everywhere reduces the volume of work and effort, its income-reducing effects are greatest in the underdeveloped countries.

Educational composition is important since income per worker is associated with degree of education. International disparity in per capita income is explainable in considerable part by disparity in educational attainments and its impact on the occupational structure. Educational composition, like age composition, also affects both saving and spending habits and thus the relative amounts in which different goods and services are produced. Per capita income is not likely to be affected, however, by these effects of education since, as long as the economy remains flexible, the pattern of production will presumably adjust to changes in consumption.

The amount of income-producing equipment per worker.[11] The movement of aggregate income is dominated by: (1) equipment or income-producing wealth; (2) technical and related forms of progress, such as increases in the division of labor; and (3) as has been shown, the magnitude of the labor force. Precise determination of the separate influence of any one of these factors is impossible. It has been estimated, however, that, with factors (1) and (3) constant, a 1 per cent increase in the amount of "capital" or income-producing wealth in use will be accompanied by an increase of around 0.25 to 0.35 per cent in aggregate net income. With factors (1) and (2) constant, a 1 per cent increase in the labor force will be accompanied by

[11] See J. Tinbergen and J. J. Polak, *The Dynamics of Business Cycles* (Chicago: University of Chicago Press, 1950), chaps. 1, 2, 10; Colin Clark, *Conditions of Economic Progress*, 2d ed. (London: Macmillan & Co., Ltd., 1951), chap. 11; E. C. Olson, "Factors Affecting International Differences in Production," *American Economic Review, Proceedings*, XXVIII (2), 1948, pp. 502–22.

an income increase of around 0.65 to 0.75 per cent. On the basis of these estimates and of the growth actually recorded in various national incomes, the forces included under (2) have been increasing national incomes in advanced countries something like 1 per cent per year.

Let us now make some assumptions that correspond fairly well with the experience of advanced industrial countries. Suppose a model country in which the productivities just described hold; in which population and the labor force increase about 1 per cent per year; in which, at full employment, national income is between a fifth and a quarter of the income-producing wealth in use; and in which this wealth increases 2 to 2.5 per cent per year, i.e., the population "saves" 10 per cent of the national income each year by transforming it into income-producing wealth. Under these circumstances the model country will increase in national income about 2.3 to 2.5 per cent per year (with technical progress contributing about 1 per cent, increase in the labor force about 0.7 per cent, and increase in income-producing wealth in use about 0.6 to 0.75 per cent). Had population and the labor force not grown, income per capita and per worker would have risen about 1.6 to 1.8 per cent per year. Instead, it only increased about 1.3 to 1.5 per cent.

Somewhat similar results were obtained by E. C. Olson in a study based on international comparisons. He found that a 1 per cent increase in the employed population was accompanied by only about 0.25 per cent increase in the national income; and that 1 per cent increases, respectively, in the total amounts of energy and livestock used, were accompanied by increases of about 0.5 and 0.25 per cent in the national income. The force of technical progress is reflected in the increase in the amount of energy utilized and possibly also in the amount of livestock units employed. Olson's study suggests that if the amounts of energy and livestock increased 2 per cent per year, per capita income would rise about 1.5 per cent, whereas if population also increased 1 per cent a year, per capita income would rise only about 0.75 per cent a year.

Population growth operates to depress the rate at which per capita income grows except when population is below the income-optimum in size. A country's population is of income-optimum size when its population is of such magnitude that, with other income-affecting conditions held constant, per capita income is as high as these other conditions permit. An increment in population may be accompanied either by an increment in the division of labor or by a decrement in the amount of equipment available per worker. So long as the first effect is greater than the second, population is below the income-optimum in size; it is the optimum size when the two effects just balance. Symmetrically, it is beyond income-optimum size when the second effect outweighs the first. Should the conditions held constant change favorably, e.g., should technology improve or the stock of capital increase, per capita income will rise, while the magnitude of the optimum may or may not change. The optimum will be increased only if, given these changes, an increase in population would make per capita income higher. Population growth may slow down the rate at which per capita income grows by increasing the number of persons among whom the benefits of an increase in wealth or an improvement in technology are distributed, and perhaps also by diminishing the rate at which wealth is increased. If a nation's wealth approximates four to five times its income and per capita income is not to fall, then a 1 per cent annual increase in population needs to be accompanied by an annual saving rate approximating 4 to 5 per cent of the national income. This saving rate would probably serve to increase per capita income about 0.3 per cent per year for some time if the population were to remain stationary.

The data presented above suggest that, given a 10 per cent saving rate and technological progress capable of increasing national income about 1 per cent per year, per capita income will increase only about 0.5 to 0.8 times as fast when a population is growing at an annual rate of 1 per cent as when it remains stationary. If, as is usually the case, capital formation is diminished by population growth (which absorbs resources that would otherwise have gone into capital formation), the decelerating influence of population growth will be even greater.

Our argument up to now has run like this: With population stationary and technical progress swelling national income about 1 per cent per year, a saving-investment rate of 10 to 12 per cent a year would put the rate of increase in per capita income at about 1.6 to 1.9 per cent. If population were growing at 1 per cent per year, the growth of total national income would rise to around 2.3 to 2.6 per cent while that of per capita income would be about 1 per cent less, or 1.3 to 1.6 per cent. Unfortunately, rates of this sort cannot long persist in a finite universe wherein compound growth is soon ended by many spatial, resource, and psychological limitations. For example, growth rates of 2.5 to 3.0 per cent per year would, in the course of a century, increase income 10.8 to 18.2 times. Therefore, the question arises: Can the raw material requirements implied by these growth rates long be met? Or will the supposedly increasing shortage of these materials make impossible the continuation for even a century of such growth rates?

The elements which compose a nation's income-producing wealth vary greatly with respect to augmentability. The labor component (perhaps 70 to 80 per cent) embodied in this wealth tends to keep pace with population growth, as do those elements which are abundant. But there remain elements for which suitable substitutes have not been found whose stock is fixed, depletable through use, or subject to markedly rising unit costs. The nonavailability of these elements on satisfactory terms will retard the growth of income even with population constant. If population should grow, there will be no compensatory offsets unless division of labor elsewhere in the economy is sufficiently increased by the increment in population.

Because of the rapid change experienced by advanced industrial societies, the empirical significance of what has been said is difficult to assess. For example, in advanced societies the relative importance of land is declining as a result of technological progress and the slowing down of population growth, yet 150 years ago the prospective shortage of arable land concerned economists and statesmen. Today, however, there is concern that the discovery of substitutes and cost-reducing technological improvements, together with the finding of new sources of supply, will not proceed rapidly enough to meet the vast and growing demands of expanding populations for higher incomes. Here it need only be indicated that growth of population makes more scarce the raw materials on whose use modern industrial society is built.[12]

State of technology and industrial arts generally. The contribution of technological progress to income growth is conditioned by a population's fundamental scientific attainments. About the influence of population growth upon scientific and technological progress there

[12] See *Resources for Freedom,* a Report to the President by the President's Materials Policy Commission, Washington, 1952.

is disagreement. Population growth, besides making possible greater division of labor, augments population density. This increase in density, it has been suggested, generates inventiveness through the intensification of social interaction, and the evocation of new needs. It is objected, however, that the relationship of population growth to technical progress is not so simple. A "need" will produce effects only if existing cultural conditions permit its appreciation. The extent and the impact of social interaction depend upon a people's culture, values, and methods of communication, as well as upon sheer numbers. Presumably a point is reached when the manner in which a population is distributed in space becomes more important for technical progress than does its size. Metropolitan populations may be more alert to inventive possibilities and developments and more receptive to their adoption because they are more specialized and perhaps more want-ridden than small-isolated-city and open-country populations.[13]

It is generally accepted that per capita income can continue to progress only in societies in which an effective "entrepreneurial" group, whether private or the agent of the state, exists and is relatively free to maneuver. While demographic factors do not have much to do with the size or the functioning of such a group, they may affect it indirectly. Insofar as class-reproduction rates are lower in the upper social strata than they are in the lower social strata, the relative numerical maintenance of entrepreneurial and similar upper groups requires considerable upward mobility, while their qualitative preservation requires some downward mobility. As a result, opportunity for advancement is continually provided, and ambition and incentive are strengthened.

Among the circumstances which generate social instability are both population pressure as such and whatever changes in population dimensions accentuate the spread between individuals' aspirations and their capacity to satisfy these aspirations. The dominant values in a society respond in various ways to population factors. When life expectancy is low, then, as Hobbes observed long ago, the time-horizons of men tend to be short and they value the present much more highly than the future, with the result that capital formation

[13] See R. K. Merton, "Science, Population, and Society," *Scientific Monthly*, XLIV, 1937, pp. 165–71; R. V. Bowers, "The Direction of Intra-Societal Diffusion," *American Sociological Review*, II, 1937, pp. 834–35.

and long-run economic planning are discouraged. Since responsible membership in a family group tends to elongate an individual's time-horizon, it can be argued that when the ratio of families to the population is relatively large the disposition, if not necessarily the capacity, to form capital will probably also be relatively large.

When natural increase by group varies greatly, with reproduction lower in the upper than in the lower social strata, (1) the values of a society may change considerably, with those of the relatively reproductive elements increasing in importance; (2) the society will be open and animated by the belief that there is room at the top; (3) the aspirations or objectives which men strive for will probably be such as to make for income-increasing activity;[14] (4) and if, as has been the case in advanced societies, there is also considerable internal migration, probably values conducive to interoccupational mobility and to economic flexibility generally are re-enforced, while those favorable to traditionalism are dissipated.

The distribution of economic activities in space. This is conditioned by distribution of population, just as that is conditioned by the distribution of economic activities. Some patterns of population distribution are more favorable than others to income production. Given a relatively static society, per capita income can be increased if individuals are ready to move from places where they produce and earn less to places where they can produce and earn more. Under these conditions a stable income-maximizing distribution of the population would presently be reached. Such a final distribution, however, is not likely to be reached in a dynamic society where the spatial distribution of economic activities and of population is greatly affected by technological and related forms of progress which necessitate further population movement. In general, such progress makes for reduction in the degree to which a population is rural or otherwise dispersed and for an increase in the degree to which it is urban and concentrated in metropolitan areas. Back of this tendency, which is not so pronounced in underdeveloped countries but very marked in advanced industrial countries, lie the various economies associated with the agglomeration of economic activities, such as the reduction of transport, communications, and related costs. Because of these economies, in-

[14] See Carson McGuire, "Social Stratification and Mobility Patterns," *American Sociological Review*, XV, 1950, pp. 195–204.

creases in per capita money income tend to be associated with conglomeration, though these increases may not prove so great as they appear when the noneconomic costs of conglomeration are taken into account.

When the spatial distribution of population differs significantly from that of economic activities, the former pattern of distribution tends to adjust to the latter. As a result there is considerable internal migration, which makes for fuller and more productive employment, since migrants, as a rule, move from lower to higher income areas. The volume of internal migration tends to fall as the distribution of population becomes better adapted to the distribution of economic activities in space, and above all, after the rural population has been reduced to minimal proportions. Even so, some migration persists since technological and related forms of change require a new distribution of economic activities in space and the rate of natural increase usually remains higher in rural and nonmetropolitan populations, where the cost of producing children and the ratio of aspirations to opportunity is lower.

The exchange relations obtaining between national economies. We shall consider here the relation between international exchange and international migration, the contribution that international exchange can make to the reduction of international disparity in income and economic development, and the dependence of growth in one country upon that in others.

The international exchange of goods and services is a partial substitute for the international movement of population which is indicated when the pressure of population upon resources is greater in some countries than in others, or when the industrial composition of population differs greatly among countries. International trade, like migration, not only would increase the production of goods on a world-wide basis but would also reduce international income inequality. In addition, it would be much less likely to depress real income in those countries which would be adversely affected by immigration. Actually, international migration can be used only in a limited degree to reduce international income disparity because the number of individuals willing and able to migrate is always relatively small and, should it increase appreciably, restrictive measures would probably be adopted in many countries. The greatest scope for migration is likely to be found in resource-rich areas peripheral to densely populated countries. Migration in such cases will contribute to the development of underpopulated lands because they will not have to bear the cost of reproducing, training, and equipping a suitable labor force.

International disparities in income and development can be most effectively reduced through diffusion of technological culture and international investment. There usually is little opposition to the diffusion of technology, differences in which account for much of international income disparity. International investment can contribute principally by acting as a catalytic agent in the diffusion of technological culture and setting strategic industries in motion. It cannot contribute much directly to the reduction of international differences in equipment per capita, for the amount of foreign investment a country can utilize is governed largely by the rate at which domestic capital is formed.[15] However, when international exchange is free and easy a country can readily adjust the composition of its capital structure to the requirements of economic development.

A considerable amount of international interdependence characterizes the economic development of nations. Each, as a rule, is not self-sufficient with respect to important raw materials and sometimes also capital. Small nations, furthermore, can maximize economies of division of labor only through the extension of international trade. It is probable, therefore, that the relationship between the members of representative pairs of economies is much more complementary than competitive. In such cases, the development of each depends upon that of the other, and the development of both depends upon the ease with which exchange can be carried on.

It is through international exchange relations that population growth in any one country makes itself felt in others. When the relationship is complementary, an increase in the population of one stimulates rather than checks the growth of population in the other. The relation is complementary when countries supply one another's re-

[15] It is enlightening to note that, according to R. W. Goldsmith's findings, foreigners had provided only about 14 per cent of the reproducible tangible wealth found in the United States in 1805, and that this percentage fell to 7 by 1850 and to 2 by 1912. Yet, in 1800–50, America's population was growing about 3 per cent per decade, land was good and plentiful, and natural resources appeared abundant.

quirements; it is competitive or substitutive when countries compete for sales and raw materials in the same market. This argument may be extended from the bilateral to the multilateral situation, and its validity would be demonstrated empirically in many instances were a larger number of smaller national states transformed into a smaller number of larger national states within which migration and exchange were free. In some instances, of course, a considerable redistribution of economic activities might take place if the barriers interposed at political boundaries were removed.

PATTERNS OF WORLD POPULATION

Characteristics of population types.[16] Because it is difficult to deal with a lengthy array of populations ordered according to some index of potential growth, it has become necessary to group populations with comparatively similar growth characteristics into a small number of classes. C. P. Blacker, for example, distinguished five pre-1940, population-growth types: high stationary, early expanding, late expanding, low stationary, and diminishing. A high stationary population is one marked by high birth and death rates which approximate each other, with the result that numbers are virtually stationary. An early expanding population is one in which natality is again high and comparatively stationary while mortality is lower and falling. A late expanding population is one characterized by falling birth and death rates, with mortality sometimes falling more rapidly and sometimes less rapidly than natality. A low stationary population is one in which mortality and natality are low and in approximate balance, with the result that there is little or no population growth. A declining population is one in which both the birth rate and the death rate are low, but the death rate is somewhat higher than the birth rate.

In the 1930's the high stationary type apparently was represented

---

[16] On the classification schemes and related materials presented in this section, see C. P. Blacker, "Stages in Population Growth," *Eugenics Review*, XXXIX, 1947, pp. 88–102; W. S. Thompson, *Plenty of People* (New York: Ronald Press, 1948); F. W. Notestein, "The Population of the World in the Year 2000," *Journal of American Statistical Association*, XLV, 1950; also, P. K. Hatt, *World Population and Future Resources* (New York: American Book Company, 1952). Table 3.1 is taken from "The Past and Future Growth of World Population— A Long Range View," *Population Bulletin*, issued by United Nations, No. 1 1951, pp. 1–2; Table 3.2 is derived from the *Demographic Yearbook*, issued at nually by the United Nations. Other materials are from this same source.

by the populations of China and several countries of Asia and Africa; the low stationary, by the populations of the United States, Australia, New Zealand, Tasmania, and northern and western Europe; and the declining, by France. The late expanding type was represented by the populations of the Soviet Union, Japan, Union of South Africa, southern and eastern Europe, Canada, Alaska, Argentina, Uruguay, Chile, Jamaica, and Guatemala; the early expanding type by populations of the rest of the world, i.e., most of those situated in Asia, Africa, and Latin America. In summary, the population of the world was distributed by types roughly as follows: high stationary, 22 per cent; early expanding, 40 per cent; late expanding, 22 per cent; low stationary, 14 per cent; declining, 2 per cent.[17]

Simpler classification schemes have been employed by W. S. Thompson, F. W. Notestein, and others. Thompson distinguishes three types of countries: (I) those in which population, while still growing slowly, is likely soon to stop; (II) those in which neither natality nor mortality has passed under "reasonably secure control"; and (III) those in which natality and mortality have been declining for some decades, with mortality declining relatively more rapidly. Notestein distinguishes three similar types. On the eve of World War II about 21 per cent of the world's population were assignable to each of Thompson's classes (I) and (III), while the remaining 58 per cent belonged in class (II).

On the basis of the experience of the past half dozen years two of Blacker's five categories may be eliminated, making his scheme similar to those of Thompson and Notestein. First, with DDT and various public health measures being introduced into many high-mortality countries, mortality is now falling nearly everywhere. Thus the countries formerly labelled "high stationary" belong in the early expanding group which now includes about 1.5 billion of the world's 2.4 billion people. Second, since 1940 mortality has fallen somewhat in countries which formerly were in the low stationary or the declining categories, while natality and natural increase have risen appreciably. These countries, therefore, need to be grouped in a category describable as "growing slowly," even though some have experi-

---

[17] In some countries population is imperfectly enumerated; in a larger number, births and deaths are inadequately reported and incompletely registered. It is difficult if not impossible, therefore, to report accurately the demographic state of a number of countries.

enced quite high rates of natural increase in the immediate postwar period.

It should be noted that when national populations are assembled in a small number of groups, regional, occupational, or other categories of each population may have characteristics and growth rates somewhat different from those representative of each group as a whole. Despite such difficulties, attempts to assemble the populations of the world into a small number of relatively homogeneous groups do make for expositive convenience.

In Table 3.1 a three-group classification of the world's populations is presented, while in Table 3.2 characteristics of several subcategories of these three groups are indicated. The major groups are (I) populations that have low growth potentials and, in many instances, are growing very slowly; (II) countries with high-growth potential populations; and (III) countries whose populations are in transition from a high-growth-potential state to one of low-growth potential. Within group (I) fall 20.2 per cent of the world's population, made up of the peoples of the English-speaking world and those of northwest-central and southern Europe. Group (III) contains 22.2 per cent of the world's population, made up of the peoples of Japan, Latin America, the Soviet Union, and eastern Europe. Within group (II) fall the remaining 57.6 per cent of the world's population, consisting of the peoples of Africa and Asia, exclusive of Japan.

Let us now consider the main characteristics of these three population groups. First, as the rates presented in column 2 of Table 3.1 indicate, during the past three decades the average annual rate of growth was about the same in groups (I) and (II) and higher in group (III). Second, the rates presented in columns 3 to 5 show that, in the absence of a considerable extension of life expectancy at birth, mortality will not decline further in group (I), whereas it will probably decline another three to six points per 1,000 inhabitants in group (III), and it may eventually fall fifteen or more points in group (II). On the mortality side, therefore, there is some potential for growth in (III) and much more potential in (II). Third, this distribution of potential is not wholly counterbalanced by the natality situation. In group (I) it is likely that natality will fall below the levels reported in column 3. Natality will decline also in groups (II) and (III), although for a time this decline may be slow in group (II). Thus the net growth potential of countries in (II) ap-

TABLE 3.1

WORLD POPULATION, GROWTH RATES, BIRTH RATES, AND DEATH RATES

Area	1950 Population (in millions) (1)	Annual Increase 1920–1950 (per thousand) (2)	Annual Rates, 1946-48 (per thousand)			Annual Rates, 1936-38 (per thousand)		
			Birth (3)	Death (4)	Natural Increase (5)	Birth (6)	Death (7)	Natural Increase (8)
World	2406	9	35-37	22-25	11-14	34-38	24-27	8-13
Low-Growth Potential (Type I)	486	9			10			5
N.W.-Cent. Europe	215	6	19	12	7	17	13	4
U.S. & Canada	166	13	25	10	15	17	11	6
So. Europe	92	9	23	12	11	23	16	7
Oceania	13	14	28	12	16	20	11	9
High-Growth Potential (Type II)	1387	8			12			7-13
Far East *	670	5	40-45	30-38	7-13	40-45	30-35	7-13
So. Cent. Asia	442	11	40-45	25-30	12-18	40-45	30-35	7-13
Africa	199	13	40-45	25-30	12-18	40-45	30-35	7-13
Near East	75	10	40-45	30-35	7-13	40-45	30-35	7-13
Transitional (Type III)	533	11			15			13-17
Soviet Union & E. Europe	287	7	28	18	10	30-34	17-21	11-15
Latin America	162	19	40	17	23	40-45	20-25	17-23
Japan	84	14	31	15	16	28	17	11

Source: United Nations.

* Excluding Japan.

pears to be very much higher than that of (I), and considerably higher than (III). This conclusion is borne out by a comparison of gross reproduction rates. In group (II) gross reproduction rates approach and even exceed 3.0 whereas, in group (I), they barely exceed 1.5. In group (III) countries, they may approach but will not often exceed 2.0. Fourth, comparison of the rates in columns 3 to 5 with those in columns 6 to 8 indicates that while mortality has fallen everywhere, natality has fallen only slightly in group (III) countries and hardly at all in group (II) countries.

It is roughly correct to say that natality and, until recently, mortality have been higher in many group (II) countries than in most of Europe's countries during the late eighteenth century. In eighteenth-century Scandinavia, which was roughly representative, the number of births per 1,000 inhabitants was in the low and middle 30's, while the number of deaths per 1,000 inhabitants was in the upper 20's. In Russia natality remained close to 50 per 1,000 in the nineteenth century while mortality averaged about 36. In the Balkans and portions of central Europe natality remained in the upper 30's and the lower 40's; mortality usually was in the middle and upper 20's. When the decline in natality in the group (II) countries gets under way, then, it will start from a level higher than that which prevailed in western Europe from 150 to 200 years ago. On the other hand, mortality will probably be lower in many group (II) countries than it was in early nineteenth-century western Europe.[18]

Data presented in Table 3.2 indicate considerable variation from group to group in the relative number of younger and older persons in the population. In group (I) countries the percentages of persons under 15 and over 59 are 25 to 30 and 10 to 14 respectively. The corresponding ranges are from 34 to 40 and 5 to 8 in group (III) countries and about 40 and 5 to 6 in group (II). Comparison of the relative number of persons aged 15 to 59 thus reveals the age composition of group (I) to be from 8 to 15 per cent more favorable to production than that of group (II). This is attributable in part to differences between the mortality of the two groups. In a life table population based upon a death rate of 12, the percentages of the population aged under 15, 15 to 59, and over 59, respectively, are

---

[18] In the United States, Thompson and Welpton estimate that natality declined from 55 per 1,000 inhabitants in 1800 to 20.1 in 1930; mortality, in Massachusetts, from 27.8 per 1,000 inhabitants in 1789 to 11.9 in 1928–31.

21.8, 60.1, and 18.1; in a life table population based upon a death rate of 23.1, these percentages become 41.1, 51.7, and 7.2.

How population types evolve.[19] Up to and including the eighteenth century, virtually all populations fell within the high-growth-potential category, though in western Europe natality was not quite so high as in present-day Asia and Africa, and in a few instances mortality seems to have been slightly lower. In the course of the nineteenth and twentieth centuries, populations situated in the European sphere of civilization which were subjected to the pressures of industrialization and urbanization underwent a number of transformations: (1) Age-specific fertility and mortality, together with crude natality, declined below eighteenth-century levels, often to less than half. (2) The age structure changed (the relative number of younger persons diminishing while that of older persons increased) and this change eventually re-enforced the impact upon natality of the forces making for a decline in age-specific fertility. (3) Intragroup differences in fertility for a time were intensified, since at first fertility declined relatively more in such groups as urban dwellers, professional families and the better educated. Then the factors making for family limitation became sufficiently diffused so that the diverging fertility pattern gave place to a converging one, and a comparatively stable pattern of small differences was again in process of being established. (4) Because the per capita demand for farm produce was comparatively constant (i.e., both price and income inelastic), improvements in agricultural methods caused the rural population to decline relatively and then absolutely. The associated drift of the population to towns and cities was accentuated by the development of urban and industrial employments, until today the number of potential emigrants in rural situations in most industrially developed countries is very small. (5) Because populations grew at different rates in different countries and because the multiplication of economic opportunities proceeded more rapidly in some countries than in

[19] On the methodology of population forecasting, including the projection of age-specific fertility and mortality and the handling of age-sex structure, none of which is treated directly in our discussion, see e.g., F. W. Notestein, *et al.*, *The Future Population of Europe and the Soviet Union*, League of Nations, Geneva, 1944. The works cited in footnote 16 deal with the subject of this subsection. We have used United Nations statistics and data compiled by R. R. Kuczynski in several of his many works.

others, the nineteenth and early twentieth century witnessed considerable international migration.[20] This was finally halted by restrictive legislation and a narrowing of differences between prospects at home and prospects abroad, as envisaged by potential migrants.

TABLE 3.2

WORLD POPULATION, AGE COMPOSITION, AND DENSITY, 1949

Area	Population (in millions) (1)	Age Distribution of Population (in percentages)			Persons (per sq. km.) (5)
		Under 15 yrs. (2)	15–59 yrs. (3)	60 and over (4)	
World	2378	36	57	7	18
Low-Growth Potential (Type I)					
N.W.-Cent. Europe............	214	24	62	14	78
U.S. & Canada................	163	25	64	11	8
So. Europe	91	30	59	11	88
Oceania	12	28	62	10	1
High-Growth Potential (Type II)					
Far East *	661	40	55	5	41
So. Central Asia	436	40	56	4	100
Africa	198	40	55	5	7
Near East	74	40	54	6	12
Transitional (Type III)					
Soviet Union & E. Europe	288	34	59	7	12
Latin America.................	158	40	55	5	8
Japan	83	37	55	8	223

Source: United Nations.
* Excluding Japan.

Not until well into the present century was the transformation between population types completed by any people but the French; it was not even effectively begun by any of the non-European peoples. At the opening of the twentieth century the west European and the English-speaking peoples were in transition, and other European peoples were beginning or about to begin the transition from a high-

[20] It is easy to exaggerate the role of migration. Around 1850 the annual number of emigrants from Europe formed about 0.1 per cent of the European population and, at the emigration peak around 1905–15, only 0.3 per cent. In the decades 1880–90 and 1900–10, immigration increased the population of the United States only about 0.9 and 0.7 per cent, respectively.

growth-potential state to one of low-growth-potential. With the exception of the Japanese, whose industrial progress placed them at the beginning of the transition, peoples in other parts of the world remained firmly in the high-growth-potential state. The first half of the present century, however, has seen many peoples besides the French complete the transition and a number move from the high-growth-potential into the transitional stage. Even so, the annual rate of world population growth continues to rise, moving from 0.29 per cent in 1650–1750, through 0.63 in 1850–1900, to 0.9 in 1920–50.

How much will a population grow in moving from a high-growth-potential to a low-growth-potential state, i.e., from one with natality in the 40's and mortality between 25 to 35 to one with natality appreciably under 20 and mortality in the neighborhood of 12 to 15? One approach is to consult the experience of countries which have undergone this transformation. The demographic history of Japan and of various European countries suggests an increase of at least 200, and possibly as much as 300 per cent. Logistic formulae suggest similar increases. Another approach is to note how fast mortality and natality have declined in the past and apply these rates of decline to particular countries. For example, G. J. Stolnitz, in an unpublished estimate, put recent Brazilian mortality and natality, respectively, at 25 and slightly over 45 per 1,000. Assuming that natality will fall gradually to 20 and mortality to 12 between 1950 and 2000, he concluded that the Brazilian population will increase from 52.1 millions to 100 millions by the year 2000, at which time it will still be increasing about 0.8 per cent a year.

In the past, both natality and mortality have declined most rapidly in those countries in which the decline began relatively late. In western Europe, once the decline got under way, the crude death rate typically fell, for sustained periods, one point every five to six years; the crude birth rate, a point every three to six years. In central and southern Europe where the decline began later, the crude death rate fell a point every three-and-one-half to four-and-one-half years, and natality a point every two to three-and-one-half years. In eastern Europe, where the decline began last, the crude death and birth rates declined still more rapidly. In New World countries, like Australia, New Zealand, the United States, and Argentina, the crude birth has fallen as much as a point every two to three years. Recently mortality declines averaging a point, more or less, every two years have been experienced in several parts of Asia, Africa, and Latin America. Accordingly, should the decline in natality not keep pace (and as yet it has not done so in much of Asia, Africa, and Latin America), natural increase may rise, at least for a time, to 1.5 to 3 per cent per year. In 50 years such rates of increase will augment a population by 111 to 338 per cent. Even a 1 per cent rate will increase it 64 per cent, and a 0.75 per cent rate will increase it 45 per cent in half a century.

According to a recent estimate made by United Nations demographers, between 1950 and 1980, the world's population will grow from 2,406 millions to between a minimum of 2,976 and a maximum of 3,636 millions, implying annual growth rates of approximately 0.75 and 1.375 per cent respectively. Table 3.3 presents the assumptions regarding growth rates for each population type which underlies this estimate. The first three columns give the actual growth rate per 1,000 experienced during 1920–50 and the high and low assumptions regarding future growth rates. The last three columns give the actual population in 1950 and the 1980 population that will result if the assumed growth rates are maintained. As a consequence of these different growth rates, the percentage which the initial low-growth-potential population forms of the world's total will decline from 20.2 to 18 to 18.4, while the initial transitional population will rise from 22.2 to 24.1 to 25.8. The high-growth-potential fraction will be little affected. If a longer period were under consideration and if the populations of all countries were developing a low natality, the proportions of the world's population falling in the low-growth-potential and the transitional groups would increase at the expense of the high-growth-potential share.

The socio-economic determinants of demographic evolution. How much a population will grow depends in part upon its age-sex structure and in part upon underlying socio-economic, growth-affecting forces. In the shorter run, the age-sex structure is important because it conditions the height of both crude mortality and natality. Crude mortality reflects the proportion of a population whose age-specific mortality is high, while crude natality reflects the relative number of women who are especially likely to bear children. In the longer run, however, changes in age-specific mortality and fertility, each of which is greatly influenced by underlying socio-economic forces, determine in considerable measure what the age-sex structure, along with crude natality and mortality, will be. It is to some of these forces that attention will now be directed.

TABLE 3.3

ACTUAL GROWTH RATES, 1920–50, POSSIBLE GROWTH RATES, 1950–1980,
AND ACTUAL AND PROSPECTIVE POPULATIONS, BY POPULATION TYPE

	Average Annual Rates of Growth (per thousand)			Population (in millions)		
		1950–1980 (hypothetical)			1980 (hypothetical)	
Area	1920–1950 (actual)	Low	High	1950 (actual)	Low	High
	(1)	(2)	(3)	(4)	(5)	(6)
World	9	7	14	2,406	2,976	3,636
Low-Growth Potential (Type I)..........	9	4	10	486	548	655
High-Growth Potential (Type II).........	8	7	13	1,387	1,710	2,043
Transitional (Type III)	11	10	19	533	718	938

Source: United Nations.

The forces which govern age-specific fertility and mortality and, through them, the growth of a country's population,[21] may be grouped into three categories: the physical environment that the inhabitants of a country or region have at their disposal; their capacity for exploiting this environment; and the level and content of their aspirations, together with the normative restraints placed around them. Each category is somewhat different now from what it was formerly. This is most strikingly and obviously true with respect to advanced industrial countries. It is also true in countries that have not undergone a great deal of change since the early nineteenth century. These countries also find themselves in a world quite different from that of a century ago, with the result that their aspirations, to some extent their environment-exploiting ability, and possibly even their physical environments, have changed.

Of minor importance, when considering the change in physical environment, is the fact that some natural resources, such as coal and iron, may have been mined until unit costs have begun to rise sig-

[21] Net immigration, which responds principally to potential migrants' anticipations respecting differences between income obtainable at home and income obtainable abroad, is disregarded since it contributes significantly to population growth only in recently settled lands.

nificantly. Of major importance is the fact that in most countries the amount of physical equipment at the disposal of the worker is much greater than formerly. For example, in the United States, R. W. Goldsmith estimates, the amount of reproducible, tangible wealth per head is now about seven times what it was in 1850. Similar changes, though of not quite the same magnitude, have taken place in many countries. Because of these changes, physical environments may be described as much more productive per capita than they were a century ago.

Capacity to exploit environment depends upon the state of technology and other determinants of the level of national income discussed earlier. In the advanced countries man has made and developed what Whitehead has called the greatest of his inventions, namely, "the invention of the method of invention." Of even greater importance is the vast reservoir of technological knowledge accumulated in the advanced countries which is available for those which are underdeveloped. If this reservoir is effectively tapped, it may become possible for the laggard countries to accelerate the rate at which their per capita incomes are growing, and to reduce greatly the spread between these incomes and those of advanced countries.

Increases in the capacity of underdeveloped countries to exploit their environment may affect population growth. First, as has been shown, it is very probable that mortality will decline more rapidly in these countries than it did in western Europe. Second, if the incomes of underdeveloped countries rise because their capacity to exploit the environment has grown, this increase in income will be accompanied by some increase in numbers unless their aspirations undergo completely offsetting modification. In most countries an increment in income tends, after a lag of time, to be devoted in some part to the reproduction and rearing of more children. As a result, natality rises and population growth is stimulated, but not enough to decrease per capita income. Unfortunately, however, considerable population growth appears to take place independently of a prior rise in income and so may lead to a decline in per capita income, except in those countries whose populations are below the income-optimum to start with.

Whereas the changes that have taken place in man's physical environment and in his capacity to exploit this environment have made for population growth, the changes that have taken place and are taking place with respect to man's aspirations and norms may eventually run counter to population growth. As yet, however, the precise impact of these changes is not clear. Incomes have risen in many countries and, for this and other reasons, natality has increased greatly. Aspirations and incomes do not change at the same rate, however, with the result that in this interval of lag, natality may first rise only to decline after aspirations have caught up with and passed income. This may be what is happening in postwar United States, for example. The aspiration adjustment process thus bears some resemblance to the process which underlies the upward adjustment of consumption following a rise in per capita income.

The aspirations and expectations of populations, together with the norms limiting the objectives which may legitimately be pursued and achieved, were somewhat differently generated in the nineteenth century when western European countries were in transition from a high- to a low-growth-potential state. Then, production dominated consumption, innovators concerned themselves primarily with production, and increases in income were brought about by the entrepreneurial class's implementation and exploitation of the environment. Since at that time income was higher in these western European countries than elsewhere, upward pressure against the existing level of aspirations had to originate largely in the urban and industrial cultures with which the rises in income were associated.

A quite different situation is at present arising in underdeveloped countries with high-growth-potentials, especially among the masses of the population. The ratio of their aspirations to their incomes often is much higher than was the case in nineteenth-century western Europe, and this ratio is being pressed still higher by a variety of circumstances. The populations of these countries live in a world that includes high-income peoples, and many members of low-income populations are aware of how well high-income peoples live. This is impressed upon them by their political leaders, anticipators of a brighter tomorrow, exponents of domestic and world revolution, and by a variety of national and international media of communication. Among the low-income peoples the attitude is developing that they have the right and the power to live very much better materially. In the low-income countries, therefore, as H. C. Wallich suggests, consumption is coming to dominate production.

As a result of these developments, two of the functions performed by the state are emphasized: (1) facilitation of capital formation and the introduction and diffusion of technological knowledge and its adaptation to local circumstances; (2) insurance that consumer's goods and services will be equitably distributed. As a consequence, the probability of inflation is greatly increased through private credit creation and government spending of more money than it takes in. This inflation, if accompanied by relatively full employment, is likely in turn to induce wage increases, especially among scarce, skilled workers and among those receiving relatively low wages, with the result that money wages outstrip real wages even though the inflation stimulates production.

What has been said may be reduced to this: The aspirations of the populations living in underdeveloped countries will be under continuing upward pressure from many sources. These pressures will be reinforced by urbanization as industrialization proceeds. While rural populations are not immune to forces making for rising aspirations, city milieus seem to intensify them. If an expanding labor organization is coupled with governmental intervention, the share of the national net product going to the masses may be increased unless firmly established ruling groups are able to appropriate much of the country's product for capital formation or the development of military strength. It is not likely, in any event, that income growth can keep pace with the growth of aspirations. Instead, aspirations will be apt to press ahead of income, and as a result the disposition to regulate family size will be widely diffused and strengthened.

Increases in the disposition to regulate family size, however, are not likely by themselves to produce a marked decline in natality even though folk methods of birth control are fairly effective. In addition, effective and suitable means for the control of births must be widely distributed. This may well be undertaken by governments in most of the high-growth-potential countries. These countries appear to be largely free of religious influences opposed to birth control, the principal exceptions being parts of Latin America and countries in the presently anti-Malthusian, Communist orbit. Moreover, the heavy expenditures required by social legislation will put those governments under pressure to reduce natality since some expenditures may thus be avoided.

Demographers have supposed that high-growth-potential countries would undergo transformation into low-growth-potential countries only under the impact of industrialization, urbanization, rising incomes, the spread of education, and the infusion of foreign standards. Even then it was argued that the transformation would proceed so slowly that population would increase by 200 or more per cent. Should this be the case, the 1.5 billion who are in a high-growth-potential state might increase to 4.5 to 5 billions in the next hundred years, assuming that enough income could be provided to prevent starvation. We can now see, however, that rising aspirations and state intervention in support of birth control may keep population growth lower than has been anticipated in the underdeveloped, high-growth-potential countries. If the populations of countries now in the transitional stage are likewise affected, their completion of the transition may also be accompanied by less growth than has been supposed. The likelihood of this slower growth occurring is increased by the fact that rural populations seem to be much more willing to regulate their numbers than has been supposed. The final answer still depends, however, upon the extent to which the State intervenes in support of birth control. Concerning the slowly growing populations the prospect is also unclear, though here it appears likely that rising aspirations will presently catch up with improvements in income and stabilize growth at a very low level.

Even on the assumption that the forces making for birth control are strengthened in the manner indicated, considerable population growth is apt to occur in the present century. Given only an over-all 1 per cent increase in the next half century, the world population will still grow to about 3.9 billion by the year 2000; even at a minimum rate of 0.75 per cent, it will reach nearly 3.6 billion. Such growth raises an additional problem. Will this increase of 1.2 to 1.5 billion be accompanied by changes in the age structure and in age-specific mortality and fertility of a sort to insure relative population stability? If not, population will continue to grow, and the Malthusian problem will remain inadequately solved.

POPULATION PATTERNS AND THE REQUIREMENTS OF ECONOMIC PROGRESS[22]

In this section attention will be concentrated upon the probable impact of population growth on countries falling in the high-growth-

[22] On the subject of this section, see M. K. Bennett, "International Disparities in Consumption Levels," *American Economic Review*, XLI, 1951, pp. 632–49;

potential group.[23] This group has a population of at least 1,450 millions and includes the countries specified in Table 3.1, together with a number in Latin America. In most of these, real income per capita and (but in lesser measure) various indicators of per capita consumption are very low. Educational attainment is low; health conditions remain poor; infant mortality is relatively high; life expectancy is much below European levels; and in many countries, especially in Asia and Northern Africa, food consumption per capita is qualitatively and quantitatively inadequate. The percentage of the population and labor force that is agricultural ranges between 60 and 75, which is greatly above the 20 to 33 level found in low-growth-potential countries. The urban portion of the population is only one-fourth to one-half as great as in Europe and America; the labor force is much less advanced and differentiated, and the average worker has at his disposal only a small fraction of the productive wealth available to workers in advanced countries.

The existence of pronounced population pressure in many of the high-growth-potential countries and its prospective intensification will augment the role of the state and make necessary great improvements in its bureaucracy and the control devices employed. Although the immediate problem in many of these countries is largely one of adopting and adapting production methods devised abroad, most of them lack a powerful entrepreneurial class. Thus major responsibility for the entrepreneurial function will probably fall upon the state.

Colin Clark, *Conditions of Economic Progress*, 2d ed. (London: Macmillan & Co., Ltd., 1951); Joseph J. Spengler, "Aspects of the Economics of Population Growth," *Southern Economic Journal*, XIV, 1947–48, pp. 123 ff., 233 ff., "The Population Obstacle to Economic Betterment," *American Economic Review*, Proceedings, XLI (2), pp. 343–54, and "Economic Factors in the Development of Densely Populated Areas," *Proceedings* of the American Philosophical Society, XCV, 1951, pp. 20–53; Kingsley Davis, "Population and the Further Spread of Industrial Society," *ibid.*, pp. 8–19. Much information has been assembled by the United Nations, World Health Organization, and other international bodies, some of which has been summarized in a *Preliminary Report on the World Social Situation* to the United Nations Economic and Social Council, April 25, 1952.

[23] The impact of population growth in the slowly growing and the transitional countries will be largely disregarded since their per capita incomes are much higher than those found in the high-growth-potential countries and are continuing to rise; since their growth is, or soon will be, under effective control; and since, with the exception of Japan and of Europe (where population growth is under effective control), they are not suffering from pronounced land shortage (see Table 3.2, col. 5).

Persisting capital shortage will probably force the state to intervene in support of capital formation while the rising aspirations of the masses may stimulate state action in support of a more even distribution of consumer goods. Because the state will be hard put to satisfy both these competing demands for resources, and because population growth tends to accentuate both types of demand, the state may well seek a partial solution in the sanctioning and the eventual dissemination of birth control as India already appears to be doing.

The decline in the relative importance of land and agriculture already experienced by some low-growth-potential countries has not been duplicated in the high-growth-potential countries. While inadequacy in the food supply is common in these countries, relief in the form of land is not available, especially in the face of further population growth. In parts of Africa and Latin America, land to accommodate further population growth is to be found in significant quantity, but this is not the case in Asia. Nor is it likely that Asia can augment its food supply appreciably through international trade, for world food production is limited by lack of land, and it is difficult to distribute much of what is produced through longer-distance international trade.[24] Continuing population growth, therefore, may make it extremely difficult to improve the quality and the per capita quantity of food available in Asia as well as in selected parts of Africa and Latin America. Nonetheless, this does not mean that the labor force in agriculture cannot be greatly reduced. The food supply depends upon the number of acres under cultivation and the yield per acre, and these depend only in part upon the man-land ratio. It does mean, however, that a rising income in countries that are

[24] In 1947, O. E. Baker, the distinguished geographer, estimated the portion of the world's land area "physically suitable for crops" at 6 to 7 million square miles, of which 4 already were in use. Bringing these into cultivation and increasing yields generally about 50 per cent per acre would increase production about 75 per cent. R. M. Salter estimated that to the 2 billion acres in crops there could be added about 1.3 billion more, distributed as follows: 900 million in South America and Africa, 300 in the northern part of North America and the Soviet Union, and 100 in Sumatra, Borneo, New Guinea, and Madagascar. Baker's estimate thus suggests that world crop acreage cannot be raised above 4.5 billions, a figure which is above Salter's. Styles of living encountered in the Western World probably will always call for at least an acre of utilizable land per person. See O. E. Baker, "The Population Prospect in Relation to the World's Agricultural Resources," *Journal of Geography*, XLVI, 1947, pp. 203–20; R. M. Salter, "World Soil and Fertilizer Resources in Relation to Food Needs," *Chronica Botanica*, XI(4), 1947–48, pp. 227 ff.

heavily-peopled and land-short apparently cannot be accompanied by a great improvement in the quantity and the quality of the representative diet. The increment in income will have to be spent otherwise. Only in parts of Africa and Latin America, apparently, can population growth be accompanied by continuing and significant improvement in the per capita food supply.

Of equal importance is intensification of the problem of capital formation caused by continuing population growth in high-growth-potential countries. Resources will be needed not only to equip increments in population but also to enable the peoples living in these countries to use the methods of production, administration, education, training, and so on, which have been developed in advanced countries. Suppose that in order to maintain per capita income in the face of a 1 per cent increase in population, the required real savings or capital formation, comes to 4 per cent of the national income. If the population were to increase by 2 per cent a year, as is now the case in many of these countries, a saving rate of 8 per cent would be required. In order to increase per capita income by 1 to 3 per cent with population constant, a saving rate of 4 to 12 per cent would be required. On the basis of these estimates, a combination of 2 per cent increase in population with 3 per cent increase in per capita income would require a savings rate of about 20 per cent. In most of the high-growth-potential countries, however, the actual savings rate is very low, averaging only about 5 per cent for the whole group in 1949!

Other methods yield even higher required rates of savings. For example, a United Nations study which aims at an annual increase in per capita income of 2 per cent, with an assumed population increase of 1.25 per cent a year, lists direct capital requirements for agriculture and industry alone at approximately 19 per cent of aggregate income.[25] With somewhat different assumptions, one gets, for the whole group of high-growth-potential countries, required savings rates of 32 per cent for 1950, 15 to 19 for 1975, and 7.5 to 12 for 2000. The assumptions used are population growing 1 per cent per year; per capita income rising 3 to 4 per cent per year; allowance of $2,500 over a fifty-year period to move each excess worker out of agriculture; allowance of a 2 per cent per year increase in the capital

[25] *Measures for the Economic Development of Under-Developed Countries* (New York: United Nations, May, 1951), especially Chap. 11.

equipment available for all other workers, with initial equipment per worker estimated at $500. The required savings rate would be appreciably lower with a stationary population; but even so, it would be high compared with the savings rates found at present in many of the high-growth countries.

The prospective contribution of international exchange to the development of high-growth-potential countries is limited but real. It can scarcely contribute greatly to the permanent alleviation of food deficits, but it can facilitate the external purchase of equipment and services required for development, at least within the limits imposed by the salability[26] of domestically produced goods and by the capacity of the underdeveloped countries to borrow and utilize foreign capital. This last point depends on the conditions surrounding the borrowing and on the rate of domestic savings which limits the utilization of foreign capital. It has been suggested that if the underdeveloped countries require 20 billion dollars of capital annually and furnish only 6 billion dollars themselves, the low-growth-potential nations could make up the difference by saving 4 per cent of their incomes. It is questionable, however, if effective use can be made of foreign capital in amounts greater than the amount of domestic savings; in fact, the effectiveness of even such an amount is doubtful.

During the past 150 to 200 years, international income disparity has been greatly accentuated by the unequal development and spread of technological culture, together with a growing international inequality in disposition and capacity to save. Before 1800, product per man-hour in the most advanced countries was perhaps 5 times that found in the least advanced countries. By now this multiple may exceed 40. Can this trend be reversed and disparity reduced? In order to see whether an affirmative answer is possible, suppose that per capita income rises 1 to 1.5 per cent a year in advanced countries and 2.5 to 4 per cent in the underdeveloped countries. Suppose further that per capita income in the most advanced country is about twenty-five times larger than in the least advanced country. This multiple would decline to 1.35 if, for a period of 100 years, per capita income rose each year by 4 per cent in the underdeveloped and only 1 per cent in the developed countries. If the two rates of growth were 3 and

[26] In the immediate future the situation of many high-growth-potential countries will be made more favorable to domestic capital formation by the improvements in the terms of trade of raw-material exporting countries.

1, the multiple would become about 3.5; if they are 1.5 and 2.5, it becomes 9.4.

Can these hypothetical patterns be translated into reality? The underdeveloped countries should be able to advance their per capita incomes faster than did the presently developed countries, for they need only adapt to the solution of their problems the technical and social means which have been successfully utilized elsewhere, and it is probably much easier to adapt than to invent and innovate. If this is the case, per capita incomes may rise in the underdeveloped countries at a rate of 50–100 per cent above that experienced in western Europe and America, i.e., they may advance for a sustained period of time at 2.5–3.5 per cent per year. Advances of this order of magnitude are not likely to be realized, however, if resources are converted into population instead of being used to transform simple labor forces into bodies of highly trained and differentiated workers and make available domestically that capital into which the technological attainments of advanced societies have been incorporated. It is principally in parts of Africa and Latin America that numbers appear to be too few and in which, consequently, per capita income has the best chance of growing rapidly.

CHAPTER IV

The Work Force

CHARLES D. STEWART*

INTRODUCTION

FOR THE UNDERDEVELOPED COUNTRIES THE PATTERN AND THE MAGNItude of the task of economic development is vividly illustrated by the changes required, if the industrialization of other countries is a guide, in the reallocation of labor.

The work force in the underdeveloped countries is largely attached to agriculture where its employment, at the existing level of technology, yields at best subsistence returns. By way of contrast, the highly developed countries typically devote a relatively small part of their labor input to primary production of foodstuffs, with most workers employed in the production of other goods and services for a growing market sustained by demands generated by a rising level of real income and domestic capital requirements. Thus, economic development in its labor aspect is seen as a task of shifting workers from agricultural to industrial or commercial employments; this involves, once development is initiated, the retraining and reallocation of individuals or, in a gradual process of change over generations, the training of new generations for work in other than traditional employments.

The experience of the United States is spectacular but not atypical. Agricultural workers comprise less than one-fourth of the work

* Assistant Commissioner, Bureau of Labor Statistics, United States Department of Labor. Coauthor (with A. J. Jaffe): *Manpower Resources and Utilization*; author: "The Definition of Unemployment," *The Review of Economics and Statistics* (February, 1950); "Labor" in *Government Statistics for Business Use* (Hauser and Leonard, eds.); "Employment Statistics in the Planning of a Full-Employment Program," *Journal of the American Statistical Association* (September, 1946) (with Loring Wood); "The Redistribution of the Labor Force" in *Economic Reconstruction* (S. Harris, ed.).

force in the more advanced industrial countries of Europe, North America, and Oceania; the percentage has declined persistently during the last 100 years, and continues to drop, in all countries where marked improvement in real incomes has occurred. In the United States, as recently as 1870, more than 50 per cent of the work force was attached to agriculture, forestry, and fishing; approximately 7 million of the country's less than 14 million work force were so engaged. During a period of rapid population growth in the next forty years, the number of such workers increased to about 12 million, but declined in relative importance to about 30 per cent of the work force. Since World War I, with marked gains in output per man and per acre resulting from progressive advances in technology, the agricultural work force decreased in absolute and relative size. By 1950 fewer than 8 million persons, representing less than 13 per cent of the work force, were required for a greatly expanded volume of agricultural production.

Except for a few notable instances, little changes have occurred in the last eighty years in the ranking of countries by degree of industrialization, if we use the agricultural work force ratio as an index of industrialization. Great Britain, a special case because of her dependency on imports for foodstuffs and raw materials, ranked first with a ratio of 12.3 in 1881 and 4.9 in 1951.[1] Belgium, the Netherlands, and Switzerland, with relatively low ratios (20- to 30 per cent) before the turn of the century, have further reduced their ratio of labor input in agriculture, and still rank high on the scale of industrialization. France, Denmark, Sweden, Finland, Austria, and Hungary also substantially reduced the role of agriculture in their economic life during this period. Relatively small changes were experienced in Italy, Ireland, and Norway and presumably in other countries for which data are not available. The United States and Germany made the largest gains during the period; Australia and New Zealand, with relatively low ratios in 1881, held their own on the industrial scale with further reductions in the percentage of the work force engaged in agriculture. Of the two late starters, Japan reduced its ratio in the course of industrialization from 84.8 in 1872 to 47.5 in 1950; and Russia reduced its percentage of workers in agriculture from 81 in 1926 to 57.8 in 1939.

[1] Data are generally not fully comparable but are sufficiently valid for illustrative purposes.

On the other hand, little if any change has occurred in the industrial allocation of the work force in the countries generally characterized as underdeveloped. Their agricultural work force ratios are generally as high or higher than the present industrial leaders were about 100 years ago, although not greatly dissimilar from those of Japan, Russia, Finland, Sweden, Hungary, and others which by reason of geography of special circumstances have since come within the orbit of industrialization. For large parts of Asia, Africa, and South America, agriculture continues to absorb the efforts of two-thirds or more of the work force. In China, Malaya, the Philippines, and other Asiatic countries, 60 to 70 per cent work in agriculture. India alone has twice as many agricultural workers as there are persons in the total labor force in the United States. (Latest data for India, for 1930, show over 100 million persons in agriculture, or 67 per cent of

TABLE 4.1

PER CAPITA INCOME AND PERCENTAGE OF WORK FORCE IN PRIMARY, SECONDARY, AND TERTIARY INDUSTRIES, FOR SELECTED INDUSTRIALIZED AND NONINDUSTRIALIZED COUNTRIES, 1925–1934 *

| Country | Income per capita (dollars) | Distribution of Work Force | | |
		Primary†	Secondary† (percentages)	Tertiary†
United States	525	19	31	50
United Kingdom	425	6	44	50
Australia	392	24	30	46
Netherlands	358	21	39	40
Germany	290	24	39	37
France	287	25	40	35
Sweden	287	32	29	39
Chile	248	37	28	34
Greece	180	44	34	22
Japan	159	50	20	30
Italy	154	43	31	26
USSR	152	74	15	11
India	90	62	15	23
China	49	75	5	20

* Selected data from Colin Clark, *Conditions of Economic Progress* and *Economics of 1960*, as adapted by Louis H. Bean, "International Industrialization and Per Capita Income," *Studies in Income and Wealth* (New York: National Bureau of Economic Research, 1946), Vol. VIII.

† Primary industries are defined by Clark to include agricultural, pastoral, fishing, and hunting industries. Secondary industries include manufacturing, electric power production, mining, building, and construction. Tertiary industry is defined as all other economic activities.

the work force at that time.) In South and Central America, according to census data for 1940, Brazil, Mexico, Peru, and Colombia taken together had 18 million agricultural workers out of a total of 27 million. For Africa, the data are particularly scanty. Egypt, however, reported 65 per cent of its workers in agriculture in 1947. Spain, Portugal, and Ireland report one-half of their work force in agriculture, and Turkey three-fourths.

The promise held out before the underdeveloped countries by the experience of the industrialized countries is a rising level of per capita income and, in consequence, the solution of a whole range of social evils associated with poverty. The relationship between industrialized economic structures and high per capita income is conveniently summarized in statistical form from estimates published by Colin Clark.

ROLE OF THE WORK FORCE IN ECONOMIC DEVELOPMENT

Except for entrepreneurial strata whose function pre-eminently is that of initiating changes in the structure of production, the work force ordinarily is not an active agent in the process of change. Economic development, however, is conditioned by the character of the work force and by the response of workers to innovations, large and small, which lead to more efficient production and increase real income; it is not at all possible without adaptation in attitudes, vocational skills, and as we have seen above, in the structure of the work force. While by definition the work force includes scientists, businessmen, public officials and others, it is convenient for present purposes to consider the work force in a more limited sense. The role of science, entrepreneurship, and the state in decisive aspects of economic development is discussed elsewhere in this volume. Too sharp a line, however, should not be drawn between these specialized strata and the remainder of the work force. Industrialization transforms the whole social structure with the result that there is growing mobility, potentially at least, between occupational and social classes.[2] Broader access to education facilitates the flow of talent into scientific research, technology, and business and governmental administration. Since shortages of trained personnel at all levels in these

[2] See P. A. Sorokin, "Social Mobility," *Encyclopaedia of the Social Sciences* (New York: The Macmillan Company, 1934), and Alex Inkeles, "Stratification and Mobility in the Soviet Union," *American Sociological Review*, August, 1950.

fields is a serious handicap to economic development, the problem of recruitment and training of such workers is an important if specialized task in the field of manpower administration.

Relation to strategic factors in economic development. In the sense of the mass of workers available for gainful employment under the direction of entrepreneurs or the State, the work force plays various roles (other than providing manpower as such) in economic development. The role may be one of active or passive resistance to changes in techniques that disturb existing work arrangements or patterns of social life. Such negative reactions, especially where they take overt and perhaps violent form, are more likely to attract the comment of contemporaries and historians than attitudes of passive acceptance; it is difficult to say whether a neutral, disinterested response is the more typical. Since history has not been free of exploitation it is to be expected that workers often have been suspicious and less than enthusiastic in their reception of change; to them, no less than to others, change represents the unknown and carries risk.

On the other hand, the response may be affirmative in nature and favorable to economic progress. Hunger, the breakdown of the old system, and the desire to escape the restraints of traditional authority often provide a push favorable to the recruitment of labor to new forms of enterprise.[3] Rational appraisal of the advantages of changes in production and the utilization of labor can provide a pull eliciting the active, enthusiastic, and constructive acceptance by workers of changes making for economic advances. Such an attitude and behavior depends upon some degree of literacy and economic understanding and, more important, upon conditions of confidence that new ways are not simply new ways of exploitation.

In the Western World the growth of the modern labor movement accompanying industrialism gave voice and a sense of responsibility and power, if not mission, to industrial workers. The conviction of exploitation gave rise to theories of class conflict accompanied, however, by appreciation of the superiority of the new forms of economic organization and acceptance of the potentialities of technology and large-scale production.[4] Greater equality of bargaining strength, to-

[3] See Wilbert E. Moore, *Industrialization and Labor* (Ithaca: Cornell University Press, 1951), pp. 77–105 and 304–8.
[4] See Eduard Heimann, *History of Economic Doctrines* (New York: Oxford University Press, 1951), pp. 152–56.

gether with social legislation, provided the basis for belief in the possibility of workers sharing the gains in productivity of the new system. Where the labor movement became mature, secure, and articulate, it became interested in sharing responsibility for national economic policies. For the less advanced countries, the facts of the historic rise in the level of living of the masses of workers in industrialized countries provide a model and an enticement.

Interrelation of changes in economic structure. The work force is not something independent or separate from the society of which it is a part. Deficiencies in the work force—illiteracy, lack of training and skills, unfavorable attitudes toward work or suspicion of change —limit the rate of industrial progress; they are at the same time consequences of the entire social milieu associated with the existing stage of economic development. Where industrial efficiency is low, the level of living is correspondingly low, not only in terms of family consumption but also in terms of health and education, public facilities, and adequacy of governmental machinery. Such countries also tend to have high birth and mortality rates. Industrialization with its higher productivity carries with it a complex of cultural characteristics, including urbanization, literacy, increased consumption and improved health and vitality, more leisure in the course of the individual life span, more effective governmental apparatus and, on the basis of available evidence, low fertility.[5] Thus industrialization, once initiated, contributes automatically to the creation of a labor force better fitted to meet the needs of modern production and in turn to contribute to increased productive efficiency.

In many respects economic development is a bootstrap operation; once started it becomes self-generating and self-supporting. Because capital is so crucial in the initial steps setting this process in motion, underdeveloped countries historically have been tempted to accept varying degrees of foreign domination in return for capital investment. The character of possible investment, in the early stages, is limited by the relative scarcity of capital in relation to labor in the

[5] See Frank W. Notestein, "The Reduction of Human Fertility as an Aid to Programs of Economic Development in Densely Settled Agrarian Regions," in *Modernization Programs in Relation to Human Resources and Population Problems* (New York: Milbank Memorial Fund, 1950), particularly pp. 95–100, and A. J. Jaffe and Charles D. Stewart, *Manpower Resources and Utilization* (New York: John Wiley & Sons, Inc., 1951), pp. 402–14.

overpopulated countries as well as, more generally, the lack of trained work force in the absence of technical education and pre-existing employments that called for and developed such a work force. Similarly low incomes and low rates of internal capital accumulation, inadequate purchasing power to support consumers' goods industries, absence of an organized labor movement and other concomitants of a higher state of development pose difficulties in the path toward an "internally dynamic organization of industrialism." Broader distribution of the fruits of economic progress appears to be a necessary condition for maximum growth of per capita income in industrialized society, in terms both of creating an expanding domestic market and providing incentives to workers to respond favorably to changes in traditional patterns of work. High profits and low wages (in Mexico, for example) favor luxury expenditures on personal services and foreign imports at the expense of possible growth of domestic industries based on mass consumption.

Premature advances in certain directions may create special problems. Sometimes extensive construction or other industrial projects, unplanned in relation to other manpower needs, results in too great a drain of male workers at the seasonal peak of agricultural requirements. Developmental programs to give direction and momentum to economic growth must necessarily provide for balanced and parallel development, including opportunities for new employments outside of traditional agriculture or handicrafts and qualitative improvement of the work force to permit them to perform efficiently as industrial workers.

The interrelation of cultural factors suggest that if the work force is to be redirected to more productive employments, it is to be accomplished not by isolated measures, important as these may be, toward the improvement of the health, literacy, skills, protection and status of workers. Rather, it can be accomplished only if these efforts are accompanied by changes in the economy that substantially alter technology and costs and affect every aspect of social life. Whether the innovations take the form of new techniques applied to agriculture, utilization of formerly unused natural resources, or attempts at comprehensive industrialization, the new investment must be quantitatively significant. Otherwise, their impact will be small, and they will be incorporated within the traditional economy, and have little cumulative effect. The dynamic possibilities of industrialism are blocked off if colonial or commercial exploitation of native man-power as cheap labor is the motivation of new enterprise, especially if accompanied by restrictions on opportunities for employment at higher levels of skills or managerial responsibility imposed for rea-sons of racial discrimination.[6] Development programs, in short, must create new effective demands for labor as well as prepare workers to meet the requirements for industrial work.

Economic "progress" for whom? Probably the interests of the gen-erality of the work force have been incorporated in the social goals of static societies within the limits of their technology to a greater degree than in dynamic societies in the early stages of change. The reintegra-tion of means and ends takes time. The carriers of economic progress, who by their innovations threaten the stability of the traditional so-cial organization, have done so ordinarily for individual or group in-terests not identical, certainly, with the interests of the masses of the population—whatever, in fact, the ultimate consequences. Economic progress conceived in the interests of the entire population—and in terms of the potentialities of an expanding technology—depended upon the emergence of democratic national states in modern times. To take a few examples from the West: The guild system promised some measure of justice but not much in the way of technical prog-ress; mercantilism manipulated economic resources, including the work force, for the power and the wealth of the State, but hampered the freedom and interests of entrepreneurs and laborers; the new lib-eralism of laissez faire, which gave rein to economic innovation and elaborated a rationale in terms of the interests of the whole of so-ciety, was brought under social control with the growth of the dem-ocratic movements.

The economic activities of national states and their nationals in colonial or dependent territories, or abroad generally, were not brought under social restraints so promptly or so fully. As a con-sequence, Westernization of less advanced areas of the world was resisted as imperialist intervention. Enterprise abroad was viewed as a possibility of tapping rich natural resources by means of a cheap

[6] See Wilbert E. Moore, *op. cit.*, pp. 131–36, and Frank W. Notestein, *op. cit.*, p. 95.

labor supply, with the native work force recruited sometimes by duress or by indirection, such as by the necessity of working for cash to pay a head tax.

Speers attributes the gap between colonial and domestic policy, in the United Kingdom, for example, to public indifference: "While the British people were fighting for progressive legislation in the form of social insurance laws, liberal trade union laws, and the like, in Britain, their apathy toward colonial matters precluded any demand on their part for the extension of these same measures to the dependent territories." [7] As late as 1929 in Britain the Colonial Development Act recited the promotion of "commerce with, or industry in, the United Kingdom" as the rationale for development of colonial industrial and agricultural resources. Not until 1940, with the Colonial Development and Welfare Act, was the welfare of the colonies themselves declared to be the main objective. Full industrialization, with maximization of demand in the domestic market of the less advanced countries, has rarely been a primary objective. Greaves concludes that "no metropolitan power has relied on commodity wants to stimulate a native labor supply." [8]

Aspirations of native populations. Despite the untoward features of Westernization, the potentialities of industrialization penetrated the consciousness of people throughout the world. The varied means of communication developed by technology carried the word of economic progress in some version even where little if any real beginnings of modernization were taking place. The spread of certain nonindustrial aspects of industrial society, as in the field of public health, or international labor standards and social legislation, through various cultural contacts including international political organization, tended to increase the tension between the promise of industrialization and the reality of "backwardness." As a result of the transmittal of the political ideologies indigenous to labor movements and the social conflicts of the Western countries, the labor movements in many backward countries, while small, were mature beyond their years. But probably no influence was so powerful as the two world

[7] Peter C. Speers, "Colonial Policy of the British Labour Party," *Social Research*, September, 1949, pp. 307–8.

[8] I. C. Greaves, *Modern Production among Backward Peoples* (London: George Allen and Unwin, 1935), p. 157; quoted by Wilbert E. Moore, *op. cit.*, p. 183.

wars. Allies were drawn from all continents, contacts of all kinds were multiplied, and resources of scarce materials were searched out and developed as hastily as possible by Western methods.

Against the background of poverty of the economically backward countries, the knowledge of the potentialities of industrialization was a ferment undermining traditional life and the stability of political order. By virtue of numbers, their disadvantageous position, and the anti-imperialist tendencies of labor movements everywhere, the work force assumed political importance in contests for power and political and economic reorganization. This was predictable even in the absence of world-wide activities of Communist Russia to exploit discontent and the historical mistakes of the formative democracies. The choice and the feasibility of the means of economic development became an imperative for political stability.

The threat of poverty to international political stability was recognized in general form in the creation of the United Nations and in the technical assistance program of the United States.

"The grinding poverty and the lack of economic opportunity for many millions of people in the economically underdeveloped parts of Africa, the Near and Far East, and certain regions of Central and South America," President Truman told the Congress of the United States in 1949, "constitutes one of the greatest challenges of the world today. In spite of their age-old economic and social handicaps, the peoples in these areas have in recent decades been stirred and awakened. . . . All these areas have a common problem. They must create a firm economic base for the democratic aspirations of their citizens. Without such an economic base, they will be unable to meet the expectations which the modern world has aroused in their peoples. . . . The preamble of the United Nations states that the economic and social advancement of all people is an essential bulwark of peace. Under Article 56 of the Charter, we have promised to take separate action and to act jointly with other nations 'to promote higher standards of living, full employment, and conditions of economic and social progress and development.' " [9]

FACTORS CONDITIONING AFFIRMATIVE RESPONSE OF WORK FORCE TO ECONOMIC DEVELOPMENT

Environmental factors conditioning positive rather than negative reaction of the work force to economic change vary in character and importance depending upon the stage of development and special

[9] "Technical Assistance for the Underdeveloped Areas of the World," *Message from the President of the United States*, June 4, 1949, House Document No. 240.

features of the particular society. A positive response on the part of the work force, contributing toward rather than hindering the process at each stage, appears most probable where, in the presence of a major change in the production function, the change in the pattern of worker relationships promises immediate advantages in the level of living and is accomplished without too great violence to the fabric of social life. Workers in the United States are accustomed to changes in techniques within a pattern of constantly changing technology; their attitudes will be quite unlike that of primitives experiencing first contacts with Westernization or that of peasants recruited for industrial production in the agricultural economies of the Orient for whom economic change means new ways of living.

Whatever the special circumstances in differing cultures and stages of economic development, a number of general preconditions for affirmative reception of change accompanying economic progress can be identified that are pertinent to problems of economic development today.

Knowledge of potentialities of industrialization. Perhaps no factor today is more conducive to the ready acceptance of economic change in whatever form it may take than the almost universal awareness of the potentialities of modern technology for production. Widespread as the knowledge of the advantages of the new technology is, understanding of the realities of the functioning of a dynamic economy, such as that of the United States, is far from perfect in even many of the more developed countries, aside from the influences of Communist propaganda. Workers as well as other strata of European society tend to reject economic changes that appear to Americans as indispensable for economic progress, partly for understandable predilections of social policy but partly also because of mistaken notions of American life. Industrialization need not follow identical patterns everywhere; indeed, its essentials can be adapted to a wide variety of institutional situations including authoritarian states. However, receptivity and adaptation to economic change can be aided by knowledge of the consequences. Much more is needed than wonderment at the undoubted technical proficiency of the machine.

Reality of advantage to the individual. The individual worker will naturally respond more favorably to new work arrangements if, on balance, the expected rewards in terms of income or other considerations appear advantageous. In Western society alternative opportunities or new situations confronting workers already industrialized ordinarily involve no great change in their ways of life; economic change represents advances along an established line. The comparative advantage of one employment as against another may be expressed in terms of relative wages with allowance for other factors. Nonpecuniary advantages or disadvantages of certain alternative employments may often be decisive, however, as where social status or prestige is involved, or where change would result in a break in personal relationships.

The balancing of alternative advantages and disadvantages is more complicated where the choices confronting workers result from radically new ways of production in the transition to industrialism. It is often suggested that workers in such situations prefer leisure to more income. What may appear to be the inefficacy of wages as an inducement, in such circumstances, is not necessarily because monetary considerations have less weight in nonindustrial cultures; more likely it is because the wage is not sufficient to compensate for the breach with old patterns of work and community life. Difficulties in the recruitment of native labor, which are often attributed to lack of aspirations for a higher plane of living, reflect instead probably a high degree of rational appraisal of the inadequacy of the wage offered. Marshall suggests the importance of the facts that "one trade is healthier or cleanlier than another, that it is carried on in a more wholesome or pleasant locality, or that it involves a better social position." [10]

The fruits of industrial progress are not always immediate and obvious to the worker; they are cumulative and to a large degree roundabout, in the form of increased purchasing power of wages and social services in the long run. Thus gains do not accrue directly to employees in firms introducing cost-reducing improvements while the innovations may result in immediate hardships to them. Obviously, this is the case when the introduction of labor-saving machinery results in displacement of workers and temporary unemployment, at

[10] Alfred Marshall, *Principles of Economics*, 8th ed. (London: Macmillan & Co., Ltd., 1938), p. 557. See Simon Rottenberg, "Income and Leisure in an Underdeveloped Economy," *The Journal of Political Economy*, April, 1952, and Wilbert E. Moore, *op. cit.*, pp. 106–13.

least for many, before absorption in other employments. Lower prices to workers as consumers is little consolation to an unemployed worker. In unionized industries increasing attention appears to be given to efforts to ease the shock effects of technological change; the problem is, of course, minimized under conditions of rising output and continuing full-employment conditions. Nevertheless, the gap between ultimate advantages and immediate impacts results in continuing resistance by organized workers to many forms of cost-reducing devices by employers, such as "scientific management" practices, piece-wage systems, speed-up of mass production lines. Organized resistance to technological improvements as such is at least quiescent in the United States and has been partly superseded by constructive appreciation of the necessity and importance for rising real wages.

Factors minimizing impact of change. For countries at the threshold of industrialization the characteristic situation is a disintegration of existing institutions under the impact of new forces while the structure of new institutions is not yet in full being. The political ferment in the Near and Far East at the present time is a consequence of growing cultural contacts and the conflict of new objectives with vested feudal and colonial interests. How readily changes can be absorbed depends, however, not only on the balance of political forces but also on the features of the society favorable to the reception and adjustment to a changing economic organization.

Adaptation may be possible as was the case in Japan:

There the archaic kinship forms and hierarchical order of society were not disrupted by the introduction of industry; on the contrary, they were strengthened and given an elaborate ideological overlay as a part of the policy of economic transition by deliberate plan and control. . . . Throughout the system, even in the larger establishments, there was a continued emphasis on paternalism of a quasi-feudalistic pattern, and on the ultimate security of the rural family structure.[11]

Thus adaptation of the work force to requirements imposed by economic change is less complicated in countries already industrialized than where a new integration in process of creation involves changes going beyond the level of technology to which the social

[11] Wilbert E. Moore, *op. cit.*, pp. 30–31.

structure is adapted. If a thorough revision of the economic and social structure has been adopted as policy by the political authority, as where today feudal institutions are being eliminated with the sanction of the State, the problem is minimized to that degree—particularly if the potential resistance of the work force arising from the new industrial disciplines and ways of work is minimized by understanding by the masses of the population that the new policy will lead to improved living conditions.

Given the technical capacity of the modern state, the adaptation of the work force to the requirements of newly emerging modes of production can be enforced with considerable efficiency, even where rewards to workers are rigidly restricted in the interests of capital accumulation for purposes of rapid industrialization. Imperial Japan and Communist Russia are examples of this. Obviously the power of the State can readily be abused. The apparatus of the State can be used to thwart resistance on the part of the work force, to manipulate with various sorts and degrees of coercion, and to win consent and enthusiasm by control of education and the means of communication. Whether industrialization is made to serve what in democratic countries are regarded as interests of workers depends upon the nature and ends of political power.

Democratic organization of workers. The democratic national state and the modern trade union movement emerged, historically, with the rise of industrialism. Although the ramifications of the interrelationship lie beyond the scope of this chapter, it may be noted that the protective social legislation of the nineteenth century was necessary to prevent the physical deterioration of the work force in the face of the excesses of the new industrialism.[12] Similarly the growth of an organized labor movement was a defensive action on the part of workers who, as individuals, were in a weaker position than their employers. In turn, this movement became a political force reinforcing democratic tendencies in the Western countries. The economic function and tendency of collective bargaining for wages—to overcome the time lag in the adjustment of money wages to changes in productivity—may be in dispute amongst economists. In any case there appears to be validity in the view that collective bargaining, by con-

---

[12] See Lujo Brentano, *The Relation of Labor to the Law of Today* (New York: G. P. Putnam's Sons, 1891), pp. 81–89, and pp. 298–99.

fronting the economic strength of the employer or group of employers with that of a collective group rather than individual workers,
completes the logical requirements of a theory of competition that
finds its social justification in a thesis of a harmony of social interests.[13] Certainly political democracy is unthinkable without freedom
of organization, if not strength of workers' organizations.

Work forces in underdeveloped countries have the protection to a
considerable degree, although imperfectly and far from universally,
of social legislation and friendly governmental policies toward trade
union organization that in Western countries had to be won over a
long period of time. To minimize the impact and exploitative tendencies of industrialization, Tawney long ago pointed to the need for
such policies if industrialization is to be acceptable. "To import western industrial techniques without importing western methods of controlling it is to prepare a disaster." [14] Indisputably the scope of labor
problems in the transition period will be limited by such safeguards
to workers' interests. Whether the importation of cultural standards
inappropriate to the stage of development or capacity of the economy
actually impedes the rate of progress, as sometimes argued, is a separate question. The problem has been a continuing one in the fram-
ing of international conventions on labor standards by the International Labor Organization. Excessively high standards have largely
been ignored in practice; the more precise question may be whether
they are enforced to the degree possible and necessary.

In any event, reformed colonialism and present-day technical assistance programs have not only fostered protective social legislation
and labor standards but also the growth of trade unionism. For example, it is declared thus in an official statement of government
policy:

Wherever appropriate the United States should encourage participating
governments [in technical assistance programs] to enact legislation promoting fair labor standards of wages and working conditions and to permit
workers to organize freely, and such other legislation as may be necessary

[13] Eduard Heimann, "On Strikes and Wages," *Social Research*, March, 1948,
particularly pp. 83–87; Lujo Brentano, *op. cit.*, pp. 115–120; and Alfred Marshall,
Principles of Economics, 2d ed. (London: Macmillan and Co., Ltd., 1891),
p. 601.

[14] R. H. Tawney, *Land and Labour in China* (London: George Allen and Unwin, 1932), p. 150; quoted by Wilbert E. Moore, *op. cit.*, p. 104.

to provide an environment favorable to the development of a free labor movement.[15]

The purpose is threefold: to win the cooperation of workers in economic development programs, to raise the efficiency of the work force, and to foster institutional bases for democratic control of economic and political policy.

RESISTANCE OF THE WORK FORCE TO ECONOMIC DEVELOPMENT

The very absence of the favorable circumstances, discussed above, constitutes limiting factors, if not sources of resistance, to the affirmative cooperation of workers to changes essential for development. Such favorable circumstances do not alone assure the ready success of industrialization, either in terms of basic economic factors necessary for initiating or for progress toward development or of the adequacy qualitatively of the work force itself. The redirection of labor to new employments involves difficulties that inhere in the nature of the transformation of the work force required by industrialization. Substantive problems of training, relocation, new disciplines, and so on, while minimized by favorable attitudes toward the new order, and varying in different social situations, remain to be solved.

Breach with the old. How difficult it is to draw workers from traditional ways of life may be illustrated by an extreme example—extreme in the sense that it is taken from within what must be regarded as a highly integrated culture, where industrialization has achieved its broadest form. We refer to migratory agricultural workers within the United States or, perhaps better, to the hundreds of thousands of subsistence farmers, chiefly in Southern states, who for all practical purposes have remained outside the market economy. The familiar characteristics of poverty, illiteracy, ill health, and large families impede transfer to productive employments. The first generation of out-migrants find complete adjustment to industrial life difficult to make and tend to return to the securities (such as they are) of their old homes whenever employment opportunities worsen in recession.

[15] "Policy Guidance Regarding Labor and Manpower Aspects of Technical Cooperation Program," Technical Cooperation Administration, U. S. Department of State, *Hearings on Mutual Security Act of 1952*, Committee on Foreign Relations, U. S. Senate, 82nd Congress, 2nd Session, March 5, 1952, pp. 742–44.

Another illustration, perhaps more important for programs of industrialization in overpopulated agricultural economies, is the diversionary effect of land reforms. This permits an alternative to forced entry to wage employments, in much the same way as the opening of the West provided opportunities for independent farming for early Americans who chose to avoid town life and employments. Whether such movement to the land contributes to economic development, or is otherwise desirable, depends upon circumstances of the particular situation; certainly it is not a direct step toward industrialization. The Mexican investigation, reported by Moore, suggests that this was one effect of land reform in that country, as indicated by the preference of workers to stay on the land, where that was possible, in one area, rather than to turn to industrial employments as in another area where less land had become available through the reform.[16]

The natural disinclination to adopt new ways of life is tempered by the degree to which loyalties to the values of the old system are maintained. As we have seen, colonialism had difficulties in alienating primitives from the attachments to their tribes where, however static and backward, tribal life constituted a satisfactory life from the restricted viewpoint of its members. Cultural contacts loosen attachments to old values, but so long as the inroads of the new are isolated or sporadic, and changes have not been absorbed into a new integration of institutions and values, they create a disequilibrium in which the old and new compete. The values and the securities of the old system must be replaced by something new if work is to have meaning or appear rational to workers and if the new system is to elicit their support.[17]

Threat to the status quo. The transition to new forms of economic organization not only threatens but requires the destruction of vested interests of many kinds. Equally for various strata of the work force, the new economy may require loss of positions of prestige and advantage if not power. Economic progress may destroy castes and vested rights to certain types of employment, or undermine the position of independent farmers, craftsmen, and artisans, or at least re-

[16] Wilbert E. Moore, "Utilization of Human Resources in Industry," in *Milbank Memorial Fund, op. cit.*, p. 59.

[17] See Georges Friedmann, "The Social Consequences of Technical Change," in *International Social Science Bulletin* (Paris: UNESCO, 1952) Vol. IV, No. 2, p. 246.

duce opportunities for employment in familiar occupations for which individual workers are trained and experienced. The consequences for the individual may be serious as in the case of technological displacement (hand cigar makers, glass blowers, and so forth), even where no fundamental change in social structure is involved. To the degree that adaptation is difficult or entails severe loss there will be resistance, even if ineffective, to economic change. Notwithstanding the passing of older forms of prejudice toward the introduction of new machinery, unionized workers in a number of industries in the United States have negotiated arrangements that apparently go beyond softening the immediate impact of technological displacement and impairing productivity; others, notably the mine workers, while winning gains undercutting the competitive position of their industry, for example, have consistently facilitated technological advances.

Inadequacy of the inducement. If the immediate material advantages of transfer to new occupations or forms of economic activity were obviously attractive to workers, much of the potential resistance due to a variety of factors would at least be lessened. There are many instances in countries now undergoing development where wages offered to workers in new enterprises considerably exceed the general level of pay in traditional employments. More typically, the circumstances of the transition are not favorable to immediate improvement in economic status. The large available supply of underemployed labor renders it unnecessary to offer wages out of line with prevailing standards. Capital is relatively scarce, and the rate of industrialization is rarely so rapid as to upset the pre-existing balance. Rational programming of economic development may favor types of expansion in the nonagricultural section using large numbers of workers in relation to capital expenditures. Thus, except where technological requirements (as in petroleum refining, for example) dictate capital-intensive forms of production, rational use of resources suggests intensive use of labor relative to capital-requiring equipment. The secular rise in real earnings is necessarily a slow process, and at best the wage inducement standing alone is relatively weak.

External domination and group conflicts. Complicating the difficulties suggested above is the fact that the influences making for economic change are to a large extent foreign in origin and, not infrequently, the direction of the new activities is in the hands of foreigners and for the advantage of metropolitan countries or foreign business interests. A growing spirit of nationalism adds a political factor to the natural suspicion engendered in such circumstances. Organized resistance in various forms of antiforeign movements is a common feature in countries seeking both economic progress and freedom from foreign domination. Political independence of the underdeveloped countries, accompanied by recognition of mutual interests in economic development on the part of the international community, would appear to be a precondition for minimizing resistance on the part of workers to modernization of backward countries.

Lack of a sense of participation in the social control of industry in the more advanced countries, particularly where the organized labor movement regards political and economic power as identical, has been a decisive social factor—whether or not standing in the way of the main lines of economic progress. Experience in continental European countries suggests that this factor is not insignificant in accounting (1) for opposition of labor to technological progress on the grounds of its unstabilizing effect on social life and in terms of business cycle fluctuations and (2) for defensive tactics, if not collaboration, in the face of cartelization policies by business that place security and stability above considerations of progress and efficiency.

Economic democracy through political, trade union, or cooperative action has been achieved to varying degrees in the Western countries. In an extreme form, co-determination—as an outgrowth of the Works Councils movement under the Weimar Constitution and perhaps later as a necessary counter to what appeared to be shrewdly devised socialization of the Russians in the Eastern zone of Germany —is a movement for labor participation in the direction and management of industry.[18] In socialized industries in mixed economies, problems arising from conflicts of interests between labor and the community at large remain, and in postwar England they complicate economic recovery and stabilization. Repression of workers, as we have seen, is possible in authoritarian states; despite the fable of the people's democracy, forced labor, arbitrary deployment of work-

[18] See Oscar Weigert, "Co-determination in Western Germany," *Monthly Labor Review*, December 1951, pp. 649–56.

ers, harsh labor laws, and restricted consumption result in various forms of passive if not overt resistance to hothouse forcing of economic development.

ORGANIZATION OF THE LABOR MARKET

"Organization of the labor market" refers to those institutional means by which adaptation of the labor supply to changes in the demand for labor is accomplished. In the market-oriented, industrialized countries the need for conscious direction of this process received belated recognition. Rationing or the allocation of workers as between employments has been viewed as part of the functioning of the market that can be left unattended by the State. Wage theory has thus been integrated in a general theory of prices to explain in common terms the utilization of labor together with other economic resources through the mechanisms of the market. Whatever the theory, governments have intervened in the process in one way or another. Certain vestiges of the past, such as the Poor Laws in England, qualified laissez faire sometimes in anomalous fashion. Modern social legislation has had important implications for the labor market, although the motivations or the objectives have usually been broader in nature. The most important continuing form of intervention has been the assumption of public responsibility for the direction of education, if not pre-job vocational training generally. Despite awareness of the relation between education and the shaping of the labor supply to serve the needs of the economy, educational policy has been guided by many other considerations and rarely closely directed to this end.

With the establishment of public employment exchanges or services in the advanced industrial countries, modern governments formed specialized agencies designed to facilitate the "organization of the labor market." Their function, first of all, is to provide insofar as possible the knowledge of the market that is presupposed on the part of employers and employees in a perfect market and, operationally, to place workers in job openings to meet the labor needs of employers. The organization of the labor market, as a conscious governmental function on behalf of social policy, is an integral part of economic policy and programming. How much is left to the play of market forces and how much is a matter of governmental administration in any given situation will depend upon the complexity of the adjustments required and the character of the existing labor market, as well as the general biases of social policy and the urgency with which active programs are viewed.

Perfect organization of the labor market would (1) minimize frictional unemployment by bringing workers and jobs together more promptly and (2) maximize productivity insofar as possible by the better matching of job requirements and the individual worker's qualifications for the job. Only in marginal ways can the efficient organization of the labor market enhance per capita income in the industrialized economies. It cannot create employment where there is no demand for labor. But as the handmaiden of economic programming in the underdeveloped countries where vast transformation of the pattern of labor utilization is essential for development, the organization of the labor market is a function of major importance.

Relationship to economic programming. If the adjustments necessary for the adaptation of the labor supply to the changing labor requirements of the economy are of a routine or marginal kind, government need take little overt action except in the direction of educational policy appropriate to the training needs of the economy and the administration of an employment service. In such circumstances, the functions of the employment service are likely to be limited primarily to job placement together with the administration of an unemployment insurance system, supplemented by some measure of occupational counseling, technical services to employers, and efforts to deal with unusual local area problems. In the United States, for example, more elaborate functions directed toward remedying structural rigidities of the labor market, as reflected in chronically depressed areas and involving relocation of the work force or industrial facilities, are likely to be regarded as exceptional and peripheral to the main functions of the employment service except in such emergency periods as war or military mobilization. More attention has been directed to problems of this kind in England and other countries than in the United States. But in countries initiating broad programs for economic development, the function of directing the organization of the labor market is hardly distinguishable from the central task of economic administration.

The organization of the labor market that is attempted in the advanced industrialized countries is ordinarily not conceived as a means of attaining changes in the economic structure or accomplishing major gains in per capita income.[19] At most it is intended to maximize employment in the given economic situation. Wherever job openings exist, the function of the employment service is to fill those jobs as rapidly as possible so that employers can go ahead with their production plans to meet market demands they foresee. Thus total output is increased by eliminating so far as possible avoidable frictional unemployment, but only within pre-existing limits of demand. However, to the extent that more workers are employed at any given moment than would have been the case in the absence of prompt filling of job openings, current incomes are thereby enhanced, and consumer demand may consequently be somewhat higher.

Per capita income may also be increased within the existing structure of technology and demand by increasing qualitative efficiency in the placement of workers. Through vocational counseling, beginning in the schools even before young people enter the labor market, and continuing to the point of placement in specific jobs, it is possible to minimize those drawbacks to efficient production resulting from workers being employed in jobs for which they are not best qualified, or at less than their highest skills. Proper job placement in this sense will add to the productive efficiency of the individual worker and to the economic process as a whole. The effectiveness of a public employment service in these objectives is limited by its own skill in job placement, by shortcomings of the educational system, by lack of complete assistance on the part of employers (particularly by discriminatory hiring practices), and by the condition of the labor market where there is less than full employment.

It is immediately obvious that the function of labor market organization is a more formidable task in countries at the threshold of economic development than in the advanced industrial countries where the task is relatively routine. For the economic changes that are required are not marginal adjustments within a slowly changing structure of production; moreover, whether or not the desired economic changes are feasible or are accomplished in fact depends to large degree upon the necessary adaptation of the labor supply.

[19] See Lloyd G. Reynolds, *The Structure of Labor Markets* (New York: Harper & Brothers, 1951), pp. 257–80, and Richard D. Fletcher, "Employment Service Program of Worker Utilization," *Monthly Labor Review*, May, 1952, pp 499–504.

Labor supply as a special factor. Redundance or shortage of particular labor in the underdeveloped countries ordinarily does not merely present a problem of adaptation of the labor supply that must be dealt with by a specialized administrative agency as in the industrialized countries, along lines discussed above. Rather, the existing supply of labor is an economic factor of primary significance and defines, we may say, the nature of the problem of economic development and the courses of action that lie ahead. Steps need to be taken to alter the economic structure to the facts of labor supply in those countries where, for example, excessive population in relation to economic resources characterizes the economic problem and explains the prevailing level of productivity. New investment is needed in the non-agricultural sectors to reduce the uneconomical application of excessive labor input on limited natural resources and thus to raise the marginal product of agricultural labor. The size of the labor supply cannot be altered in the short run, and population may even increase to complicate the problem of development as a result of initial efforts toward development. In Ceylon, for example, a mosquito control project, part of a comprehensive developmental plan initiated during the prewar and war years, resulted in a natural increase of population from seventeen or eighteen per 1,000 to twenty-seven per 1,000 in 1948. Even if fertility declines during the process of industrialization, as is generally the case, mortality rates typically decline faster. Thus in Chile the natural increase in population rose from six per 1,000 in 1905–09 to seventeen in 1947.

In the absence of changes in technology, rational use of labor under existing conditions may result in limited increases in total output while per capita output actually declines.[20] It is quite conceivable for

[20] Economists of the International Labor Organization describe the cumulative adjustments to use labor more intensively in agriculture, with the consequence of decreased output per head, thus: "First, changes may be made from the less labour-intensive crops to those which require more labour. This type of shift has recently been noticeable, for example, in Mexico, where population pressure is beginning to be felt. Secondly, in some cases, the successive subdivisions of holdings may render the adoption of more intensive labour techniques not only more profitable but even necessary. As the family income declines, the cultivators are compelled to use more human labour to replace animal labour. Thirdly, with the growth of population the area under cultivation may be extended steadily to include less fertile land and land with more difficult access to the supply of water; and, as a rule, the less favourable the land for cultivation, the higher are the labor requirements per unit of area. . . . It is mainly through these various ways of raising agricultural labour requirements that up to a certain stage the increased

the work force to be adapted in more or less optimal fashion to other economic factors, including the prevailing technology, without full utilization of the work force or economic growth. A stationary state, by definition, is one in which real income does not increase over time.[21] Either retrogression or progress is more likely in reality. If the supply of labor stands in an unfavorable relationship to the stock of capital and natural resources, the line of development is more likely to be in the direction of decreasing per capita income than a stationary equilibrium. Chronic redundance of labor does not invite efforts to improve technology in agriculture.[22]

The organization of the labor market is inseparable from the general problem of economic development. For economic development to take place in the underdeveloped countries, whether overpopulated or underpopulated, the work force must be utilized in conjunction with advances in technology, ordinarily requiring increasing capital investment and more extensive use of natural resources where available. Special problems of labor market organization, accompanying and facilitating economic development, must be conceived and dealt with in the framework of necessary changes in the economic structure.

In the overpopulated countries there is typically a redundant supply of labor employed in agriculture at less than full levels of utilization, and the problem is to create conditions for employment in more productive employments and to affect the transfer of workers to those jobs. The problem is different and perhaps not quite so difficult in the underpopulated countries such as are found in South America: Because of shortages of capital and the use of backward technology the work force is employed at low levels of productivity but there is no excess of population in relation to land or other natural resources. While the essential problems of economic development are otherwise much the same, a growth of population in these countries pre-

population has been able to find productive work on the farm despite the rise in the ratio of agricultural population to cultivated land." But as population pressure is intensified, additional increments of labor (in the absence of capital investment or improved agricultural methods) yield successively smaller increments to output, if any at all. (International Labour Office, Action Against Unemployment [Geneva: 1950], p. 131.)

[21] J. S. Mill, Principles of Political Economy (New York: Colonial Press Edition), Book 1, Chapter 11, p. 169.

[22] See Karl Brandt, The Reconstruction of World Agriculture (New York: W. W. Norton & Company, Inc., 1945), pp. 333–36.

sumably would be favorable for raising per capita income by virtue of the possibility of more advantageous specialization and enlargement of the market.[23]

Modernization of technology by means of technical assistance and presumably larger capital investment per worker is the common problem of economic development in over- and underpopulated countries alike. The large population base in the overpopulated countries renders the problem of financing economic development, expressed in terms of per capita investment, a difficult one even if not complicated by the need for finding capital for expected population increases. Such countries are caught in a circle of low productivity and low net domestic savings. Experts reporting to the United Nations in 1951 indicated that the problem of the underpopulated countries is somewhat less difficult than that of the overpopulated; for although annual per capita investment requirements are estimated to be somewhat higher because of the capital needs for more productive use of workers in agriculture as well as for industrialization, per capita income and savings are higher. For the overpopulated countries, although population increase is projected at a lower rate than in the underpopulated countries, the experts estimated that five times the present rate of accumulation of savings would be required to raise per capita national income by 2 per cent annually through investment for increasing agricultural yields and providing nonfarm employments for an increasing proportion of workers.[24]

Problems of labor market organization. Purely technical problems of labor market organization are difficult to disentangle from general economic problems of the economy. This is the case even in the industrialized countries; it is more obvious in countries seeking to industrialize. Each has its special range of problems. The major cause of disorganization of the labor market in the industrialized countries is the fact of cyclical variations in the demand for labor. Depending upon the degree of fluctuation in the level of employment, certain institutional arrangements, such as unemployment insurance, can ameliorate the situation. Cumulative disorganization, resulting

[23] *Cf.* Frank W. Notestein, *op. cit.*, p. 92.

[24] "Measures for the Economic Development of Under-developed Countries," Report by a Group of Experts appointed by the Secretary-General of the United Nations, New York, May, 1951, pp. 75–80.

from urgent competition for the reduced number of jobs and the consequent pressure upon wage levels and workers' incomes, can be minimized by a guarantee of specified levels of unemployment compensation for a specified length of time. Workers have a period of time to seek comparable job opportunities, and are not forced to accept employment at less than their experienced skill level. Employers can count on maintaining their work force without the prospect that their workers have dispersed in various forms of casual work. Minor fluctuations can thus be accommodated.

Constant changes in the pattern of demand, both seasonal and secular, and in labor requirements resulting from technological innovations, present problems susceptible to some degree of solution. Here the problem is one of placement in other available job openings requiring in many instances comparable experience and skills, or retraining where the individual worker's skills are no longer required. The problem is complicated if the available demand for workers with the skills possessed by the temporarily unemployed are in other areas than the place of residence. Considerable interarea and interregional migration takes place for a variety of reasons; but in no country has it proved easy to overcome the difficulty of space in the matching of jobs and workers. Only in a few relatively skilled or highly paid occupations does a national labor market exist in the United States. The problem appears to be equally difficult in countries where distances are less, but home attachments perhaps stronger, than in the United States. Better educational planning to the end of more versatile vocational training or anticipation of future trends in the labor requirements of the economy can minimize disparities between workers' qualifications and changing job requirements.

Problems of this kind can be handled with some success by well-organized public employment agencies through a variety of familiar services to workers and employers.[25] The employment exchange itself is of central importance. Increasing attention is directed to the dissemination of information and labor market studies designed to inform both workers and employers of both national and area trends with respect to the demand for labor and the availability of workers. Considerable progress has been made in recent years in the United States in local labor market analysis and in vocational counseling or occupational outlook studies. Similarly, the employment

[25] See Richard D. Fletcher, *op. cit.*

services and related institutions have made gains in analysis of skill requirements of individual jobs and of job family relationships, as well as testing of aptitudes for jobs requiring elements of various skills. Again it must be noted that full success is hardly attainable and little success is possible under circumstances of large-scale unemployment. One other limitation needs to be noted. Job placement remains a primary function of such agencies. American experience indicates that an employment agency staff must devote first attention to day-by-day work load. Beyond this, the staff may be used to improve knowledge of the labor market and better utilization of the work force. Other than counseling, however, no one has suggested as a practical matter attempting to service employed as well as unemployed workers—that is, to make it a general objective of an employment service to inform workers employed and unemployed alike of all job openings and to throw employed and unemployed alike in competition at all times for jobs both vacant and filled. This would appear to be the ultimate length to which an employment service could go to approximate a perfect market for labor, but one that is hardly feasible.[26]

Other identifiable problems susceptible to some degree of solution include those of casual, seasonal, and migratory workers. The problems overlap, and all are rendered more difficult under conditions of less than full employment. Casual work as a social problem is in large part the result of marked irregularity in the demand for labor in a general situation of slack demand for labor. If there is a long continuing situation of less than full employment, employers are permitted or perhaps encouraged to rely on a float of "underemployed laborers, no one of whom is out of work continuously but all of whom are employed only a part of the time." [27] Some ameliorization is possible by institutional arrangements of one kind or another. Decasualization of dock workers has been the subject of international conventions and efforts at solution. Strong union organization has helped in a number of situations, as in the garment trades, although unionization in such circumstances is ordinarily difficult. Efforts to deal with the problem have usually included central employment exchanges, sometimes through the union hall, or through

[26] Cf. Lloyd G. Reynolds, op. cit., pp. 271–73.
[27] Paul F. Brissenden, "Casual Labor," Encyclopaedia of the Social Sciences (New York: The Macmillan Company, 1932).

public services, as well as effort to regularize the demands for labor, if possible, in one way or another. Full employment is the surest remedy in urban centers, for by assuring alternative employments to otherwise casual workers employers cannot fall back on a reservoir of unemployed workers to provide workers to meet peak needs.

Where the irregularity in the demand for workers is primarily related to seasonal factors, as in agriculture or commercial canning, there is little opportunity to rearrange the time pattern of demand. Some regularization has been attained in industries, where the irregularity is one of consumer demand, by means of regularizing production by building up and running off inventories, but this is often costly. The problem of meeting peak needs, including seasonal, has been increasingly met in some industries and areas by reliance on women workers who enter and withdraw from the labor market as the occasion requires, although this has not been free from difficulties. In other situations, practices have developed involving urban employment of farm workers during peak periods in factory employment which coincide with low points in agricultural needs.

Seasonality in agriculture has been partly met by a built-in flexibility of labor supply on the family farm whereby housewives and school-age members of the household are available for seasonal needs. Commercial farming, however, requires large numbers of seasonal workers who cannot be provided from local sources. This fact, combined with the fact of underemployed population in many agricultural areas, has led to elaborate patterns of large-scale seasonal migration of agricultural labor to meet successive peaks in labor requirements on various crops in different parts of the country. Much has been done to supervise and regulate this migration, which in the United States involves foreign as well as domestic workers, but the system is open to many abuses and remains a major social problem. As part of this picture, the Commonwealth of Puerto Rico is attempting to regularize employment of its cane sugar workers not only by industrialization of the island but also by a systematic and controlled flow of agricultural workers to the mainland during the off season.

The range of labor market problems in the developed and underdeveloped countries overlap but in many respects are quite different. They merge, as has been noted, with the basic problem of economic reorganization and development. Cyclical fluctuations are less important but the inherent seasonality of agriculture makes large-scale underemployment a characteristic feature of the underdeveloped countries. Industrialization is per se the means by which fuller utilization can be achieved and productivity increased. The training of workers and the shift of workers to places of industrial employment, which are elements of labor market organization, is an integral part of the massive task of redeployment of men and resources in the drive for higher levels of per capita output and consumption.

Economic planning may be conceived and expressed in population and manpower terms. Programs for industrialization may be planned with reference to estimates of excess agricultural population for which job places need to be found in industrial employments and as a measure of capital requirements. The form industrialization takes may turn upon considerations of how limited capital resources can be most economically rationed to maximize output of the work force as a whole. Investment will be required in agriculture as well as industry to raise the level of living of the farm population and to obtain food production for workers diverted to industrial employments. In some cases, large industrial projects may draw so much manpower away from agriculture that too few are left for peak agricultural needs. Thus manpower surveys may be an essential tool for economic planning. Similarly economic programing will have to take account of increased demands for consumer goods to avoid international balance of payments problems in connection with needs for capital equipment and possible inflationary pressures, as well as the objectives of an internally dynamic economy. From this point of view, handicrafts may need some measure of protection, especially in view of the temptation to resort to such workers as a more readily available supply of workers for new industrial employments than untrained agricultural workers.

The selection of means for providing entrepreneurial direction for economic enterprise, whether in private or public spheres, falls within the field of economic policy and strategy. Yet the availability of entrepreneurial personnel is hardly distinguishable from the need for recruiting and training professional and skilled personnel at somewhat lower levels of responsibility. Economic programs cannot go ahead unless workers with requisite skills at all levels are available in the numbers and in the places where they are needed. The very decisions as to what plans and projects are to be pursued may depend upon estimates of availability of trained personnel.

Recognition of manpower aspects of economic development has led underdeveloped countries to devote considerable effort in duplicating institutional arrangements of the more advanced countries. In this they have had the aid and encouragement of international agencies and technical assistance programs of other countries. These efforts have ranged from modern systems of social legislation, such as protective labor laws and social security systems, to encouragement of trade union organization. The establishment of some form of employment exchange or labor offices to perform functions comparable to those of the advanced countries is attempted wherever governments actively pursue development programs. Quite commonly, attention is given to the needs for training professional and technical personnel, for apprenticeship and other training programs for skilled workers, and for health and community facilities. Manpower surveys are a common feature of efforts to deal with problems of internal and international migration to accomplish relocation of population as required for developmental programs or to relieve population pressures. Social research of all kinds has been stimulated through technical assistance programs to provide factual data to guide economic programing. By way of illustration, one interesting line of demographic research is directed toward the prediction of population growth resulting from or accompanying changes in economic and social structure under the impact of industrialization.

In addition to specific functions of training, job placement, administration of unemployment insurance and other social security programs, and enforcement of protective labor legislation the government labor agencies can contribute to the solution of a variety of economic developmental problems. Decisions with respect to the location of industry need to be made with regard to special concentrations of surplus labor or, where surplus labor is not particularly localized, effort may be required to decentralize industry to minimize the problem of relocation of population. Similarly, decisions as to what industries should be favored by developmental and capital investment programs ought to take into account the effect of technological displacement of workers. The International Labour Office suggests the need to mitigate technological unemployment where handicraft industries play an important part, as they do in many countries, in the production of manufactured goods; this may be done, to begin with at least, by developing modern industries along lines complementary to rather than competitive to the handicraft trades.[28] The problem of seasonal unemployment in agriculture can be dealt with effectively only by the closest collaboration between economic development and manpower agencies. Employment during the course of a year may be extended by creation of new rural industries, by the introduction of mixed farming, by utilization of agricultural workers in planned conservation programs, and in public works and other capital expansion programs. Many of these measures suggest the need for aid to internal migration and, in some cases, temporary migration to adjoining countries. Permanent migration of excess population to other countries, while difficult, is one of the approaches or partial solutions to chronic conditions of overpopulation in relation to scarce resources, and one requiring cooperation between national and international agencies.

The varied tasks of labor market organization in relation to problems of economic development in the less advanced countries are posed by the special circumstances of the individual situation. To a greater degree than in the developed countries these tasks are operational aspects of the central economic problem of allocation and combination of scarce and abundant resources toward the objective of increasing the productivity of the economy in the interests—in democracies—of the welfare of the whole population.

[28] International Labour Office, *op. cit.*, pp. 162–67.

CHAPTER V

The Formation of Capital

JOHN A. BUTTRICK* [1]

Definitions and Concepts

THIS CHAPTER IS CONCERNED PRIMARILY WITH THE RELATIONSHIP BEtween the capital and income of a nation. More particularly, it will explore the connection between changes in the amount of capital and changes in the flow of income.[2] Historically, such additions to the productive capacity of an economy have been one of the most important ways by which per capita income has been increased. What determines whether a small or large fraction of current production is devoted to capital formation? What are the consequences for society of varying the amount and type of capital and of changing the rate of its formation? Of the societal changes over which there is some measure of control, which encourage and which hinder capital formation? It is with such questions that we shall deal.

* Associate Professor of Economics, University of Minnesota; Fellow, Foundation for Advancement of Education, 1952–53. Author: "The Inside Contract System," *Journal of Economic History* (Summer, 1952); "The Economist and the State," *Review of Economic Studies* (Fall, 1951).

[1] The author wishes to thank the Fund for the Advancement of Education for the fellowship awarded him during 1952–53 during which time this chapter was written. He also would like to thank for their comments on an earlier draft of the chapter: Professors Tibor Scitovsky, Hayden Smith, Lorie Tarshis, and Richard Weckstein. The author is, however, responsible for any shortcomings or errors.

[2] In most of this chapter, so that the role of capital formation may be isolated for separate consideration, changes in population will be ignored, i.e., population will be assumed to be constant. As a consequence, per capita income will be a fixed fraction of total income, and the two terms may be used interchangeably. For the same reason, this chapter will largely ignore international aspects of capital and investment.

The theory of capital formation is complex and highly developed. Like all theories, its understanding depends upon a set of definitions and a carefully worked out analytical framework. It is particularly important to understand these because words like capital, investment, and income are used in common speech to represent a variety of concepts. In real (as opposed to money) terms, capital may be defined as part or all the stock of goods in existence at a particular moment while income (or product) refers to goods and services which are produced during a period of time. Some of these, such as food, medical care, or an automobile ride, are used up soon after being produced but others, such as roads, machinery, or buildings, are constructed with an eye to facilitating future production. Loosely speaking, this latter portion of current output is referred to as "investment," while the term consumption is reserved for the former. Capital and its several components, then, are "stock" concepts while income and its subcategories are "flow" concepts.

As investment goods are completed, they become part of capital so that the process by which they get manufactured is called "capital formation." During any period, however, many items which were in existence at the start, disappear; some are worn out and discarded, some are destroyed by fire or explosion, others die or are eaten. In order to get an accurate picture of the amount by which capital has actually changed, only net amounts should be considered. In other words, the things which disappear must be subtracted from those which are produced.

While in its widest meaning capital refers to the collection of everything in existence, including consumer goods, natural resources, and even human beings, in this chapter we shall concentrate only on certain classes of things.

First, we shall be interested solely in "scarce" goods and services, i.e., those which can be obtained only by giving up something else in exchange. Second, we shall ignore things over whose creation we have no control, e.g., indestructible features of land. Third, we shall, by and large, disregard things which are expected to yield satisfaction directly rather than indirectly, e.g., durable and nondurable consumer goods which are owned by households. Finally, human beings and the knowledge and skills associated with them will be excluded. Thus the concept of capital to be used here includes all scarce, reproducible goods which are expected to yield up satisfaction indirectly to some person in the future (although they may also be providing satisfaction now).[3]

In our complex society it is important to distinguish between real capital and its mirror image which is the mass of paper claims representing ownership of capital. We know that for every automobile there is a title of ownership, for every house a deed, and for every bag of groceries a bill of sale. In any society the titles of ownership are there by implication; they tend to be explicit whenever an owner fears someone may dispute his claim, or whenever it is expensive to prove again that he owns a given piece of capital. In this chapter, the words capital and investment will be used only when referring to real things.

The act of defining capital has solved the next problem, that of identifying the flow concepts needed, such as investment, depreciation, and consumption. Because investment is defined as "addition to capital," identification of those things which are capital also tells us what things to call investment. Depreciation and capital loss have similarly been tied down since they are the "using up of capital." Definition of investment in turn enables us to rid consumption of conceptual difficulties. Goods and services produced during a given period will either be consumed or added to capital; in other words, consumption goods are noninvestment goods. At various times certain subcategories of capital, investment, and consumption will be considered; if the basic distinctions already mentioned are kept in mind, these should not prove bothersome.[4]

Problems of measurement and valuation. Even the relatively restricted subcategory of capital with which we are concerned consists of a wide variety of dissimilar objects: various sorts of machinery, tools, buildings, inventories, transportation facilities, and the like.[5]

---

[3] Other chapters in this volume deal with other portions of capital. For example, Chapter VII will consider consumption which is the using up of those things owned by households; Chapter II dealt with natural resources, i.e., items which have a relatively long life and cannot be easily reproduced; and Chapters III and IV discuss various attributes of population and the labor force.

[4] For a good, brief discussion of these definitional problems, see United Nations, *Measurement of National Income and the Construction of Social Accounts*, 1947. Appendix by Richard Stone, especially Chapter VII.

[5] Notice that the purchase of a bond or stock is not investment nor, on a national level, is the purchase by one person of final goods which were previously in the possession of someone else.

The flow of real goods and services also consists of heterogeneous items. While the definitions given impose a modicum of homogeneity on the things included, this does not help very much in the problem of measuring the "amount" of capital, consumption, or investment. However, the solution of this problem was discussed at length in the introductory chapter and the appendix thereto; it need not be considered in detail here. In general, measurement of capital is analogous to measurement of income, i.e., the money equivalents of all things included in the given category are used to obtain a list of values which can be summed up. For this reason, all the difficulties of understanding and evaluating income figures are also present in estimates of capital. There are, however, some special problems attached to the valuation of goods which have a long life but typically pass through a market only once—a description which fits many capital items.

In the earlier discussion of income measurement it was assumed that prices accurately reflect the desires of consumers. Even in the case of those goods and services which are used up soon after they are produced, this may not be a very good supposition. It is still more difficult to assume, when valuing a railroad or a public utility which was constructed, say, twenty years ago, that the prices then paid reflect the worth of the property to consumers today. To see what is involved, consider the factors which lead a producer to purchase a piece of machinery. If he actually buys a new machine, he must think his profit will be greater for doing so. He is thus comparing a flow of expected future income with the cost of obtaining the capital which will yield this flow. The size of the income flow depends upon what will happen to receipts on the one hand and costs of operation on the other. It is the difference between these which he compares with the purchase price to calculate the rate of profit on his investment. At best, though, he can only make a rough estimate of these future receipts and costs. Technological change, shifts in the desires of his customers, changes in the labor force and raw material supplies may well show him to be quite wrong; hindsight will probably indicate that he was either too pessimistic or too optimistic in his forecasts. Yet, it is his estimate of future profits which will, and must, determine how much he is willing to pay for the machine now.

Furthermore, his decision can be influenced by events which seem to have no connection with these immediate factors. If the government, for example, were to engage in a bond-selling campaign and lowered the price of its bonds to make them more attractive, the prospective machine purchaser would then be able to earn more money by "investing" in government bonds than was the case before. Consequently, the estimated rate of profit on the machine would look less attractive, and he would be willing to buy only if its price dropped.

On the one hand, then, the buyer's maximum price for the machine is that at which his expected rate of profit just equals the alternative return if he put his money elsewhere. On the other, the seller has a minimum price, that which gives him just enough to pay his factors of production (including himself) what they could earn elsewhere. At the margin, given enough buyers and sellers, the stresses of this bargaining situation tend to balance out and the price of the machine (or any other capital item) equals the buyer's maximum and the seller's minimum. In other words, the flow of expected profits, divided by the price, and properly adjusted for risk and uncertainty, just equals the interest rate obtainable in the market. In the absence of various "imperfections" in the market (construing the word very broadly), then, the price of a capital item does reflect its worth to the consumers at the time it is purchased.

Now, with the passage of time, the expected stream of future revenue will fall as the capital item gets closer to the end of its useful life. As the ability to produce income diminishes, so should value; the question is by how much. If there were a foolproof method of estimating depreciation, the price of a capital good could be reduced by the amount of depreciation which has taken place since it was purchased. The new and lower value would then tell us how much the good is worth today. However, in the real world of changing techniques and tastes, plagued by inflations and depressions, depreciation changes in an almost whimsical fashion.

Conceptually, depreciation is "the difference between the total value of the goods comprising that original stock [of capital] as it is at the end of the year and the value which would have been put upon the initial stock at the beginning of the year if the events of the year had been correctly foreseen, including among those events the capital value at the end of the year." [6] The estimate of the depreciation made by the accountant who uses some rule of thumb

[6] J. R. Hicks, "Maintaining Capital Intact: A Further Suggestion," *Economica*, N.S., Vol. IX (1942), p. 177.

based on initial price and estimated length of life will, under the circumstances, be wrong with regrettable regularity. Nonetheless, capital goods are valued according to these rules of thumb until things get so far out of line that the errors are glaring. Then a drastic revaluation takes place, usually with the assistance of bankruptcy, receivership proceedings, or the accountant's *deus ex machina* of "good will." While this is an unsatisfactory arrangement, we are hard pressed to find a workable alternative.

Those readers who are convinced that the satisfaction of the consumers provides, in general, an improper basis for judging the relative value of goods and services will have become more and more distressed as this section proceeded. It is true that substitution of a set of absolute values for market prices would eliminate most of the problems raised here. It is also true that consumers are increasingly revealed to be inconsistent and confused in their choices. Few would be willing to argue that they are always competent to determine what is good for them. When it is further realized that the actions of today's consumers will determine, in large part, the sort of goods and services available for tomorrow's population, one is still more hesitant about using prices as the basis for assigning values to capital and income.

When this has been said, however, what are the alternative methods? Any other procedure would have to employ a set of values established by somebody. Each of us would have confidence in such arbitrary values only if they coincided with our own. However, if each of us made independent calculations as to the relative worth of those goods and services which we were interested in buying, the composite values found by combining our independent calculations would look very much like market prices. Thus the use of imputed or actual market prices as value indicators rests on the "democratic" assumptions that an individual is, in general, a better judge than someone else of what will give him satisfaction; an individual should be able to change his mind as to what he wants frequently; and actual behavior is a better indicator than verbalizations of what an individual's preferences are.

Even if one agrees with these assumptions, it can still be argued that prices are poor indicators. However, the argument would then have to be that the market is, in some cases, an inadequate mechanism to express or compute the values which exist. This, indeed, is the point of view presented in most of this book. It is the reason why attention has been paid in the introductory chapter and else-where to the need for "adjusting" market prices in various ways. It is especially important to keep this in mind when considering capital goods, since typically they will last a long time.

The limits to investment. Let us now concentrate on the component of the spending stream which is of primary interest to us, namely investment. Under what circumstances can it be increased and what are the limits to the total amount possible during a given period? Discussion of how much investment is or ought to be under-taken will be postponed until after these limits have been described, since there is little point in advocating levels of capital formation which are unobtainable.

The amount any individual saves (adds to his capital) during any period depends upon two things; the amount of money he re-ceives during the period (his income) and the amount he pays out for goods and services (his consumption expenditures). Only if he takes in more than he spends will he be able to increase his stock of capi-tal. For most people in the world today, the accumulation of capital means real deprivation—it is only the fortunate few who have in-comes large enough to permit an adequate standard of living and still leave something over at the end of the year. This applies equally to a nation. If we limit ourselves to the time period within which invest-ment is being undertaken, investment goods, in real terms, are purchased at the expense of consumption or potential consumption. The word "potential" is included because an economy may be operat-ing at less than capacity, i.e., it may be possible to produce more than is being produced with the natural resources, labor, and capital available. Thus the limits to investment during a given period depend upon the potential output of goods and services and the proportion of this which must be in the form of consumption items. If the consumption flow is reduced too much, total potential output will drop, since the various factors of production will not all be willing or able to work for nothing.

Figure 5.1 will illustrate these relationships.[7] The vertical axis measures the output of investment goods during a given period, while consumption goods and services appear along the horizontal

[7] This diagram owes much both to discussion with Hayden Smith of Stanford and to P. A. Samuelson's "Final Comment" in *The Impact of the Union,* D. McC. Wright, editor (New York: Harcourt, Brace & Co., 1951).

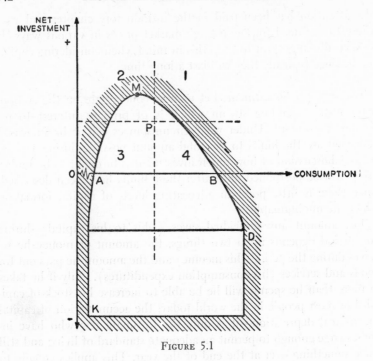

FIGURE 5.1

axis. Investment may be either positive or negative since it is possible to use up existing capital as well as add to it. The shaded area outside the boundary line represents joint outputs of investment and consumption which cannot be achieved, given the resources and knowledge presently available. In this diagram very small amounts of consumption are considered to be unattainable since they could be achieved only if some of the population were eliminated. The distance OA represents the amount of consumption goods necessary to keep the labor force working just hard enough to maintain the capital stock. If additional capital is desired, workers would have to be given more goods so the boundary curves to the right as it rises. It would also be difficult for an economy to make only consumption goods, since some factors of production are so specialized or immobile that they will be idle if not employed in the manufacture of investment goods. In addition, as more and more productive resources are devoted to the production of one or the other class of goods, costs will increase, i.e., to get more of a particular sort of goods in any economy facing scarce resources, increasing amounts of other goods must be foregone. Thus the boundary of the attainable curves downward from its peak (at M) as consumption output increases. OD is the maximum quantity of consumption possible during a given period. This amount is made up of two components: current output of OB plus those of the existing capital goods which can be transformed into consumers' goods. Most of the stock of capital (OK altogether), however, is in a form which makes it unsuitable for direct use by households.

The total output of any economy may be represented by a point located at the appropriate place on the diagram. Let us suppose that the economy we are considering is at P which, being well inside the boundary, indicates that potential output is not being achieved, perhaps because unemployment exists. Changes in the way resources are used (or misused) may be represented by movements into one or another of the four zones marked off by dash lines. Only a shift into zone 1 will increase the output of both types of goods or, at the borders, provide more of one sort of good and no less of the other. Zones 2 and 4 include shifts in which an increase in the output of one sort of good is made at the expense of the other while zone 3 represents a smaller amount of both. These four zones exist regardless of where the economy happens to be. If it were at M, however, all of zones 1 and 2 would lie in unattainable regions; if it were on the boundary somewhere to the right of M, shifts into zone 1 would be impossible until such time as the capital stock was increased.

Starting from point P, we can see that investment can be increased by (a) using partially or wholly unemployed resources to increase investment without cutting into consumption—indeed consumption may even expand at the same time (which would be a movement into zone 1); (b) reducing the output of consumption and using the resources thus freed for the production of investment goods (a movement into zone 2); (c) introducing technological change or increasing the quantity of some or all of the resources available to the economy (pushing outward the boundary of the attainable). It is important to remember that the existing stock of capital is one of the resources which determine the position of the boundary line. Therefore, if net investment is greater than zero, *ceteris paribus*, the boundary drawn for ensuing periods will be farther out, and vice versa.

It must be pointed out that the diagram does not relate directly to the satisfaction which a society's members receive from the operation of their economy. A given output will provide more or less satisfaction depending upon such things as the distribution of the output and the tastes, level of aspiration, and size of the population. Thus, while the maximum investment possible is at M, this does not necessarily mean that the economy "ought" to be there; it is entirely possible that more consumption than this is preferable. In general we can say, however, that the output which will yield the largest amount of satisfaction will fall on the boundary line somewhere between M and D so it is primarily this segment which interests us here.

In order to make useful the concepts presented above, some rules are needed to tell whether there is a "gap" between actual and potential output in a given economy at a particular time, i.e., whether P is on the boundary or inside it. Some way is also needed to judge the consequences of a reduction in the flow of consumption goods. If the output attributable to each factor of production (human or nonhuman) is considered and it is supposed that after moving one of these factors from its present occupation to a different one, total income (output) rises. Then, and then only, will it be possible to increase investment without decreasing consumption.[8] Of course the process of moving a factor of production is not costless. During the period when the movement is being accomplished, the factor's output will drop toward zero and additional output will probably have to be spent. For example, transformation of domestic servants into factory workers may involve spatial movement, job training, and the construction of new housing near the factory site. Such costs are part of investment.

Following this line of argument, then, three general reasons for a gap between actual and potential output may be identified: (1) The existence of simple, *involuntary* unemployment is a clear indication that an economy is producing less than possible. Unfortunately, however, such unemployment is not altogether easy to lo-

---

[8] In making this statement, as will be seen, voluntary and involuntary unemployment are treated as "occupations," and "leisure" is classified as a consumption good.

cate in a particular case although as a mass phenomenon it is clearly recognizable. On the one hand there is the number of persons (or other factors of production) who are actually seeking employment; on the other is the number of job vacancies in existence. When the difference between these two magnitudes is at a minimum, involuntary unemployment does not exist. Typically this will not be the same as zero unemployment since, in a changing economy, there will be persons out of work in one occupation or part of the country while job vacancies exist in another.[9] (2) The existence of *hidden* unemployment provides a second class of cases. It exists if a reduction in the number of workers (or other factors) in a given occupation or industry would either leave total output unchanged or result in an increase of output. There is good evidence that the labor of a considerable portion of those on farms in several underdeveloped nations is submarginal in this sense. In India, for example, it has been estimated that upward of 25 per cent of those in agriculture could be removed without causing any decline in agricultural output. (3) Finally there is a *poor allocation* of the factors of production if, as a consequence of moving a factor from one occupation to another, the output gained is greater than the output lost. This last case actually covers the previous two and includes "frictional" unemployment as well. The leisure "produced" by the person involuntarily unemployed has a zero value. Society also places a zero or negative value on the output of the worker whose employment is "hidden." In each case, if alternative occupations could be found, there would be an increase in total output.

We have argued that a "gap" exists whenever the output which could be produced with given factors is worth more than the output actually being produced. Thus if some consumption goods are less valuable than the investment goods which could be produced instead, the potential output represented by this difference between consumption and investment is automatically a part of this "gap." From this it follows that a given gap may be made larger or smaller by suitable manipulation of prices as well as by reallocating factors of production.

[9] Such residual unemployment. referred to as "frictional," is a necessary consequence of changes in such things as technology, the location of production or of markets, the tastes or income distribution of the population. Unfortunately, it hardly helps the person without work to be told that he is frictionally rather than involuntarily unemployed. Other measures of involuntary and frictional employment could easily be constructed, but this one will serve our purposes here.

The prices which are, or would have to be, paid for something may be altered by government action as well as by changes in private demand and supply conditions. By making some items more and others less expensive, the value of total production can be varied upward or downward. To illustrate, take an economy which is producing at capacity; then suppose that more investment is desired. If the government were to tax certain classes of people, they would spend less. This would enlarge the gap and thus free some resources which the government could hire directly or indirectly with a portion of the tax receipts. The new spending pattern would result in a different set of prices in which investment was worth more and was therefore encouraged.[10]

Elimination of the gap between actual and potential income. What are the conditions responsible for the gap and how may their effect be mitigated? Starting with the misallocation of the factors of production, the remedy is quite clear: Shift factors into uses where their output will be higher, and continue doing so until further increases in output are impossible. This is so simple that one wonders how any misallocation can exist for very long. People will surely move to those occupations and geographical locations in which they can produce and receive more. From this point of view, we are driven to look for barriers which prevent the requisite mobility. These turn out to be considerable: The social and political structure may make it extremely difficult for a factor to leave its present occupational or geographical position. There may also be barriers to entry into certain occupational or geographical positions. Of course, immobilities similar to these may be created simply by ignorance of the possibilities available or because the required knowledge is accessible only to the few.[11] For example, in a caste-ridden society, an individual may not be free to move out of the position in which he was born. More generally, the training given each person by his early upbringing, the educational system, and so forth, coupled with inherited abilities,

---

[10] Although couched in terms of total investment and total consumption, clearly this discussion also applies to one particular sort of investment versus another. If extra roads have a higher value than more mining equipment, for example, a gap will exist until the patterns of resource allocation and valuations coincide.

[11] Similar barriers may of course exist in the product markets where, by reflection on the factor markets, they would have similar consequences.

set limits to the positions in society open to him. On the other side, those at present occupying given positions in society may be able to screen out what they consider to be undesirable entrants. At the limit, monopoly may be so strong that scarcely anyone new is permitted to enter a given occupation, geographical area, or industry.

In the case of general involuntary unemployment, the nature of the "barrier" which prevents those who are out of work from finding employment is again easy to identify. The economy is able and willing to produce more than the population is able or willing to purchase. Insofar as people are prevented from buying more by a lack of purchasing power, this barrier may be removed by arranging matters so that more purchasing power is given those who will use it. Devices by which this can be done will be discussed later; suffice it to say here that this aspect of the gap is easier to eliminate than the one created by the types of immobility mentioned above. Finally, if a campaign to do away with both involuntary unemployment and misallocation of resources were successfully instituted, the unnecessary portions of hidden and frictional unemployment would also disappear. Indeed, in one interpretation it is legitimate to ignore them as separate phenomena, since, by definition, they cannot exist independently.

Societies differ widely in respect to the barriers which prevent the achievement of their potential output, but a few general remarks can still be made. Systems of reward and punishment found in the real world fall along a continuum. At one end, a person receives goods and services, as well as prestige in his peer group and status in the wider community, depending upon who he is, i.e., upon events over which he has relatively little control. At the other extreme are reward systems which "pay off" according to what a person does, i.e., rewards and punishments depend on events over which the individual possesses a large measure of control. Mobility will obviously be greater in societies which conform more closely to this latter type. To be accurate, however, a reward system of the "what one does" type is a helpful but not indispensable condition for economic development. For example, it is possible for a society to move toward the achievement of its potential even if all the existing members are frozen in whatever positions they occupy and the parents' standing determines that of their children. The number of persons occupying the relevant positions could still change through births and deaths; in the course of time, misallocations would be corrected if births exceeded deaths in every occupation or geographical area which had too few members, and vice versa.

While many of the barriers which have been erected in various societies appear to rest on deep cultural relationships, others are more easily removed. The construction of a system of cheap transportation is one obvious way of increasing the mobility of both factors and products, given the willingness to move. Transportation also helps in another way by greatly widening the markets available to each factor, each product, and each producing and consuming unit. A school system, job training programs, and information schemes for owners of productive factors and consumers have similar consequences. All such changes will enable the gap between actual and potential income to be narrowed and may also push outward the boundary of the attainable. Thus they will make it possible to increase investment greatly.

Extensions of the use of money and explicit titles of ownership fall in this same category. Both facilitate trade, permit savings to be accumulated in the form of paper claims rather than real things, and thus encourage real investment. Their use permits capital to be in one place while the person who holds title is in another. They make it relatively easy for an individual to change the composition of his assets, since the ownership of a given piece of capital can be split among several persons as is done, for example, with a corporation's stock. To appreciate the importance of this development for investment and economic growth, consider the manner in which individuals save in a country like the United States in contrast to India. In the United States one adds to his personal assets by accumulating pieces of paper (e.g., money, stocks and bonds, insurance policies, and mortgages), while the items of capital represented are used by others in the process of production. In India, on the other hand, it has been much more common to find persons saving in the form of jewelry, gold, and the like, with the titles implied and the capital items unavailable for the use of producers. There is no need to dwell on the necessary role of government in this process, but it is clear that without some means of settling disputes over ownership in a consistent and therefore predictable manner, the widespread use of explicit titles would be impossible.

The "Proper" Level of Investment

The determination of the proper division of total output between consumption and investment, i.e., where along the boundary line (in Figure 5.1, page 142) the economy "ought" to be, depends upon a comparison between the costs and the benefits of investment. Even though we may be unable to quantify all the costs and benefits, a listing of the factors which must be considered should prove useful to those concerned with national investment policy and planning.

The benefits and costs of investment. For an individual the problem is simply stated. The "cost" of adding to capital consists of doing without those things which could have been purchased with the money which went into capital instead. On the other hand, the "benefit" of having more rather than less capital comes from the additional consumer's goods which can, as a consequence, be purchased in the future. A careful person would try to compare these costs and benefits before deciding what portion of his income to set aside each year in savings. If he felt the costs were not worth it, he would put aside less, and vice versa. Only if the costs of having more capital just equal the benefits will he be doing as well as possible.[12] This is admittedly a difficult calculation to make; not only do both costs and benefits involve subjective judgements, but the benefits will accrue some time from now, while the costs must be borne immediately. For most of us a bird in the hand is worth two in the bush primarily because we find it difficult to predict and visualize the future. Nonetheless, no matter how difficult the task of equating the costs of adding to capital with the benefits, explicitly or implicitly we must do exactly this in order to reach a decision.

These same considerations apply to the decisions faced by a nation regarding its capital formation. Costs relate to the actual or potential consumption goods which could be produced if investment is not undertaken; benefits refer to the additional consumption potentially available in the future if investment is undertaken. Costs and bene-

---

[12] It might be argued that it would be better if benefits exceeded costs. However, if the benefit of owning an extra (marginal) unit of something were greater than the cost, one's satisfaction would be increased by purchasing it. Only when benefit just equals cost will one's satisfaction be unaffected by the purchase. This, then, is the point at which to stop buying; the point at which satisfaction is at a maximum.

fits are thus related to two sorts of behavior on the part of society's members—saving and investing. In a simple, subsistence economy the same person is both saver and investor, and the two decisions are intimately connected. Even in such an economy, however, it is possible to separate analytically the function of investing from that of saving and to relate benefits to one and costs to the other. In more complex societies, a major portion of the saving decisions are made with one set of considerations in mind, while decisions to invest are made in a different context and for a different purpose. Playing an intermediate role between these two decision-making functions are banks, investment houses, insurance companies, and the like.

If we look at the cost side, it is reasonable to suppose that people would save more if the rewards for doing so increase. From this it follows that there is some rate of payment—a sort of interest rate—which would be just sufficient to prevent the members of society from either using up or adding to the existing stock of capital. It would not matter if some were induced to save while others dissaved so long as, in the aggregate, the nation's net saving were zero. This would be a situation in which consumption was just equal to total output minus depreciation. Whatever this hypothetical interest rate may be, it gives us a measure of the nation's "time preference" (its preference for goods in the present rather than the future). Its magnitude depends upon how badly the savers want goods and services now instead of in the future, although it will also be affected (among other things) by the distribution of income and wealth. For instance, if income were distributed more unequally, saving would probably rise even though the interest rate remained the same. Generally, we would expect this rate to be greater than zero although it could be negative if people were willing to pay for the privilege of saving. But even in this case a different and probably higher rate would be required to extract a larger amount of savings.

The "pure" cost of investment may be measured by the difference between this hypothetical rate which is required just to keep capital intact and the interest rate necessary to bring forth enough saving to equal the amount of investment being undertaken. If we assume that people do not reduce their consumption without compensation, this difference would increase as investment became larger. There are reasons to suppose, however, that this might not occur immediately. In a wealthy country the interest rate required to extract a given amount of savings will be less than in a poor one, just as the rich find it easier to save than the poor. And, since investment increases the wealth of a country, it may reduce the interest rate associated with a given level of saving. In addition, individuals who are saving now in an attempt to amass a lump sum by some future date may save less whenever the interest rate rises. Higher interest means larger incomes for the recipients so that more will be saved with a given cut in consumption.

Before considering the costs of investment further, let us examine the benefits. These also depend on the wealth of a country and the amount of investment being undertaken and may be expressed as a ratio between two sums of money, i.e., a percentage, just as were costs. Thus, if adding $1,000 worth of machinery to an existing stock of capital increases the annual potential output of consumers' goods by $200, the "marginal potential revenue" (MPR) of the investment will be 20 per cent. If the machine had cost $2,000 and output increased $200, the marginal potential revenue would be 10 per cent. Under conditions of full employment and decreasing returns, the price of machines would rise if more of them were being made. It would cost more to draw additional factors of production from other industries into the manufacture of the machines, and the equipment-making industry itself would be operating near capacity so that its costs would rise as output increased. Thus the MPR would fall with every increase in the pace of investment.

The amount of capital in existence also influences the MPR. So long as there are no changes in technology or in the other factors of production, typically the MPR will drop with every increase in the stock of capital. This is just a further application of the principle of decreasing returns; if more and more units of capital (or any other factor) are used in the production of a given commodity, *ceteris paribus*, additional units will cause output to grow by smaller amounts. Indeed, if capital were increased by a large enough amount, additional units would add nothing to total output and might even reduce it. This reasoning will lead to faulty conclusions, however, whenever the supply of other factors of production or the state of technology change. An increase in labor or the supply of raw materials, for example, will raise the marginal product of existing capital, and thus the MPR, by making capital (relatively speaking) more scarce. An increase in the labor force would very likely also be accompanied by an expansion of the market for consumer goods which would reinforce the increase of the MPR. Improvements in technology or in the skills and perseverance of labor and management will have similar effects.

As a country grows, then, there are two sets of pressures on the MPR of investment which work in opposite directions. Increases in wealth and in the proportion of total output (income) going into investment will tend to lower the MPR. On the other hand, growing technical skill, discoveries of new sources of raw material, and an expanding population and labor force will tend to raise it. In the typical underdeveloped country these last forces might be expected to dominate initially, so that with economic growth the MPR will first be high and may only begin to drop after a considerable period of time.[13]

In addition, it is important to remember that changes in the level of output, in capital, or technology which occur in one part of the economy may influence events in other parts. An increase in the population of one town may so swell demand for, say, electricity that a larger and more efficient power plant becomes profitable. As a consequence, the cost of providing electricity (and the price) will fall, which may bring new industry to the town. This in turn may make the construction of additional transportation facilities and housing attractive. On the other hand, the entry of new employers may bid up the price of labor for the older firms both in the area and outside, while the new goods and services being produced may cut into the markets of firms located elsewhere.

From the vantage point of the nation, then, we must take account of all these effects when calculating the MPR of a particular investment. Not only is this a complex technical problem but it is conceptually difficult because, at the time a given investment is undertaken, the changes in output attributable have not yet taken place. The best we can do is make an estimate of future output which unavoidably will be an uncertain one. This requires a modification of our conceptual apparatus. The initial (uncertain) estimate of future output must be transformed into a "certainty equivalent." As an example of one way of doing this, suppose we calculate that there is one chance out of ten that our estimate of output for next year will turn out to be wrong. Then, to obtain a certainty equivalent, we could

---

[13] However, see the discussion on pages 154–5, *infra*.

use this probability to reduce our estimate by 10 per cent. Since we are presumably more uncertain about events which lie still further into the future, the proportion by which estimates for future years should be reduced would form an increasing series.[14] Without some such adjustment of original estimates, there would be no way of handling such events as war or political change which influence the MPR by making investment more risky. Because the future typically appears very uncertain in an underdeveloped country, we can guess that the MPR will be smaller there.

Achievement of the proper level of investment. Once both costs and benefits have been expressed as ratios they may be compared in a way which will enable us to find the "proper" level of investment. First of all, there will be advantages to increasing the amount of capital (i.e., the benefits of investing will exceed the costs) whenever the marginal potential revenue of investment is greater than the interest rate which indicates the nation's time preference. Second, the MPR of investment will probably decline as the pace of investment increases. In contrast, the interest payments required to induce people to engage in positive saving will most likely rise as saving increases. Thus at some level of investment these two ratios, which express costs and benefits, will reach equality.

Figure 5.2 will illustrate these relationships.[15] The horizontal axis measures amounts of saving and investment which might take place in a given period. The vertical axis is graduated in percentages so that the marginal potential revenue of investment and the interest rate necessary to bring forth the required savings may both be pictured. In the diagram it has been assumed that when no net investment (or net saving) is being undertaken, the interest rate is zero while the MPR is much greater. In technical terms this means that the time preference of the nation is assumed to be zero and the

[14] This method of "correction" is somewhat unsatisfactory because the data are not (and probably will not be) available for making the required probability calculations. It is as if we had to calculate the chances of a seven coming up on the next roll of a pair of dice when we did not know how the dice were loaded and when the degree of loading could be changed on each roll without our knowledge. There are other methods of adjusting for uncertainty but most face this same difficulty.

[15] This diagram and the surrounding discussion were suggested by Tibor Scitovsky, *Welfare and Competition* (Chicago: Richard D. Irwin, Inc., 1951), pp. 216–26.

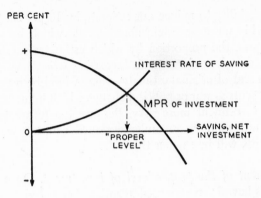

FIGURE 5.2

marginal product of capital is positive. As the amount of investment undertaken increases, the MPR falls for the reasons mentioned earlier. At the same time, the interest rate required to obtain increasing amounts of saving is assumed to rise.[16] The intersection of these two curves shows the level of investment (and savings) at which costs just equal benefits, i.e., the "proper" level of investment. It is easy to see that this equality will occur at a high level of investment if (1) the marginal product of capital is much greater than the interest rate which is required to persuade savers to maintain the capital stock; (2) the MPR declines slowly with every increase of investment; (3) the payments required to make people forego consumption increase slowly or decrease for a time as saving (and investment) rise.

The concepts developed with the aid of this diagram are most useful in pointing out differences between so-called underdeveloped and advanced economies. Since the underdeveloped country possesses relatively little capital, the marginal product of capital will be high. Taken alone, this means that the proper amount of investment will be larger. With a small stock of capital, however, the production of very many investment goods in a short time will probably be difficult and, therefore, expensive. As a result, the MPR of investment will fall off rapidly as capital formation proceeds, which tends to

[16] These particular assumptions are not necessary since the crucial intersection would occur even if the interest rate fell, so long as it fell at a slower rate than the MPR. It is also entirely possible for the intersection to occur in the second quadrant which would simply mean that negative amounts of investment and savings were involved.

counteract the influence just mentioned. In addition, consumers in a poor country with a small stock of capital will likely have to be liberally rewarded for cutting back the amount of goods and services they consume, which also tends to keep the amount of investment down. Finally, insofar as the consequences of investment are more certain in the advanced country, the MPR will fall less rapidly there and more rapidly in the underdeveloped one.

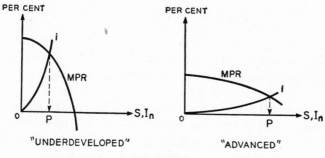

FIGURE 5.3

Two somewhat exaggerated versions of the diagram just presented picture the situations described. The proper level of investment (OP) may well be much larger in the advanced country even though the marginal productivity of capital is considerably lower because of the difference in the shapes of the two sets of curves. In summary, then, there is no particular reason to suppose that the underdeveloped country should (or will be able to) undertake a great deal of investment just because it possesses a small amount of capital.

What, then, is the likelihood that the "proper" amount of investment will be achieved? In the real world, savers typically must not only be rewarded for saving (not consuming) but must also be induced to relinquish control over their stock of assets. Safety and liquidity are sacrificed by the saver when his accumulated savings are put in a form suitable for investment, and this sacrifice must be recompensed. From a societal point of view, however, this extra payment, which appears as a higher interest rate, does not represent a real cost of abstaining from consumption. Society as a whole can only save by increasing the stock of goods in existence; it can never save by simply amassing titles to ownership or hoarding money. Thus, so long as savers are paid to surrender safety and liquidity, a higher interest rate than is "proper" usually will be required to obtain a given amount of savings.[17] Those who like institutional arrangements whereby decisions to save and invest are made through the operations of a decentralized market will consider this extra payment a negligible cost for maintaining free-enterprise capitalism. Others will point to different institutional arrangements which would permit this particular cost to be eliminated.

Whether or not the curve labeled "interest rate for saving" bends upwards more abruptly than it "should," there is another reason why an improper amount of saving (and investment) will probably be forthcoming. In the diagram, the pure time preference of the population was assumed to be zero. It is usually more than this in the real world; most people seem to view the future through the wrong end of a telescope and so overvalue the present, which means that a zero interest rate would not call forth enough saving even to maintain the capital stock.[18] The question is what sort of time preferences ought people to have? If we argue quite plausibly that this generation of society is neither more nor less important than future generations, then the reward for consuming no more than is being produced currently should be zero. If this is granted, then the intersection of the two curves in the diagram will not occur at the "right" place because a higher interest rate will, in fact, be required to maintain capital. If, with hindsight, the future turns out to be more important than the present, then the intersection is of course even farther from its proper place.

The behavior of real world investors reveals similar discrepancies between what is and what "ought to be." In calculating whether or not to engage in capital formation, potential investors consider the benefits they will gain from the possession of additional capital rather than the benefits which will accrue to society. Obviously these may not coincide: (1) A monopolist will charge a price higher than his costs, even if "normal" profit is included among these costs. To maintain this price (and his monopoly profit), output must be restricted.

[17] These remarks must be modified when dealing with situations of rapidly changing prices whether or not there is full employment, when the "proper" rate of interest may well be greater than the actual rate.

[18] This factor would be partly mitigated by an "improper" distribution of income. With an income (and wealth) distribution which is very unequal, for example, more would be saved, although this is not certain in all cases.

But a smaller output implies a smaller amount of capital and investment.[19] (2) In the case of a glue factory or a tannery, private gain
will again exceed public benefit, at least to the extent that those living nearby are disturbed in their daily lives by smells and discom-
forts emanating from the factory. (3) On the other hand, investment in sewerage systems, schools, highways, and the like are
examples in which social benefits are greater than private. Indeed,
to obtain desired quantities of such goods, consumers have had to by-
pass the market and use political devices instead. (4) Finally, while
both society and the individual investor discount their estimates of
future benefits for uncertainty, there is no reason to think that each
will use the same discount factors. Insofar as private investors are
more pessimistic than is indicated, they will invest too little, and vice
versa. The fact that society's life span is longer than that of any member suggests that the discount factor appropriate to society will generally be the smaller. For this reason also, then, investment may be
less than is proper.

There is evidence that in many underdeveloped countries the cases
in which social benefits exceed private will dominate those in which
private are greater than social. The first person who constructs a factory in a given area will have to bear particularly heavy costs. Labor
recruitment and training programs will be needed, along with housing, sanitation, and police protection; transportation facilities to
bring in raw material and deliver finished goods will also have to be
constructed. In contrast, the second or third person who builds a factory can take advantage of the "external economies" which the initial
investor has installed. The private costs of the first investor thus include what amounts to a subsidy which is available to those who follow. Unless offered real protection from threat of competition by the
physical and social situation or by government, it is easy to see why
the original factory might never be constructed.

In conclusion, then, the proper amount of investment will be
forthcoming in the real world only by coincidence. There is no
mechanism in the typical market economy which will automatically
cause investors to respond in the manner indicated by the MPR in

---

[19] This reasoning has to be modified when the assumption of constant technology
is removed since there is evidence that some forms of monopoly make innovation
easier and that, in turn, innovation increases capital formation.

Figure 5.2 (page 154). Our analysis of the behavior of real world savers increases the likelihood that the amount of investment will be improper. By definition, this means a misallocation of resources between the production of consumption and investment goods perhaps accompanied by unemployment or inflation. The analysis so far undertaken, however, does not tell us which of these possibilities will occur. This will be dealt with next.

The "Actual" Level of Investment

In order to find out how much investment will actually take place requires looking at what people do rather than at what they ought to do but don't. In other words, what are the factors which determine the actual level of capital formation? In order to identify the relationships which determine this level, a thumbnail sketch of the manner in which income and investment are related will be presented. Then certain crucial aspects of the process will be explored in greater detail. While some individuals and firms may decide to save because they have made a prior decision to invest, we shall consider primarily the more complicated situation in which the two acts and the two decisions are largely separate. We shall also consider explicitly only an economy in which money is used to facilitate exchange and in which a large proportion of the things people desire are obtained with money or money substitutes.

Imagine an economy, then, which consists only of consuming units (individuals and houeholds) and producing units (business firms), i.e., we are disregarding for the moment the existence of both government and the rest of the world. During any period, these firms pay income to the households in the form of wages, dividends, rent, interest, and so forth, which is either spent or saved. In turn, the firms receive money from the sale of goods and services they produce. If at the end of the period we subtract the amount spent by the households for consumption from both their incomes and the outpayments of firms, we find two residuals. One is clearly the saving which was undertaken by households in the form of increases in their bank accounts, holdings of insurance, stocks, bonds, etc. The other is that portion of the firm's outpayments which was spent to get investment (nonconsumption) goods produced. The amounts of these two flows will be equal if the firms paid out to workers, managers, raw material, suppliers, and owners all they received, since then the income of the households would be just another way of viewing the firms' receipts.

This equality between saving and investment can be kept even if the firms retain some of their profits (or incur losses) by redefining saving to include such undistributed earnings. Indeed, stretching the concept of saving in this manner can easily be justified by arguing that firms act as agents for their owners and so save for the households whenever some profits are retained and dissave whenever losses take place. Definitions of the sort just adopted also enable us to equate consumption expenditures with the market value of the consumption goods and services produced during the period, and similarly with expenditures for investment. Thus investment will always turn out to be the same amount as saving for any period, and the total value of all production will be the sum of consumption and investment.

In an *ex post* or "actual" sense, then, saving is equal to investment by definition. This does not mean, however, that the amount people expect to save at the beginning of a period will be equal to the amount they will actually save, nor to the amount which the firms plan to invest. But if *ex ante* or "planned" savings and investment are not the same, how is it that they are equal *ex post?* The answer becomes clear when we consider what would happen if the firms were to increase their investment. Soon households would find themselves with additional (and unexpected) income since extra investment means that more workers are employed and more raw material is being purchased. This unexpected income would not be spent immediately; thus it would constitute the extra saving needed to match investment. In time, of course, some of it would be spent but when this happened consumption would rise and inventories fall. A decline in inventories is disinvestment, no matter whether it is planned or unplanned, so investment and saving would still be equal in the *ex post* sense.

In the situation just discussed, the initiating force was an upward change in investment. Because of this, money income, which is the same as the value of total output measured in existing prices, rose enough so that sufficient saving was generated to equal the new, higher investment. If a decrease of investment had started things going, income would have fallen instead. Again, however, savings would have been brought into equality with investment, although in a rather unfortunate manner—at the expense of income and employ-ment.[20] While this explanation of the manner in which investment and income are related is incomplete, it does focus attention on several important relationships. Investment is one component of national income (output) so that a rise in investment immediately shows itself in more income. In addition, an increase in income will, under most circumstances, lead to more spending by someone and this will very likely induce additional investment. Thus investment is one of its own determinants since it is one component of income.

The marginal propensity to consume and the accelerator. To make sense of this complicated cause and effect relationship, let us trace out the consequences of a dose of exogenous investment spending. Suppose the management of a large firm borrows from banks or government $10,000,000 which then goes into new capital. As this money is spent, not only will the incomes of households rise but their expenditures will also increase. The relationship between changes in income and the induced changes in consumption—called the "marginal propensity to consume"—is crucial to an explanation of the process by which the initial investment spending affects the level of income. For example, if the typical household spends one-half of any additional income (a marginal propensity to consume, or m.p.c., of 0.5), when the $10,000,000 ends up in the pockets of workers, stock-holders, raw material suppliers, and others, it will cause consumption to increase by $5,000,000. But this secondary spending also means enhanced incomes so it will induce still more spending, and so on. The total increase in spending, therefore, will be the sum of a diminishing series: $10,000,000 + $5,000,000 + $2,500,000 + $1,250,000 + . . . = $20,000,000. On the other hand, should the m.p.c. be 0.9 instead of 0.5, as might be the case in an extremely poor country, income would instead increase like this: $10,000,000 + $9,000,000 + $8,100,000 + $7,290,000 + . . . = $90,000,000.[21]

---

[20] A change in consumption, as will be seen in Chapter VII, could equally well be the generating force. A government surplus (or deficit) or a change in the current balance of trade could also initiate changes of the sort described.

[21] The mathematically inclined reader will know that the formula for an infinite geometrical progression is being used:

$$a\left(1 + r^2 + r^3 + \ldots + r^n + \ldots\right) = a\left(\frac{1}{1-r}\right),$$

where: a is the amount of initial investment,

and $r < 1$ is the marginal propensity to consume.

Of course, this will not be a permanent increase in income because as soon as the investment which started things off ceases, the process described will go into reverse and the flow of spending will begin shrinking. This may be seen by replacing the plus signs with minuses in the above series. Even if the process were to continue in the manner indicated, there is nothing about the mathematics which tells us that the value of money will remain unchanged.[22] For instance, if the economy were operating close to capacity at the start, we would be describing an inflationary movement in which the value of money became smaller with every rise in money income. In addition, there is no particular reason to suppose that the m.p.c. will remain constant throughout the time required to complete the sequence of spending-receiving-spending. (Actually, a small change in income seems to have negligible effects on the m.p.c., although there is some evidence that a substantial increase may lower it.) If the m.p.c. is high, the entire economy will have an inflationary bias and be generally unstable, whereas a nation with a low m.p.c. will react sluggishly to primary changes in spending. The magnitude taken by the m.p.c., therefore, provides a way of predicting the "leverage" of an initial change in income whether it is caused by new investment or some other component of income. The m.p.c.'s of countries for which we possess data range from something like 0.5 up to 1.0, with underdeveloped countries generally falling higher on the scale, as one might expect. Occasionally during periods of extreme inflation or civil unrest the m.p.c. has exceeded 1.0, which indicates that people are changing their spending by more than their incomes change. Since the various segments of each country's population have different m.p.c.'s, an alteration of the income distribution will very likely affect the national m.p.c. For example, in most societies wealthier families have lower m.p.c.'s than those who are poor, and urban families fall higher on the scale than rural. Thus if the same income were redistributed in favor of poor, urban residents, we would expect the national m.p.c. to rise. The national average would also change if the value-attitude system of the population were to alter from one, say, which emphasized "keep-

---

[22] Throughout the discussion which follows the reader is asked, for the most part, to assume that the supply of money and credit will expand and contract enough for the indicated income changes to take place. In other words, we shall pay little attention here to the problem of where the money comes from during an expansion or where it goes when income contracts. Actually, this assumption seems to fit many economies tolerably well.

ing up with the Joneses" to one of "keeping ahead of the Smiths." Little imagination is required to think of still other changes which might affect the m.p.c. This whole subject will be discussed more fully in Chapter VII.

Having considered the effect of a change in income on spending, the impact of a change in spending on investment must next be examined. To do this, knowledge of another ratio is needed—that between a change in sales and the consequent change in investment. Sometimes referred to as the "accelerator," this ratio depends upon (1) the relationship between capital plant and the salable output which it can be used to produce, given the other appropriate factors of production; (2) the manner in which businessmen's expected profit rates are affected by a change in sales since, presumably, investment is undertaken because someone thinks it is profitable to do so. Ignoring the second of these for the moment, let us concentrate on the capital-output ratio. Imagine a firm whose sales are rising which requires machinery worth $20,000 to produce an annual output of $5,000. In each of the years during which sales increase, the firm, in order to maintain this necessary four-to-one ratio, will invest an amount equal to four times the increase in its sales plus whatever is needed to replace old machinery as it wears out. As soon as sales level off, however, the firm's investment will drop to the replacement level. Should sales decline, there would be unused machinery so that it would not even be necessary to replace worn out units, i.e., disinvestment might take place. If the capital-output ratio had been six-to-one, changes in investment would have been magnified, whereas a ratio of one-to-one would have resulted in smaller movements. Thus a large accelerator means that a country's capital goods industries, and indirectly the entire economy, will be particularly subject to fluctuations in income and employment.

The level of a nation's technological development sets broad limits to the accelerator; traveling on horseback requires a fraction of the capital needed to travel by automobile or railway. Similarly a given output of energy supplied by an atomic pile will require more capital than if it had come from coal-driven generators or ox-driven water wheels. While, in general, the advanced country will have a much larger average accelerator than one which is underdeveloped and, typically, agricultural, empirical evidence indicates that this ratio is not nearly as constant as the m.p.c. The accelerators found in various parts of a given economy may be of quite different sizes, which means that an increase in the demand for one sort of commodity and a decrease in the demand for another (or simply a difference between rates of increase or decrease) may cause a nation's accelerator to vary considerably over a short period.

Furthermore, the capital-output ratio may change even in the absence of technological innovations. The management of a firm which is making a certain product must select one production method from among all those available. Of these it will presumably choose the cheapest, *ceteris paribus*, in order to maximize profit. Since production methods differ in respect to the quantities and proportions of the various factors of production used, the selection will be made with an eye on the prices and expected prices of these factors. Thus a change in prices, as well as a change in technological knowledge, can affect the accelerator. If the cost of machinery were to rise, for example, this might lead businessmen to shelve plans for expansion and instead run existing facilities on a three-shift basis; if wages of skilled labor increased, it might become profitable to install more roundabout and capital-using production methods. This means, among other things, that a change in the pace of investment may itself cause the accelerator to change. Increased investment will raise the demand for any factors which are specialized in the production of capital goods. As a result, their prices will rise *vis-à-vis* those used in consumption-oriented industries. The new set of prices may lead to the choice of a different production method involving a different capital-output ratio; it will also initially create a tendency to shift factors from the consumption to the investment sector of the economy. Thus increased investment definitely will affect the accelerator unless the production of consumption goods, whose output is curtailed when investment increases, were to require factors in the same proportions and quantities as do investment goods.[23]

Patterns of interaction in the short run. Only if our knowledge of the accelerator and the m.p.c. are combined can the reciprocal relation between investment and income be examined. Again, assume an economy consisting only of households and firms in which $10,000

---

[23] A representative reference on the marginal propensity to consume and the accelerator is Alvin H. Hansen, *Fiscal Policy and Business Cycles* (New York: W. W. Norton & Co., 1941), pp. 264–88.

investment takes place in "period one." (A period is an arbitrary length of time, say, approximately one month.) This initial investment is not repeated and is the result of events which occur outside the highly simplified model of the economy which we are using. Perhaps it is traceable to the ("exogenous") process of invention and innovation in areas of technology or tastes, or to government action; it could be a new power plant, highway, or cellophane factory. In any event, suppose that the people who receive this $10,000 wait to spend it until the next period and then spend half (the m.p.c. is 0.5). In this simplified world businessmen are induced to change their stock of capital whenever a change in total spending occurs and by the same amount. However, they do not get around to this until one period after spending changes, e.g., if the difference in total spending from period one to period two were $5,000, "induced" investment would rise in period three by $5,000 (thus, the accelerator is 1.0). Total spending (or income) is, of course, just the sum of the consumption and investment which occurs within a given period.

Under these restrictive assumptions about the nature of the economy, the accompanying table shows the manner in which investment, consumption, and income change over time. The values of consumption, investment, and income in the base period have been ignored, in order to concentrate attention on the effects of the initial investment. Thus minus signs mean there is less consumption or investment than there otherwise would have been, while plus signs mean the opposite.[24]

To follow the steps of this "model," notice, for instance, that the change in total spending, from the first to the second period of $5,000 induces investment to change by an equal amount in the third period. The third period also finds the consumers increasing their spending by $7,500, which is just half as much as their income was in

[24] For the mathematically inclined, the model presented here could be written as follows:

$$Y_t \equiv C_t + I_t + E_t$$
$$C_t = a Y_{t-1}$$
$$I_t = b(Y_{t-1} - Y_{t-2})$$
therefore, $$Y_t = (a + b) Y_{t-1} - b Y_{t-2} + E_t$$
$$Y_{t+1} = [(a + b)^2 - b] Y_{t-1} -$$
$$b(a + b) Y_{t-2} + (a + b)$$
$$E_t + E_{t+1} \text{ etc.}$$

where: Y, C, I, E refer respectively to changes in income, consumption, induced investment, and exogenous investment; and the subscript refers to the period, a is the m.p.c. and b the accelerator.

This is a modification of the model presented by P. A. Samuelson, "Interactions Between the Multiplier Analysis and the Principle of Acceleration," *Review of Economic Statistics*, Vol. XXI (1939), reprinted in *Readings in Business Cycle Theory*, editor, G. Haberler (Philadelphia: The Blakiston Co., 1944).

the preceding period. Since there is no more exogenous investment, total spending in the third period is simply $5,000 plus $7,500 or $12,500. When we move to the fourth period, induced investment has dropped to –$2,500, the amount by which income fell between periods two and three. Consumption has also declined but by much less, being half of the third period's income. In the fourth period, then, total spending is –$2,500 plus $6,250, which is $3,750.

TABLE 5.1

Period	"Exogenous" Investment	"Induced" Investment	Consumption	Income*
0	$0	$0	$0	$0
1	+ 10000.00	0	0	+ 10000.00
2	0	+ 10000.00	+ 5000.00	+ 15000.00
3	0	+ 5000.00	+ 7500.00	+ 12500.00
4	0	− 2500.00	+ 6250.00	+ 3750.00
5	0	− 8750.00	+ 1875.00	− 6875.00
6	0	− 10625.00	− 3437.50	− 14062.50
7	0	− 7187.50	− 7031.25	− 14118.75
8	0	− 56.25	− 7059.38	− 7115.62
9	0	+ 7003.21	− 3557.81	+ 3445.31
10	0	+ 10560.94	+ 1722.66	+ 12282.59
11	0	+ 8837.28	+ 6141.30	+ 14978.58
.	.	.	.	.
.	.	.	.	.
.	.	.	.	.

* Rows will not add to totals in all cases because of rounding.

This example is quite arbitrary, not only because different values could have been selected for the marginal propensity to consume and the accelerator, but also because different "reaction times" (the length of time households and firms take to react to changes in their incomes) could have been used. Nonetheless, it provides the beginning of an explanation as to why levels of investment and consumption (and therefore income) change. Furthermore, the example points up a basic idea: that the level of total spending can change, even though the behavior of the units making up the economy does not. It is clear that income variations can be explained by assuming appropriate changes in the behavior of households, firms, and government. But it is perhaps not so obvious that changes in output may occur even though consumers consistently spend a constant portion of extra income and businessmen always react by investing an amount equal to a constant fraction of every change in sales.

The other important thing to notice about this example is that the last three columns portray a business cycle. While this is the result of the particular magnitudes chosen for the m.p.c. and the accelerator, most realistic pairs of values lead to a cyclical pattern in which, as in the mathematical model, investment fluctuates more widely than consumption. Thus we have an explanation—almost too enticing in its neatness—of both the "cause" of the business cycle and the reason why capital goods industries go through more severe ups and downs than industries producing consumer goods.

This crude model also suggests that national economies may be classified according to the values of their m.p.c.'s and accelerators— e.g., if either of these ratios were larger than was assumed, income would have changed in explosive fashion, and vice versa. An m.p.c. greater than 1.0 would create inflationary pressures great enough to swamp the cyclical pattern entirely; if accelerator and m.p.c. were very small, fluctuations would also disappear but, in this case, because of the economy's sluggish responses. It is possible to argue that as a country develops, it will pass from the stage in which a very high m.p.c. dominates and business cycles are fragmentary to the sort of situation portrayed by our mathematical example. Before we can be sure such easy generalizations are legitimate, however, the model must be considerably refined. Two sorts of modifications are called for: those required to identify the nature and causes of the business cycle and those needed to deal with long-run changes of the sort associated with economic growth. Although these modifications overlap, let us take them up in order.

Refining the model. The model provides no way of distinguishing between changes in real and money income. Only if the price level were constant would the income fluctuations of the mathematical example represent changes in real income. We know empirically that as income rises, any unemployed factors of production tend to be absorbed into the economy. As the gap between actual and potential output narrows, the task of finding and fitting the dwindling supply of unemployed factors into jobs becomes more difficult. Finally, the rise in income takes itself out wholly in rising prices and, if income continues to increase, inflation will sweep everything before it.[25] The danger of this happening depends upon (1) the size of the

[25] Similarly, when income falls, there will first be a drop in employment and then prices will start to fall in response to shrinking expenditures for consumption and investment.

initial gap between actual and potential output, (2) the relationship between accelerator and m.p.c., and (3) whether or not the accelerator and the m.p.c. are modified sufficiently by the change in income itself.

In a country with an accelerator (or a m.p.c.) very much larger than that used in our model, total spending would soon exceed capacity to produce, i.e., the income rise would become progressively larger or a series of explosive fluctuations in income would occur. On the other hand, a nation with a smaller m.p.c. (or accelerator) would experience a series of dwindling fluctuations which would finally disappear unless injections of exogenous investment initiated new cycles. In the latter case, the size of the gap between actual and potential output at the start would be important while in the former it would be overshadowed by the underlying, explosive character of the economy. The income changes just described, however, will modify the magnitudes of the m.p.c. and the accelerator, and this will in turn modify income.

As was suggested earlier, the accelerator is partly determined by the expected rate of profit, which is influenced by changes in the level of income, and by the rate of investment itself. On the upswing of a cycle, when investment and income are both mounting, expected profits (and the accelerator) will first rise, reflecting the optimism engendered by increased sales, and then fall in response to the rise in the prices of investment goods caused by the approach to full employment.[26] Thus, the upswings pictured by the model may hit a sort of "ceiling" before being curtailed by the leveling off of consumption. On the downswing, changes in the expected rate of profit are also important. Businessmen will not disinvest at the rate suggested by the model if they think their idle plant and equipment will be needed again in the future. Maintenance of such facilities together with new shocks to the system caused by exogenous investment may well, therefore, act as a "floor" to the downswing.[27] In other words, at this point in the cycle, induced investment may be overshadowed by capital formation which is caused by a different set of forces.

[26] There is some recent empirical evidence, however, that profits will just continue to rise along with income, although special circumstances may have been responsible.

[27] See J. R. Hicks, A Contribution to the Theory of the Trade Cycle (New York: Oxford Univ. Press, 1950), especially Chapter VIII, for a discussion of the "floor" and "ceiling."

Somewhat similar modifications in the simple theory are required because the households' behavior may also change as income varies. Changes which do occur in the short run can be traced largely to expectations of price changes. If a price increase leads people to expect a further rise, they will buy more goods and services now and less later on. Such "self-justifying" expectations affect investment in two ways: Firms will find their sales increasing, which will raise the expected rate of profit and thus investment. On the other hand, a smaller proportion of income will be saved so that the cost of obtaining investment funds may increase. The income rise, however, will largely swamp this last effect. (If prices had dropped initially, the consequences of the expectational factor would be reversed.)

Variations in the length of time it takes consumers and investors to react to changes in their environment also modify the path of income and investment. Briefer reaction times speed up the entire pattern of fluctuations and, as we might expect, they do shorten as the rate of increase of income rises. This means that whenever inflation is approached, it will be approached faster and, when depression is in the offing, the economy will become progressively more lethargic.

Changes in the rate of interest will also affect investment directly and indirectly. A potential investor with a given sum of money at his disposal presumably looks around to see where he can get the largest rate of profit and invests there. If he discovers a use for his money which promises a very high return, he may well share the prospective profit with others by borrowing money from them and paying interest in return. If his calculations are accurate, this will be to his advantage since he will collect for his foresight the difference between the total profit and the amount he has to pay out in interest. Because he always has the alternative of loaning his money rather than using it himself, he will not invest at all unless the expected profit rate exceeds the return obtainable by loaning his money, i.e., the market rate of interest. Thus, as we saw in the section on the proper level of investment, a low rate will bring forth, *ceteris paribus*, more investment than a high one.

This implies that the interest rate is determined by the behavior of those who wish to borrow (investors) and those who wish to lend (savers). In other words, the rate of interest will be compatible with the amount of saving and investment being undertaken since the same forces determine both simultaneously. In the real world,

however, the interest rate is influenced by actions of ir
credit institutions, such as banks, saving and loan assoc
usually a number of government agencies. Taken all t
institutions can loan money which was not previously ..
households. Indeed, a very large part of what is used for mon.,
in every advanced economy consists of checks drawn against a
set of numbers on the books of some financial institution, i.e.,
it has no physical counterpart in dollar bills or coins.[28]

The use of credit in place of coins means that the supply of money
available for investors can be expanded or contracted with considerable ease. As income rises, managers of the credit institutions will
find it easier to make loans, and may well be enticed by the profit
possibilities into expanding the money supply. At such times, therefore, the interest rate will not rise so much as it otherwise would and
additional investment will take place, whereas during a downswing
the situation would be reversed. In other words, the behavior of the
banking system will change during the business cycle in a manner
which reinforces the movements of investment and income. Ultimately, of course, there are limits to the elasticity of the money supply, depending on the maximum velocity of circulation possible and
the laws governing financial institutions. Typically, however, the business cycle starts downward, for reasons already examined, before these
limits are reached.

In summary, then, interaction between the marginal propensity to
consume and the accelerator provides an explanation of why income
and investment change over time. The simple relationships of the
mathematical model, however, must be modified to take account of
those changes in accelerator and m.p.c. which are induced by the very
fluctuations in income they "cause." These may be located by looking at changes in reaction times, interest rates, and in expected prices
and profits.

Widening the model. Modifications of the basic model so far considered do not enable us to look much beyond the short-run confines
of the business cycle. This does not mean that such a model is of no
use in explaining changes which occur over longer periods of time.

---

[28] Those readers who are surprised by this statement should review the section
on money and banking in a textbook such as P. A. Samuelson's *Economics: An
Introductory Analysis*, 2nd. ed. (New York: McGraw-Hill Book Co., 1950).

On the contrary, the relationships which have been isolated and identified as being important in an understanding of the economic system's cyclical behavior are also of crucial importance for an interpretation of the longer sweep of history. In any case, it will be the short-run success or failure of a development program which will matter to most people since, as a famous economist put it, "in the long run we are all dead."

For purposes of long-run analysis, however, the model must be viewed in somewhat different perspective. First, the institutional framework, which could be treated as a constant for a period of time as short as a business cycle without violating reality too much, may undergo drastic changes as time passes. Indeed, this will often be one of the purposes of a development program. Second, the magnitudes of such ratios as the m.p.c. or the accelerator may show discernible trends when longer periods are considered. This section and the next will deal with these possibilities and their consequences for economic growth.

As intermediate financial institutions develop and the use of credit is extended, there will be a tendency, *ceteris paribus*, for the interest rate to start declining. This will not only encourage investment in general but will also change its direction. Typically, the more durable a given piece of capital the more expensive it is initially and the longer it takes to recapture the funds required to build it. A drop in the market rate of interest will therefore encourage long-lived capital while a rise will discourage it. Credit institutions, as we saw earlier, also enable savers to keep their assets in a liquid form while permitting investors to borrow for longer periods of time. With adequate policing by government, the existence of such institutions also reduces the risk which a saver unavoidably takes whenever his assets are in the hands of others. Both of these effects will reinforce the movement of the interest rate downward. Increases in the amount and changes in the composition of capital will not only push outward the boundary of the attainable but also will probably raise the accelerator and create price and profit expectations which are generally favorable to further investment.

Exogenous investment provided the initial shock which started the fluctuations of investment and income described by interaction of the m.p.c. and the accelerator. It was also largely responsible for the "floor" to income and output mentioned earlier. To separate investment into two categories enables us to concentrate on that portion of investment which can be explained by prior changes in spending i.e., induced investment. In some ways, however, this is a disadvantage because it covers up the fact that economics cannot now adequately explain a considerable portion of government's investment or that occasioned by such events as war; the discovery of new sources of raw material; technical and managerial inventions; or changes in the size, skills, and desires of the population.[29] Nonetheless, this unexplained investment has profound consequences for the economy as even our simplified model suggested.

In some cases, the record from the past is clear enough to permit extrapolation of a historical trend which will influence this sort of investment, as may be the case, for example, with population, growth of credit facilities, changes in the skill and age of the labor force, or even the discovery of some sorts of minerals. When this can be done, the appropriate investment series can at once be inserted into the column of the model labeled "exogenous investment" (see Table 5.1, page 165) and the consequences in terms of income, consumption, and induced investment quickly perceived. In other cases, even this makeshift solution is not available and explanations must await a more profound synthesis of various social and physical sciences. In such cases, we can only assume that the residual, unexplained investment varies in a random fashion, i.e., it becomes larger and smaller in an unpredictable manner. As soon as this step is taken, the income-investment model will show quite complex patterns of fluctuation. Each (random) change in exogenous investment will create its own cycle, and these will overlap, sometimes reinforcing, at other times contradicting, one another.[30]

The explicit introduction of random elements into the theory has a special advantage for those interested in improving our understanding of the process of economic development. To illustrate, suppose that data on the various required relationships from some particular economy are inserted into the fully modified model and that the resulting time paths of income, investment, and consumption are

[29] Consumption should also be divided into exogenous and induced components in order to handle variations caused by such things as population or tastes. This is done in Chapter VII, while a discussion of technological change is found in Chapter VI.

[30] See, for example, G. H. Fisher, "Comments on Stochastic Macro-Economic Models," American Economic Review, Vol. XLII (1952).

plotted. This "predicted" pattern may then be compared with actual income statistics covering the same time period. Insofar as the discrepancies between these two patterns are non-random, they will offer clues to important relationships which have been overlooked or misinterpreted. If the model used for predicting is a good one, the discrepancies will be relatively small and random; if they are not, the model needs revision.

The general theory outlined in this section of the chapter provides us with an explanation of why the level of investment changes as well as an understanding of the connections between investment and income. The theory is general in the sense that it can be used to explain a wide variety of investment and income patterns depending on (1) the values which are inserted for such relationships as the m.p.c. and the accelerator; (2) modifications of such relationships caused by the behavior of the model itself as expressed by price and profit expectations and the interest rate; (3) the nature of outside constraints like the floor and ceiling mentioned earlier, development of credit facilities, growth of population, and so forth; (4) refinements introduced to make room for random elements; and (5) actions taken by government and the influence of other economies.

This knowledge of the determinants of investment and income may be put to work in several ways: It can be used to explain past changes in total output and its components. It enables us to isolate the relationships which must be known in order to predict the future course of the economy and, as more data on these crucial relationships become available, it will permit actual predictions. Finally, it provides a powerful government with a set of weapons which can be used to change the future course of the economy.

RATES OF GROWTH: ACTUAL VERSUS PROPER

Now that both proper and actual levels of investment have been discussed, more attention may be paid to the fact that investment means a growing stock of capital, a widening of the boundary of the attainable, and greater current output. If such changes are expressed as growth rates, it becomes possible to compare the actual with the proper.

Should some exogenous investment occur during a depression period, two things will happen. First, as we have seen, the extra consumption induced by this investment, plus the investment itself, will move the economy in the direction of "full employment." Second, investment will make it possible to produce more goods and services in the future with the same number of workers. If the second effect is stronger than the first, then as soon as the investment is completed, there may be even more unemployment than there was originally. There is evidence that this has occurred in countries where both the accelerator and the m.p.c. were small. In such economies, the push toward full employment would be weak, i.e., the initial investment would result in a relatively small increase in income. On the other hand, if the m.p.c. and the accelerator were large, then there would be a rapid approach to full employment and an overshooting of the mark with inflation as the consequence.

Achievement of the proper growth rate. These two extreme cases suggest that there is some rate of increase of investment which will be just enough to maintain full employment over time. To isolate this crucial rate, we need to bring back into the discussion a concept developed earlier, namely the marginal potential revenue of investment. This, it will be remembered, is the numerical relationship between a change in potential output (income) and the investment which brought it about. We can now see that it bears a family resemblance to the accelerator, which tells how much investment will be induced by a given change in income. Indeed, if the accelerator is small in magnitude, then the MPR, *ceteris paribus*, will be large because the capital-output ratio is common to both. In other words, if a large change in sales will induce a small amount of investment, then a little investment will enable the economy to produce a great many more goods and services. Actually, the relationship between MPR and accelerator is not quite so mechanical and rigid as these remarks suggest. This is primarily because the accelerator refers only to the induced portion of investment whereas the MPR relates to exogenous investment as well. One is backward looking while the other is focused on the future.

To lend concreteness to the search for a happy medium between an economy which does not produce all that it can and one which constantly faces inflation, let us use a numerical example. Suppose we have an economy which is at full employment in the initial period with total income (output) at 100, net investment 15, and consumption taking the remaining 85. Assume further that the marginal propensity to consume is constant at 0.85 and that the MPR is 0.33 (i.e., the increase in potential output in a given period is one-third of the amount invested). In terms of Figure 5.4, which is similar to the diagram on page 154, this means that the intersection indicating the "proper" level of investment occurs at P.[31]

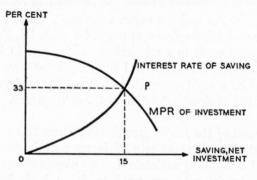

FIGURE 5.4

While investment of 15 assures full employment in the first period, what level of investment will be consistent with it in the next? Since the MPR is 0.33, net investment of 15 means that potential output in period two will increase to $105 = 100 + (0.33 \times 15)$. In order for this potential output to get produced, total spending must also equal 105. Consumption can be counted on only for $89.25 = 85 + (0.85 \times 5)$, which means that net investment must rise to 15.75. If full employment is to be achieved throughout the process of expansion (still assuming the m.p.c. stays at 0.85), in the third period investment must increase to approximately 16.54, in the fourth period to about 17.36, and so forth. This is a 5 per cent rate of growth for investment and also for income.[32] A table of compound interest tells us that with such a growth rate, investment (and income) will quadruple in less than twenty-nine years, which suggests that maintenance of full em-

[31] In the following discussion, it is assumed that the best allocation of total investment among various uses is achieved, i.e., as between several alternatives, those with the highest MPR's are selected.

[32] This is not an unrealistic growth rate for a short period. The United States, over the past fifty years, has managed to average between 3 and 4 per cent; Mexico and the U.S.S.R. in recent years seem to have hit better than 7 per cent; China and India, before the recent changes in governments, however, scarcely kept pace with increases of their populations.

ployment over long periods of time may become a difficult matter.[33]

A diagram, with income plotted on the vertical axis and time on the horizontal, may help to summarize these relationships. The family of curves (only some of which have been drawn) labeled "5" shows

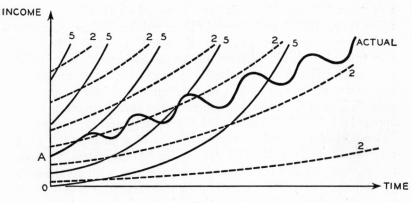

FIGURE 5.5

the path of income and investment over time if the growth rate required for full employment were 5 per cent, and initial income was at the various levels indicated on the vertical axis. In contrast, the family of shallower curves indicates the path of income and investment if the rate of growth were only 2 per cent. The wiggly line labeled "Actual" shows the path taken by a hypothetical economy's income. Initially, the m.p.c. and MPR of this economy were such that full employment meant a 5 per cent growth rate. Thereafter its path shows generally higher rates during the upswings of the cycle and lower ones during downswings, while over the years it has not achieved even 2 per cent growth.

As the reader can see by inserting different values in the mathematical illustration above, an increase of the m.p.c. would shift the economy to one of the family of curves representing a lower growth rate. A drop in MPR has comparable effects while a decrease in the size or vitality of the labor force (or other factors of production)

[33] Representative references on the "growth problem" are E. D. Domar, "Expansion and Employment," *American Economic Review*, Vol. XXXVII (1947); and S. S. Alexander, "The Accelerator as a Generator of Steady Growth," *Quarterly Journal of Economics*, Vol. LXIII (1949).

would counterbalance an increase in potential output brought about by investment and thus work in the same direction as a rising m.p.c or a falling MPR. In these terms, let us ask whether the generally declining growth path of the "actual" economy pictured on our graph is compatible with full employment in the long run or, instead, means stagnation. This question boils down to one of whether the structural ratios (m.p.c., MPR, and the work-leisure ratio) will alter sufficiently with the passage of time to change the growth rate required for full employment so that it conforms to the "actual" growth rate. In the short run it will not, so the cyclical pattern of actual income undoubtedly means alternating periods of deflationary and inflationary pressure. Sudden and fluctuating changes in the crucial structural ratios appear both intuitively and realistically unlikely, and the mathematical model of the previous section tells us what to expect if these ratios are relatively stable. Disregarding the cyclical pattern, however, and concentrating on the trend of income instead, what are the prospects that more gradual changes in the structural ratios will occur as a nation develops and what direction might such changes take?

Concerning the labor force the historical record is mixed. Undeniably in the West with economic development (and increasing income) the length of the work week has been reduced, i.e., leisure has increased. On the other hand, the percentage of the population "gainfully employed" has risen along with levels of skill, education, and health. In western nations this second cluster of factors so far seems to be dominant, although this may be reversed in the future. From the point of view of the presently underdeveloped country, then, the potential growth rate, *ceteris paribus*, will probably be even higher than a simple examination of the m.p.c. and MPR suggest. For an advanced country like the United States it is probably safer to assume that changes in the labor force on balance will have negligible effects on the potential rate of growth.

Evidence on which to base future guesses concerning the m.p.c. is also mixed. With the beginnings of economic development, population typically increases, a rural-urban movement starts, the market widens, patterns of emulation develop, and the complex of socio-psychological factors called "tastes" undergoes changes. Generally, these work in the direction of increasing consumption. In opposition, an "entrepreneurial" value-attitude system favoring frugality and "keeping capital intact," together with rising incomes and the growth of credit institutions, tend to lower the m.p.c., as does the fact that income and wealth often become more unequally distributed during initial stages of development. After a time, the pressures towards higher per capita consumption unquestionably will dominate, unless vigorous political restrictions are imposed. As development proceeds, such factors as wider communication, greater spatial and social mobility, and the emulative drive may well produce sociopolitical pressures which favor greater income equality and push up consumption still further. At a still later stage, declining population growth, increased political and social stability, together with increasing incomes and wealth, may stabilize consumption. Finally, although this is more difficult to say, the strength of the value-attitude system associated with the "protestant ethic" may decline so that the (by then) large quantity of liquid assets held by the population may appear quite sufficient. If this happens, consumption may once again increase by as much or more than income. On balance, then, consumption may keep down the potential growth rate during both early and extremely late stages of development, while in the wide middle range it probably has negligible effects.

The only other possibility depends upon changes in MPR, but here too evidence is contradictory. To the extent that economic growth is associated with increases in the wealth and technological development of a nation, it has already been argued that the accelerator will increase, which means a decreasing MPR with the passage of time. Any decline in the interest rate, increase in entrepreneurial "optimism," or reduction of uncertainty would reinforce these changes in the physical capital-output ratio. There are some reasons to suppose, however, that this may not happen automatically. For example, investment which incorporates technological change may render obsolete some of the existing stock of capital, and some new products may require less capital to manufacture than did the products which they replace. Fewer facilities are needed to maintain and repair the newer fabrics, and passenger transportation by air can be provided with less capital than similar transportation by rail. Such developments will keep the MPR from becoming larger but it is difficult to guess their net impact. Whichever way one reads the evidence, it is difficult to argue that changes in the MPR (or in the labor force and the m.p.c.) will be always just sufficient to achieve and maintain full employment over time. In other words, there is little reason to expect that a given, steady rate of growth will be automatically achieved.

On the one hand, this discussion implies that the future cannot be viewed with equanimity. On the other, it suggests that government policy could be designed to achieve the objectives of the potential growth rate implied by the (changing) magnitudes of the economy's labor force, m.p.c., and MPR. It must be pointed out, however, that almost any government action will affect the potential rate of growth as well as the level of actual income. Redistribution of income accomplished by raising taxes for some people and giving subsidies to others, for instance, will have some effect on the m.p.c. and the amount being spent for consumption. It will therefore change the level of actual income, the amount of investment required for full employment, and thus the potential growth rate. Variations in government expenditures for battleships or post office buildings will have similar consequences.

Application to underdeveloped and advanced economies. The theoretical apparatus constructed in this and previous sections has been designed to fit a wide variety of situations and economies. This means, as we have seen, that empirical information must be incorporated in the theory before it can be used for purposes of explanation or prediction. To illustrate these remarks further, let us consider "typical" underdeveloped and advanced economies.

A so-called underdeveloped economy usually has a relatively high average m.p.c., at least, in comparison to one of the countries bordering the North Atlantic. The underdeveloped nations also appear to have relatively high MPR's (low accelerators). Knowing only this, it is possible to say something regarding the course of economic growth and capital formation. Starting with the short run, we know that in any economy exogenous investment, or indeed an increase in any component of total spending by itself will create an inflationary pressure. If there are mobile and unemployed factors of production, this will result in additional output, otherwise it will lead directly to higher prices. In an "advanced" country, however, the higher accelerator will likely produce alternating periods of inflation and depression in the manner illustrated by the mathematical model examined earlier. The "underdeveloped" nation will also find that prices tend to rise with investment but, in this case, the high m.p.c. (unmodified by a large accelerator) is primarily responsible, so the inflation is much less apt to be followed by a depression. Historically, the pattern of business cycles has been associated with those industrialized nations in which government has played a passive role; this, we now see, is to be expected.[34]

Let us abstract from the cyclical pattern and look at the long-run growth prospects in our two model economies. As was suggested earlier, the advanced country's MPR is relatively low. Nonetheless, it is large enough to cause difficulties because the m.p.c. has at most a slow upward drift and the proportion of the population in the labor force probably will not decrease sufficiently. Even a 2 per cent growth rate means that extremely large income increases will be required to maintain full employment after a time. In the underdeveloped country the MPR itself appears to be quite high, which means that small amounts of investment will yield high potential growth rates. When coupled with the fact that productive factors are relatively immobile, this explains the presence in underdeveloped countries of "hidden" unemployment. Investment widens the gap between actual and potential income by raising the productivity of labor in occupations connected with the investment. Demand for workers in other occupations and places falls and, if movement does not occur, this means additional unemployment. Although both countries might find it difficult to achieve their potential output, the manifestations of these difficulties would be quite different.

A further contrast between these two economies lies in the magnitudes of investment and income involved. If 20 per cent of current total spending were devoted to investment in such a country as the United States, it would amount to about $65 billion; the same percentage applied to the much lower national income of India, for example, would result in only $4 billion of new capital goods. Under these circumstances, the MPR in the United States would have to be

[34] These statements, like all predictions, rest on certain assumptions and would have to be modified if they were not approximated in the real world. For example, if our "underdeveloped" economy consisted entirely of self-sufficient units, consumption would automatically be curtailed whenever investment rose. Since we supposed that the accelerator and the m.p.c. did not undergo any drastic changes as inflationary pressure mounted, the predictions also rested on a whole series of subsidiary assumptions regarding such things as changes in the labor force, technology, distribution of income, and expectations regarding prices and profits.

approximately one-sixteenth the size of India's before potential output would increase by the same absolute amount in each country. Unquestionably, India's MPR is nowhere near that much larger. By itself, this explains why economic development is apt to be more rapid in the advanced country than in the underdeveloped one in the absence of government action.[35] The man in the street expresses the same thought when he says, "Him who has gets."

We can see that a policy designed to prevent both depressions and inflations which is appropriate for the advanced country will be most inappropriate for one which is underdeveloped. In the United States, for example, assuming a peaceful world, the objective might be to put upper and lower limits on investment to cut down cyclical fluctuations, coupled with the encouragement of consumption (including leisure) so that the potential growth rate will decline. In a country like India, on the other hand, the m.p.c. is already high enough to give an inflationary bias to the economy whenever investment occurs. There the aim might be to encourage the mobility and increase the skills of labor so that this high MPR will lead to increased output rather than hidden unemployment. While such policies would reduce inflation, unquestionably it also would be important to keep consumption from rising. Since mobility and consumption are probably related, a more realistic aim for the underdeveloped nation would be to compare the increase in potential output caused by greater mobility with the increase in consumption necessary to get factors moving, and then adopt a policy which would maximize the difference between these—which would be investment.

So far, achievement of a given growth rate has been discussed largely in terms of aggregate investment. The subsidiary problem of getting a "balanced" growth has been bypassed with remarks that of all possible investments, those with the highest MPR's should be selected first. In any program of capital formation, whether centrally planned or directed through a decentralized and impersonal market, a given investment project depends for success on complementary production elsewhere. Not only is it necessary for the goods produced by the new capital to be demanded by consumers but also the various factors of production required in manufacture must be forthcoming. In both cases, proper timing is essential. For the underdeveloped

[35] In this connection, see also the argument on pages 152 ff. *supra*.

country, particularly, this means that investment will probably have to take place in clusters if any part is to succeed. For example, a steel mill requires the simultaneous construction of coal and iron ore mines, of a transportation system, and the existence of a market for finished output.

Any investment program will initially create bottlenecks in some parts of the economy while gluts will occur elsewhere. The elimination of these indications of imbalance depends upon the existence and mobility of requisite productive factors and the demand of intermediate and final consumers. If the possibility of international trade is ignored, then the availability of certain raw materials or of labor possessing particular skills sets an upper limit to the rate and type of capital formation which can be achieved during a given period. In other words, the flexibility of the various sectors and industries of the economy determine the flexibility of the whole. This limit was implicit in the earlier formulation of the "boundary line of the attainable;" it was the reason so much attention was paid to methods by which barriers to factor mobility could be eliminated. Clearly, it is also implicit in the discussion of the over-all growth rate required for full employment.

In the advanced economy this question of balance can, in large measure, be ignored, since each separate investment outlay will be an insignificant fraction of existing capital. Furthermore, the country is wealthy enough to absorb mistakes without undue sacrifice of living standards. It is otherwise with the underdeveloped nation which is building from a small capital stock. Such considerations, together with the real dangers of rapid population growth, have led many to argue that, for the poor country, a little investment may be a dangerous thing and that a massive, many-faceted effort is needed before living standards can be raised permanently. Others point out that cheap international transportation and world trade mean that any small country can easily import those items which are needed for its investment program and can similarly depend on foreign markets when it comes time to sell finished goods. In view of the restrictions which many nations impose on foreign trade and the historical instability of world markets, however, most underdeveloped countries will probably wish to explore the possibilities of achieving balance internally.

The Impact of Government

The fact that major portions of the national incomes of many countries in the world today are attributable to government activity underlines the importance of government's role in the process of investment and the formation of income. A powerful government is able to extract purchasing power from or inject it into an economy in ways not open to households and firms. In addition to ordinary buying and selling, it can tax or hand out subsidies and gifts; it has unusual powers of borrowing and lending; and it can cause money to be created by manipulation of the banking system or by resort to the printing press. In this section, particular attention will be paid to policies which, if adopted by government, would affect the amount and direction of investment.

Starting with the outpayments of government, it is clear that government can add to its own stock of goods (and thus invest) simply by purchasing more during the year than it sells and uses up. The amount and type of capital formation which can be accomplished by this method seems to be limited only by the minimum amount of consumption and private investment which households and firms must be permitted if the particular government is to remain in power. A less direct but analogous method is the use of government funds for the subsidization of private investors and potential investors. We need only consider the many ways in which subsidies may be distributed to see the policy flexibility possible. Loans could be provided at low or even negative interest rates to anyone guaranteeing to invest in a given sort of capital good; outright gifts could be made to certain classes of consumers which, when spent, would induce the firms receiving the money to invest; or government might construct certain facilities itself and give them to private industry. If a government owns any considerable stock of goods, e.g., stockpiles of "strategic" materials, deposits of oil and coal, or timber stands, private investment can be influenced by the way and the rate at which such goods are distributed.

The inpayments of government, which consist of taxes, borrowing, and sales, provide still other opportunities for manipulating the economy. An increase in the personal income tax, for instance, will reduce consumption or saving and thus affect investment. By drying up some saving, it initially forces the interest rate up, while its effect on consumption reduces the receipts of business. (If the tax is progressive, saving will bear most of the burden.) Thus there will be a double reduction in induced investment (and income), although if investment falls enough the interest rate may not actually drop.

In addition, the income tax turns out, at the margin, to fall on work and leisure. Above a certain level it probably causes reductions in the labor force by lowering the reward for additional work. At still higher levels it may actually force people to increase the number of man-hours worked if they are to maintain customary living standards. Investment will also be affected via this channel since a change in man-hours offered for hire will change the cost of producing investment goods. Finally, most income taxes change the distribution of income. If the tax is progressive, for instance, purchases of "necessities" will rise at the expense of "luxury" goods, which will affect the profitability of investment in facilities designed to produce these different types of goods and, for this reason, the composition of investment.

A tax levied on a specific commodity, to take another example, clearly drives investment out of the industry being hit. To the extent that consumers escape the tax by shifting their purchases, some additional investment will be induced in industries making non-taxed goods. Those households who pay higher prices in order to buy the taxed commodities will have less income remaining for other purposes, including saving, and this, *ceteris paribus*, will affect investment by putting pressure on the interest rate. A tariff is a special case of a tax on a specific commodity. It differs from that just considered because many of the negative effects on investment occur in the exporting country, whose sales fall as the export flow dries up. In contrast, most of the positive effects are reserved for manufacturers in the country levying the tariff. A great many other possibilities for influencing investment become obvious when we remember that subsidies are simply negative taxes and generally have reverse consequences. A reduction in a given subsidy would be the same as a rise in a comparable tax, and vice versa.

In addition to being able to take money out of the economy by taxation, the government may also borrow. In this way it can decrease (selectively or generally) funds which would otherwise become available for investment. Since the government does not need to show a profit, it can always successfully compete with private business for loanable funds by lowering the price of its bonds, i.e., raising the interest rate. It can offer bonds for sale only to certain classes of buyers just as it can refuse to make loans for certain purposes. Such changes in the cost and availability of credit clearly may be used to alter investment.

Now that some of the items which might appear on the two sides of a government table of in- and outpayments have been considered, it requires little imagination to envisage the vast number of "combination policies" which are possible. For example, government might, during a given year, raise certain taxes, lower others, increase a few subsidies, auction off some oil rights, and build a new railroad.

So far, no mention has been made of the relationship between total inpayments and outpayments. Varying the difference between the two totals opens up still other opportunities for affecting investment. If the government on balance takes money out of the economy, i.e., runs a surplus, this will create deflationary pressure, while a deficit will push the economy towards inflation. This is easy to see when we remember that taxation generally reduces the size of the spending stream, while expenditures by government (or anyone else) increases it. The connection between a deficit (or surplus) and changes in the level of investment are fairly obvious. Indeed, the the oretical model which occupied our attention earlier was designed to show just this connection. The path of investment and income produced by the interaction of accelerator and multiplier could as easily have been initiated by a government deficit as by exogenous investment.[36]

Should inflationary pressure continue after full employment has been reached and prices rise, this may well change the behavior of both households and firms in a way which encourages investment both directly and indirectly. Not only will firms find themselves with un-

---

[36] In real rather than money terms, however, there is a difference. As a consequence of exogenous investment, there will be additional capital as well as extra consumption and the investment induced by it; in the case of a deficit, the effect on real income comes only from induced consumption and investment. This just means that to achieve a given increase in total investment a larger deficit will be needed. We are ignoring the problems faced by a government which runs a continuous deficit and so builds up a large debt. These problems, however, are quite different from those encountered by a firm or household which operates in the red.

expected profits because prices are rising, but their sales may swell as consumers purchase more in anticipation of further price increases. Inflation will also change the distribution of income. Those whose incomes are fixed, such as pensioners, "white collar" workers, bondholders, and other lenders, will suffer while those whose incomes are more directly tied to profits gain. Insofar as profit takers are innovators and business managers, investment will be encouraged by this shift in income distribution. It will tend to make them more prosperous and optimistic and, in addition, their social status may be enhanced as well. However, inflation can also create a situation which encourages commodity and real estate speculation. And this will not always be favorable for investment.

Other quite different devices are also available to a strong government which wishes to influence capital formation. Those mentioned in the last few pages have been tied to government's expenditures and receipts, but the government can affect the entire social and economic climate which surrounds household and firm in other ways. For example, laws governing property and job rights can be changed, rationing and controls over prices of products and factors can be instituted, and new and different systems of rewards and punishments can be inserted into the economy. The government of an underdeveloped country may find it necessary to tamper with the existing structure of society in just such ways to speed the growth process. Because of this, the cluster of institutions and behavior patterns which permit and encourage the private market to function as a regulator of economic activity deserve special mention.

The impersonal competition which characterizes the unconscious cooperation of the "free enterprise" system solves many of the communication and allocation problems which would otherwise plague a host of administrators. Within limits it transmits the wishes of spending units to producers and encourages the movement of factors away from occupations which are not in demand. Although it heavily penalizes those who ignore the signals, the private market mechanism holds out large rewards to successful innovators. It is of great assistance to any development program, and a government might well wish to promote its use. Thus it becomes important to increase the scope of the market by improving transportation, extending the use of money and credit, increasing factor mobility by eliminating barriers to entry and exit, and by encouraging the dissemination of information about conditions of supply and demand. For this same reason, it is also important to perform in other ways those functions which the private market can only fulfill defectively, if at all. For instance, some prices may need adjustment so they will reflect all costs and benefits, not just private; the distribution of income and wealth may have to be changed so the economy's reward system will more nearly coincide with the population's wishes and the requirements of development; provision must be made for the production and distribution of so-called community goods. And, almost more important for the purposes of this chapter, there is the special need to regulate the flow of investment and to maintain high levels of employment and income.

Problems of a country in the process of development. By way of review, let us consider some of the problems faced by an underdeveloped country in its search for more capital and larger per capita income. This exercise will also be directly useful since elimination of these problems will undoubtedly be part of a developing nation's policy objectives. In the "typical" underdeveloped country most of the existing population live in rural areas and are close to the subsistence level even though there is considerable hidden unemployment. Birth and death rates are high. The distribution of income and wealth is quite unequal and the few wealthy landlords and businessmen oppose any governmental policies which they feel will damage their position in the society. This group controls significant supplies of productive factor, can make entry into crucial industries difficult, and does virtually all the private saving. The government is weak, although increasing in power, and cannot lightly step on these groups who possess social prestige and economic strength. Markets are restricted in scope because of a severe lack of transportation and communication, and relatively little use is made of money and paper claims to ownership.

The existence of hidden unemployment means that the level of income can be raised without resort to outside aid. Before these underemployed factors of production may be used for capital formation, however, some way must be found of removing them from agriculture. A number of socio-psychological as well as physical barriers to mobility have to be eliminated and suitable rewards (and punishments) provided. Although agricultural output will not drop with the removal of the hidden unemployed (their marginal productivity in agriculture is zero or less), the agricultural goods will continue to go to those still connected with the farm. If those producing the new capital are to eat, this ownership tie must be severed and the necessary consumer goods shifted spatially along with the factors. Further, if the construction of capital goods requires an urban setting, such facilities as housing, stores, sanitation, police protection, and highways will also have to be provided.

An additional and major complication remains. The death rate of the agricultural population may drop as the number of those engaged in agriculture is reduced. Since there is no reason to suppose the birth rate will also fall, such an event might doom the entire undertaking. Either the standard of living of those on the land or of those who have been shifted would have to fall, and this might mean starvation for some.[37]

There is still the problem of actually getting the additional plant and equipment constructed. This means (1) using domestic factors to construct it; (2) expanding the output of goods which can be exported and then exchanging them for the desired capital items; or (3) exchanging the exported goods directly for the additional consumers' goods which are ultimately desired.[38] National pride and fear of losing sovereignty if the economy becomes too dependent on outside sources for critical commodities may well rule out method (3) and tip the scales slightly in favor of the first method. On the other hand, a cost comparison made for the short run would probably reverse this order, although in the long run this is more doubtful. Consider, for example, the costs of importing capital goods. In addition to the purchase price, these include transportation from the country of manufacture, installation charges, and the costs connected with maintaining, recruiting, and training labor and the owners of other factors of production. In contrast, the cost of obtaining plant and equipment domestically include all but the first two of those just listed plus the cost of actually constructing the capital. And additional plant and equipment would be needed to build the desired facilities which involves the maintenance, recruit-

[37] Reasons why the death rate would fall under such circumstances while the birth rate would not were discussed in Chapter III, *supra*.

[38] Here we are ignoring the further possibility of intergovernment loans, gifts, etc. See Chapter VIII.

ment, and training of additional productive factors. (Part of this last cost as well as that of the necessary primary industry should be allocated to investment produced in future periods, although it would have to be borne at the outset.) [39]

The complex of problems which have so far plagued our hypothetical, developing country may be solved in several ways. Some sorts of investment, such as rural highways or drainage ditches, can be constructed without moving factors very far from their present locations; training is not required and provision of food and housing is automatic. In such cases government can get the needed labor by levying a tax which may be paid by working so many hours, while the purchase of simple hand tools (capital) is not too expensive. Many high priority investments, however, are not of this sort and more "civilized" methods are required.

To obtain the necessary money for more ambitious projects, saving must voluntarily rise or be "forced" either by increased taxes or inflation. The first of these is unlikely; the second, difficult and for the most part politically unwise. We are left then with inflation and those taxes which are hard to identify, easy to collect, or those which can be placed on unpopular groups. Taxes levied on the export-import trade, the infant wholesale business, and certain luxury or socially unacceptable commodities fit these requirements. A small head tax and graduated license fees collected from those engaged in unpopular and undesirable activities would also serve, as would a levy on any funds removed from the country for other than specified purposes.

Whereas a tax structure of this sort, coupled with inflation, would tend to drive factors out of certain occupations, additional measures would undoubtedly be needed to increase factor mobility. A traditional but expensive method is to raise the incomes of those producing desired investment goods. More forceful devices, such as giving certain groups a choice between the armed forces or specified occupations, are also available. Education, which probably increases mobility and skills in the long run, can be provided in exchange for a year or two of government-directed employment. In many cases an information service and gifts (or loans) to cover the cost of moving and job training may be sufficient.

---

[39] This discussion is incomplete because such things as balance-of-payment difficulties and terms of trade between nations have been ignored. In this connection, see Chapter VIII.

When it comes to building the new capital goods, a similar range of devices are available. In this connection, we have already mentioned direct construction by government and the use of various sorts of subsidies. These could range from low-interest loans, gifts, and tax rebates to franchises, patents, tariffs, and other monopoly privileges. Many of such measures mean either raising government expenditures or lowering receipts. Thus they place additional strain on the tax structure or involve further inflationary financing.[40]

One of the costs of investment to be considered when deciding both the total amount and its composition is inflation itself. Since even moderate inflation may change the value-attitudes of the community's members, as well as prices, expectations, and the distribution of income, the evaluation of its costs is a value-laden problem of higher order. Without attempting to solve this problem, those investment alternatives which increase factor mobility, make use of relatively plentiful and inexpensive factors, and those promising quick returns in terms of increased output of consumer goods will minimize inflation. Insofar as the underdeveloped country finds it more difficult than an advanced one to estimate future needs and conditions, an additional reason is provided for encouraging approximately these same categories of diversified new capital goods. Such remarks just mean that those investment projects undertaken at any time should have the highest MPR's of all those possible.

To illustrate the sort of calculations required, consider some of the consequences of agricultural investment which raises productivity so that the same output can be produced with fewer workers. If population has not increased, this means that total agricultural income may actually fall while its distribution will probably become more unequal. There may even be a tendency for the m.p.c. to fall. Hidden and partial unemployment may be transformed into the full-time variety and, by inducing a rural-urban movement, this may make recruitment of an industrial work force easier. All this assumes, of course, that appropriate investments are being undertaken outside agriculture. In fact, after a time it might be possible to increase other sorts of investment without inflation since the changes in agriculture, taken separately, would have deflationary consequences for the economy. The other possibility is that the greater agricultural productiv-

---

[40] If foreign loans or gifts are available, this will pass some of the inflationary pressure to the foreign country and so help prevent threatened domestic inflation from getting out of control.

ity be used to produce exportable, farm-grown commodities which would be directly exchanged for the industrial products needed to raise living standards. One possibility does not exclude the other.

Once our underdeveloped country has managed to get well started on the process of capital formation and living standards have begun to increase, other problems arise—problems which are now being faced by more advanced nations. Consumer goods must be distributed so as not to interfere with continued capital growth. The return from their sale must be enough to "justify" the investment already undertaken, yet consumption must not increase so much that the flow of saving required for further investment is dried up.[41] This is no mean accomplishment. The successful distribution of most mass-produced articles depends upon a large market, and this may require a more equal distribution of income. Certainly it means a widening of the physical extent of the market and consequent extensions of the use of money. (A more equal distribution of income may also have been necessary to induce the factor movements discussed earlier.) The marginal propensity to consume of underdeveloped countries is high, even given their present distribution of income and wealth. In addition, the m.p.c. for new, mass-produced goods may be higher than for traditional goods and services so that the changing composition of output may also push up consumption. To the extent that this rise in the standard of living takes place, it may cause the death rate to drop with a consequent population upsurge which will mean further consumption. (Of course, this population upsurge may have begun earlier for reasons already mentioned.)

Once the hidden unemployment which made the initial capital formation possible has been eliminated, additional factors for investment must come from those released by saving. For this reason, an expanding market for consumer goods is not an unmixed blessing. We have now come full circle and are once again discussing the problems which concerned us in the earlier section on rates of growth. The first problem facing our developing country is how to control consumption so that inflation will not occur. Later on, however, as the country's stock of capital swells, the rate of increase of

---

[41] Of course, the market for these consumers' goods need not be a domestic one. They can be exchanged in the international market for additional capital goods, and so forth.

consumption may slow down. This, as we have already seen, may lead to depression.

Devices available to a powerful government which wishes to lower or raise investment have already been discussed. Similar measures are clearly available if the government wants to change consumption. By modifying the composition of investment and consumption as well as by influencing the supply of labor even more dramatic changes in the flow of real income and the rate of growth may be achieved.

Theoretical Framework for Policy

If our objective is the achievement of a proper level of invest-ment and the growth rate this implies, it is necessary in every period to (1) identify this level, (2) measure the divergence between it and the amount actually being added to capital, and (3) adjust the "actual" so that it coincides with the "proper," by environmental manipulation or direct intervention. This, however, provides little help for the administrator who has to make detailed and specific decisions.

We know that it is not particularly easy to determine the proper level of investment. Only under conditions not often found in the real world will the market place provide indicators which are directly useful. Not only must the market indicators be adjusted for known defects but agreement must also be reached as to whether society's time preference ought to be zero; whether the cost of supporting the set of institutional arrangements which lie between the acts of sav-ing and investing is worthwhile; and what constitutes a proper dis-tribution of income and wealth. It will also be remembered that a similar range of intangibles exists on the investment side; namely, in ascertaining the divergence between the actual and the required mar-ginal potential productivity of investment.

Problems of values again rear their heads when it comes to deciding how the total amount of investment ought to be distrib-uted among the various sectors of the economy. To know that new capital should be allocated so that any other arrangement would re-sult in a smaller addition to total output is not particularly helpful unless there is some way of comparing the benefits of more capital in this place with more in that. Here also the market test of profita-bility provides a defective and inadequate measuring rod. Social benefits and costs may not coincide with private, and investment which facilitates community goods output will be quite ignored. As yet, however, ways of measuring accurately the relative desires of the population for community goods have not been invented, nor have methods been devised for putting social and private benefits and costs in common terms. In many cases, it is difficult to ascertain the direction of the divergence, let alone its magnitude. In an underdeveloped country, the problem of determining the proper level of investment in both total and specific senses is particularly hard. Not only is the market in such a country spatially limited but, in comparison to advanced nations, a much smaller proportion of factors and products pass through it regularly. Thus, there are fewer prices to use as value indicators and these probably bear a more remote relationship to the population's wishes.

If we grant that our mythical investment administrator is interested in increasing the welfare of the country's citizens and if the welfare of the whole community depends upon the welfare of each of its members, what must enter into his calculations? [42] He requires a method by which (1) each member of the community will be able to indicate any change in his welfare (subjectively calculated), and (2) changes in the welfare of one individual may be related to changes in that of another. Suppose that the quantity of a given sort of capital is increased. As a result, some of the community's members benefit while others are made worse off. The introduction of mechanical cotton pickers in a region which employed great numbers of hand pickers, the construction of power projects such as TVA, or merely an increase in the number of machines making shoes are cases in point.

Now, a set of hypothetical taxes (and subsidies) can be conceived such that if they were collected (and paid), all members of the community would be no better and no worse off than they were initially. By definition, then, these subsidies and taxes are equivalent respectively to the full social costs and benefits of the investment which have already been discussed. If the administrator calculated that more would come in from taxes than went out in subsidies, he would be reasonably certain that he had selected a beneficial investment.

---

[42] In making this statement, we may disregard those members who are unborn (or have died), since there is no conceivable way by which they can make their wishes known. This does not mean, however, that living members may not pay attention to what they think would be the wishes of other generations.

And if the algebraic sum of these taxes and subsidies could be found for each of the many investments possible, then the administrator would be able to reach a decision as to what ought to be done by choosing those whose net benefits were greatest (however, see the next paragraph).[43] It should be noticed that this analytical approach may be widened to include the over-all choice between consumption and investment as well as that between different sorts of investment.

Once an investment project has been tentatively selected, the next problem is the distribution of these net benefits, i.e., what is the administrator to do with the real (positive) difference between the hypothetical compensating taxes and subsidies? His objective is clear: to distribute it so that the initial distribution of income and wealth, plus that added, will be closer to what is "proper" than could be achieved by any other possible distribution. This will not be easy since at present it seems impossible to identify a distribution of income which would generally be considered proper. Not only does each person tend to think he deserves more, but the well-being of society's members depends in part on the distribution of benefits itself. One individual may gain satisfaction simply because he is better off than someone else. At first glance, it might seem that calculation of the net benefits of the various investment policies could, in any event, be separated from distributive problems. This, however, is not the case; the size of taxes (or subsidies) necessary to leave a person just as well off as he was before depends upon how much that person had. Consequently, weights must be attached to the hypothetical taxes (or subsidies) to be paid by different individuals; the size of the weights being determined by the divergence between the benefits initially possessed by the various individuals in comparison with the share they "ought" to have had.[44]

By this time, it is clear that the proper level of investment must be determined in fairly arbitrary fashion. There are no formulae which enable policy makers to reach decisions without making value judg-

[43] Technically, this hypothetical, algebraic sum would have to be calculated after subtracting the real costs of calculating the hypothetical taxes and bounties plus the hypothetical cost to the economy and its members of seeing that the hypothetical compensations were collected and paid.

[44] For a recent survey of "welfare economics," the topic discussed in the last few pages, see Kenneth E. Boulding, "Welfare Economics," in A Survey of Contemporary Economics, Vol. II, B. F. Haley, editor (Homewood, Illinois: Richard D. Irwin, Inc., 1952).

ments and guessing about the future. In practice, the customary procedure is to set a "target" for investment policy consisting of so
much more of this sort of capital by some future date and so much
more of that; the various quantities being chosen with an eye to the
political power possessed by government, the size of the gap between
actual and potential output, and a set of value-attitudes regarding
the calculation and distribution of benefits and costs which are not
stated explicitly.

The next step in policy formation—that of predicting the path
which will be taken by actual investment—is, as we have seen, technically difficult. But these difficulties are of a different order from
those which have just been discussed. They can, in principle, be overcome by gathering appropriate empirical data and fitting them into
the appropriate economic model.[45]

The social scientist is also of use when it comes to the final
step in policy determination: The selection and design of policies
which will change the actual level of investment in some predetermined fashion. Knowledge of the real world and the way its component parts react to changes in their environment may be used to
predict the consequences of a given action by government, as well as
what would happen if government did nothing. This ability to predict obviously can be turned inside out and used to isolate the actions required to achieve desired results, i.e., if the consequences of
a given government action can be predicted, then it is possible to
say that given consequences will follow the adoption of certain policies. In practice, however, the scientist will not possess complete information about the real world nor be sure which of several
competing theoretical models to employ. The best he can do under
these circumstances is make "probability" statements of this form:
There are eight chances out of ten that this objective will be achieved
by these policies. (Any sort of prediction, however, must also be
stated in this manner and for the same reasons.)

To employ social science in such a way is cause for both hope and
alarm. Knowledge of how to change the actual level of investment

[45] This model must take account of the fact that predictions themselves may
influence the behavior of the economic units which are part of the model. For
example, knowledge that economists predict a depression of a certain magnitude
may cause the behavior of firms and households to change in a manner which will
vitiate the initial prediction. In contrast, the natural scientist can properly assume
that his atoms and amoeba know nothing of his predictions.

is of little use until government possesses considerable power. Yet, such a government is able to disregard the wishes of its citizens within wide limits and instead design investment policies which will lead to "improper" objectives. Almost more alarming in its implications is the fact that a strong government can, with known techniques, modify the desires of its citizens. And there is nothing in the analysis developed which tells us whether these will be better or worse than those they replace. Still, the acceptance of such risks seems to be the price which must be paid in order to gain the power to achieve certain objectives. It seems that we must choose between alternatives, none of which we really like.[46]

Unwillingness to assume such risks has led many to oppose virtually all actions of government designed to influence economic development. Instead, they prefer the unhampered price system, coupled with private property, as a regulator of economic activity. This chapter has been more eclectic in approach. Many things the decentralized and impersonal market can accomplish remarkably well; others, as we have seen, it does poorly or not at all. By pointing to various ways in which government might intervene, we have implicitly taken a middle road between those who fear every intrusion of government into the economy and those who advocate total government direction. In cases where the private market is only slightly defective or where the choice between it and more authoritarian measures is a matter of indifference, we would argue for the market place. Our guiding principle has been the maximum satisfaction of the whole population, both now and in the future.

[46] The implication of the last few pages might seem to be that the social scientist *qua* technician is not permitted to make any statements either for or against a given set of objectives. This is not quite correct. In order to deduce a policy, the scientist must work with a set of objectives which are both internally consistent and sufficient for the job. Since he will be unable to proceed unless the objectives given him meet these requirements, it is his proper function to point out any respects in which they fall short of these requirements.

CHAPTER VI

Entrepreneurship and Technological Change

YALE BROZEN* ¹

AT THEIR 1952 MEETING, THE GOVERNORS OF THE INTERNATIONAL BANK for Reconstruction and Development and of the International Monetary Fund studied the contention that they were playing *Macbeth* without Macbeth. The International Bank, the Technical Assistance Administration of the United Nations, the United States Technical Cooperation Administration, and other agencies were making efforts to raise income levels in sections of the world dissatisfied with their economic status. Capital was being supplied to these areas; training programs for the development of special skills were under way; technicians versed in devising ways of improving methods were available. But a vital spark necessary to catalyze technological advance and economic growth was missing. The entrepreneur had been neglected.

Fashion seems to rule as strongly in the world of economic policy as in that of women's dress. One area of policy, in particular, has seen a startling change of style in the last decade. In this period, the convention of attacking the problem of poverty by remolding dis-

* Professor of Economics, Northwestern University. Author: "Social Impact of Technological Change," *Journal of Engineering Education* (Nov., 1950); "Value of Technological Change," *Ethics* (July, 1952); "Adapting to Technological Change," *Journal of Business* (April, 1951); "An Alternative Program for Maintaining Farm Prosperity," *Current Economic Comment* (May, 1953); *Textbook for Economics*.

¹ I am indebted to the Rockefeller Foundation and to the Graduate School at Northwestern University for grants which made possible the research on which this paper is based. The Trusteeship Division of the United Nations and the United States Department of State gave their cooperation in providing opportunities to interview informants.

196

tribution has given way to the policy of attacking poverty by increasing production.

During the last 150 years, fashion in policy for attacking poverty has come full circle. When Adam Smith wrote his *Inquiry Into the Wealth of Nations*, the problem of distribution was thought important, but only to the extent that different patterns of income division might affect rates of population growth and accumulation of national wealth. In the succeeding century, the center of interest gradually shifted. The problem of what determined the division of income among classes and, climaxed by the Marxian analysis, what this might do to the relationship among classes, and what might be done to it, took the center of the stage.

There were always those who claimed that poverty could be alleviated only by increasing production. The pessimistic aspects of classical analysis and the views of Marxian enthusiasts came to dominate, however, reaching their peak of popularity after the difficulties of the early 1930's. The iron law of wages, which held that wage rates would always be at subsistence levels except during periods of temporary disequilibria, and the Marxian dogma, that the rich would grow richer and the poor poorer as a consequence of industrialization, seemed to preclude any solution via the route of increased output. Experience in the depressed 30's was regarded as final corroboration.

More recent experience has brought the circle around. English postwar attempts to eliminate poverty by redistribution ran head on into the brutal fact that there must be a larger income to distribute if the poor are to become less poor. In the late 1940's, it became apparent that improvements in the lot of the lower one-third could go no further if changes in the division of income were the only method open. The English Labor party began, for this reason, to shift its policy from one of concentrating on the redivision of wealth and income to one of pressing for increased output. Similarly, heightened concern with the underdeveloped areas of the world furthered the idea that only by increasing production could "adequate" incomes be provided.

We have rediscovered the elementary principle, which was always kept in the foreground by the policy makers of the late eighteenth and early nineteenth centuries, that labor, capital, and natural resources are necessary to produce an income in any area, but not sufficient in themselves. We are again aware that, to increase income improvements in technology are required as well as supplies of factors of production, although demands for a moratorium on science were heard only a few years ago. Innumerable cases may be cited where better methods could increase, or have increased, production. With the present supply of labor and capital used in the hand loom industry in India, for example, output would be increased 30 per cent by substituting the fly for the throw shuttle. Technological advance has increased food production 46 per cent in Etawah, India, in the last few years, with little change in the supplies of productive factors.

The Role of the Entrepreneur

In bringing into use the techniques which will wring an adequate income from a group of resources, someone has to make the decisions required to institute new methods in place of old. These decisions may be made by members of legislative committees, cabinet members, heads of government enterprises, and other such government officials, or they may be private individuals operating with nongovernmental resources.

Since the major spheres of production have been in private hands in Western civilization, most innovations have been made by those controlling ultimate decision-making power in private enterprises. Another reason for this state of affairs is the fact that the kinds of persons who have been selected to fill government posts were less likely to be innovators than the kinds of persons who started new private enterprises.[2] Also, government service has not provided an environment conducive to innovation.

Regardless of whether decisions to innovate are more likely to be made by those in government or private enterprises, some group must not only be available but also be willing and able to make such decisions. Otherwise, economic growth will not occur.

In this chapter, the extent to which entrepreneurship is necessary to bring about improvements in technology and productivity will be examined. We shall find that other types of decision makers may do the job, but they are less likely to do it as efficiently as entrepreneurs

[2] See David Riesman, *The Lonely Crowd* (New Haven: Yale University Press, 1950). Also, F. H. Knight, *Journal of Political Economy*, December, 1938, pp. 867–69.

checked and goaded by competition. We shall find that even with a supply of entrepreneurs, advances in the technology employed will not necessarily occur. A certain type of entrepreneur is required. Also, certain types of market arrangements are needed in order to transmit pressure to lagging enterprises from those which introduce more economical arrangements. We shall examine the circumstances necessary to produce the required type of entrepreneur and to transmit pressure to others. Finally, we shall examine technology itself and determine what types of technology are appropriate at different stages of development and what types of technological change are most economical in moving toward and promoting higher income levels.

Economic development is so intimately tied to entrepreneurship that entrepreneurs have been defined as those who institute "new combinations." [3] A new combination may involve a new product, a new method of production, development of a new market, the utilization of new sources of productive factors, or a new form of organization. Although this definition emphasizes the dynamic role of entrepreneurs, it does not take into account the important function of risk taking or assumption of the responsibility for the results of decisions. As practically every decision to initiate new combinations involves an element of risk, it seems more appropriate to define the entrepreneur in terms of both the innovating and risk-bearing functions.

Those who institute new combinations (i.e., put resources to work producing new products or who recombine resources using different techniques to produce an old product or who enlarge old organizations or establish new organizations to produce a good) may or may not be entrepreneurs. If the men who institute "new combinations" bear no responsibility for the results, they are innovators but not entrepreneurs in the sense of our definition. If control of a producing enterprise is vested in a group of nonremovable directors with salaries independent of their success, control and responsibility are split, and there is no locus of entrepreneurship.

Entrepreneurs may or may not undertake a managerial role in their enterprises. The essential feature of their control is the conscious exercise of ultimate power in the selection of persons to fill

[3] See Joseph Schumpeter, *Business Cycles*, New York, McGraw-Hill Book Co., 1939, p. 103.

the managerial role. They may make no other decision except to hire one manager rather than another.[4] They do, however, bear the responsibility for managerial decisions in that they bear the losses or receive the profits resulting from a decision anywhere in their enterprises.

In a society with no need or desire for change, entrepreneurs or others who might institute new combinations are unnecessary.[5] If men wish to go on doing the same jobs and consuming the same goods in traditional ways, and if those filling the different occupations reproduce at rates just sufficient to man jobs as they fall vacant, no change in resource use or patterns of combining resources will be necessary. Neither new decisions nor entrepreneurs for the purpose of making new decisions will be required.

It is not in the execution of an existing plan, but in decisions as to the introduction of new plans that undertaking [entrepreneurial] genius [finds] its chief employment. As pioneer the undertaker [reaps] his proudest gains; and as pioneer he [carries] on in the tradition of Adam Smith's hero, who bestowed increasing opulence on mankind through the extension of the division of labor.[6]

Even where new decisions are wanted in order to make use of additional productive factors, new techniques, or to change the quantities or types of goods produced, they may be made by persons who do not bear the responsibility for results. Entrepreneurs are necessary only to the extent that we want to make changes as efficiently as possible. That is, only to the extent that we want change not simply for the sake of change but in order to get a greater yield of wanted ends are entrepreneurs required.

Suppose, for example, nonremovable directors with salaries independent of success were in charge of productive activities. New decisions necessary to make use of additional facilities or to introduce new techniques could be made, but they would not be motivated in the direction of greatest efficiency. The directors would make changes in the operation of their organization when they feel them to be necessary and worth making. However, there would be little motivation

[4] F. H. Knight, *Risk, Uncertainty, and Profit* (Boston and New York: Houghton Mifflin Co., 1921), p. 291.

[5] M. Dobb, *Capitalist Enterprise and Social Progress* (London: George Routledge and Sons, 1926), pp. 19–20.

[6] N. Kaldor, "The Equilibrium of the Firm," *Economic Journal*, March, 1934, pp. 60-76.

to choose those product mixes which best serve consumers or to choose resource combinations which minimize cost (maximize product from the available resources).

The marriage of control and responsibility is an effective device for promoting efficiency. Where those with any control of production, whether managers or production workers, receive a fixed compensation which is little affected by the quality or quantity of their work, efficiency is likely to suffer. John Stuart Mill argued that fixed, customary wage rates are not conducive to efficiency since the man who turns out more product is paid no more than the one who turns out less. The main motivation of both managers and workers on fixed salaries is either to minimize their work[7] or to do those things which interest them in a hobby sense.[8] However, even if it became a hobby to minimize costs and produce the products most preferred by consumers, there would be no check on mistakes and no automatic selection process for removing those less capable in making a success of this hobby. If directors bear no responsibility for the decisions they make (i.e., no penalties for mistakes or rewards for success), it is exceedingly improbable that such decision-making would be as efficient as that of entrepreneurs who are subject to the pressures of a competitive market.[9]

It is often argued that in fact managers rather than entrepreneurs control large enterprises, even where they are privately owned. In this situation, it is assumed, little difference is to be found between managerial direction of government enterprises and of large private enterprises.[10] However, there is a competitive check on the

[7] A *Pravda* editorial of April 15, 1941, for example, praises a section of the Soviet invention act of March 5, 1941, designed to circumvent bureaucrats and *procrastinators* "who tried to brush off inventors like pestering flies." Cited by F. Hughes, "Incentive for Soviet Initiative," *Economic Journal*, September, 1946, p. 415.

[8] F. H. Knight, *op. cit.*, p. 361.

[9] Such completely state owned and operated systems as the Russian have been forced to recognize the necessity of an entrepreneurial type of control to increase productivity efficiently. Peter Drucker writes of Russian industrial executives receiving bonuses for lower costs or increased output. See "Stalin Pays 'Em What They're Worth," *Saturday Evening Post*, July 21, 1945.

[10] Bert Hoselitz has presented an excellent analysis of differences in managerial behavior under various forms of private and state control, together with the implications of this for the problems of underdeveloped areas. "Entrepreneurship and Economic Growth," *American Journal of Economics and Sociology*, October, 1952.

activities of a private enterprise. Also, managers in a private enterprise with torpid stockholders are subject to the possibility that if their enterprise is less profitable than it could be, a new entrepreneurial group may obtain control by purchasing the stock at a depressed price and replace lackadaisical with aggressive management. Since ultimate control and responsibility lie in the hands of owners of voting stock, entrepreneurial groups who have ideas for improving efficiency can get those ideas into operation by obtaining a stock interest. They are motivated to do so since rewards will follow the improvement of efficiency.

Many government and other nonprofit enterprises are measured by such numerous and inexact criteria, and often by criteria which have nothing to do with the avowed objectives of the enterprise, that there is no real check on their managers except for the most flagrant and obvious abuses. Although a theft of stamps is dealt with readily by the United States Post Office, failure to provide services worth their cost and provision of services costing far more than they are worth result in waste which not only meets with little objection but also may even bring commendation.

Entrepreneurship and Technological Advance

The role of the entrepreneur in advancing technology has such an intimate connection that many entrepreneurs have been mistakenly designated as the inventors of the devices they successfully brought into general use. Robert Fulton is thought of as the inventor of the steamboat, although there is a record of about thirty steamers built before the *Clermont*.[11] He was not the inventor, but rather the entrepreneur who took prior inventions and put them to practical use. Samuel Morse was the founder of a telegraph company, not the inventor of the telegraph. Von Sommering was telegraphing electrically in 1809, almost three decades before Morse built his system. Thomas Edison was successful in bringing the electric lamp into general use as much because of his entrepreneurial talents as because of his inventive genius.[12]

In studying the history of invention, we are struck by what ap-

[11] W. Kaempffert, *Science Today and Tomorrow* (New York: Viking Press, 1939).
[12] H. C. Passer, *The Electrical Manufacturers, 1875–1900* (Cambridge: Harvard University Press, 1953), pp. 78–128.

pears to be the greater difficulties of bringing an invention to economic fruition than those of overcoming the initial technical problems. Neither the ability to invent nor the mere act of invention produces an economic device or persuades people to use the device in place of less economic methods. After invention, there is frequently a long period of development in which a promoter-entrepreneur who has faith sees to it that "bugs" are eliminated, the design brought to the point where it is economical to use, and methods of manufacture devised which can produce the device at sufficiently low cost to make it worth producing.

The work of the inventor or the discoverer in such changes is only the first step. If the change is to descend from the realm of theory to that of practice, the adoption and introduction of the invention or the actual exploitation of the discovery will have to be arranged. This is a quite distinct matter from the invention itself, and is by no means the simple matter which the words imply. It will need the combination of two rather subtle qualities about which at present we have little precise knowledge. First, it will need the intuitive quality of choosing between numerous alternatives and choosing the right one, a quality which will require a certain power of imagination—the power to grasp and to conceive future possibilities. Second, it will need a certain courageous self-confidence—confidence enough to make the choice, and courage enough to force it into effect even in the face of opposition and when there is very little scientific basis to render the outcome anything but extremely uncertain. Bitterest scepticism before making a choice, persistent and unerring faith in the choice when it is made—these are both necessary if decisions are to be the right ones, and if the enforcement of them is to be carried to success. In social life this quality is essentially the creative quality. The loss of it spells stagnation, however bright may be the genius of science and however great the devotion of those who toil.[13]

The case of the lithomat method of duplication provides a recent experience demonstrating the essential role of the entrepreneur.[14] Around 1934, J. E. Gilligan conceived an idea for a lithographic plate made with paper which could be used for office duplication. He interested an engineer and a papermaker in developing plates and paper and an office equipment manufacturer in furnishing capital. These people became discouraged in 1936, but Gilligan continued experimentation on his own until 1939. He found other sources

[13] M. Dobb, op. cit., p. 33.
[14] J. K. Butters and J. Lintner, Effect of Federal Taxes on Growing Enterprises (Boston: Harvard Graduate School of Business Administration, 1945), pp. 167–87.

of capital at that time, and finally began making commercial sales in 1941. Operations were unprofitable, and further capital had to be raised. As the result of the faith and efforts of Gilligan and of others who became associated with him after 1941, material problems were worked out, and the lithomat method was finally brought to the point of economic feasibility in 1943. Nine years of promotional effort by Gilligan were required to bring into use a new duplicating method. During this time, the method was examined and rejected by experts in the field, some of them working for office equipment companies which were seeking similar methods. Gilligan's entrepreneurship was the main force which made the new technique for economic duplication available and pushed it into wide use.

The main charge against enterprises lacking entrepreneurial control is not that they delay the introduction of new techniques or that they make mistakes. Entrepreneurs, too, are often slow and make mistakes. But the cost to the society of their actions is kept small where a check is imposed by the necessity of meeting a market test, especially when the market is competitive.

The Quality of Entrepreneurship

It seems that control of production by potential innovators is necessary for generating technological advance in the most efficient way. However, is this sufficient for advance? Judging by experience in many sections of the world, it is not. Peasant proprietors in India, for example, have continued to farm in traditional patterns for centuries, with little improvement in methods.[15] English businessmen in some industries are notorious for such poor performance that it

---

[15] This should not be taken to mean that the *typical* Indian peasant never introduces a new product or technique. M. Marriott, reporting on his observations in the area of a village about 100 miles from New Delhi ("Technological Change in Overdeveloped Rural Areas," *Economic Development and Cultural Change,* December, 1952), writes:

"Although this area had seemed at first to be very backward and unchanging I was struck soon afterwards with evidence of a great amount of recent development. Indeed, the very existence of a population problem implied that there had been extensive recent technological expansion and change. . . . Farmers in my village were cultivating potatoes, corn, tomatoes and a strain of improved cotton, all of them imported from America. . . . A home-made seed drill was being used for sowing wheat in place of the broadcasting by hand which had been traditional. Big, hand-cranked, rotary iron chaff-cutters were cutting half of the fodder eaten by village animals. A gasoline flour mill was grinding one-third of the village grain and beginning to replace the stone querns formerly used in every house."

was easy for those industries to show better performance after nationalization. Something more than control of activity is required.

Clarence Danhof's classification of types of entrepreneurs points the way to the something extra required.[16] His classification is:

1. *Innovating entrepreneurship*, characterized by aggressive assemblage of information and the analysis of results deriving from novel combinations of factors. Men in this group were generally aggressive in experimentation and exhibited celerity in putting attractive possibilities into practice.

2. *Imitative entrepreneurship*, characterized by readiness to adopt successful innovations inaugurated by innovating entrepreneurs. (In American agriculture of the period ranging about 1830, Groups 1 and 2 were often derogatorily termed "book" farmers.)

3. *"Fabian" entrepreneurship*, characterized by very great caution and skepticism (perhaps simply inertia) but which does imitate when it becomes perfectly clear that failure to do would result in a loss of the relative position of the enterprise.

4. *Drone entrepreneurship*, characterized by a refusal to adopt opportunities to make changes in production formulae even at the cost of severely reduced returns relative to other like producers.[17]

Innovating and imitating entrepreneurs are required for efficient technological advance. In order to have more than an occasional innovator, however, constant entrance of new entrepreneurs seems to be necessary.[18] Inventions may appear which are worthwhile, but they frequently are not adopted or are adopted as slowly as in nonentrepreneurially controlled units if established firms are the only outlets. The outcome of a "bet" on a new method or product is very uncertain. As a consequence, even decision makers with the best interests of the public in mind would turn down, and have, many of the innovations which are of major importance in our economy today. *Future* stated the case very well when it said:

Any public body must be selective and conservative. The history of industrial progress shows that radical innovations have usually been established without help from the leaders of the industry and often in

[16] "Observations on Entrepreneurship in Agriculture," reported by R. Wohl in *Change and the Entrepreneur* (Cambridge: Harvard University Press, 1949).

[17] The "drone entrepreneur" is not fulfilling his social role, because he refuses to assume any innovating function.

[18] A report on the *New England Economy* (Washington, D.C.: U. S. Government Printing Office, 1951) indicated that "A survey of a cross-section of more than one-hundred manufacturers' establishments in the post-war years indicates that *new* manufacturing activity in New England grows primarily by the establishment of *new* small firms." p. 83 (Italics supplied).

defiance of the collective judgment of industrial and professional opinion. New industries are created by men who are ready to put their shirt on the horse of their choice. Established firms and State corporations are perfectly justified in refusing to back their fancies with their shareholders' or taxpayers' shirts, for most entries for the industrial stakes are non-starters and also-rans.[19]

Frank Kottke, in his study of *Electrical Technology and the Public Interest*[20] stated thus:

When the innovation is crude and has obvious shortcomings the (leading) concern may be a bit too ready to conclude that the idea has little prospect of commercial success. It cannot be only chance that the Western Union interests underestimated the telephone, that the Telephone Company was slow to appreciate the possibilities of radio, that it remained for newcomers to bring out the inexpensive table model radio receiver, that small concerns made the first F. M. transmitters while a local network was the first commercial enterprise to install them.

The necessity for easy entry by the *novus homo* into an industry, to turn inventions and research findings into innovations, is illustrated by an experience in the pharmaceutical industry. An American chemist, Russell Marker, discovered that *cabeza* (the Mexican sweet potato) was a source of inexpensive material suitable for the synthesis of hormones. After a futile effort to sell the technique to the American drug industry, Marker founded his own firm in order to get his research results into use. His firm was successful not only in using *cabeza* for this purpose but has since developed many other drugs, produced at a cost far below that of methods previously used.

Where innovators are present, but control over production is largely in the hands of the Fabian and drone class, there may still be little advance in the average technology of the society. To get industry-wide advance, a mechanism for transmitting pressure from the innovators to the latter two classes is necessary. In English industry, for example, we often find technological leaders who can teach lessons to any firm in the world existing side by side with firms which not only lag behind their own leaders but are behind the relatively most backward firms of their type in other countries. The reason for this stems primarily from the cartelized organization within

[19] "Wanted: Realism in Research," *Future*, February–March, 1951, p. 30.

[20] *Electrical Technology and the Public Interest* (Washington, D.C.: American Council on Public Affairs, 1944), p. 77.

England of the industries in question. Technological leaders do not take customers away from laggard firms through price cuts or aggressive selling because of the quota systems used in some industries and because of a strong tradition of a "gentleman's agreement" in others. Much the same condition exists in France where firms refuse to grow any more rapidly than the availability of retained earnings allows.

To get technological advance efficiently and at an economic rate requires, then, more than a supply of innovating entrepreneurs. A mechanism must operate for transmitting pressure from them to the Fabian and drone classes which will serve to convert drones into at least Fabian types. Preferably, it should serve to convert both into the imitative type. Where drones refuse to convert, the mechanism should eliminate them (not as people or as suppliers of resources, but as entrepreneurs) and bring into being new entrepreneurs.

One danger in selecting a mechanism for eliminating drones, however, is that it may leave the innovating entrepreneur with the only, or the dominant, firm in his industry. An innovating entrepreneur may successfully bid resources away from drone entrepreneurs.[21] If he becomes dominant, his monopoly position may slow the rate of advance in the industry. Preferably, an industry should have several innovating entrepreneurs, each of whom is also frequently an imitator of the successful techniques of the others who are innovators. A sufficient condition for technological advance is the presence of an innovating entrepreneur and a mechanism for forcing the efficient changes he introduces into the entire industry. A necessary condition for continuing advance is a mechanism for preventing domination of an industry by any one firm.

Factors influencing the supply of innovating entrepreneurs. An entrepreneurial group or fund of entrepreneurship spurs advance only if it includes innovating and imitating entrepreneurs. Thus the problem becomes one of generating these types where they are now lacking. An examination of some differences between societies in which they do and do not exist offers useful clues to the development of a solution. An examination of how they have come into be-

---

[21] In Kenya, for example, ". . . The aggressive and successful initiator of the new idea . . . purchases (land) from the less efficient, and thereby, displaces him." "Kenya's Land Problems," *The Times British Colonies Review*, Autumn, 1952.

ing historically is also helpful, as is an analysis of why they have ceased to exist in some areas.[22]

Three aspects of relationships among members of societies seem to be outstandingly different in societies possessing large supplies of innovating entrepreneurship and those possessing relatively little. These are designated by Levy as the cognitive aspect, the membership criteria aspect, and the substantive definition aspect.

The cognitive aspect may be regarded as the rationality of a society in its expectations as to how members should choose the action to be undertaken when considering how to use capital, what person to hire for a job, how to design a product, or in making other choices. Action is here defined as rational to the extent that *objective and subjective ends of action are united.* Choices made on the basis of reasoning in terms of attaining a maximum of an *avowed* end are regarded as rational. A society may be regarded as nonrational insofar as it is *institutionally expected* that reasoning about action will proceed primarily in terms of what is justified by custom or transcendental powers regardless of the empirical effects. In Nazi Germany, for example, Einsteinian theory was rejected not because of its empirical validity, or lack of it, but because it was Jewish. Another instance of nonrationality is that of public power projects or publicly financed steel plants which somehow get located in the home districts of particular politicians, although economic considerations would dictate their location elsewhere. In these cases, those who control these choices may well be rational, but their subjective ends are different from the avowed end of such endeavors. These projects are supposed to produce a maximum amount of steel or power, but the persons who choose locations select those which ensure tenure in office or personal gain of some other kind.

In terms of the membership aspect, relationships may be regarded as more or less universalistic or more or less particularistic. A society is purely universalistic if members of its various organizations are chosen in terms of criteria such that: (1) the criteria are germane to the purpose for which selection is made and (2) no individual is institutionally barred from possessing or acquiring the necessary

---

[22] The discussion in this section is drawn in part from M. Levy's "Some Sources of the Vulnerability of the Structures of Relatively Non-Industrialized Societies to Those of Highly Industrialized Societies," in *The Progress of Underdeveloped Countries*, B. Hoselitz, editor (Chicago: University of Chicago Press, 1952).

criteria. Their membership relationships are particularistic to the extent that choice is made on the basis of "who a person is" instead of on the basis of "what he can do." If people are chosen for certain jobs on the basis of family connection or political affiliation where these criteria are not relevant to the performance required, the relationship is particularistic. If people are chosen for engineering jobs on the basis of engineering skill, on the other hand, rather than on the basis of friendship or family connections, the relationship is universalistic.

In terms of substantive definition aspects, a relationship may be regarded as more or less functionally specific or functionally diffuse. A relationship is functionally specific if the rights and obligations of the relationship are precisely defined and delimited. The typical "business contract" is usually functionally specific, while the relation-ship between family members is typically diffuse.

The societies possessing large funds of innovating entrepreneurship seem to be those in which relationships are predominantly rational, universalistic, and functionally specific. This might be expected since, where tradition or supernatural powers exhibiting themselves in the form of omens irrelevant to a choice determine the time of planting, choice of crops, or method of cultivation, it is unlikely that innovations will appear. Innovations would be sacrilegious. Also, if positions are filled on the basis of "who you are," it is improbable that the best qualified persons will be chosen.[23] And if relationships are functionally diffuse, an innovator will find, for example, that the more he produces, the more demands will be made on him by distant relatives or officials, with the consequence that the incentive to innovate is considerably diminished.

Related to the mores of choice as a determinant of the amount of

[23] *The New England Economy*, for example, ascribes management weakness in the firms in some communities to "lack of opportunity for individuals from all groups in the community to rise to supervisory positions. In the past, but fortunately not to the same extent currently, those with control in the textile and shoe industry did not provide opportunities for individuals irrespective of social groupings to attain management positions. This reflected in part the general social and economic stratification of our textile and shoe communities. We have also been told that New England textile firms have not and are not recruiting their reasonable share of able graduates from the leading textile schools. In fact, it has been widely questioned whether New England firms generally are as enterprising as they should be in picking up potential executives and supervisory talent from the local universities." (Washington, D.C.: Government Printing Office, 1951), pp. 81–2.

enterprise (in the sense in which we are using enterprise—i.e., innovation and imitation) is the *Weltanschauung* characteristic of a society. Its world view in terms of its goals and ethics, its beliefs about the "rightness" of change, and whether the idea of change occurs to its members will profoundly influence its fund of innovating entrepreneurship.

Bursts of innovation have followed religious change in the past.

. . . the most important innovation in any society is the *idea* of innovation itself, for this represents the "Rubicon" between the traditional stationary type of society, in which each generation repeats the pattern of its elders, and the "economic," dynamic society in which innovation becomes an accepted and profitable role. A strong case can be made for the claim that the principal historical agency bringing about this critical change is a reformation (or revolution) in religion, that this liberates the society from its previous equilibrium. . . . Once iconoclasm has succeeded in the most traditional and "sacred" area of life, once "free enterprise" has been successful in religion, the spirit of innovation seizes upon all other areas of life.

What in our western society we call *the* Reformation is of course only one among many. The period of rapid innovation which followed the rise of Mohammedanism is another and spectacular example. Within Christianity itself the monastic reformations—especially of the Benedictines and Cistercians—paved the way for the economic development of medieval Europe.[24]

In addition, the ethics religion teaches in terms of right goals and right behavior may inhibit or assist the growth of entrepreneurial activity. The Protestant ethic with its emphasis on temperance, frugality, hard work, and honesty is justly credited with an important role in the flowering of enterprise in Western Europe. The Mohammedan ethic, which legitimizes misrepresentation and sharp practice, has inhibited enterprise in the Near East.

The amount of individual decision-making may be influenced by religion in ways which inhibit the development of entrepreneurs. If a religion teaches that the individual must leave theological decisions to a higher authority, the habit of leaving decisions to such authority may make him less capable of becoming a decision-maker in the economic sphere. The emphasis of Protestant teaching on the individual's responsibility for his own salvation and on his right to interpret the Bible for himself helped create the decision-making frame of

[24] K. E. Boulding, "Religious Foundations of Economic Progress," *Harvard Business Review*, May–June, 1952, pp. 35–6.

mind important for the development of a fund of innovators. The Quakers carried individual self-determination of faith to an extreme, and it may be for this reason that they have made such a disproportionate contribution to commerce, industry, and finance.

The early history of the British iron and steel industry can be written without going outside The Society of Friends, and from the time of Edward Pease, the founder of the world's first railway, the Stockton and Darlington, Quakers provided a number of distinguished railway magnates.

"Making and saving money, and enjoying a reputation for integrity, Quakers were entrusted with other people's money. They became bankers, at first in a small way, later (as a result of inter-marriage) in a big way. They can claim to have founded two of the Big Five of the banking world, Lloyds and Barclays.

Quaker-founded firms in several industries are household phrases in Britain today; in beer, Truman Hanbury Buxton and Co. . . ; in matches, Bryant and May, Ltd.; in biscuits, Huntley and Palmers; in tea, Horniman and Co. . . ; in starch, Reckitt and Sons. Finally and perhaps most famous, there is the chocolate and cocoa trinity, Fry of Bristol, Cadbury of Birmingham, and Rowntree of York.[25]

In the past, innovating entrepreneurs frequently came from classes barred from advancement to prominent positions through normal channels, such as the civil service, the military, or the clergy. The disproportionate number of non-Anglican entrepreneurs in England of the seventeenth and eighteenth centuries, for example, may in part be accounted for on the basis of the church membership requirement for advancement through the usual channels.[26] Men of education and means, precluded from the normal outlets for purposive activity, turned to the commercial and industrial world.

As K. E. Boulding has indicated, however,

. . . a perfectly fluid or homogeneous class structure may not be the most conducive to economic progress. One of the problems of economic progress is that of encouraging people to become "innovators." Not only is the innovating ability a naturally scarce one, but even where it exists, its possessors are frequently unwilling to exercise it, in view of the risks and troubles involved. If then, the class structure of society is completely fluid, so that there is equal opportunity for all to enter the easier-going

[25] See "The Society Called Friends," *Future*, II (2).

[26] The ranks of non-Anglican entrepreneurs in England were also swelled by the migration of Huguenots from France before and after the revocation of the Edict of Nantes. Also, we must not discount the role of the Protestant ethic, although it is not clear to what extent it was a cause and to what extent a consequence.

professions, there may not be sufficient talent diverted into industry and trade to ensure a proper rate of progress.[27]

On the other hand, historical experience with the benefits of the lack of fluidity must not lead us to raise social rigidity into an absolute virtue. A little may help; too much may hinder. Rigidity may be carried so far that it freezes potential innovators in their status or it prevents them from sharing in the fruits of their innovations or even punishes them, with the result that innovators will be unable or unwilling to come forth. To quote again from Boulding, "In French society before 1789, as in Russian society before 1917, power and property were concentrated in the hands of a small, pleasure-loving and irresponsible aristocracy. Consequently, the creative abilities of the masses found no opportunities for expression, while those that had the opportunities usually had no creative abilities." [28]

Social structure not only affects the quantity of entrepreneurship, but it may also have marked effect on the quality or kind of entrepreneurship and management. As indicated above, the kind of entrepreneurship in operation will influence the rate of technological advance. If the social structure is such that it filters into entrepreneurial ranks only those who will play a Fabian or drone role, little technological advance is likely.

Where entrepreneurs inherit their roles and are not subject to the pressure of "upstarts," aggressive innovation or even quick imitation is unlikely to be an entrepreneurial characteristic. Possessing status as a birthright, they do not have the drive for success that motivates the new man; and they may also lack ability. At best, such men will be Fabian entrepreneurs. Their drives are likely to be in the direction of status obtained other than as an entrepreneur; they are likely to select managers who can help them fulfill these other aspirations, rather than those who can wisely direct their enterprises. Perhaps it is fortunate for the efficiency of American enterprises that business success usually conveys social status to the successful businessman and, sometimes, even political preferment.

English experience exemplifies this point. Social status was a perquisite of the aristocracy and the landed gentry. Business success was a step in the direction of social status only in that it provided the

---

[27] *Economics of Peace.* (New York: Prentice-Hall, Inc., 1945), pp. 90–91.
[28] *Ibid.*, p. 89.

means for an aristocratic education and for the purchase of an estate and title. British businessmen had their sons educated in the tradition of "gentlemen" and thereby unfitted them for entrepreneurship. They used capital which might have gone into their businesses to purchase the estates of the profligate aristocracy. They or their descendants appointed managers who had position rather than ability.[29]

Even where entrepreneurs attempt to use ability as a criterion, they may fail to recruit innovating management if they are not sufficiently active in their own business to take a chance on anything less than perfectly safe selections. Being inactive, they may not recognize unconventional qualities and may be unwilling to use people who have not been thoroughly trained for the position under consideration. Such an attitude arises because they are not close enough to their concerns to be able to check any wrong directions that unconventional personnel may take.

An example of recruitment apparently based on ability which fails to produce innovating management is provided by industries which train management "from the ground up." The tradition of putting all executive and engineering trainees in the "shop" with the provision that they compete on equal terms with others (as in the United States steel industry) repels much potential innovating talent. Alternatively, this method of training and selection thoroughly grounds the potential talent in the prevailing techniques and current views on method with a consequent stifling of freshness and originality.

In contrast, Warren Scoville's study of the *Revolution in Glassmaking*[30] indicates that mobility of talent between industries provides cross-fertilization conducive to rapid technological advance. R. S. Sayer, recounting the factors leading to the invention of a new heavy loom in 1925, tells us that "This invention came from a young engineer who claimed that his success was because of his newness in the field and the fact that he was not obsessed by tradition

[29] D. S. Landes has pointed out that in France ". . . a good business was always a stepping stone to a career in the government service, possibly even to ennoblement or marriage into the aristocracy. . . . the *affaire* was never an end in itself but the means to an end. The obsession of the entrepreneur with the enterprise as such, which Sonibert finds so common in America and Germany, to all intents and purposes did not exist in France." ("French Entrepreneurship and Industrial Growth in the Nineteenth Century," *Journal of Economic History*, May 1949, p. 53.)

[30] Cambridge, Mass.: The Harvard University Press, 1948.

enabled him to plan a new type of loom construction from the floor up!" [31]

In summary then, the availability of a supply of innovating entrepreneurs seems to depend on the constant entrance of "new" entrepreneurs. Indeed Schumpeter argues that "innovations are always associated with the rise to leadership of New Men" and that old entrepreneurs or those who inherit the role seem to become Fabian in their outlook unless constantly "pressured" by new firms.[32] They attempt to monopolize their area of activity and, if they succeed, relax in the comfort and security of an assured business which need not adapt and progress in order to provide a desirable level of income. This seems to occur especially where the social structure is such that those with status live a feudal style of life. Then the drive of entrepreneurs "to accumulate and to expand their enterprises is . . . counteracted by the urgent desire to imitate in their living habits the socially dominant 'old families,' to prove by their conspicuous outlays on the amenities of rich life that they are socially (and therefore also politically) not inferior to their aristocratic partners in the ruling coalition." [33]

GENERATING A SUPPLY OF INNOVATING ENTREPRENEURS

Realizing the importance of "new men" for the problem of enlarging the fund of the kind of entrepreneurs who will bring about an increased rate of technical advance, we are confronted with the task of determining the conditions necessary for getting these new men. The principal conditions required for their entrance seem to be the presence of goals realizable by entrepreneurial activity which are socially acceptable, free access to capital and labor supplies, a supply of "promotable" people, and no artificial restrictions on entrance to an industry (equality of opportunity). These may all be illustrated in reverse by examining situations where they are absent.

Share cropping tenantry illustrates the effect of diminished incen-

---

[31] "The Springs of Technical Progress in Britain, 1919–39," *Economic Journal,* June, 1950, fn. 5, p. 283.

[32] . . . new productions functions do not typically grow out of old businesses—if a new man takes hold of an old firm, they may—and hence . . . their insertion proceeds by competing old ones out of existence or by enforcing transformation of them. (Schumpeter, *op. cit.,* pp. 96.)

[33] P. A. Baran, "On the Political Economy of Backwardness," *Manchester School,* January, 1952.

tives on the rate of technological advance. Since increases in output must be shared with the landlord, the incentive to make improvements is reduced. Where, for example, the cost of putting into operation an improved technique is more than half of the increase in production that results, a 50–50 tenant does not find it worth his while to use the better technique. A fixed rental system, perhaps with provision for postponement of payment in bad years, would promote technical advance by leaving extra production brought about by such advances in the hands of the people who introduce them.[34]

In some cases, the incentive system is so badly out of gear that it has reduced the supply of entrepreneurship. The experience of American Indians in the nineteenth century illustrates how the entrepreneurial spirit may be reduced and even killed. Because of the disappearance of the buffalo, Indians were advised to establish enterprises to support themselves. Many did so. However, those who developed ranches or created farming enterprises had their lands confiscated by the whites when the productivity of seemingly barren land was demonstrated. The Indian soon learned that the only reward for enterprise was to be herded to some more remote and barren reservation. The tradition of the apathetic Indian was not long in being born.

It is important from the point of view of incentive not only that material rewards but also that social prestige be given successful entrepreneurs.

Thus, in feudal or aristocratic societies where power is inherited rather than earned, and where little respect is accorded to wealth which has been created in the first or second generation, the energies of ambitious men are not attracted so much to the production of wealth as to the acquisition of skills which may secure entry into the strongholds of power—to the acquisition of military skill, or the skill of the hunt, or the skill of the lawyer or priest. In such societies, the production of wealth is frequently held in contempt as a profession for well-bred young men.[35]

The entrepreneurial spirit is often present in persons who lack capital. If they can save enough to assume the risks of an enter-

[34] See *Land Reform: Defects in Agrarian Structure as Obstacles to Economic Development* (New York: The United Nations, 1951) for a thorough discussion of this issue.

[35] *Measures for the Economic Development of Underdeveloped Countries* (New York: The United Nations, 1951), pp. 13–14.

prise and are allowed access to the balance needed to found a business or to enlarge their firms, they become additions to the supply of entrepreneurship or can exert pressure on Fabian and drone entrepreneurs. Thus unless entrepreneurs have ready access to capital, the entrepreneurial spur to economic growth is hampered.]

French supplies of entrepreneurship, for example, are restricted by a lack of capital. Bright young men of ambition, talent, and imagination who are born to families without established wealth and position find the capital markets barred by lack of family connection or lack of an inherited business. To get ahead, they must either get an education which fits them for the professions or the civil service or they must enter politics. As a consequence, the supply of new entrepreneurs is slim in France, and the number of innovations correspondingly small.

This shortage of risk capital serves to explain in turn, at least in part, why France has so often failed to appreciate its own inventors. From Lebon's discovery of gas lighting at the turn of the eighteenth century, through Girard's spinning machine, Sauvage's screw propeller, and Verguin's accomplishments in artificial dyes, to Tellier's refrigerator and beyond, the list of innovations which originated in France only to find their quickest and greatest development abroad is quite impressive.[36]

The difficulty of the would-be entrepreneur in France stems, in part, from conservative business tradition. Since a borrower might not be able to repay and might lose his business in case of a depression, French businessmen, believing as they do that the quickest road to success is the slow but sure one, have financed their businesses with their own capital or that obtained from relatives and friends. A tradition of borrowing as a normal method of financing business has not developed. Since established firms do not seek outside capital, and potential suppliers of capital have not been built up in the course of the normal activity of business, new firms and would-be entrepreneurs have no source to which to turn for capital except to those with whom they have close personal connection. If they lack such connections, then there is little hope for them.

Not dissimilar difficulties have been encountered in the United States. In mid-nineteenth century, banks in some areas of the United States would lend only to commercial enterprises. Manufacturing firms found that the lack of credit facilities inhibited their

[36] D. S. Landes, *op. cit.*, p. 51.

activities and made it difficult to raise capital when necessary to institute new methods. In mid-twentieth century, farmers interested in practicing soil-conserving ideas found banks unwilling to lend for this purpose. The impasse was not broken until the value of such practices was thoroughly demonstrated and redemonstrated. Even lending on chattel mortgages for the purchase of agricultural machinery was not accepted by banks, despite the prior example of the bankability of loans on trucks and automobiles, until farm equipment companies conducted an intensive educational campaign.

The necessity for free flow of capital to private firms in order to generate a supply of entrepreneurship conducive to optimum rates of development has been pointed out by the International Development Advisory Board in its report, *Partners in Progress*. The suggestion was the spur which led to the discussion among the governors of the International Bank and the International Monetary Fund reported in the prologue to this chapter.

In asserting the necessity for a free flow of capital to private firms, we are thinking only in terms of improving the allocation of the existing fund of capital. If the flow of capital can be increased, as well as its allocation improved, the rate of advance in productivity will be even greater. Aubrey has pointed out in his study of *The Place of Small Industry in Economic Development* that the introduction of improved equipment which would amortize its cost in a month is barred by a lack of capital. Even such small amounts as 140 rupees for a semimechanical loom are frequently beyond the reach of the individual handicraftsman.[37]

In some underdeveloped areas, entrepreneurship is stifled by the inability to recruit labor. Workers are tied to the soil, or cannot move to new occupations because of caste restrictions, or are bound up in family cooperative systems. Even where these conditions do not prevail, union restrictions may prevent recruitment of additional people when skills are scarce. Since a new enterprise has little appeal to those already holding protected jobs with established firms, the new firm finds it difficult to obtain the needed skills when union apprenticeship and color rules restrict the supply.

Artificial restrictions on entrance to industry slow development of innovating and imitating entrepreneurial talent. Africa provides

[37] Henry G. Aubrey, "The Place of Small Industry in Economic Development," *Social Research* (September, 1951), p. 15.

some examples of this, although restrictive schemes abound elsewhere. Licenses are required for pioneering and for establishment of certain enterprises in Kenya, Tanganyika, and Uganda. Qualification for licenses is based on experience and capital. As a consequence, only conventionally trained persons can start businesses. The shoestring operator and the unconventional person are barred; many of these would fail but some are more likely to be innovators than the normally selected groups.

In French West Africa, cartel-type restriction is found. A case exemplifying this is provided by the experience of a French miller who was unable to start business until he purchased the burned-out assets of a defunct milling firm. On the basis of the defunct firm's historical share of the market, he was finally permitted to operate.

Development of "promotable" people. A supply of "promotable" people is essential as a pool from which new supplies of management and new entrepreneurs may be drawn. By "promotable" people, we mean those who have acquired the skills required for managerial and entrepreneurial decision-making and have learned to make decisions in connection with the use of these skills. Other writers usually refer to the middle class as the provider of entrepreneurial seed, and there are differences in the supply of entrepreneurship and rate of technological advance between different areas which occur when there are differences in the size of the middle class. The state of São Paulo, Brazil, for example, was settled by Jesuits who "frowned upon slavery, tried to protect the Indians, and sought to create, not great plantations, but permanent settlements of free men cultivating small holdings." [38] Although not completely successful in their aims, the Jesuits did establish the first middle class in Brazil at a time when the balance of the country had only masters and slaves. This may be one of the key factors in the rapid advance of São Paulo, which has over 40 per cent of Brazil's industry.

Africa provides an example of how not to develop "promotable" people and warns of methods which must be avoided if maximum economic growth is to be promoted. Governmental and trade union policy in some areas of Africa reserve the right to use certain skills for preferred groups. Also, it bars entry into some of the businesses

[38] M. L. Cooke, *Brazil on the March* (New York: McGraw-Hill Book Co., 1944), p. 56.

where entrepreneurial skills might be acquired on a simple level and thereafter be transferred to other, more complex, activities. Africans are prevented from occupying supervisory positions which might fit them for higher management and entrepreneurial roles. As a consequence, the supply of entrepreneurial talent is drawn very largely from a restricted group. While this group supplies many persons to fill entrepreneurial roles, nevertheless, the restriction chokes the supply and slows development.

The importance of giving skills to people in order to develop a fund of entrepreneurship is illustrated by the activities of persons who acquired new skills through their training in the armed forces in World War II. Africans who were trained as lorry drivers and mechanics have founded bus lines, transport companies, and repair shops since their discharge. In this case, it should be emphasized that restrictions on entry into the bus business imposed by government franchise grants were either broken or were nonexistent. Otherwise, there would not have been the flowering of this type of enterprise with the valuable training it has given to entrepreneurs. Development of the air freight and passenger business in the United States following World War II teaches the same lesson.

The positive results flowing from a program for developing "promotable" people may be seen in the work of the Arabian-American Oil Company. Starting with nomadic Bedouins, who knew little more than how to keep a few animals alive in the desert, Aramco first trained them for fairly simple tasks. From the most promising in the group, men were then selected for technical and supervisory training. Finally, some became contractors on simple jobs, such as digging cellars with Aramco's assistance in arranging for the purchase of equipment and the development of sources of capital for their operations. As they gained experience, they expanded operations and moved to more complex tasks. By purchasing local supplies, Aramco has also developed domestic enterprises which have received no direct aid. With the growth of supply of "promotable" people, new enterprises are being founded, producing items ranging from ice and laundry services to furniture and houses.[39]

In order to develop "promotable" people, areas launching industrial development should lean toward certain types of organization ·

[39] E. Muller, "Social Upheaval in Arabia," *United Nations World*, September, 1952. Condensed in *Reader's Digest*, September, 1952.

and techniques of production. Although early stages of development may require organizations in which there is close supervision, because of the lack of skilled personnel, this should be relaxed as quickly as possible. The early stage of close supervision should be regarded as one in which supervisors primarily train rather than supervise. Supervisors should explain why certain methods are used and their relationship to the whole undertaking. They should avoid simply telling people under their direction what to do.

The difference in the two approaches may be illustrated by M. Opler's criticism of the approach used in a medical dispensary established by American missionaries in India.

> On one occasion I brought an Indian villager to a medical dispensary established by American missionaries. The American doctor in charge diagnosed the case as malaria and prescribed a course of atabrine tablets as treatment. The only directions to the patient had to do with when to take the pills.
>
> On talking over the matter with this villager, I learned that he had no idea that mosquitos had anything to do with malaria. He owned a mosquito net but used it only when the mosquitos became too annoying and not out of fear of contracting disease. This man was certainly "aided" by the services at this American clinic; in fact, he was cured temporarily by the treatment. But few will hold that this kind of technical aid is enough. The person helped remained unconscious of his problem and unable to prevent a repetition of his sickness. Needless to say, he could communicate nothing useful about the matter to others. Yet this man was very intelligent, quite receptive to new ideas, and a leader in his caste and village. It is obvious that malaria and this kind of treatment could exist side by side for hundreds of years.[40]

After the learning stage has passed, supervision should be reduced to a minimum with as much decision-making as possible being placed in the hands of the individuals doing a job. Similarly, jobs should be broadened to the point where individuals do something more than constantly repeat a single, robotistic motion. They will learn quickly to think for themselves and will become the sort of people who can be promoted and, perhaps, even reach the stage of being able to start their own enterprises.

To minimize detailed supervision, techniques of production and organization must be selected which lend themselves to minimizing supervision. In a functionally organized manufacturing operation, for

[40] Harris Foundation Lectures, *Report*, B. Hoselitz, editor, Chicago: University of Chicago Press, 1951.

example, where all lathes are grouped in one center, milling machines in another, grinding machines in still another, with a foreman assigned to each, supervision will be detailed. Each workman will be performing a task like every other worker under the same foreman. With a flow organization, where lathes and milling and grinding machines are all in one center, the foreman will be unable to supervise in detail, since each man will be performing a different task. He can do little more than co-ordinate. As a consequence, more of the decisions on detail will be made by the men doing the jobs. It has been found that, under these circumstances, many more "promotable" people are developed.[41]

The role of government in generating innovating entrepreneurship. The creation of a supply of innovating entrepreneurs seems to be less a matter of generating the spirit than of removing barriers to outlets for the spirit. Yet, it may be necessary to take positive steps where social custom and structure have made the innovating spirit rare. There are, however, methods of going about this which may result in less, rather than more, productivity.

The early experience of the Japanese textile industry provides an experience of this negative sort. To get the industry going, the Japanese government gave subsidies to textile operators. Textile firms were started, but their owners were persons with the political connections necessary to get the subsidies. They were not enterprisers who raised productivity, and their firms were able to live only because of the subsidies they received. Fortunately, innovating entrepreneurs who did not have the required political connections also entered the industry. Since they were not subsidized, their success depended on their ability to make appropriate decisions in choosing techniques of production, buying fiber, and selling their product. Efficiency in these firms was greater than in the subsidized firms, since those who were unable to reach high efficiency were quickly removed by their inability to obtain a sufficient return to pay enough to hold the resources they were using. The field was left to the efficient and the subsidized firms. After the subsidy was reduced, the

[41] See James C. Worthy, "Organization Structure and Employee Morale," *American Sociological Review*, April, 1950, for an excellent discussion of the effect of factors such as span of supervision and degree of specialization on the kind of people produced.

market eliminated all but the efficient. An entrepreneurial selection system based on political connections did not bring into being a technologically competent industry. A market selection system, which gave the best returns to the most competent entrepreneurs and which penalized the less competent, resulted in a more productive industry with higher income for the society.

One of the first steps required in some areas, both to create a free flow of capital and to give incentive to entrepreneurial activity, is a change in the land tenure system. In some areas of Africa, land is held in the name of chiefs for tribal benefit. Individuals do not have a right to any particular piece of land and cannot sell the land they happen to be working or borrow on it. It does not even pay the African in these circumstances to build the fertility of his soil by fertilization or crop rotation, since he cannot be sure of having the same piece of land in succeeding years. In some areas where clan and family communalism prevailed as little as ten years ago, individual ownership has emerged. However, it has not yet been legalized and farmers do not have access to credit facilities.[42] Individual ownership should be legalized by registration of land holdings and issuance of titles in order to give this access.

Government aids for increasing the supply of innovators should largely take the form of gathering intelligence concerning techniques, markets, prices, and costs, together with the establishment of a tax, property, and monetary atmosphere which does not inhibit entrepreneurial activity. Where capital markets are not free, aid in creating such markets may be necessary. The break up of monopolistic financing and the development of laws making it possible to float securities serve this end.

In some cases, it may be necessary to ease the entry of foreigners into a society in order to get innovating entrepreneurs. The simple fact that persons from outside the culture have not been habituated to the usual patterns of production and distribution gives them a fresh view which may enable them to see opportunities. If they are of a type to seize an opportunity, they become additions to the fund of innovating entrepreneurship.

Wherever significant entrepreneurial activity is taking place in South America, foreigners in the areas seem to be sparking the effort. Philip Bradley has pointed out that:

[42] "Kenya's Land Problems," *op. cit.*, p. 15.

The three places economically most forward-looking in the whole area are Monterrey in Mexico; São Paulo, Brazil; and Medlenna in Colombia; in all of which there is a significant "foreign" stimulus. Over the long term, Argentina reveals the efficiency of such activity. According to its census of 1938, 65 to 70 per cent of all Argentine industries were controlled by first-generation immigrants.[43]

The United States, too, has benefited from the activity of foreign entrepreneurs. It had the advantage of constant importations of people during the nineteenth and early twentieth centuries who had the entrepreneurial spirit and replenished the fund of entrepreneurship built up earlier. Instances may be cited such as the migration of Samuel Slater, with the secrets of cotton manufacture, and of the Schofields, with the plans for woolen mills. In the nineteenth century, a group of German families migrated to the United States who founded breweries, printing plants, and optical, chemical, and piano factories.

Early Mexican experience is instructive on another score. It provides an instance of government sponsorship of new enterprises which to some extent negates the Japanese experience. To help in the founding of the textile industry in Mexico, the government imported machinery and gave financial assistance to new enterprises. These failed; yet, in their failure, they provided the seed for later, successful firms. Knowledge of the industry and its techniques was acquired and personnel was trained, which eased the way for other firms. Perhaps the lesson to be drawn is, not that government programs which are economic failures may be good, but that information about methods of production is the most efficient aid which can be given. Perhaps the intelligence services may go as far as a governmental research program designed to discover the adaptations needed for the local scene. Brazil is offering this sort of intelligence to its pioneering farmers with good results.[44]

Perhaps the most important requirement for generating a supply of innovating entrepreneurs is the provision of entrepreneurial security. This consists as much of freedom as of protection and is, perhaps, improperly labeled security. What is necessary is the avoidance of unnecessary, inhibiting risks. While protecting the entrepreneur from

[43] Reported by R. Wohl, *Change and the Entrepreneur* (Cambridge, Mass.: Harvard University Press, 1949), pp. 41.

[44] Willard Price, *The Amazing Amazon*. New York: John Day Company, 1952.

these, he is left the freedom, or obligation, to take "the ordinary and legitimate risks of doing business." These consist of "risks of investing in the wrong places—risks of demand changes, of technical obsolescence in plant facilities, and of guessing badly only because too many others guessed the same way." [45]

The security required for development of maximum entrepreneurial activity can only in part be provided by the state. It can prevent banditry, make property secure, stabilize tax rates and aggregate demand, and prevent aggregations of power large enough to reduce an entrepreneur's freedom of action. Primarily, entrepreneurial security must rest on public acceptance of entrepreneurship as good. If the public regards every change in a price or a wage rate as an iniquitous action taken by a "greedy" entrepreneur or the consequence of collusion (assuming none exists); if it regards entrepreneurs as fair game in any damage suit, feeling that they should be "involuntary Good Samaritans"; if profit is thought to be "unfair" or something that comes only from buccaneering activity; if the employment of labor is regarded as exploitation—then entrepreneurship is likely to languish. Only if people feel they have a stake in permitting entrepreneurs maximum freedom and that both parties can benefit from a trade, will it be possible to have the necessary entrepreneurial security. Perhaps this might be summed up by saying that people must realize that "the straightest, perhaps only, road to social security is via entrepreneurial security." [46]

Summary and conclusion. Efficient technological advance, i.e., the development and use of techniques which will do most to raise productivity and increase income, requires a supply of innovating entrepreneurs checked or goaded by a free market. While innovation and imitation will occur in government enterprises and in other enterprises not guided by an identifiable entrepreneur, the process will likely be less efficient, will fail to approach the optimum rate and kind of change as closely, and will thus contribute less to raising income.

Not only is a supply of innovating entrepreneurs necessary for efficient technological change; it is necessary for efficient use of

[45] Henry C. Simons, *Economic Policy for a Free Society* (Chicago: University of Chicago Press, 1948), p. 146.

[46] W. T. Easterbrook, "The Climate of Enterprise," *American Economic Review*, May, 1949, p. 329.

additional resources as they become available. In the words of M. Abramovitz, ". . . labor supply, resources, existing capital, and the state of the arts only create a potentiality for capital productivity, while it is enterprise which performs the miracle of transforming potential into effective productivity. A substantial part of the explanation of differences in the level of investment between developed and undeveloped countries, among advanced economies, and between different stages in the progress of any single country, is to be found in the size, energy, and scope of operations of the entrepreneurial or business class." [47]

If innovating entrepreneurship is essential for efficient increases in productivity, then the development of conditions which will generate and maintain a supply is also essential. The first step in this direction seems to be that of obtaining people who are not bound to the traditional patterns. Historically, they seem to have come from two sources—foreigners and minority groups not permitted to participate in the traditional patterns of achieving social success. The Chinese in Malaya and Burma and Indians in Tahiti and East Africa exemplify the role played by foreigners; Protestants in seventeenth- and eighteenth-century England and Parsees in India, that played by minority groups.

Outsiders to the tradition of a society cannot or will not function, however, if the rewards for entrepreneurial activity are not safe or if tradition opposes such activities as buying and selling for a profit, lending or borrowing, or making decisions on the basis of pecuniary measures. If an employee's wage cannot be reduced when his productivity fails to equal his wage (as in the case of Italy where employers cannot reduce wage rates or lay off their work force), or if services must be provided at prices which fail to cover costs because of legal or ecclesiastical regulation rather than because of entrepreneurial error, then entrepreneurship cannot function, will fail to start where it does not exist, and will wither where it does. In general, the greater the amount of regulation of entrepreneurial activity by means other than competitive markets, the smaller the supply will probably be.

Avoidance of governmental regulation, with the selection of entrepreneurs provided by competition, is the negative side of the problem of generating innovators. On the positive side, governments can

---

[47] "Economics of Growth," A *Survey of Contemporary Economics*, Vol. II, B. Haley, editor (Chicago: R. Irwin, Inc., 1952), II, p. 158.

take steps to ease the problem of raising capital. The passage of laws relating to securities, rights of security holders, and business structure, which are conducive to a flow of capital from suppliers to users, is important to the development process. Provision of capital, if the capital market is very imperfect, is another important aid. Probably the greatest impetus could be given to the private flow of capital into enterprise by the creation of or publicizing of conspicuous examples of successful profit making. Perhaps the ready grant of access to natural resources would not only provide conspicuous examples of profit making but would also provide natural capital to enterprises which could then be turned into other kinds of capital.

Where other measures, such as provision of intelligence on opportunities, favorable tax and property laws, and provision of capital, have failed, government may undertake enterprises itself. Where it does so, however, it should be done with the attitude of the promoter who intends to start a business but does not intend to stay in it. Once an enterprise is started, entrepreneurs should be found or trained, if necessary, to take over. If a government enterprise remains in a field, entrepreneurs will be very unlikely to feel that the industry is worth entering in competition with an enterprise which has such special status.[48]

SELECTION OF TECHNIQUES AND SEQUENCES OF ECONOMIC GROWTH

In discussing the necessity for the creation of a supply of innovating entrepreneurs, we have tacitly assumed that technological change would increase income and that it would be desirable for a society to have technological change. Some sorts of technological change do not, however, represent advance nor contribute to a rise in income levels. The argument for the use of entrepreneurs for selecting and instituting change is partly based on the assumption that they will more often select the right changes and will less often be able to maintain the wrong changes than other kinds of innovators.

Entrepreneurial selection of techniques. There is little question that, in terms of income effect, entrepreneurs will select the right changes, if they are checked by competitive markets in a properly

---

[48] This is not the place to discuss the proper sphere of government enterprise, but there are instances where only governments can efficiently provide certain services. National defense is an example.

framed private property system. They cannot bid resources away from other uses and long hold them with an inferior technique if they must pay as much for those resources as they are worth in other uses. As a consequence, the personal resources of entrepreneurs using an inferior technique will dwindle or, at least, fail to increase as rapidly as they otherwise would. Entrepreneurs interested in maximizing their return will soon realize that they are failing to do so and take action to stop the inferior use of resources. Henry Ford, for example, found that using resources to produce Model T's was yielding a smaller return than could be earned in other uses. To avoid the loss of his personal resources, then, he redesigned his product, although he also felt that the Model T should be produced. The competition of Ford's rivals, then, forced him to stop using an inferior technique (of product design) and shift to a more productive one.

When a sufficient supply of innovating and imitating entrepreneurship exists, we can depend on entrepreneurs to select proper techniques in terms of income effects. We find some situations where undesirable *value* effects occur, however, unless the framework of choice is properly constructed.

Assuming the primary value is the right of every individual to choose his own goals and life patterns, as long as this interferes with no other person's choices, a necessary condition for the avoidance of undesirable value effects is a device for permitting the choices of the people to determine the outcome. In some cases, the terms of choice are such that individuals do not have the maximum freedom possible among all the values involved and are precluded, therefore, from choosing the optimum combination. When people are forced to make a single decision which encompasses several areas (although the areas could be separated), an undesirable value outcome may result. Choosing more product, for example, may also mean choosing a method of production whose inherent values are inferior.

Some critics of machine technology, for example, point out that the cottage method of production has values which perish in factory production. They argue that mill work is more productive for reasons which lie outside the choice between cottage and mill production. If capital markets were reorganized, co-operatives for the purchase of materials and sale of product set up, and technical education made available, hand production could compete with mill operation.[49] If

[49] R. G. Kakade, A *Socio-Economics Survey of Weaving Communities in Sholapur* (India: Gokhale Institute of Politics and Economics. Publication No. 14).

the choice between more productive forms of cottage industry and mill work were available, then people could, if they preferred, avoid sacrificing certain values that are lost in moving to mills and yet engage in more productive work.

However, the suggestion that entrepreneurs will select the best techniques in terms of income effects, but not in terms of value effects, is usually overstated. Insofar as values associated with work other than income are important to people, the firms which offer values such as desirable work surroundings can recruit their work force at less expense and force other firms to adopt similar policies or lose their labor force. Japanese industry, for example, found it difficult to persuade people to give up values associated with rural life. The shortage of labor in the cities forced firms to locate small shops in the countryside in order to get production.

A similar movement is taking place in the United States. Where labor feels that the extra income is not worth the sacrifice of country living, concerns which could use their labor more productively (in an end-product sense) at urban centers are finding it profitable to move to small towns. The lower labor cost offsets the extra expense.

Sequences in technological development. A full-blown industrial society of the type found in northeastern United States cannot be erected on a peasant, agricultural society in a few decades. Long historical processes are required in which the society goes through several stages of technological development.

In general, societies must proceed from simple to complex techniques—from activities which require no "external economies" and little pre-conditioning of the labor force, in terms of discipline and skill experience, to those which do; from those which satisfy local needs to those which are attuned to more and more distant markets; from those which require little more than local resources and simple techniques to those which require much capital.[50] These rules of thumb may be summed up in terms of three primary criteria for the selection of industries and techniques which will or should be de-

---

[50] These are essentially rules of thumb which should not be elevated to the rank of absolute principles. Obviously, capital, for instance, should be placed where it produces the greatest possible marginal social product. This may justify some very capital intensive investments in countries very short of capital. The issue is thoroughly discussed by A. E. Kahn, "Investment Criteria in Development Programs," *Quarterly Journal of Economics*, February, 1951.

veloped in an area at any given stage of progress. These are (1) locational factors, (2) priority of needs, and (3) time sequence.

The locational factor as an element in the developmental pattern would lead to the selection of resource-oriented industries, which can capitalize on some resource relatively abundant in the area, and market-oriented industries, for whose product a local market exists. The second element points out that the pattern will be conditioned by barriers between the area in question and others. High barriers dictate that priority of wants and local supplies of the kinds of resources (capital and skilled labor) that might otherwise immigrate must rule. If no barriers exist, then only the nontransferable resources and transportation economies in supplying the local market (that is, the first set of determinants) would dominate. Finally, the time sequence of the developmental pattern is important. Industry using low-level skills and suffering little from the lack of external economies should be found first. Industries using high level skills and dependent on external economies can then follow.

Value, as well as economic, criteria must be allowed to rule the direction and rate of development. Change must not be so rapid that it destroys the basic social agreement (consensus) required for the continuing functioning of the society. Also, change which destroys accepted life patterns and goals with such rapidity that new ones do not have sufficient time to spread through the society may result in personality disorganization, apathy, and anomie. Under these circumstances, irresponsible leaders may find it easy to seize control, with what may be ugly consequences for world peace or, at least, for the future of the society in question. Change must proceed on a step by step basis, each step preparing the way for the next, avoiding the creation of goal vacuums or power vacuums in which irresponsible elements may find opportunities.

External economies and capital supply in the sequence of change. The proper sequence of industries and techniques in the process of economic growth will depend in part upon the relationship of "external economies." As industry grows in an area, individual concerns can shed functions to their gain and contribute to the founding of separate and new industries which, in turn, may make further industrialization possible. As the fishing industry in tropical Monrovia grows, it may finally produce enough fish to supply immediate needs with enough left over to be quick-frozen for off-season and other markets. A refrigeration plant may then become economic, but it will have to produce its own power. Perhaps diesel or gasoline-engine driven compressors will serve it. As other concerns begin production, it may finally become economic to build a central electric power plant. The resultant cheapening of power may then lead to manufacturing or other operations which could not be founded if expensive self-produced power had to be used. A priority in the development of industry may be dictated, then, with those consuming little power or using an abundant domestic resource coming first, while those consuming much power without any offset through economies generated by use of an abundant local resource must wait until the advantage of external economies in the production of power makes their operation economic.

One of the possible determinants of the sequence of development is the priority of needs. The industries which serve a local market frequently should be the first developed. This may have the advantage of assisting in developing local entrepreneurship at a simple level which requires no knowledge of the problems of long distance transport and foreign exchange and marketing. However, the underdeveloped area in the modern world need not concern itself with developing industry according to the priority of wants as long as interregional commodity flows are not barred. For it, resource patterns, technology, and markets are the appropriate determinants of its growth. It is more efficient to engage in a land-intensive industry such as iron-ore mining in an underpopulated area like Labrador, than it is to grow food. Foodstuffs can be obtained at less expenditure of resources, under the pattern of available techniques, by mining and exchange with other areas.

Usually there is a problem of balance in the development of industries directly serving local wants, along with those indirectly serving them. One of the first problems that has arisen in Africa, for instance, in the process of industrialization is an imbalance between agriculture and industry. As people have been withdrawn from agriculture by mining enterprises, food shortages have developed; the balance between food production and population was destroyed by the withdrawals. Imports of food become necessary, then, in early stages of industrializations, until agricultural productivity is improved. Industrialization, perhaps, should be accompanied by, or even preceded by, an agricultural revolution. In the African case, the techniques for increasing agricultural production in the area in question had not been introduced when the withdrawals began, and several years of work since have failed, as yet, to affect production sufficiently to improve the food supply. Difficulties with native diet and health are being encountered as a consequence.

In attempting to bring about agricultural advance, let us say, simply for the purpose of releasing children from the necessity of labor in order that they will have time for schooling, the problems that arise may take the form of proper use of capital. Assuming the crops cultivated are suitable, power machinery such as tractors with attachments and harvesters might be brought in. This is likely to be a mistake for two reasons. First native skills may be inadequate for the comprehension of the operation and maintenance of complex power equipment and the supporting service and repair organizations may be missing. More important, this may be gross misuse of capital. Suppose, for example, that three hundred pedal-operated threshers and three hundred steel hoes could be purchased with the capital required for one power unit and harvester. Suppose the latter enabled one farmer to increase his output tenfold from four hundred to four thousand bushels of grain, then a net increase of thirty-six hundred bushels would result. If the hand tools requiring the same capital enable three hundred similar farmers to each increase his output ten per cent, the gain would amount to twelve thousand bushels. If only enough capital is available to purchase one power set, it might bring far greater returns if spent for hand tools instead. Not only may it be a more efficient use of scarce capital to spend it for simple tools, but the simple tools also have the advantage that their manufacture and repair is simple. By teaching the use of simple hand tools, a demand may be created which can become the basis of a local industry.

It becomes especially ridiculous to allocate capital for such capital-intensive techniques as power farming, which is primarily labor saving rather than output increasing, when an area suffers from "disguised" unemployment. Some family farm systems, such as those in India, permit everyone to share in the family pot, although some of the members have a zero marginal productivity and the farm is overstaffed. It has been estimated that as many as ninety million people could be removed from farming in India with no decline in total output. As long as labor is immobile, the only effect of power equipment would be to increase the amount of disguised unemployment. This was well expressed by a 1950 discussion at the Asian Center on Agriculture and Allied Projects.

From a broader point of view, it may be difficult to justify the use of tractors merely as saving of expense in terms of labour, because in a large project or in a nation employment must be found for the available manpower. It is no real advantage to save half of your own labour, for example by using a tractor, if you have no means of converting the time saved into income. It is no clear advantage to save the labour of a great many landless labourers, unless there is some way of giving them another opportunity to make a living. When industrialization or cottage industry has developed far enough, one may not need to worry about that aspect of the problem so seriously, but at the present time it would conceivably create a serious social problem.[51]

Instead of labor-saving equipment of the kind used in Europe and the United States, the need in most underdeveloped areas is for output-increasing equipment which is capital saving. An example of this is the use of the bullock-drawn grain drill in India. Present seeding methods require more capital invested in seed than the drill method would. Since seed is not dropped evenly nor placed at a uniform depth, much seed is lost. With a drill, less seed would be used, less capital would be required, and a better crop would be produced.

The resource pattern and choice of techniques in the sequence of change. Industries which are well suited to the situation of the usual underdeveloped area which lacks capital, labor skills, managerial skills, and entrepreneurship are of two kinds: (1) those which will attract foreign entrepreneurs and enterprises able to provide the missing developmental essentials and (2) those which can operate on a small scale, using simple techniques requiring little capital; those using labor of low skill; and those requiring only meager managerial and entrepreneurial skill. Foreign enterprise is largely useful and will respond in those cases where a resource is abundant in the area and scarce in the world and which requires skills and organization beyond existing native ability. The oil industry in Iraq and iron mining in Liberia are modern examples of this type. Some types of plantation operation fall into this pattern as well. Where crops can be produced and marketed, and perhaps even processed, on a small scale, it is pref-

[51] *Formulation and Economic Appraisal of Development Projects* (New York: The United Nations, 1951), pp. 775.

erable that native enterprise be spurred in order to develop local supplies of entrepreneurship.

In general, in early stages of development, the enterprises which are of a type calculated to develop entrepreneurship should be encouraged. Those which are small, use rudimentary production techniques, and give immediate returns are most likely to accomplish this at the earlier stage. Larger-scale enterprises using more complicated techniques and yielding distant returns must wait for a later stage when simple entrepreneurial skills and attitudes have been learned.

The evolution may be thought of as from the simple to the complex. Simplicity may be measured in terms of: (1) finance, (2) production, and (3) return. In terms of finance, the simple enterprise is the small one which needs only the capital its owner is capable of furnishing. Larger enterprises which require partnership and borrowed capital are at the next stage of complexity in terms of finance. Still larger ones, which must use the corporate technique to mobilize capital, or riskier ones, which must use limited liability devices, are the most complex.

In terms of production, the simplest enterprise is the commercial firm which does little more than increase value by exchange, i.e., by creating "place" or convenience or "service" utility. As it comes to encompass the creation of more extensive "time" utilities, with the attendant increase in risk (or increased hedging operations required to eliminate risk), a higher level of complexity is reached. The enterprise which engages in simple processing operations creating "form" utility may be termed even more complex, since it must not only carry on the usual commercial operations but also manufacturing. To some extent, the amount of commercial operation in a manufacturing enterprise may be minimized by production on contract for a commercial enterprise. To this extent, simple processing may arise alongside simple commerce. At a later stage, complex manufacturing may be undertaken. In terms of historical movement, we often find the peddler becoming a retail merchant, later a wholesaler, and finally a manufacturer. Many Brazilian textile operators, for example, had their start as peddlers. As they amassed capital and skill, they moved on to the more complex level of enterprise.

The third dimension of complexity—immediacy of return—may be illustrated in agricultural terms. Farmers who are used to waiting a season for the return from their effort do not readily take to a tree crop for which they must wait five to ten years for a return, even where capital markets are well enough organized to furnish interim loans for living expenses. By educating them first to a two or three year crop such as viniculture, the next step to the five to ten year tree crops may be eased. Immediacy of return is also of importance in the choice of commercial and manufacturing enterprises. Capital turns more quickly in some commercial enterprises than others. The step to some levels of manufacturing enterprise is difficult where the proportion of fixed to circulating capital is large. Where the proportion is reversed, the next step is easier.

At all these different levels of complexity, there must be a supply of labor skills to support the entrepreneur. It is easy enough to start as a peddler or as a one-man retail shop; but as operations expand, skills are required which the entrepreneur may find difficult to teach. He may even lack the required skills himself. Thus the development of laborers qualified for the various levels of operation is a necessary concomitant for the success of increasingly complex enterprises.

The textile and shoe industries have served as skill educators and inculcators of work discipline in many underdeveloped areas within the United States, as well as abroad. A typical sequence of development begins with these industries as the first step. Remember, however, that the preconditioning step appears to be the growth of commercial enterprise which trains managers and entrepreneurs, who then find it less difficult to move on to supervising more complex manufacturing operations which need distributing skill as only one component in an array of skills. Commercial enterprise teaches not only a skill, but also a frame-of-mind essential for successful management of complex enterprises where it is sometimes more difficult to realize the necessity of adapting to market realities.

Choice of technologies is not only conditioned by the skills available, but it is also a conditioner. By choosing industries in which the techniques used are such that low-skilled people can be trained in a short time to the level required, the labor force can be skilled upward, first through the training, and then through the work experience. Succeeding generations easily grow up to the higher skill level, since it becomes a part of the cultural atmosphere. The new generations, in turn, can be taken to still higher levels. .

In the United States, for example, the textile industry started in New England with simple techniques. As skill levels rose, industries requiring higher level skills began bidding labor away from the textile mills using lower skills. Metal working industries and machine makers, for example, bid for such labor. Even within the textile industry, the mills producing finer materials and using more advanced methods bid this sort of labor away from less advanced mills and those producing coarser materials. The mills using low-skill labor succumbed not only to the bidding away of their capital and labor by those who could use it more productively, but they also lost their markets for coarse materials to new mills in the Carolina Piedmont. These mills played the same role in this area as the earlier mills in New England had. Now that finer spinning and weaving and other industries are coming into the Piedmont, it is suffering a similar fate. Mississippi is now playing a role relative to the Piedmont that the latter played relative to New England.

The shoe industry has undergone a similar history in New England. Missouri and Arkansas are now becoming centers for producing cheaper shoes, and the shoe factories in other regions are shifting to higher quality output.

Optimum techniques in different areas at given levels of development. In trying to determine the technologies appropriate to areas beginning their development, and contrasting these with those appropriate in areas in other stages of development, it is not easy to make generalizations. Resource complexes differ not only at different stages of development, but from area to area. The United States and Canada began their development with abundant natural resources and scarce labor and capital. India and Egypt, by way of contrast, have abundant labor, but land is scarce. Capital in use is also scarce, yet the latter countries are less in need of additional capital than they are of entrepreneurs to use the capital they have.

Both Western Europe and the United States are at an advanced stage of development. While Europe has a longer history of development, the United States has, in some respects, reached a more advanced stage. Only a few decades ago, the United States was importing capital from Europe. Since World War I, the situation has been reversed. Europe today is relatively long on labor and short on capital and land. The differences in the relative availability of resources show in the technologies most efficient in each. In the United States, for example, machines are ruggedly designed to minimize maintenance (labor being scarce and capital relatively abundant). European machines are lighter, require more maintenance, and use less material (natural resources) in their construction and more labor. Swiss water wheels of given power ratings in hydroelectric projects, for instance, run at twice the speed of the larger United States wheels. Although the material requirement is less for their construction, the Swiss wheels require much more labor since tolerances are closer and balance finer. Similar labor in the United States is relatively much more costly than the extra material required for United States type constructions.

Conclusion. The appropriate technology for an area depends on its resource patterns and its markets. Part of its resource pattern is the quality and skill of its labor force. Since a relatively unskilled population cannot be propelled from low- to high-level skills in one generation without the investment of prohibitive amounts of capital in training and education,[52] and since there would be little use for the skills without even more prohibitive investment in equipment, the techniques appropriate for an advanced economy are inappropriate in an area beginning its development. By using techniques which are skill- and capital-saving, national income is benefited more than through the use of seemingly "advanced" techniques, and, in addition, the scene is prepared for further advance.

Even the methods used in some areas which use relatively little skill and capital are not appropriate "as is" for other areas in similar stages of development with similarly scarce labor and capital. Differences between areas always necessitate adaptations, and appropriately so.

Appendix to Chapter VI

A graphical method for analyzing and selecting techniques of production. It has been emphasized that the technique appropriate for an industry depends upon the resource constellation available in the area in which it operates. This point may be demonstrated by the use of the graphs described below. These graphs are also helpful in selecting appropriate techniques.

---

[52] The United States was fortunate in its development period in that it could import large numbers of people who had skills. The importance of this is indicated by a statement, attributed to Corrado Gini, that the saving of the cost of education to the United States by mass immigration from Europe was as large as the total sum of capital formed up to the time of World War I.

The techniques available for the production of any commodity may be represented by rays on a graph whose axes represent the different factors which may be combined to produce it. To keep the graph simple enough to reproduce on a two-dimensional sheet of paper, let us assume a single commodity is produced with the aid of only two factors of production, which we will call labor and capital.

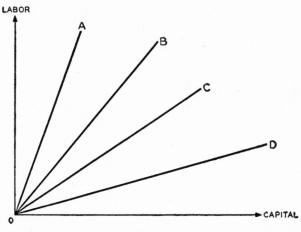

FIGURE 6.1

Each technique may be represented by a single ray. The different points on a ray represent different levels of production which can be attained by using different amounts of the factors, although always in the same proportion. Figure 6.1 shows four techniques, represented by rays A, B, C, and D. We can select a point on each of these rays which shows the amount of labor and capital required to produce, with that technique, say, one thousand units of product. The line joining these points is called an iso-quant; that is, a line showing the resources required to produce the same quantity of product with the techniques pictured at whatever ratio we wish to use in combining resources.

We may wish to use a combination of factors which falls at some point between those called for on any ray. In that case, the combination can be obtained by using the techniques shown on the rays lying on either side of the point representing the combination in question, assuming the rays show all the feasible techniques.

The actual amounts of factors available to an economy can be represented by a point in the plane of the graph. If the point happens to fall on ray A, this is the technique which will yield maximum product. For example, if the amounts of labor and capital available are *a* and *b*, as shown in Figure 6.2, then technique A will yield the

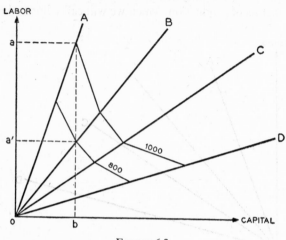

FIGURE 6.2

maximum amount of product. If we were to use the more capital-intensive technique B, we should be able to employ only the amount *d′* of the available labor as a consequence of the limited amount of capital available. We should find ourselves operating on the eight hundred rather than the one thousand unit iso-quant.

This represents the sort of mistake that has frequently been made in overly ambitious developmental programs for underdeveloped areas where capital is very scarce. If these areas would at first employ what may seem to be primitive techniques, instead of trying to imitate the techniques employed in highly industrialized, capital-rich areas, they would attain higher levels of national income.

With the aid of this graph, we can see that technological change may occur in either of two ways. In the first case, a change in the relative abundance of different resources may direct movement from, let us say, technique A to technique B. For example, suppose that the supply of capital increases to *c*. Then, as we can see from Figure 6.3, the economy should shift to the use of techniques B and C instead of technique A.

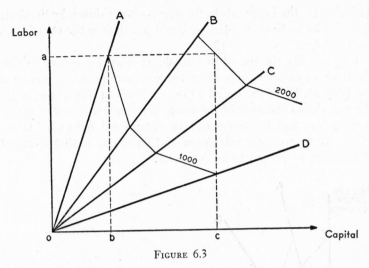

FIGURE 6.3

In the case of a change in resource availabilities with no change in technological possibility, change will occur through a shift to already known techniques which employ relatively more of the now relatively more abundant resource. Technological change may also occur without any change in the available resources. If new techniques are developed, this will alter the position of the iso-quants. Suppose, for example, a new technique, shown as C' in Figure 6.4, is developed.

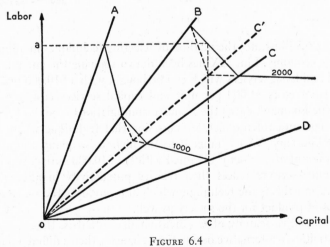

FIGURE 6.4

This changes the iso-quants to the new positions shown by the dotted lines. Under these circumstances, it will pay to drop the use of C and use C' instead.

To generalize the use of this graph, we must know how to select the resource combinations when the economy produces more than one product. With the use of a "budget line" (a line whose slope is the negative of the ratio of the resource prices), the correct resource combination and technique can be determined for each industry. The correct resource combination and technique is that where the budget line is tangent to an iso-quant.

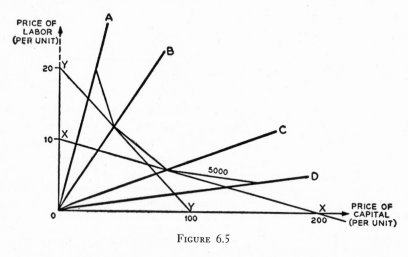

FIGURE 6.5

Figure 6.5 illustrates the method of selecting techniques in a multi-industry economy. Line XX has been drawn showing the amounts of capital and labor services which can be bought with a $10,000 budget when labor costs $1,000 per unit and capital services cost $50 per unit. The iso-quant shows the resource combinations required to produce 5,000 units of product. By choosing that technique where the budget line (line XX) is tangent to the highest iso-quant, the maximum amount of product is obtained with the $10,000 outlay. If prices of resource services reflect their relative productivity in alternative occupations, this is the technique which also produces the maximum amount of product for the society as well.

If the relative scarcity of resources changes (that is, their relative productivities in alternative occupations change), then a different combination should be used. If new prices for labor and capital come to prevail at $500 and $100, then the new budget line YY will show the amount of resource services which can be purchased with a $10,000 budget. In this case, technique B will yield a larger amount of product for $10,000 of resource services than technique C. If, again, relative prices of resource services correctly reflect their relative productivities in other industries, the use of technique B will result in the maximum possible contribution to total income.

CHAPTER VII

Consumption Patterns

JOSEPH P. McKENNA*

CONSUMPTION OCCUPIES A UNIQUE POSITION IN ANY DISCUSSION OF economic development. In a society based upon individual choice, it is the goal of economic activity and of development. In an authoritarian society in which the goals are set by the leaders, consumption might be considered a necessary evil, a cost of carrying out some program. However, we are concerned with societies which place emphasis upon individual choice and make the future consumption of individuals the objective for development. Of course the cost element is not absent in such societies; since productive capacity is limited in every country, a large output of consumer goods will leave few resources free for investment. On the other hand, if total consumption is low, investment will be low as well and economic development will lag. Thus consumption is one of the principal factors determining the pace of development.

By changing the level of consumption as well as its pattern, it is possible to influence the magnitude and direction of investment activity. An understanding of the circumstances under which consumption will change is, therefore, crucial knowledge for anyone interested in the process of development. Such understanding is necessary for predicting changes in the level of income and it will also increase our ability to control economic growth.

As the word implies, consumption means the actual using up of goods and services in the satisfaction of human wants. Food is consumed when eaten; the services of a barber are consumed when administered. In the case of other products the concept is more trou-

* Associate Professor of Economics, University of Minnesota; Consultant, Office of the Technical Staff of the United States Treasury.

blesome. When does one consume a book which is purchased, read once, and never again removed from the bookcase except for occasional dusting? Is an education consumed during the years one is a student, or throughout life?

Beyond such conceptual difficulties, there are problems of measuring consumption which are even more critical. It is hard enough to gather statistics on the sales of food, without trying to collect records of what is eaten and when. These brief remarks indicate why statisticians usually define consumption as the purchase of any goods or services by one who will finally use them for satisfying human wants (i.e., by a consumer).[1] Although this does not exactly meet the ideal definition of consumption, it does have the advantage of being measurable with no more guesswork than is normal in economic statistics. While this definition will be used throughout this chapter, it will sometimes be necessary to remember the difference between it and the ideal definition. In underdeveloped countries, for example, this difference is typically very large because a considerable amount of goods are produced and consumed in the home without ever going through the market, where they can be measured. (Brazil attempts to include these goods in consumption, but the statisticians of other nations have been less bold.)

In recent years the governments of many countries have provided their citizens with such community goods and services as parks, band concerts, police protection, and armies. Such things clearly improve the current well-being of the population and should be classified as consumer goods. They are, however, community consumer goods and so are different in kind from those customarily classified under consumption. The increasing proportion of total income devoted to their purchase in many countries today makes it essential for us to consider their place in the pattern of consumption and their role in economic development.

A definition of saving poses no problems on a conceptual level since it is simply that portion of income which is not spent for consumption goods. In common speech saving often refers to a particular *stock* of assets which one may accumulate; in the present context, however, we are speaking of the disposition of part of the income

---

[1] In the case of houses, consumption is measured by use, not purchase. They are treated differently because they are especially expensive, long lived, and regularly available on a rental basis.

flow. Thus purchases of securities or life insurance, repayment of debts, or accumulation of cash are just different ways of saving. While the form which saving takes makes a considerable difference in various situations, for the present we will concentrate on consumption and treat saving as the residual portion of income.

CONSUMPTION AND ECONOMIC DEVELOPMENT

We now return to the problem of the relationship between consumption and economic development. If a society is fully employed, there is a maximum output which it can produce, and if this output is taken by consumers, then there will be nothing left for investment. Under these circumstances, an attempt to purchase goods for investment purposes will serve to drive prices up, since total supply will be less than demand. The postwar experience in the United States and many European countries provides an example of a combined demand for consumption and investment which exceeded productive capacity. The resulting inflations give ample proof of the effects on price of the excess demand and underline the fact that consumption and investment are competitive in a fully employed economy. If the society is not fully employed, however, clearly investment can be increased with no loss of consumption, because it will be possible to expand total output by hiring unemployed workers and renting unemployed equipment. Indeed, in such a case, consumption might even increase along with investment. The classical economists, writing in the early nineteenth century when there was generally high employment, never considered this aspect of the problem but were greatly concerned about the competitive nature of consumption and investment.[2]

In Chapter V we saw that the "proper" amount of investment is determined by its marginal potential revenue and the marginal social sacrifice involved in saving. It is obvious that the latter is directly related to consumption, for saving is defined as income less consumption. However, the marginal potential revenue (MPR), is also related to consumption. In the economic sense, the productivity of any capital good depends on the market where its output is sold and valued. Since most of this output goes for consumption, productivity depends upon consumption patterns. A given investment will be

[2] With the notable exception of T. R. Malthus who called attention to this problem in the 1820's.

worthwhile only if demand rises by enough to "justify" it. Earlier it was also pointed out that a developing society can maintain full employment over a period of time only if investment and income grow at an annual rate which depends upon the marginal propensity to consume (m.p.c.) and the MPR. If it is possible to alter consumption and thus the m.p.c., then this strict rate of growth may be changed.

It is clear that investment will not always be exactly the amount required for full employment. Investment, as we have seen, takes place in an amount that will be profitable to the investor. Ordinarily it will be high only in an expanding market, or at least in a wide one. If we distinguish between those investments which are merely duplications of existing capital and those which introduce new products or processes, it is apparent that the duplications are profitable only when the market is expanding by an amount sufficient to take up the increased output. This is quite clearly related to a growth in consumption.

The case of new inventions or new techniques is less clear. At first glance these appear to be uninfluenced by consumption. A new invention may appear at almost any time, depending upon the luck and skill of the inventor. However, an invention may lie unexploited for years before being introduced into the economic process. Thus it is necessary to examine the forces behind the process of innovation, as well as those behind invention. Innovation requires wide markets, where it is easy to find customers. Expanding markets are even better, for then it is not necessary to supplant existing firms who would be apt to retaliate as demand for their goods transferred to the newer product.

We can now restate the principle by which consumption and investment are complementary and competitive. It is the demand for investment which is complementary with the demand for consumption; the supplies are competitive, since consumption and investment bid for the same factors of production. Now consumption itself tends to move upward and downward with income. Thus if consumption becomes too small, there will be a decline in income and therefore less need for further investment. If consumption becomes too large, it may lead to inflation, and in the short run, less investment will be possible because of the strain on resources.

We may conclude, therefore, that for a given society with a given historical background and a given set of investment opportunities, there is an optimum rate of consumption which is neither "too large" nor "too small." This optimum rate is just high enough to encourage a suitable rate of investment, but also low enough so that there will be enough free resources to permit this amount of investment. Obviously this amount of consumption will change from year to year as new investments make possible a larger national output. Yet in the short run a society must avoid both unemployment, which makes investment seem unprofitable, and inflation, which makes it too expensive, in order for national output actually to increase in the long run. This is the same problem in different words which was just discussed in terms of rates of growth.

The effects of consumption upon total spending have been discussed at some length, for it is through this route that consumption exercises its most important immediate effect upon economic development. Less immediate but no less important is the relationship between consumption and the size and efficiency of the labor force. Malnutrition is often a contributing cause of disease, thereby raising the death rate and reducing the size of the labor force. Even if malnutrition-bred disease does not kill the workers, it will impair their efficiency. Food is the largest single part of consumption in most countries. Other types of consumption are also important for the same reasons. Obviously greater consumption of medical services by households will increase the effectiveness and size of the labor force, as will better housing and clothing. In malarial areas, government consumption of insecticides would perform the same function. Greater consumption of educational services will tend to increase the availability of managerial and technical workers while consumption of drugs and alcohol would tend to lower the effectiveness of the labor force.

Beyond these effects of specific kinds of consumption, the over-all level and rate of increase of consumption contributes to the general effectiveness of the labor force through its impact on workers' morale. However, a rapid shift to a high level of consumption may tend to lower the amount of work offered by a given labor force. As income and consumption rise, less labor may be offered since the value of additional consumption to the worker will be lower, while the value of leisure will rise.

Consumption patterns also tend to alter government expenditures, for the government is often forced to provide services which are complementary with consumer purchases. If consumers wish to use automobiles, government must provide roads; if consumers insist on certified food products, government must provide inspectors. In addition, consumption tastes are sometimes expressed through the ballot box rather than in the market place. In such cases, government provides services because the electorate prefers that method to individual purchase. Even in nondemocratic societies, government is often moderately responsive to such consumer demands, though the channels of communication are less direct.

Having established the important relationship between consumption and economic development, it is necessary to examine in some detail the determinants of consumption. This is vital for predicting the future path of development as well as for understanding what has happened in the past. Those interested in changing the economy's rate of growth and developmental pattern are also forced to examine these determinants. In the first place, it is clear that a change in investment, the balance of trade, or government expenditures will have repercussions in the area of consumption which may be important for development. In the second place, changes in consumption, which by definition can only be brought about by changes in the determinants of consumption, may serve as initiating or encouraging forces in the growth process. An ability to control one or another of these determinants, then, may make it possible to influence the entire process.

DETERMINANTS OF INDIVIDUAL CONSUMPTION

Since the publication of Keynes' *General Theory*,[3] it is customary to concentrate first on the relation between income and consumption. This is not because Keynes and Keynesians were such bad social scientists that they thought income alone determined the level of consumption. However, it did seem reasonable, both a priori and on the basis of the available statistical evidence, that changes in consumption could be satisfactorily explained by changes in income alone. A satisfactory explanation in this sense means that a moderately close prediction (say one with a five per cent error) may be made without considering other factors. This implies that the other

[3] John Maynard Keynes, *The General Theory of Employment, Interest, and Money.* (New York: Harcourt Brace & Co., 1936.)

factors are either of minor importance, cancel one another out, or do not change substantially during short periods of time.

It is legitimate to ignore variables which change but slowly if one is dealing with short-term analysis, as Keynes was. It is not satisfactory to ignore them in a study of economic development; indeed we are especially concerned with changes that may take place over decades. The industrialization of Russia, for example, began just after the revolution, was interrupted by World War II, and is not complete now, thirty years later; and this is an example of rapid industrialization.

Even in the short run, economists no longer neglect other determinants so readily. One reason is that many, dissatisfied with certain policy implications of Keynesian analysis, have turned to the study of other variables to seek justification for alternative policies. The second and more important reason is that such analysis gave very bad predictions of consumption in many countries during the period following World War II. These failures motivated an elaborate re-examination of the determinants of consumption.[4]

Therefore, we will examine the effect on consumption of many variables. First let us consider those which affect the consumption of individual households. Next will come the problem of aggregation: adding these individual actions to obtain national totals. Finally we will discuss the effect of government actions on individuals and on the totals. In these sections we will discuss only total consumption and leave the discussion of specific types of consumption until later.

Income. Although we have indicated that income is not the sole determinant of consumption, it is nevertheless probably the most important single factor. Prices, wealth, tastes, needs, and all the other factors which we will consider color the decision, but income provides the funds and thus limits the amount of consumption possible.

If families have needs or desires for consumption and for saving, one would expect additional income to be divided in some manner between these two categories of uses. It was from such reasoning

---

[4] See, for example, *Review of Economic Statistics* articles by Bassie, August, 1946; Katona and Likert, Bean, Friend, Bennion, and Brady, November, 1946; Hagen, May, 1947; Woytinsky, and Koffsky, February, 1948 for a sample of this discussion. Other journals produced a similar number of articles.

that Keynes deduced the famous psychological propensity making consumption increase as income increases, but by less than the change in income. Factual evidence confirms this relationship for individual households, as is demonstrated in Table 7.1, which gives the average income and average consumption of families in each income bracket.[5] Notice that the change in consumption between two adjoining brackets is always less than the change in income. This ratio of increased consumption to increased income is the marginal propensity to consume. For example, the increase in income between the $1500–$1750 bracket and the $1750–$2000 bracket is $217. The increase in consumption is $172. Therefore, the marginal propensity to consume between these brackets is the ratio of 172 to 217, or 0.79.

Since any increase in income which is not consumed is saved, the increase in saving between these brackets is $217 minus $172 or $45. The marginal propensity to save then is the ratio of 45 to 217, or 0.21. Clearly the sum of these two propensities must always be 1.00. Keynes estimated the marginal propensity to consume for all the households taken together in such nations as England and the United States as just over 0.6. For poorer countries, changes in consumption might be expected to just about match changes in income. In such countries, the average household finds that it can barely support itself at a subsistence level even by spending its entire income. So many needs will be left unfilled that saving will seem insignificant.

In richer countries where saving and assets are common, income determines how much a family will want to consume, but does not absolutely determine how much it can consume. In such countries, many economists have suggested, therefore, that some form of normal income is best for predicting the relationship between income and consumption. This implies that households maintain consumption for a time after income drops and push up their consumption in anticipation of a future rise in income. Others, who point out that habits linger after circumstances change, argue that past income is more important than current income. Past income may be important for another reason in a relatively wealthy country. For example,

<hr/>

[5] These particular statistics, from the *Consumer Purchases Study of 1935–36*, were chosen because the large sample gives a better picture of behavior in the upper income brackets.

a family whose income has recently fallen may own a car (or a house) and feel that it is better to keep the car than to dispose of it, although a car would never have been purchased had income always been at its present low level. In general, a family with money "sunk" in certain consumer durables may continue spending to maintain and use these durables, although the durable will not be replaced when it is finally worn out.[6]

To summarize then, current income is important in determining current consumption, but its influence is modified by past income history and expected future income. Realizing the practical difficulties of gathering appropriate data on expectations, we might decide to use a combination of current income and highest previous income as the determinants of current consumption. This is a special case of a "habit" theory, implying that consumers try to maintain the highest previous level of consumption, subject to the restrictions of current income.[7]

Distribution of income. If income were equally distributed, we might consider the consumption of a typical individual and multiply it by the total number of individuals, for all would be identical with respect to income, and other differences might be expected to average out if the group were large. This cannot be done because incomes are distributed quite unevenly in all countries, with the large bulk of persons falling in the lower income brackets.

One of the phenomena observed from budget studies is that the marginal propensity to consume falls as income increases. Table 7.1 also shows these relations for 1935–36 for the United States based on the *Consumer Purchases Study.* Other studies show similar results. Thus the effect on consumption of a rise in income will depend upon the distribution of that increase. Let us illustrate, using the figures of Table 7.1. If an increase of a million dollars in national income were distributed equally among 4,082 families in the $750–

---

[6] This is similar to the argument that a firm will maintain old equipment if average variable cost is less than average revenue but will replace it only if average total cost is less than average revenue.

[7] James S. Duesenberry, *Income, Saving, and the Theory of Consumer Behavior.* (Cambridge, Mass.: Harvard University Press, 1949), J. R. Hicks, *Value and Capital.* (New York: Oxford University Press, 1939.) Margaret G. Reid, in *Saving, Inflation and Economic Development.* (Minneapolis: University of Minnesota Press, 1953.) See also footnote 4 for some of the statistical studies.

TABLE 7.1

ANNUAL INCOME AND CONSUMPTION OF UNITED STATES FAMILIES, 1935–36

Income bracket	Average income*	Average consumption	Marginal propensity to consume†
Under $500	$310	$466	.76
500–750	625	707	.84
750–1,000	872	914	.87
1,000–1,250	1,117	1,127	.78
1,250–1,500	1,361	1,316	.79
1,500–1,750	1,608	1,512	.79
1,750–2,000	1,825	1,684	.73
2,000–2,500	2,215	1,968	.68
2,500–3,000	2,707	2,302	.63
3,000–4,000	3,381	2,729	.56
4,000–5,000	4,364	3,276	.49
5,000–10,000	6,775	4,454	.39
10,000–15,000	11,024	6,097	.53
15,000–20,000	16,707	9,134	.28
20,000 and over	36,950	14,822	

Source: National Resources Committee, *Consumer Expenditures in the United States.* (Washington, D.C.: Government Printing Office, 1939.) The last column was computed by the author.

* Adjusted for personal taxes.
† The increase in consumption between these brackets divided by the increase in income.

$1,000 bracket, it would raise them from an average income of $872 to $1,117. If their marginal propensity to consume remains constant, we would then expect their consumption to increase from $914 to $1,127, an increase of $213 per family, or $869,466 total. If the same million dollars were distributed among 235 families in the $5,000–$10,000 bracket, it would raise their average income from $6,775 to $11,030, just above the average for the next bracket. We should expect their consumption to increase from $4,454 to about $6,100, an increase of $1,646 per family, or a total of only $386,810. This is less than half of the increase when the million was distributed in the lower brackets. (The choice of 4,082 families and 235 families, respectively, was made so that the increase should bring the average income up to that of the next higher bracket. No other significance attaches to these numbers.)

Too much reliance should not be placed on the exact results obtained from statistical techniques such as that just employed, because it hardly seems reasonable to suppose that a family whose income increases will, after the increase, behave exactly like those whose incomes were previously at the higher level. Enough has been written about the *nouveaux riches* to suggest that they will not spend as they did before their incomes rose. If everyone in the society moved up together, the situation would be different. In such a case, one would stay in the same group and social influences would remain relatively constant.

This discussion of distribution gives only an introduction to a complete study of the problem. The marginal propensity to consume varies among individuals in the society for many reasons other than differences in income. In general, the marginal propensity to consume is higher for young families than for older ones, higher for urban families than for rural ones. We would expect these results, for younger families still are acquiring consumer durable goods and have less pressing needs for saving than older ones. Similarly, since rural families have fewer contacts with higher income groups than city families, we should expect them to have a lower marginal propensity to consume. These expectations are borne out by further analysis of budget studies. Therefore, if we wished to know the exact effect upon consumption of an increase in income we should need to know all the characteristics of the recipients, age, rural-urban status, and income class.

This initial concentration on income seems justified by its importance in determining the amount of total consumption. More basically, however, it is labor, land, or some other resource, rather than income, which households spend. The wage earner has a certain amount of time available with which to satisfy his desires for income and leisure. After making this decision he determines the portion of income to be spent currently and the portion to be set aside for the future. Since these decisions are interrelated, if anything occurs to increase his desire for consumption goods, we might expect that it would be at the expense of leisure as well as saving. Thus, if there were special consumption desires, one might work longer or harder, as well as cut down on saving.

On the other hand, technological advance, a change in consumer demand, or variation in the conditions controlling the supply of resources can easily result in more income going to some segments of the society. This permits people to satisfy their customary wants with less effort and obtain more leisure. Some plantation owners in Latin America and the West Indies have found that their employees have made just this choice. The employers' final solution was to make available stocks of European goods for the workers to buy. Only after consumption tastes changed was additional labor offered. This is a case where consumption did not depend upon income as much as income upon consumption. As Simon Rottenberg points out, discussing this thesis for the West Indies, "If the doctrine is true, an important objective of public policy ought to be to raise the level of aspiration for income *and for the goods and services for which income exchanges.*" [8]

Wealth. A household's consumption will be affected by its existing wealth; that is, the stock of assets, both real and monetary, which it holds. Even in poorer countries where most families have few assets of either kind, this relationship may be important. The richer members of the population do have assets, and it is these people who do most of the saving. At a given income level, a family will wish to own a certain stock of durable goods such as a house, a car, or major appliances. Very few couples can afford to purchase a complete stock immediately after marriage, and the process of accumulating these durables may take ten, twenty, or more years. Since the statisticians define consumption of such durables as taking place at purchase, a family's consumption will be high during the early years and then decrease as the durable goods are used up. (Of course, if we could spread the value of the consumption evenly over the life of the assets, then consumption would increase as the family uses up more durables.)

The effect of an increasing number of durables is, however, not altogether in the direction of lower consumption. As we have already seen in a different connection, many durables require certain additional expenditures. The most familiar are those associated with an automobile or a house, where the costs of repair and operation may, over the years, add up to a considerable fraction of the purchase cost. In most countries there is not a sufficient number of such durables to make this reverse effect of real assets on consumption important. In the United States, however, it is entirely possible that

[8] Simon Rottenberg, "Income and Leisure in an Underdeveloped Economy," *Journal of Political Economy,* LX, No. 2, April 1952. (Italics mine.)

an increase in the stock of consumer durables may, on balance, even increase consumption. The effect of a change in the stock of monetary assets (i.e., money and claims to money, such as bonds, other loans, and equity in insurance policies and retirement programs) is quite different. Near money, such as jewels and precious metals, as well as holdings of common and preferred stock and real estate seem to affect consumption in about the same way. (Here we ignore any income derived from asset holdings.)

Most people increase their stock of monetary assets (i.e., save) because they have some definite purpose in mind—retirement, education for children, safeguards against emergency, or the eventual purchase of some large durable, such as a house. The larger the stock of money assets on hand, the more nearly these goals can be met without additional saving. Thus the possession of such assets lowers the value of additional saving and consequently raises consumption. Of course, if the household is following a saving program with a definite purpose in mind, the increase in its assets will follow as a natural result, and one should not expect any alteration in the program as a result of the increase.[9] However, if the asset increase is a result of a windfall, such as winning a lottery, one would expect a downward revision of the saving plan. Only under the unlikely assumption that mere ownership of this wealth induces a "miser complex" will consumption be reduced.

In this discussion of the influence of asset holdings on consumption, it must be emphasized that we are talking of changes in the total stock of assets, not merely of changes in ownership. In any society some households are selling real or monetary assets which others are buying from them. Only if one of these groups is quite different from the other, will such transactions lead to a change in consumption. For our purposes, it is variation in the total stock which is important.

For most people in poorer countries, discussion of asset holdings is unimportant, for they have none. Any circumstances which reduce income will typically reduce consumption an equal amount. Only for the wealthier classes, the landlords and entrepreneurs, are asset holdings an important factor. In general, we might expect them to be affected by changes in their assets much as people generally are in

[9] James Tobin, "Asset Holdings and Spending Decisions," *American Economic Review Papers and Proceedings,* Volume XLII, No. 2 (May, 1952).

a wealthy country, with the possible difference that the "miser complex" mentioned above may be somewhat more important for countries in early stages of development than for more advanced ones. As the process of development leads to higher incomes, the wealth owned by households typically increases also. For very rich countries, this may introduce a considerable measure of instability into the economy, as was demonstrated by the sudden buying of consumer durables financed by the sale of monetary assets in the United States following World War II.[10]

Need for saving. A family has definite desires for saving, as well as for consumption. There is a desire to save for contingencies and for expected expenditures in the future. In general, there is a tendency for an individual to spend enough and save enough so that he gets the same satisfaction from both the last dollar saved and the last dollar consumed. Any additional income received will also be allocated between saving and consumption in this same manner. If it were all allocated to spending, this would lower the marginal satisfaction of spending below that of saving, making it preferable to increase saving. Thus, we conclude that any additional income will be directed toward both saving and consumption. This serves as further evidence that as income increases, consumption will increase, but by less than income.

As we have noted before, the greater the stock of assets, the less will be the need for saving, since more of the family's needs can be taken care of without further saving. This is obviously true of monetary assets: it is also true that real assets (consumer durables) can lessen the need for saving, for their ownership permits one to use their services without further expenditure. A family which owns a home, completely furnished and with a small garden, is obviously better prepared against retirement or loss of income than a family without them.

This may seem at odds with our previous statement that consumer durables lessen the need for consumption. The answer is that a family with such durables receives their services and thus in reality has a higher income than its cash receipts would indicate. Since we

[10] James Tobin, "Relative Income, Absolute Income, and Savings," in *Money, Trade, and Economic Growth: Essays in Honor of John Henry Williams.* (New York: The Macmillan Co., 1951.)

measure everything in money flows, statistically this higher real "income" is treated as a reduced need for consumption and saving.

Where a family saves to provide for its children, increased family size will increase the need for saving. This is true whether the object is an education, a dowry, or a start in business. However, these additional desires for saving come at a time when needs for consumption have increased. The net effect of these increases in both directions is problematical.

Development of insurance plans will have a great influence upon the needs for saving. If there were no medical insurance available, for instance, every family would feel a need to build up enough assets to cover its maximum medical needs, not the average. Similarly, if retirement insurance is available, the average amount saved will be lessened by the expected mortality. If unemployment insurance is available, the risks of income loss can be spread. Thus in every case, insurance makes it possible for a family to obtain suitable protection against contingencies by saving the average amount, rather than the maximum. In general, most "rainy-day" funds are not fully needed. If the risk can be shared, this unnecessary saving can be reduced.

Prices. The effect of prices on consumption will be felt in various ways. It is immediately clear that higher prices with income and monetary assets fixed will have somewhat the same effect as a drop in income and monetary assets with prices fixed; namely, lower consumption. The effects of price changes, however, are more complicated, since they may create expectations of future changes. If prices are expected to increase significantly, people will buy more consumption goods in order to make their purchases at the lower level, to the extent that they can finance these purchases out of asset holdings or borrowed money. Such effects will be most noticeable for durable and storable commodities; least for highly perishable ones. The extreme case may be observed during runaway inflation, when consumers try to spend money as rapidly as possible, with the expectation of further price increases tomorrow. Conversely, expectations of lower prices will persuade many consumers to postpone purchases as long as possible.

In recent years, much discussion has centered on the effect of a drop in both prices and money income on consumption. Such a decline makes monetary assets more valuable in terms of purchasing power. Thus there is reason to expect consumption in real terms to increase, although the amount of money spent will decrease.[11] If a fall in the price level leads to an expectation of a further fall, however, this analysis will be invalid. Furthermore, if people suffer from a "money illusion," they will not be apt to revalue their assets in terms of their increased purchasing power; and if prices are expected to return to the higher levels which prevailed before, people will act as if these assets have not increased in value. Indeed in this case, the pressure to save might actually be increased, since consumers are trying to accumulate funds for use at a price level higher than the current one. Finally, many forms of saving are contractual (e.g., an insurance policy). Such contracts are stated in terms of dollars and are not automatically adjusted every time the price level changes. Therefore, when prices and incomes fall, the amount of money available for consumption will fall by more than the price level. One might expect a readjustment of these contracts if the new price and income level persists for a long period of time, but the immediate effect would be to decrease consumption.

While this discussion of the relationship between changes in prices and changes in consumption emphasizes the complexity of the problem, on balance, a general rise in prices typically increases consumption, and conversely. It is otherwise, however, when a rise in the price of some particular goods is accompanied by a corresponding drop in the price of other goods or services. If these changes are thought to be permanent, consumption of the now cheaper goods will generally expand at the expense of those whose prices have risen. While statement of such changes of course presumes that incomes and the desires of the consumers have not changed, it also presumes something about the nature of the goods in question. It has long been recognized that some commodities are noticeably "rich man's goods," while others are purchased mostly by the poor. Should it be a rich man's goods whose price had dropped, its possession would no longer be so prestigeful and sales might even fall off.

This distinction between rich and poor man's goods is important in another connection too. While a change in the real income re-

---

[11] A. C. Pigou, "The Classical Stationary State," *Economic Journal*, 1943; "Economic Progress in a Stable Environment," *Economica*, 1947, reprinted in *Readings in Monetary Theory*, (New York: Blakiston Co., 1951.)

ceived by households will almost certainly change total consumption in the same direction, it will be otherwise with the various clusters of goods and services which make up the total. An increasing income per capita will benefit those who produce luxury goods at the expense of those sectors of the economy geared to the production of so-called necessities. Changes in the distribution of income towards greater inequality may have similar consequences. The importance of such facts for the successful planning of a development program is clear.

Credit. The classical economists laid great stress on the role of the interest rate in determining the levels of consumption and saving. According to these theories, consumers were persuaded to save either more or less by changes in the interest received on savings. Later discussions showed that it was not clear whether a rise in the interest rate would increase or decrease the amount of saving. A higher interest rate means a better return, but less saving each year is required to attain any given savings goal.

The interest rate would presumably be most important to a rich man, whose savings are relatively large. Such a man can often live on the income from his capital and might be expected to react to the price of that income. People of more moderate means save primarily to build a fund which they expect to spend at some future time. For such groups the income from assets is relatively small. A man with an annual income of $5000 might have accumulated assets of $1000. At 5 per cent this sum yields an income of $50, or 1 per cent of his annual income. A rise in the interest rate to 6 per cent would change his annual income by an insignificant $10. In the underdeveloped world which the classical economists knew, most saving was done by the rich, and the analysis naturally concentrated on the factors which were important to the rich. In the England and America of today, a large proportion of saving is done by moderate income groups, for whom the interest rate is less significant.

Furthermore, as countries such as England and America have become more wealthy, there has been an increase in the importance of consumer durable goods. Many of these are very expensive and purchases are often made on credit. Changes in the terms on which this credit is available, particularly the requirements as to down payments and the length of the loan, may take over the role previously assigned to changes in the interest rate.

It is quite probable that the classical emphasis on the interest rate still fits underdeveloped areas. For these areas, the general level of income is so low that most saving must come from the rich. In many of these countries, interest rates are both higher and more variable than in western countries and thus more important.

The interest rate does have one important role, whatever its relation to saving. *Ceteris paribus*, a higher interest rate will induce people to hold more of their assets in income-yielding securities, rather than in idle cash or jewels. Clearly this incentive to use assets for productive purposes is a necessary condition for economic development. It is not clear, however, whether an interest-rate-induced change in asset structure will affect consumption patterns directly. If investments are made primarily in bonds, which have a relatively stable dollar value, the effect on consumption will be about the same as holding cash. On the other hand, if the investments are made in stocks, one would expect less reaction on the part of consumers to price changes, for the value of stocks is apt to change with price. This effect on asset structure is probably the most important role of the interest rate on the behavior of households, at least in advanced countries.

Needs and tastes. The foregoing factors, income, wealth, prices, and interest, are important in determining the level of consumption in the short run, as well as over longer periods. In contrast, the next few pages are devoted to factors whose influence is felt only over the long run. This is not because they are less important, but because they change much more slowly.

Needs are almost impossible to distinguish from tastes. Individuals often talk about necessities as if they were subject to simple objective classification, although the word usually implies only that the speaker values the particular commodity highly. One might define necessities as food, clothing, and shelter. But what kind of food? Some years ago, several economists amused themselves by computing the cheapest way to get a diet containing all necessary food elements.[12]

[12] George J. Stigler, "The Cost of Subsistence," *The Journal of Farm Economics,* Volume XXVII, No. 2 (May, 1945).

In 1951, such a diet for a family of four could have been provided for about $300 per year. Actual average expenditures for such a family in 1951 were about $1600 per year in the United States, and a diet of exotic delicacies could easily cost $5000 per family. Similar ranges could be provided for clothing and shelter.

It may be that the most satisfactory method of distinguishing between needs and tastes is in terms of the response of demand for particular foods and services to changes in income as was just done in the previous section. Another way to describe the same thing is to say that necessities are those items which a family would struggle to retain even though its income falls. This implies that the final judge of what is a necessity for a household is the household itself, a point of view which is justifiable with the great majority of goods and services.

But if it is possible to list only an insignificant number of goods which everyone must have for biological survival, we must search elsewhere for an explanation of people's wants and desires. For the purposes of this chapter, however, it is sufficient to discuss how tastes or desires change, rather than concern ourselves with the entire learning process by which each of us is trained to live in a given culture. The most important single way by which tastes change seems to come from a household's relations with its neighbors. The ownership and consumption of certain goods by one family often change the tastes of other members of the group. In some cultures, these changes are based on simple rivalry or emulation, as exemplified in "keeping up with the Joneses." In other cultures, people may be motivated by a desire to maintain a preferred status by "keeping ahead of the Smiths." This latter may be especially important in affecting the conspicuous consumption patterns of the highest income classes in poorer countries, although those close to the top may be motivated by emulation of similar people in more advanced economies. Since the income distribution in many of these countries is very unequal, those at the top of the scale may find no Joneses and few Smiths, and thus they are able to maintain their social status by spending a small portion of their income. Where this is true, the "miser complex" mentioned earlier may possibly develop.

These are real changes in taste, regardless of motivation, for they lead to different consumption patterns even when income and wealth are fixed. Changes in taste may also take place because a neighbor's ownership of certain goods demonstrates their value. Simple demonstration might bring about a similarity of consumption patterns for a social group even without emulation, and the effect of such demonstrations may spread rather widely.[13] Some of the pressures for higher consumption in underdeveloped countries clearly come from comparison with the "Western standard of living," as transmitted by mass media of communication and contact with tourists and troops from more advanced countries.[14] This may be especially bothersome to officials in these countries who may find much of their dollar exchange going for American shoes, movies, or other consumer goods, rather than for the machinery desired for development.

Another factor in the development of tastes, especially in advanced countries, is advertising, whose virtues have been so vehemently affirmed and denied. At a minimum, however, advertising tends to shift people's preferences toward the output of manufactured goods, since it is in these sectors of the economy that wide markets (and therefore advertising) are most profitable. This should create stimulus to new investments in machinery and stimulate economic development. The advertising industry in the United States takes much of the credit for the great development of large-scale mass production. Although these claims are overstated, they probably contain substantial elements of truth.

A further effect of advertising has been to encourage the splintering of a single market into markets for individual brands. To the extent that each seller has a partial monopoly through his brand, he is encouraged to restrict output. Such restrictions may discourage further investment by these firms and possibly encourage needless investment by other firms which wish to enter the industry.

Advertising may have other effects which are especially important to those interested in the future of democracy. The constant impact of advertising may standardize the tastes of the population, rendering them more homogeneous and thus making political democracy easier. However, either unquestioning acceptance or complete cynicism resulting from continued exposure to advertising might leave the population more susceptible to demagoguery.

[13] Duesenberry, *op. cit.*

[14] Horst Menderhausen, discussion on "Growth in Underdeveloped Countries," *American Economic Review Papers and Proceedings*, Volume XLII, No. 2 (May, 1952)

With these and other factors operating to change tastes, their stability is a rather striking phenomenon. The explanation lies in the fact that sheer habit plays an important part in their determination. (Advertisers are aware of this and direct much of their effort toward inducing an initial purchase of their product.) Thus while tastes change rather slowly, for the course of economic development, changes in taste may be very important.

We discussed earlier the importance of wide markets in simplifying the introduction of new products. In addition, some change in tastes is necessary before a new product will be accepted. The processes by which these changes come about are only slightly understood. A part of the change may be induced by advertising. Indeed, one of the best arguments for advertising is its special role in developing such new demands and thus making innovation successful.

Once a few people have been persuaded to try the new product, perhaps because of simple curiosity, perhaps in an attempt to gain social prestige, the demonstration effect may operate to spread both knowledge of and desire for it. Under not too unusual circumstances, this could lead to a snowballing of demand of very sizable proportions for the product. Given fixed incomes, however, any increase in preferences for new goods will, of necessity, mean a decrease in the demand for older, competing goods. An explanation of the rise in favor of the new way thus also explains the decline of the old. Of course the advertisers hired by those manufacturing the older, competing goods may successfully persuade people that both prestige and utility are unique attributes of their products and that only the ill-informed and ill-bred would buy the new goods.

Even if changes in taste occur, they will not always be translated into purchases. Many innovations occur in the area of durable goods, replacing other durables. In such cases, the change in taste will be translated into purchase only if the obsolete goods are sufficiently worn out to be replaced. If one did not have the older asset, one would buy the new goods if the expected satisfaction exceeded the satisfaction to be derived from alternative expenditures of the purchase price. If one already has a competing asset, one must weigh the *increase* in satisfaction against the entire cost, less what the old one will bring in the secondhand market. If the innovation is only a slight improvement, the purchase will not be made until the old asset declines further in value.

An important factor in the acceptance of new products is the general attitude of consumers toward new products. In countries where new products appear regularly, customers expect, and even demand, innovation. (American advertisers exploit this by continued use of "All New," "Latest Scientific Discovery," and similar phrases.) In countries where change is relatively rare, new products are apt to be treated with skepticism. The effect of this upon economic development is that innovation is easier in those countries which already have a high level of development, more difficult in backward areas.

Community consumption. As societies evolve, their members form associations to carry on certain functions for the group. The oldest such association is government, which was originally formed to provide for defense and the administration of justice.

In addition, private clubs and associations have grown up for all purposes—social, cultural, benevolent, and economic. These associations resemble government, as well as organizations which perform similar functions for hire. For example, a mutual aid society performs certain of the functions of an insurance company. There is, however, one principal difference between these associations, including government, and private companies. The individual consumer has much less freedom of choice with the association. Private firms offer a collection of services which the individual may buy or not as he chooses. The associations ordinarily offer membership with all its privileges as a package, with but little freedom to accept certain privileges and not others. This involuntary nature is most extreme for government, but it is present in all such associations.

One effect of the growth of organizations, then, is to decrease the flexibility of consumers' expenditures. To the extent that consumers commit themselves to membership, they lose the right to allocate the funds represented by membership fees. This inflexibility is increased by the element of social pressure which is often attached to such associations. Since many are partly social in nature, many people will prefer to remain in the group even if their income changes, although they might change their purchases if these were on a completely voluntary basis. It is also possible that this element of social pressure may result in higher consumption.

Another aspect of the growth of associations is that of a change in the direction of consumption expenditures. In general, the basic items of consumption can be provided by recourse to the regular markets. Thus the simpler items of food, clothing, and shelter are seldom provided by associations. It is only for goods which are either too specialized or too vast for individual entrepreneurs to provide that it is necessary to form associations to carry out the desired end. Specialized eating clubs are often formed to provide gourmets with food of a type which is not feasible in a commercial restaurant. At the other end of the scale, philanthropic undertakings are usually entrusted to associations. A similar development is the recent growth in the United States of private associations devoted to various sorts of research.

An even more obvious case of the change in direction of consumption is the special case of government. The government is called upon to perform just those acts of consumption which are not feasible for individuals by themselves, the primary example being military defense. As the society has become more complex, many more such activities have been added to the governmental portion of consumption. As a society becomes richer, provision of more "community" goods becomes possible. With greater complexity, the range of individual action is increasingly restricted, and the need for associations therefore becomes greater. It is no surprise, then, to find the role of private associations and government in consumption expanding as economic development proceeds.

Government and individual consumption. Knowledge of relationships which have just been discussed between consumption by individual households and incomes, wealth, prices, tastes, and so forth, can be put to use in various ways. First, a given historical change in consumption of the sort, say, which might accompany economic development, can be explained by locating those determinants which were responsible. Second, should a national administrator wish to influence consumption in some particular fashion, then manipulation of one or another of these determinants would be required to achieve his objectives. Some of the ways by which this can be done were mentioned in earlier chapters; additional methods will now be discussed. A government administrator, however, is not limited in his attempts to control consumption to manipulation of the sort of determinants which have just been considered. Indeed, the most obvious influence of government is its role as a provider of community goods and services. In this case, spending decisions are removed from the direct control of the individual members of the society. And government can vary within fairly wide limits the amount it spends on such things as parks, education, or health and welfare measures. Furthermore such expenditures will influence the expenditures of households for individual goods and services.

Another method open to government is taxation, and it is this which will next be considered. While, in practice, changes in taxes are usually closely related to changes in government expenditures, there are good analytical reasons for treating these two processes separately. Every dollar of tax—regardless of the sort of tax—is equivalent initially to a dollar less of income for someone. Thus, in general, any taxes will result in lower consumption. Similarly, a change in distribution of the tax burden will affect consumption like a redistribution of income. Ignoring their effect on investment or government expenditures, the only "exceptions to the rule" of treating taxes as a simple decrease in income are those taxes which discriminate between consumption and saving or consumption and leisure. An income tax needs no special consideration; a general sales tax does. A sales tax tends to have the effect of raising the general price level, usually by less than the tax, for a part of the tax may be absorbed by the producer. If the tax is expected to be permanent, it will act as a price rise; if it is only temporary, there will be a tendency to postpone purchases until after the tax is removed. A selective sales tax, such as a tariff or an excise tax, will tend to redirect consumption into different channels, but will have less effect on over-all consumption. After all, such taxes can often be avoided by buying nontaxed goods.

Some taxes levied on assets, such as a property tax, are directed against saving. Others may be designed to encourage saving. It is somewhat doubtful, however, that any permanent tax has any long-run effect of altering the decision to save rather than consume, for most savings are designed to be consumed eventually and thus ultimately do not escape a consumption tax. If the consumption tax were progressive, it might encourage smoothing out consumption over the years, since thus a lower average rate would be paid.

Most modern tax systems tend to put the greater burden on higher income and thus are called "progressive." Such taxes permit a higher rate of consumption than would a tax system which distributed the burden more evenly. As was seen in Table 7.1, upper income families have a lower marginal propensity to consume; thus their loss of a dollar in taxes will decrease consumption by less than the loss of a dollar to lower income groups. Conversely, regressive taxes, which put the greater burden on low incomes, tend to discourage consumption.

Certain activities of the government may lower the need for saving. For example, a comprehensive program of social security will reduce the amount of savings needed for retirement or for periods of unemployment. A program of universal health insurance would decrease the need to save for possible medical care. Government aid to education will lower the need for saving to provide for schooling. Such programs are not, of course, free. Often, however, they are similar to insurance and lower the total need for saving in the same way by spreading the risks over all the population, making each individual save (through taxes) only the actuarial cost, rather than requiring that he save against the maximum.

It is doubtful that government can substantially lower the total consumption requirements in the same general way it can lower saving needs. Here there is no actuarial element to reduce total cost. There does remain the slight possibility that cost will be less if the government purchases all of certain consumption goods, rather than leaving matters to individual purchasers. Cost may also be lower if government uses its taxing power to reduce certain sorts of advertising or to redistribute income. In effect, such redistribution takes place if the government provides services for one group but pays for them with taxes on a higher income group. Government can also use direct persuasion and become an "advertiser." Encouragement of social and spatial movement, which may be desirable on other grounds, will probably raise consumption.

It is, however, possible for the government to alter actual consumption even though it finds it difficult to alter needs. Rationing of goods will clearly lower consumption, as will excise taxes. Similarly, use of the police power may alter consumption by refusing to permit sales of certain products, such as drugs or obscene literature.

The government might affect the general level of consumption by its control over the money supply. If the government pursues a policy of moderate inflation, one would expect prices and incomes to rise. This means that the real value of money assets would decline and consumption (in real terms) along with it, unless the price rise created expectations of further price increases. Actually, of course, an inflationary program would probably result in greater consumption since price expectations would be drastically changed. Just the opposite would happen if the government were to establish a long-range deflationary program.

The last important effect of government activity is the direct relationship of specific government programs and specific personal consumption. Automobiles require roads to operate. Thus a government program of road building will increase consumption of automobiles and gasoline. Government programs providing cheap electricity will increase the use of electrical appliances. Other programs might have similar effects, although not so obviously. For example, a national park system might increase the consumption of items associated with outdoor vacations.

CHANGES IN CONSUMPTION PATTERNS AND ECONOMIC DEVELOPMENT

In this section, we will examine the historical patterns of consumption as income has increased, and summarize certain conclusions which have been reached. Statistical illustrations will be based on United States data primarily because this is one of the few countries with reasonably good estimates as far back as 1869. All dollar totals will be stated in 1929 prices.

Patterns of individual goods and services. As real incomes have increased over the years, there has been a steady decline in the importance of nondurable goods. The data are summarized in Table 7.2. As consumption expands, this category expands less slowly because most "necessities" are nondurable goods. The fact that people consider them necessities means that as incomes decline, consumption of these goods declines little. Conversely, as incomes increase, consumption of these goods increases but little. Nevertheless, for the United States this still remains the most important single category of consumption.

Meanwhile, there has been a steady increase in the importance of durable consumer goods. This development, however, has been associated with two factors which may not be repeated in other times and places. During the period under examination, many household

TABLE 7.2

CONSUMPTION AND PERCENTAGE DISTRIBUTION OF COMPONENTS FOR THE
UNITED STATES, BY SELECTED DATES

Year	Annual per capita consumption (1929 dollars)	Percentage Distribution of Consumption			Ratio of government expenditures to national income‡
		Nondurables	Durables	Services	
1869–78 *	185	62%	9%	29%	11%
1919–28 *	550	53%	11%	36%	16%
1950 †	900	48%	14%	38%	21%

* Simon Kuznets, *National Product since 1869.* (New York: National Bureau of Economic Research, 1946.)

† *Survey of Current Business, National Income Supplement,* 1951 ed. (Washington, D.C.: Government Printing Office, 1951.)

‡ Since it is not possible to estimate government consumption for the earlier periods, this ratio is given instead to indicate the trend of government expenditures.

appliances were invented and marketed, especially those for the kitchen, and the automobile was introduced and sold on a mass basis. Throughout this eighty-year period, the share of services in total consumption also grew, although a considerable portion of this increase has been statistical, rather than actual.[15] National income measurements are based upon market transactions and so, in particular, ignore services of housewives. If a housewife begins to send out laundry rather than doing it at home, there will be an increase in purchases of services. In many cases, there has been no increase in services actually performed, but only a movement out of the home.

The increase in the production of durable goods, as well as in services performed commercially, is in part the result of the increased emancipation of women and the increased demand for leisure by housewives. The adoption of household appliances accelerated the disappearance of domestic servants, while increasing mechanization opened many factory jobs to women, made them more attractive, and raised women's productivity in such jobs. The increasing bureaucracy which accompanied the growth of large-scale enterprise expanded the number of clerical jobs, at which women are usually superior to men. These changes decreased the supply of women for domestic service and helped women gain social emancipation. While

[15] See also, P. T. Bauer and B. S. Yamey, "Economic Progress and Occupational Distribution," *Economic Journal,* Vol. LXI (December, 1951).

it is possible that this emancipation might come at different periods in the economic development of other countries, historically the two have been concurrent and are probably functionally related as well. We may therefore expect consumption of both durable goods and services to increase more than income when income increases.

One should expect a continuation of these changes in advanced countries and duplication of them in underdeveloped countries, since they involve forces which are likely to continue into the future. It should come as no surprise, then, to find that in the course of economic development there is a decline in the relative importance of agriculture (which produces mainly nondurables) and a shift of resources into the heavy manufacturing and service industries, both urban industries. The effects of technological change in agriculture would accentuate this shift.

In discussing income and consumption, we commented that consumption desires might affect the willingness to work. Such has been the case in the United States. Much of the potential increase in goods and services has been forgone in favor of a shorter work week. In 1850 the average work week in nonagricultural industries was sixty-eight hours. By 1920 it had fallen to forty-eight hours, and by 1950, to forty hours, a decline of forty per cent in the last hundred years.[16]

Government consumption. The last column in Table 7.2 suggests the increase which has taken place in the share of government in consumption. While the statistics for 1950, in part, reflect the increase in government spending associated with the cold war and, during the last half of the year, with the Korean fighting, even if these activities were subtracted, the government portion of total consumption would still have shown an increase over the earlier periods. This illustrates again the growing need for group consumption as our society becomes more complex.

With advancing incomes have come other developments which have altered consumption and behavior patterns. High per capita income is possible only with large-scale production and specialization of function.[17] Although not an inevitable consequence, large-scale

[16] J. Frederic Dewhurst, *et al.*, *America's Needs and Resources.* (New York: Twentieth Century Fund, 1947.)

[17] With international specialization, this large-scale production could be in another country.

production has usually been accompanied by increased urbanization. Increased specialization and division of labor has made every individual more dependent upon the complex working of the entire system. While such changes have been deplored by many, the effect which interests us here is that the increased complexity of an advanced society contributes to the growth of group or community consumption. As people become more interdependent, more reliance must be placed upon associations, both private and governmental, to do those things which individuals cannot do alone.

A secondary effect is that consumers have been forced to spend a portion of their income overcoming the disadvantages of urbanization. In 1950, local public transportation (street cars, buses, taxicabs, and commuter trains) took over two billion consumer dollars in the United States. The additional cost of private automobiles used for shopping and transportation to and from work can only be guessed. In this and many other ways, the growth of cities has created many necessary costs not directly contributing to personal satisfaction. For this (and other reasons) simple comparison of total consumption in different periods and different countries is not a suitable measure of relative welfare, even if the totals are corrected for differences in price.

Applications to advanced and underdeveloped economies. We may now review the material covered in this chapter and apply its lessons to two types of economies, "underdeveloped" and "advanced." In areas with little capital equipment, the bulk of consumers usually have incomes so low that they are unable to satisfy even their basic needs. If they had assets or credit resources, they would be dissavers. For all such low income groups, consumption will tend to equal income, and the marginal propensity to consume will approach one. Such a situation makes accumulation impossible, unless those few in the higher income brackets can finance it.

A society in such a situation can raise its living standards only by very drastic means. Some growth can often be achieved by the use of improved techniques with minimal investment, but such increases in income will soon be matched by an increase in consumption and there will remain no surplus for capital formation. A ruthless tax program by the government might lower consumption enough to permit use of some resources for investment. The government might also finance new investment by inflating the currency, but this would have almost the same effect as a tax program. Such a program for development is a bitter one for humanitarians to accept, for it means further lowering the standard of living of a people already at bare subsistence.

It is little wonder that many people search for ways to finance development without such drastic inroads upon consumption. One such possibility is the use of foreign gifts and loans of capital equipment. These loans could be repaid in later years, when incomes had risen enough as the result of the increased capital equipment to permit saving. This is like the case of the college student who borrows money to finance his education and repays the loan from the increased earnings which his education brings. The analogy breaks down, however, when we consider the magnitudes of help involved. The student can borrow all the money required to complete his education, but no country can borrow all its capital equipment. Kuznets estimates the reproducible wealth of the United States on December 31, 1938 as 288 billions (in 1929 dollars),[18] over two and one-half times the national income of that year. No lender could provide such vast sums, and the United States is a small place in comparison to Africa or Asia.

Let us examine the effect of a foreign loan of some smaller amount of capital. If the net income from the use of such capital equipment goes to low-income consumers, consumption will increase and leave no resources free for further investment. However, if some portion of this income can be siphoned off, either to the government or to the wealthy, it may provide resources for further investment. The profits from these investments, in turn, might provide further sources of investment funds.

Another way to increase investment has been suggested. Our earlier discussion indicated that consumption and investment are competitive only if there are no unemployed resources. It is possible that there may exist hidden unemployment; that is, workers whose marginal productivity in present occupations is very low, or even zero. If these workers could be transferred to other occupations the

[18] Simon Kuznets, *National Product since 1869*. (New York: National Bureau of Economic Research, 1946.)

total income might be increased without first decreasing consumption, although special programs would probably be required to keep consumption from rising.

Aside from the possibilities available if the work of the hidden unemployed can be utilized, the primary problem for underdeveloped countries is that consumption and investment are competitive. Any increase in income will be matched by an increase in consumption, leaving no more resources for capital formation than before. Since restriction of consumption is, for this reason, important to underdeveloped countries, let us go through the determinants of consumption to see ways in which a government may provide for development by limiting consumption.

No effective action through assets is possible, since most of the population have none. Since the principal effect of price changes in lowering consumption is through the effect on assets, this route will also be ineffective. Nevertheless, by raising some prices and penalizing the holding of some sorts of assets, steps can be taken to encourage investment in productive assets. If the few wealthy can be persuaded to make such investments, rather than speculate in real estate or commodities, the chances for development will be enhanced. Further, such policies would also encourage saving by those whose incomes rise as a result of development. Special tax programs might assist in this allocation.

Changes in income and thus consumption can be effected through taxation of sales or income. If this could be done without detrimental political repercussions, it would be even more effective in underdeveloped countries than in advanced ones, since the marginal propensity to consume is almost unity.

Changes in taste, particularly for new products, are an important part of any program for economic development. It will usually be both impossible and undesirable to provide a development program which increases all goods uniformly. Therefore the consumption pattern must be altered to fit the changing production pattern, or the development program will bog down with unsalable surpluses in the midst of poverty. An active price system can do much of this job, but before such a system can be constructed, the set of traditional prices and price-relationships must be broken down. Price controls might assist in establishing a changed set of prices, but the psychological effect might be against a free-price system. The psychology of free prices is possibly the most important aspect, so one should be reluctant to hamper its development. Advertising may also be necessary, especially to call attention to products which have not been part of the consumption pattern.

Special care must also be directed to suppressing tastes for imported or exportable luxury goods, since the nation will wish to keep exports high and consumption imports low in order to purchase machinery and other tools of development. Import duties plus excise taxes on exportable commodities will assist this program, for consumers who attempt to avoid these taxes can do so only by saving or redirecting their purchases. Subsidies on the substitute goods might also help, and, as a last resort, the government might use direct controls, such as rationing. This problem of directing consumption into appropriate channels may be even more difficult than keeping the over-all level of consumption from rising too rapidly.

The possibilities of equalizing the distribution of income and wealth have often been discussed as a primary goal of development. Unfortunately, however, the immediate effect of such redistribution will be to increase total consumption and decrease saving. In addition, such redistribution might destroy incentives, especially if entrepreneurs and potential entrepreneurs thought that it were to be a continuing process or a possibly recurring one. For both of these reasons, such redistribution might be a blow to a program of economic development. Nonetheless, this does not mean that wealth should never be redistributed; it is clearly important to put certain assets, especially land, into the hands of those who will use them more efficiently. When this is done, however, it should be made clear that it will not be repeated.

War destruction has lowered the capital equipment of many European countries and forced them to lower levels of per capita incomes. For these countries, much of the foregoing analysis holds. Marshall Plan aid has served as the help from abroad to assist in investment, but stringent consumer restrictions have also been necessary. Among major Western nations, only the United States emerged from the war with high productive capacity. This capacity has permitted tremendous net investment and high consumption levels simultaneously.

Countries with high per capita income are seldom faced with such severe competition for resources between consumption and investment. Instead the problem may be to find enough demand to keep the economy employed. A society can enjoy the riches to which its capacity entitles it only if consumption plus investment are high enough to permit full employment and no "misallocation." As consumption falls off, more investment is required to achieve full employment, but the less profitable investment seems. In the past, a sufficient number of special circumstances have arisen to create an adequate amount of investment and keep depression an unusual event. Among these circumstances have been the growth in population, development of new areas and resources, and exploitation of inventions. These offered opportunities for profitable investment, even without changes in current consumption. Many economists feel that such times are behind us, and only a continued high level of government expenditure will maintain full employment.[19]

There is no need to discuss whether such "stagnation" threatens the United States at present, since it is sufficient for our purposes that such a possibility exists, either now or in the future. The model of economic growth discussed in Chapter V illustrated this possibility. We should therefore consider whether the society contains any automatic corrective mechanism and what sorts of governmental actions would alleviate the problem, with particular reference to consumption. Let us therefore consider a simplified case where consumption is growing too slowly to provide great stimulus to investment, where investment outlets are scarce, and saving at full-employment income is greater than investment. These conditions are assumed to be long run; that is, not part of a business cycle movement. We are here concerned only with such changes in consumption as will remedy the situation.

Advertising may play a part in a positive, as well as a negative, sense. As manufacturers see the decline of the producers' goods market, more of them will attempt to shift to the output of consumer goods and advertising pressure will be increased. As investment opportunities diminish, there will be fewer outlets for saving and advertising by savings institutions will decrease.

We have also seen that increased use of government or private insurance may decrease the total amount of saving required of individuals. As investment opportunities decline, insurance companies

[19] Alvin H. Hansen, "Economic Progress and Declining Population Growth," *American Economic Review*, XXIX, No. 1, Part 1, March 1939.

may turn more to sales activity in an attempt to maintain profits, putting their funds in government bonds or even keeping them idle. Thus it is possible that consumption might rise enough to bring full employment. This process is apt to be quite slow, and impatient politicians (and their constituents) may insist that the government take stop-gap action to speed the process.

Among the stop-gap programs, increased government expenditure for goods and services is perhaps the simplest. If these expenditures are chosen wisely, they may even speed the process of adjustment by individuals, for many types of government programs are complementary to private consumption. Among such "consumption-inducing" expenditures are highways, hydroelectric plants, and national parks. A general decrease in taxes or an increase in various transfer payments would give consumers money to spend, thereby increasing consumption. Special taxes on savings might serve to increase consumption still more. To the extent that the new patterns of savings and consumption become habitual, a part of the effects of such changes in the tax structure might remain even if the old taxes were reinstituted.

The government might also help to speed up the system's natural adjustment process. It might, for instance, insure against those risks which private companies cannot handle. Foremost among these is unemployment, for no private company can afford to pay out large sums to a majority of its policyholders at the same time. To give quite a different example, a continued policy of rising prices might contribute to the decline of saving, for consumers would expect their accumulated assets to be rendered worthless by the inflation.

If it chose, whenever unemployment became severe, government could eliminate the need for any adjustment by creating and spending sufficient money for various group purposes, such as increased expenditures for schools, medical care, and parks, as well as substantial capital investment in roads and school buildings. However, it is quite possible that make-work projects undertaken primarily for the purpose of providing employment would be less in value than equal expenditures by consumers. For this reason, if a way to full employment by private spending exists, it is usually preferable to increased government expenditures. It is for this reason also that many economists prefer a general tax reduction program, leaving the decision as to how additional money should be spent in the hands of consumers.[20] We have thus seen that even for the extreme case which we have assumed, there is a possibility that consumption will rise enough to provide full employment. In any case, government programs could be designed to assure an adequate level of demand. Therefore, possible stagnation need hold no terrors, even if it is in prospect.

Underdeveloped countries, then, will be most concerned with programs to limit and direct consumption in order to free resources for investment. Advanced countries may be concerned with limiting consumption in some periods, such as wars and reconstructions, but will more frequently need programs to encourage consumption. Methods are available for both purposes, but governments in underdeveloped countries will probably need to intervene directly, while in advanced countries they may be able to influence consumption indirectly through the market. In any case, a knowledge of the factors influencing consumption will be essential to the development of rational economic policy.

[20] In addition, of course, the government might undertake investment directly, or encourage private investment, either at home or abroad.

CHAPTER VIII

The Migration of Capital, People, and Technology

JOSEPH N. FROOMKIN*

INCREASING THE LEVEL OF REAL INCOME PER CAPITA AT AN ACCELER-
ated rate, which is presumably the objective of economic development, can be brought about by a number of methods. This chapter
will consider three closely related factors, which, although they often
originate outside a given economy, may contribute to its development: movements of capital, people, and technology. The role these
factors play in the process of economic growth will be indicated first.
This discussion will then be followed by an evaluation of their possible contributions to economic growth, especially in underdeveloped countries.

An increase in the level of real income takes place when the productivity of labor increases. This will occur whenever it is: (1) used
more sparingly in conjunction with other factors of production such
as land and capital,[1] (2) applied more judiciously in conjunction
with the existing supplies of land and capital, or (3) recombined
with increased stocks of land and capital. Modern economic theory
conceives of the traditional factors of production not so much as
having different attributes, but as stimulants to production which are
interchangeable at the margin. Thus, while it is impossible to grow
wheat by substituting more capital for all the land, an increase in
the production of wheat may be achieved either by increasing the

---

* Research Associate, International Program in Taxation, Harvard University
Law School. Formerly Research Associate, Bureau of Applied Social Research, Columbia University. Economic Affairs Officer, United Nations.
[1] The word capital is used throughout this chapter in the conventional economic
sense; i.e., any stocks of goods are referred to as capital.

amount of capital (through the use of better machines or more fertilizer) or by increasing the application of labor (more careful harvesting). The introduction of technology into the consideration of the effect of productive factors on the level of life is nothing but a belated acknowledgment that there may be different optima in the recombination of resources, depending upon the level of technological development.

This chapter will be mainly concerned with the international movement of these determinants of the level of production and with the way these movements may change the level of income of under-developed countries. It is fitting to start with the most common phenomenon in international economic relations, the relationship of foreign trade to economic development.

FOREIGN TRADE AND ECONOMIC DEVELOPMENT

Foreign trade takes place because countries are differently endowed with productive resources and have varying climates. A certain country can produce a particular item with application of fewer units of certain resources than the rest of the world, while another country, in turn, is more efficient in the production of some other commodity. With limited production capabilities in both countries, the command of their residents over goods and services will increase if each country specializes in the production of only a few commodities and then trades with the other. Even a country which is less efficient than the rest of the world in the production of all commodities would still gain by specializing and exporting those commodities in which it has the least comparative disadvantage; i.e., is relatively less inefficient in their production than the rest of the world.[2]

Advantages of foreign trade. Foreign trade benefits all countries which engage in it by bringing about higher per capita incomes throughout the world. The following advantages are probably the

[2] No detailed explanation of the basis for foreign trade is offered here. It can be found in any standard text on the subject. For a clear treatment of the subject see Stephen Enke and Virgil Salera, *International Economics* (New York: Prentice-Hall, Inc., 1947), Chapters 1 and 5. For a more advanced treatment see Jacob Viner, *Essays in the Theory of International Trade* (New York: Harper & Brothers, 1937), Chapters 7–9. For an excellent summary of the theory of foreign trade see Lloyd W. Metzler's essay on this subject in a *Survey of Contemporary Economic Theory* (Philadelphia: The Blakiston Co., 1948).

most important for an underdeveloped country: (1) It enables a country to complement an incomplete industrial or agricultural structure and permits its citizens to diversify their consumption over a series of commodities which would not be available otherwise. (2) It tends to equalize factor prices and results in a more efficient allocation of resources, which is one of the most important prerequisites to an increase in living standards. (3) It enables a country to buy machinery and capital equipment which it could not purchase otherwise, and it establishes the mechanics for the repayment of interest and principal of capital imports.

A country with a low standard of living will feel much more acutely than a developed country the losses in productivity caused by an absence of specialization, which could be realized by the exchange of commodities in world trade. For example, during World War II, the United States was cut off from its main source of rubber supplies, and diverted part of its productive facilities to the manufacture of synthetic rubber. This necessitated using more resources than had been hitherto used in manufacturing commodities to exchange for Malayan rubber. The resulting loss in command over goods and services would have been critical if per capita national income had not been relatively high. Even in the United States this loss would have been acutely felt if previously unemployed resources had not been brought into use. Also, such a transformation in production is only possible in a highly developed country where there is sufficient "know how" to manufacture substitutes. An underdeveloped country without these advantages has to forgo many commodities completely unless it participates in international commerce.

Not only does foreign trade bring within the reach of an underdeveloped country a wider assortment of goods and services, it also brings about a more efficient arrangement of productive factors within the economy. This happens not only because of the exchange of commodities in which the country is more efficient, but also because of equalization of factor costs between countries, which could take place otherwise only through the more cumbersome migration of labor and capital. By way of illustration, let us assume that country A is underdeveloped because of a shortage of capital, and produces two commodities, cotton and wheat, with cotton requiring the application of more capital per unit of production than wheat. Assume, further, that the rest of the world also produces only these two commodities. It is probable (and here we must make a transition from the discussion of foreign trade in real terms to the more realistic discussion of foreign trade in money terms) that if country A is brought into the orbit of foreign trade, it will be undersold in cotton, which takes so much of the scarce and high-priced factor (capital) to produce, but will be able to offer wheat for sale to the rest of the world. What will happen to the cost of the factors of production in country A? If the amount of land and labor has not changed, and the demand for capital has declined because of a change in the pattern of production, the price of capital will have declined as well, moving nearer to the international price. The same process will, on an international scale, tend to equalize rents and labor.

The net result of this readjustment should be higher aggregate incomes throughout the world. Since the proportion of labor, land, and capital will move nearer to their optimum, the marginal returns to labor must increase. This will result in higher per capita incomes for the majority of the population, even though the share of the capitalists, as well as their real income, will decline. This, of course, is the simplest possible explanation of the equalization of factor prices under the unrealistic assumption that there are only two factors of production and that these are not complementary. Also, no analysis has been given of the cases when changes in factor prices affect the supply of the factors concerned. Actually, however, a more refined analysis would show that our basic conclusions are still correct.[3]

The last benefit from international trade accruing to an underdeveloped country arises from the fact that such trade familiarizes foreigners with its currency and economical prospects. International movements of currency are a prerequisite for imports of capital and repayment of past borrowing, as well as for the servicing of debts.

---

[3] Cf. Lloyd W. Metzler, *op. cit.*, p. 238 [appraisal of Bertil Ohlin, *Interregional and International Trade* (Cambridge, Mass.: Harvard University Press, 1933)]. An elegant theoretical construction by S. F. James and I. F. Pearch entitled "The Factor Equalization Myth" (*The Review of Economic Studies*, Vol. XIX (2) No. 4, 1951–52, pp. 111–120) has shown that this is not necessarily so. By discarding the assumption of homogeneous production functions throughout the range of the process in which both countries are identical and by introducing a number of commodities, the authors showed that factor prices are not necessarily equalized by foreign trade. Professor P. A. Samuelson, commenting on this article ("A Comment on Factor Price Equalization," *ibid.*, pp. 121–122) admitted the validity of the argument, but argued that reality is better mirrored by the simpler analysis.

The movements of a country's currency in and out of the accounts of foreign banks, foreign central banks, etc., in the course of years develops a familiarity with its currency. Foreigners come to appreciate its problems in meeting payments at certain times of the year, and they usually are willing to lend money to the country during a seasonal drain if there are good prospects of receiving repayment during the next period of influx of foreign exchange. This is especially true in the case of underdeveloped countries, which often export such seasonal commodities as coffee or cocoa.

This familiarity (which central and private banks of foreign countries gain in handling the currency of a given country) gives an added advantage should the country wish to establish a long-term credit. Its approximate position in relation to the world economy is already known to foreign bankers. The composition of its trade with the rest of the world and the prospects of the development of that trade in future years are also periodically appraised by these foreign financial institutions. When the request for a loan is presented, the time spent on investigation and inquiry is thereby considerably shortened.

Limitations of foreign trade. Up to this point the discussion of the advantages which result from foreign trade has been conducted in the simplest possible terms. We have implicitly assumed that the size of a country in relation to the rest of the world has nothing to do with the distribution of the benefits of world trade, that full employment is prevailing at all times in all countries, and that production is conducted under conditions of constant costs. To make the discussion more realistic, these assumptions must be relaxed.

A small country selling a commodity in world trade, for example, is to a great extent at the mercy of economic conditions in other parts of the world. If, as may be the case, it is a small supplier of a widely consumed staple, the price it receives will depend on the production of the same commodity in other countries, as well as the demand for its products in the international market. Both are beyond the small country's control.

Variations in supply of many commodities may be quite considerable from one year to another. A good harvest in one region may result in materially cutting incomes in competing areas. In the long run, new productive capacity or the development of substitutes may have still more serious repercussions. China, for example, has been especially hard hit by substitutes, as in the case of pig bristles, which have been largely replaced by rayon fibres, and by competition from other countries, e.g., silk manufactured in Japan and tea grown in India.

Changes in the levels of economic activity in the consumer countries may also adversely affect world prices and bring about repercussions in the supplier's economy, even if the latter is a fairly important supplier of a particular commodity. For example, Bolivia's economy is keyed to exports of tin. Changes in the price of tin in more industrialized countries are thus a strategic factor affecting Bolivia's development policy and prospects. It may even be argued that Bolivia would be better off with a more stable national income, even at a lower real level, if it could in this way avoid the perpetual ups and downs caused by changes in tin prices.

Once the full-employment assumption is discarded, the effects of foreign trade on aggregate employment of the underdeveloped country becomes of critical concern. There is usually much hidden unemployment in such countries, especially in farming and small-scale retail business. Hence it is most important to determine the effects of foreign trade on employment and vice versa. The task of doing this will be simplified if a few concepts are introduced first.

The payments of a country for imports and its receipts for exports can be visualized in the form of a balance sheet, usually referred to as the "balance of trade." If all the financial transactions with foreigners are included, such as payments and receipts of interest, dividends, transfers of capital, and payments for services like shipping and insurance, the balance sheet is referred to simply as a country's "balance of payments." The prices paid to foreigners, and those received from them for exports, when compared over long periods of time, are referred to as "the terms of trade" of a country. These terms of trade, of course, both affect and reflect the balance of payments.

Empirical studies of foreign trade have shown that the elasticities of demand for imports by most large countries are low. This means that in the event of a decline in the demand for imports by large countries, the underdeveloped countries cannot increase the volume of receipts from foreign trade without considerable deterioration of the prices received for their exports. At the same time, it has been found that the demand for imported goods by underdeveloped countries is also relatively inelastic. This means that even an increase in the prices of imports because of, say, currency depreciation, will reduce demand for them very little. If the balance of payments on current account of an underdeveloped country has been affected adversely by a change in some other part of the world, for example, causing exports to fall relative to imports, it cannot hope to remedy the imbalance without either a tremendous deterioration of its terms of trade, i.e., a sharp drop in the foreign price of its exports, or a reduction in the level of its employment. Either of these events will, in turn, cause a decline in its demand for imported goods.

The final position of equilibrium will be reached after some time, when the "multiplier effect" of the initial decrease in exports and the counter decrease in imports have worked themselves through.[4] The foreign trade multiplier works in the following manner: (1) a decline in exports will cause domestic employment to decline somewhat; (2) this drop in domestic employment in its turn will cause a decline in the demand for imports; and (3) this will bring about a decline in employment abroad, which, in turn, will cause a further drop in the demand for the country's exports. After some time, the cumulative effects of these declines will work themselves out, and a new position of equilibrium will be reached. The extent of the decline in a given country and in the rest of the world will depend upon the propensities of a country (and of the rest of the world) to import and export, i.e., how much a change in the level of income will cause their demand for imports and exports to change.

With this complex chain of cause and effect in mind, another argument has been raised against an expansion of foreign trade. In certain not unlikely situations, an increase in the demand for the exports of an underdeveloped country may cause its purchases abroad to increase by more than the original rise in exports. This would leave the

[4] The multiplier is the change in the national income induced by an exogenous change in some component of income. Algebraically it is represented thus: $\triangle Y = \frac{\triangle K}{s}$ where $\triangle Y$ is the change in income, s is the marginal propensity to save, and $\triangle K$ is the exogenous change. The same mechanical analysis has been applied to the repercussions of foreign trade. In these cases the simplest form of the expression would read $\triangle Y = \frac{\triangle K}{s + m + f}$, where s is the marginal propensity to save, m the marginal propensity to import, and f is the foreign "repercussion factor." For further analysis see Fritz Machlup, *International Trade and the National Income Multiplier* (Philadelphia: The Blakiston Co., 1943).

citizens of the country with less money to spend on domestic products than before the increase in foreign trade took place and would actually cause domestic employment to fall.

In addition to these hazards, some doubts have been raised as to whether foreign trade will contribute under all circumstances to the long-run productive capacity of a country. It has been argued that a country with a comparative advantage in an industry, or series of industries, operating under conditions of constant or increasing costs, and a comparative disadvantage in industries with decreasing costs should refuse to specialize and engage in foreign trade. Some economists have prophesied that such a country's aggregate income would be smaller if it did permit foreign trade.[5]

Actually such an outcome is possible but far fetched. Any country engaging in trade and operating under increasing cost conditions will, in all probability, find that at some point it becomes uneconomic to give up more of the increasing-cost commodity in exchange for the decreasing-cost items. This would encourage the development of domestic supplies of commodities produced under decreasing costs and provide a more or less automatic check against specialization. It is only under conditions of extreme inflexibility of resource use, when no productive alternatives are open, that an underdeveloped country runs into the danger of over-specialization.[6] This danger arises less from the possibility of production being carried on under conditions of increasing costs than from the domestic effects of variations in the level of incomes in other countries. Studies in the terms of trade of underdeveloped countries have not revealed any set trend in the prices of commodities which such countries buy and sell abroad.[7]

Conclusion. An underdeveloped country must consider the benefits that it would derive from foreign trade in the context of all the dy-

---

[5] See F. D. Graham, "Some Aspects of Protection Further Considered," *Quarterly Journal of Economics*, XXXVII (1923), pp. 199–216 for a mathematical proof of this proposition.

[6] See Viner, *op. cit.*, p. 482.

[7] Cf. *Relative Prices of Exports and Imports in Under-developed Countries* (Lake Success: United Nations, Department of Economic Affairs, December, 1949) with Walt W. Rostow, *The Process of Economic Growth* (New York: W. W. Norton, 1952). The conclusion of these studies is that there are cycles in the terms of trade of countries. The studies do not agree on the duration of the cycle. This is due to the necessarily poor data which have to be used for intertemporal comparisons spanning many years.

namic factors which play a part in the formation of aggregate wealth and income. With no restrictions on foreign trade, will domestic employment and income be increased? What are the long-run prospects of exported commodities? These questions have to be answered before restrictions are placed on foreign trade. A country which desires economic development is likely to answer them in such a way as to encourage foreign trade because development can take place only if there is a rearrangement of the factors of production. It has been shown that foreign trade encourages the rearrangement of these factors of production in a more efficient way. Hence, within certain limitations already noted, foreign trade is likely to benefit rather than impede the forces which favor economic growth.

The Role of Capital Transfers

Conditions prevalent in underdeveloped countries are characterized by: (1) a small capital investment per capita of population, (2) immobility and inflexibility of the factors of production, and (3) underemployment of resources, especially labor. Many of these conditions are basically caused by initial shortages of capital, which may, in turn, become cumulative in effect. For example, at times labor does not have a chance to reach new jobs in the market sector of the economy because of shortages of some strategic capital expenditure, such as roads or education. Shortages of capital may contribute to low levels of income, which, in turn, may keep domestic savings below the amounts needed to create the necessary base for economic growth. For this reason capital imports are often looked upon as one way of implementing a development program, providing more jobs for the underemployed, or increasing the productivity of those who are already employed in the market sector.

Imports of capital will probably cause movement in both directions. Those persons who had been busying themselves only part of the year in seasonal occupations will be able to find more permanent jobs once the capital stock of the country is increased. At the same time those workers who had been employed in the market sector of the economy, once they are provided with more productive machinery, will be able to increase their output. If capital imports are substantial, the secondary effects of the expenditures of the workers may also give a considerable spurt to the service industries and thus cause a further increase in employment. At the same time, the new and larger demand of the workers for goods may encourage invest-ment in consumer goods industries and thus cause a further increase in output. Thus the magnitude and direction of the capital imports determine whether living standards and employment patterns are changed sufficiently to encourage the introduction of a modern tech-nology.

An indirect effect of the increase in capital formation and in-creased living standards may be to increase the birth rate so as to neutralize any tendency toward increased per capita income. It has been suggested, however, that if capital could be applied intensively to one segment of the population at a time, the increase in birth rate could be avoided, and the problems of overpopulation reduced.

These remarks are predicated on the assumption that an increase in the productivity of the workers will be accompanied by an increase in their standard of living and that this will reinforce the forces favor-ing economic development in the country. If this does not occur, the majority of the population may very well remain outside the scope of the market economy, and attempts at development will fail unless rigorously controlled by government.

Foreign capital movements. Before much was known about the elasticities of demand for imports in creditor and debtor countries, or the influence of income levels on foreign trade, it was assumed that international capital movements came about almost automatically. It was argued that countries where capital shortages existed would be granted loans by the capital-rich nations. Then, as soon as the bor-rowers' industries were developed, the interest and principal of the loan would be repaid. Time and again, the example of the United States' evolution from debtor to creditor country has been cited in this connection. While the United States did change from a debtor to a creditor country during World War I, this occurrence neither confirms nor refutes this argument. More commonly in modern times countries have rid themselves of external debt with the help of un-usual circumstances such as a war, repatriation payments following war, or a revolution, accompanied by repudiation of all foreign debts.

Whatever the ultimate solution, in the short run a debtor country must recognize the problems of repayment. A nation which is bor-rowing capital may find it difficult to increase its exports without an unfavorable shift in its terms of trade unless certain drastic conditions, such as the destruction of productive equipment or a spectacular increase in consumption, take place in the creditor nations. Borrowing money abroad and repaying it is not always easy. This is important for both lending and borrowing countries to remember when considering foreign trade and loan policy designed to promote industrialization.

Actually, there is little reason to expect that international capital movements by private lenders will become a crucial factor in sponsoring economic growth in underdeveloped countries. This kind of lending reached its peak during the late nineteenth and early twentieth centuries, when international financial transactions took place within a framework characterized by relatively stable exchange rates and with little or no government interference.

At the apex of the period of "orthodox" financing, immediately preceding World War I, the total volume of international loans was estimated at forty-four billion dollars. The principal lenders and borrowers, and the amounts outstanding are reproduced in Table 8.1.

TABLE 8.1

INTERNATIONAL INVESTORS AND BORROWERS IN 1914
(in millions of U.S. dollars)

	Investors	Borrowers
United Kingdom	18,000 ⎫	
France	9,000 ⎪	
Germany	5,800 ⎬	12,000
Belgium, Netherlands, Switzerland	5,500 ⎭	
United States	3,500	10,000
Canada		8,500 ⎧
Asia		6,000 ⎪
Africa	2,200	4,700 ⎬
Latin America (incl. Mexico)		2,300 ⎪
Oceania		500 ⎭
Total	44,000	44,000

Source: International Capital Movements during the Inter-War Period (New York: United Nations, October, 1949), p. 2.

It should be noted that even as of 1914 nearly one-half of the foreign investments were distributed among the so-called developed countries of Europe and the United States and Canada. Especially significant is the fact that the principal lenders at that time were European countries, and that some 30 per cent of the investment

was redistributed among themselves. This occurred notwithstanding the fact that capital stock per capita was much lower in underdeveloped countries than in the borrowing European countries.
The propensity of capitalists to seek investment in economies similar
to their own is well demonstrated by these figures.

Important changes in the creditor-debtor pattern of the major
countries of the world took place as a result of World War I. The
most important was the emergence of the United States as a creditor
country (a lender of funds rather than a borrower), both on government and private accounts. Britain, France, and Germany were
forced to divest themselves of an important part of their investment
during the war in order to pay for supplies, while both German and
French investors were hard hit by the defaults of Russia, the Balkan
states, and Turkey.

The period between the two World Wars breaks down into two
fairly distinct phases. The first, from the end of the war to the depression of 1929, was characterized by payment difficulties of European nations resulting from war debts and by large short-term lending
by the United States, especially to Germany and other European
countries. The second phase, which started with the depression, was
characterized by competitive currency depreciation, defaults, blocked
currency, barter agreements, and the like. During this period the
gold standard was abandoned as a goal of international financial policy. The restrictionism and increase in government controls, which
began as a result of the depression, further discouraged private foreign investments. The volume of savings in developed countries
shrank with the decline in the national incomes, and the prospects
of foreign lending appeared rather dim with wholesale defaults occurring in debtor areas.

The main disequilibrating factor in the post-depression world was
the abnormal flow of funds to the United States, which interest rate
differentials and outright prohibition could not dam. Short-term
funds took refuge in America from continuous devaluations and political uncertainties in Europe. The flow of funds to underdeveloped
countries was practically halted during that period.

The rise of protectionism and interventionism. Sanctioning of non-
repayment and lapse of servicing of foreign loans by the governments
of most debtor countries during the thirties was due to the deteriora-

tion of the terms of trade of their main exports and the slackening of demand for primary products. These factors had an adverse effect on the trade of all countries but were especially serious in underdeveloped areas. An additional incentive to establish a moratorium on foreign debts by government decree was that at least one-third of the foreign lending had been made on government account. Countries whose revenues from taxation dwindled considerably were reluctant to service external debts through deficit financing. They did little to encourage the repayment of foreign obligations by private citizens.

Abandonment of the gold standard, currency devaluations, and export and import controls were all government measures designed to minimize the effect of the depression on domestic economies and to provide insulation against unfavorable events taking place in the rest of the world. Departure from the gold standard allowed governments a greater leeway in the manipulation of their currencies in order to alleviate unemployment at home. These measures dealt a blow to the confidence of foreign lenders in the borrowers' currencies.

Many countries during this period were faced by an imbalance in foreign payments caused by a decline in the demand for their exports relative to the domestic demand for imported goods. Unless further deterioration of the terms of trade was to occur, imports had to be limited, which usually meant the imposition of direct import controls. Not infrequently, an attempt was made at the same time to protect local industry by increasing tariffs, thus giving a stimulus to home industries and apparently increasing domestic employment. When these measures did not achieve the desired results, they were frequently followed by outright restrictions of imports.

A tariff or the licensing of imports can remedy the balance of payment difficulties of a country only if the imbalance is caused by minor spreads between domestic and foreign costs. The experience of the 1930's showed that the balance of payment difficulties were more serious. Licensing of all foreign transactions and, finally, controls over all movements of capital came about only after various countries realized that changes in exchange rates could not help. The underdeveloped, as well as some of the developed, countries, therefore, attempted to insulate themselves against depressions by restricting foreign trade through keeping the domestic price level above that of other countries and by the imposition of tariffs.

The net effect of these various measures was unfavorable to the flow of international investment. Uncertainty over exchange rates discouraged foreign lending. Moreover, import restrictions by developed countries hampered export industries in raw-material-producing areas and further lessened the possibility of repayment of principal and interest on loans. Finally, even though most import restrictions exempted the importation of capital goods, the establishment of new industries became more difficult. This was because certain complementary commodities which play a secondary part in capital investment were not similarly exempted, including, for example, such things as lubricants, typewriters, and comptometers.

Once these steps had been taken, it was not easy to return to conditions which would encourage a free flow of goods and funds among nations. For many countries, the restoration of free exchange rates could only be accomplished by a reduction in their general price levels sufficient to bring their costs in line with those of other countries. Not infrequently, the only way to bring about such a deflation was for the government to impose heavy taxes or to restrict its expenditures, including those for development. A further complication involved the status of industries which had been encouraged by tariffs. Such industries would find it difficult to meet foreign competition without continued protection.

Foreign investment after World War II. It is not astonishing that foreign capital, prior to World War II, was not directed to the development of domestic industries in underdeveloped countries. As a report by a United Nations committee put it: "Countries—particularly in the Far East, Africa, and Latin America—appear not to have been profoundly influenced in their economic development by capital imports; they remained outside the international economy and their foreign trade remained at a low level." [8] Furthermore, no spectacular movements of private capital to the underdeveloped countries took place either during World War II or in the immediate postwar period. It is true that during the war, a number of underdeveloped countries accumulated sizable balances in New York which were the unspent counterparts of payments for materials used by the United

[8] Report by a group of experts appointed by the Secretary-General of the United Nations, *Measures for the Economic Development of Under-developed Countries* (New York: United Nations, Department of Economic Affairs, 1951), p. 4.

States during the war effort, but these balances were soon depleted after 1945.

The lack of interest on the part of private investors in the United States, and to a lesser degree in Great Britain, in foreign lending may be explained in part by the existence of more favorable investment opportunities at home. The returns to capital in the developed countries have not moved towards the vanishing point, as predicted by a number of pessimistic economists during the thirties. On the contrary, returns on venture capital following World War II continued at least as attractive as they had been during the twenties. World War II strengthened the position of the United States in world affairs and caused Great Britain to become a debtor nation. (In 1945 Britain had nearly four billion dollars of foreign assets and slightly more than five billion in foreign liabilities.) In general, the countries which previously had been leaders in foreign investment have had most of their funds tied up in domestic reconstruction. American private investment, largely for reasons already mentioned, did not assume the role of foreign lender.

The underdeveloped countries, at the same time, are reluctant to contract debts which would require repayment at fixed intervals in the currency of the lender. Changes in the terms of trade or in the demands of foreigners for their exports could put extremely harsh strains upon their economies during periods of business depression. In the case of very underdeveloped areas, transfers of capital and the repayment of profits may claim a considerable part of the national income. Thus in a number of African countries from one-third to one-half of the value of exports goes to pay the claims of foreign investors. Since the market sector of those countries consists chiefly of the export and import trade, such financial obligations weigh rather heavily upon them.

The aggregate value of net private foreign investment in the world since World War II has amounted to slightly more than 500 million dollars a year. Most of this money has been invested in the extension and promotion of oil properties with very little going into industrial investment. The outlook for private investment was characterized in 1951 by one group of experts as follows:

Private buying of foreign government bonds, . . . at one time, the largest category of foreign investment, has now virtually ceased. The European capital markets have had little capital to spare . . . [and have] been prohibited by their governments from undertaking foreign lending. The New York market . . . has still not recovered from its shock in the 1930's when some governments suspended payment on their borrowing in the previous decade.

Practically all the private foreign investment now taking place is direct investment in undertakings which are effectively controlled in the capital exporting countries. Most of it represents investment in subsidiaries or branches of firms established in such countries. . . . About 70 per cent . . . has been going into petroleum. . . .[9]

Minimum standards for capital investment. A series of minimum standards have to be met if foreign investment as an aid to development is to be stimulated. Especially if the investment is to be conducted on private account, the returns to capital in the underdeveloped countries will have to be made safer than they are now. As a minimum, foreign investors must be guaranteed that they will: (1) get fair treatment under the laws of the country, (2) not be discriminated against in the application of regulations, taxation edicts, etc., and (3) have some assurance that their autonomy in the management of the enterprise and in the disposition of their assets will remain unaffected by subsequent government action.

Even these conditions are far from being realized by a great number of underdeveloped countries. The governments of these countries have an ambivalent attitude toward foreign investment. While they feel that foreign investment is necessary for the advancement of their citizens, they also feel that the investment should be received on their own terms, which are apt to be rather harsh. They often act as if the foreign entrepreneur should suffer for the privilege of being in the country: they try to force him to pay higher wages, hire native labor to participate in management, and hold the threat of nationalization over his head most of the time.

Unfortunately, even in those instances where foreign investment does take place, foreigners in underdeveloped areas are frequently consciously discriminated against in the allocations of quotas or licenses for foreign currencies. Profits repatriation clauses in commercial treaties are often unclear and allow for interpretation by the officials in charge of disbursing foreign exchange permits. Thus an underdeveloped country may arbitrarily set a percentage of the capital invested as "normal" profit and fail to allow repatriation of any larger sum, notwithstanding an intervening domestic inflation. Or a

⁹ *Measures, op. cit.*, p. 80.

government may not permit the repatriation of profits on reinvested earnings, claiming that foreign exchange had not been brought into the country for that particular investment.

Thus it is not astonishing to find, as Table 8.2 shows, that only three out of seventeen foreign dollar bonds of Western Hemisphere nations were selling at par or above. American investments in nine countries were quoted at discounts ranging from 50 to 89 per cent.

TABLE 8.2

AMERICAN INVESTMENTS IN FOREIGN DOLLAR BONDS
MARKET AND PAR VALUES, 1945
(year-end data; in millions of dollars)

	Market Value	Par Value	Market Value as Percentage of Par Values
Canada	1,250.0	1,165.6	107
Dominican Republic...	3.3	3.2	103
Panama	9.7	9.7	100
Argentina	50.3	51.4	98
Haiti	2.2	2.3	96
Uruguay	12.0	13.7	88
Brazil	65.1	111.6	58
Cuba	9.7	10.4	56
Guatemala		.8	50
Colombia	31.1	63.1	49
El Salvador	2.1	4.6	46
Costa Rica	1.0	2.9	34
Chile	24.8	86.2	29
Peru	10.9	38.4	28
Mexico	7.7	32.1	24
Bolivia	5.7	38.4	15
Ecuador	8.1	.9	11

Source: U.S. Department of Commerce, International Transactions of the United States during the War, 1940–45 (Washington, D.C.: Government Printing Office, 1948), p. 215.

The policy of underdeveloped countries toward foreign enterprises is at other times highly inconsistent with repressive measures in force against existing foreign investors: sometimes the entrepreneur is promised, and actually receives, tariff protection; often he is made a monopolist in the country where he established the industry. Such privileges are usually given without any concern for the actual rate of return which the industry will get in the underdeveloped country. A similar type of inducement is the tax exemption provision which a number of underdeveloped governments give to newly established industries. This inducement, however, is not successful in attracting foreign capitalists when they have to pay higher taxes in their own country on the profits realized in the underdeveloped country. It may aid in recapturing the capital of domestic nationals who have held it abroad, and who may be induced to bring it back because of tax exemption.

In summary, if private foreign investment is to be increased, the governments of the underdeveloped countries must take steps to make such investment attractive, at least as desirable as investment is in developed countries. One of the crucial considerations in this connection is the problem of convertibility. Domestic investment is always in the currency of the investor, so that the convertibility problem does not arise. If, on the other hand, an underdeveloped country were to assure convertibility for the funds of foreign investors, this would commit it to a series of policies which, on the whole, it might consider detrimental to its welfare. For example, it would be forced to keep its currency in line with the valuation placed upon it by the international money markets and would probably have to abandon many forms of government intervention in the economy.

Private capital exports. What is the future of private capital exports? The answer to this question depends on the form and extent of government, and government-sponsored, lending which will take place in the near future. If there is no sensible increase in the amount of government lending, it is probable that the difficult payment position of underdeveloped countries will remain what it is today for a number of years.

Under these conditions, private capital exports will remain small, in the vicinity of one billion dollars a year. In the case of underdeveloped countries, these capital flows will be mostly oriented as hitherto into export industries. Under present conditions, therefore, the profitability of establishing consumer goods industries in underdeveloped countries and of repatriating profits seems to be much too uncertain.

On the other hand, if large-scale government-sponsored international lending does take place, the future of capital exports will depend on the attitude of the borrowing countries towards private foreign investors. The low rates of interest at which these loans will have to be floated might put such investors at a disadvantage in competing with enterprises financed by intergovernment loans. On the other hand, such lending will probably reduce the regulation of foreign capital flows by the governments of underdeveloped countries and thus make private investment in them less risky.

The future of foreign capital investment will be determined by the role played by the government of the underdeveloped country in development. If it limits itself to assisting production in a limited number of fields, such as natural monopolies, there will be sufficient scope for foreigners elsewhere in the economy, and private foreign and domestic capital will compete for newly created markets on a basis of equality. On the other hand, should the availability of cheaply borrowed funds be extended to all sectors of the economy, foreign entrepreneurs will have to offset their disadvantageous position by more efficient productive methods. Under the second alternative, the flow of private funds abroad is likely to be much less than under the first.

Foreign loans and the problem of distribution. If large scale flows of capital sponsored by an international authority are to be considered, the effects of these flows of capital on the social structure of the recipient country, and the distribution of wealth and income therein, cannot be ignored. Once the flows of money are in the hands of private individuals, and their direction is determined by the profit motive, an excuse may be found not to regulate these flows. Rationalization for the absence of such regulation in the past has been made on the ground that loans were on private account and that free interplay of the forces of the market would bring about an "optimum" distribution of wealth and resources over the world. Lenders were assumed to be able to evaluate the risks of loans and not to need any governmental aid or regulation. The possibility that high risk would act as total deterrents was not considered relevant.

The lending of money by an international authority, which would place a levy upon the developed countries of the world to provide money for investment in their more underdeveloped partners, puts the problem in a different setting. If the money is advanced at very low rates of interest and with flexible repayment requirements, it will, in effect, be partly a gift to the recipient countries. The citizens of the countries advancing the loans may insist on the right to a voice in determining the manner in which funds are spent.

Historically, the value judgments of the lenders have certainly been reflected in the conditions accompanying the money. Thus the agency to be devised must be well suited to formulate these conditions. For these reasons, loans and grants by an international authority will probably be made with provisions that make it mandatory for the underdeveloped country to accept certain Western standards of justice in the allocation of their resources and the resulting distribution of income. Thus the underdeveloped country must not favor any given group at the expense of some other, especially because of political considerations. If the borrower country is to distribute the money through a special bank, the bank must take great care to see that the money is lent to the group most likely to contribute to the welfare of the country.

The experience of subsidized lending in underdeveloped countries has not been too happy to date. Lending has usually been distributed through ordinary banking channels, with the customary commercial standards of vendibility being applied to judge loan applications. Frequently this resulted in the rich getting richer and the poor remaining poor. Often the money so borrowed was used to drive out competition or consolidate monopoly, rather than to expand the aggregate volume of production. Little attention was paid to the character of the proposed production processes and the need to sponsor the more capital-intensive endeavors.

Underdeveloped countries in their attempts to achieve economic development are ordinarily faced with the problem of creating a new entrepreneur class. The lending of development funds to established owners is only a partially satisfactory solution to this problem. It may narrow the distribution of property, while historically, dynamic progress in productivity has been accomplished under conditions of social mobility. However, denying loans to those already propertied, and distributing them to the unknown and inexperienced in order to sponsor a new entrepreneurial class imposes the risk that funds may be used inefficiently. Nor is the practice of establishing and running enterprises by the government and financed through foreign lending entirely satisfactory. The government may be unable to obtain and retain the best managerial talent, and governmental domination of industry, as well as other spheres of the economy, vests it with powers which may make it inflexible and render it dictatorial.

Most underdeveloped countries will have to use three methods of distributing ownership rights to new capital investment, if investment on a large scale is ever to come about. They will have to balance judiciously the distribution of the borrowed money between investment in government-run enterprises, preferably for "natural monopolies," such as railroads and power plants; allocate some of the borrowed money to establish capitalists, especially in the case of larger projects requiring a great deal of management experience; and take a gamble on technically trained and inexperienced persons for smaller projects.

Such a policy is likely to be satisfactory to the developed lending countries, especially the United States and Great Britain, who are the most promising lenders. These countries subscribe to the principle that, though enterprise should be rewarded, great inequalities of income must be reduced. To implement these requirements, the borrowing government must then use fiscal policy to reduce inequality. Improvement in administration, through the migration of foreign firms and institutions, will make for the possibility of implementing this redistribution of income so as to satisfy the standards of foreign leaders.

Government exports of capital. The breakdown in foreign lending has given birth to a number of institutions in the international lending field. Foremost among these is the International Bank for Reconstruction and Development, formed in 1947. The record of the Bank, seven years after its establishment, shows that the concept of the founders has been too narrow to enable this organization to engage in a development drive. The lending of the Bank has been circumscribed by its unwillingness to provide money in speculative development activities. The directors of the Bank should be commended for their restraint in dealing with funds borrowed on the open market but, at the same time, the narrowness of their activity should be deplored.

Shortly before World War II, the United States inaugurated the Export-Import Bank for the purpose of lending funds to foreign governments for development activities. After the war the Bank granted a number of loans in connection with Economic Cooperation Administration activities and has assumed an increasingly important role in international capital movements. However, it is not an ideal instrument for international economic investment largely because credit lines for the Bank are authorized by Congress, and the larger the credit lines, the more likelihood there is that conditions, influenced by irrelevant political considerations, will be attached to the loans. Furthermore, the Congress is often unaware of long-range development objectives and is swayed, as every national legislative body usually is, by short-run considerations. This in no way denies, however, the need of some policy requirements set forth by lenders.

The important movement of goods and services from the United States was in the form of lend-lease and military aid to its Allies, which amounted to as much as fourteen billion dollars a year during 1943 and 1944 and did not fall much below five billion dollars in any of the war years. This was an important innovation in the technique of moving goods abroad. True, the bulk of the supplies sent were of military nature, but still a considerable part consisted of consumers' goods used by the army and by the civilian population. The United Nations Relief and Rehabilitation Administration and later the European Recovery Program, which at its peak cost the United States government nearly five billion dollars a year, showed that the government transfers of goods and equipment as a technique of exporting were firmly entrenched.

A long-run solution to the problem of foreign financing of underdeveloped countries lies in the formation of an international agency, yet unborn. This agency may take the form of an International Economic Development Board or Bank. It should be managed by delegates and experts from a number of countries who would review and decide upon the needs of various underdeveloped countries, and upon the way loans or grants are to be raised in the developed countries.

The advantages of such an international agency would be: (1) an ability to float its bonds, or to assess contributions on a number of developed countries, and (2) broad participation by a number of nations in its management, thus removing the stigma of imperialistic investment from foreign funds. The establishment of such an agency would be a real step toward promoting the integrated economic development of the underdeveloped areas of the world.

TRANSFERS OF POPULATION

Since movements of capital are not likely by themselves to establish a balance of the factors of production which will equalize incomes throughout the world, let us turn to movements of people and examine under what conditions they will contribute to such balance. Theoretically, given the small stocks of capital in underdeveloped countries, it would appear that their present populations are much too large in comparison with those of other countries. Thus, bringing a balance between capital and people would require considerable population transfers between countries.

Historically, the mass migration of persons has played an important part in the process of economic development. This occurred during the time when the populations of the more developed nations of the world were growing at a fast rate and it was necessary for large numbers to emigrate in order to maintain living standards. Not only were people attracted by prospects in the new countries, but they were forced out by conditions in the old. As would be expected, those who actually migrated were the younger and more enterprising members of the population who were able to finance the move. It is certainly possible to argue that such a group was unusually well qualified to contribute to the development of a new country.

The kind of mass migration of Europeans that occurred prior to World War I is not likely to be repeated. The birth rate in all European countries has been declining, and whatever gains have been achieved in the reduction of the death rate, which accounted for the spectacular increase of the population in the course of the past three centuries, have already been reflected in population figures. A further increase in the life span of the average European will be reflected more in the preponderance of old people in the population, rather than in a reduction of infant mortality.

These facts lead to the inescapable conclusion that, unless Europe wishes to depopulate itself in favor of the less developed areas in the world, such as South America, parts of Africa, and Australia, there is little prospect of any large-scale migration. Despite an upward spurt in the birth rate since the end of World War II, only Italy and Holland have been willing to part with their citizens, and Holland has been attempting to place its migrants in developed countries.

The more developed the European country, the more desirable its labor is to the underdeveloped country. Not only will its workers possess needed skills, desirable work habits, and experience, but they may also bring valuable capital. The government of a developed country, however, is more likely to have a full-employment program in effect and be reluctant to part with its skilled workers. An advanced country provides various advantages not available in an underdeveloped country, such as free schooling, social insurance, and other free or subsidized goods and services. Thus a worker has very little incentive to leave the country at a time when employment opportunities are good, and, during the periods of depression in the more advanced countries, the under-industrialized countries are even less likely to have jobs open. As we have seen, these countries are usually producers of primary goods and feel the effects of depressions much more acutely than their developed neighbors.

Even a life of comparative hardship, such as has prevailed in England since the end of World War II, has not induced much migration. The emigration of workers from Great Britain has been far from spectacular, and it has been mostly directed to member countries of the British union rather than to underpopulated, underdeveloped areas.

Selective migration of skilled workers may have a different effect on the process of production than mass movements of people or transfers of commodities and capital. In the past, immigration of skilled workers has certainly created a favorable climate for certain investments. The silk industry of France, for example, owed its start to the encouragement given Italian silk weavers to settle there. A still better known example is the migration of French cotton weavers to England.[10]

The migrants brought with them enough capital to affect the money market and the industrial outlook in the France and England of their day. This is not the case with such migrants today. The very large size of major industries has made it necessary to spread ownership widely. Indeed, if the largest single owner were to emigrate and take his equity with him, he would not be likely to change the economy of either country as much as did the typical emigrating merchant-craftsmen of the seventeenth or eighteenth centuries. The entry of many countries of the world into the industrial era has reduced the possibility of one country basically affecting the industrial face of another through the transfer of persons.

In any event, selective migrants to underdeveloped countries in the

[10] See Warren C. Scoville, "Minority Migration and the Diffusion of Technology," *Journal of Economic History*, XI (1951), pp. 347–66.

twentieth century are not likely to be numerous, and those who do move will come in most cases from countries where there is a surplus agricultural population. Such migration will probably be spearheaded by younger persons, who have been detached from the soil for a short period of time, usually by serving in the army. While comparatively unskilled in relation to the labor force of the country they are leaving, they will probably possess much more technological knowledge than the average resident of the country to which they migrate. Thus, they will typically settle in the cities of the new countries and form the core of the industrial work force.

The number of emigrants is further reduced in the modern world because receiving countries allow only certain classes or types of persons to settle within their borders. Even the United States, where unskilled migrants would soon be expected to acquire valuable skills, has been unwilling to permit immigration on a scale comparable to that of the late nineteenth and early twentieth centuries. Thinly settled areas, such as countries in Latin America, have been highly selective with respect to their choice of immigrants. A recent survey of immigration rules and policies revealed that these governments are willing to permit the entry of only certain categories of migrants, and these of particular racial stocks.[11]

The majority of these countries are apparently not planning to industrialize their countries with the help of foreign-born labor. On the contrary, they are attempting to utilize immigrants to increase agricultural production. In Asia, where most of the countries are overpopulated, strict rules have been established to discourage immigration. In Burma, for example, even foreign technicians are not permitted to reside over a certain length of time, and it is incumbent upon them to train native replacements. The British colonies in that area, of course, admit all British and Dominion subjects, but they tend to keep out others.

Perhaps the main reason why most underdeveloped countries have reservations about the desirability of admitting foreigners in large numbers is the fear that foreigners may come to dominate the cultural life of their country. Such apprehensions have been voiced by community leaders in such areas as Australia, South Africa, and, re-

[11] Malcolm J. Proudfoot, *Population Movements in the Caribbean* (New York: Columbia University Press, 1951). See especially Part III.

cently, around the Arabian peninsula. They have only to recall the colonization of their own countries to buttress their arguments with historical examples.

The development of Israel, especially since independence was achieved in 1947, superficially belies the thesis of this section, that large-scale migration is unlikely to affect the economies of under-developed countries. However, the contradiction is more apparent than real. The Jewish migration was under Zionist auspices, swelled by persecution, and backed by important capital inflows. Although the Israelis have managed admirably to create employment opportunities out of a vacuum caused by the Arab exodus, immigration has been so heavy since 1945 that the inflow of capital (roughly estimated at $200 per capita) was not sufficient to keep the standard of living of former non-Arab Palestinians at the pre-World War I, or even World War II, levels.[12] Nonetheless, the case of Israel does demonstrate how a country with few natural resources can make an attempt at establishing fairly high standards of living, provided certain conditions are met. Israel had a ready reserve of disciplined labor in the new arrivals from Europe, and some capital with which to put the labor to work.

The experience of Israel is the principal modern example of migration induced by persecution, drastically affecting the economy of the area into which the migrants moved. It cannot, however, be taken as a prototype of desirable population inflows into underdeveloped countries since the original residents of the country were not integrated with the migrants.

This writer dislikes conceiving the possibility of more migrations in the future like the one to Israel. Rather, he would feel that the migration policies of underdeveloped countries should encourage the arrival of certain groups of workers, planned in accordance with the employment opportunities in the countries concerned.

The restrictions placed by underdeveloped countries on the employment of foreign technicians and administrators seems unreasonable in the light of their urgent need for capital, and the time limits set for the replacement of key personnel by natives often discourage

---

[12] Recently Dutch migrants to Brazil were permitted to take $750 per capita of equipment with them to help them in their resettlement from Dutch to Brazilian farms. This sum would permit the Dutch to apply modern farm methods in their new homesteads. Resettlement, as this example shows, is an expensive proposition.

foreign investment. Peoples of the underdeveloped countries must decide whether they are going to take the chance of having their industry dominated by foreigners or take the chance that foreign capital will pass them by, or, almost as bad, be mismanaged when invested.

Lastly, it cannot be overstressed that a shortsighted view of migration can be disastrous. The original occupation of the migrants may have little to do with their later career orientation. Thus the Chinese and the Indians who migrated to the South Seas as agricultural laborers and made the plantation economy possible, later moved to the cities and eventually played a critical role in the establishment of light industry in that area. The role of the Chinese in the market sector of Thailand has been pivotal. "Big oaks from little acorns grow"— given the space and time to grow, of course.

Effect of migration on investment and saving. We have already indicated that persons who migrate under modern conditions are not likely to bring with them significant amounts of capital or technology. We shall discuss in this section the effects of migration of persons on saving and investment in their adopted country, touching also upon the attraction to the foreign investor of a country which has a high rate of immigration and urbanization.

Theoretically, an influx of people into a country or the influx of rural dwellers into a city is likely to increase the marginal product of capital. There is more inducement for entrepreneurs to invest, and eventually, as the new workers become receivers of income and spend their wages, there will be a correspondingly greater demand for goods. Even if the population movement has been from village to city, and there has been no increase in total population, an increase in money wages and demand for urban, capitalistically produced commodities is likely. Many of the rural dwellers had not, hitherto, entered the market economy, so their demands for manufactured commodities will be larger now than they were before.

An important consideration in this connection is the effect of changes in the composition of the labor force brought about by the process of economic development upon the marginal productivity of investment. In the first place, the abundance of labor and newly created purchasing power create anticipations of profits and raise the subjective marginal productivity of capital, thus encouraging investment. Foreigners are more likely to make direct investments in a country where all the conditions for undertaking a given type of manufacturing process are already present and business conditions are favorable.

Migration to urban areas is also likely to encourage the mobilization of savings which can be used for investment. The movement of rural dwellers into the city places them within reach of modern savings institutions. New urban residents are, or usually can be, interested in saving more through such institutions as postal savings, savings banks, or even a bond drive with lottery provisions.

Foreign migrants are even more promising potential savers and investors than rural migrants. They are ordinarily more highly skilled and, with higher earnings, are able to save a larger percentage of their income. They are also more sophisticated, however, and will not take part in organized investment unless convinced that their savings will not be dissipated by currency depreciation. Thus, a propaganda campaign and an effort to stabilize the currency over a period of years becomes of paramount importance if their savings are to be mobilized.

The same foreign migrants are also more likely to be enterprising investors, because they come from countries where the industrial organization is more complicated. For example, the enterprise of Chinese migrants to the South Seas, as compared to the easy-going population of those areas, is so well known it hardly needs retelling. Indeed, the trade and light industry in Thailand (Siam), the Dutch East Indies, Malaya, and, to a lesser degree, the Philippine Islands are still largely in Chinese hands.

The crucial determinant in the orientation of savings patterns of immigrants is the power of assimilation of the recipient country and the capacity of the migrants to be assimilated. It has often been felt that the Chinese are the most difficult to assimilate, because they are bound to their country of origin. It was estimated that during the 1920's as much as 200 million dollars were sent back to China by former migrants. Large movements of capital to the "old country" are also made by Italian immigrants, who habitually remit a large part of their savings to support relatives in Italy.

Clearly, however, the orientation of the migrants is not hereditary and depends upon the environment in the country of immigration. If the migrant group is made to feel apart because of ethnic differences, such as the Chinese in the United States or the Philippines, or bars are placed to their assimilation because of language difficulty, as in the case of West Indians in some Latin American countries, the immigrant is hardly at fault. Wherever there is little race prejudice, as in Peru where the sizable Chinese minority is being assimilated, the remittance problem has decreased. Similarly, in the United States, with the more rigid enforcement of the minimum education requirements, young Italians have been easily exposed to the naturalization process and are less apt to be oriented towards the "old country."

Some investment at the outset of a program of economic development will go into the building of housing, roads, etc. In a highly developed country such expenditures have very large secondary effects, especially if such activity is undertaken during a period of underemployment, since the building industry is very cycle-sensitive. The multiplier effect of these expenditures is likely to be quite pronounced in an underdeveloped country as well. Consequently, the government and financial institutions in that country must take care to channel these secondary effects into domestic consumption and investment. A disproportionate increase in imports of consumer goods will nullify the original impetus towards increasing incomes.

The migration of capital, as well as of people, will, of course, affect domestic saving. For example, if the foreign capital is invested in a particular industry, the net saving in the economy of the underdeveloped country during later periods will depend upon the extent to which profits of the industry are either repatriated or reinvested domestically. If they are repatriated, even though they are later used to buy machinery abroad and expand the industry, the net effect of the investment on levels of employment and income will be much smaller than if the machinery were manufactured at home. If used abroad, the employment effect is similar to that of extra investment upon an economy with a high propensity to import.

If, on the other hand, the influx of capital is channeled through an indigenous financial institution, more of the money invested will be spent locally, assuming it is feasible to use only a relatively minor proportion of the funds abroad. Further, secondary expansion throughout the banking system, which is felt more readily in a country whose banking system is relatively more closely interconnected than that of developed countries, will provide it eventually with an even greater volume of domestic funds to be loaned out in the fu ture. Finally, a financial institution is likely to have better facilities than an individual investor for appraising the prospects of local industry, trade, and agriculture, and thus may be better able to gauge the potential contribution of these to economic development than a newly arrived foreign investor.

THE MIGRATION OF TECHNOLOGY

In a world where it has become increasingly difficult for people and capital to move freely, the migration of technology may well hold the greatest promise for the future growth of underdeveloped areas. Indeed, a familiarity with the economic history of the more advanced countries indicates the significant role technology has played in their growth. We need only imagine what economic life would be like without steam, electricity, and petroleum or other sources of power, railroads and highways to transport products and people, the extensive use of metals in both capital and consumer goods, or modern methods of organizing production and business to realize the impact that technical innovations have had over time.

Even in advanced countries, as was pointed out in the preceding chapter, the gap between the "best methods" and the ones in current use may be large. In underdeveloped countries this gap is, of course, ever so much greater. In many instances the introduction of relatively simple techniques, such as improved seed or tools involving little capital, may bring about substantial increases in output. Knowledge and adaptation to the requirements of more advanced techniques offer further possibilities, even with limited domestic supplies of better capital and labor.

Advanced countries have been marked by the number of technical innovations that their citizens have contributed. The discovery of important new processes does give a certain initial advantage to the country of origin, but, fortunately for less advanced areas, it is not necessary to be an originator in order to secure the benefits from advanced technology. This was not always so. From the Middle Ages well down into the nineteenth century, special skills, formulae, and productive processes were carefully guarded secrets, handed down from generation to generation or transmitted through the training of apprentices in particular crafts. It was a part of national policy, particularly during the seventeenth and eighteenth centuries, to prevent the spread of techniques into other countries by prohibiting the migration of skilled craftsmen. The fame of Samuel Slater, who memorized the construction of power-driven spinning machinery before migrating from England to America in 1790, illustrates this proposition.

The modern world, with a few exceptions such as the development of atomic energy, presents a quite different picture. The growth of the physical sciences has been accompanied by the training of thousands of skilled individuals, chemists, physicists, biologists, and engineers of all types, capable of applying the accumulated knowledge of the past to the task of increasing production and improving its quality. Textbooks, scientific journals, and popular articles make the latest development or application of scientific principles available on a world-wide basis. A growing number of manufacturers, especially in the United States, are proud to show visitors their establishments. Owners of patents are ordinarily willing to license them to anyone who shows promise of returning attractive royalties, while machine builders have long sought foreign outlets for their products.

This does not mean that there are no limitations on the transfer of knowledge or of advanced techniques embodied in improved machinery. The problem of patents is still vexing on occasion. Apparently some individuals in underdeveloped countries cannot reconcile themselves to paying royalties, although they are quite willing in many instances to pay for machinery which includes a royalty payment in its price. There have been frequent complaints that manufacturers have agreed not to sell the most advanced equipment to underdeveloped countries but, instead, have limited sales in those areas to antiquated machines. It has also been suggested that international cartels, controlling particular kinds of manufactured commodities, have taken steps to limit the expansion of production facilities in undeveloped areas. This has been done by various predatory practices, such as nonlicensing of patents, competitive buying of raw materials, and price cutting in domestic and foreign markets.

It is doubtful, however, whether, on balance, the restrictions on the migration of technology are very important. As far as technology is concerned, the underdeveloped areas of the world are largely free to draw on a common fund of knowledge and techniques. Their problem is not one of availability. It is one of working out the difficulties of effective transmission from one environment to another, adapting particular techniques to given resource patterns and social institutions, and initiating changes in domestic resource patterns and institutions that will make technology more effective in contributing to economic growth. The magnitude of the problems involved depends upon the speed with which new techniques are introduced and the extent to which customary work habits, living conditions, and the like are disturbed. These points are brought out clearly by the experiences of various countries in their attempts to introduce industry into essentially agrarian or raw-material-producing economies.

During the period between the two wars, great stress was laid on the leadership requirement for technical change, such as might be provided by engineering training and the organization of management teams. Foreign technicians were called on to give this kind of leadership, and many nationals received technical training in Europe and the United States.

The experience of native technicians trained abroad was not always a happy one. Governments and local entrepreneurs tended to show some preference for foreign experts, although their efforts in this direction were tempered by the realization that a number of natives who had been similarly trained were not employed according to their specialty. Thus, Mexico promulgated a law in 1933 to the effect that immigration of foreign technicians would be prohibited unless it was shown that an effort to recruit Mexican technicians had been unsuccessful.

This preference for foreign experts was not always based on the superior qualifications of these technicians, but rather on the intimate "know how" which is acquired by persons reared in a mechanical environment. Foreign technicians seem to appreciate more fully the need for enforcing rules and procedures which assure the success of a productive process. Native engineers and technicians are more likely to be lax and compromise with local habits and customs and impair the effectiveness of an unfamiliar type of capital-intensive investment.

By the end of the 1930's, it had gradually become clear, however, that technical leadership was not enough to ensure effective industrialization. More and more it was realized that transition from artisan to factory production was no easy step in industrialization but involved basic changes in the structure of the economy and in the attitudes and habits of the people. The industrial, as opposed to the artisan, type of production of new industries in underdeveloped countries depends for success on a certain attitude of the workers toward the job. If the workers' desire for the amenities of life have been awakened and if they have been accustomed to purchase new commodities, they are more likely to stand the disciplines imposed by the mass-production process.

Actually, this had been realized in part at least by many employers who had appreciated for many years that a different kind of worker was desirable for work in a factory, as contrasted to a craft establishment. Selection of prospective workers for new enterprises in underdeveloped countries has commonly been made with this in mind. In a number of South American countries, preference in hiring was given to men wearing workmen's caps; in China a worker in the waiting line for a job, wearing tennis shoes of a Western pattern, was more likely to be hired than one in native shoes. The worker who has assumed urban habits is preferable to one who has not, since these habits are a signpost showing a willingness to accept foreign technology.

An assault upon the productive forces of the country and a campaign to increase the productivity of the population has to be conducted along the lines of changing the form of production. The widely held belief that in a country where labor is abundant there is little need to introduce capital-intensive techniques is not as popular as it was before World War II. Rather, it has been suggested, the introduction of advanced methods of production should be attempted at once, instead of being preceded by intermediate stages of semi-artisanal production. In some cases, at least, the new process of production must be taken over in its entirety, exactly the way it is conducted abroad, if it is not to be a failure. The attitudes of the population crucial to the successful acceptance of the new technology are much more likely to be brought about if a modern process of production is introduced. Not only will an increase in the population's command over goods and services make them more willing to bear the discomfort of the discipline required by the new technological process, but it will also give them the necessary physical stamina to withstand the demands made upon workers by an assembly-line type of production. The secondary effects of a spectacular increase in productivity are also very important, even if only a small proportion of the population is affected. If the standard of living of the population rises, it is likely that the younger generation will be allowed to spend more time in school and be better prepared to function in a complicated industrial society.

The introduction of a new type of machinery in an underdeveloped country is likely to be accompanied by a number of varying manifestations on the part of workers. In a large industrial Chinese city, workers were known to bribe their supervisors for the right to work on a new machine. On the other hand, if the installation of a new machine is followed by an industrial accident, its acceptance may be greatly retarded by a mere chance occurrence. The entrepreneur may also face a number of problems unknown to his counterpart in developed countries. Servicing new machines may be expensive or totally impossible and may require a complicated series of arrangements to insure their smooth operation.

To make sure that the transfer of technology is a success, an underdeveloped country must not only transpose the physical layout of a plant from abroad, but must also make sure that the organizational makeup of production is accepted as well. A number of industrialization projects have failed because of the mistakes made in coordinating the various phases of production and distribution. The failings may occur through bad planning of the various steps of production. Thus, a steel rolling mill may be built without attention to the capacity of the smelting works which it is to service, or no provisions may be made for the distribution of the product once it has been manufactured. The experience of foreign producers in locating production facilities is just as important as the physical layout of the plant.

Another pitfall which must be avoided if transfers of technology are to be a success is the subversion of the character of institutions adopted from the more advanced countries. One of the more important contributions which advanced countries can make to the development of other countries is the adaptation of techniques of financing. Central banks, commercial and agricultural banks, and the institution of the corporation may all contribute substantially to the development drive, on condition that their character is not changed once they are removed to another country. Despite the adoption of laws patterned on those of the advanced countries, an agricultural bank may limit itself to lending only to large landholders, and a corporation may be used as an instrument to circumvent financial responsibility, rather than to facilitate the mobilization of funds. Not only the organization of institutions, but their functioning too, must be closely watched.

With an ever-growing awareness and consciousness of leaders in underdeveloped countries, such subversion is now less likely to occur. The unprecedented facilities for the dissemination of ideas, such as newspapers and magazines, as well as the relative ease of travel, which encourages contact and exchange of ideas between peoples in the twentieth century, are reflected in the larger amount of technology which is being successfully transmitted. Not only are technical magazines widely circulated, but the mores of persons in different countries are made familiar to residents of other countries, either through personal contact or through the literature or movies which are brought to them. Motivation for the assimilation of foreign technology is often due to the knowledge which a worker acquires about the standard of living in advanced countries through inspection of advertisements in popular publications.

The transfer of technology may also be emulated by personal contact between persons of advanced and underdeveloped countries. While there is no denying that they are important, they are not pivotal in the transference of technology. The effect of the long residence of United States soldiers in the South Sea islands during World War II is wearing off quickly, despite the fact that the natives could not but envy the wealth and the equipment of their wartime visitors. Unless there are certain prerequisites which can make development possible, such as a minimum amount of education, sources for capital formation, and the presence of certain institutions, mere contact with foreigners is not sufficient to ensure the transference of technology.

Introduction of technology by migrants is likely to be more lasting and more important. In the first place, the migrants remain in the country for longer periods of time; secondly, they often establish productive enterprises patterned after those in advanced countries. Even then, the influence may not be a profound one, unless their methods are widely copied or they submerge the native group by sheer weight of numbers. Capitalistic production in one sector of the economy has often survived for long periods of time side by side with primitive methods of production of the same commodity.

In summary, it can be said that the introduction of foreign technology to an underdeveloped country has to be done after careful planning and consideration of the capacity of the country to accept such new technology. It would seem more advisable to adapt current forms of technology to the requirements of that country, rather than to start it out with antiquated machinery or out-dated institutions. The planning of methods in transferring technology has made large advances during the decade of the Fifties, when special missions have been sent to underdeveloped countries to study methods of transferring new techniques to bolster production.

FOREIGN AID AND THE OUTLOOK
FOR THE DEVELOPMENT OF UNDERDEVELOPED AREAS

Given that movements of persons are to be at a minimum and that technology is allowed to migrate comparatively freely, the development of modern-type industries in underdeveloped countries must rest primarily on domestic accumulation of capital and capital imports. It has already been indicated that unless a program of development is carried out on a fairly large scale, there is very little chance of breaking the vicious cycle of low levels of consumption and investment in these areas. But what is the desirable level of investment in underdeveloped countries, and how much of this investment will have to be contributed by foreigners? These two questions have to be answered before any foreign-sponsored program, or indeed any program, of economic development is undertaken.

In answer to the first question, a group of United Nations experts, who met in 1951, set as their goal the rather modest increase of the national income of underdeveloped areas by two per cent per annum and arrived at a figure totaling fourteen billion dollars. One assumption underlying this calculation is that the present level of its national income is a good indicator of the capacity of the underdeveloped areas to absorb new capital.[13] Although an oversimplification, the lack of statistics in underdeveloped countries precludes a more exact estimate of aggregate investment needs.

The next question to ask is how much of this investment can be generated domestically and how much will have to come from foreign aid. The same United Nations experts did not believe that the underdeveloped countries will be able to raise internally any sizable portion of the moneys necessary for development and felt that about three-quarters of the sum will have to come from foreign sources. If some additional saving induced by new investment or forced by gov-

[13] See *Measures*, etc., *op. cit.*, Chapter XI.

ernment action occurs in underdeveloped countries, we may justly hope that such will be used to speed the program beyond this unspectacular two per cent increment.[14]

Foreign investment at the rate of fourteen billion dollars a year has also found favor in different quarters. For example, one author has argued that a foreign lending program equal to the peak annual United States export surplus of World War II, i.e., the excess of the value of all goods sent abroad over the goods shipped to the United States, is justifiable on the basis that the strengthening of underdeveloped countries is as effective a deterrent to communism as the armed forces of the United States.[15] If a conflict between the United States and the Soviet Union and its satellites is not to occur in the near future, investment in economic development of about twenty-five per cent of the military budget of the United States of the early 1950's—about fifteen billion dollars—does not seem unreasonable. Nonetheless, a figure of fourteen or fifteen billion dollars a year, or any other amount for that matter, must be mentioned only as a target with reservations, though there is no denying that the level of foreign lending or aid to underdeveloped countries must be much higher than the one billion dollars a year invested abroad in the period between World Wars I and II.

The sum to be invested will depend on the ability of the underdeveloped countries to make plans and generate the necessary conditions to facilitate the absorption of capital into their economies and the requirements set by the capital-exporting nation for repayment. Suppose, first, that the capital transfer is made in the form of a gift, since this will permit concentration on the proper balance between imports of investment goods and imports of consumer goods. New productive facilities cannot be constructed and staffed without withdrawing workers from other parts of the economy: thus domestic production of either consumption or export goods will be reduced and their prices will rise. This means both the creation of inflationary pressure and an unavoidable change in the population's consumption patterns. To the extent that such events are detrimental to the development program, then, some portion of the funds available

[14] Involuntary saving, resulting from a decline in consumption due to a rise in prices, is likely to take place if the underdeveloped country undertakes a vigorous investment program, disrupting existing supply and demand relationships and causing shifts in the relative, and probably the absolute, price level.

[15] Benjamin A. Javits, *Peace by Investment*. New York: Funk & Wagnalls, 1950.

from the foreign country must be used to import consumption goods. But this in turn means that fewer investment goods can be purchased abroad.

In the short run, the presence of underemployment in the economy will mitigate, but not eliminate, this problem. Geographical immobilities of labor and the length of time needed for training new workers make it difficult to expand the size of the industrial labor force with any considerable speed. In the course of time, however, as a larger and larger portion of the population is drawn into the market sector of the economy, greater flexibility in the composition of production will become possible.

Should the underdeveloped country be the recipient of a loan rather than a gift, the same set of problems will still have to be faced. Under these circumstances, however, particular attention will have to be paid to the relation between exports and imports in view of the need for amassing funds for the payment of interest and principal. The special problems thus created will serve to limit the amount of capital the country would be willing to borrow to that which can be serviced by the excess of exports over imports estimated for future years.

It is now necessary to consider in greater detail the factors influencing the division of imports financed by the foreign gift (or loan) between investment and consumption goods. It will be necessary to change the distribution of consumption goods available both from domestic and foreign sources so as to penalize those who are either unnecessary for the development program or who oppose it. At the same time, those groups which are needed for continued economic growth must be rewarded. Rewards, however, need be no greater than sufficient to bring about the desired movement of workers into the investment sector of the economy and the desired creation and encouragement of an entrepreneurial group. Penalties, on the other hand, cannot be so great as to strengthen the forces of opposition. They must also be evaluated in terms of the further objective of increasing the scope of the market sector of the economy for both products and factors.

Such a balancing process will clearly involve a considerable amount of trial and error to fit particular social and political situations and the nature of the changes taking place in these aspects of the total society. Under some circumstances, total consumption will need to be raised, as well as redistributed, as might be the case if the levels of health, nutrition, and sanitation of most of the population were very low. Under other circumstances, a change in the pattern of distribution accompanied by no change, or even a drop, in the total amount of consumption will be sufficient.

Questions regarding the design of consumption policy will be complicated by the presence of inflation and the need for achieving rather soon a "favorable" balance of trade, as would be the case if the foreign capital had come in the form of a loan rather than a gift. A certain amount of inflation does provide an opportunity to penalize groups whose incomes are relatively fixed without resort to direct controls over income or taxation, and this group may well include many of those unessential to the success of the development program. Further, since an upward movement of prices increases the profit possibilities for businessmen, it will encourage such domestic investment as may be in line with the program of development. It will also, however, cause consumption to rise, and this will increase the inflationary pressure. A continuous and rapid upward movement of prices may encourage a shift of potential entrepreneurs into speculation in real estate and commodities and into other activities not required for development. Further, the fact that it will eliminate the rentier group who may be supposed to oppose the program may not be too significant, since the size of this group is typically small in underdeveloped countries.

As a consequence of domestic price increases, the demand for imports will expand as foreign goods become relatively cheaper, while foreign demand for exports will decline. This will create the need for control measures in the export-import sector of the economy. The magnitude of this inflation-created problem will depend, in part, on the sort of goods being exported. If the underdeveloped country has been shipping out such resources as lumber or iron, which are needed for domestic investment, control will be less difficult than would be the case in a country exporting such staples as cotton or coffee. To the extent that underemployment exists in the export industries, however, changes in the pattern of exports and imports may themselves be part of the development program. While a certain amount of inflation may make achievement of this objective easier in terms of possible repayment difficulties in the future, the total volume of exports should, if anything, be increased relative to imports.

Summary

If large sums of money are to be invested annually in the economy of a country, certain forces within the economy have to be put into motion to promote the efficient absorption and utilization of the new capital. Of these, the borrowing of foreign technology and skills, which is necessary to further this absorption, has already been noted.

The success of an investment program depends in the final analysis on the attitude of the population toward change. Since an investment and development program must necessarily be supported by the people of the country in which it is undertaken, the population must be willing to enter the industrial labor force, submit to the discipline of the mass-production system, and attempt to reorient its consumption pattern in such a manner as to liberate a larger part of the national income for the purpose of investment.

Certain attitudes and administrative techniques are prerequisite for economic development. An attempt to create a favorable climate for the acceptance of values necessary for the function of the market economy and the techniques for the orderly administration of such an economy have received considerable attention lately.

For example, the Point Four program sponsored by the government of the United States is strongly oriented in this direction. The program does not provide investment funds for underdeveloped countries, but is designed to aid them with technical assistance to eliminate bottlenecks to economic development. Sometimes the bottleneck is a disease, such as malaria, and then public health teams are provided to eliminate it by eventually curing and making more of the population capable of systematic labor. At other times, the bottleneck is the lack of technical knowledge necessary to control agricultural pests or build a dam.

The United Nations' research and technical assistance program began by disseminationg information of this character to the underdeveloped countries. Its principal task is thus to facilitate the search of underdeveloped countries for foreign experts; in its more ambitious projects, however, the program has contributed to the integrated approach of preparing a backward country for economic development. It is significant that these broader studies have frequently pointed out the need for changes in attitudes and techniques rather than for simple doses of capital.

The story of the mission to Bolivia is a case in point.[16] A number of experts in a variety of fields ranging from agronomy to public finance were dispatched to Bolivia in 1950–51 to make a survey of its economy, at the invitation of the Bolivian government. After a thorough investigation of the conditions prevailing in the country, the mission recommended a reform of public administration as the first step necessary to promote economical development. Members of the mission felt that remedying the shortcomings of the administrative system would itself be a powerful stimulant to the savings and investment program of the country. In their opinion, the absence of a stable and efficient regulatory system was the chief obstacle which prevented Bolivia's economy from increasing per capita incomes at a faster rate.

This approach demonstrated the importance of having certain functions of government to encourage persons to participate in the development process. If business is subject to arbitrary levies from government, if accumulation of property is not regarded as a desirable end in itself, and if stability and traditionalism are placed above the Western concept of business "success," then the prospects for development are poor.

The same concern for these preconditions of economic development was voiced by the group of United Nations experts mentioned above who pointed out:

There is a sense in which rapid economic progress is impossible without painful readjustment. Ancient philosophies have to be scrapped; old social institutions have to disintegrate. . . . There cannot be rapid economic progress unless the leaders of a country at all levels—politicians, teachers, engineers, business leaders, trade unionists, priests, journalists—desire economic progress for the country and are willing to pay its price, which is the creation of a society from which economic and political privilege has been eliminated.[17]

In summary, then, the movement of any considerable amount of foreign capital into the economy must be accompanied by fairly drastic changes in the structure of the society. Too much change will create difficulties which make development impossible, while too little will have no lasting effect on the economy.

[16] *Report of the United Nations Mission of Technical Assistance to Bolivia* (New York: United Nations, 1951).
[17] See *Measures*, pp. 15, 16.

CHAPTER IX

Cultural Factors

FRANCIS L. K. HSU*

BASIC CONCEPTS

TWO CONCEPTS WILL BE MOST IMPORTANT TO THIS CHAPTER: CULTURE and economic development. The term "culture" refers to human behavior which is learned. Culture consists first of all of social organization through which members of the society are grouped together into such entities as family, community, and state. Second, it consists of the particular ways in which members of the society react to one another. Here we have such things as chivalry or the penal code, the Bill of Rights or religious values. Third, every culture is based upon some language spoken or written or both. And finally, every culture contains some artifacts, usually known as its material aspect, such as houses or canoes, supersonic planes or the atomic bomb, which can survive long after the human beings sharing the culture have become extinct.

All of these together make up what we ordinarily understand as being a way of life. When we speak of "culture" we are referring to some or all of these component parts. They do not exist in a haphazard manner but are interrelated and tend to form a more or less consistent whole. Each culture pattern, then, tends to be consistent in two ways. It is consistent historically. That is to say no culture pattern comes "out of the blue"; it is invariably the result, or the descendant, of some cultural ancestry which has existed before and which has given it form and direction. A culture pattern is also consistent horizontally. The different contemporaneous component

* Associate Professor of Anthropology, Northwestern University. Author: "Suppression Versus Repression: A Limited Psychological Interpretation," *Psychiatry* (August, 1949); *Under the Ancestors' Shadow; Religion, Science, and Human Crisis; American and Chinese: Two Ways of Life.*

parts tend to dovetail or support one another. For this reason no culture pattern can completely break from its past, just as none can for long harbor two violently opposing tendencies without civil war or revolution. But no civil war can last forever. When the battle dust has settled, the emerging culture pattern may represent a big or small break from the past, but it is never completely different from it. In most cases, of course, culture patterns evolve more slowly and their continuity with the past is easily recognized.

The term "economic development" may be defined as an increase in per capita real income. In this sense man achieved economic development when he changed from simply gathering food to agriculture, or from complete dependence upon rainfall to artificial irrigation, for such changes insure to man a more certain and abundant supply of food. In the present connection we must, however, broaden this definition a little for two reasons. First, the purpose of this volume is not to analyze man's development in the Stone Ages or in his Oriental or African aspects, but rather his transition from noncommercialized activities to commercialized ones. Second, and more important, while increases in per capita real income may be measured quantitatively, there are unmistakable reasons to believe that the transition from agriculture or nomadism to commercialization has important qualitative aspects. For example, this transition cannot be achieved unless a change of mental outlook occurs toward work and enjoyment of leisure.

Each human being has two facets to his standard of living: objective and subjective. The first consists of the actual conditions of existence to which he has attained. The second consists of those things which he would like to enjoy whether or not he is presently enjoying them. Different individuals within a given society or in different societies vary widely not only in their actual conditions of existence but also in what, if possible, they would like to enjoy. When a Chinese farmer has become well to do, he has tended to put the farm in the hands of tenants so that he can lead the life of an absentee landlord. But he does not usually wish to sell his land in favor of some other form of capital, nor is he prepared entirely to lead the new style of life which his wealth now permits. Instead, he will remain frugal and regard filial duties to parents as a part of the order of nature; he will continue his accustomed ceremonial and social activities, though he will now spend more money on them. He may build a bigger house, but his new home will be merely a more extensive version of the traditional house. He may construct a more impressive graveyard, because he still regards this as one of the most important achievements of any man. He may even buy some imported items from New York or London, but he cannot afford to neglect the festivals and obligations of the community in which he lives. This is an example of a quantitative increase in the real income of a person, not accompanied by a subjective demand for a different (and higher) standard of living. Changes of this kind might have characterized man when he invented a new stone-polishing technique or when he first turned from hunting to nomadism. But they went along slowly, each step taking thousands of years, and they certainly need not automatically lead to industrialization.

American pioneers in the New World presented a different spectacle. They were not content to develop a mode of life like that at home. Nor were they interested merely in achieving the upper-class style of life known in Europe. Americans did not merely want more of something of which they had less before, they wanted more of, as well as many other things very different from, that which their parents and grandparents had known.[1] This is an example of a quantitative increase in the real income of a people boosted by a subjective demand for a different standard of living. Such changes usually occur much faster than the strictly quantitative kind related earlier, sometimes within a single generation. This subjective demand for a higher and different standard of living is the foundation of impetuses to change which originate within the society, as distinguished from those pressures to change which come from outside.

Cultural Factors Favorable to Economic Development

The importance of cultural factors to economic development has often been neglected and this has led to serious errors in thinking.[2] A significant example of this is the usual linkage between pop-

---

[1] The new environment, with its greater abundance of resources, certainly helped this development. But, as will be made clear in this chapter, the environmental factor was secondary.

[2] The discussion in this chapter will be primarily concerned with large literate societies such as those of Europe and Asia. For an extensive study of the relationship between culture and economy throughout the nonliterate world, the reader is referred to M. J. Herskovits: *Economic Anthropology* (New York: Alfred Knopf, 1952).

ulation pressure and economic development. It has been argued that one of the basic reasons for the Industrial Revolution in England was the Enclosure Acts which, by forcing people off their land, compelled them to seek employment in factories. One widely accepted theory of military aggression is based on the effects of population pressure; only yesterday the Germans and the Japanese both advanced their need for living space as the *raison d'être* for warlike activities. A recent book that is based on this theme and which has gained wide attention is Josui de Castro's *The Geography of Hunger*.[3] What Castro and other like-minded scholars fail to see is that people may not react aggressively at all to population pressure. A striking example concerns the Chinese. Though pressed chronically by overpopulation and a scarcity of land, they have neither given themselves to invention nor to aggression. Instead of producing an inventive, or even commercially aggressive, spirit, the conditions of China seem to have induced in a majority of its inhabitants an even greater desire to stay where they are in spite of the fact that this means a further reduction of an already low standard of living.[4] For this reason Chinese farmers and city folk tend to regard land with a sentimental attachment that is beyond economic advisability. For the same reason the frontier regions of China, including Formosa, have been slow in their colonization. Of those who did migrate to these regions, a very substantial number periodically returned to their old home towns or retired there after they had made their "fortune." Others sought at least to strengthen their ties with their ancestral communities through donations to clan temples, hospitals, and schools. Furthermore, it is significant that in spite of the extensive coastal areas of China which have been subjected to contact with the West, most Chinese immigrants who settled in Europe came from only a few counties in Chekiang province; most Chinese in the South Seas came from a few counties in Fukien and Kwangtung

[3] Boston: Little, Brown & Co., 1952.

[4] The role of Communist China in the recent Korean conflict may appear to contradict this observation. The truth of the matter is that military ventures under ambitious leaders have been frequent in Chinese history. But such ventures were never followed up (as noted later) by aggressive waves of immigration and colonization. Whether Communist indoctrination has succeeded in changing Chinese orientation sufficiently more than did Western capitalist impact to have made drastic differences in this picture, time alone can tell. It must be remembered that so far only a few years have passed since the Communists have taken over, whereas the actual historical test requires decades if not centuries.

provinces; and the ancestors of the great majority of the Chinese in Hawaii and the continental United States came from five adjacent counties whose total area is smaller than metropolitan Los Angeles.

For convenience, the cultural factors favorable to economic development may be grouped under three headings, according to the three basic elements of an economy, as (a) those favoring the availability of savings, (b) those favoring the utilization of resources, and (c) those favoring the availability of labor.

The availability of savings. Among factors favoring growth and accumulation of capital are patterns of income distribution, consumption, and saving. For capital to be available for industrial purposes there must be a certain concentration of income, whether this concentration is based on genuine surplus over the needs of the society or on deprivation of some sections of the population by actions of others. This concentration may come about through the inheritance rule of primogeniture, through outright exploitation, such as slavery and tribute to a ruler, or through profitable trade.

Habits of consumption are equally important in helping or hampering the growth of capital. The most relevant element here is consumption for reasons other than those of physical preservation or utility, known as "conspicuous consumption." For social or ceremonial purposes such as weddings, honoring of the gods, or debutante parties, peoples in many parts of the world are known to spend themselves poor. Where such conspicuous consumption is high, capital is not easily formed. On the other hand, in societies where thrift is considered a virtue or it is customary to save for old age, then the supply of funds available for capital formation tends to be greater.

The last important element is the pattern of saving. If people do not indulge much in conspicuous consumption, or if they still have anything left after much conspicuous consumption, what do they do with what is left? They may hoard it in caches, which practice is better than conspicuous consumption. The growth of capital is facilitated if there is some customary channel such as co-operatives or banks which can make funds available for investment. Short of co-operatives or banks, some regularized pattern of borrowing and lending at interest may be of some help. Even high usury rates, though they tend to break the debtors in the long run and "kill the goose," may be helpful to economic development if the usurers can be persuaded, in their own interests, to invest in productive channels.

The utilization of resources. This leads to a consideration of the cultural factors which induce the utilization, as distinct from the mere availability, of resources. From the point of view of economic development, the accumulation of wealth, however great, is a passive asset. Unless there are cultural forces which press this accumulated wealth into productive investments, such as factories, roads, and mines, it is of no consequence. In precisely the same sense, the mere presence of natural resources will not help economic development unless there are cultural factors favoring the aggressive exploitation of them.

The American Indians came to the New World at least twenty thousand years ago. They found two continents as laden with mineral wealth as did the Pilgrims much later. But the American Indians exploited little of those resources and mostly led an existence not too far different from their Asiatic ancestors. Many European peoples, on the other hand, went to far corners of the earth looking for what they wanted when they failed to find it at home. The availability of the resources did not encourage the former, while their absence did not discourage the latter. What differentiated the American Indian's approach to the resources from that of the European was the factor of culture.

Culture affects the utilization of resources in diverse ways. Where the land and natural resources are communally or state owned, their availability for industrialization may depend upon whether the consent of the chief or the governing body can be secured. If resources lie in territories which people regard as unexploitable because of ancestor worship or because of other supernatural reasons such as geomancy,[5] then their utilization may be impossible, or can be achieved only after long delays.

The most important element in this connection is, however, technology, without which exploitation of the resources can never be ef-

[5] This may be described as the earthly counterpart of astrology. Instead of the idea that the movements and junctions of the heavenly bodies determine the individual's fate, geomancy is built on the premise that the location and geographic configuration of one's house, ancestral graveyards, and village have strong effects on his chances of success, failure, life, and death.

fective. Technology may of course be imported as it was by continental European countries from England in the early days of the Industrial Revolution and by many non-Western countries and Russia during the past two hundred years. All of these countries have received from one or more industrialized nations either machinery or technical advice or both. This cultural borrowing has evidently facilitated the utilization of resources in the recipient countries, greatly in the case of Russia and Japan.

But can importation of technological equipment and knowledge be adequate for purposes of a lasting economic development without indigenous science and invention? The answer probably depends upon the kind of economic development which is needed or planned. If the economic development desired is a slight raising of the standard of living or a short-term alleviation of poverty or malnutrition, then importation of technology is probably sufficient. But if the economic development desired is of a more permanent nature, aiming at a substantial growth and expansion of the economy, then there must be native cultural forces making possible an indigenous development of science and invention. This was what happened in all the European industrial countries which initially borrowed from England. This has also in part been true of Japan.

The availability of labor. There are several cultural factors favoring the availability of labor. First, after producing the requirements for the maintenance and continuation of the society, under its traditional standard of life, is there a surplus in the working population? Alternatively the question may be put thus: If we were to open up avenues of employment other than those previously existing in the society, what portion of the labor force could we get without endangering the basic mode of existence of the society? Second, even if there is a surplus, can members of the labor force go anywhere freely, as dictated by the needs of economic development? People may be unwilling to leave their home villages for social reasons, or they may have a taboo against crossing water or using certain types of transportation. Or they may simply not be in the habit of seeking work anywhere except in their immediate circle of familiarity. Third, will the available labor force be willing to work in factories where men or women have to obey a rigid routine of hours and conditions of work, and where the individual worker handles but one of the many different production processes? Will it be willing to go through the necessary trouble of learning the appropriate skills? Will it stay in the factory for a reasonable length of time and not create a problem of rapid turnover?

In addition, some previous exposure to formal education may facilitate matters although, as noted later, this is not essential. Then, if the prestige pattern among the people in question is founded on material gains, and the latter can be more or less freely acquired, it may make economic development easier than if their basis of prestige lies elsewhere and wealth is restricted by caste or inheritance. Finally, the question of vertical and horizontal social mobility is important. There may be a great deal of actual mobility, or there could be much less of it, but it is essential not only that there be the idea that some mobility is possible, but also that such a possibility should obviously not be precluded by some caste or rigid class structure. Where both the possibility and the idea of mobility are present, people tend to be more easily attracted by new avenues of advancement than otherwise, even though such conditions do not automatically lead to aggressive economic attitudes.

From the above it seems clear that all explanations of economic development, or the lack of it, on such bases as an "interest in material things" or the "relative preference for leisure" are bound to be superficial. However broadly the term "leisure" is defined, it is hard to see any significance in such a statement, since it is like saying that people do not want to work because they prefer not to work. Human beings of any cultural heritage will not refuse to work if there is, in their eyes, reason for the trouble. Conversely, if they decline to work, it is because they can get their satisfactions elsewhere, not because of their "love of leisure." For instance, the assertion that reservation Indians simply have no desire to improve their economic condition is founded on the observer's ignorance of the real reasons for their lack of enthusiasm for economic betterment.[6]

THE NATURE OF HUMAN CONDUCT

However, economic development of a society is only one aspect of its general development. Therefore, not only are those cultural fac-

[6] See Ralph Linton, "Culture and Personality Factors Affecting Economic Growth," in Bert F. Hoselitz, editor, *The Progress of Underdeveloped Areas* (Chicago: University of Chicago Press, 1952), pp. 76–77.

tors favorable or unfavorable to economic development interrelated, but the entire question of economic development must be considered in the total framework of human conduct, and cannot be treated separately from it. The logical starting point of inquiry into man's conduct in economic activities is, then, the basic nature of man's existence itself.

In addition to his own psychology and physiology, every human being has to deal with two environments. One consists of material heritage from the past, such as architecture and technology, and natural environment, such as vegetation, climate, and minerals. The other consists of human beings who stand in kinship—marital, economic, social or political relationships—to him.

While it may be impossible to state precisely the exact importance of either of these environments, there are good reasons why the human environment is much more important to man than the physical. The individual begins life by complete dependence upon other human beings. During infancy this dependence chiefly centers around food and bodily protection. What he does gradually learn is that one, such as the mother, or several persons, including aunts, grandmothers, or some in-laws, are his answer to all problems, because they administer to his needs and respond to his cries. To the infant the most crucial sources of his discomfort or satisfaction are such individuals who may administer to his needs and answer his cries. He is ignorant of the sources of his food, or even its variety, but will accept or reject, or like or hate, the food depending upon who feeds him and how he is fed.

As the infant grows, he learns to differentiate between the animate and the inanimate, between animals and human beings, and between some human beings and other human beings. In becoming conscious of a wider and wider universe the maturing individual has essentially to integrate his new experiences with what he has known before. That is to say, at each step of the individual's growth he interprets the new by projecting the old. He may have become independent of human beings, such as parents or siblings, but he is likely to substitute other human beings such as wife, children, or friends.

It is not enough that a person be just adequately fed and comfortably clothed. He must also have parents who love him and others with whom to live, play, and work. It is not enough, as he grows older, to have a wife or husband. The normal thing is for each person to desire a wife or husband of whom the person can be proud before neighbors, friends, and the world at large. To achieve a desirable place among fellow men, most human beings are willing not only to endure hardships originating from the physical environment but even to accept self-destruction. A girl may purposely starve herself in order to achieve a "good figure." A man may give up his job, his rice bowl, in the interest of an ideal which he holds dear. The extreme examples of such actions may be found in the Hindu widow who throws herself on her husband's funeral pyre or the soldier who, exceeding the call of duty, dies for his country.

The individual's concern about others need not be motivated by any noble purpose. Unless we assume some unlikely instinct for self-deprivation or destruction, and unless we can make hermits, great thinkers, or lunatics out of the majority, we must admit that the most basic concern of man is other men. This is why in all societies we have ideas of honor and decency. This is why we have taboos and religions. It is to control and regulate relationships between men that we have ethics and laws. As human beings have left their animal ancestry, their problem of existence has become a group matter, and their most basic concern is not the direct satisfaction of their individual impulses in the physical environment, but the satisfaction of these impulses through finding the most appropriate place among their fellow men.

THE INTERNAL IMPETUS TO ECONOMIC DEVELOPMENT

While man in all societies is concerned with other men, differing patterns of culture cause him to regard others in different lights. In this respect, the contrast of China with the West is most illuminating. The Chinese culture pattern has as its central theme what may be described as mutual dependence among men. At the core of this pattern lies the tie between parents and their male children. Economically, all sons have the unquestionable duty of economic support of their father, just as the father's possessions automatically and equally belong to the sons. There is no question of inheritance in the Western sense of the term. For even if the elder were to make a will in the interest of someone else, it would have no validity against the long-established custom. Socially, the bond between the two generations is just as striking. The Chinese proverb has it thus: "In the first thirty years of a man's life, one looks at the father and respects the son, while in the second thirty years of a man's life, one looks at the son and respects the father." That is to say, while the son is young, his father's social status determines his place in society, but when the son has grown up and the father has become old, the son's status determines that of the father.

This automatic father-son bond is the basic link between all generations. It is the foundation of all other relationships within the primary groups, such as the family, the clan, and the community. It even serves as a model for wider relationships, such as those between teachers and their pupils, employers and their employees, and rulers and their subjects. It is, however, within the primary groups that the individual Chinese has his inalienable place in life. He can be very competitive when necessary to better himself and his father. But in so doing he has to follow the footsteps of his forebears or deviate from them according to the established routes of advancements, which meant in the past scholarship and officialdom. Even in Republican China the traditional competitive routes for enterprising young Chinese broadened but little. Their center remained the professional community. Once having made the entry, the ambitious young man sought opportunities in bureaucracy. The lesser alternatives included teaching, preferably in colleges, but also, tolerably, in high schools. Very few of the graduates from modern Chinese schools went into business and industry and fewer still into work involving any manual capacity.

When an individual has improved himself, his parents, his clan, and his community will shine with him, for, through the pattern of mutual dependence, his honor is theirs. But he does not have to do these things if he does not care to. His worth as a human being does not depend on accomplishment of them. Nor is there much stigma attached to failure even though failure is undesirable. Through the pattern of mutual dependence, his misfortune or failure is theirs too. In fact, they are in a sense regarded as being responsible for his misfortune or failure.

This relationship is especially clear in certain features of Chinese religion. According to Chinese ideas, in ancestor worship, the condition of descendants is invariably related to the behavior, imagined or real, of one's ancestors. A successful man owes his success to the

merits of his ancestors, just as a man who has failed owes his failure
to the demerits of similar forebears. For example, the son of a thief
may become a prominent member of government. If this happens, the
people will say that even if the father had been a thief, he must have
been a good thief, who most likely stole from the rich and gave his
loot to the poor, for how else would he deserve a descendant of this
stature? In the same way as the father-son bond serves as the foundation for all other human relations, the merit-demerit connection between ancestors and their descendants is extended beyond the kinship sphere. For example a man's success will be explained because
his family graveyard is well located or because his native village or
district has the "Wind and Water" for prosperity. An individual is
merely the agent of these forces which predetermine his chances in
the world.

A Chinese who has failed or is in economic distress will be most
happy if friends and relatives appear on the scene and lend him
money or render him all necessary help. These benefactors can from
then on count on his good will and his determination to repay them
in the utmost of gratitude as long as he lives. If he does not, he will be
avoided as a scoundrel. Furthermore, a Chinese who has been so
helped will feel no embarrassment at all in letting the whole world
know about it. He has nothing to hide when he is acting according
to his culture pattern of mutual dependence.

The culture pattern of the West is the exact reverse. Details vary
from one European country to another, but the central theme of
this culture pattern is individualism. We do not know the exact time
when this pattern first emerged in the West. There are good indications that, even as early as the Greeks in the fifth century B.C., the
rudiments of individualism were already present, at least among the
small nonslave portion of the population. Certainly by the sixteenth
or seventeenth century A.D. individualism was already a firmly and
widely established fact in the West.

There has been some confusion among anthropologists and sociol-
ogists in their description of some non-Western peoples in this regard.
One hears of the statement that the Manus of the South Seas are
like Puritans or that the Chinese are among the most individualistic
in the world. But individualism is to be differentiated from self-
interest or self-seeking activities. Self-interest and self-seeking activi-

ties are to be found in all human societies,[7] but the characteristic Western individualism is founded on the assumption that the individual, any individual, has certain inalienable rights that are born to him or God-given. The basic expressions of this assumption are freedom and equality. Under these tenets, parents and children, employers and employees, rulers and subjects are at least theoretically equal, and any barriers, whether they be human, customary, or traditional, are in the final analysis to be removed if they are found to be stumbling blocks to the exercise of freedom on the part of the individual. Under the same tenets, each individual should be his own master, rising or falling not according to his ancestry, not through the help that he may receive from others, but purely because of his own efforts.

Consequently, the Westerner's success is individual, and his triumph is great; but his failure is also his own and his misery extreme. If he succeeds, the whole world is at his feet. Even his wife and children are among his worshippers, for the benefits he bestows on his wife and children are signs of his success. Conversely, if he fails, the world has collapsed for him. There is a distinct danger that his wife may leave him and his children will be disillusioned with him. His anchorage in the world beyond his immediate family is even flimsier.

The Westerner must have success because he has no retreat. A Westerner who has failed or is in economic distress may not decline help from friends and relatives at the moment, but, in the normal course of events, he will feel thoroughly uncomfortable because they have seen him at his worst. There is nothing more ruinous to an individualistic person's self-respect than to fail and so be dependent upon other human beings. Therefore, he will not only entertain little lasting gratitude toward his benefactors, but what he is likely to show them in return is resentment and often withdrawal from otherwise satisfactory friendships.[8]

Thus for the Chinese success is desirable. But if he lacks success, he

---

[7] Francis L. K. Hsu, "Incentives to Work in Primitive Communities," *American Sociological Review*, VIII, 6 (1943), pp. 638–42.

[8] A projection of this Western psychology is one basic reason why many Americans caution against foreign aid. According to this view such aid can buy only ill will later on. What these critics should realize, however, is that their worst fears are much more likely to come true in Europe, where individualism prevails, than in China, Japan, Korea, and other Asiatic countries characterized by the pattern of mutual dependence.

still retains his inalienable place in the primary groups, wielding his authority as father and fulfilling his filial obligations as a son. Since personal success or failure is relatively unimportant to their basic security because their anchorage among fellow men is firm and unshakable, the Chinese tend to lack the determination and the desire to grind forth toward remoter goals. On the other hand, with Westerners, since success or failure is vital to their very security because each individual stands or falls alone, they are inclined to go every inch of the way in the spirit of the last battle and to persevere even though all odds seem to be against them. For what they lack in a strong anchorage among fellow men, they have to make up by controlling the physical universe.

Economic consequences. Once these differences are understood, we are in a better position to deal with their specific consequences in economic development. One of these is the limits placed on methods of excelling over fellow men in China in contrast to their much greater variety in the West. The individualist handles his own affairs and takes his own consequences. As soon as he reaches majority, he enjoys exclusive material possession, exclusive contractual powers, and the right to build his own career as he pleases. In his competitive efforts he is therefore relatively free from tradition, parental authority, or communal demands to stay within certain pre-existing limits. If his father is a wine merchant, he may take up law or become a clothier. Or if his father is devoted to politics, he can spend his time on scholarship or religion. In short, there are many avenues open to him.

It is not alleged that Westerners, in their search for self-improvement, are entirely free from restraints by men and custom. But given a social climate in which the older people are on the defensive, each new generation tends to deviate more or less from the one before. Consequently, those Westerners who are aggressive can more easily try the unbeaten path and make something of it because of their culture pattern of individualism. Their counterparts in China can hardly do so with any hope of public sympathy. How closely the generations in China have been tied to one another is well expressed in the Eastern saying that what is good enough for the father is good enough for the son. Given a framework in which the elders and the ancient traditions are inviolate, there tend to be fewer individuals who are able and willing to deviate. Even when they do attempt to better their elders, they are inclined to follow the well-trodden ways, with the result that fast changes of any kind are hard to achieve.

For this reason neither the idea nor the actual possibility of mobility, whether vertical or horizontal (a question we briefly touched on previously), induced the Chinese as a whole to develop an aggressive economic spirit characteristic of their European brethren, which expressed itself in mercantilism and in the Industrial Revolution. Thus although the Chinese could move upward, he was content to move within the shadow of his ancestors. He did not rear to free himself from the rein of tradition. Similarly, while Chinese rulers had many times, historically—under the Han (202 B.C.–A.D. 200), T'ang (618–906), and Yuan (1260–1368) dynasties, etc.—conquered vast expanses of non-Chinese territory, Chinese colonizers who took advantage of the economic opportunities thus made possible by their conquering armies were few. Furthermore, to the previously noted fact, namely, that a majority of the Chinese, though hard pressed for bare necessities at home, made no attempt to go to the South Seas or the Western world after the sea lanes became open, must be added another, that they were even slow in populating the outlying areas of China, such as Manchuria or Formosa.

Some common fallacies regarding economic development. In discussing the cause of lack of industrialization in China, Max Weber came closer to the truth than any other scholar when he pointed out that it was the nature of Chinese human relationship with its Confucian ethics which was responsible. But Weber was both guilty of ethnocentrism and wide of the mark when he characterized the forces which held back Chinese economic development as "irrational," in contrast to those "rational" forces which propelled the capitalistic history of the West.[9] Our analysis makes it clear that neither variety of forces may scientifically be described as more or less rational or irrational than the other. Each individual acts to find his security according to the cultural premises of his society. The

[9] Max Weber, *The Religion of China* (Glencoe, Ill.: Free Press, 1951). First published as essays in 1915 in *Archiv für Sozialwissenschaft und Sozialpolitik.* Before his death in 1920 Weber revised these for book publication. Present English translation is by Hans H. Gerth.

Chinese are oriented toward finding their best security among fellow men in the primary groups because their culture pattern of mutual dependence makes such satisfactions honorable. The Westerners search for their best security in the control of things because their culture pattern of individualism makes all social relations temporary. If one is characterized as "rational" then the other one too must correspondingly be regarded as "rational."

The same error in thinking has been applied to attitudes toward experimentation. Consider, for example, the following quotation:

> Where it has been learnt, human beings are experimental in their attitude to material techniques, to social institutions and so on. This experimental or scientific attitude is one of the pre-conditions of progress. The greatest progress will occur in those countries where education is widespread and where it encourages an experimental outlook.[10]

An objective study of the *actual* lives of diverse peoples in the world, including those of the West, reveals that human beings are remarkably "non-experimental in their attitude . . . to social institutions" in spite of "education." How willing is any people to make a drastic change in its family organization? How ready is any people for a drastic alteration of its attitude toward sex? Even the obviously "experimental attitude" of Westerners with reference to "material techniques" does not necessarily come from any true scientific evaluation of the evidence. It is more attributable to a pattern of life in which science has become the "sacred cow," and scientists and technicians (including doctors) have taken over the important place occupied by medicine men and diviners in other societies.

In this connection we need only to review the many commercial products, from cigarettes to beds, that are advertised and consumed in terms of alleged qualities specified in statements like "Scientists say . . . ," or "Doctors all over the country have agreed. . . ." A few scientists or thinkers may be completely experimental toward certain things, but the majority of the people buys this or that product or does this or that, not because they know or have thought through the intricate processes involved, but because it is their custom or habit to follow the advice of the "scientists," the "doctors," Hollywood stars, etc. There is nothing unusual about this. For all human beings, in their day-to-day existence, are guided very little by a scientific atti-

[10] See *Measures for the Economic Development of Under-developed Countries* (New York: United Nations, 1951), p. 13.

tude and very much by faith. No one can eat in a restaurant without faith that the food is not poisoned; no one can drive on busy highways without faith that other drivers will obey the traffic rules. This picture is rendered more complicated by our emotions. Even the relatively small number of scientists and thinkers are never above emotional involvement. These few individuals may be "scientific" about a few things, such as the value of π, or the distance between the Milky Way and the remotest star, or even the characteristics of the American government, but on other matters they are just as subject to "unscientific" prejudices, preferences, loves, or sorrows as the next man.[11]

Within their cultural premises, all peoples, regardless of education, are capable of being somewhat "experimental" toward certain desired objectives. Within a cultural framework of mutual dependence, the Chinese tend to be "experimental" in ceremonial and ritual matters by staging bigger and better weddings or funerals, or by building more impressive and costly graveyards and clan temples. On the other hand, given the cultural framework of individualism, Westerners tend to be "experimental" in their attempts to control the material universe by flying faster or extracting more copper ore. The Western reaction to the suggestion that one can be "poor and happy by being dependent" is likely to be as negative as the Chinese reaction to the suggestion that one can be "rich and satisfied without heirs and relatives." In either instance the culture pattern limits the sphere of satisfaction which in turn determines the objectives toward which a people will assume an "experimental" attitude. The objectives which will motivate the Chinese to be "experimental" all center around the strengthening of mutual dependence among men, but the objectives which cause Westerners to be "experimental" tend to fall in the sphere of conquest of the physical universe.

[11] The relationship question between scientific modes of thought and magical thinking in human behavior is treated in some detail in F. L. K. Hsu, *Religion, Science and Human Crisis* (London: Routledge, Kegan Paul, 1952). There is a customary tendency to equate the word "experimental" with the word "scientific." This is not quite correct. Being scientific involves clearly defined hypotheses, definite procedures of testing them, and the discarding of the whole works if the hypotheses fail to stand up to the testing. On the other hand, being experimental may not require any clarity or precision in the action taken or the ideas behind them. It may simply be a matter of a person in need of a pair of gloves shopping around for the most suitable pair, or one who desires a loan writing to all relatives until he gets it.

Imagination, science, and economic development. What really distinguishes the West from the East in this regard is the quality, extent, and intensity of Western imagination as contrasted to that of the East. Here we come upon another popular fallacy to the effect that the West is materialistic, while the East is spiritual.[12] But no people is too "otherworldly" to be interested in material things. Anyone who has any first-hand contact with nonindustrial peoples of the East or Africa will realize that, if it comes to bargaining for better material advantage, Chinese or any other allegedly "spiritual" folk are perfectly capable of taking care of themselves. For whether we define spirituality as otherworldliness or an emphasis upon the sight unseen, its most basic ingredient is imagination. Here is where the West has excelled the East in quality and variety, as well as intensity.

Compare Western painting with Chinese or Japanese painting. No one would deny that Oriental masterpieces are great art. But one unmistakable characteristic of the first is its emphasis on emotions, phantasy, and other subjects which are not easily or directly open to the senses, while typical of the latter is its unemotional matter-of-factness and its lack of concern for variation and originality. An Oriental painter could achieve great public acclaim and fame by being known as the best imitator of a well-known master of, say, the fourth century A.D. On the other hand, the play of imagination in Western art has gone to such extremes that many of the modern productions have not without reason been compared with individual dreams or even lunatic whims.

Western literature is equally in contrast to Oriental literature. Nearly all novels in the West dwell in part or whole on the introspective aspects of the characters portrayed. In fact, many such a novel is based on the mental picture of a single individual. These Western literary qualities are as far removed from those of the Orient as are the two poles of the earth. Oriental novels practically never deal with introspection, if with any mental life at all. What they mainly do is to depict man and events entirely in terms of external action.

Art and literature are strong reflections of reality. For the same East-West contrasts are to be found in almost every aspect of life in

---

[12] This was most certainly what the previously mentioned United Nations authors had in mind when they declared that "lack of interest in materials" may also "be due to the prevalence of an otherworldly philosophy which discourages material wants." (*Op. cit.*, p. 13.)

the two worlds, from marriage to religion and from philosophy to politics. Although shortage of space here precludes any extensive documentation of this point, its origin is not far to seek. The Western flair for imagination comes from the loneliness in Western life to which American writers, from James T. Farrell and Thomas Wolfe to Sherwood Anderson and Carson McCullers, have mostly or even wholly devoted their literary talents. The lack of compulsion among Easterners, especially the Chinese, to penetrate the unknown is due to the absence of opportunities for such misery in their midst, a fact made equally clear by writers of their fiction. Loneliness is inevitable where human relationships are but transitory and where each individual is the master of his own success or failure. Conversely, loneliness is practically impossible where the concept of privacy is absent and where even marriage and support are arranged and assured by parents.

However, this Western loneliness, though sometimes terrible in its consequences on the mind of the individual, is the fertile field which has nourished Western imagination, which in turn is the basis of Western science and invention, the most essential ingredients of economic growth of the Western type. What distinguishes the Oriental attitude is not spirituality, but the emphasis on human mutual dependence which, though eliminating loneliness, curtailed imagination, limited scientific interest and achievement, and gave the people no incentive to embark on the unbeaten path. We thus come to a position very different from that which is popularly held; namely, that Western materialistic achievements, instead of being opposed to spirituality, were actually based on a degree of spirituality unknown in the East.[13]

The several factors outlined do not, of course, work singly. They buttress one another to make the differences much greater than they would separately have been. Thus the Chinese culture pattern not only promoted little imagination, but even those who had a flair for imagination found it hard to do what their imagination would lead them to do. Furthermore, even if they were free to follow their imagination, the security in their human relationships would prevent them from entering into such pursuits with an emotional drive, curi-

---

[13] For a fuller exposition of these views, including the connection between spirituality and materialistic achievements, see F. L. K. Hsu, *Americans and Chinese: Two Ways of Life* (New York: Henry Schuman. 1953), Chapter XIV.

osity, and a feeling of urgency and determination—characteristic of industrial empire.

The differing ways of life of the Chinese and Westerners can also directly encourage the growth of capital or make it scarce. Here we hit upon a paradox. On the one hand, the Chinese seem to be among the most frugal peoples in the world. Parents admonish their children to eat every grain of rice in their bowls; neighbors frankly censure one another for signs of extravagance. This emphasis on frugality is even typical of the relatively well-to-do in most villages and small towns. Yet on the other hand, on all ceremonial occasions, the usually frugal Chinese tends to forget his frugality. In his monumental work on Chinese agricultural economy, J. L. Buck shows that many farmers went into debt in order to purchase food and to meet the cost of birthdays, weddings, and funerals. The average cost of a wedding was about four months' net family income, while the customary funeral cost, about three months' net family income.[14]

The reason why the Chinese engages in conspicuous consumption to this extent is that he owes it to others—parents and relatives, friends and fellow townsmen. He has, therefore, little leeway in determining the extent to which he disburses his surplus. And even if he possesses no surplus, he still is forced to engage in conspicuous consumption because the latter is essentially ceremonial in nature, not personal; hence the character and the degree of the individual's expenditures are commanded by his established place in the community. No one expects to raise his class-standing by conspicuous consumption, but to the Chinese dissipated wealth tends to be much less important than disrupted human relationships. Hence, for such purposes, the rich may spend themselves poor, while the relatively poor often do not hesitate to make themselves even poorer.

In indulging in conspicuous consumption the Chinese do not stand alone. Peoples all over the world engage in it in one circumstance or another. But to the individualistic West conspicuous consumption is largely personal and only incidentally ceremonial. It brings prestige to the individual himself, and it is a token of class standing at the moment as well as an index of movement upward. Consequently, he is not only careful about expenditures which do not contribute to this personal sense of triumph but, when necessary,

[14] *Land Utilization in China* (Chicago: University of Chicago Press, 1937), pp. 466 and 468.

also finds it a relatively simple matter to economize. The neighbors may gossip about the fact that he did not take his midwinter trip to the Riviera, that his wife is now assisted by one servant instead of two, or that the daughter's wedding was a rather small affair. But an explanation that business comes before pleasure, that the son's departure for college made two servants unnecessary, or that the doctor advised a quiet wedding because of the wife's well-known nervous condition is usually sufficient to subdue the rumors. Conspicuous consumption in the West need not, therefore, be a drain on accumulated savings if the individual decides that the funds could be used to better advantage elsewhere.

The differing ways of life of the Chinese and Westerners affect the individual in the two societies from birth to death. The contrast is especially sharp at old age. At the threshold of old age the individualistic Westerner is threatened with loss of employment, leading to the loss of economic independence, or at least the likelihood of a lowered standard of living, but has nothing in sight except himself with which to meet these dark problems. His individualism makes dependence upon his children out of the question, and if he is forced to such dependence, it is a matter of extreme shame. On top of this he is further faced with social oblivion. His children, whether single or married, may have drifted away. Even if they are near, he has no important place in their scheme of things. At best he is an object of toleration; at worst he is plainly unwanted.

The result is that the individualistic Westerner must exert all his energy toward security for his old age. Even if there is no danger of poverty and starvation, he must meet the threat of social isolation. Only if he possesses great talents will he enjoy continued importance among his fellowmen. More usually he must compensate for old age by the accumulation of wealth, or by devices such as social security, pensions, and annuities. Shorn of permanent human relationships, he finds wealth one substitute which tends to assure him of a degree of attention.

The mutually dependent Chinese oldster has no such worries. He has no fear of unemployment. Long before he becomes physically incapacitated he has already retired to live thenceforth on the fruits of his youngsters' labor. It is not uncommon to hear a Chinese elder gloat to his friends and relatives, or to anyone who cares to lend an ear, over the fact that he had a hard time when he was able-bodied but that now, since his children are grown and doing well, they have provided him with everything that he has ever wanted. As to his social importance, he gains it by leaps and bounds as the years advance, rather than suffering from its diminution. Since in the normal course of events the majority of human beings are likely to be endowed with male descendants, the Chinese has relatively little pressure to forge ahead continuously, either for the purpose of supporting himself and his wife or for the purpose of insuring a respected place among his fellowmen.

This Chinese and Western difference is faithfully reflected in the individual's relationship with the supernatural. The Chinese worships many gods, and he will frankly ask these gods for specific favors. There is a god of measles whose function is to see that the worshipper or his family will not get measles if he makes the necessary offerings and sacrifices. For similar reasons there is a goddess of fertility, an agricultural god, a god who controls locusts, a god of wealth, a god of literature, and a myriad of others, all of whom function under one supreme ruler of heaven. The Chinese attitude is summarized in such sayings as "We depend upon Heaven for food," or "Heaven and faith will determine the course of events." The individualistic Westerner's God acts quite differently. He loves, He creates, and He rewards and punishes, but characteristically the Western mottoes are "God helps those who help themselves," or "Pray to God and keep your powder dry."

Having his inalienable and psychologically comfortable place among men, and being equipped with supernatural forces on whom he can unashamedly depend, the average Chinese has no need to be perpetually acquisitive toward things, to risk his life by attempting to scale the highest peaks and to fathom the deepest ocean, or to venture into a physical world which may be hostile and unknown. It is in this context that we can understand the Confucian dictum that "When parents are living one does not travel far away." It is in the same context that we can understand why many Chinese willingly engage in conspicuous consumption beyond their economic capacity. Finally, this context also explains such a popular Chinese attitude as "Wealth is treasure of the nation. Every family can keep it only for a period of time. It must be kept circulating." Such a relativistic attitude toward wealth is truly remarkable when we consider the poverty of the Chinese as a whole.

Having but a precarious place among men and being under the tutelage of a God who will not help him unless he exerts himself to the utmost, the average Westerner is compelled to be relentlessly acquisitive toward things, to conquer new worlds, to reach the North Pole, or to fly in the stratosphere. He must do these things in order to assure himself of a degree of security among his fellowmen, for apart from what he can do or can possess there is no other way in which he will be continuously loved or even appreciated. This is why Emerson wrote so glowingly on self-reliance. This is why, although since the Industrial Revolution the West has experienced a material prosperity unknown to the Chinese, the calculating rich, or even the kind of character made immortal by George Eliot's Silas Marner, is much more commonly met in the West than in the East. For to control wealth, whether it be the symbolic money, or wealth-producing tools, such as a factory or corporation, or natural resources, from land to minerals, is the Westerner's chief road to maintaining his importance among his fellowmen—his basic source of self-respect.

Cultural differences within the West. Although the Western culture pattern described thus far applies both to Europe and to America, there are certain observable differences between them.[15] The principal difference between the English way of life and that of the Americans is to be found in the difference between individualism and self-reliance. Basically both concepts are similar. The idea of inalienable right born with each individual is inherent in both; so are the ideas of freedom and equality. But while English individualism was most clearly expressed in terms of political equality and freedom, American self-reliance is intimately tied up with an insistence upon economic and social equality and freedom as well. A qualified individualism and a qualified equality and freedom have prevailed in England, but what has fired the zeal of Americans is a stark self-reliance with its extreme emphasis on complete equality and com-

---

[15] See, e.g., James Bryce, *The American Commonwealth* (2 vols.; New York: The Macmillan Co., 1910); Alexis de Tocqueville, *Democracy in America* (2 vols.; New York: Alfred A. Knopf, 1948); D. W. Brogan, *U.S.A.: An Outline of the Country, Its People and Institutions* (London: Oxford University Press, 1941); Harold Laski, *The American Democracy* (New York: Viking Press, 1948); Geoffrey Gorer, *The American People* (New York: W. W. Norton & Co., 1948); Henry Steele Commager, *The American Mind* (New Haven: Yale University Press, 1950); David Riesman, *The Lonely Crowd* (New Haven: Yale University Press, 1950).

plete freedom brought about in part by the favorable ratio between population and resources. The English therefore tend to take class-based distinctions in wealth, status, manners, and speech as a matter of course, while Americans are inclined to resent them. This is not to say that all Americans enjoy the complete economic and social equality in which they believe, but the important thing is that in American life this complete equality is more firmly insisted upon and given more exuberant expression.

This insistence on complete freedom and equality is helped, in the first place, by the fact that economic opportunities are more abundant in the United States for the average individual than they are in any other country in the world. In addition, the many from-rags-to-riches stories, legendary or true, do stimulate American imagination and vindicate American faith in the reality of unlimited economic future. The emphasis on social equality is even more extensive in the American way of life. In its widest expression it appears as the pattern of informality. Ceremonies become brief; customs and traditions tend to be overrun by considerations of love or convenience. Even the parent-child relationship, that relationship in which every individual learns his cultural beginnings, has no clearly defined pattern. The instability of the marital bond is too well known to need elaboration.

Undoubtedly these are strong statements of attitude which, in fact, must vary somewhat from individual to individual. Exceptions to the described pattern can easily be found. But all social norms are subject to variation from individual to individual. There are many Americans who do not vote, in spite of the fact that it is the pattern for all Americans to vote. There are many Americans who do not go to church, although the over-all importance of religion in the country is undeniable. There are also Americans who deviate from the pattern of monogamy. There are, finally, Americans who refuse to join the armed forces or send their children to school. In each case the deviations or exceptions, instead of destroying the over-all pattern, only serve to highlight it.

Greater stress on the independence from all bonds and traditions unavoidably leads to a greater instability of human relationship and therefore to a stronger sense of insecurity[16] on the part of the individ-

---

[16] To some readers the term "insecurity" will have an unpleasant ring because it sounds abnormal or bad or at least not quite good, just as the term "security" will

ual. The only assurance of security is possession of economic goods. The result is that the European pattern of acquisitiveness, of which R. H. Tawney so ably wrote,[17] has in America reached a new height. Helped by the superabundance of resources in the New World, America has achieved a new kind of production and a physical standard of living the ceiling of which is not yet in sight. This greater aggressiveness toward material gains is a necessary accompaniment of a greater insecurity due to greater instability of human relationships.

DIFFERENTIAL REACTIONS TO EXTERNAL PRESSURES FOR CHANGE

So far we have only dealt with the question of internal impetus to change. We have seen how individualism is the foundation of this impetus and how, when European individualism became American self-reliance, this impetus correspondingly increased in momentum and intensity. From historical and anthropological data, it seems certain that individualism or self-reliance as a way of life is found nowhere except in the West. This fact is undoubtedly the most basic factor underlying the origin of the Industrial Revolution in England and its rapid spread in the other Western countries, as contrasted to its slow adoption in a majority of non-Western nations.

No one who looks at the facts can say that all non-Western peoples are alike; in fact they show a great diversity. But one thing which links most or possibly all of them vis-à-vis the West is their lack of emphasis on inborn and inalienable rights of the individual and in their absence of the ideas of freedom and equality. With few exceptions the individual in these societies is tied to family, neighborhood, clan, community, or other primary groups to a degree not found in the mainstreams of Western life.[18] And since the individual in most of

---

have the reverse connotation. This is unfortunate. The nature of human culture is such that to live like a human being is to feel more or less insecure. Human beings who are completely secure are the dead and buried. Among other creatures that feel completely secure we may include oysters under the sea or worms in a dunghill. It is insecurity that has enabled human beings to achieve the cultural heights (family, religion, government, science, art, literature, economy, etc.) which are characteristic of man. The point of the discussion in this chapter is that the elements of some cultures promote a greater degree of insecurity than those in others, and that this difference can be demonstrably related to differences in economic development between them.

[17] *The Acquisitive Society* (New York: Harcourt, Brace & Co., 1923).
[18] Walter Goldschmidt voices essentially the same view in his article "The Interrelations between Cultural Factors and the Acquisition of New Technical Skills," in Bert F. Hoselitz, editor, *The Progress of Underdeveloped Areas* (Chicago: University of Chicago Press, 1952), pp. 139–140.

these societies normally can assure himself of a degree of importance among his fellowmen he tends, not unnaturally, to have little compulsion to venture out into the wider and more unfamiliar world. In other words, the non-Western peoples, as a whole, lack internal impetus to economic development.

But although most non-Western culture patterns lack internal impetus to economic development, they may nevertheless react differently to external influences making for change through contact, pressure, or conquest. The differing reactions of China and Japan under Western pressure bring out this contrast.

The patterns of life of Chinese and Japanese peoples are similar and, in many ways, even identical. Both peoples enjoy strong family and kinship ties; the majority of both live in small communities; both are strongly influenced by Buddhism; both emphasize similar class differences; both were ruled for many centuries by an aristocracy headed by an emperor; and both value Confucian ethics. But while both peoples came under intensive Western pressure in the nineteenth century (China since 1841 and Japan since 1853), China remained economically miserable, politically helpless, and militarily impotent for a century, whereas Japan became a first-class industrial world power in less than seventy years. The respective histories of some corporations in the two countries are symptomatic of the wider differences. The China Merchant Navigation Company in China started at about the same time as the Nippon Yusen Kaisha in Japan, with no apparent disadvantage in initial capital and equipment. By 1930 the Japanese firm had big steamers sailing all oceans and for some time holding the blue ribbon of the Pacific. The Chinese company, by that time, had dwindled into a concern with little more than a dozen river boats plying the Yangtze. Why did the two peoples, though sharing a similar culture pattern, behave so differently under Western contact?

One obvious difference between them is the existence in Japan of primogeniture, as in England and early America, whereas the Chinese rule has always been equal division of inheritance. This difference probably led to two results. First, primogeniture enabled the Japanese to accumulate capital, so that when Western pressure began, they had more of an economic foundation than the Chinese with which to start industrializing. Second, since primogeniture severed all but the oldest male heir from the family inheritance, it could foster a sort of need on the part of other males to leave home and search for their fortunes elsewhere. This was most certainly the basic reason why Kyoto was the largest city of the entire world c. 1700; the same fact also unquestionably contributed to the labor stability in modern Japanese factories.

Primogeniture, alone, does not explain the Sino-Japanese differences. The effect of Japanese primogeniture on labor supply was by no means as great as it would at first appear. For while the rule gave the oldest male heir the exclusive right to inheritance, the other sons did not have to leave the estate unless they chose to. In the absence of the Western pattern of self-reliance, this choice was possible because those who had in some way to rely upon their oldest brother felt no necessary sense of embarrassment. Even when Japanese left their homes, they looked, not for complete independence, as would their Western brethren, but for wider human ties, after the pattern familiar to them within the families in which they were reared. In fact Westerners, with their self-reliance, would have left home even in the absence of primogeniture. What the Japanese, with their mutual dependence, wish to do away from home is to fortify their ancient traditions even more, and on a wider scale, in order to restore to themselves that satisfaction of which primogeniture deprived them.

The complementary factor in the situation, I think, is to be found in the different ways the Chinese and the Japanese are related to their respective governments. To the Chinese, his primary groups represented by the family, clan, and community are his all. His wider activities toward material gain or political glory are motivated and limited by his relationship with these primary groups. Occasionally a Chinese general or civil official did die to defend the government, thus putting the interests of the wider political allegiance above his allegiance to the primary groups. But as a whole this was rare, and what we see in China for at least the last two thousand years was that the individual sought examination honors or political offices, or engaged in other activities away from the primary groups, chiefly for the purpose of bringing honor, prosperity, and aggrandizement to the family, lineage, clan, and community. Within these primary groups, the community is least important and the clan is a little more so, while the direct lineage or the joint family is most basic to the individual. These primary groups are welded together to varying degrees by ancestor worship. Universally, all Chinese worship their lineal ancestors at least three generations back, if not five. In most parts of the country the Chinese also worship at their clan temples, in which the most honored place is occupied by an ancestor from whom all members of the same clan claim descent. Then, in many scattered areas of China, there exists many communities or villages known as the "Wang family village," or "Chang family village," etc., and inhabited chiefly by descendants of one common ancestor. But outside of these units the Chinese have little feeling of kinship or *esprit de corps* with each other. The Nationalist administration tried for many years to modify this pattern without significant success. The Communists are trying to accomplish what the Nationalists failed to do, and more, but the ultimate consequences of their actions remain to be seen.

The case of Japan is very different. To the Japanese his primary groups such as the family and community are also important. He obeys their commands, and it is his duty to see that they prosper. But the Japanese, because of his need for a wider object of mutual dependence as a result of primogeniture, maintains a relationship with his emperor, and all that the emperor stands for, which is thoroughly unfamiliar to the Chinese. The Japanese emperor, instead of being considered someone outside the primary groups, is actually very intimate with the people. And this intimacy was buttressed from time immemorial by the pattern of Japanese ancestor worship. Like the Chinese, the Japanese worship their lineal ancestors. But unlike the Chinese, the ancestors of Japanese emperors are also worshipped by the common people as their own. It is in this context that we can understand why the Japanese emperor is considered to be the direct descendant of the mythical sun goddess who was also the procreator of the Japanese islands, as well as the Japanese people. No Chinese emperor or dynasty ever even attempted to make such a claim. The Chinese emperor's ancestors were worshipped by the emperor and the emperor's family in a special temple. As far as the Chinese people were concerned, they were like ancestors of another family, to be worshipped only by members of that family.

The extension in Japan of the primary group to include the relationship between the emperor and the people was what, in my view, saved the Japanese government and its modern industrializing efforts from the kind of civil wars and corruption which plagued the Chinese political machinery and ruined Chinese chances for economic modernization. Two kinds of fact seem to support this theory. First, the Japanese beliefs and practices gave the Japanese imperial dynasty a stability which assured it an unbroken rule over the Japanese for at least fifteen hundred or more years, whereas the Chinese pattern of ancestor worship and relationship with the political ruler at least in part explain why no Chinese dynasty ever lasted for more than three or four centuries. The Chinese civil wars during the first half of the twentieth century were simply a modern version of the interdynastic strifes by which China has been periodically disrupted, but from which Japan has always been free. Yet, both the Chinese and the Japanese families have held together under modern pressure and have not been seriously affected by the kind of disintegration characteristic of the West.[19]

Second, since the Japanese government is merely a sort of extended primary group, it is natural that the kind of loyalty characteristic of such groups should have been extended to the relationship between the emperor and his subjects. When the values and controls prevalent in the primary groups are extended to the relationship between the emperor and the subject, bureaucratic corruption should be as rare as corruption in the family and the small community.

Conversely, though it is perfectly conceivable that relatively fewer large estates existed in China than in Japan, because of the absence in the former of the custom of primogeniture, it is clear that this was not why China failed to industrialize rapidly under Western pressure, while Japan did. The Chinese government, like that of the Japanese, invested heavily in many lines of industrial endeavors. In fact modern Chinese industries, from mining and railroads to shipping and armaments, were primarily begun and owned by the government, usually with funds borrowed from foreign powers. The trouble was that these funds soon found their way into private pockets because of nepotism and corruption, while any industry and commerce located outside the foreign concessions was soon reduced to naught by civil wars. The reason is not obscure. Since the Chinese government, unlike that of the Japanese, is outside the primary

[19] There have been many unfounded statements as to how revolutionary were the changes which came upon the Chinese family. On closer scrutiny it becomes clear that such statements are usually no more than projections of Western conditions into the East. See Hsu, review of Marion J. Levy, Jr.'s *The Family Revolution in Modern China*, in *Scientific Monthly*, Vol. LXXI, No. 4 (October, 1950), pp. 279–280, and again in Vol. LXXII, No. 3 (March, 1951), pp. 201–203.

groups, it becomes a fair target for the loyalists to the family and community, who must enrich the latter at the expense of the former. The truth of the last observation is especially borne out by the fact that Chinese business houses, usually governed by the same factors of loyalty characteristic of the primary groups, have never been troubled by the kind of corruption traditionally synonymous with Chinese bureaucracy.[20] For what made the Chinese connive or engage in corruption in government was their negative attitude toward their ruler and his regime, but what prevented them from taking a like view toward their private businesses was their positive relationship with such businesses, which they considered their own, or which were owned and run by people whom they considered their own, or in which misbehavior would cost them the loss of their respected places in their all-important primary groups.

The customs of primogeniture and a primary-group-type relationship between the state and the people were among the most basic reasons why the Japanese met the industrial challenge of the West extremely well, while the Chinese proceeded but little in that direction. However, for these very reasons, the Japanese industrial structure was built on a foundation very different from that of the West: in the West, it was built on individualism and free enterprise; in Japan, on the same feudal system which bound the society for centuries.[21]

---

[20] For a detailed discussion of the contrasts between Chinese government and Chinese business, and the reasons for them, see Hsu, *Under the Ancestors' Shadow* (New York: Columbia University Press, 1948), pp. 226–228.

[21] Elsewhere I have taken up some of the points raised by F. S. C. Northrop in his *The Meeting of East and West* (New York: The Macmillan Co., 1946); see Hsu, *Americans and Chinese*, Chapters VIII and XIV. Here it will be sufficient to point out that Northrop was right in stating (p. 419) that the "Japanese were the only Oriental people to become a nation of the Western type quickly." In fact he could have rightly extended his statement and said the Japanese were the only non-Western people succeeding so well. He was even right in attributing (p. 420) this phenomenal success partly to the existence in Japan of a "feudal, hierarchic medieval society with its Emperor and privileged select orders." But he was in error in giving a major credit to Japanese Shintoism, that conglomeration of old Japanese beliefs, which he erroneously compared with monotheistic religions of the West; but he gave no credit to Japanese ancestor worship, which is the link between the Japanese emperor and his people, a link that the Chinese ruler and his subjects lacked. Northrop seems to have failed to see that neither Japan's modern political state nor her modern economic development was rooted in the same basic psycho-cultural forces which propelled Western nationalism and industrial revolution.

ECONOMIC DEVELOPMENT: GENUINE AND SPURIOUS

The foregoing pages show that industrialization can come about as a result of forces within a society, which motivate it to push toward a higher standard of living, or of pressures outside the society, which more or less compel it to acquire a greater acquisitiveness. In the former situation, individual initiative is essential. In the latter situation, at least in Japan, individual initiative, founded on primogeniture and loyalty to the emperor patterned after primary-group relationships, is basic.

But some readers must have looked in vain throughout the foregoing for detailed discussions similar to those now under way on ways and means for fitting certain new techniques, from the power plow to modernized dairying, into the existing cultural framework of the industrially backward peoples. This was no oversight. Piecemeal introduction of a given new technique may be successful here and there, in one connection or another, but without the fundamental forces which propel changes (of which the economic change is one variety) as a whole, such innovations are not likely to take root. They may even fail to last for long, much less to grow from there.

The point becomes clearer when we realize that most of the previously existing habits, customs, values, and even technical tools or skills of all nonindustrialized societies must be considered hindrances to industrialization. From this point of view, preindustrial Europe was as handicapped as the rest of the world. In fact most of the European hindrances were even identical with those prevailing elsewhere. Europe had much conspicuous consumption in the Chinese style; it had known much hoarding in caches because banks were unknown; its poverty was extensive, and the poor suffered much in the hands of usurers; and it was a feudal society in which the peasantry was tied to the land and to its seigneurs. Contrary to popular misconceptions the European labor force at first reacted to machinery and factory in very much the same negative way that European entrepreneurs have subsequently encountered in Africa and Asia.[22] The literacy rate was very low, for public schools were unknown. As to beliefs in the supernatural, they were deeply involved with witchcraft, with folk beliefs, such as that the sowing of seeds should be done at new moon, and

---

[22] English manufacturers, visiting continental countries toward the end of the eighteenth century, thought German and Italian laborers unfit for industrialization.

with the doctrine of predestination, as in Calvinism, which is not basically different from that which the Chinese believed up to the time of their contact with the West. Furthermore, Europe even had for a long time a guild system similar to that of the Chinese. And most Europeans at the time of the outbreak of the Industrial Revolution lived, like the Chinese much later, in villages or small towns in which primary face-to-face relations were essential.

The fact is, however, that the Industrial Revolution began and flourished in Europe *in spite* of these and many other hindrances to economic development, but it has so far failed to take firm root in any non-Western country except Japan, in spite of Western pressure, example, encouragement, and leadership. How plainly industrialization failed to take root in Southeast Asia is emphatically stated by Hubertus J. Van Mook:

> The age-long influence of the West . . . failed, with only few exceptions, to instill its economic activity and enterprise into the minds and habits of these peoples. The Western apparatus of finance, commerce, and production remained an alien, undigested and indigestible element in Southeast Asia. It had created institutions, means of production and communication and a stability far beyond the achievements of the past, but it had hardly awakened a new economic initiative or industry. . . . The social solidarity, the public spirit, and the economic energy that were necessary for a vigorous resurgence were lacking.

Samuel P. Hayes, Jr., who quotes the above, rightly points out that "This is true of much of South Asia, Latin America, and the Near East as well (with some notable exceptions) . . . ," but he fails to go any further with it, being content with the vague statement that "all these attitudes (which have prevented a new economic initiative) may turn out to be logical deductions from historical experience and existing institutions, or they may be habits carried over from previous eras, or they may be rooted in projective systems involving personal anxiety feelings." [23] The fact is that since economic development of the industrial kind was not prevented in Europe by the many hindrances which also are present in the non-Western world today, we shall fall far short of our objective if we continue to dwell on these apparent "hindrances" and ignore fundamentals. Our analysis of the fundamentals leads us to the inevitable conclusion that the pri-

[23] "Personality and Culture Problems of Point IV," in Bert F. Hoselitz, editor, *op. cit.*, pp. 215–216.

mary force of industrial development is the human need for conquest of nature in order to compensate for insecurity among men. In the absence of an internal impetus in its complete Western form, the next best cultural foundation for industrialization would seem to be that of the Japanese. Here the pattern of mutual dependence and a certain insecurity due to primogeniture joined forces to extend unity of kinship to the relationship between the state and its subjects. The result is a culture pattern that, though failing in the first place to develop internal impetus on its own, responded adequately (certainly as far as economic development was concerned) to external pressures from the West.

The industrialization of the West and of Japan gives us what may be termed genuine economic development, which will, once set in motion, propel itself regardless of the external circumstances. Therefore, we are inevitably led to the conclusion that insecurity born of Western individualism is the best nourishment for that acquisitive spirit toward the physical universe which makes genuine economic development possible. A secondary insecurity, like that arising in Japan out of primogeniture, together with a pattern of mutual dependence between the state and its subjects, helps to sustain the economic development once the impetus is applied from outside. Short of these types of cultural situations, the best which can be achieved under tutorship and aid from without would seem to be a sort of spurious economic growth. This is a kind of development which owes not only its inception, but also its implementation, wholly or primarily to a foreign power or regent.

Spurious economic development through implementation by a foreign power is exemplified by that which prevailed in colonial India, partially noted in Chapter XII. Spurious economic development through the rigid control of a single individual is best shown by the present condition of Bahrein, a tiny oil-rich archipelago in the Persian Gulf, off the coast of Saudi Arabia. An American reporter states that twenty-five years ago the sheikdom was infested with disease and was poverty-ridden and terribly ill-governed. Today, after a quarter of a century of able direction by an Englishman, but with no outside economic help, the country is healthy, prosperous, and peaceful —a paradise in the Middle East.[24] This phenomenal success was not

[24] See James Bell, "He Said Forward! to the Backward," *Life*, XXXIII (November 17, 1952), pp. 156–174. The British Information Service at New York City,

simply due to the fact that Bahrein is favorably located as a transshipping point amidst the oil and pearl riches on both sides of the Persian Gulf, or because Bahrein has oil resources attractive to foreign companies. The English regent wields unquestioned dictatorial powers, and he provides what he considers good for the Bahreinians, such as schools, hospitals, and modern conveniences. He prevents what he considers not good for them, such as anti-Semitism, and he censors their only press. There is no indication of any rising Bahreinian economic, or even political, initiative.[25]

The role of the strong man. This does not mean, however, that all non-Western peoples, in order to achieve self-sustaining economic development, must necessarily also develop either a Western type of individualistic competitive system with economic reward as the basic incentive, the Japanese type of feudal structure centered in loyalty to the emperor, or continued foreign colonial control or tutelage. Industrial psychologists have found that economic reward, even in the West, must at least be partially supplemented by other incentives. For instance, American industries are advised to promote the factory as a "family" and reward workers in part with stock instead of cash. In any event, both the Western and the Japanese types of social organization are the end results of centuries of tradition which cannot be achieved in relatively short order, while colonialism or foreign regency is everywhere in disfavor. In their places, and as a matter of expediency, some type of dictatorship by a native strong man or an oligarchy appears to be unavoidable as an instrument to economic development. What peoples living under dictators or despots lack in individual initiative, the state compensates for by resolute leadership. What they lack in private capital formation, the state provides through revenue or foreign loans. What they lack in incentive to

---

after looking over this article, informed me that, "In general, the facts related appear to be correct," although it was "unable . . . to establish its accuracy in detail."

[25] It is not without interest that, in the *Life* magazine report, only the pictures of two "prominent" Bahreinians appeared beside one of the sheik: a director of boys' schools and an accountant in charge of the government bookkeeping system. There may be some Bahreinians who figure aggressively in their country's economic and political life, but this is not clear from the magazine article referred to. From what I know, this kind of spurious economic development also characterizes most of Bahrein's bigger neighbors—notably Saudi Arabia.

work, the state helps to supply by indoctrination of new values or reorientation of old ones. What they lack in efficiency, the state makes up by strict control and planning.

The principal drawback is that the dictator or the despot or his advisors may not be interested in economic development and may retard it. Take, for example, the differences in economic development between two princely states in India: the prosperity of Mysore in the south and the poverty of Patiala in the northwest seem to be largely attributable to the differences in their respective rulers. Should a dictator and his cohorts decide to act rashly, they may lead their followers to quick disaster. For example, the fates of Germany and Italy might very well have been quite different if Hitler had been less impetuous and Mussolini more far-sighted. Lacking the necessary socio-cultural foundation for genuine economic development, peoples who have made economic gains under foreign colonialism or native dictatorship will have little assurance that the trend is permanent.

This conclusion seems to cast a dark shadow over the future of the Point Four type of program. It appears to show that, at best, such a program will lead to economic developments of the spurious, and therefore transitory, kind while its usual results are much less impressive. Such pessimism is ultimately unwarranted. Spurious and genuine economic developments are not antagonistic. A Point Four program, well organized and adequately directed, may well lead many industrially backward peoples from spurious to genuine economic advances. As we observed previously, human beings are remarkably plastic. If the Western acquisitive spirit was a result of cultural conditioning and not of biological heredity, then all peoples can, at least theoretically, be conditioned likewise.[26] The failure of the peoples of the South Seas and elsewhere to develop an aggressive spirit of enterprise in spite of intensive Western pressure may be partly due to the fact that under the yoke of colonialism the natives were deprived of the necessary incentives and conditions for such a development. Now that colonialism is on its way out, at least in Asia, we may possibly expect the picture in the next century to be different.

[26] The fallacy of overzealousness toward non-Western culture patterns and consequently of regarding them as being rigid and totally resistant to Western technology has been pointed out by Walter R. Goldschmidt in "The Interrelations between Cultural Factors and the Acquisition of New Technical Skills" in Bert F. Hoselitz, editor, *op. cit.*, p. 150.

Strong man: East and West. There are, however, two important things to be noted. First, of course, not all dictators act alike. Western dictators, reflecting the individualistic tendencies of their peoples, are more inclined toward aggressive economic policies. Their Moslem or Eastern counterparts, in line with the relative lack of such tendencies among their subjects, are more likely to settle for the *status quo*, unless they are under Western pressure and are convinced that their very existence or that of their subjects is endangered.

The second thing is even more crucial. The strong man in an individualistic country will not only tend to make aggressive designs, but he will have a stronger hold on his people than his counterparts in countries where the pattern is one of mutual dependence, or at least nonindividualistic. As has already been indicated, the more individualistic the way of life, the greater the individual's insecurity. When human beings are threatened with insecurity, they will try to fortify themselves with more human bonds or hope to buttress their human bonds with material acquisition. Conversely, where human beings find their places in their primary groups satisfying and inalienable, because of their pattern of mutual dependence, they will have little need for wider entanglements and little or no compulsion to improve their ancestral standards of living.

We have seen how the effect of this difference in human relations was at the roots of the separate Chinese and Western economic developments. What we must now demonstrate is that the secure human relationships of the Chinese and the insecure human relationships of the Westerners mean that the hero, or the "great man," possesses wholly different powers among the two peoples. In the West, insecure human relations will spur the majority to look for more permanent anchorages in the wider human society. A hero, or a "great man," at least partially fulfills this basic emotional need. Accordingly, Western heroes are ardently supported by many (just as they may be vigorously hated by many others), are showered with flowers, confetti, and kisses, have volunteers working for them, and must make many personal appearances before the public to renew their rapport with them. Their pictures are everywhere. Their relationship with their followers is a positive and personalized one: the followers look to them for leadership in practically everything. If the heroes smoke a *Camel*, their more devoted followers are likely to favor no other brand. If the heroes pronounce the Jews objectionable, their fol-

lowers are likely to add force to anti-Semitism. If the heroes champion Christianity, their followers will take up the Cross. It is not suggested that such a hero will be able to make his followers do all the
things he wants them to do, even totally contrary to their wishes.
But there is little doubt that he will be able to wield great power
among his followers.

The Chinese, because of their secure primary groups, have little
emotional need to become involved in the wider society. Consequently, between the Chinese heroes or great men and the common
people there is always a deep status barrier symbolized by residences
fenced in by high walls, numerous bodyguards, enclosed sedan
chairs, and absence of any personal contacts with the people, whether
in private audiences or meetings. The higher the rank and the
prestige, the more such barriers and distinction. Before the Revolution of 1911, the emperor and high officials were never to be seen
by the people. Possession by any of his subjects of a personal like-
ness of the emperor was tantamount to treason. His name was never
to be pronounced or written by the common people. Sometimes,
somewhere, some great local official was such an object of gratitude by the local people that, upon his departure, the people turned
out en masse to see him off. The stories, some legendary and some
true, would have it that sometimes the people, old and young, even
wept to express their loss of him. But, significantly, the followers, if
such they were, were never intimate with their hero or great man.
They showed such signs of welcome or farewell because he, as a great
man way above them, had been able to do things beneficial to them,
the common people. After he left they might even build a special
temple to house his effigy, to be worshipped year after year with in-
cense, candles, and food offerings; however, the relationship was
never a positive emotional tie, but merely a passive liaison in which
status difference took the place of personal intimacy. The hero or the
great man exercised his superior abilities and powers in behalf of
the common people and they, as his subordinates and dependents
with much less to offer, were duly grateful. They would not aspire to
what he had done or was going to do.[27]

---

[27] This Chinese pattern of hero worship has not changed materially in modern
times. There have, however, been some superficial signs of Western ways of hero
worship. For example, prior to World War II, portraits of Chiang and Sun hung
everywhere. Their names graced many boulevards and parks. Chiang made many

All these facts serve to emphasize that, while a strong man in a non-Western country and a strong man in the West may share certain superficial similarities and fulfill some identical roles, their respective influences over their followers tend to be drastically different. If this analysis is at all correct, a Western dictator will be able to mobilize his followers for good or for evil, for economic or political pursuits, much more easily than his counterparts elsewhere. This fact has obvious, important implications for China's future development, economic and otherwise, under the Communist regime.

The one over-all conclusion which may be drawn from this analysis is that, though the breach between spurious and genuine economic development may be shortened by outside aid, it seems safe to assume that this shortening process can be more easily and more rapidly accomplished in most underdeveloped Western countries, from Greece to Mexico, than in most underdeveloped Eastern countries, which share a common way of life with China, from Korea, Indochina, Burma, Thailand, and Malaya to, possibly, Indonesia. India and the Middle East, by physical traits and cultural characteristics, are not Oriental, although often the Middle East, and India, always, are erroneously defined as such. Nor are they entirely Western. Japan, on the other hand, is thoroughly Oriental. But because Japan was the only non-Western nation which became as aggressive as the West, some Western characteristics which she does not possess were attributed to her. Besides the kind of error which Northrop made, the Japanese government before World War II was usually termed a dictatorship. This view received a special boost because Japan was allied first with Russia and then with Germany and Italy. But the Japanese government was never a dictatorship in the Western sense of the word, either militarily or politically speaking. The basis of Japan's success vis-à-vis the West in modern times was due, as we have seen before, to her culture pattern of a solidarity of kinship extended to embrace loyalty to the dynastic state. Japan shows little of the Western type of hero worship. The Japanese reverence to their emperor is much closer to that of the Chinese, previously described.

personal appearances. But these external changes did not alter the essential relationship between the Chinese and their leaders because of lack of a strong psychological identification. The result was that, when it was clear that the Nationalist forces were losing out to the Communists, most of his onetime supporters went over to the other side with great haste. See Hsu, *Americans and Chinese*, Chapter VI.

No single Japanese, from Prince Ito to some of the most powerful generals, ever came even close to the kind of public acclaim, personal distinction, or dictatorial powers which Mussolini and Hitler had in their respective countries. The most that can be said is that Japan, before World War II, was under a sort of "dictatorship" by the military as a whole, in which, however, the lower echelons had as much "pull" as their superiors, which latter were often presented by the former with *faits accomplis* and had no alternative but to support the action of their subordinates. Furthermore, the whole military "dictatorship" was at least theoretically subject to the wishes of the emperor, even though the latter, by tradition, did not often exercise his prerogatives. The result of this pattern of mutually dependent relationships was that no one felt completely free to act. Even if an individual acted on his own, he might have to commit *hari-kiri* as a means of escaping the dilemma between individual wishes and the mandate of the society. No one was exempt from this dilemma. Japan's colossal economic development before World War II was, therefore, not the result of action by one or two strong men, but was rooted in the many features of the Japanese culture pattern outlined previously. For this very reason, we have even less rational basis for hoping to arrest Japanese aggression by eliminating a few so-called war criminals than we would for altering the future course of German aspiration.

CHANGING THE CULTURE

The thesis that has run through the foregoing pages is that economic development has, historically, been inseparable from a high degree of individual insecurity. We must now examine how this condition may be brought about in underdeveloped areas where it is absent.[28]

Anyone concerned with the question of implementing any kind of aid program to underdeveloped societies which will promote a rapid and self-perpetuating economic growth must face the facts. In the capitalist societies, individual insecurity is based on individualism and primogeniture, which weaken the primary human relationships. In the hope of compensating for this insecurity, the individual fortifies himself with economic goods, or the symbols of their possession. Under the circumstances, economic development is not only self-

[28] I am much indebted to Harold F. Williamson and John A. Buttrick for their stimulating comments while this section was being completed.

perpetuating, but tends to gain momentum because the individual has to "keep moving in order to stand still."

As a way of promoting conditions necessary for economic growth in non-Western societies, this is impractical. It took Europe ten centuries or more to produce an individualistic orientation of life which bore economic fruit two hundred years ago, and there does not seem to be any way in which a similar orientation could be generated in a matter of years, or even decades. Yet in the modern world, any nation which hopes to take several centuries to evolve its orientation undisturbed is simply unrealistic. Moreover, any society which has not had primogeniture will find attempts at quickly instituting it resulting either in apathy or revolt.

The Communists have demonstrated an alternative method of inducing insecurity, which has underlined their industrial successes, at least up to the present. The key of Soviet economic successes is also insecurity of the individual. In place of primogeniture, they have instituted collectivism and nationalization. In place of individualism, they have maintained a secret police and a system of mutual watchfulness which enable few, if any, to be entirely certain of self or place in the scheme of things. The result is, if we overlook certain differences and examine instead the basic mechanism upon which the society works, an economic development which is impressive both in speed and in scale, at the expense of the individual who also has to "keep moving in order to stand still."

There are serious difficulties in using this model to promote economic development. Popular misconception notwithstanding, the Soviet program has been carried out within a culture that is essentially Western in character. It was part of the Russian tradition for the individual to identify himself with the state or a wider group than the family, to exuberate in religious and missionary zeal, and to regard persecution as inherent in the order of society. It is reasonable to doubt whether the same model will work as effectively or as quickly in societies where these and similar characteristics are absent. At the same time it should be noted that, among the Chinese cultural factors favoring a considerable degree of economic development under the Communist rule, at least in the near future, we must name two that are quite opposite to those operative in Russia: (a) a lack of direct opposition to, and indeed a traditional expectation of, state control or at least direction in many matters; and (b) the need for a strong government which stabilizes the currency and protects industries and commerce from strangulating interferences by the ravages of the military, the irregularities of bureaucracy, and the competition of foreign powers under unequal treaties. In addition to these two factors, we must note a third which is similar to that found in Russia and the rest of the West, at least in effect. World War II has further shaken the family and communal structures among increasingly large numbers of the Chinese population—a process already under way through a century of Western impact. The firm hands of the Communist regime have now come in to accelerate the process yet, at the same time, encounter the yearning of the individual for mutual dependence. The state gives direction, absorbs losses, and shares profits and glory with the individual in a manner reminiscent of that which previously existed between him and the primary groups. Moreover the state, however stable, is bound to be impersonal because of its size and complexity. This, together with secret police, brain washing, and introduction of new systems of competition, cannot but generate a good deal of individual insecurity—that quality which has aided economic growth in other lands. These forces may not precipitate an industrial revolution of the magnitude of those in Soviet Russia or the capitalist West, but they may result in enough economic growth to give the country a new look. Even if this model should work with a considerable degree of success in non-Western societies, such as China, the cost in violence, misery, and social upheaval would be great. By its own admission, the Chinese Communist regime has caused the liquidation of millions of human beings. Furthermore, it is hardly conceivable that any government inviting foreign economic aid will do so with the express purpose of overthrowing itself—invariably the central step counted upon in the Communist formula.

There is a third way of engendering the necessary cultural conditions for economic development which involves neither the long historical processes of capitalistic free enterprise nor the negation of the individual characteristic of the Communist planned society. This comes somewhere between the two extremes. The insecurity necessary for economic growth will be generated by a system combining state control with individual initiative.

More specifically, we must assume at the outset that most of the people in the society which we hope to change are not hostile to the program and that such society has a government which is more or less stable—whether it be a somewhat democratic organization, or one under the thumb of a single strong man, or an oligarchy. Given these conditions, it should be possible to introduce a development program which starts with a project that fulfills some long-felt need, such as a dam, an irrigation scheme, well-digging, a factory, or road-building. From past experiences in the East, and more recently in South America, we know that such a project, with its promise of monetary reward and a chance of obtaining a mode of existence that is somewhat more comfortable than before, will usually succeed in attracting a native labor force, even though the condition of the latter may not be all that is desired according to Western standards.[29] However, it will be a labor force, and it will be subject to gradual education and influence toward the improvement of its permanence and efficiency.

The next problem to be tackled is that this initial attraction to the laborers, who will naturally have come from the bottom of the social ladder, will also be attractive to those who are much better off. Here the government will do well to initiate a mild inflation, say of ten or fifteen per cent. Inflation will cause hardship to the middle classes, especially the higher-leveled wage-earners and most salaried people. A mild inflation will push many of the fixed-income, white-collared workers into trading and other entrepreneurial activities. It must be

[29] Those who know something about the South African Union may contradict this statement. It is to be recalled that European entrepreneurs had at first little success in getting Africans to work in the factories and mines, and that, at one time or another, the Africans had to be forced to accept such work by means of the head or hut tax or other arbitrary methods. The African situation seems to me to be due to two factors, neither of which applies to the Orient or to South America today. First, when the European entrepreneurs went to work in South Africa, it was at a time when Western products and the physical comforts that they entailed were not generally known. Today, throughout all my travels in the East, I do not know of any villager who is not fascinated or attracted by some Western inventions. Second, South African natives live in a world such that their oppression by the Europeans becomes so much more obvious under active contact in factories and mines than in their own home reserves that they simply have been reluctant to subject themselves to such greater discomfort. That the latter is not imaginary is shown by the fact that some South African industrialists have reportedly been bothered by many native workers tending to forget everything they learned in several years, after a brief stay back in the reserves. The people who observed such difficulties have been attributing this to the native diet and have been looking for remedies therein. But a simpler explanation is probably that human beings tend to forget what they least want to remember.

noted in this connection that the inflation must be mild and not a runaway one. In the latter case, people would simply become panicky and not seek to enter relatively permanent forms of enterprise. On the other hand, inflation by itself cannot generate increasing economic development. If nothing is done beyond a mild inflation, a society of peddlers (to use an extreme metaphor) may be the result.

The next step is to revise the tax structure to favor those who move vertically or horizontally. The one may be instrumental to the other, but at any rate both are calculated as expressions of the individual's dissatisfaction with the *status quo* and his desire to improve himself. Vertical movement may mean climbing the wage ladder or improvement of one's position by a change, say, from being a technician to a manager of some sort. Horizontal movement may include going from the traditionally sanctioned occupations to newly introduced ones, as well as leaving the ancient homesteads and venturing into new frontiers, either for the exploitation of the land or for the utilization of new resources.

The revision of the tax structure or the institution of new tax measures must not be too drastic, so as to avoid the possibility of a revolt or a revolution. The eventual aim of such measures may be to strengthen primogeniture in inheritance, but this will take a long time and must be done gradually. While these measures are under way, the existing system of rewards by honors must be revised so as to add attractions to new forms of incentive. The change would be aimed at introducing new varieties of achievements as objects of reward, rather than new forms of the reward. That is to say, if the government has been giving medals to those who rear big families, it may be advisable to give similar recognition to those who have produced most in the factories. Or if the government has been conferring honorary doctorates upon individuals for filial piety, let it also confer similar honors on those who have conquered especially knotty problems in the new frontier.

There is no question but that such honors will provide effective incentives. America uses this form of reward a great deal, especially in war, while Soviet Russia has extended its use to a much broader area of human activity, especially to that of production. The major precaution that a government which hopes to use honor as a means of increasing incentive to work must take is that the honor thus conferred must be meaningful with reference to traditional aspirations, and that the number of recipients of such honor at any given point of time must not be so numerous as to render it worthless.

Along with these developments there needs to be an increase in consumer goods to meet the newly acquired wealth. At any rate, as the initial industrial project gets under way, some new goods will be produced locally. The government must see to it that some goods are imported which are not produced locally. Money, without increased consumer goods, will not only cause more inflation than desirable, but may also cause a loss of continued interest in the new developments on the part of the native population. It is not expected that the level of consumption in such a society will be as high as that in the United States, or even that all of the results of growth will be available in the form of products immediately available for consumption. Capital has to be provided if there is to be further expansion in the economy. Therefore, honor and other considerations must take a part of the place of the demand and enjoyment for goods, at least in the initial stages of the experiment.

Thus far, education has not been mentioned as a means of furthering economic development. The omission has not been due to any oversight. Education, as such, cannot be of much help in promoting economic development unless the process is already under way and people have reason to accept its utility. As the previously mentioned measures begin to take shape, a system of formal education, both of the liberal and the technical kinds, will help to turn out new leaders and new technicians for the society's economy. Furthermore, as the economy develops, there will be indigenous means to finance the new education. An educational program started with foreign aid before there is any sign of economic development will lack the foundation for its continuation and also run the risk of being opposed later by the natives as an alien effort designed to indoctrinate supporters for foreign interests.

This middle-of-the-way program, though possessing certain advantages over both the capitalist and the Communist routes to economic development, is not without its own complications. For this reason, those who think of a Point Four type program as a form of magic which will change an entire economy without much effort are unrealistic, but those who expect its effects to be limited to the economy alone, and to be wholly in the desired direction, may be greatly surprised. For example, the new developments as outlined above could well play into the hands of an indigenous dictator who would use them to further his own ends, to oppress his people even more than before, or to use his newly acquired economic strength to further his own aggressive ambition on weaker neighbors. In this way, a society that formerly presented a negative threat to world stability by its poverty and misery may have afterwards turned into a positive threat by its aggressive nationalism, backed up by its newly found economic and, possibly, military strength.

Or the aid program may lead to the overthrow of the strong man or to an active revolution of some kind. It may be that the changes in custom, religion, and other beliefs necessary for economic development are unpalatable to a majority of the people. Positive steps to reduce the rate of population growth, the curbing of ceremonial spending, or the modification of property rights may represent costs too great to accept. It is possible, of course, that the overthrown strong man will be replaced by another or by a new governing body more favorable to world stability. The trouble is that no such assurances can be made. Similarly, a revolution may move in a direction more congenial to the recognition of the importance of more individual liberty and to orderly internal adjustment. Again the trouble is that no such eventuality can be guaranteed. Here another complicating factor must never be lost sight of.

The United States, for example, is actively carrying out a Point Four program in industrially backward societies, many of which have shown signs of leaning toward Communist Russia. It is absurd to assume that the Soviets will do nothing in return. Every intelligence has its counterintelligence, and every weapon its counterweapon. It is highly unrealistic and foolish for the West to assume that there is no Soviet counterweapon to any Point Four program.

We thus must realize that any foreign aid program is no small venture to be carried out with petty cash, that it takes more than a spark plug to build a machine. If aid is carried through well, adequately and wisely, it *may* bring desirable results both to the givers and to the recipients. If aid is carried out badly or inadequately, it can lead to consequences that are much worse than if there had been no aid at all. Or the latter eventuality may result from circumstances beyond control.

Once economic development gets under way, however, and as people eat and live better than before, they may have less desire for revolt or revolution. Or the threat of revolt or revolution may serve as effective checks against any dictator or oligarch too bent on aggrandizing himself. Strong men in every country need not be egotists or megalomaniacs; they may be altruistically inclined. Jawaharlal Nehru of India and Kemal Atatürk of Turkey are two outstanding altruistic leaders who will go down in history as individuals who placed their respective people's interests above those of themselves. There is little doubt that an aid program under the leadership of this type of man will have a good chance of success.

A feasible aid program should probably aim at a moderate level of economic development, in all or in a majority of the industrially backward regions, to a level higher than those prevailing in the East and in Africa, but not as high as those found in more advanced nations of the West. But even this moderate aim will require a program much more extensive, and prolonged over a much longer period of time, than most politicians, scholars, and average citizens currently envisage. To make such a program work toward desirable ends, furthermore, Americans and Europeans alike must abandon their feeling and obvious attitude of superiority toward the rest of the world. A century ago such a feeling and attitude probably would have aroused little antagonism, because the world was in much less close contact and because Western ideas of equality and freedom had much less meaning to a majority of the non-Western peoples. Unfortunately, as the demand for universal equality and freedom increased, Western conviction of its superiority seems to have increased. This attitude can only alienate the peoples whom Westerners have helped or hope to help. Neither the magnitude of the task nor the difficulty of psychological reorientation should blind us to the stakes involved. To the extent that the present tensions of human existence, in which strife and bloodshed are part of the everyday picture, can be relieved by economic development it will be more than worth the cost.

Concluding Thoughts

The present problems of the underdeveloped areas are certainly primarily economic in form if not in source. That is, social-cultural attitudes have resulted in little or no material development. A broadened and enlarged development program which looks toward, not only an immediate increase in standards of living, but toward developing attitudes which will sustain this development after the external aid is withdrawn, will surely be worth while. It will be worth while too in that it will provide an outlet for energies and talents in the West which are either blocked at present or may soon be. But if we think the opening of these new frontiers is a final answer for all concerned, we may be doomed to disappointment. We may find that a not far distant future contains new problems, tensions, and crises in no small measure attributable to the very success any large-scale aid program might achieve.

What we need to realize is that economic development alone will fail to solve the world's problems, and, if pursued for its own sake, will certainly multiply them. For in spite of their impressive economic development and their enjoyment of a standard of living that mankind has never seen before, Western nations are today plagued with more terrible problems than ever. The characteristic social-cultural attitudes which have enabled Westerners to work so zealously to reach their present economic heights are at the same time generating new discontents and fresh demands for greater and better satisfaction. Such discontents and demands as a whole cannot be met except by unlimited economic expansion. In a world of limited resources (whether we take the conservative or the liberal estimates), unlimited expansion is certainly not the permanent road to general prosperity and peace.

The success of development programs depend upon how well we succeed in placing them in their proper context: We must have such programs to raise the level of material welfare of the economically *underdeveloped* non-Western world, so that the immediate discontent due to poverty, disease, and starvation will not serve the cause of totalitarianism. But what we need even more is perhaps another but different kind of aid programs to strengthen the human ties in the economically *overdeveloped* Western world, so that the restless individualism, insecurity, and competitiveness will not drive mankind to impossible economic demands and ultimate destruction.

CHAPTER X

The Role of Government

HERMAN FINER*

The Economic and the Political

ECONOMIC DEVELOPMENT MAY BE CONTEMPLATED FROM EITHER OF two standpoints. Economic institutions, in themselves, freely established and run by individuals and groups—voluntary associations—may be thought of as logically distinct from the state. Alternatively one may start with the state and look at the factors in *its* economic development. But, whichever approach is adopted, the state (that is, government) is assigned a role.

It is necessary to formulate the nature of government, and then to define economic institutions, in order that the role of the latter may be concretely sketched.

Government is the agent of society, politically organized. Society is composed of the spontaneously arising groupings of men for purposes that they consider worth pursuing. The values men seek are numerous and of the greatest variety: support of the United Nations, the production of aluminum, the enjoyment of nudity, the collection of coins, dancing, dramatics, education, religion. These values are not purely intellectual—the groupings are *will*-organizations; that is, they drive to secure their values, either by getting allies to defend them from enemies or by making other people conform to behavior like that of their own members.

Such societies make up the whole of society, which we may now limit to the nation, though for some purposes, particularly economic development, the whole world may be viewed as one society. The nation is the society which embraces all the lesser societies within the

* Professor of Political Science, University of Chicago. Author: *Theory and Practice of Modern Government; America's Destiny; Road to Reaction; T .V. A.: Lessons for International Applications.*

frontiers as settled by international law[1]—or as some have said, within any one customs barrier!

In a long process, lasting over thousands of years, families, groups, clans, tribes, cities, and principalities have arisen, developed, died down, coalesced, fought, and migrated. Ideas of truth, beauty, wisdom, science, and worship have developed, originated by prophets and teachers and spread by their followers. A hierarchy of values has emerged in the nations—something like a national *conscience*—to insure order, justice, and the enduring unity of the whole society against external aggression and to minimize violence within. This general spirit of interpersonal behavior is partly economic, but it is also noneconomic (that is, religious) in its ethics. Nations are marked by their different emphases on the militaristic, the aristocratic, the theocratic, or the democratic, and the consequent character affects the importance attached to economic development and the possibilities of its progress.

The pattern of values forming a system, in which some are given high place and others lesser rank, necessitates the establishment of authority, since all people cannot have their own way in everything, completely without conflict and force. In the course of long evolution, the principle of the legitimacy of such authority (that is, the right of those in power to say what kind of rights and duties should prevail and for whom) has come to be partly or wholly democratic.[2]

This right to determine mutual claims among individuals and groups is embodied in a constitution, whether written or unwritten, and in statutes and judicial decisions. A constitution embodies the distribution of authority among various agents. This society of societies, nation-wide in extent, that exerts authority to command in the name of the whole nation's supremacy, is called the state. The institutions that act in its name, as a more or less rational system, such as (if it be democratic) a congress, a president, the several states, and so on, constitute the government. The government, then, is the day-by-day maker and executer and judge of the laws which set out in detail the mutual rights and obligations that citizens and groups of citizens must render to each other in the name of the authority of the state.

[1] See Robert M. MacIver, *The Web of Government* (New York: The Macmillan Company, 1947).

[2] Herman Finer, *Theory and Practice of Modern Government* (New York: Henry Holt and Company, 1949), Ch. I.

The relationship between government and the economy becomes clear. The economy consists of one phase of men's activities and interests in society: that concerned with producing goods and which is torn out of the body of all the other phases of man's existence, religious, artistic, philosophic. It is helpful for the enthusiast for economic development to think of the nation, as did Hobbes, as an "artificial Man," for such a concept will stress the interdependence of all the phases on one another. Their severability is conceptual rather than practical. In the Soviet Union the economy is an integral and indistinguishable part of the government, except by conceptual analysis.

Thus, in this peculiar aggregation of human minds and wills that makes a state, the economic is but a part. In some countries it is a large and predominant part; in others and in other times, it may have a subordinate place in the ingredients of a good life. In some places, religion or a secular world outlook embodied in custom may frown on economic acquisition, as did the Christian in the Middle Ages.[3] Full Buddhism would condone economic acquisitiveness only to the point at which life is to be barely sustained—and economic development in countries where this attitude prevails will be difficult to achieve: Krishna teaches, "The Good is *not* to act!"

The economic and the noneconomic in man affect each other. They live in a changing and developing super- and subordination. The state is a powerful instrument of this continuous change. The state is partly fashioned of the economic and noneconomic by the changing balance; and, insofar as the agents of the government exert the appropriate leadership—that is, are *ahead* of society in conceiving new objectives and plans of execution—government contributes to the change.

The economist must by no means underrate the force of political will and pressure emanating from all the noneconomic phases of the human spirit. These help shape the answers to what goods shall be produced, by whom, by what means, at what pace, who shall get the goods, and what shall be conserved for future generations. Such shaping operates through political pressures, where the sovereign power (the highest political authority, with the supreme power of

---

[3] Richard H. Tawney, *Religion and the Rise of Capitalism* (London: Murray, 1926); and Max Weber, *The Protestant Ethic and the Spirit of Capitalism* (London: Allen & Unwin, 1930).

physical coercion) is competed for by votes, if the polity is a democracy. The manner of developing the economy, insofar as government is concerned with it, must be markedly different in a democracy from the ways of the other extant states. Some are feudal; some, semidictatorial; some, primitive tribal; and some, like the USSR and its satellites, almost totally dictatorial. Some are called democracies, but are actually military or aristocratic cabals which hold on to power and act until violently overthrown by another faction.

Laissez faire is merely a phrase of degree, not of the absolute annulment of the activities of government in directing, controlling, or regulating the economic activities of society. The classical economists were substantial political activists.[4] History exhibits no society, ever, in which the purposes of acquiring wealth, the degree to which energies are devoted to it, and the method of its production and the principles of its distribution have not been markedly controlled and ruled by political principles; that is, by the views of the highest good, and by political processes, or government.

Historic evolution, itself the product of geography, climate, the development and fortuitous rise of mind, invention, and leadership in ideals, confronts us today with an immense variety of politico-economic systems. The economic developer who is in the seat of government must take account of the historic datum: what is left to development by spontaneous acts of individual and group entrepreneurs, and what has come to be habitually regulated and undertaken by government or the community in primitive political forms, or regulated by hard and fast custom. He will have to decide whether it is possible to introduce the technology necessary for a given economic project into the particular setting, and how far, by what means, and at what speed it is possible to change the setting.

In the Western nations, a high freedom has been won in economic life. But this has been possible only with the ascription to government of some crucial functions. These are the powers to protect and mold property rights, though the basis of private property is deeply rooted. There is the defense of contracts by the state, without which force, fraud, and violence might be called in to regulate economic relationships. There is the power to tax, including the objective of "the general welfare." The state has a "police power"—that is, the

[4] Cf. Lionel Robbins, *The Theory of Economic Policy in the Classical English Economists* (New York: The Macmillan Company, 1952).

right to protect the public safety, health, and morals, and to promote public convenience and prosperity. The state takes action against restraints of trade. It curbs liberty of development that interferes with consumer interests in businesses affected by a "public interest." [5] The economy is a blend of free enterprise, governmentally regulated, and government enterprise. This mixture exists everywhere; for economic development, the blend that suits the problem to be solved in each specific place, that is viable there, is crucial. In developing parts of Africa, government cultivates the soil, while peasants sow and reap.

The devices used by government in the West for economic development have relied on the motivation of self-interest in the individual, which produced a tremendous force for production and remarkable ingenuity in its service. This must never be forgotten by those who plan development, and it deserves constant emphasis, since it affects judgment regarding what shall be entrusted to the private sector and what to the public sector of economic activity.

Yet the private enterprise method of economic development also has its drawbacks:

1. A monopolistic tendency on the part of all producers, for their own profit and security, which may well lead to sluggish effort and "featherbedding." In the words of J. R. Hicks, one of the principal advantages of monopoly is "the quiet life."

2. An unwillingness to have government use tax funds or loans to execute economic projects of: (a) collective value, such as roads, harbors, bridges, health measures, and education, the benefit of which is widespread and the allocation of the cost of which is not personally imputable; (b) collective value, where, however, the private entrepreneur does not, for reasons good to him, undertake the risk of a valuable societal enterprise, and where it would be simply misanthropic to waste existent resources in goods, invention, and innovation of a managerial type to a dogma of private enterprise—works of conservation, drainage schemes, and such hydro-electric projects as the T.V.A.

3. An unreadiness to allow for the enduring nature of the national economy and therefore to provide adequately for its future wealth. This neglect leads to galloping consumption of natural resources, like the fertility of the soil, and forests, coal, and oil, with no care for replacement. It is admittedly difficult for the government to know what standard to

[5] United States Mutual Security Agency, *Report for the Public Advisory Board*, current numbers; Merle Fainsod and Lincoln Gordon, *Government and the American Economy*, 2d. Rev. Ed. (New York: W. W. Norton & Co., Inc., 1941, 1949).

apply in allowing or decelerating production and consumption now as compared with the future, and who should decide this—whether private persons or the state.

4. A serious economic damage being perpetrated as an unplanned consequence of economic decisions made individually. Misplacement of factories destroys beauty spots. Thoughtless creation of industrial communities with housing, schools, and utilities at the cheapest rate for industrial purposes and by individuals who later abandon them has occurred.

5. Whole branches of economic enterprise developing at their own pace and with their own self-regarding aims: banking, agriculture, commerce, home investment, and foreign investment. These establish governmental assistance for themselves as well. They are, of course, to a considerable extent intermeshed. Yet the disharmonies of the great sectors of the economy, and of the millions of individual firms within each, have proven to be serious by causing slumps and booms of a destructive nature.[6]

Therefore, some agency must provide against the shortcomings of the system. It must:

1. Set an optimum output rather than accept the idea that the wealth of the nation is properly the total of the products arising from the spontaneous action of free entrepreneurs and labor;

2. Avoid or mitigate disharmonies of a cyclical character;

3. Furnish information leading to the more rational allocation of resources to more clearly perceived objectives, seeing that individual firms have limited knowledge, limited resources, are limited in scale of operations, and may be content to go slow after a certain income has been secured;

4. Intervene for the purpose of strengthening competition all through the economy in the face of cost-increasing monopoly;

5. Supply safeguards against waste of resources, both material and human;

6. Supply collective or "indiscriminate-benefit" goods: defense, communications, education, health measures, etc.;

7. Undertake economic development neglected by private enterprise, even when such enterprise is encouraged and assisted by government.

This is a formidable program. It has become politically inevitable, particularly in democracies, and more recently in underdeveloped lands where the population has awakened to the values of democracy and the benefits of a high standard of living under the impulse of science and technology.

[6] J. M. Keynes, General Theory of Employment, Interest and Money (New York: Harcourt, Brace & Co., 1936); Roy F. Harrod, The Life of J. M. Keynes (London: The Macmillan Company, 1951); Temporary National Economic Committee Final Report (Washington, D.C. U.S. Government Printing Office, 1939).

The problems involved in this program are far easier for the developed countries than for the underdeveloped, because long experience offers its lessons. Insofar as the latter have any advantage, it lies in the government's freedom to plan and act unobstructed by vested interests.

THE ADAPTIVE AND ACTIVE ROLES OF GOVERNMENT

Government. To produce, incentives are required. Whatever the motivation of development, whether military strength, religious philanthropy, or material well-being of diversified kind that satisfies manifold individual and social values, such motivation must be built on, organized, and made durable. There must be order in space and order over time.

Whether the government is completely or partially the entrepreneur of development, it will need to take a total view. Its ideas, if not its own activities, must be all-embracing, even if only to indicate where it shall not act. This is so, whether the government is to start development *de novo* or whether it is to enter correctively. It must represent the idea of a desirable society, and this in tune with the value-traditions of the existent society; assess the economic goods and services (that is, the actual projects) to serve those values; determine the relative importance they have in substance and their priority in time; fit these to the human and nonhuman resources; and, in proportion to the potential flexibility of these, adapt them. To discharge these obligations implies the possession of much power.

This is what has been accomplished over the centuries in the developed economies, and without a plan made prior to that development, or struck off at one given moment and adhered to throughout all vicissitudes. This intricate interlacing of motives, incentives, and science stands as an example from which underdeveloped lands may benefit, but which must be made conformable to their culture and resources.

Economic development requires the hitherto indicated apparatus and procedures of laws and a constitution to give direction and assure men of the benefits commensurate with the efforts and sacrifices the development program promises to entail. It requires also an appropriate administrative system to follow through with the plans laid down in the laws. Such a government must offer society these services if it desires to stimulate economic development: order, justice, police, and defense; rewards commensurate with ability and application in production; security in the enjoyment of property, which may be of extremely varied character; testamentary rights; the assurance that business convenants and contracts will be kept; the provision of standards of weights, measures, and currency; and stability of the governmental system itself, to maintain the sense of order and future calculability of expectations and duties.

It is not difficult to appreciate what a strain such basic requirements must set up in the Far East (except Japan) where the millennial culture of loyalty to the joint family, filial piety, and vague religious intuitions rule, rather than wide-scale, impersonal, determinate laws of science and of super-family government!

It is proper to comment on two further strategic factors in the role of government in economic development: democracy and area. In the short run, a strong and undemocratic government and a complaisant people might conduce to quick and sound economic development. It would depend on the ability of the governors and their willingness to be objective and uncorrupt and un-self-seeking in their management. In the long run, and perhaps even in the short run, the danger of corrupt and egoistic misuse of power and profits, and the expectation that the energies and ability of the people will be withdrawn, commend democratic government and administration. But this system entails a division and limitation of authority and much consultation before decisions can be made and fulfilled. In any event, it may be better to plan development in the democratic way rather than in the undemocratic, even with all the friction and loss the former involves.

The areas of the nations (or of African tribes) were never evolved to be self-sufficient economic units giving the maximum return for the work expended and resources employed in them. All areas of development must look beyond their own frontiers for a better market, sources of raw materials, and division of labor than their own area allows. They have so proceeded by the alternatives of political expansion and a unitary state; by federalism, as in the United States, Canada, Australia, and elsewhere; by uninhibited international trade; by customs unions; by preferential tariff arrangements; and so on.

The assumption of economic development by government offers advantages which may be inferred from the summary of the shortcomings of private enterprise already given. But government, when it becomes an entrepreneur, is not exempted from the technical necessities of successful economic behavior.[7] If it wishes to be successful, government must fulfill these conditions: possess or acquire the sentiments and creative force to enterprise; possess or acquire the material resources necessary; and establish or improve its administrative machine to convert will, energy, and resources into work done. Such government is itself the main element in a society's "intangible capital," like the population's physical health, its literacy and knowledge, and its mores of honesty and alertness. This "intangible capital" may be far more important to economic development than any or all of the tangible projects at any time planned and needing large amounts of capital to build. The possession of a vocabulary may be more important than a road through a valley.

In order to avoid inevitable repetition in what follows, something more may be added regarding the potential weaknesses of government in economic development. Government is nothing but a disposition of men and procedures, and is prone to all the weaknesses of men when collectively engaged in a common task. Of these, three stand out, as demonstrated by experience:

(1) Government is in competition with other forms of collective enterprise as regards the knowledge at its disposal. In some cases it can be more objective, produce more valid generalizations, and even be more accurate. In other cases, it must be inferior to the detailed, realistic knowledge on the spot of millions of individual firms. But there is a point where the individual firm is blind as to distant repercussions of its policies and egotistically negligent.

(2) Free enterprise depends on the incentive of private profit. It can be intense and of tremendous productive drive. But we know that monopolistic tendencies come into play. This hurts the possible aggregate of welfare producible with given resources. Often the incentive of good work fully performed, as one's career and life purpose, is visible in those who serve the government. Nothing miraculous in the shape of altruism needs to be postulated—merely the professional devotion of men of the same average ability and character as those who are in private enterprise, and who are not operating for profit but for an assured salary. Perhaps the more speculative of enterprises seem to be ideal for the private entrepreneur; yet we know

[7] Herman Finer, *Municipal Trading* (London: G. Allen & Unwin, Ltd., 1941), first and last chapters.

that many great enterprises with much risk attached to them are neglected by private enterprise. They are left to the patriotic professional motivations of government, which is prepared to take a longer-run view.

(3) Economic development requires that its *objective* conditions be fulfilled—that is, the logical requirements of the development stemming from the technological conditions it poses and the human and material resources appropriate to it. Among other things, it requires that personal, religious, "partisan" ideological prejudices be ignored, or indeed, suppressed. Government, whether formally or informally representative, labors under difficulties in this respect. It is subject to a multitude of pressures not to be objective.

The work force. The work force is profoundly influenced by government when it provides education and information, in addition to the effect on work habits produced by the stability and honesty or otherwise of government in its own practices. This has already been referred to as "intangible capital."

Education, first, cultivates basic intelligence and skill without regard to any specific occupation. The high productivity of Danish agriculture has been ascribed to its adult education instituted in the twentieth century.[8] Underdeveloped lands have very far to go in such matters as these. They might learn from the experience of French-Canadian workers during World War II who found themselves at first unable to obtain work in the war-stimulated Canadian factories as compared with their non-French kinsmen, because they had not had enough elementary education to learn to read a blueprint. A real service was rendered to the economic development of India by the British Government which supplied the common language of widest use. Lands of mixed scripts and languages are at tremendous disadvantage. Second, wide education opportunity, paid from taxes wholly or in part, is not only a potent factor in increasing productivity, but also in developing versatility and mobility of labor. It also reduces class inequalities that may stem from hereditary status.

Third, educational opportunity inculcates general values in a way of life and co-operativeness among those who are or will be co-operating agents in economic development. A kind of consensus as to what is worth while is developed, in which values are formulated

[8] Richard W. Livingstone, *The Future in Education* (New York: The Macmillan Company, 1941).

and brought into conformity with one another. In underdeveloped countries, such education is basic to a change-over from tradition and belief in miracles to an understanding of the technical, objective, and measured conditions of economic enterprise, a scientific and non-superstitious or sentimental frame of mind, and a desire for welfare. Such education can be used to inculate the notions of law and or-der, property, the sanctity of contract, devotion and integrity on the job, regularity and punctuality of attendance at work, exactness and meticulous accuracy, and the importance of the constitutional basis of state life. Education furnishes something of what the Physi-ocrats called "enlightenment" (*évidence publique*), regarding the "natural order"; that is, the nature of the economic factor in human endeavor.[9] They regarded this as an indispensable function of govern-ment, fearing that without it their policy of extreme *laissez faire* would result in the mutual frustration of millions of individuals, each seeking his own selfish advantage. They sought for enlightened self-interest, the kind of self-interest that is not destructive of its own claim to continuance, as monopoly might be, in which freedom would destroy freedom by fostering fraud, breach of contract, laziness, or uninventiveness.

Education is recommended as a means of bringing labor and cap-ital to a sense of responsibility to each other and to the whole econ-omy. The alternatives are friction, conflict, and waste in development, or the assumption by government of activities hitherto conducted in the private sector of the economy. Such education would concern itself with several of the most serious disharmonies in the economic sys-tem. These are: the selfish interests of occupations competing against each other; the inability of consumers and firms to secure information about the market; the hereditary (caste or class) or accidental privi-leges that prevent operation of "the career open to the talents," so depriving the whole of the economy of the ability available. The third of these poses an especially serious problem in the so-called feudal or tribal economies.

Then education, even at the general level, also affords vocational guidance and selection for occupation.[10] It is at school, especially if mass populations are in attendance, in play, and in classroom com-

[9] Herman Finer, "The Development of State Activity," *Theory and Practice of Modern Government* (London: Methuen & Co., Ltd., 1932), 2nd Ed.

[10] B. C. Hayes, *et al.*, *The School Follows Through* (New York: National Edu-cational Association, 1941).

petition and grading (frequently counter to existent occupation and social standing of parents) that children are assessed, guided, and given opportunities. Increasingly, aptitude and inclination are matched to labor needs and future economic requirements. In the Soviet Union, which no longer ago than 1918 was an underdeveloped country, the drive for planned industrialization and modern agriculture has been ferocious, and the very opportunity of schooling has been made the selective and attractive factor among the whole formerly illiterate people. Furthermore, its system of education has been deliberately couched to innoculate the work force against Marxian theories which would have been inimical to economic development, theories such as the communistic idea of "to each according to his needs," instead of "to each according to his production," and that the government is not rightly entitled to levy a surplus out of the proceeds of industry for its political and administrative services.[11] The doctrine of foreign aggression is also an education in motives to produce according to governmental plan.

A limiting factor to this immensely valuable economic aspect of education is the existing inequality of income and class distinctions. Such distinctions have been the mixed consequence of historic conquests, of superior force, of accidentally obtained privileges perpetuated by the law of succession or the political franchise, of religiously established caste systems, as well as of superior ability and dedication to economic enterprise. They tend to place persons of much ability below the economic roles they could best fulfill and to leave others in economic positions which they cannot efficiently develop, though such are in receipt of a high income. It is equivalent to the "ploughing-under" of brains. Furthermore, much economic misery and tension in the conduct of industry or agriculture are attributable to the widespread and undiagnosable dissatisfaction with life issuing from pursuit of an intensely disliked occupation, for which the money reward becomes the only attraction and, therefore, the chief contention.

Governments improve the work force by vocational training at public expense and have learned in two wars how to make possible transfer to new occupations as these displace decaying ones.[12] This

[11] *Higher Commission on Education of Soviet Union on Education in Economics* (New York: International Publishers, 1948).

[12] *Vocational Training of Adults* (Geneva: International Labour Office, 1949).

is the answer to technological unemployment of some kinds, and it receives increasing attention by governments. It is also the answer to the problem of those lands in Asia, Africa, the Middle East, and Latin America, where, though technically employed, something like one-third or more of the population could be transferred from their agricultural pursuits to other work without causing a fall in agricultural production.[13] But training would be necessary if they were to be transferred to other occupations.

Beyond this, it is noteworthy that developed economies, more especially those of northwestern Europe, Britain, and the United States, are alert to two special requirements: the development of scientific and technological work forces by expert investigation of future developments, and the institution of scholarships through such agencies as the National Science Foundation,[14] grants to universities and colleges, and the organization and honoring of scientific workers who are in the public service. The recent establishment of international productivity teams, composed of employers and workers of mixed nationality,[15] is a noteworthy attempt to improve the ability of the work force, not least in industrial organization and managerial method. The Technical Assistance activities of the United Nations[16] is an international activity of the kind discussed here, and is of special service to the underdeveloped lands.

In the underdeveloped lands, it has now become accepted that a fundamental of their economic planning must be all sorts of educational preparation. The proportion of their development funds going into education attests to this.[17] They are faced with the problem of the "mass-education" type started by the British in their African colonies and which enables an immediate modest start to be made on the improvement of local agriculture and handicrafts, with some raising of the standard of living or doing something more elaborate and

[13] United Nations, *Measures for Economic Development of Under-Developed Countries* (New York: Columbia University Press, 1951).

[14] John R. Steelman, *Science and Public Policy* (1947).

[15] United States Mutual Security Agency, *Reports for the Public Advisory Board* (Washington, D.C.: U.S. Gov't. Printing Office).

[16] Robert Mack, *Coordination Among National and International Agencies in Development of Underdeveloped Economies* (New York: Citadel Press, 1953). W. R. Sharp, *Technical Assistance Program* (Chicago: Public Administration Service, 1953).

[17] Public Affairs Institute, *Policy and Program for Success*, Washington, D.C. (1950), see p. 36 for a proposed proportioning of development expenditures.

expensive. The problem is one of timing and resources and what may be termed the earlier or later resort to the cumulative effect of economic gains from education for even more education once development gets under way.

Finally, many countries now have a long history of government employment services, starting first in local charitable and private agencies, then developing to labor union agencies, and culminating in governmental and nation-wide organization. This is because the tremendous width and complexity of the national labor-market necessitate a single system, with the resources and authority to coerce, if necessary, available only to the government. In its modern form, this is a flexible and decentralized, telepathic clearing-house of immense economic benefit, especially where the labor force, as in the United States, is highly mobile. The employment services are coordinated more or less with the government administrative departments responsible for the economic surveys. The latter are of most effectiveness where, as in a strained economy like the British or the German, the allocation of resources, especially investment, is closely planned year by year, or as in the Soviet Union, where planning for economic development is almost totally in the public sector. Careful economic planning would be especially important in underdeveloped countries where resources are being marshaled and authoritatively allocated in a development plan. A crude form of this exists in "labor compounds" of Africa.

Before leaving this subject, two things may be emphasized. The full potentialities of the government's role in economic development through the education of the work force are nowhere completely exploited. A little more expenditure could bring large and increasing returns in national output. Furthermore, no country in the world has as yet carried universal economic enlightenment to its maximum potential in the reduction of useless economic conflict.

Yet, education and employment services are ineffective if the complementary resources are not also available for the willing worker; nor can a farmer be created merely by making him the gift of a farm. In African development, contemporary tensions represent the conflict between primitive men claiming hereditary tribal ownership of the land and foreigners with three centuries of science and "know-how." In developing its economy, government is bound to make a decision as to whether the work force may work at its own discretion as regards hours and risks to life, limb, and health, or whether to set limits to this. It would be possible to push ahead faster with economic development if no such limits were enforced. It is true that the goods and services thus produced ought to be appraised, keeping the cost of the damage done to people in mind. Experience has demonstrated that, left to themselves, without the leadership of their own fellows or of their government, most workers, in order to get more money, are prepared to assume risks that are unwise, even wittingly ignoring safety regulations in dangerous coal mines. Some are prepared to conduct "unfair" competition against fellow workers who are unwilling to suffer the dangers and disagreeability of certain kinds and times of work. Many do not appreciate the dangers to which they may be exposed; others are driven to wear out their lives, pressed by economic necessity. Employers are prepared to use their economic dominance and consumers to ignore the cost in health of workers. Here are choices which require at least a lead from the government. Once a high standard of living is attained, the additional earnings of more danger or fatigue or boredom become less compelling. The experience of the development of Great Britain in the first half of the nineteenth century, of Japan in the twentieth century, and the Soviet Union since 1926, shows that speed and massiveness of development at certain stages is attainable hardly otherwise than by two generations of long, hard, and dangerous work. The knowledge of safety at work has increased to a point where the loss of production by its application has been much reduced compared with fifty or a hundred years ago. The new economies may be the benificiaries of this knowledge.

The more dignified of the workers, and soon the conscience of the majority of the nation, revolted against human self-destruction and exploitation. A series of statutes beginning with the British Health of Morals of Apprentices of 1802 broadened out to limit the work of women and children and then of men for more than a certain maximum of hours and in dangerous conditions in all industrial countries. The establishment of the International Labor Office in 1918 [18] was the result in part of a revolt against the idea that "labor is simply a commodity." Its purpose was to civilize production by inducing all nations to make treaties to establish such factory legislation, and to

[18] Francis Wilson, *Labor in the League System; a Study of the International Labor Organization in Relation to International Administration* (Calif.: Stanford University Press, 1932).

confute the objection that the lands of sweated and dangerous trades would capture the markets from their rivals who had higher costs of production.

Economic development can be quicker and more substantial where people work longer hours up to a point—the experience of the wars and the aftermath in the devastated and stricken countries demonstrates this. If economic development is designed among other things to provide people with more leisure, this objective may conflict with a desire for a higher material standard of living. In some lands, the tradition is fast-set that leisure is of very high value. But in some others, it is a choice that is hardly a choice, for no competing economic goods have been offered for which leisure might be enthusiastically exchanged.

In some planned economies of the dictatorial type, like Mussolini's Italy, the Nazi regime, and the Soviet Union, similar protections of the workers to those mentioned, are established, though not under the impulse of the workers' political power. Otherwise the dictator encounters passive resistance. In such economies, the government also has complete dominion over the mobility of labor. Economic development is to that extent facilitated. Thus, the government of the Soviet Union experienced no very great difficulty in uprooting surplus populations from the land and bringing them to the factory areas, for it had command of all productive instruments, including the land, and unchallengeable coercive force at its disposal (although food supplies did prove inadequate). British planning authorities during the post-World War II redevelopment of the economy were obliged to proceed by persuasion and reasoned argument. A disposition to stay in the neighborhood of one's birth or settlement, connected with family or friends, is very strong in many parts of the world, especially in those that happen to be underdeveloped—a vicious anti-development circle is here noticeable. In India, looking to a modernization of the economy, Prime Minister Nehru has suggested the need to draft young men for certain types of "essential labor."

A well-known method of restricting the size of the labor force is that of legal apprenticeship regulations, established by the associations of workers in a particular craft. The traditional cultures, coinciding with the underdeveloped economies, where domestic industry and handicrafts are the rule rather than mass production, high specialization, and division of labor, are especially hidebound by apprenticeship, and often further surrounded by family mores. Government swept many of these away in the modernized economies because they were obstructions to development, although some still flourish by informal arrangement, as a perversion of the original purpose of apprenticeship. Generally, government sets up qualifications and licensure for certain professions (physicians) and occupations (engineering of certain kinds), where the damage done by unqualified practitioners would be irremediable. It requires registration or licensure by the state or state-approved professional bodies, and this is a consequence of the territorial gap between producer and consumer that has opened with division of labor, or what has been called indirect production.[19] Government abolition of apprenticeship and its own licensure for competence are factors favorable to economic development, since they free for innovation, discourage feather-bedding, and demand genuine skill, certified by qualified judges.

A government bent on economic development must solve the problem of co-operation among the owners and managers of capital and the work force. It is almost as involved in the difficulties of this problem when it acts only as adapter, as when it is actually the employer. For the issue of the justice of the wages of labor as compared with the profits of capital affects the zest of the entrepreneur, the readiness of the investors to stake their resources to develop agriculture and industry, and the willingness of the workers to do an "honest day's" work. The issue arises as acutely in the various sharecropping and rental arrangements of the lands of still fairly primitive agriculture, awaiting development by modern methods of farming and fertilizing, as it does in the already well-developed lands of progressive manufacturers.

No obvious objective test of the comparative value of capital and labor, and therefore of the proper shares that should go to each, exists. Utterly free competition would suggest these shares, but it does not exist. Competition is least free in the underdeveloped lands where hereditary ownership and the hereditary semiserfdom of the laborers is prevalent, and where, also, the owning class is rarely enterprising, but spends its time and money in idle pursuits, often as absentee land-

[19] National Education Association, *Statutory Status of Six Professions* (1938).

lords. Nor would free competition have the ability to give the proper share to the proper people by any inherent logic. It might merely furnish the least inacceptable distribution.

The consequence is one of constant pressure and strain and sometimes of lawless conditions, including murder, in the attempt of both sides in the economy to improve their lot. The increase of production is often forgotten in the battle for distribution. In some underdeveloped countries, revolution has been provoked by the failure of the traditional owners to reform. This has come about under the impulse of the demand for a higher standard of living learned from other nations and spread by the mass media of communication, or through the example of the soldiers of the developed countries who have passed through those lands. The latter case is most notable in the effect of the Middle East's position as a supply center during World War I.

Government's role in economic development in this context is: (a) to reduce hostility between capital and labor, (b) to avert losses of production through strikes and lockouts, especially when a stoppage in one industry has a disproportionate effect through the whole of a closely knit economy, and (c) to give labor a sense of responsibility for increasing output, and both parties a realization of the damage their internecine strife does to the public at large.

These aims are met partly through legislation giving labor rights to combine for collective bargaining, and including pressure, as in strikes on notice and picketing, and through assisting the achievement of equal bargaining power[20] through conciliation services managed by the government and, in some branches of the economy, the outlawing of strikes altogether—light, power, water, transport, and firefighting.[21] It is difficult to understand the logic which justifies the separate treatment of these as compared with coal, steel, food, and so on. Indeed, in some countries where the problem of economic development is tight—that is, where social security funds, social services of magnitude, and planning are perforce micro-arithmetically formulated—the workers have themselves come to appreciate the unwisdom of stoppages of work for improvement of pay and conditions. In such

[20] Charles O. Gregory, *Labor and the Law* (New York: W. W. Norton and Co., Inc., 1949). Hilary Marquand, *Organized Labor in Four Continents* (New York: Longman, Green & Co., Inc., 1939).

[21] Morton Godine, *The Labor Problem in the Public Service* (Cambridge, Mass.: Harvard University Press, 1951).

countries they aid development by co-operating with the government on persuasion that the plan requires good behavior. For such propitious conduct, a long period of political and economic education is required, including the creation of educated and public-spirited labor leaders. This has its implications for the advantages of encouraging democracy as one part of a plan for achieving economic development.

How can the workers be associated with the actual conduct of the firm and the industry, without their becoming obstacles to development? It has been found that in experiments of producers' co-operatives, the problem of objective work discipline is hard to solve: the workers give themselves the benefit of the doubt when extra exertions are required. This can slow down economic development. Germany has a long experience, and Britain some, of associating the workers in management by the legal establishment of Works Councils. It has been of little effect in spurring development, for the workers have no property to venture and so to back up their will, nor have they the appropriate managerial skills. Some of the work force are antipathetic to comanagement because they hold that it diminishes their independence in fighting for better conditions. The Soviet institution of collective farms is in this class; however, free co-operatives associate the workers with management equally, without the disadvantage of coercion.

The inexorable need for entrepreneurs in private industry with freedom for innovation and discipline is well established by experience, and a government that conducts development needs them as much as private enterprise. The Soviet's spasmodic attempts to subordinate its managers to party factory rank and file were damaging.

Labor can be as monopolistic as any employer. One way to secure its sense of responsibility is the British: through the development of a political party that is largely the party of the workers. It is then hard for them to claim that the party's considered policy that labor must subordinate itself to the objective technological and administrative conditions of progress is unjust. The American way is to reach a temporary equilibrium by an open fight: it is the way of much lost wealth.

So far we have considered only tension between employers and workers. But the occupations form pressure groups sometimes, when the workers and capital in an industry connive together at the expense of the consumers and of all other occupations whose cost of production depends on what they must pay to those who supply them with services, raw materials, or semiprocessed products. One of the ways to prevent the clashes inherent in the chain reaction of strikes of occupation versus occupation and to try to secure an all-round view of the economy is the institution of the governmental apparatus and procedures of Economic Councils, as in Germany, France and the corporative structure of Fascist prewar Italy. Subordinate to the popularly elected representative assemblies, these are forums in which the economic interests meet each other, to discuss and appraise the government's economic, social, and financial proposals. An alternative is the council and lobbying arrangements of the less organized countries.[22]

The problems just discussed are variants of the problem of producers' control of production. If the producers dominate the market, will the consumer be the master of production? The consumer may be represented by the government, or the market unorganized by the government. Such a market will provide for the protection of consumers' interests if it is responsive to their demands. Otherwise they must rely on bringing pressure through politics or by forming associations like consumers' co-operatives.

Full employment. The Charter of the United Nations commits the signatories to "full employment and rising standards of living." The commitment is paralleled in the United States Employment Act of 1946 and equivalent documents in other countries, not to speak of the Soviet Union's constitutional guarantee of "the right to work."

The relationship of a government's responsibility for full employment to economic development faces at the outset the sentiment that prompted these commitments: the revulsion of the work force against prolonged unemployment, which creates the personal demoralization of themselves and their families. The development of the economy may clash with the moral demand for a job. For the organization of the economy, within the nation and internationally, may make it liable to depressions, and there may be phases of planned development (technological change) when many workers must be laid off. The government then must make up its mind how far it can carry its plan of development, while it is politically pressed to see that

[22] Herman Finer, *Theory and Practice of Modern Government*, Rev. Ed. (New York: Henry Holt and Company, 1949).

every man has a job. It may be forced to slow up development in order to reduce frictional unemployment.

Assuming a target of, say no more than five per cent unemployed, the measures available are: fiscal and monetary policy; control of the volume of private investment; the planning of public investment; the encouragement of consumption; sustaining and developing markets; and stabilizing the economies of private producers.

What gives concern here, as it does in any broad planning, is the pressure of choices between the available policies whose nature is highly political. The end is full employment (not necessarily a benefit for every interest!), but the benefits and burdens of each chosen policy have secondary effects of conflicting moment to the welfare of a nation's various classes and occupations. To aid in the solution of such problems, all advanced countries have established governmental machinery for continuous vigilance. The United States established the Council of Economic Advisers, reporting to the President half-yearly, and instituted a Joint Committee of Congress on the Economic Report, to consider, discuss, and analyze, with the aid of its own economic experts, the recommendations and diagnoses in the Presidential document.[23] Linked with the Council, through the President, is the Federal Reserve System and the Treasury, not to mention other government departments whose co-ordinated efforts may be required to offer further factual surveys and eventually to take action.

As with all governmental action in economic development, where the government has partly or wholly displaced private entrepreneurs, the value of this system depends on the ability of the experts entrusted with vigilance and measurement, the intelligence and fortitude of the politicians, and the patience of big industry, big labor, and big farming. Where the system is democratic, the advantage is enjoyed that, once a decision has been made to the general satisfaction, the conduct of the plans is smooth. But the difficulty lies in the jockeying of the competing interests before Congress and behind the scenes of the Executive, and of public threats to act regardless of opinion. It depends on the courage of the politicians, the wage boards, and the rest of the agencies to take the necessary measures when their authority extends to this, though they may displease their voting clien-

[23] E. G. Nourse, Papers and Proceedings, *American Economic Review*, May 1950. E. G. Nourse and B. M. Gross, *American Political Science Review*, April, pp. 283–295.

tele. Full-employment planning and economic-development planning requires independence of mind on the part of the plan-makers and administrators, and the nation-wide clienteles need educating as to the technical significance of such independence. The state of mind indicated is heeded in dictatorships, as well as democracies, insofar as making plans and laws is concerned, but the process comes easier to the government. The administration is as difficult, even if more coercion is applied.

The British planning system, involving the cabinet, the interconnected economic, statistical, and other secretariats, the planning staffs, and the departmental and interdepartmental planning councils, may be taken as a good working model that reveals the principles involved in the government's role as entrepreneur in multipurpose development.[24] It exemplifies the fact-finding, situation-analyzing, and forecasting functions connected with the top decision-making cabinet of political leaders skilled in political values and persuasion. They are rather more successful than their American counterparts because the politicians and the parties are more sober, less partisan, more civic-minded, and better instructed, and because the line of authority and responsibility runs clear and unbroken, up from the electorate (well-organized in the continuously operating political parties), through the legislative assembly, to the admixture of executive direction and legislative leadership embodied in the cabinet. Also, a larger sector of the economy is directly controlled, and some directly owned and operated, by the government. The American institution of the separation of powers was designed deliberately to prevent the gathering of political power by the government and to leave it to the individuals. Its planning is wasteful of money and official health, even when things are accomplished.[25]

The traditional budgetary methods of government have been much reformed as a result of such substantial governmental responsibility for a stable and advancing economy. Modern nations produce each year, sometimes more often, a national economic budget— a survey, statistical account, and interpretative analysis of the size and use of the whole complex of national resources. This is an indispensable

[24] Herman Finer, "The Central Planning System in Britain," *Public Administration Review*, Autumn 1948, pp. 237–249.

[25] J. D. Millet, *The Process and Organizations of Governmental Planning*. (New York: Columbia University Press, 1947).

instrument of comprehension, as well as of social criticism, of plans. It has necessitated a reorganization of statistical services of the various governments and the greater employment of economic analysts. The Economic Report of the President in the United States, the annual Economic Survey in Britain, and the occasional reports on the progress of their Five-Year Plans in the Soviet Union, are examples of this twentieth-century type of budgeting.

Influencing consumers. A government interested in the development of an underdeveloped economy, will, like the entrepreneur anywhere, need to pay attention to marketing. Indeed, a marketing system which brandished goods and catalogues of purchasable commodities before the population might awaken the incentives to produce and to steady work discipline. This is scarcely more than saying that economic development marches on the cupidity of consumers. In the Chilean attempt at modernizing its economy, the utilization of the immense fish resources on its long coast depends on the popularization of fish-eating. This parallels the action of the French government in the eighteenth century to popularize potatoes. These are direct marketing and advertising activities of the government; to be successful it must employ the art of salesmanship or fail.

Government taxes in order to provide collective goods, including defense, to sustain and stimulate the economy counter-cyclically, to promote equality, and to encourage or discourage specific kinds of consumption. In combination, these various forms of taxation can intentionally promote economic development. First, aggregate consumption by free discretion of the consumer is modified. The government takes resources away from the consumer and, instead, itself spends. It may spend on its own chosen objects of development, the basic utilities for instance, or it may spend on consumption which the consumer would have freely bought, though perhaps not in the same quantities; for example, education and health. Perhaps the government can do this better because it is a large-scale organization. But some of the liberty of the individual is lost and this must be reckoned as a cost, according to the value it has for the individual. But, it must also be added that, even if government did a worse job technically than the *sponte acta* of individuals, in some underdeveloped economies the general need for raising the standard of living is so great and private enterprise so lacking, that a start has to be made by the government. The government has the problem of carrying the mass of the people along a new pattern of consumption, without the weakening of their incentive to produce.

In compulsory social security, the government has ordained an object of consumption on which the consumer might not have spent money—owing to ignorance or lack of self-respect or self-control. The government in enforcing a long-run view on the short-run mind of the consumer is attempting to maximize welfare over time. It is thereby reducing the present flexibility of the consumer's budget. Since taxation (whatever its form) for social security affects the timing of consumption, it may be integrated with anticyclical measures. The funds can be raised or lowered to meet the need for more or less free purchasing power on the market. Government must exercise great foresight to avoid an ill-balanced consumption pattern. For example, diets may deteriorate because money has been paid into social security. Even in the United States, the personal consumption statistics suggest that, if more were spent on health than on cars, drink, tobacco, and beauty parlors, the cause of economic development would be advanced. In lands afflicted with malaria and various insect pests and bacteria, attacking the body, the lungs, the blood stream and especially the eyes, government intervention is urgently a prelude to development. Nor is that all; government-instituted medical services are indispensable to the spread of knowledge of birth control in order to cope with overpopulation.

The government may powerfully affect economic development by the degree of progressiveness of its taxation. The wealthy may be forced out of the luxury and near-luxury markets, and workers and other resources may thus be released for the comforts and needs of the middle and working classes. The price pattern is thus freed from distortion caused by inequality. Yet, as John Stuart Mill pointed out, the incentive to produce may be weakened by excesses in taxation policy. The system of income tax and death duties in countries like the United States, Britain, Sweden, Germany, and so on, have powerfully affected consumption patterns between classes.[26]

What the taxation policy should be, in general outline, to spur on economic development in backward economies, may be inferred from British and Russian policy. In the former, by stiff luxury taxes,

[26] S. Kuznets and R. Goldsmith, *Income and Wealth of the United States* (Cambridge, Eng.: Bowes & Bowes, Publishers, Ltd., 1952).

rising in some cases to one hundred per cent of the price, home consumption of goods was reduced for war purposes and, subsequently, to cut down the consumption of foreign goods and domestic goods which could be exported, thus helping to close the dollar gap. The alternative would have been direct governmental restriction of supplies. In Russia,[27] free consumption is drastically curtailed in the interest of plans for swift and massive industrialization. It is achieved largely by fully planned allocation of resources and of the amounts of the various goods to be produced, as adjusted by the pre-planned taxes which each planned industry must provide.[28] Authority fixes the amounts and kinds of civilian goods for present consumption. It has been said that the government of Russia regards the present generation as the "manure of the future." It is not too difficult to keep people in this status if they have known no better alternative. But the Russian government also uses the propaganda of "foreign aggression" to keep incentive alive, direct violence if "norms" are not produced, and the menace of a criminal charge of sabotage for production failures.

Economic development requires capital. One way by which it may be produced at home is by deferring consumption and paying taxes or lending money to the government. British development in the nineteenth century was stimulated by the presence of a mass of poor without the immediate power to get more of the product of industry for themselves, a *laissez faire* government dominated by the owners of property, and the surplus wealth of the upper classes, who were sufficiently puritanical to save as a matter of duty. The Russian people are today subjected to the same abnegation, and the policy rings with the familiar slogan that "progress is the reward of abstinence." One of tropical Africa's most serious problems is the spendthrift frenzy of the natives at times of marriage and other festivals.

Subsidies to consumers supplement taxation as a means to governmental egalitarian policy. They spring from public sympathy with poverty and from patriotic shame. The subsidies take the form of money or kind. Money subsidies may be direct allowances or aids of price reductions. Britain has subsidized the price of some goods, like

[27] William B. Reddaway, *Russian Financial System* (New York: The Macmillan Company, 1935).

[28] A. E. Baykov, *The Development of the Soviet Economic System* (New York: The Macmillan Company, 1947).

meat, bacon, milk, bread, and eggs, to provide even the poorest workers and pensioners with the minimum supplies for health and productive efficiency and, especially, to assure the welfare of their growing
families—the state's future labor force. The government purchased
the supplies and sold them to distributors at less than cost, allowing
the price to be this cost plus the distributors' permitted profit. The
administrative difficulty lies in the need of a large body of officials
and rationing. What government should do in this case depends on
the condition of economic inequality, the consumption habits of each
country, and the ability of administrative personnel which it has at
its command, and on the relationship of these to its plan of development.

The very conditions that dictate rationing render its administration
difficult. Wholesale and retail distributors need watching; black
market operations must be detected and punished; thefts may occur;
ration coupons ought to be assigned but they are costly and liable
to forgery. Under some circumstances, the stimulation of extra
production that might be bought with higher incomes is slowed
down. The fixing of ration prices is a laborious compromise, as is
the fixing of the date of dismantling controls.

Some subsidies may be given in kind. During the depression, the
United States government distributed surplus crops by way of relief. In Britain, children at school are given meals. In future depressions, governments may be impelled to place large orders of such
goods as boots, shoes, and hose for distribution as free gifts.
Government-subsidized housing, on low credit terms or low rentals,
or bonuses to contractors, are also subsidies to consumers. An alternative method of subsidizing families is by direct payment in the
form of subsidized prices in the family allowance. "The chief cause
of poverty is children," was the sloganized theory of such allowances.
Such policies have been widely practiced on grounds of health,
raising the standard of living of the poor, and, as in Britain and Chile
(through the Development Corporation), furthering the development of new areas and industries.

Available consumption schedules reveal two things: variations in
the patterns of consumption at different income levels, and the mold-
ing of the pattern when government revenues and expenditures affect the distribution of income, prices, and the amount of social services and various community goods. The main peaceful instrument of

income re-distribution is progressive income and death or estate duties, whereby, as in Great Britain where the tendencies have gone furthest, inequality is strongly reduced through two or three generations.[29] This policy is in the very "furnace" of politics of class conflict. It concerns the redressment of inequality down through the middle class and the skilled workers to the unskilled, and not merely the "rich" and the "poor."

Governments interested in economic development face two problems in such egalitarian policy. Ceteris paribus, the greater the equality, the less will be saved. The fact that in well-developed economies investment is mainly made by corporations from undistributed profits makes little difference. Secondly, entrepreneurial zeal may be weakened by high taxation. Men may not invent or innovate or fatigue themselves if government takes the cream. But, it is alternatively argued, men will strive for a target of income after taxation, and therefore a high tax may well stimulate, rather than discourage, enterprise. The empirical data for a determination of the relative strengths of these forces in a given situation do not exist.

Evaluation of advantages of a given income distribution goes back to a problem of economic analysis: whether the satisfactions of any one person are comparable with those of another person, whether the marginal satisfactions of identical consumption patterns are interpersonally comparable. Many now argue that, though every individual has his own system of tastes, and the imputation may be rough, we will not go far wrong in assuming the equality of utilities among different persons; hence, the basic principle for consumption policy and egalitarian taxation is still Bentham's:

This addibility of the happiness of different subjects, however, when considered rigorously, it may appear fictitious, is a postulatum without the allowance of which all practical reasoning is at a stand. . . .[30]

Influencing investors and innovators. There are four possible ways of overcoming monopolies, so as to give access to investors and innovators into an industry and enforce enterprising development on the firms in control of production.

Suits may be instituted in the ordinary courts under common law

---

[29] Hugh Dalton, *The Inequality of Incomes* (London: P. S. King, 1920).
[30] Jeremy Bentham, *Manual of Political Economy Works*, Bowring Edition London (Edinburgh: Tait, 1843) Vol. III.

prohibitions of restraint of trade. Until recently this was the procedure in Britain, and it was ineffective. Such was American practice until the Sherman Act of 1890.[31] Ineffectiveness sprang from lack of definition of monopoly and absence of a special agency of the government to watch continuously and to bring suits.

Second, it is possible to make inquiries into monopoly by an agency set up by the government, as in Britain at present. If monopolistic practices are found, the agency, after endorsement by Parliament, declares the practices unlawful. Publicity is expected to set an end to restrictive practices. If not, civil actions can be taken against the monopolist, with fines and imprisonment as the sanction. The "public interest" is the test of monopoly: efficient production and distribution; efficient organization of industry and encouragement of enterprise; fullest use and best distribution of men, materials, and industrial capacity; and development of technical improvements and markets. This method was used in preference to the American way of trying to "bust" trusts by a "series of legal Armageddons" with not very much effect, and the Federal Trade Commission's attempts to deal with dynamic situations by "cease and desist" orders that soon become irrelevant.

American experience since 1890 has suggested to some that monopoly seems to bring with it deliberate or by-product forces that buy inventions and innovations in order to sterilize them; that protect against new energies, ideas, and rivals; that make possible the sustaining of an unnecessarily high cost of production or give an undue margin of profit to the monopolist; and that continue inferior and sluggish service to the consumer. In order to get rid of such forces, government would need not only a far larger staff of officials than has actually been provided, but an apparatus of inquisition, research, detection, and prosecution—almost as large as the total staffs of the monopolists. This is what creation of *free* competition would entail. For the ways of the monopolist—of labor as well as of capital—are subtle, ingenious, and secret; moreover, effective co-operation may come without any formal agreements—such is the evidence before the courts. But it is important for government to count the cost before it seeks perfection in its policing. Some apparent imperfections are economical.

[31] Milton Handler, *Study of Construction and Enforcement of the Federal Antitrust Laws*, T.N.E.C. Monograph, No. 38 (Washington, D.C.: U.S. Government Printing Office, 1941).

It has been argued that, in spite of immense concentration in industry and commerce, enough rivalry by like firms and by competing products still holds monopoly in check.[32] Nonetheless, by far the larger part of American prices are "contrived prices," that is, made by firms who dominate the market.

The difficulties of "trust-busting" have caused many reformers to demand outright ownership and management of monopolies by the state. Several countries have done this for municipal utilities, since the geographical nature of the monopoly presents strong grounds for ownership. It was not merely the consumers of water, gas, and electricity who demanded protection, but also manufacturers and merchants whose own economic ventures were threatened by gouging prices and the possibility of strikes.

Some utilities, like railroads, telecommunications, and so on, may be alternatively run by the government or especially regulated as to their services and charges through government agencies like the U. S. Interstate Commerce Commission, and the Federal Communications Commission. The government here is entangled in the inner processes of the industries themselves and the problems of quality, development, and a just return to work force and investors. However, at the very least, close vigilance by the government is a vexatious stimulus to the entrepreneur.

Perhaps there is a place for governmentally condoned monopoly on the same plane as the protection of infant industries. Where development is urgently desired, and funds and brains must be especially encouraged and given the assurance of time in which to execute the plans as the technology of the projects requires, government has its role. The Elizabethan monopolies in industry and foreign trade; the German and Japanese monopolies; the quasi-monopolies of the development corporations of newly-developing economies at the present time—all are cases in point. The vigilance of the representative institutions, and the public, and the opinion leaders in the politics of the country is indispensable to their good administration.

Interest rate and price level as influences on investors and innovators have already been referred to in preceding chapters. The power to play upon these has come, in almost every country in the world, to be vested to a major degree in a central bank. It is of lesser moment

[32] J. K. Galbraith, *American Capitalism, The Concept of Countervailing Power* (Boston: Houghton Mifflin Co., 1952).

whether this is instituted as a nationalized bank, under the aegis of the government treasury, or by a legally instituted private banking system, as in the United States, where there are strategic controls of its credit operations and solvency exercised by the Federal Reserve System supported by the Treasury. In either circumstance, the economy as a whole is the point of reference. Underdeveloped countries which are embarking on a well-knit plan, bringing home and foreign resources to bear on multipurpose programs, would need to concentrate their credit resources and controls in some such way.

"Wildcat" speculation and innovating exhilaration are toned down by the raising of interest rates and the sale of government bonds to take money off the market. A general intimidation magnifies the effect. The factual situation at the moment of intervention presents the central bank with the problem of either using the interest rate (which is not usually so large a part of total costs for big business as to be a harsh deterrent to innovation) or direct raising of the bank reserves, so restricting credit. For encouragement of investment and innovation, the reverse process is applicable.

The underdeveloped economies are usually in lands where government is distrusted for historic reasons and where, therefore, considerable funds are hoarded. As a stimulator of economic development, it is desirable that government get these hoards released. Experts have recommended that government borrowing at high interest be tried, but deferred until development projects are going enterprises.

Long-term interest rates have powerful effect on projects requiring heavy capitalization—construction for industry, commerce, residences, and heavy machinery and equipment. The rate is related by the entrepreneur to the real productivity of his investment. If money is plentiful, there is more to be spent on consumption, thus creating demand for the capital and new ideas and effort which the inventive and ingenious entrepreneur makes available. The effect, in a regime of low interest rates, is to provide a large volume of money, and so an environment of optimism for the investor and innovator.

It is necessary to emphasize the political difficulties of the administration of the whole battery of alternative and complementary credit devices and money-market operations needed to influence economic development. The effects of any move may be so far-reaching and specifically affect the welfare and need for adjustment of the various firms and groups in the community that all the pressure groups bring their tactics to bear on politicians and officials.

Furthermore, this particular aspect of the government's role in economic development illuminates the basic need of *stability* in government. We mean the continuous existence of government; free of insurrection; the solidity and continuity of career administration, not too frequent elections; and, even then, no brusque reversals or amendments of fiscal and monetary policy. The market must exist toward which the entrepreneur is moving, with his funds saved or borrowed at a price, his work force gathered and paid, his plant rented, and so on, when the finished goods have at last been made. It is government that must give the guarantee that, when the entrepreneur has paid all the prices, he will be able to sell at a reward. The government must keep the societies in the nation in being, and to do so, it itself needs stability and continuity.

A government that finds development unusually urgent, may consider the above-mentioned methods insufficiently strong to implement its plan according to its timetable. It may have to be the entrepreneur itself, gathering its means through taxation, patriotic loans, forced loans, foreign loans for military promises, or strict import restrictions.[33]

Influencing population and resources. It is difficult for a government to increase or decrease its population for purposes of economic policy, even in the long run, especially if it be concerned with the work force for a projected number of diverse enterprises. Fascist and Nazi experience demonstrates that government devices such as public praise, lower taxation for large families, family allowances, improved public health, even encouragement of illegitimacy, caused at most a small rise in the population over and above the increase spontaneously adapted to the culture and the general state of economic welfare.

Overpopulated, underdeveloped countries face the problem of reducing their birth rate, especially as health measures reduce mortality among infants, if they are to raise their per capita income. In some places, it seems a hopeless problem. Its magnitude may be appre-

[33] Herman Finer, *Chilean Development Corporation* (Montreal: International Labour Office, 1945).

ciated from the Bombay Plan for the economic development of India, where it was necessary to plan for the threefold increase of production over some thirty years in order to achieve a twofold increase in per capita income. Experts do not despair.[34] They believe that the spread of health education and the development of the medical services will assist the control of births, and that general education and economic hopefulness will commend it. Government is obliged to counteract cultural and religious creeds that applaud large families or frown on deliberate birth control. *Laissez faire* in the population-increase of the underdeveloped lands of the world is the supreme welfare-destroyer.

Migration is a drastic possibility in the hands of government, whether it permits freedom of admission or is selective or generally limitative. The economic development of the United States, and other such open lands in the nineteenth century was decisively furthered by the immigration of people who brought with them their education, their specific skills, a desire for economic improvement, their clothes, and in some cases their trade tools. They came equipped with the intangible capital of development, and with capital of a concrete kind in many cases—the savings of the European continent.

The rise of nationalism has, in the twentieth century, either closed most lands seriously to immigration or made them strictly selective as to race (not necessarily favorable to economic development) or the possession of capital and skills desired by the government to implement an economic policy. Within commonwealths, like the British, French, and Dutch, migration is governmentally sponsored. Hitler's Germany, Mussolini's Italy, and the Soviet Union pursued the policy of not letting their people leave; they wanted a large population for military purposes or were afraid of the political consequences of disclosure of their internal affairs. Nationalism in underdeveloped lands threatens to oust the foreigner with "know-how."

The essential and long-run objective is the maintenance of the optimum population, insofar as this does not come about by the spontaneous adjustment of numbers to the economic potentialities of the area. The optimum is here defined as the maximum per capita return from the total elements of the economy—soil fertility, scientific and technological ingenuity, existent skills, the specialization and division

[34] Milbank Memorial Fund, *International Approaches to Problems of Underdeveloped Areas* (New York: Milbank Memorial Fund, 1948).

of labor, and so on. Government may further this objective by benefiting specific groups as distinct from the rest of the population and at the latter's sacrifice for a time in order to get development under way. For instance, the surplus population of a given area may be clothed and equipped and educated and then placed to colonize neglected areas, as in the policy of Tsarist Russia over the centuries.

At any rate, it is much in the power of government to encourage and promote the increase of skill of its population, to discover and build complementary resources, and to nurture invention and innovation. Patent legislation and financial assistance to persons of ability assist in these purposes. A more recent experiment is the sending out of considerable numbers of young men and women from underdeveloped lands to the factories and laboratories of the developed ones, and being assisted in this by the international political agencies. International rivalry is less of an obstruction than might be thought probable—at least in the Western world. It is noteworthy that the lands of underdeveloped economy pursue a policy of sending their young men abroad to become experts and limiting the numbers of foreigners who may act in managerial positions in their industries.

To conserve is to counteract the waste of resources, especially the primary ones, like the soil, forests, and similar endowments that take many years to replace—mineral deposits, water, fish, and other animal life. But a government is faced with the invidious problem of defining "waste." If it leaves the economy to private individuals, it allows society to take the risk that private motivation may, as has happened in many countries and especially the United States, result in using up exhaustible or nonreplaceable resources in a relatively short time, for what may be regarded as trivial values of present consumption. The United States has been groping since the beginning of the twentieth century toward the principle that the processes of extraction shall impair at the minimum, if at all, the access of later exploiters to the reserves (thus in coal mining, or oil extraction) or shall replace the fertility or the products of the soil and water (timber, grass, roots, nitrogen and phosphorus, fish, and game) currently lost in the process of taking the annual produce.[35] Current American and long-practiced European policies of conservation convert at least the younger and larger producers from short-sighted exploiters into conservers and im-

[35] J. R. Whitaker and E. A. Ackerman, *American Resources, Their Management and Conservation* (New York: Harcourt, Brace & Co., 1951).

provers of the resource-base. For this, a very large apparatus of preventive, punitive, and educative procedures are employed.

Since waste is often due not to avarice but to ignorance, a government policy of resource surveys is essential to rational economic development. What is obtained is a necessary basis for what is to be developed at home and what must be obtained from abroad. The more developed governments have long had governmental geological surveys, land utilization surveys, engineering corps to explore and estimate such resources as water power, bureaus of marine biology, wild life observation stations and censuses, and so on. For the greater part of the world in area, such agencies and activities are still not established. A large part of the prospecting has been undertaken by national and international firms for particular products: coal, tin, tungsten, oil, uranium, and so on. Resource surveys have been spotty. Even a country as advanced as Canada was only truly awakened to this truth during World War II. In this respect, the specialized agencies of the United Nations have an important service to perform, for the more advanced nations may be of inestimable benefit to the underdeveloped ones.

Influencing foreign trade. The extension of foreign trade, based on comparative costs and a world-wide division of labor, increases world production. Government plays a major role in this phase of economic development because it is responsible for the national defense, because foreign private investment is hazardous, and because the less powerful nations have revolted against eighteenth-century militant imperialism and nineteenth-century colonialism and dollar diplomacy.[36] Private investors in foreign countries fear expropriation. But much governmental action has been in the direction of hindering, rather than encouraging, international trade as steps have been taken to utilize export and import controls such as subsidies, tariffs, cartels and commodity agreements, investment, and monetary policy.

Tariffs have been imposed because of urgent pressure from capital and labor, for their own specific benefit, or on grounds of military strength or the independence of the nation from supplies of other

[36] J. A. Hobson, *Imperialism: A Study* (1938). Parker T. Moon, *Imperialism and World Politics* (New York: The Macmillan Company, 1928). Eugene Staley, *War and the Private Investor* (New York: Doubleday Doran and Co., Inc., 1935).

nations.[37] It has been advocated that certain "key" industries ought to be fostered for defense, at least while they are still "infant." In practice, it has proved hard to remove the props. Less efficient industries are maintained at cost to the consumer.

Policies promoting national self-sufficiency have been instituted, such as synthetic rubber production in the United States. Latin America, underdeveloped, has stimulated native industries of iron and steel, cement, and metal processing, for this same reason, instead of buying from the most efficient producers. They lose as consumers more than they gain for defense purposes or in national pride, for they can hardly prevail against big nations—yet their envy and pride are directed more toward their own more comparable neighbors. Further, they are proud that they can manufacture as well as the renowned industrial nations. This causes underdeveloped countries everywhere to entertain grandiose ideas of industrialization, and to be tempted to undertake works far too expensive for the stage at which they now are.

Home industries and agriculture are protected and are required to employ nationals against competition from advanced development elsewhere. This is another species of monopoly and has its usual effects. Intense nationalism fosters protection which private interests exploit for their own advantage. An artificial economic structure is built. It is not because the government exists that tariffs come into being, but because economic groups use government as a cat's-paw. They have riddled the political process with specious pleas of national advantage and perverted reason.

Where other national economies produce at less cost, the home entrepreneur asks government for tariffs in order to equalize the costs of production. The consumer is mulcted of the advantage of lower costs. The producer in the protected country loses markets in the lower-cost rival's territory. The least efficient producers are subsidized at the cost of economic development.

Governments are also impelled by the plea of high and stable employment to impose tariffs. It is, of course, difficult to transfer workers from one industry to a new one when the former loses the support of a tariff. But unemployment assistance nowadays eases adjustment.

[37] F. W. Taussig, *The Tariff History of the United States,* 7th Ed. (New York: Putnam, 1923).

The tariff merely keeps workers in less efficient work. The better reasoning is to maintain national economic stability by the most abundant and stable international trade, made so by the appropriate international monetary devices and domestic purchasing power stability.

The remedy for tariff fallacies—including import quotas, export subsidies, international cartels, and the procedural variations of tariffs —and the short-sighted egoism of pressure groups is enlightenment. The exposure of lobbyists, and public debate in the legislative assemblies (as during the passage and renewals of the U. S. Reciprocal Trade Agreements legislation), are steps in this process of effective enlightenment, for this might strengthen political parties as advocates of free trade.

To all general rules of good policy, governments are obliged to make temporary exceptions. Two of this nature may be mentioned. A country like the newly developing Israel may twist its economy, both as to productive development and its close correlative, consumption, to obtain dollars for dollar-purchasable supplies, or to receive deliveries from a German government as reparation for past despoliation of its Jews. Or, as in the United States, large-scale production in agriculture is fostered when the government buys surplus quantities (raising the income of farmers) and sells them abroad at prices that undercut foreign producers. Intense nationalism is the continuing cause.

International cartels are arrangements of producers to frame the market to suit themselves and limit competition. A constructive justification is the desire to counteract the producers' ignorance of the intentions of their rivals in relation to the total market, which causes ruinous spells of over- and under-production. Various governments favor such arrangements when they protect against instability that may spread to the whole economy.

Governments are strongly tempted to regulate and subsidize agriculture by means of the special instability of the incomes of primary producers (e.g., the American government's farm parity program), and this, in turn, by international commodity agreements. They allocate foreign markets and fix prices by international agreement and control domestic production accordingly. Hitherto, however, unlike the objective of cartels,[38] the purpose of the agreement has been the

[38] G. W. Stocking and M. W. Walkins, *Cartels in Action* (New York: Twentieth Century Fund, 1946).

expansion of the market. Coffee, tea, sugar, tin, rubber, and wheat agreements are typical.[39] The objective is production regulated by knowledge of the world market and producers' intentions and, hence, stability over the years. It could, however, be stability with rising production and reduced costs of production and, hence, lower prices.

An underdeveloped economy, making plans for economic development, would jeopardize its success if it failed to enter such agreements. The potential relationship with the plans of the Food and Agricultural Organization, the International Bank for Reconstruction and Development, and the International Trade Organization,[40] not to mention the economic co-operation and security planning agencies of the wealthier countries, needs no further stressing.

Dollar diplomacy and Point Four. Well-developed economies need customers, fields for investment, and sources of raw materials. Underdeveloped economies need capital, technical knowledge, and management. Their complementary interests before mid-nineteenth century were furthered by such state-supported corporations as the British East India Company; after about 1850, largely by private enterprise.

While the economic advantage of such arrangements to both partners was immense, private investors could not bring roads, dams, warehouses, commercial institutions, mining, railroads, street cars, and resource-processing means to underdeveloped countries without the question of sovereignty being raised. The laws and customs of other countries, most of all those where village or tribal economy prevails, with joint ownership of land, and which is bound up with ancient religions, nonindustrial values, and ethnocentric family and tribal ties, are not smoothly adaptable to the incursion of foreign businessmen and ideals. In any case, the power of the state is required for the protection of economic enterprise, if only to maintain contracts and secure property. The dollar and the pound moved into other countries along with diplomatic support and the power of the national flag of the investing country. For about two centuries the incomers intervened in the internal governmental affairs and social development of the country in which they invested, supported occasionally by intimi-

[39] Joseph S. Davis, *International Commodity Agreements* (1947). *Intergovernmental Commodity Control Agreements* (Geneva: International Labour Office: 1943).

[40] William Adams Brown, *The United States and the Restoration of World Trade* (Washington, D.C.: Brookings Institution, 1950).

dation, armed intervention, or fomented revolution.[41] Rivalry between the diverse investing nations stirred up further trouble. The price paid to the investor was overly beneficial to him. Yet, in spite of ex post facto complaints by the later generations of the countries so developed, the recipient economy was markedly advanced.

The underdeveloped economies learned, however, that the historic priority of northwestern Europe and the United States in industry was no natural monopoly confined to the harbingers. Their nationalism developed; they resented their colonial status; and they wished to be liberated from the condition of being raw-material countries (nitrates and copper from Chile; silver from Mexico). Intellectuals and businessmen demanded the right to replace foreign investors, technicians, and foremen. Some of the countries confiscated the foreign investments; others bought them at forced selling prices; while still others forbade further investment, except on much more favorable terms. The freeing of management for their own nationals was more important to them than a low rate of interest, even if thereby they paid a higher price for goods and thus slowed down the rate of economic development. The governments of the investing countries became more and more ashamed of the charge of "imperialism." Furthermore, anthropological observers, inside and outside the underdeveloped countries, made all parties concerned more sensitive to the changes in the cultural habits of the native populations and raised the question: Is economic growth worth the loss of traditional values? If an African ceases to have cattle, he has lost the currency that buys a wife!

These various factors and the state of international politics after World War II, together with the universal longing for a world-wide international economic system, brought about the establishment of the many specialized agencies of the United Nations, and the specific national contributions of America, Britain, and Holland toward economic development above all. Most of the activities of these and other agencies have been labeled Point Four.

As set out in President Truman's message on economic development, January 20, 1949, Point Four promised the application of scientific advance and industrial progress to underdeveloped areas, particularly to the lifting up from inadequate food, disease, and igno-

[41] S. F. Bemis, *Latin American Policy of the United States* (New York: Harcourt, Brace & Co., 1943). H. N. Brailsford, *The War of Steel and Gold* (London: G. Bell and Sons, Ltd., 1914).

rance of that half of the world's population that lives in economic misery. This would be accomplished by making available technical knowledge and capital investment, so devised and controlled as to benefit the peoples of the various areas, and by guarantees both to the foreign investors and the interests of the local populations.

Through the International Bank for Reconstruction and Development, whose capital is put in shares by the signatory countries, large sums are lent directly, or loans in the market are guaranteed. There is similar assistance through other agencies of the United Nations and the funds of particular countries. Supplementing investment and knowledge are mixed teams of experts and directors which visit each others' countries to develop better budgetary methods, statistics, and administration and improve productivity.[42] Long-term plans are produced by each country, assisted and encouraged by experts from the advanced lands.

The amount of capital needed is tremendous. The amount contributable by the backward economies is trivial, since it must be wrung from a standard of living hardly above that of a crude subsistence. Long-term capital is the key; it is the role of governments, rather than the private investor, to provide it and of the recipient government to plan its use.

POTENTIALS OF GOVERNMENT'S ACTIVE ROLE

Consumer and saver. The day of the free market with thousands or millions of private individual firms, each not so large as to displace the power of competition excessively, is over. Modern national governments spend from one-fourth to more than one-third of the total national income. It is doubtful whether this figure will ever decrease, even when the more crucial threats of aggression have died down. In the underdeveloped economies, the whole task of development begins with the government as the dominant saver and consumer.

No private economic corporation has ever been close to attaining such power to animate, direct, stimulate, or narcoticize economic development. In addition to financing, as already suggested, government can acquire funds by the sale of goods it produces, through power,

[42] United Nations, *Formulations and Economic Appraisal of Development Projects*, Books I and II (New York: Columbia University Press, 1941); T. R. Mack, *Coordination of International Aid and Socio-Economic Development* (New York: Citadel Press, 1953). Walter Sharp, *International Technical Assistance* (1953).

transportation, communications, fuel, and so on. This is especially the case where industries have been nationalized on a large scale.

The effect is immense. The government bids against private bidders. It is a powerful determiner of prices. It faces the problems of timing, of how to stagger its purchases, and how to relate this to civil consumption, in terms of the seasons of the year and the cycle of years. This is closely related to its budget, to the national debt, and to private saving and investment.

This powerful position, fraught with the power to destroy as well as create prosperity, has necessitated attention to planning agencies. In every country there is a top nexus of economic advisers, security resources councils, and so on, closely geared with the chief executive, the administrative department, and the legislative assembly. Political parties have been forced to make themselves more expert technically, either by governmental inquiry bodies or by their own intraparty research councils. The problem of administrative co-ordination of the various departments of governmental activity was never so urgent as now, even as the nascent world economic agencies have needed special co-ordination through the Economic and Social Council of the United Nations.[43] A plan of development must be integrated and its executers must be specialized experts: success depends on the integration of knowledge and departmental coherence continuously until the fulfillment of the plan in time.

Government, not only a great consumer, is also a saver; its methods are a combination of taxation and borrowing. Its full potential here is the total annual product of the nation. But there is a point at which the work force and the managers and investors will rebel against taxation and saving: it depends on the ability of the government to convince its constituents of the value of the uses to which the proceeds will be put and of the fact that the administrative cost is not wasteful, as compared with the goods obtainable by free spending and the very value of freedom from control itself.

Insurer and producer. Modern economists have found it indispensable to require their governments to engage considerably in substantial lending, guaranteeing and insuring activities.[44] These fall into

[43] Herman Finer, *The United Nations Economic and Social Council* (Boston: World Peace Foundation, 1946).

[44] M. Fainsod and L. Gordon *op. cit.* Hoover Commission on the Reorganization of the Executive Branch of the Government.

well-defined categories: loans and guarantees of provisions for housing and farms, crop insurance, foreign investment, and loans for business operations and economic development.

What is the rationale of such activities? Some of the ventures are long-term, where private enterprise cannot take the risk over such time because its own interest may be ephemeral or its members not courageous or foolhardy enough. Or, as in underdeveloped countries, private entrepreneurs may be ignorant or prefer to go out hunting, or being idle, or taking part in religious festivals, or leading a military life. In other cases, government can find the funds much more cheaply than private investors because it can call up capital through taxation, by inflation, or by spreading the risk involved. In still other cases, as in a project like the TVA covering several segments of a number of states, the exercise of sovereign authority is necessary to get areas evacuated or, as in underdeveloped countries, to transfer populations and to keep native work forces in compounds and under police control. Such authority can hardly be entrusted to private individuals.

Government may not actually undertake such works itself, but merely guarantee the risks run by private entrepreneurs. This helps reduce the number of employees of the government and simplifies its machinery and processes. It also tends to obviate political favoritism in the selection of who shall or shall not receive government credits and avoids the problem of shady intermediaries between government and entrepreneurs. In underdeveloped lands, government insurance and loan activities are essential to defeat exploitation by money-lenders.

There are and can be many variations in government investment. For example, the Chilean Development Corporation (government-owned), acts in part by investing funds obtained from tax funds, while private entrepreneurs match the funds so provided. Initially, the government has a wide control of the management of the industry. As soon as the industry is strong, government generally sells its shares to private buyers and then puts the proceeds into a new industry according to the plan it has formulated.

Producer. Many governments now own and manage industries and agricultural ventures. The reason has been suggested in part in the treatment of government investment. Inequalities of property and income in some countries have also become so stereotyped as a class structure that pressure for careers open to talent eventuated in government ownership, since government could be held to responsibility. Moreover, certain "key" industries are held to be basic to the whole economy, and it is expected that government ownership will outlaw strikes in them. Other reasons for nationalizing are general planning and international security.

The United States has traveled least in this direction; the Soviet Union, most; other countries, like Britain, France, and Italy, have instituted government management of the municipal utilities and a few "key" industries.

The nationalized industry, if it is to be efficient, must respond to the conditions of successful economic management as must any private firm. The name of government bears only this extra magic which that of private business does not—that there may be a certain awe and majesty about it. On the other hand, it is, according to time and place, liable to be reviled and mis-served, precisely because it represents authority. A low prestige of government, due to past inefficiency or corruption or self-seeking, robs it of good servants. The inner difficulty is to provide men with the incentives of innovation and invention in a government-owned monopoly, when the surrounding professions are both competitive and high-paid and bear social prestige. Furthermore, the control of government-owned agencies is, in the final resort, either committed to elected representatives or to their own consciences. They may be clever and sensible enough to trust their experts, but that too has its dangers since the experts may interfere with partisan intention. If they do not stimulate, the expert directors' routine may freeze innovation. Moreover, clear-cut competitive accountancy enabling the ascription of responsibility for good or bad management and activity is reduced, by hypothesis. And, where, like the TVA, government runs an agency which is multipurpose, it is difficult to pin responsibility on one of the activities without another being entered as an alibi, and the ascription of costs to each beyond dispute is impossible. However, these dangers have to be set against the inefficiencies of private enterprise—ignorance, throttling of competition, fraud.

Resource-owner and innovator. Some nations claim all mineral, power, and water resources and the land for the government and proceed by direct management or licensing to private firms, or co-operatives. Economically, this involves the problems already noted in the discussion of managing industries, regulating monopolies, and developing backward economies. Will direct exploitation by government yield better results than licensing or partnership of some form with private enterprise? It depends on the answers to the political and administrative questions suggested at the beginning of this chapter and restated in the section on government as producer.

Sometimes, governments like the British have bought resources (coal) from the landlords because these neither had the incentive nor the temerity nor the technical means at their disposal to exploit the resources to their economic maximum.[45] Their mores could not be adapted properly to the foreign competition, new technology, and long-term planning required due to the obsolescence of equipment and structure of the mines. In some underdeveloped countries, there is an analogous pressure for government ownership; in places like Chile, Egypt, southern Italy, and so on, the large landowners underutilize their land and are not interested or expert enough to develop their produce as available technology allows.

Government as innovator has a great field in the provision of works that benefit the whole of society, as in regional development like the TVA or the Punjab drainage area. These help both the individuals in the area and the entire nation. In these cases, the government's "brains" have been added to that of the private entrepreneurs in other parts of the economy. What may be done may be inferred from the ingenious multipurpose economic development of Chile, using more brains and research and patriotic incentives; in the atomic energy projects that have been developed through mass organization of scientists and technicians, long-term research, and highly expensive plant; and in the Rural Electrification Administration, with its philanthropic incentive, its stimulation of enterprise, its long-term risk-taking, and its education of the rural consumer in farm and household economy.

GENERAL OBSERVATIONS

The competence of government. Capitalism, or private enterprise—sometimes called economic decentralization—is a system of administration; government in the economy is an alternative system of ad-

[45] Henry T. Rose, *The British Coal Industry* (New York: The Macmillan Company, 1951).

ministration. The difference lies in their incentives and organization. The former are based on the "self-love" of the entrepreneur. Self-love is creative, but it can also be obstructive, of economic development. The process of social development may cause the entrepreneur to take rather more altruistic views of his objectives and measures—and education might make him more competent, for his vision unaided cannot extend very far, even when he combines with others. The moral pressure of the community may develop this considerably further. In the advanced countries the churches have shown an interest in such changes.

The process is slow, and government has been forced to assume responsibilities. What of the difficulties of public administration? The first is that of personnel where potentialities are bounded only by ability to decide what kinds of skill it needs—the character required to conduct an enterprise; the ability to pay the pecuniary and prestige rewards to the right numbers of men and women; and then, the maintenance of morale and inventiveness and a spirit of continuous innovation by rewards, punishments, and leadership.

Next, economic development through government depends upon the right solution to the choice of organization; that is, the specialization of functions, their departmentalization, and the proper technical centralization of authority and decentralization of discretion for operations, as also the marshaling of the minds and interest of all the workers for the information and animation of the directors.[46] Such organization may require, for example, a fair freedom on the part of the government-owned corporations.[47] The natural—that is, the geographical and technological—conditions of each project must be met by personnel and organization.

The potentiality of the government's role depends on these factors, but also upon satisfying the consumers. What means could be substituted for the free market of consumers who spur on the producers? It may be assigned to the legislators, whether representatively elected

[46]Herman Finer, *The Road to Reaction* (Boston: Little, Brown and Company, 1945). Barbara Wootton, *Plan or No Plan* (New York: Farrar & Rinehart, Inc., 1935). F. A. Hayek, *Road to Serfdom* (Chicago: University of Chicago Press, 1944). Lionel Robbins, *op. cit.*, and *The Economic Problem in Peace and War* (New York: The Macmillan Company, 1947).

[47] William A. Robson (ed.), *Problems of Nationalized Industries* (New York: Oxford University Press, 1952). C. H. Pritchett, *The Tennessee Valley Authority* (Chapel Hill, N. C.: University of North Carolina Press, 1943).

or dictatorially appointed, to lobbying groups, to the political parties, and to nonpolitical associations of consumers impinging on the legislative assembly and the executive agencies. Governments are in the process of improving such devices.

Democracy, where conflict is free, and a program of development must await compromise, is a precarious way of life. The answer lies in limiting the role of government to that minimum revealed by previous analysis to be necessary. In general, the burden of proof should rest on the government. This is no counsel of inertia, but of more dynamic degree.

Customary motivations. John Stuart Mill long ago suggested that the various nations differed markedly in their economic motivations. More recent sociological and anthropological study has provided ample confirmation of the extent to which economic development is tied up with the totality of the culture. No series of illustrations can be offered within the present space. But attention must be drawn to the fact that (a) for economic development of the Western sort, profound cultural changes would need to be brought about in most other parts of the world, and that (b) such has happened in the Western world itself over the centuries, but is now possible rather more swiftly because the example of cause and effect is before those who have developed a desire for a higher economic standard of living. Some cultures regard economic acquisition as not worth their while; some have caste systems that make a modern factory system impossible; while in some, peasant morale pertains, making it difficult to secure steady work-discipline and the acceptance of reprimands from foremen.[48] In India, the constitution at once guarantees both "equality of status and opportunity" and also the various cultures! But one of these must give way. The climate may in some places make government or any other agent ineffective in securing high economic development, but in some places, the spacing of work shifts may solve climatic problems.[49]

[48] K. F. Helleiner, "Moral Conditions for Economic Growth," *Journal Economic History* (Spring 1951), Vol. XI, No. 2, pp. 97–116; S. D. Clark, "Religion and Economic Backward Areas," *American Economic Review* (May 1951), Vol. 41, pp. 258–68. B. F. Hoselitz, "Entrepreneurship and Economic Growth," *American Journal Economics and Sociology* (Oct. 1952), Vol. 12.

[49] Sydney F. Markham, *Climate and the Energy of Nations* (New York: Oxford University Press, 1944).

One element of culture is nationalism. This has driven the world into an economy of national economic development or the development of congenial blocs. But, enmity reduces the effectiveness of world organizations for development. Within the blocs, there may be free arrangements, as in the Western world, or the Soviet-style plan enforced on satellites by a compulsory gearing of production and consumption to the Soviet economy under threat of national extinction altogether.

Nationalism may stimulate production and invention, but it enhances the role of government therein. The result is to distort both the national civil economy and the maximum economic development of the material and human resources of the whole world.

The Atmosphere of Development and Forms of Government

It has been shown that if a government is to encourage economic development, it must be able to tax, to borrow, to control the money supply, to initiate industry, to subsidize, and so on through many more complex operations. This has involved the functioning of a carefully articulated set of political and administrative institutions and mores. On previous pages we have suggested certain basic conditions these institutions must fulfill in order to promote economic growth—such, to repeat, as stability of government, continuity and objectivity of administration, the proper area of government, appropriate centralization and decentralization, and so on.

These very institutions and the attitude of mind of those who operate them have been the product of a social atmosphere—the spirit in society that they were needful to society's values and purposes—and, at the same time, once in being, they help to sustain and develop that very spirit to fit the development of the economy as its needs are unfolded in experience.[50]

The line between society and government is a formal one, after a certain period of operation and adaptation. The provision of atmosphere becomes a most important function of government, not least in the matter of economic development. An illustration suggests the relationship. In the early years of the TVA, the problem to be solved was the swifter or slower eviction of the private electric utilities from

[50] W. R. Espy, *Bold New Program* (New York: Harpers & Brothers, 1950). W. W. Rostow, *The Process of Economic Growth* (New York: W. W. Norton and Co., 1952).

the channels of distribution of the power which the TVA was to produce. One element in the board of directors of the Authority insisted that government could not proceed in a struggle against the utilities by ignoble means, on the plea that a government contributes to the welfare of the people not only by what it does for them but by the decency of the means it uses. This policy would inevitably have slowed the progress of the Authority, and those who held to the values indicated were willing to accept this consequence.

Let us consider, then, more broadly, the provision of the atmosphere of economic development by government and the kind of government, democratic or other, that might best accomplish this.

What can "atmosphere" mean in the present context? It must mean prevalence of a desire for a rising standard of living that has a high priority among all other values. The desire must represent not a mere wish or dream, but a determination as strong and sustained as the economic projects demand to make the sacrifices of habits, culture, and so on required for success, and included in such submission is the responsiveness to the will of the government acting as economic entrepreneur. In India and China, the family and philosophy of the universe would have to be fundamentally changed from intuitive norms of a Taoist (or Brahman) kind to Western logic, mathematics, and science.

This desire and determination has in some places been developed chiefly by the rise of an acquisitive spirit in society, even if government has been infected by it, and in some places by government taking the lead. A glance at the respective experiences is important.

In England, the birthplace of modern industry and capitalism, the late eighteenth and early nineteenth centuries saw the transformation of the Protestant ethic into economic endeavor.[51] The spiritual values of salvation were couched in terms of success in industry on earth, and "good works" for heavenly merit were translated as the producing of goods. There followed steady, exacting work habits by the entrepreneurs, considerable personal frugality, and the idea of saving for investment purposes, with the attendant doctrine that interest was the reward of "abstinence," and an incentive for economic development in the interests of the next generation.

This spirit acted mainly through the landless middle classes,

[51] Richard H. Tawney, *The Sickness of an Acquisitive Society* (London: Allen & Unwin, 1920).

through small trader's and a merchant class, which, though con-
demned by the aristocracy, nevertheless were not subjected to remaining what they were in their humble origins by any rules of caste,
but, instead, benefited from social mobility.[52] Moreover, the age-long
practice of colonial trade and rule produced a spirit of economic development and of a certain callousness of the developers towards ancient manners and customs.

The ruling class was partly, but subordinately, one of merchants.
Yet the mercantile spirit triumphed because wealth is seductive to almost all men, because wealth assists political power, and because all
men could appreciate that great national wealth meant success in arms
and foreign policy.

Hence, the government itself took on the complexion of economic
entrepreneur, though the earliest activity was the demolition of ancient rules, such as that of apprenticeship, reversal of a too-kindly
benevolence to the destitute, and a sweeping away of a mass of antiquated and inefficient central and local administrative arrangements.
Soon, the new industrial and commercial upper *bourgeoisie* came
largely into the highest offices of government and continued the work
of freeing economic enterprise from old trammels. In addition, they
established some positive institutions to spur on, and yet reduce the
uncertainties facing, the entrepreneur; they established the joint-stock
principle in order to reduce the risks taken by the entrepreneur and
regulated the banking and currency system to avoid susceptibility to
crisis.

Industry was thus allowed to take the lead, and more so when wide
circles of the population became convinced that the wealth and
strength of the whole country (this is the element of national pride or
patriotism that is enlistable) was good. For some decades, the government was willing to give industry free rein by breaking down the obstructions, excepting the laws relating to contract, inheritance, and
fraud. Even the laws protecting agriculture were repealed in the interests of commercial freedom and to encourage markets for manufactures through such a policy.

The education of the time corresponded to the economic purposes:

[52] T. S. Ashton, *The Industrial Revolution* (London, New York: Oxford University Press, 1948); S. E. Finer, *The Life and Times of Edwin Chadwick* (London: Methuen & Co., Ltd., 1952); J. H. Clapham, *Economic History of Modern
Britain* (Cambridge, Eng.: The University Press, 1930–38).

it was Protestant, and it placed the emphasis on character and self-help.[53] The principle of "less eligibility" tended to force able-bodied persons out of the workhouses, where their destitution had hitherto been relieved. It took many years before governments so motivated entered to rescue men, women, and children from excessively long hours and employment in dangerous occupations.

These governments were not democratic in the full sense. They did not represent the mass of the working population, but mainly represented the entrepreneurs.

In the economic development of the United States, after the federal Constitution was set up, the regulating activity of government was at its very minimum, for the prevailing atmosphere was one even more vigorously and crassly acquisitive than that of England of the same era and lasted so for much longer. Avoidance of the invidious sense of the well-known term "robber-barons" is desired when it is applied to the economic pioneers in America; yet the sense of rapacity cannot, in all scientific candor, be ignored.[54] The quintessence of Protestantism, when secularized, was individualism under the steam of "life, liberty, and the pursuit of happiness," with the minimum of religious and social restraints, for the Constitution guaranteed also freedom of worship and did not permit the establishment of a state church. The country was peopled by those who came from other lands to be well off economically and to escape from class rigidities. The opportunities were so immense as to turn the God-fearing Puritans into the sharpest and most uninhibited traders[55] and manufacturers. But how can such individualism of property and enterprise be produced in communities today where land is held in common?

Government became practically an absentee, except when it gave gifts of land to settlers and provided some so-called internal improvements—roads, posts, and river and harbor works. The "atmosphere"

[53] Charles Birchenough, *History of Elementary Education* (London: University Tutorial Press, 1914). Samuel Smiles, *Self Help* (1871); *Thrift* (1859); *Duty* (1880). (New York: Harper).

[54] *The People Shall Judge*, two vols., Univ. of Chicago Social Sciences Staff (Chicago: University of Chicago Press, 1949). S. E. Morrison, and H. S. Commager, *The Growth of the American Republic* (1950), Vol. I & II; bibliographies are valuable.

[55] George A. Graham, *Morality in American Politics* (New York: Random House, 1952). Paul H. Douglas, *Ethics in Government* (Cambridge, Mass.: Harvard University Press, 1952). British Government Report (H.M.S.D.) *Intermediaries Between Business and Government*, 1950.

it condoned and did not interfere with included freedom of the entrepreneur, rewards to the successful, private charity to the failures, the prestige of economic success (there were no titles of nobility), *caveat emptor*, and the maximum decentralization to the states of their feeble powers of economic regulation and assistance. Even the Bank of the United States was abolished after it had been founded. And in the middle and later decades of the nineteenth century the U. S. Senate and the state legislatures were to a large extent the creatures of the ironmasters, the railroad and oil magnates, and the financiers. The government was forced into a high-tariff policy.

Tremendous economic development followed. But some of the terrible economic and social evils of no-government are being paid for today by the entrance of government to do a repair job on wasted resources, etc.[56] Social Darwinism condoned the cruel disregard of humanity and ethics.

At one stage, then, and in some places, according to the prevalent spiritual dispositions of society, a government may do best by staying out of the picture of economic development and by giving the uninhibited entrepreneurs free rein—making itself their agent as and when they like. At a later stage, the economy may become so complex, as in Britain and the United States, both domestically and as regards foreign markets and investments, that its regulative, knowledge-providing, integrative, and compensating power is the very condition of the stable progress of the economy.[57]

Japan since 1870, Tsarist Russia after the seventeenth century, imperial Germany, and the Soviet government more recently are, on the contrary, examples of economies in which government played a great initiating and active entrepreneurial role, helping to establish "atmosphere."

Both Japan[58] and Germany entered the modern industrial era with strong and nondemocratic systems of government. In the first case, Japan had maintained a feudal system of agriculture over many centuries, and in the second, Germany had in the seventeenth century practiced state control and ownership of agricultural, mining, and in-

[56] President's Research Committee, *Recent Social Trends in the United States*, (New York: McGraw-Hill, 1933).

[57] Herman Finer, "Politics and Economics," *Theory and Practice of Modern Government* (London: Methuen & Co., Ltd., 1932).

[58] John H. Clapham, *Economic Development of France and Germany*, 4th Ed. (Cambridge, Eng.: The University Press, 1936).

dustrial enterprises through its own skilled bureaucracy and had not been substantially converted to the ideas of *laissez faire* or unbridled acquisitiveness by either the French Revolution or the doctrines of Adam Smith.

Japan began economic development faced with maturing industrial economies elsewhere and a high progress of invention. Her government realized that if she were now opened to the influences of the world, she would then have to be militarily strong, and this depended in large part on industrial strength. But Japan had a servile, docile, hard-working, and religious-minded population. The government and the high aristocracy and its tycoons became the main instrument in transforming the country, through the type of education and through a deliberately planned policy that embraced government subsidies to selected industries, the unscrupulous copy of foreign inventions, the energizing of entrepreneurs by government propaganda and the grant of national honors, and the fostering of a kind of economic envy and contempt of foreign competitors. It has been argued that the Japanese benefited from the idea of authority incarnated in the sun-god, and that this made it easy to transfer authority to the *zaibatsu*, the financial oligarchy.[59]

In Germany, the government undertook a similar role, with the advantages of a better educated population, a great commercial tradition, a splendid culture, an extraordinarily expert bureaucracy, and a respect for the rule of law. Here a conscious partnership between government and the upper *bourgeosie*, based on the strength and the military and colonial hopes of the former, the quest of greatness and the aspirations of the latter for economic wealth and national prestige, fostered economic development. The rivalry with England; the propaganda for colonies and a "place in the sun"; the glorification of Germany, the fatherland; and an activist policy in world affairs—all brought the population to a high state of enterprising tension. There followed the modernizing of the commercial and industrial codes of law, the encouragement of invention, the subsidizing of industrial research, and one of the finest systems of general education—especially scientific, technological, and commercial instruction—the world had

[59] F. S. C. Northrop, *The Taming of the Nations* (New York: The Macmillan Company, 1952). William A. Lewis *et. al., Attitude to Africa* (Hammondsworth, Eng.: Penguin Books, 1951). William M. Macmillan, *Africa Emergent* (New York: Ryerson Press, 1938).

ever seen. A severe hardness in economic life broke down the older virtues of kindliness and good-natured dreaming where they had flourished and gave rein to Prussianism which had heretofore been chiefly operative in the bureaucracy and the army.[60] The cult of *Tüchtigkeit*, high, objective competence and "rational" organization (the word "rationalization" stems from German economic development, as does *Planwirtschaft*, the planned economy), became the top value, and government promoted it fully. Both these governments persecuted and tried to suppress labor unions and socialism as contrary to the interests of the entrepreneurs of economic development.

As for the Tsarist Russian government, they attempted the job of colonizing the vast spaces of Russia with different means and spirit from those of the similar conquest of the frontier of America by Americans.[61] In Russia, a government prevailed which was secularly and religiously absolute and admitted of practically no social development of any kind, unless sanctioned or initiated by the government. With a servile, intimidated, apathetic, and superstitious population, a government might have proceeded to offer education and enlightenment. It preferred compulsorily to consign whole villages or army groups to distant places for agricultural settlement, and to establish its own workshops, and it left the general task of economic development of the land to the nobility, with enslaved peasants as their workers. An Asiatic mentality kept this system almost intact until the sixties of the nineteenth century. Then the government built railroads [badly] and alternately encouraged industry and commerce and corrupted them.

Perhaps the most important service of the Soviet regime to Russian economic development is not the actual things it produces, but its emancipation of the masses from the Tsarist regime; the spreading of education and the very idea that education is desirable (even though it may be warped by wrong economic and world-political ideas); the overthrow of the superstitious element in Russian religion and education; the animation of the population to mobility, social and territorial; the sponsoring of the idea of careers open to talent; the inflaming of economic acquisitiveness; and adoption of the principle of pay

[60] Werner Sombart, *Modern Capitalism*, 1930.

[61] B. H. Sumner, *Short History of Russia* (New York: Reynal & Hitchcock, 1943).

graded to production. These are permanent and essential ingredients of economic development. The authoritarian political and economic structure may, of course, be destroyed by the very posterity of the generations which have been used by the Soviet dictatorship, in their own words, as "the manure of the future."

In general, the economic structures and dynamics so developed were not planned at one single moment, nor were the governments or social services and organizations that interplayed with them. Yet the process of development was not an entirely blind one or one without deliberate policy for at least a few years ahead. Sometimes the day's work was done with statesmen or individual entrepreneurs, conscious that it was but the work of a day and the best they could do or wanted to do; sometimes, as with the case of the Hamiltonian policy of manufacture and the tariff, a longer, almost a timeless, development was postulated.

Whether the development policy was highly directed or less so, an adjustment occurred between the standard of living, possible and aimed at, the size of the population, the occupational distribution (where mobility was possible), and the educational system. In the free-government countries, it was appreciated by society and government that, for a stable, uninterrupted economic development, not operating under violent coercions among the work force or the entrepreneurs, all involved in the productive process must be able to get what they work for, to get what they thought themselves worth compared with their abilities and effort, and be allowed to keep such products for themselves or freely dispose of them. They had to be assured that the goods and services they wanted to buy or sell, the businesses they wanted to start, or the markets they anticipated would not be arbitrarily closed off by the action of society or government.

These desiderata required that the government do nothing as an adapter or entrepreneur of economic activity except to supply the framework of law and order, the guarantee of the sanctity of contract, and so on, and that here it must be very strong in order to avoid chaos and violence. Or, if government did undertake some degree of economic enterprise, that then it must also be powerful and objective. These two terms have already been used and explained. Where governments both interfered and were not powerful but simply authoritarian and not objective but ignorant and corrupt, economic life not only stagnated but was a disgrace to human spirit—such was Tsarist Russia, and such are present examples among the underdeveloped economies.

It is doubtful whether any economy can develop, whether by government impulsion or under the free energy of individuals, without at least a high degree of representativeness in the government—that it be representative of the people at large. Even the Soviet Union's economy has had to admit (though probably with reluctance for political-dictatorial reasons) a highly representative part for the people and the agencies of representation.[62] The entrepreneur must *know* as much about his work force as he can—its tastes, capacities, and amenability to discipline and education; however, having allowed them to represent what they want and are, he may still try to bend them through institutions that are not *responsible* to the people in the sense that these may choose and throw out their governors by free election. The Mussolini system of dictatorship, with an economy geared to welfare as the dictator conceived it and strongly marked by military preparation, could not avoid a representative arrangement of men and women grouped in the associations of workers and employers (syndicates, *sindicati*) and joint representative bodies of both of these, the corporations.[63] The individual firms in modern industrial nations have learned the same lesson as to the need for representation of the mind and force of their workers, and governmental legislation has assisted this, because the continued loyalty and work discipline of the work force is essential to development. Schumpeter has placed considerable stress on this theme in considering the future of capitalism and in assessing the inroads of Marxian values on the present-day work force. The underdeveloped economies everywhere are beginning their progress in a world from which the excitements of democracy cannot be banished. It is a moot point whether life-service will satisfy the sophisticated.

Now candor requires the admission that in some cases the populations are so feeble in health, so uneducated, so illiterate, and so primitive that centuries might go by before any hand was set to substantial economic development unless government intervened in an autocratic manner. Such situations exist in various parts of Africa; for

---

[62] Barrington Moore, *Soviet Politics—The Dilemma of Power* (Cambridge, Mass.: Harvard University Press, 1950).

[63] Herman Finer, *Mussolini's Italy* (London: V. Gollancz, Ltd., 1935).

example, among the Berbers. These may be admirable peoples and cultures with many pleasant and picturesque features—but economic development has its own demands. Gold Coast farmers believed that liberation from British rule would permit them to keep their diseased cocoa trees. They soon learned otherwise. If it happens that the leaders of society are more conscious of economic desires and of the uses of acquired material welfare and also are superior in knowledge to the general body of the people and to that degree in which time is of the essence in getting a higher income, then an autocratic leadership will be the technique of economic development, whether it come in the form of "government," or in the societal tolerance of individual entrepreneurs.

If such development is conscious—if conditions allow it to be conscious and controlled, not blind and jittery—then for the long run of economic development, wisdom would ask that the autocracy be (a) benevolent and (b) consultative or representative. The first quality would seek to persuade by a sharing of benefits rather than by slave-driving, and the second, to educate, not merely by attendance at school or through propaganda, but by shared experience of the actual process of success and failure in development. The native prime minister of the Gold Coast was forced by the prospect of national ruin in a few years to decree the destruction of diseased cocoa trees and a replanting with healthy ones: long-term welfare against shortsightedness. Perhaps the greatest merit of the American way during the nineteenth century was that the greatest number of people was involved in the deepest first-hand experience of what economic development under *laissez faire* actually meant and demanded—its successes, failures, rewards, and deprivations.

A land that is poor in resources may, even though it is rich in culture and skill, find itself forced to a regimented economy if it wants to make fast economic progress, and according to the measure in which it wants a high standard of living.

There is no royal rule applicable to *all* nations at all times regarding the government that will give them economic welfare, totalitarian or democratic. The economic circumstances and the demand for values other than economic welfare determine whether either of these, or what extent of mixture, is necessary, and for how long.

It is extremely difficult to make over a nondemocratic polity into a democratic society with a government to order in a short time, if this should be thought to be a major condition of economic development. Democratic government means the election and rejection of governments for shortish periods of tenure by the people, the formulation and sanction of policy by free discussion, and reliance on self-leadership and *self-control* by the masses.[64]

Democracy seems also to be a solvent of certain rigid social forms that may inhibit economic development. For a democratic government that relied for its morale and impetus on a democratic spirit would be secular and rational regarding traditional values and economic pursuits. For example, religious piety, founded as it is in many parts of the world on assumptions of mysticism and even witchcraft, could not resist free discussion. Under a democracy free inquiry might well dissolve such obstacles to economic co-operation and education as might be imposed by the operation of a caste system or a profession like the priesthood. Money-lending, with its high prestige as compared with domestic manufactures, and tradition-bolstered landlordism would be on the defensive. Democratic nations would require an accounting of certain practices that are not favorable in the long run to economic development—if democracy includes the principle of equality—because favoritism and nepotism would come under attack and the demand would be made for the "career open to the talents." Sooner or later, the assets of production, like the land, would be judged by whether their management inured to the "public" or only to private welfare. The various traditional customs that limit territorial and social mobility would break down. New prestige might be given by a democratic society to the creators of wealth and their ruthlessness in sweeping away all the "sacred cows" if the masses were left free to hear all opinions and choose "rich milk rather than such sacred cows" when the facts are put before them early enough in their education to permit an effective choice.

But this sounds like a nondemocratic society pulling itself out of its social characteristics "by its own bootstraps." If a nation is tradition-bound, religion-bound, culture-bound, and primitive-economy-bound so hard and fast over the centuries, so that it has a feudal, slothful, and arrogant nondemocratic government, or a set of dirty, diseased witch-doctors, how is it to be changed so that it becomes democratic

[64] J. S. Mill, *Considerations on Representative Government* (New York: Henry Holt and Company, 1867).

by act of its nondemocratic government? The hard cake of custom has to be broken, and it can be broken by the incursion of economic invaders—and this is nondemocratic, at any rate for some time—or by some kind of revolution within the country from one or another level of the population.

It is necessary to repeat that the temporal situation of some lands makes Western democracy ineffective as an instrument of economic development. Something like the benevolent revolution and temporary autocracy of Kemal Atatürk in Turkey[65] and, possibly, the action of General Naguib in Egypt, are required as the initial thrusts to secure the rational freedom from fatalism and the opium of doctrines of immortality that destroy economic impetus. Kemal Atatürk was even obliged to begin by demanding that everybody *take a name(!)*; that censuses be instituted; that written characters be modernized; that women be emancipated; that the religious authority of the Mohammedan caliphate be ejected from all civil affairs; and that the fez be discarded in favor of hats (compare Werner Sombart's theory of the relationship between economic development and "rational" costume! The village stagnation of China has been laid partly to its pictographic, nonsyntactical language.) Moreover, a "democratic" constitution was set up which, though not responsible in the Western sense, nevertheless was representative and initiated a regime of political education of the masses destined in the end to produce responsible government. It took a revolution by a truly modernized and popularly benevolent patriotic leader to overthrow the corruption and stagnation of centuries and so release the energies and brains of a vigorous people for economic development. The "atmosphere" of economic development was here supplied by a few men whose values gave it, and a Western pattern of humane values, supremacy over the traditional religious pattern, and since they felt strongly enough to abhor the patience of centuries, revolution was their initial step.

To appreciate the relationship between government and economic development and to enable some judgment to be formed concerning whether the circumstances in which a democratic, an autocratic, or

[65] International Bank for Reconstruction and Development, Mission to Turkey, *The Economy of Turkey* (Washington, D.C.: International Bank for Reconstruction and Development, 1953).

totalitarian, or some "mixed" form is more propitious to it, a glance at two experiments in economic development will be appropriate: the economy of the Soviet Union and the American TVA.

It is reasonable to suggest that the economic progress made since 1918 in Russia could not have been made with anything short of the measures like the Soviet government has taken. However much one may detest Soviet dictatorship and the political bestiality of the men in the Kremlin, politically and internationally, this does not touch the problem of whether total over-all production has increased. The managers of the Soviet economy set various economic goals;[66] they created institutions to achieve them, with remarkable ingenuity and steady, tenacious thought. They then adapted the institutions to the changing goals to repair the mistakes they had made. They ridiculed or abolished old, functioning customs, religious and otherwise. They poked public fun at and deplored such Russian beloved characters as Oblomov, a good-natured but absolutely bone-lazy character in Goncharov's famous novel of that name. They brought home to the people that their economic pace was henceforth no longer to be that of the Song of the Volga Boatmen. By unflagging and nationwide propaganda, they animated the populace to a desire for economic welfare and the need for self-improvement and work discipline. They broke into agriculture with the tractor and experimental station, and even the new collectives were made into collective educational organizations. The Russian educational system was adapted to a highly modernized, science-animated society and industry. Economic mobility was encouraged through the selection of *cadres*; that is, the officer-type, schooled and groomed leaders of battalions of workers and officials. These leaders were specially trained to act as pioneers in economic development and to further the education of the rank and file. They supplied high social prestige for the outstanding modernizers and the champion producers in all the local communities.

They also established a representative system of government, which, while denying the masses the authority to determine policy, nevertheless enabled the Soviet top entrepreneurs to understand better what policy was actually feasible. This also aimed to draw more and more

[66] A. E. Baykov, *Economic Development of Soviet Russia*, 1948, David Lilienthal, *Democracy on the March* (New York: Harper & Brothers, 1944). Joseph Stalin, *Leninism*, 1942. *Reports of the 19th Congress of Communist Part(y) of Soviet Russia* (1953).

of the masses into economic and political experience designed to take the terrible weight off the shoulders of the few at the top, to offer some assurance of a perpetuation of the development they had arbitrarily started, and to produce the illusion of democracy. They proceeded with a tremendous pressure of coercion to extract the maximum of work from their people for the minimum of present-day consumption in order to establish the essential fixed-capital works and the intangible capital which would bear fruit later on.

It is difficult to believe that the democratic-bourgeois Russian revolution could have achieved this enormous economic progress under its own tenets of individual liberty, competing political parties, and free trade unions *in this length of time*, though, had the people been guaranteed the freedom of choice among values so available, they might freely have *chosen* this way or might have preferred a different balance of values.

The Tennessee Valley Authority was established in a mature economy of a democratic society by democratic means. But in relationship to the valley itself, it is an authoritarian organization; that is, it was established not by a respresentative or responsible *local* electorate, but by "Washington." [67] Yet, to conform to American democratic expectations, though it set up no "responsible" councils, it carried out its plans wherever they had an effect on local mores, welfare, education, and enterprise after consultation with representative, though nonelected, persons, with the land-grant colleges, and with members of the local governing institutions of state, city, and county. Its first directorate deliberately included a Tennessee personage of educational and agricultural development reputation. For the rest, it was plausibly argued that its democratic responsibility was sufficiently guaranteed by the location of the board of directors in the midst of the valley's inhabitants, and by the ability of these inhabitants to speak to Congress, which was the master and the financial provider of the Authority. A free press, the right of free association, and the habit and resolution of democratic and local government among the people of the valley made the directors and administrative officials of the Authority careful of the opinion of the area.

But without the incursion of the Authority from the outside, the

---

[67] Phillip Selznick, *T.V.A. and the Grass Roots* (Berkley, Calif.: University of California Press, 1949). David Lilienthal, *TVA—Democracy on the March* (New York: Harper and Brothers, 1944).

great progress now visible would not have been made; the various works would perhaps never have been undertaken. A plan of works, to take many years to complete, had to be made on the basis of exacting engineering and social research. That plan demanded a large total investment, that all of it as wanted should be available, and that the continuity of operations be assured. The relationship of agricultural, river transportation, and hydroelectric purposes had to be determined by expert authority. These works involved the coercion of inhabitants, who desired to remain on the land to be flooded, to the extent of their relocation—even cemeteries were relocated. (This is a species of ancestor-worship, most troublesome in primitive economies.) But the choice of remaining on the reservoir land was not allowed.

The inhabitants of the area required a re-education regarding (a) the use of electric power on their farms and homes, (b) better farming methods, (c) conservation, and (d) the introduction of industrial processes. The Authority found it necessary to undertake such education, in part through its own officers, in part through the county agents and influencing of the local public educational authorities. Even in the board of directors there was moral objection to industrialization. A change in eating and work habits was fostered. Careful consideration for the terrain and the means of the farmers stimulated the invention of electric and other equipment of special design. Attention was paid to better general education and to the improvement of health administration. The Authority was chosen by the President of the United States from "dutiful" men in a land of spoils, political favoritism for appointments was legally prohibited, and the morale of the work force was created and sustained by an enlightened system of joint consideration of working conditions and pay and by fair practices over work-force grievances and misdemeanors.

Here, then, is a second way to give an impetus to economic development.

Clearly, there is no sovereign single way: the atmosphere of confidence, security, and enterprise is to be created and maintained by democratic or "mixed" methods attuned to the time, place, and social circumstances, depending on what is determined to be achieved and the noneconomic values people are prepared to sacrifice, and whether the time element in the policy of development is such as to be able to rely on education and persuasion or must take the path of coercion.

Only when the projects envisaged are known, and their cost in labor and other resources determined, can the price they exact in terms of the amount of power and the type of authority be discovered, and these again will indicate the extent to which the individual person must be remodeled and must remodel himself and his social and cultural relations to become an instrument of economic progress.

Whatever kind of government takes up the task of economic development, in the degree in which economic welfare is wanted, it must mitigate the rigidities of caste and class, promote and defend the rights of property and free disposition, and see that the laws are administered without fear or favor to any man. Society itself will need to demolish such social and cultural obstacles before or after government leadership takes control.

Whatever the type of government, its role in economic development should be conducted on certain proven principles in order to guarantee long-run success:

1. Development should be undertaken, but not on some costly, sensational scheme of a utopian kind, regardless of the culture and the human and technical preparedness therefor. It should rather be built up gradually, piece by piece, to fit the developing capacities and values of the people, and to take advantage of each new lesson that the experience of an already achieved project demonstrates. Development undertaken against the will of the masses risks demolition and, even more, a lack of cheerful, energetic co-operation. Much is required of the work force and the consumers as factors in economic development—their acceptance and cooperative obedience and present sacrifices for the future. Coercion is expensive to organize, chokes the energies of the directing and planning minds, and is very costly to make successful. If responsible co-operation is to be obtained (and it is indispensable), then not too much must be asked all at one time.

2. The political arrangements should allow for the reconsideration, the amendment, or the dismantlement of projects shown by experience to be mistakes, as a whole or in part. The way out and the way back should be kept open: in a democracy by the process of election and in a dictatorship by an open mind in the governing group. Human vision in social and economic processes on any scale is far from omniscient. Dependence on the periodical process of election enforces an open mind on the part of public authorities and keeps the mind of the electorate open. A change in course may conflict

with important invested resources; nevertheless, any government that preferred to cover up its errors would be "throwing good money after bad."

3. A "fulfillment" organization is needed; that is, a continuing agency or agencies to make sure that the development progresses according to plan and to watch for inevitable signs that a change of course is needed. In some countries it will properly be an organized system of committees of the legislative body standing outside the executive agencies. In other systems, it would take the shape of groups and committees appointed by the dictatorial clique, like the fulfillment agencies of the Soviet Communist Party, to verify assiduity, detect sabotage, and stimulate managers and workers.

4. The task of education in all its forms ought to be unremitting.

5. One part of such mass education lies in the maximum local decentralization of management consistent with a high (but not necessarily a perfectionist) technical efficiency. This is in order that many people may be drawn in to manage, and criticise the management of, development, and to learn thereby, in practice, the relationship between the ends of economic development, the values obtained and lost through it, and the relevant ways and means of obtaining it.

6. The best education for economic development is democratic government. Such government ought to be instituted or broadened at the earliest possible moment, on the famous principle that "a cure for the troubles of liberty is more liberty." But not all peoples are ready for full, Westernized democracy. Self-government will come first in any full form to a few thousand educated and wealthier persons. If these are patriotic, it will be shared in benevolent leadership with the masses. At some subsequent time, the basic conditions of a genuine democracy will have spread among even larger groups and will consist of a desire for self-government, a willingness to accept its chores and to exercise self-control, as well as impulses of leadership, and an elementary education in the shape of literacy, and the intelligence to listen and learn from political and economic experience.

PART II

CASE STUDIES IN
ECONOMIC DEVELOPMENT

Introduction

THE PRECEDING CHAPTERS HAVE DEALT WITH THE FACTORS RESPONSIBLE
for economic growth largely in an analytical and topical fashion. In
contrast, the authors of the following chapters have presented case examples of the development process in different institutional settings.
This last section of the book, then, has been designed to reveal the
manner in which the various factors interact to produce or inhibit
economic growth.

A glance at the map in the *Foreword* will put these three areas
of the world selected for case studies in perspective. India's annual
income per capita, as the frontispiece diagram shows, is extremely
low even by Mexican or Japanese standards. These countries, in turn,
are still poverty stricken by standards of the West. The recent
history of Japan and Korea provides a unique laboratory in which
to explore the relationship between economic development and
population changes. The fact of Japan's spectacularly rapid industrialization is well known; the somewhat unexpected population
changes which accompanied this industrialization are not so familiar.
Yet an understanding of these changes and their implications is most
important for those concerned with the economic growth of other
heavily populated, underdeveloped areas. India, on the other hand,
provides an example of an area which has failed to achieve its
potential for a long period of time, while Mexico, the other case
example, has shown remarkable growth possibilities, especially during the past decade and a half. A comparison of these countries'
recent history may, therefore, enable us to identify and evaluate the
potency of factors responsible for development. How important has
been the resource base; have elements of the culture influenced
the process; and what role has government played in each case with
what consequences? It is with such questions in mind that these
last chapters should be read.

The choice of relatively underdeveloped countries for detailed consideration was deliberate. Most of the world falls in this category and it is in these areas that the question of how to achieve rapid and sustained growth is most pressing. This by no means implies that problems of development do not face the wealthier nations bordering the North Atlantic. The history of the economic growth of such countries is better known, however, and a number of accounts are readily available to the interested reader.

CHAPTER XI

Japan and Korea: Population Growth

IRENE B. TAEUBER[*][1]

THREE CENTURIES AGO THE POPULATION PROBLEMS OF ASIAN LANDS were relatively simple. Asia then had only one-third the number of people who now secure a limited subsistence from its crowded rice lands, its dry plains, and its eroded hills. As elements of the culture of the West expanded eastward, the stability and order of centralized governments and controlled economies replaced the civil strife and the hazardous inefficiencies of the existing self-sufficient groupings. Export crops were introduced and subsistence increased. The force of epidemics was limited and mortality declined, but, as the life in the peasant villages proceeded in the routine of the centuries, the number of children born was not decreased proportionately.

As numbers became superabundant, governments sought solutions by extending irrigation projects, improving agricultural techniques, and redistributing people. This economic development was appropriate to the life of the peoples, and it proceeded through the movement of technical assistance and capital from the "advanced" to the "backward" peoples. Then as now there was a general evasion of the

[*] Research Associate, Princeton University Office of Population Research. Specialist in the demography of underdeveloped areas, particularly Africa and the Far East.
[1] Major portions of this material for Japan have been published previously in the following articles by the author: "Population Increase and Manpower Utilization in Imperial Japan," *Milbank Memorial Fund Quarterly*, XXVIII, 3 (July, 1950), pp. 273–293. "Population Growth and Economic Development in Japan," *The Journal of Economic History*, Fall, 1951, pp. 417–428. "The Population Potential of Postwar Korea." *The Far Eastern Quarterly*, May, 1946, 289–307. Portions of these articles are reproduced here with the permission of the Milbank Memorial Fund, New York University Press, The Science Press, and The Far Eastern Association.

431

elementary fact that population cannot increase indefinitely within a finite area. It was more comfortable to evade than to wrestle with the fundamental contradictions of an expanding technological culture whose ultimate welfare problems increased with its economic efficiency and its humanitarianism. Yet analysis of the historical developments in area after area reveals these contradictions. Order, economic development, and medical technologies permitted the decline of death rates, while ancient ways of living and thinking among the peasants kept birth rates at or near the levels which had been essential to biological and cultural survival in earlier centuries.

Technical and financial assistance in economic development for the countries of Asia are today recognized as international responsibilities. Their justification lies in political, economic, and humanitarian goals for recipient and donor nations alike. There are critical differences between this contemporary movement and those that preceded it under imperial auspices, but the basic similarities are sufficient to raise serious questions concerning long-run consequences. Many students of the East, and probably most demographers, suspect that economic action taken without reference to the problems of population growth may lead only to the maintenance of more people at the same all-pervasive level of poverty. Other students see today's potentialities for human subsistence so expansible as to make the problem of man's numbers one which requires only minor adjustments in the foreseeable future. Hence it becomes essential to search within the experience of the past, and particularly that of Asia, for experience that will permit analysis of the demographic correlates of economic development.

The classic historical example of economic development and population increase in the East is the Japanese Empire. In Japan itself, industrialization proceeded within an Eastern culture that remained sovereign, while it extended its area of political hegemony and economic utilization to include other Asian peoples. This economic development was based primarily on an interpenetration of subsistence agriculture coupled with production for the export market. In Japan the transformation was indigenous in the sense that it was planned, directed, and implemented by Japanese. In the countries of the Empire the transformation was guided by the civilian elite of an alien culture under a system of political and economic colonialism. Japanese and colonial peoples alike were counted in censuses that were extraordinary in accuracy and comprehensiveness. Thus we have not only the experimental situation for the analysis of the relations between population increase and economic development in various cultural and economic settings but the demographic data that permit controlled and impersonal analysis as well.

The basic hypothesis underlying the analysis of Japanese experience is that there are demographic correlates of industrialization, and that these correlates are relatively independent of the nonmaterial aspects of the culture in which the industrialization occurs. The question may be phrased rather bluntly as follows: Could the experience of European peoples from the Industrial Revolutions to the present have been used to predict the population development of Japan in the century from 1850 to 1950? Further, can the experience of an industrializing Japan be used to predict the nature, if not the magnitude, of the changing balance of births and deaths in the great cultures of the mainland as they too move toward the industrial economy? A portion of the answers may be found in the trends of growth in the agrarian colonial areas as contrasted with those in the industrializing home country during the Imperial period. If declining fertility is a correlate of industrialization, the fertility should have been lower in industrial than agrarian areas, and the rate of decline in fertility should have been roughly proportionate to the extent of the industrialization. We shall explore the data bearing on these hypotheses later. There is a deeper problem, though, and one that complicates analysis and limits generalization. If declining mortality, declining fertility, and the transition to slowing growth occurred with industrialization in Japan as in the West, can one therefore assume that the same demographic consequences will follow comparable economic developments in the former colonies and in other areas of the East? Was premodern Japan typical of the other great rice cultures of the Pacific littoral in those aspects relevant to the feasibility of industrialization, the postponement of deaths and the limitation of births?

In order to suggest the pitfalls to an analogy between Japan and other Asian areas, we shall begin our report with a brief résumé of the premodern history of Japan. We shall follow with a summary statement of the interrelations between population increase, urbanization, and manpower utilization, with emphasis on the late Imperial period, roughly from 1920 to 1940. Then in order to keep the presentation within manageable proportions we shall use Korea as a testing ground for the generalizations derived from Japanese experience.

People and Economy in the Historic Development of Japan

The broad pattern of Japanese population and economic development was inherent in the location of the islands which lay in the outer path of the diffusing culture of China. Sometime in the last millennium b.c., elements of Chinese Bronze- and Iron-Age culture reached this peripheral region on the Asian frontier. Agricultural techniques and iron implements permitted the groups who possessed them to push back the still neolithic peoples who lived by hunting and fishing. Simple developments in trade and communication paralleled the transition to rice agriculture. Ships moved from Kyushu to Korea, and from Korea came sericulture, weaving, ceramics, carpentry, and leather processing, together with luxurious articles of gold and silver, jewels, and rich textiles. Refugees from the dynastic wars of the mainland brought not only techniques and products but literature, writing, and Buddhism.

Cultivation of the soil permitted an increasing population that in turn generated pressures for the cultivation of greater areas and the improvement of yields. Territorial expansion, population increase, and migration weakened the political and social controls of the pseudo-consanguineous clan structure, while central political control was threatened by the rise of powerful local chieftains. A government that was an unstable coalition of clan leaders, a population whose increase and mobility made the concept of the clan a fictitious survival, and an imported culture of literature, philosophy, and aspirations unrealizable at existing levels of production and distribution could not coexist indefinitely. The resolution of this early crisis might have come through the reappearance of localism or through an indigenous reintegration of power. There was an alternative, however. The culture of China had produced rice agriculture, sericulture, metalworking, Buddhism, and Confucianism. Now, in the dynasties of Sui and T'ang, it evolved an integrated governmental and social structure to facilitate the centralized functioning of an economy and a culture more extensive, more populous, and richer than that of the Japanese.

The Taiko Reforms of 645–650 a.d. provided the official basis for the creation in seventh-century Japan of a replica of the culture of the

T'ang dynasty. All lands and properties were declared the property of the state, with sustenance grants given to the overtly dispossessed persons of rank. Communication and transportation facilities were developed in the area under state control, with a centrally appointed bureaucracy administering the country on a territorial basis. Registers of population and land were to be established as the basis for an initial distribution and a periodic redistribution of land in relation to family size and composition. In theory taxes on commodities replaced those on labor, although all areas owed contributions of post horses, weapons, and men proportionate to the number of households.

There was great activity in the centuries that followed the Taiko Reforms. In the areas under central control, an elaborate bureaucracy reached down through provincial governors and district chiefs to the headmen of the villages and the small groups of households. Extension of the cultivated area, improvement in yields, and population increase proceeded together, sometimes one and sometimes another advancing more rapidly. Correlated with them went a northward push that gave the central government control of all Honshu by the end of the tenth century A.D. Severe demographic maladjustments were thus postponed, but they could not be averted. The theory of Taiko provided for the periodic redistribution of *ku-bunden* (subsistence rice fields) in relation to family size and composition. If this provision had been equitably and universally applied, population growth would have been rapid, for the subsistence available to the marginal consumer would have increased. There is some indication that such in fact was the effect of the land reform in the regions where it was carried out. While the area of stability was increasing, and agricultural techniques were improving, land available for redistribution soon became inadequate for all the claimants. The periods of time between allotments were increased, and the amount of land allotted per household was reduced, but still there were complaints that the rice lands were inadequate. By the early years of the eighth century, the government was ordering the transfer of families from the older provinces to the frontier areas where they could extend the cultivated acreage at the same time that they served as palisade guards against the unpacified aborigines. These movements were slight in view of the magnitude of the needs, though, and so the Great Council of State became concerned with the population problem. The councilors planned vast reclamation projects that would double the cultivable land of the country, but managerial ability and capital funds were too limited for massive governmental operations. Motivations for private works were limited because redistribution removed individual and familial profit as stimulants to development.

The economic problem in Japan was not the simple one of producing a quantity of food that would maintain the people equitably. Instead, a proliferating aristocracy generated material demands beyond the productive capacity of the countryside at existing, and even improving, technical levels. The luxury of the capital city meant increasing demands for extraction of product from the peasants. Social imitation complicated the problem because lesser peoples in the capital and the provinces developed standards of living beyond the crude ones of the past. By the beginning of the tenth century, the tax structure was a complex system that left little alternative to peasant or provincial noble other than to attempt to escape it. As the apparatus of the central government deteriorated, the *shoen* [manors] increased in numbers and in power. Disintegration into localism again threatened.

In the centuries of struggle that followed, new consolidations emerged in the form of the hierarchical vassalage of feudalism. As a form of organizing the people and resources of the state, feudalism continued for some seven hundred years, from the earliest government at Kamakura in the twelfth century to the last at Edo (Tokyo) in the nineteenth. During these centuries, the Japanese economy developed from a simple and largely fragmented one that supported six to nine million people to a unified and fairly complicated one that supported thirty million people. The period was not homogeneous with reference to political order, however, and population growth followed no regular pattern, either of change or of stability. From the late twelfth to the late sixteenth century there were alternate periods of order and conflict, of centralism and localism. The resolution of the problems of instability and disorder came in the late sixteenth century with the formation of the Tokugawa shogunate [*baku-fu*]. The police state established by the Tokugawa shoguns survived with slight political changes through almost three centuries of relative seclusion from the outer world.

According to well-established interpretation of the data, population fluctuated irregularly but with a generally upward trend during the centuries of halting political and economic advance, roughly from the thirteenth through the sixteenth century. It increased rapidly during the first century-and-a-quarter of the period of seclusion when peace and generally enlightened agrarian policies resulted in simultaneous increases in the food supply and decreases in the chances of death. Then, from the first quarter of the eighteenth century to the middle of the nineteenth century, population remained relatively unchanging. The results of official counts and fragmentary vital statistics apparently attest the existence of this period of approximate stability. Two types of arguments are adduced to explain it. One, economic in orientation, finds here a population that has increased to the physical limit permitted by subsistence. The other, crudely psychological in nature, attributes stability of numbers to abortion and infanticide. If the former interpretation is substantiated, we have a documented Malthusian situation. If the latter interpretation is substantiated, it follows that the demographic development of modern Japan is atypical of the past growth of Western peoples or the potential future growth of Eastern peoples, for Japan would have begun the process of industrialization with a low and consciously controlled fertility. The birth rate rather than the death rate would have been the variable governing growth.

Analysis of the prolific quantitative and verbal descriptive materials available indicates that the presumed stability of numbers in the presumably unchanging agrarian economy of the late Tokugawa period is mythological. It is true that numbers had increased until population was extraordinarily dense on the land, considering the technical levels in agriculture and related segments of the economy. However, the dynamic sections of the society and economy were urban and commercial rather than rural and agrarian. The shogunate required the *daimyo* [feudal lords] to spend alternate years of residence in Edo and to leave their families as hostages for their return. Cities developed as centers of conspicuous consumption, with the extractable rice and other commodities of the countryside moving by road and ship to these concentrations of people, wealth, and handicraft production. Financial and commercial classes rose to equal and even exceed the landed barons in their ownership and control of resources and facilities other than land. The economic structure of the shogunate was crumbling under the impact of a commercial revolution even before the black ships of Admiral Perry "opened" the country to the West.

The appearance of stability in the population of Japan during the last century-and-a-quarter of Tokugawa government was likewise fictitious. There were quite divergent rates of change in the various regions of the country over periods—years or decades in length. Numbers fluctuated sharply as great famines and epidemics decimated sections of the country, or years of good crops and relative freedom from epidemic brought the population to or beyond the levels previously attained. A slow and halting increase seems to have begun sometime in the early years of the nineteenth century, as the commercial and handicraft revolutions gained impetus. Whatever the rate of population change, it represented the balance of a high death rate and a high birth rate. Abortion and infanticide occurred, but, if they had been as general as the spectacular accounts assume, a population subject to the hazards that existed in eighteenth- and early nineteenth-century Japan would have declined precipitously rather than changed slowly and rather erratically.

The interrelationships of factors in the presumably changeless police state of the Tokugawa were complex indeed. The accumulating frictions generated by demographic and economic change within a political structure resistant to change undermined that structure. In a superficial sense, population was a passive factor in the internal transformations of economy and society. The high and fluctuating death rates of peoples subject to periodic famines and epidemics, the infanticide practiced by families without resources to provide for children, and the movements of the dispossessed and the adventuresome into cities and the frontiers of settlement—these were products of a fixed agricultural production at a time in which substantial population increase was still possible. If the factors responsible for economic inadequacy are analyzed, however, the coincidence of enforced political stability and an alteration in social structure that was the product of, and tended toward, social and geographical mobility emerges as a basic incompatibility. Scrutiny of the feudal period from the initial consolidation of the Muromachi *baku-fu* at Kamakura to the eclipse of the Tokugawa *baku-fu* at Edo indicates that the population factor was a powerful compulsion to change.

Any given political, economic, and social structure impinges on the conditions under which people live, the quantities of food and the necessities available, and the aspirations and motivations that influence their activities. Mortality, fertility, and migration continually create new populations whose size, composition, distribution, and dynamics are the facts, the opportunities, and the problems of the political and social order and the system of production and distribution. A changing population dictates a balance of the forces of change throughout economy and society. If that balance does not occur, or occurs in ways inconsistent with the population dynamics generated by the economy and the society, population emerges as a pre-eminent problem. This is what occurred in the last centuries of the period of seclusion.

Somewhat comparable conclusions flow from an analysis of the role of the population factor in the great cycles of integration, flowering, and decline in Chinese culture and economy. In China, as in Japan, there could be no permanent balance between people, production, and social structure because the traditional familial and reproductive mores of the culture remained largely intact among the peasants. Amelioration of living conditions resulted in a population increase that imposed pressures on the stability of the politico-social system. Progressive economic development and improving levels of living require a precautionary limitation of population growth that proceeds through fertility, rather than limitation through death—the appearance of great devastations itself attests the failure of the society of the period to achieve a reasonable relationship between population and economy. The demographic dilemma was inherent in all economic development in the East that was based on the improvement of the traditional agriculture within the traditional social structure. This was true of premodern Japan and for the other cultures and economies of the East that were Chinese or derived from China.

INDUSTRIALIZATION AND THE DEMOGRAPHIC TRANSITION IN JAPAN

The opening of Japan to the West, and the power-oriented state that followed the Meiji Restoration, brought an expanded and more intensive agriculture and an accelerating industrialization that moved a once-peasant people cityward. Mortality declined during the early decades of modernization. Fertility changed more slowly, for the resistances of an ancient and integrated rural culture were buttressed by the resources of a state whose pre-eminent goal involved the creation of political and economic power within an oligarchic social structure. The forces generated by the industrialization process were more compulsive than those that had evolved in the agrarian world of the past.

The conservative forces of a society continuous for millenniums could not achieve that segmentation of culture and personality implicit in the coexistence of a changing economy and a stable social system.

It was impossible to base the industrialization essential to power on an illiterate peasantry. And a former peasantry, educated, concentrated in cities, subject to the pressures of a pecuniary economy, and exposed to the potentialities of that economy for material advancement and psychological liberation, questioned if it did not evade the obligation of abundant parenthood. The first three quarters of a century of controlled modernization produced appreciable declines in death and birth rates. By the thirties, fertility was falling more rapidly than mortality.

Mechanical projection of population trends was tempting, and many "predictions" were made. Although they varied in the complexity of their mathematics, all assumed continued declines in fertility and mortality, without explicit consideration of the social and economic developments required for the achievement and support of the numbers forecast. The majority of these estimates indicated that the population would increase to some 90 million by 1960 and reach a maximum of perhaps 100 to 115 million near or after the end of the century. Eventually the people of an industrialized Japan, like those of an industrialized West, would cease to increase. Moreover, as contrasted with the West, the period of transition would be shortened and the total increase of her population would be less. Japan would take a century and three-quarters to achieve a new stability of numbers at low birth and death rates, and population increase would be threefold or fourfold.

If we examine the transformations in the geographical distribution and the internal structure of the population, the situation in Japan is comparable to that in the West. The proportion of the population that was rural declined with relative consistency from 1872 to 1940; the *number* of people in the rural areas changed little between 1872 and 1930 and declined thereafter. Cities and nonagricultural employment absorbed their own natural increase and the major portion of that of the rural areas beyond maintenance requirements. Youths left agriculture and the rural areas, adjusted early to the relatively greater economic opportunities and the freer social atmosphere of the cities, founded their own families at considerably later ages than would have occurred in the ancestral villages, and limited the numbers of their children to correspond more nearly to the realities of a pecuniary economy. Declining fertility and hence the solution to the problems of growth created by modernization appeared to inhere in urbanization, itself an essential correlate of industrialization. Residential and occupational movement away from the peasant village and its agrarian activities was the overt manifestation of the cultural and psychological transformation that marked the "Westernization" of the Japanese and their escape from the economic difficulties of increasing numbers.

Population increase. The people of Japan numbered 30 million in the middle of the nineteenth century; 35 million at the time of the Meiji Restoration. By 1920 there were 56 million people; in 1940 there were 73 million (See Table 11.1). Increases of this order of magnitude are difficult to comprehend. The increase of 17 million in two decades was greater than the population of the Philippine Islands in 1939 and as great as that of Korea in 1920. It would have peopled an empty Japan with 115 persons per square mile. Each year there were three-quarters of a million additional claimants to the products of the Japanese economy.

In Japan, as elsewhere in Monsoon Asia, population increase occurred among a people already densely settled in relation to the size of the land and existing techniques. In 1920, the number of persons per square mile of total area was 380; in 1940, it was 500. These are crude figures, for Japan is a land of mountains and turbulent rivers, where only one acre in six is cultivable. If we make our assumption of equal distribution somewhat more realistic and allocate the people to the land that was cultivated or regarded as available for cultivation, we secure density figures that are startling. In 1920, in this country still predominantly peasant, there were almost 2,500 people per square mile of cultivable land. If the 17 million people who were added to the Japanese population between 1920 and 1940 had been equally distributed over the cultivable land, there would have been 740 additional persons on each square mile—a total of more than 3,200 persons per square mile.

Citation of rates of population increase, density figures, or other population statistics for Japan as measures of the demographic transformation of the Japanese people ignore an essential characteristic of that transformation: its integral relationship with economic and po-

TABLE 11.1

POPULATION INCREASE IN THE JAPANESE EMPIRE, 1920–1940
(Total population of each area)

Area	1920	1925	1930	1935	1940#
	Population (in thousands)				
The Empire.........	77,729	84,279	91,421	98,934	105,226
Japan	55,963	59,737	64,450	69,254	73,114
Outlying Areas.......	21,766	24,542	26,971	29,680	32,112
Korea *	17,264	19,523	21,058	22,899	24,326
Taiwan...........	3,655	3,993	4,593	5,212	5,872
Karafuto..........	106	204	295	332	415
Kwantung†	688	766	956	1,134	1,367
South Seas‡.......	52	56	70	103	131
	Increase (in thousands)				
The Empire.........		6,550	7,142	7,513	6,292
Japan		3,774	4,713	4,804	3,860
Outlying Areas.......		2,776§	2,429	2,709	2,432
Korea *		2,259§	1,535	1,841	1,427
Taiwan...........		338	599	620	660
Karafuto..........		98	91	37	83
Kwantung†		78	190	178	233
South Seas‡.......		4	13	33	29
	Per cent increase				
The Empire.........		8.4	8.5	8.2	6.4
Japan		6.7	7.9	7.5	5.6
Outlying Areas.......		11.3§	9.0	9.1	7.6
Korea *		13.1§	7.9	8.7	6.2
Taiwan...........		9.2	15.0	13.5	12.7
Karafuto..........		92.4	44.9	12.5	25.0
Kwantung†		11.8	24.8	18.7	20.6
South Seas‡.......		7.8	23.7	47.3	27.9

Source: Kōjima, Reikichi, "The Population of the Prefectures and Cities of Japan in Most Recent Times," *Municipal Problems Pamphlet* (*Toshi mondai pamfuretto*; Tokyo) No. 41 (1941); translated by Edwin G. Beal, Jr., in *Far Eastern Quarterly*, III, 4 (August, 1944), pp. 313–362.

* A "special survey" rather than a census was taken in Korea in 1920.

† The Kwangtung Leased Territory alone is included in this compilation. The South Manchuria Railway Zone, formerly a part of the Empire, was attached to Manchukuo in 1937.

‡ Nanyō-guntō, the South Sea Islands received as a mandate from the League of Nations.

§ Since the special survey taken in Korea in 1920 was probably an undercount, the increase between 1920 and 1925 may be overestimated for Korea and hence for the Outlying Areas and the Empire as a whole.

litical expansionism within and outside the three main islands that were utilized at the end of the feudal period—Honshu, Kyushu, and Shikoku. In the late nineteenth century the island of Hokkaido was occupied in a northward thrust that carried the Japanese up through the southern part of Sakhalin Island. Next expansionism turned southward and the Ryukyu Islands were added to Japan; Taiwan, to the Empire. In the early twentieth century, the drive to economic and political advance was diverted toward the mainland and the Kwantung Leased Territory, the South Manchuria Railway Zone, and Korea were added to the Empire. The South Sea Islands, which imperial Germany had once held, were acquired after World War I as a mandate from the League of Nations and added to the Empire in fact, if not in legal right.

Japanese moved outward to the islands of the Pacific, across the narrow waters to northeastern Asia, and eventually southward below the Great Wall (Table 11.2). In 1920 there were 726,000 Japanese in the colonial areas outside Japan, including the military; in 1940, there were 1.7 million, excluding the military. This was internal redistribution in a sense, for it was movement under the Japanese flag. Migration beyond the area of Japanese sovereignty but within the area of political hegemony increased sharply during the thirties. In 1920 some 580,000 were beyond the legal boundaries of Japan. In 1940, the number abroad had increased to 1.9 million, of whom 820,-000 were in Manchukuo and 365,000 in occupied North China. This redistribution of the Japanese reflected a complex adjustment of social and economic pressures at home and economic opportunities abroad. The main concentrations remained in Japan, though, for here lived 99 per cent of the world's Japanese in 1920 and 97.5 per cent in 1940.

The relevance of population increase to economic and political transformation cannot be assessed easily from the statistical data on the maze of movements and countermovements that produced the internal redistribution and the external increases portrayed in the preceding tables. It can be deduced in hypothetical form, however, if

---

NOTE TO TABLE 11.1

‡ The censuses of 1920–1935, inclusive, were *de facto* enumerations of the populations of the various areas. In 1940 the enumeration of the general civilian population was *de facto*, but members of the armed forces and persons attached thereto wherever they might be, whether within or outside the Empire, were allocated to the place of enumeration of their nearest of kin.

we proceed as if all colonials and aliens are expelled from Japan on October 1, 1920, and the home islands are sealed as they had been throughout the centuries of Tokugawa control. Let us suppose that within this stable and isolated universe births and deaths occur at the age-specific rates that characterized the actual population of Japan from 1920 to 1940. We shall limit the analysis to men and assume that each enters the labor force at the age of fifteen and remains in it continuously until death or retirement at sixty-five. Furthermore, there is no increase in economic opportunities, and no job is vacated, except by the death or retirement of its holder. Japan's population problem thus becomes, by definition, the increase of her manpower between the ages of fifteen and sixty-five, for adjustment techniques, whether economic, political, or demographic, are ruled out. Under

TABLE 11.2

THE INCREASE IN THE NUMBERS OF THE ETHNIC JAPANESE, 1920–1940

Area	Number of ethnic Japanese (in thousands)			Per cent increase in ethnic Japanese		
	1920	1930	1940	1920–1930	1930–1940	1920–1940
The World	57,191	65,766	75,372	15.0	14.6	31.8
The Empire*	56,611	65,149	73,500	15.1	12.8	29.8
Japan†	55,885	63,972	71,810	14.5	12.2	28.5
Outlying Areas*	726	1,177	1,690	62.1	43.6	132.8
Korea	377	527	708	39.9	34.3	87.8
Taiwan	164	228	312	39.0	36.8	90.2
Karafuto	103	284	395	176.3	38.8	283.7
Kwantung . . .	79	118	198	50.0	68.1	152.0
South Seas . . .	3	20	77	476.8	292.3	2,163.0
Foreign Countries‡	580	617	1,872	6.3	203.4	222.5

Source: Publications of the Cabinet Bureau of Statistics, Japan (Naikaku tōkei-kyoku, Nihon; Tokyo).

1920: *Descriptive Summary of the 1920 Census* (1933), Appendix.

1930: *Final Report of the 1930 Census* (1938).

1940: *Census of 1940*, Selected tables. (Microfilm copy, Library of Congress, Washington, D. C.) The number of Japanese in foreign countries in 1940 is based on a compilation from Japanese sources, modified where census or registration data permitted more accurate estimation.

* Excluding the South Manchuria Railway Zone, which became part of "Manchukuo" in 1937 and hence technically outside the Empire.

† Ethnic Japanese only, i.e., excluding natives of the Empire and aliens.

‡ Including the South Manchuria Railway Zone, which had a Japanese population of 81 thousand in 1920 and 107 thousand in 1930.

these assumptions there would have been 180 Japanese entering the labor-force age for each hundred vacancies created by death or retirement. One hundred of these 180 potential entrants would be utilized; eighty would find no place within the stationary economy. In other words, 45 per cent of the annual increment to the number of men in the productive ages would be surplus. Given the validity of the assumptions underlying the computations, this would have been the measure of Japan's demographic difficulties.

Economic transformation. The economic transformation of Japan in the three quarters of a century from the Restoration to the Surrender was a movement away from agricultural self-sufficiency toward an industrial and commercial economy dependent on the world market alike for the purchase of its raw materials and the sale of its finished products. At the beginning of the twenties Japan's industry was predominantly textile, cocoons and silks tying the agricultural and the industrial segments of the economy together in dependence on the vagaries of taste and the fluctuating purchasing power of American women. The twenties were a period of growth in the traditional pattern. However, the depression of the late twenties and the early thirties shattered the world's demand for Japan's silk and cotton textiles. Poverty spread in ever-widening circles from the employees in the textile mills to the small farmers who supplemented agricultural production with the cultivation of mulberry trees and the raising of cocoons. The depreciation of the yen, increasing efficiency in organization, and controlled sales restored Japanese products to the world markets, but only at the heavy price of depressed wages at home and increased accusations of "dumping" abroad. World trends toward economic autarchy, controlled trade, managed currencies, and the political manipulation of economic relationships seemed to threaten the economy of a nation that required trade to survive.

The response of Japan's leaders to a constricting outer world and cumulating internal friction was an outward surge that carried the Kwantung armies into Manchuria and established a Manchu emperor on a puppet throne. The decade of heavy capital investment thus initiated resulted in the establishment of an economic and military bastion from which the Soviet Union could be held while China below the Great Wall was invaded. In Taiwan, Korea, and Karafuto there was forced industrialization somewhat comparable to that of

Japan's early post-Restoration period. Economic "progress" occurred, but it was a by-product of military expansion and preparation for further expansion.

The immediate demographic consequence of the economic transformations of the interwar decades was the urbanization of the population structure. The villages and the smaller towns became producers of children, exporters of youth, and havens for the aged. The maturing youth moved toward the cities and nonagricultural employment in such numbers as to create an urbanization seldom paralleled in the history of the West (Table 11.3).

Between 1920 and 1940 the population of the cities [shi] increased from 10.1 to 27.6 million, while that of the rural areas [gun] remained virtually unchanged (from 45.9 to 45.5 million). Fewer than 5 million people lived in cities of 500,000 and over in 1920; 14.4 million lived in such cities by 1940. In relative terms, the population living in communes of 10,000 or less declined 3 per cent during this twenty-year period, while that in cities of 100,000 and over more than trebled.

The urbanward movement was predominantly from the rural area to the large city or the great metropolitan center. In 1920 over two-thirds of the total population lived in communes of less than 10,000 population; less than half lived in such communes in 1940. In 1920 one out of twelve lived in a city of 100,000 or more; in 1940, one in five lived in such a city. All the provinces of Japan contributed substantial portions of their natural increase to the great metropolitan cities of Tokyo, Yokohama, Nagoya, Osaka, Kyoto, and Kobe. In fact, for the interwar decades as a whole, the net migratory gain of the seven metropolitan provinces (Tokyo, Kanagawa, Aichi, Osaka, Kyoto, Hyogo, and Fukuoka) was greater than the net migratory loss of the remaining forty provinces of Japan, because these provinces attracted not only Japan's own provincials but also the immigrants of the Empire.

The economic force that underlay urbanization was industrialization, including under that broad term the expansion of manufacturing industry and the facilities and services necessarily associated with it, as well as the increasing efficiency of primary production that accompanies advances in techniques and facilities. The human aspect of this industrialization was the changing allocation of the labor force. Agriculture, forestry, and fishing declined in relative importance,

TABLE 11.3

THE URBANIZATION OF THE POPULATION STRUCTURE OF JAPAN, 1920–1950

Year	Total	Population by size of commune				
		Under 10,000	10,000– 29,999	30,000– 99,999	100,000– 499,999	500,000 or more
		Numbers (in thousands)				
1920....	55,391	37,720	6,570	4,348	2,127	4,626
1925....	59,179	37,681	6,736	6,021	2,538	6,203
1930....	63,872	37,951	7,613	6,827	3,876	7,605
1935....	68,662	37,303	7,992	5,849	4,873	12,645
1940....	72,540	35,999	8,188	7,062	6,907	14,384
1944....	72,120	34,019	7,897	8,361	8,173	13,670
1945....	71,998*	39,460	11,654	9,869	5,045	5,969
1946....	73,114	38,482	11,366	9,801	6,389	7,076
1947....	78,101†	38,690	12,130	10,492	7,778	9,011
1950....	83,200	38,294	12,441	11,139	10,136	11,190
		Per cent				
1920....	100.0	68.1	11.9	7.8	3.8	8.4
1925....	100.0	63.6	11.4	10.2	4.3	10.5
1930....	100.0	59.4	11.9	10.7	6.1	11.9
1935....	100.0	54.3	11.7	8.5	7.1	18.4
1940....	100.0	49.6	11.3	9.8	9.5	19.8
1944....	100.0	47.2	10.9	11.6	11.3	19.0
1945....	100.0	54.8	16.2	13.7	7.0	8.3
1946....	100.0	52.6	15.6	13.4	8.7	9.7
1947....	100.0	49.6	15.5	13.4	10.0	11.5
1950....	100.0	46.0	15.0	13.4	12.2	13.4

Source: Bureau of Statistics, Japan, Population census of 1950 (4 vols.; Tokyo, 1951), Vol. I, Total Population, Table, p. 25.
  * Including 1,627 not distributed by area.
  † Including 932 not distributed by area.

while manufacturing, commerce, transportation, and communication increased (Table 11.4). The maintenance of a relatively unchanging population in agriculture was accompanied by a rapid increase in both the numbers and the proportions of the people who secured their livelihood from sources other than agriculture. In 1920, ag-

TABLE 11.4

ECONOMIC UTILIZATION OF THE POPULATION OF JAPAN PROPER: INDUSTRIAL CLASSIFICATION OF THE GAINFULLY OCCUPIED, 1920, 1930, AND 1940

Number (in thousands)

Status	Total population			Males			Females		
	1920	1930	1940	1920	1930	1940	1920	1930	1940
Total	55,963	64,450	73,114	28,044	32,390	36,566	27,919	32,060	36,548
Armed Forces*	250	243	1,694	250	243	1,694			
Civilian Population	55,713	64,207	71,420	27,794	32,147	34,872	27,919	32,060	36,548
Unoccupied	28,702	34,830	38,937	11,057	13,360	15,142	17,645	21,470	23,795
Occupied†	27,011	29,377	32,483	16,737	18,787	19,730	10,274	10,590	12,753
Agriculture and Forestry	14,128	14,131	13,842	7,750	7,735	6,619	6,378	6,396	7,223
Fishing	558	568	543	517	515	476	41	53	67
Mining	425	316	598	328	271	529	97	45	69
Manufacturing and Construction	5,300	5,876	8,132	3,716	4,428	6,178	1,584	1,448	1,954
Commerce	3,188	4,906	4,882	2,158	3,406	3,006	1,030	1,500	1,876
Transportation and Communication	1,037	945	1,364	975	907	1,214	62	38	150
Government and Professional	1,192	1,762	2,195	884	1,369	1,515	308	393	680
Service	655	802	709	71	92	39	584	710	670
Miscellaneous	528	71	218	338	64	154	190	7	64

Per cent of gainfully occupied

Status	Total population			Males			Females		
	1920	1930	1940	1920	1930	1940	1920	1930	1940
Total	100.0	100.0	100.0	100.0	100.0	100.0	100.0	100.0	100.0
Agriculture and Forestry	52.3	48.1	42.6	46.3	41.2	33.5	62.1	60.4	56.6
Fishing	2.1	1.9	1.7	3.1	2.7	2.4	0.4	0.5	0.5
Mining	1.6	1.1	1.8	2.0	1.5	2.7	0.9	0.4	0.5
Manufacturing and Construction	19.6	20.0	25.0	22.0	23.6	31.3	15.4	13.7	15.3
Commerce	11.8	16.7	15.0	12.9	18.1	15.2	10.0	14.2	14.7
Transportation and Communication	3.8	3.2	4.2	5.8	4.8	6.2	0.6	0.3	1.2
Government and Professional	4.4	6.0	6.8	5.3	7.3	7.7	3.0	3.7	5.3
Service	2.4	2.7	2.2	0.4	0.5	0.2	5.7	6.7	5.3
Miscellaneous	2.0	0.3	0.7	2.0	0.3	0.8	1.9	0.1	0.5

riculture absorbed slightly more than half those reporting themselves as gainfully occupied; in 1930, it absorbed slightly less than half; in 1940, it absorbed only 43 per cent. This is an understatement of the economic transformation, though, for it is distorted by the number of women who are reported as gainfully occupied in agriculture. If men alone are considered, the percentage gainfully occupied in agriculture was 46.3 in 1920, 41.2 in 1930, and 33.5 in 1940.

The declining fertility of the Japanese was largely a by-product of industrialization and urbanization or, more specifically, of the development of industrial employment and urban ways of living. Economic developments in agriculture were accompanied by rising levels of living and increasing age at marriage, but marital fertility remained almost as high as it had been in the past. Industrial developments in the rural areas, such as the great textile mills with their factory dormitories, had little discernible impact on fertility. Moreover, the women who labored at household industries in the *ku* of a world metropolis such as Tokyo reproduced at levels more comparable to those of the peasants than to those of the urban women of the central districts or the elite residential areas of Tokyo. The demographic transition did not follow economic development or industrialization per se, but rather that industrialization and urbanization which involved altered ways of living, working, and thinking. Small factories and household industries in the rural areas may have led to the more adequate utilization of rural manpower and higher levels of living for rural families, but they also helped to perpetuate the rural way of

---

NOTES TO TABLE 11.4

Source: Publications of the Cabinet Bureau of Statistics, Japan: 1920: *Reports of the 1920 Census*, Section on All Japan, "Occupations" (1929). (Reallocations to produce as much comparability as possible with the later classifications of "occupied" and "unoccupied.") 1930: *Reports of the 1930 Census*, "Occupations and Industries" (1935).

For 1940 data: United States Strategic Bombing Survey: Manpower, Food, and Civilian Supplies Division: *The Japanese Wartime Standard of Living and Utilization of Manpower* (Washington, D. C., 1947), Table PP, p. 124.

* The armed forces in 1920 and 1930 included only those present in Japan proper who could not be allocated to another category of the occupational (1920) or industrial (1930) classification. In 1940 the armed forces were reported by their closest civilian relative and include armed forces and persons attached thereto, wherever stationed.

† The unemployed are included, classified according to the industry of the usual employment.

living and the rural values that were such basic factors in the demographic imbalance of the modernizing state.

The general conclusion of our analysis of Japanese experience prior to World War II is that the demographic transition occurred with industrialization in the East as in the West. The differences were in the speed and the detailed structuring of the transition, not in the fact of its occurrence. The critical questions with reference to other areas in Asia involve the possibilities for industrialization and its magnitude, rather than the existence of a demographic impact should massive industrialization occur. Japan's transition appeared successful indeed to the demographers and the statesmen by the end of the interwar decades. In fact, by 1940 the Japanese had become seriously concerned about the possibility of slowing growth and ultimate decline in numbers. They saw their country as the England of the Far East, with responsibilities for continental leadership far beyond her limited man power. The population that had served as a rationalization for expansion was now viewed as inadequate for the responsibilities anticipated from that expansion.

War and postwar. The population generated by three-quarters of a century of economic development survived in major part to achieve some adjustment in a truncated land with leveled cities, destroyed industries, returned servicemen, and repatriated civilians. The goal of reagrarianism proved fantastic; economic policy gradually shifted toward restoration and further industrialization. The birth rate surged upward to the level of a decade and a half before; the death rate moved downward to Western levels under the impetus of the welfare and public-health activities of SCAP. The rate of natural increase rose to the highest level in Japanese history; the surplus of births over deaths reached 1.75 million in 1949. Total population enumerated in the census of 1950 was 83.2 million. Deeply pessimistic Malthusianism spread throughout Japan. People were moving back to the cities, however, and by 1952 the developing employment opportunities outside agriculture were again reducing the labor force in agriculture. The birth rate fell sharply as economic difficulties in agriculture and increasing employment in cities contributed to the motivations for a limitation of births. Legal facilities for abortion and contraception furnished the means.

Rapid increase in the numbers of adult men and women will continue for decades in the future. If deaths remain at the level of 1948 and there is no movement to or from Japan except the repatriation of some five to six hundred thousand persons between 1947 and 1953, the number of men in the productive ages between fifteen and sixty will increase from some 22 million in 1947 to some 31 million in 1967, a growth of over 40 per cent in twenty years. This increase in the coming decades will be larger both absolutely and relatively than that which occurred in the twenty years between 1920 and 1940.

To predict the distant future of either economy or population would be foolhardy. The pattern of the demographic future lies in the evolving complex of forces that include economic development, individual attitudes, familial values, social structure, political orientation, and international relations. However, the fact and the realization of population growth again constitute a powerful motivation for forced expansion, with the possibility of an economic disequilibrium that may again mold political forms in ways which are hazardous for the peace of the Pacific region.

KOREA[2]

The interrelations between the Japanese and the Koreans can be traced back to the legends of the age of the gods; continuing interrelations are an inescapable consequence of geography. We are concerned here not with the economic and social demography of Korea *as Korea*, but rather with the reaction of the Koreans to the type of economic development that occurred during the period of Japanese hegemony, from 1910 to 1945. The experience of Japan indicated that declining fertility and the lessening rates of increase that avert ultimate demographic tragedy are associated primarily with industrialization and urbanization and that economic development per se results in no social changes adequate to lessen appreciably the population increase that has been generated by the associated changes in mortality. If this conclusion can be generalized beyond Japan, then there should have been declining mortality and increasing rates of population growth in Korea, with only slight declines in fertility prior to the last decade of the imperial period when industrialization

[2] Portions of this material have been presented previously in the following article: "The Population Potential of Postwar Korea," *The Far Eastern Quarterly*, May, 1946, pp. 289–307; it is reproduced with the permission of The Far Eastern Association.

and urbanization became policies and facts for Korea also. If we are to argue that the differences between Japanese and Korean demography in the decades of imperialism are correlates of the differences in economic transformations and modes of living, we must assess the similarities and differences in the premodern balance of births and deaths as between Japan, Korea, and a generalized Far Eastern type culture which is basically Chinese.

People and economy in the historic development of Korea. Korea's early history was generally comparable to that of Japan in those basic forces of resources and culture that determined the balance of births and deaths. The Neolithic culture of the early peoples was similar to that of South Manchuria, the Maritime Provinces of Siberia, and Japan, but by the last millennium B.C. the diffusing Bronze and Iron culture of China had reached Korea. The transitional Neolithic peoples of southern Korea, referred to in the Chinese records as the "San Han," began to receive the agricultural techniques of the southern Chinese during this period, while the Chinese province of Lakliang brought the brilliant culture of the Han Dynasty to North Korea. Native kingdoms replaced the Chinese colonies and the Neolithic groupings of the early historic period, but the culture of China remained a major force. Korea received the economic developments, the political forms, the social structure, and the intellectual values of China and in turn transmitted them to Japan.

A language and a culture which were specifically Korean developed during the twelve hundred years that separated Silla's acquisition of peninsular domination in 668 A.D. from the abdication of the last Yi emperor of Korea in 1910. The Buddhist temples, monasteries, and pagodas built during the three hundred years of Silla's hegemony indicate the expansion of the economic base, the flowering of the culture of the elite, and the continuing influence of China. In the Koryo period (935–1392), there was further development of Buddhist culture and scholarship, but the invasions of the Mongols and participation in the Mongol attempts to invade Japan were major economic deterrents. In 1592, the Japanese invaded Korea as the initial step toward the conquest of China. There were seven years of devastating and generally futile war before the Japanese forces were withdrawn and Japan herself moved toward the extirpation of Western influences and the retreat to seclusion. Korea was soon forced to accept the suzerainty of the Manchu. Then from the seventeenth to the nineteenth century Korea withdrew into a seclusion as complete as that of Japan.

In the period of seclusion there were critical differences in the economic and social histories of Korea and Japan, differences that were to permit Japan to seize the developments of the West for indigenous industrialization and force Korea into colonial status. Political factionalism, economic stagnation, and Confucian conservatism characterized Korea while agricultural, commercial, and industrial revolutions were transforming the lives and increasing the numbers of European peoples. Korea entered the modern world at the middle of the nineteenth century with the intellectual equipment and the technology of sixteenth-century Asia.

In Japan the centuries of seclusion had involved the maintenance of peace, the extension of agriculture, and, during the early period, rapid population increase. A commercial revolution involving both a substantial merchant class and a pecuniary economy was well advanced by the time of the opening to the West. The leaders of the Restoration turned toward the West to learn its techniques of industry and power, and they guided Japan cautiously along paths that would insure the achievement of economic and military power without jeopardizing political independence and social stability. In Korea, on the other hand, the last decades of isolation involved dynastic friction, social disorganization, and a deepening poverty. Here there was no great development of cities, no rising merchant class, and no intellectual awakening. Instead, the landed aristocracy retained authority, handicraft industries were limited, and intellectual life was dominated by the sterility of late Manchu China. During the early decades of contact with Western peoples there was vacillation on policy, with continuing reliance on China and a general procrastination and ineptitude in political and economic matters. This reaction against the encroaching culture of the West had occurred in Japan also, but in Korea delay was more serious.

By the final quarter of the nineteenth century, Japan's forced industrial and political expansionism was oriented toward the mainland of Asia, and Russia was endeavoring to expand her economic and strategic spheres of influence in the Far East. The imperial struggles led, through the Sino-Japanese war of 1895 and the Russo-Japanese war of 1905, to the annexation of Korea by Japan in 1910.

Long cycles of population increase and contraction comparable to those of China apparently characterized the evolution of the Korean people. It is probable that year to year changes in numbers were quite irregular and slight by modern standards. Crude agricultural techniques and vagaries of climate and rainfall made yields precarious, while the wasting of the land through deforestation and erosion resulted in a continued shrinking of the effective resources base. Malnutrition must have been ever-present and famine a continuing hazard. Little knowledge of medicine or public health existed to lessen the mortality from recurring epidemics. The absence of efficient internal protection and continuing civil disorders added further to the hazards of existence.

The positive controls of which Malthus spoke operated at such high intensity that ethnic and cultural survival would have been jeopardized had not all the familial and group values been oriented toward the reproduction of the population. Early and almost universal marriage, the high prestige of the fertile wife, aversion to abortion, and the supernatural sanction of a folk religion which demanded sons were cultural mechanisms which favored maximum fertility and hence group survival. They were a heritage of the historic culture to modern Korea.

Population increase in the modern period. In the traditional Korean economy and culture, population change represented the difference between a high birth rate and a fluctuating death rate. A necessary consequence of the economic and political control of the country by the Japanese was a decrease in the death rate, due in part to the lessening of the hazards of disease and in part to an increase and regularization of the food available for the support of population.

The family and reproductive patterns of the Korean peasant remained relatively untouched by the partial diffusion of those elements of Western culture transmitted via the Japanese imperial system. Agriculture and the service and handicraft industries remained the principal occupations. Cities existed, but in 1930 they were primarily administrative and service centers for an agricultural hinterland. Modern factory industry was not only limited but so geographically concentrated as to minimize diffusion. Only one-fifth of the people were technically literate in the sense that they reported themselves as able to read and write either Korean or Japanese. The conditions directly affecting marriage and the bearing of children remained essentially as they had been prior to the Japanese period. Marriage occurred at an early age and was almost universal. In 1930, 66 per cent of the women aged fifteen to nineteen and 96 per cent of those aged twenty to twenty-four were married. Only one-fifth of one per cent of the women aged fifty and above remained single. Few women worked outside the home, even in agriculture. Abortion and infanticide had never become folk techniques of population control as they had in late Tokugawa Japan. Instead, the sterile woman received contempt, while the mother of sons received the approbation of family and community.

Crude birth rates throughout the census period of the twenties and thirties remained over 45 per 1,000 total population. Gross reproduction rates were at least 3.5 in 1925, 1930, and 1935; net reproduction rates were 1.8 or above. The population crisis inherent in the maintenance of increase at this level was averted temporarily by the increased employment opportunities in and outside Korea that were consequent on Japanese industrial and military activities. This utilization of Korean labor in the industrialization of Japan and Manchukuo lessened, but did not eliminate, the increase of the Korean people within Korea. Numbers expanded 24 per cent between 1925 and 1940, and the absorption of this increase within the limited economy of Korea was difficult. The accumulation of people in the rural areas continued in the 1925–1930 period. Then, between 1930 and 1940 there was substantial economic development. In this decade the total male population of Korea, including the Japanese, increased 13.5 per cent, but the number of persons engaged in agriculture declined almost 10 per cent. The number in industry increased 44 per cent. By 1940, 28 per cent of all gainfully occupied Korean men reported an occupation other than agriculture, and 10 per cent of the population lived in cities. Redistribution within the country quickened as the youth of the rural areas moved cityward and the crowded southern people moved northward for employment in the growing industrial centers. In the five years between 1935 and 1940 the total population of Kyonggi-do, which included Seoul, increased 17 per cent, while that of strategic Hamkyong-pukto increased 29 per cent. Four rural provinces lost in total population: Ch'ungch'on-namdo, Cholla-namdo, Kyongsang-namdo, and Whanghae-do. By 1940, 9 per cent of all Koreans were living in a province other than that in which they were born, and this proportion rose to 13 for the migrant ages between twenty and thirty-four.

If the expansion of the Japanese economic and military system had continued without war or depression, the movement of Koreans outside Korea and the growth of cities within the country might have signalized the end of the period in which population increase tended to result primarily in accentuation of the man-land-production problems of the rural areas. Eighty per cent of the internal increase of 3.2 million between 1925 and 1935 was absorbed in the rural areas. The next five years, on the other hand, saw 85 per cent of the increase of 1.3 million absorbed by urban areas. Three facts are basic to assessment of this achievement. First, in the period between 1935 and 1940, the total natural increase of the Koreans in Korea was 2.4 million. Over 900,000 migrated, leaving 1.4 million within the country. Thus cities absorbed only 48 per cent of the total natural increase. Second, both emigration and urbanization were by-products of Japanese policies for the development of Korea. Third, this first rough approximation to adequate utilization of the increasing population occurred sixty-five years after Korea signed the first trade treaty with Japan, and thirty years after Japan achieved effective control of the peninsula. In Japan, where economic development was indigenous and oriented toward the achievement of national power, if not of individual welfare, the rural population remained relatively unchanged from the Meiji Restoration to 1930 and declined thereafter. The entire natural increase was absorbed in cities and nonagricultural employment and, prior to 1930, there was little net loss through movements from the country.

The demographic expansion of the Koreans reflected an imposed, rather than an indigenous, development. An alien managerial, professional, and technical group was responsible for the transformation of the submarginal economy of old Korea into an expanding economy that maintained a greatly increased population and yielded sizable export surpluses. The Japanese in Korea numbered 443,000 in 1925 and 707,000 in 1940. While they were a tiny proportion of the total population, in 1944 Japanese civilian men in Korea included half the college graduates of the country and over two-fifths of those who had some education beyond the elementary school level.

The perspective of 1952 contributes toward a generally pessimistic assessment of the late prewar developments of the Korean population,

TABLE 11.5

THE KOREAN AND JAPANESE POPULATION OF KOREA BY URBAN
AND RURAL RESIDENCE, 1925–1940

Population	Numbers (in thousands)				Per cent change		
	1925	1930	1935	1940	1925–1929	1930–1934	1935–1939
Total	19,523	21,058	22,899	24,326	7.9	8.7	6.2
Urban	850	1,190	1,606	2,821	40.0	35.0	75.7
Rural	18,673	19,868	21,293	21,506	6.4	7.2	1.0
Koreans	19,020	20,438	22,208	23,547	7.5	8.7	6.0
Urban	608	890	1,245	2,377	46.4	40.0	91.0
Rural	18,412	19,549	20,963	21,170	6.2	7.2	1.0
Japanese	443	527	619	707	19.0	17.5	14.2
Urban	221	268	334	435	21.3	24.6	30.2
Rural	222	259	285	272	16.7	10.0	−4.6

Source: Censuses of Korea. [In Japanese.] 1925: Tables of Results, pp. 492–576. 1930: Reports of the 1930 Census, Provincial Volumes, Table 10. 1935: Reports of the 1935 Census, Provincial Volumes, Table 11. 1940: Summary of the Results of the 1940 Census, Table 7.

particularly if the comparisons are made with Japan or the industrialized countries of the West. However, analysis of the demographic status of other underdeveloped areas indicates that the Korea of 1940 had moved farther toward the solution of the strictly demographic problems that accompany economic development than had any other region in the Asian colonial world of the prewar period. Japanese and Korean demographers noted the similarities in the population dynamics of the Western countries, Japan, and Korea. They assumed that Korea would repeat the history of Japan, just as Japan was repeating the history of the West. Let us assume for the moment that this argument was valid, and that the prewar world of East Asia had remained intact. In 1940 there were 26.2 million Koreans in the northeast Asian region, almost twice the number there had been in 1910. Recapitulation of the Japanese demographic transition would have yielded some 80 million Koreans before increase ceased. Even the demographers of Korea had difficulty viewing this prospect with equanimity.

Analysis of the dynamics of mortality and fertility within Korea during the twenties and the thirties of this century reveals the same relationships as existed in Japan and the countries of the West. Mortality had declined throughout the country because life was desirable to all and the saving of life was an expressed policy of government. Family and child-bearing involved following accepted ways and the achievement of sons and the succession of the generations. There were no government policies here except those of the quiescence and ignorance that operated to slow whatever dynamic elements were diffusing throughout the country. Birth rates were lower in more prosperous areas and in cities and were higher in rural areas. The groups of low fertility were so small a proportion of the total population, however, that national fertility remained relatively unchanging, except insofar as the pressures of the industrializing society caused marriage to be postponed. There were no evidences of fundamental differences in the responses of Koreans and Japanese to the altered conditions of living and working in industrialized areas and great cities. Differences inhered in the quantitative impact of the forces of transformation, rather than in any qualitative differences in the response of the people to them.

CONCLUSIONS

Japan constitutes one case study in the demographic correlates of modernization of a predominantly industrial type, albeit a peculiarly significant one. Japan's historic culture was Eastern. Her industrial and urban transformation was thus divorced from a base in the non-material culture of the West, except insofar as specific elements were deliberately selected for imitation or diffused through more informal mechanisms. Japan was shrouded in the quiescent seclusion of the Tokugawa *baku-fu* when Europe awakened in the Renaissance and the Reformation. Japan, again, had no Protestant ethic whose interconnections with the evolution of capitalism could be debated and no church whose familial pronouncements implemented the Pauline philosophy. Yet here, within the East, the demographic correlates of industrialization were roughly comparable to those in the West.

The population growth that accompanies indigenous and comprehensive industrial development and the slowing of that growth through a progressive limitation of child-bearing are alike products of the changes in ways of living and thinking that are both precondition and product of industrialization. The relations of culture and demography proceed through the intermediation of the economic process itself. Political stability, a disciplined labor force, and rapid capital accumulation are necessary aspects of substantial industrialization. Cultural factors exert a major influence on the extent and the speed of the economic transformation, for there are cultural preconditions to native economic transformations and cultural limitations to imposed transformations. As industrialization extends over time and expands over wider segments of a nation, declining mortality and declining fertility become necessary consequences of the accompanying economic pressures and cultural stimuli. But industrialization regarded as economic, political, or social process is in turn modified by the changing dynamics of population. The relationships are complex; the particular constellation of factors that produced the population growth of imperial Japan will not be duplicated in detail elsewhere. The fundamental fact, though, is that experience within the East corroborates the hypothesis deducible from Western experience: substantial increase in the size of the total population is a correlate of industrialization, but the social and psychological transformations implicit in industrialization result eventually in a lessened rate of reproduction and a slowing population growth. Given the technologies and the basic values of the twentieth century, both population growth and the ultimate slowing of that growth are predictable consequences of the industrial and urban transformation of agrarian cultures.

If this experience of the one nation in Monsoon Asia that has achieved a substantial degree of industrialization can be used to project the future of the other cultures, industrialization and urbanization will lead eventually to declines in fertility that will first lessen, and then eliminate, the growth that accompanies modernization. There are, however, two major uncertainties. The first concerns the validity of the assumption that the East will achieve internal order, increasing agricultural productivity, and an expanding industrial economy. The second is the supposition that, even under these circumstances, international movements, frontier expansion, urbanization, and declining fertility can operate rapidly enough to permit an accelerating decline in mortality such as that which accompanied the industrialization of the West and Japan.

In Asia, numbers are so great and the pressure of people on subsistence so intense that time is crucial. Asia cannot afford to permit the transition from high to low fertility to evolve as a by-product of the pressures and the stimuli generated by the urbanization process.

Levels of living, perhaps existence itself, for a large portion of that half of the world's people who live within Monsoon Asia may depend on the rapidity of the cultural developments through which numbers are related to the economic potentialities for their support within the familial social structure of the rural areas themselves. If these cultural developments occur, then economic development based on agricultural improvements, small industries, and the preservation of the traditional values can proceed without the demographic hazards that now appear to lie ahead.

CHAPTER XII

India: A Colonial Setting

HELEN B. LAMB [*]

BASIC FACTORS CONDITIONING INDIAN ECONOMIC DEVELOPMENT

SINCE INDIA IS AN EXAMPLE OF ARRESTED ECONOMIC DEVELOPMENT, THE Indian story provides a significant case history of the difficulties and obstacles in the way of development. India is a vast subcontinent with a great and ancient cultural tradition of its own. In preindustrial terms India has been well developed for a long time—highly skilled craftsmen, intensive agriculture in the northern river valleys, and considerable concentration of wealth in the hands of local potentates and of the bankers who financed trade in luxury goods and the personal and military expenses of the princes. It was the wealth of India which incited Western European commercial groups, already expanding beyond their own frontiers, to vie with each other in an effort to capture as much of the Indian trade as possible.

With British penetration and conquest, the drive for change in India came from without. This fact has had profound results for Indian economic development because British interest, not Indian, has determined the pace and direction of Indian economic development. After England's industrial revolution, the British dream for India became that of a vast market for British manufactured goods and a source of food and raw materials for the West. As Thomas Bazley, president of the Manchester Chamber of Commerce, testified before the Parliamentary inquiry of 1840:

[*] Research Associate, Center for International Studies, Massachusetts Institute of Technology. Author: "Rockefeller, U.N. Reports, Highlight Point IV," *Foreign Policy Bulletin* (August 31, 1951); "The Development of Modern Business Communities in India," *Labor, Management and Economic Growth* (1954); *Industrial Relations in the Western Lettuce Industry* (thesis), mimeographed by the Department of Employment Relations in the State of California, 1943.

In India there is an immense extent of territory, and the population of it would consume British manufactures to a most enormous extent. The whole question with respect to our Indian trade is whether they can pay us, by the products of their soil, for what we are prepared to send out as manufactures.[1]

The British were not looking for any magic formula for all-round economic growth. In fact, British merchants in the eighteenth and nineteenth centuries showed little prophetic interest in the problems of twentieth-century economists. They were looking for markets and sources of raw materials, and within limits they got them.

What would have happened had the British not come to India is anyone's guess. For a long time it was customary in Great Britain to speak of chaos as the alternative to British rule. And it is quite possible that without British rule the Indian subcontinent would today contain not two countries but, like the European continent, many more—some more advanced, others less so. Certainly had the British not been there, the impetus for developing a complementary type of economy would not have emerged to anything like the degree that it did.

For Britain, however, the development in India of an economy complementary to Britain's own was less urgent than the maintenance of political control in India—no mean feat, considering that the British were never more than a tiny minority of less than 200,000 in a population which numbered 388,000,000 in 1941. To obtain, and later to maintain, domination in India, the British relied on the well-known tactic of divide and rule, a policy made initially easy by the fact that Indian society had long been split into two quite antithetical cultures, the Hindu and the Moslem, and by the fact that the British arrived on the scene just when the Mogul empire was disintegrating in the face of local chieftains who were rising in various parts of India. After conquest, the British continued to balance one religious group against another, to organize the Indian army on communal and territorial lines, thus perpetuating sectional animosities, and, most important, to retain the princely states apart from British-administered India, thus preventing India's unification.[2]

[1] Quoted in R. P. Dutt, *India Today*, rev. ed. (Bombay: People's Publishing House, 1947), p. 105.
[2] Before the Indian Rebellion of 1858, British policy had been to attack, infiltrate, and undermine the finances of princely states, preliminary to their absorption

Just as the British put maintenance of political power first, so in recent years the growing Indian nationalist movement also put the elimination of British political power ahead of economic development. The main energies of India's future leaders—lawyers, economists, writers, politicians and industrialists—were for more than a generation poured into the struggle for independence. Until it was won, Indians could scarcely tackle the problem of development and discuss economic issues free from unproductive political controversy and invective.

Furthermore, the Indian attitude toward development has been ambivalent, partly because India has not yet tasted the fruits of economic development in greater general well-being. Development has been so slow in India that population increases have tended to outstrip, or at least to keep pace with, rising (total) national product, even though the rate of population increase has been moderate.[3] In addition, along with the desire to oust the British politically, came the wish on the part of many Indians to reject the factories, railways, and materialistic values which the British had imposed on India. One way for a subject people to throw off the mental shackles of inferiority and subordination to their rulers is to invoke a past age of independence. Gandhi, with his appeal for a return to the simple life of the spirit, of few wants, handicraft industry, and village self-sufficiency, was doing just this by telling Indians to be themselves rather than poor imitators of the West. So strong was this aspect of Indian nationalism that it was not until 1938 that the All-India National Congress came out unequivocally for rapid economic development and industrialization

---

into British India. The rebellion, representing in part the protest of recently subdued princes against British rule, brought a change in policy. The presidencies—those parts of India which had come under direct British rule—were united into British India (three-fifths of the area and three-fourths of the population of India), and thereafter the British undertook to maintain the remaining six hundred princes as nominal rulers in their own domains. The British Raj protected them from each other, from themselves, i.e., from their own worst excesses (a British resident standing by to direct and advise them), and from their own underlying populations, to obviate the possibility of economic and political reform movements springing up from below. These principalities scattered throughout India provided Britain with friendly fortresses, since the princes owed their economic privileges and very existence as nominal rulers to their British protectors.

[3] Between 1871 and 1941 India's population grew at the rate of 0.6 per cent per year, about the world average and considerably less than the rate of population growth in Western Europe and the United States. K. Davis, *The Population of India and Pakistan* (Princeton: Princeton University Press, 1951), pp. 26–27.

as the only effective way to cope with India's poverty. The chief forces moving the Congress in this direction were the left wing, under the leadership of S. C. Bose, and the small group of rising Indian industrialists who wanted vigorous state support of industry; this policy collided with the traditional British view of India as a market for British manufactured goods.

The relegation of economic development to second place, at least in procedure if not in importance, came out clearly in the hands-off attitude of Indian Congress leaders toward the princely states. One of the major stumbling blocks in the way of economic development was the existence of numerous small states, too small to be viable economic units, run by autocratic princes who habitually spent a large portion of state revenues on their own luxurious living and did little if anything to raise income levels.[4] The states, being interspersed through British India like a checkerboard, stood squarely in the way of administrative integration of India.[5] Many of the smaller principalities were really little more than estates where the princes as glorified landlords had complete authority over their tenants. The few large states, relying on customs duties as an important source of revenue, effectively blocked the obvious path to national integration.

Yet Congress leaders for a long time did nothing to build a popular movement in the states or to agitate for economic integration of the states with British India. This abstention was partly based on expediency and tactics; Congress leaders wanted a united front of *all* Indians, including the princes, against British rule. And it was partly a matter of pride and sentiment; the best-run Indian states, such as Baroda, Mysore, and Travancore, were pointed to by Indians as demonstration and proof that Indians could govern India right away, not at some remote time in the future when they would finally be judged "ready" for self-government.

Indian Economic History

The economic history of India under British domination falls into three main periods: (1) 1750–1850, the period of conquest and con-

---

[4] Productivity in both industry and agriculture was lower in the states than in British India. See the series of charts in the publication of the Office of the Economic Advisor, Government of India, S. Subramanian, *Statistical Summary of the Social and Economic Trends in India* (in the interwar period) (1945), pp. 1, 5–6, 7–11.

[5] In statistical terms the states represent large gaps in our information about India, having either no statistics or less complete statistics than British India.

solidation under East India Company rule, (2) 1850–1914, the development of India as a producer of food and raw materials, and (3) 1914–1947, the period of political transition and economic stalemate.

1750–1850. Though the East India Company, a private British trading company with monopoly rights to the trade between England and India, began doing business in India in 1600, it did not become a territorial power until after 1750. From then on, the conquest and consolidation of British power in India took place under the impetus of the Company's economic interests, with the early years of the period marked by plunder and extortion. As the Marquis of Salisbury remarked in 1797 (according to the records of the East India Company), "The primary object of Great Britain, let it be acknowledged, was rather to discover what could be obtained from her Asiatic subjects, than how they could be benefited." [6] The later years of this period witnessed the gradual transfer of power from the Company to the Crown (consummated in 1858).

This period saw some slight development of India's raw materials for export and a shift from being, on balance, an exporter of handmade manufactured goods to being an importer of British textiles and metalware, though in quantitative terms foreign trade was still slight. This shift, resulting from a combination of British mercantilist policies and the impact of the British industrial revolution on the prices of these articles, was accompanied by a persistent and growing excess of exports over imports on current account, popularly known as "the drain." During this period there appears to have been no appreciable flow of capital into India and at times some liquid funds were drained away. The British, however, did lay the groundwork for a private enterprise type of economic development by initiating important institutional changes such as the alienability of land; British right to own land; freedom of contract; the introduction of British courts to enforce law, order, and contractual rights; and the removal of numerous obstructions to trade. In economic terms the period ended in 1848 when British capital came to India to build the first railway.

1850–1914. This was a period of considerable economic growth under the impetus of Britain's search for markets and the West's de-

[6] Quoted in William Digby, *Prosperous British India* (London: T. Fisher Unwin, 1901), p. 266.

TABLE 12.1

INDIA'S EXPORTS, IMPORTS, AND BALANCE OF TRADE, 1913–1914

(millions of rupees)

Country	Exports	Imports	Balance
United Kingdom	580	1,170	− 590
Other countries of the British Empire	360	110	+ 250
Total British Empire	940	1,280	− 340
Europe	840	300	+ 550
United States	220	50	+ 170
Japan	230	50	+ 180
Other foreign countries	250	150	+ 100
Total Foreign Countries	1,550	550	+1,000
Grand Total	2,490	1,830	+ 660

Source: B. N. Ganguli, *Reconstruction of India's Foreign Trade* (Bombay, London: Oxford University Press for Indian Council of World Affairs, 1946), p. 20.

mand for India's raw materials. The growth was greatly stimulated by the opening of the Suez Canal in 1869; by the new network of railways, which opened up the interior to trade and stimulated Indian coal production; and by the building of India's major irrigation works. This period saw the rise of India's first modern industry, cotton and jute textiles.

The opening up of India resulted in a rapid expansion of her export trade from an estimated 560 million rupees per year in the 1860's to

TABLE 12.2

TOTAL VALUE OF IMPORTS BY COMMODITIES

(average 1910–1914)

Commodity	Value (millions of rupees)	Percentage of total value
Textile manufactures (mostly cotton)	617.9	40.3
Metals	165.7	10.8
Metal manufactures	153.5	10.0
Sugar	135.9	8.9
Oils, minerals	38.7	2.5
Others	420.8	27.5
Total	1,530.5	100.0

Source: H. Venkatasubbiah, *The Foreign Trade of India 1900–1940* (Bombay, London: Oxford University Press for Indian Council of World Affairs, 1946), p. 28.

2,242 million rupees per year in the period 1909–1914 (uncorrected for the changes in price level). Both the destination and the composition of this trade indicate that the dream of British manufacturers was being fulfilled. The destination of India's trade suggests that India had become more important to England as a market for British goods than as a source of raw materials for British industry. In 1913–1914, 60 per cent of India's imports came from Great Britain, whereas only 25 per cent of India's exports went to Great Britain; yet, to be sure, India's exports to other areas helped to maintain the prevailing multilateral trading system of the London metropolitan economy.

TABLE 12.3

TOTAL VALUE OF EXPORTS BY COMMODITIES
(average 1910–1914)

Commodity	Value (millions of rupees)	Percentage of total value
Cotton, raw	337.4	14.8
Rice	278.1	12.2
Seeds	254.0	11.1
Jute, raw	239.8	10.5
Wheat	142.8	6.2
Tea	134.1	5.9
Hides and skins, raw	104.6	4.6
Jute manufactures	210.3	9.2
Cotton manufactures	112.8	4.9
Hides and skins, dressed or tanned	43.5	1.9
Others	425.6	18.7
Total	2,283.0	100.0

Source: H. Venkatasubbiah, op. cit., p. 28.

The commodities heading India's import list came largely from Britain: 90 per cent of her imported cotton manufactures, 87 per cent of her metal manufactures, and 66 per cent of her metals. The only important imports originating other than in Great Britain were oils, minerals, and sugar.

To effect the opening up of India and the consequent expansion in foreign trade, British capital poured into India. According to the estimate of Sir George Paish, British investment in India and Ceylon in 1909–1910 was £365,399,000. He considered this to be about 11 per cent of Britain's entire overseas investment and estimated its distribution as shown in Table 12.4. Measured in per capita terms, however,

TABLE 12.4

BRITISH INVESTMENT IN INDIA AND CEYLON, 1909–1910

Government bonds	£178,995,000*
Railways	136,519,000
Tea and coffee plantations	19,644,000
Rubber	4,610,000
Mines	3,531,000
Banks	3,400,000
Commercial and industrial	2,647,000
Miscellaneous municipal bonds, tramways, telegraph and telephone, gas and water, electric light and power	16,053,000
Total	£365,399,000

Source: Sir George Paish, "Great Britain's Capital Investments in Individual Colonies and Foreign Countries," *Journal of the Royal Statistical Society*, Vol. 74, 1910–1911, p. 186.

* About two-thirds of total public debt in 1910, the total being composed as follows: 74 per cent railways, 12 per cent irrigation, and 14 per cent ordinary, i.e., unsecured debt. (Of the remaining third of the public debt, that held in rupees, British residents in India held about one-half.)

this investment was not large. British investment in Canada, Australia, and South Africa came to £55 sterling per inhabitant, whereas in India it amounted only to £1.2 sterling per inhabitant.

Indian statistics are unfortunately too incomplete to provide any reliable over-all measure of Indian economic growth. Comprehensive statistical data on national net income and its distribution, aggregate productive wealth and its composition, and the like are outgrowths of economic development—a valuable by-product of development. It is no accident that these statistics do not exist for India.

Nonetheless it is possible to reach some guesses on the basis of the data we do possess. India was able to sustain a larger population than previously, which already indicates growth if we assume living standards did not decline.[7] The excess of exports over imports in value terms grew steadily, along with increases in the exportable volume of specific commodities, such as cotton, tea, wheat, and jute. It is hard to see how this could have taken place unless the Indian economy became both less self-sufficient and more productive. The rise of new

[7] See the discussion of various conjectures as to per capita income in India in "India's Economic Development since 1850, as Illustrated by Statistics: Part 1, National Income Statistics," Social Science Research Council, *Conference on Economic Growth in Selected Countries*, April 25–27, 1952, proceedings to be published.

modern industries suggests a more productive economy, though this rise was to some extent at the expense of traditional handicraft industries. Land area under cultivation increased (some of this increase reflects improvement in agricultural statistics[8], and the land under irrigation increased. Finally there has been considerable growth in the apparatus of government. When all this is said, however, it must be emphasized that the growth which did occur could not have been great; the scanty data available all bear this out.

1914–1947. War and partition have enormously complicated India's situation, but the basic problems of Indian economic development emerged before 1940 and became the subject of widespread discussion and study. While in some ways the period 1919–1939 is confused and difficult to analyze, state policy toward Indian industry took a new course. Government indifference, if not hostility, to Indian industry was replaced by official concern for industrial development as a result of the plight of India and England during World War I and the growing influence of Indian industrialists. Free trade gave way to some degree of protection and new industries sprang up under its shelter, though not to the extent of priming the pump of real industrial integration and all-round expansion of the economy. (See the discussion of Indian employment below.) Industry became slightly more diffused; there was more Indian participation in the modern sector of the economy; steel production increased; imports of consumer goods, notably cotton textiles and sugar, fell off, and imports of producer goods increased.[9] Although all these changes indicate some development, agriculture, India's basic industry, appeared to languish.[10]

Because of the relatively low productivity of agriculture, growth of population and consequent rise in the consumption of agricultural products, and the impact of the world depression on prices, Indian ex-

[8] The net area covered by professional survey increased from 552 million acres in 1901–1902 to 679 million acres in 1936–1937. G. B. Jathar and S. G. Beri, *Indian Economics,* rev. ed. (Madras: Oxford University Press, 1939), Vol. I, p. 164.

[9] For a good account of the changes in India's industrial pattern and their impact on India's foreign trade, see N. S. R. Sastry, *A Statistical Study of India's Industrial Development* (Bombay: Thacker & Co., 1943).

[10] See the charts on agricultural production in the paper by Daniel Thorner, "Indian Economic Development since 1850." This paper was prepared for the Social Science Research Council, *Conference on Economic Growth in Selected Countries,* held April 25–27, 1952, proceedings to be published.

ports of agricultural commodities, which had been mounting for decades, began to decline.[11] In addition, the composition of the export trade shifted. Raw material exports replaced food, while manufactured and semimanufactured exports remained about the same.

TABLE 12.5

INDIA'S FOREIGN TRADE IN COMMODITIES

(in millions of rupees)

Years	Imports	Exports
1900–1901 1904–1905	836.2	1310.1
1910–1911 1913–1914	1530.5	2283.0
1919–1920 1923–1924	2540.4	2863.4
1935–1936 1939–1940	1502.2	1808.5

Source: Venkatasubbiah, op. cit., p. 28.

This forty-year period was marked by first a gradual, then a sharp, increase in prices, followed by a decline; by 1940, prices were roughly equivalent to those of 1914. It is clear, comparing the figures for these two years, that India's export capacity had fallen off, while her total imports remained about the same.

RESOURCE USE

Like those of many underdeveloped countries, Indian resources, human and material, have not been fully utilized. Even India's land, despite the pressure of population, has not produced anything approaching its potential capacity for food and raw materials. Underdevelopment appears to go hand in hand with underutilization. We discuss below the use of India's resources and the various forms which underutilization takes, whether as the result of idleness, wastage, or combination of resources in such proportions as to impede full utilization.

Development hinges primarily on a community's ability to make use of what resources it has, rather than on the presence or absence of

---

[11] George Blyn, "Indian Trade: Secular Trends," unpublished paper written in 1952 for a seminar, University of Pennsylvania.

particular resources, important as these may be. In fact the absence of particular resources can on occasion be an incentive to development. One thinks immediately of the lack of cultivable land in Japan.[12] Germany's development of synthetic oil and raw materials for the textile industry is another case in point, though to be sure, this type of creation of resources requires considerable previous development. In the early period of industrialization, the presence of iron and coal in proximity to each other has been an important precondition of development. While India possessed some coking coal and high-grade iron ore near each other in the Bengal-Bihar-Orissa triangle (see Figure 12.1), no steel was produced until 1913 and then only in small

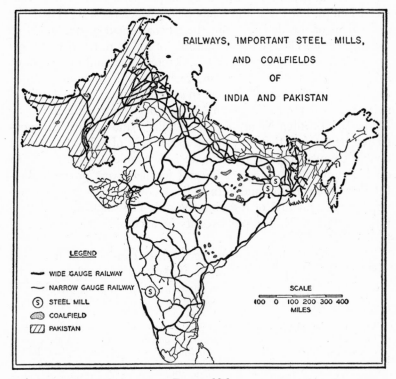

FIGURE 12.1

[12] Japanese population density per square mile of arable land was 1,500 in 1870, far above the 1940 figure in British India of 602 per square mile of cultivated land (the estimates are from K. Davis, *op. cit.*, p. 219).

amounts. The presence or absence of particular resources in India will necessarily condition the country's future development. But the Indian experience to date has been one of not using what resources it has.[13]

Land use. Land in India is underutilized in several respects; output per crop per acre is low due to the lack of essential components— water, fertilizer, good seed, and agricultural techniques—and to the declining fertility of Indian soil. Two counteracting tendencies have been going on simultaneously. New land has been brought under cultivation by irrigation and clearing, improved agricultural practices such as use of better seed have raised output per acre in certain commercial crops, but the soil in many places is deteriorating. There are many signs of this deterioration: the encroachment of the Desert of Kutch, erosion, silting and waterlogging of soil from faulty canal irrigation, increasing salinity of the soil, deforestation, and the spread of kans grass—all of which cause land each year to become marginal or to go out of cultivation altogether. In some cases kans-infested soil has reduced wheat production from 750 to 170 pounds per acre.

The lack of intensive utilization of India's land is further demonstrated by the fact that only about 15 per cent of cultivated land is double cropped, though the climate is favorable in many areas to double cropping if enough water and fertilizer were provided. Furthermore, much of the land in India lies fallow, an obviously slow and unproductive method of restoring the soil. The small size and fragmentation of cultivated plots results in a considerable wastage of land in boundaries.

Statistics on Indian land use reveal that considerable new land could be brought under cultivation if the cost of clearing could be met. Though we have no figures on land use for about one-third of prepartitioned India (the unsurveyed area amounted to 348 million

[13] Our main emphasis in this section is on resource use. For a detailed analysis of the impact of partition on Indian resource potential, see C. N. Vakil's book, *The Economic Consequences of Divided India* (Bombay: Vora and Co., 1950). Estimates of potential resources of the Indian Union with respect to power, coal, and iron are given below. Vakil gives the allocation under partition of India's natural and man-made resources, transportation facilities, factories, land use, crops, irrigation, forests, banking, and so on. One of the most important effects of partition has been the economic disorganization it has caused, since the two areas complemented each other economically. This disorganization obviously raises serious questions as to future trade and peace in the area.

acres in 1936–1939), it is safe to assume that this land, the property of persons of privileged tenure, or located in the more backward states for which no statistics are available, was less intensively utilized than the surveyed land in British India and in the more advanced states.

TABLE 12.6

INDIAN LAND USE, 1936–1939

(millions of acres)

Total area surveyed	660
Not available for cultivation	121
Forest areas	88
Available for cultivation	451
Uncultivated	112*
Fallow	59
Sown once a year	244
Sown twice a year	36

Source: Vakil, op. cit., p. 153.
* Susceptible to cultivation if cleared, restored, irrigated, etc.

The fact that land resources have not been more intensively utilized in India despite increasing population pressure is traceable in part to the magnitude of the task of clearing the jungle, building roads, ridding large areas of malaria, terracing and contouring land, and in some instances providing water. It also involves the cultural complex of the Indian countryside which is discussed below.

Forestry resources. Though India possesses substantial forest reserves, much of what the statistics list as forest is actually sparsely wooded grazing land. Reckless deforestation took place until the British in 1855 embarked on a policy of forestry conservation. Since then Indian forests have been conserved rather than developed. India's forestry resources are very unevenly distributed—Bihar and Orissa being at one extreme with only 3.6 per cent of the area in forests in 1937, while Assam, a frontier and little-settled province, had 37.6 per cent forest area. Development would require the building up of fast-growing woods in areas which are deficient, thereby supplying the villages with wood for tools, building supplies, and, above all, firewood. Moreover, a far more vigorous and scientific exploitation of the remote forest regions, such as Assam, is indicated. This exploitation in turn would require organization, capital funds, equipment, roads, the building of new communities, and subsidiary industries to utilize the by-products of wood. As it is now, most of the total value of forest products is left unused even in those areas where lumbering is significant.

Wastage of agricultural products. As in many other underdeveloped countries there is considerable wastage of the products of agriculture due to insects, pests of all kinds, and lack of adequate storage facilities. The Industrial Commission *Report* in 1919 pointed out the small recovery rate involved in the traditional methods of processing India's agricultural products, especially in the extraction of oil from seeds and of *gur*, a kind of sugar, from sugar cane.[14] This is true also of the tanning of hides. In addition, while India's huge cattle population is used for power and milk, they are able to give very little of each because they are so underfed. The neglect of fodder production is a relic of the days when India was not overpopulated and cattle were able to fend for themselves; it provides another instance of the persistence of an extensive, rather than an intensive, type of agriculture. Perhaps the most spectacular example of wastage of agricultural products is the use of manure for fuel instead of fertilizer, largely because of the unavailability of firewood.

Fishing resources. Like many underdeveloped countries, India makes little use of her fishing resources. Even the exploitation of a resource as free as the fishes of the sea requires organization, capital, landing facilities, and refrigeration and canning equipment. The Indian Union's annual catch comes to 3.4 pounds per capita. For the 135 million Indians who are not vegetarians to obtain even a quarter of the protein they need from a native fish industry, expansion is clearly needed.

Mineral resources. The First Five Year Plan summarizes the Indian Union's position with regard to minerals as follows:

Coal, iron ore, manganese ore, mica, gold, ilmenite, and building materials are produced in India in quantities of real importance to industry

[14] Government of India Industrial Commission 1916–1918, *Report* (1919), pp. 33–36, 341–353.

and other sectors of the economy. Other minerals of which India possesses good reserves are bauxite, industrial clays, steatite, chromite, atomic energy minerals, refractory minerals and abrasives. The more important minerals, supplies of which are inadequate for any large industrial development, are sulphur, copper, tin, nickel, lead, zinc, graphite, cobalt, mercury and liquid fuels. Except for these India is endowed with the basic mineral and power resources needed for industrial expansion though, in relation to the population, the reserves compare unfavourably with the important mineral regions of the world.[15]

TABLE 12.7

COMPARATIVE PER CAPITA NATURAL RESOURCES IN DIFFERENT
COUNTRIES AND AREAS

Countries	Coal and lignite reserves, coal equivalent (tons)	Water power at ordinary minimum flow (h.p.)	Iron ore metal content (tons)	Arable and other cultivated land (acres)	Pastures (acres)
West Continental Europe	1,510	0.20	31.4	1.09	0.47
East Continental Europe	980	0.10	4.1	1.34	0.51
Soviet Union	6,300	0.46	94.0	2.35	5.70
United States and Cuba	17,000	0.25	48.0	2.66	4.40
Canada and Newfoundland	37,300	2.27	217.1	5.04	6.78
India	66	0.10	5.9	1.29	0.52
China	546	0.05	1.4	0.55	1.78
Japan	227	0.10	0.4	0.23	0.11
All countries listed, average	3,000	0.16	24.6	1.30	2.10

Source: A. J. Brown's *Industrialization and Trade* (London: Royal Institute of International Affairs, 1943), reproduced in Government of India Fiscal Commission, *Report* (1949–1950), Vol. I, pp. 118–119.

Since discovery is never very far ahead of use, however, it is quite possible that India may find she has considerably more mineral resources than would now appear. The Fiscal Commission *Report* reminds us: "Geological exploration in this country has been hitherto more extensive than intensive; even so, large areas of the country still remain to be mapped." [16]

[15] Government of India Planning Commission, *The First Five Year Plan*, a draft outline (1951), p. 139.
[16] Government of India Fiscal Commission, *op. cit.*, Vol. I, p. 117.

Power resources. The Indian Union has no oil. Good-quality coal is limited and mainly concentrated in Bihar and West Bengal. It may be as much as 5 billion tons, of which only 2 billion can be used for coking coal; India has also some 60 billion more tons of low-grade coal. Much of her good-quality coal has been wasted through inefficient methods of extraction and by the use of her limited coking coal for other purposes than making steel.[17] Indian coal output is only about 30 million tons per year. In contrast, India has a great water power potential: installed capacity in 1948 was 500,000 kilowatts, whereas potential capacity has been estimated at between 30 and 40 million kilowatts; however, only about 6 per cent of the water that flows annually through India's rivers is utilized.[18] The greatest power potential is located in remote regions such as the Brahmaputra River in the Eastern Himalayas, where power development awaits the building of communities and industries to use it.[19] Thus future multi-purpose irrigation and power projects will be more expensive, and it will be necessary to build extensive reservoirs for water storage in southern India, where the flow of water throughout the year is extremely uneven.

TABLE 12.8

RELATIVE DEVELOPMENT OF HYDROELECTRIC POWER IN
VARIOUS COUNTRIES OF THE WORLD

Country	Water power . potential (million kw)	Water power developed and installed at present (million kw)	Water power developed as percentage of potential at present
Soviet Union	100	22.4	22
United States	45	14.5	34
Canada	38	7.7	20
Switzerland	4.5	2.4	67
Japan	20	5.8	30
Australia	3	0.3	9
India	30–40	0.5	1.5

Source: Table 7, Government of India Fiscal Commission, *op. cit.*, Vol. I, p. 30.

[17] Government of India Planning Commission, *op. cit.*, p. 142.
[18] Government of India Fiscal Commission, *op. cit.*, Vol. I, p. 30.
[19] H. V. Sieveking, "Hydro-Electric Development in India," *Indian Finance, Engineering and Transport Number*, 1950.

Transportation. In a country the size of India, with such great variation in products due to climatic differences and with raw materials so unevenly distributed, development hinges to an unusual degree on transportation facilities and transport policies. While India's railway network (a total of 42,000 miles in 1940—see Figure 12.1) is among the largest in the world, it is underdeveloped as compared to those of Western countries in terms either of trackage per thousand inhabitants or trackage per square mile of territory. Nonetheless it is overdeveloped as compared to the degree of development of the rest of the economy.

Total road mileage in British India in 1936–1937 amounted to 306,700 miles, of which 82,300 were metaled and 224,400 were dirt. Of this total, the 237,900 miles maintained by district and local boards had in general been allowed to deteriorate. Though southern India is better served than northern India, there is still an acute need for building roads to feed the railways, and thousands of villages are without roads. Under East India Company rule, roads were built largely for military purposes. Subsequently roads were built to meet the needs of the civil population, but road building was not pushed, especially in the case of roads running parallel to, and thus competing with, railways.

The development of water navigation, especially in North India, was also neglected by the British, again possibly because of their desire to minimize competition with the British-financed Indian railways. Many rivers in the South Indian peninsula are torrents during the monsoon but shrink to puddles at other times of the year, and cannot be used for navigation. In North India, however, there are 26,000 miles of navigable waterways. To round out the picture of transportation, India has a deficiency of natural harbors, particularly in the south; virtually all of India's foreign trade passes through Bombay, Calcutta, Madras, and Karachi (the last now capital of Pakistan).

Use of India's industrial equipment. One might expect that in underdeveloped countries, due to the undoubted shortage of capital, what little capital equipment there was would be used overtime, with factories running two or even three shifts. This has not been the case in India, save for short periods during the wars when the demand for textiles was high and it was impossible to import new textile ma-

chinery. The jute industry, effectively organized into the Indian Jute
Mills Association and catering to foreign markets, has frequently resorted to limitation of output. Between 1926 and 1936, members of
this association introduced the 40-hour week and sealed off anywhere
from 10 to 15 per cent of the looms in order to prevent overproduc-
tion.[20] India's other big modern industry, cotton textiles, has also had
excess capacity, particularly in Bombay after the industry began moving out of Bombay into up-country towns in lower-cost areas, nearer
to markets and sources of raw materials. In the twenties, the Indian
Tariff Board denied the cement industry a protective tariff on the
grounds that the trouble with the industry was that capacity had out-
run consumption. (Since then both consumption and capacity of
cement have steadily mounted.)

Underutilization of existing capacity, in India as elsewhere, reflects
in part a lack of effective demand. K. N. Raj, in his study of Indian
central banking, pointed out that deficit financing in the period September 1939 to March 1942 had a salutary effect since it increased
production of Indian industry with a minimum of price disturbance.[21]
However, agricultural production, in which the factors of production
are notoriously immobile, did not respond to deficit finance and inflation. In assessing the presence of "overcapacity," it must be borne
in mind that "expansive" fiscal policies were never tried in India except during wartime, when the limited shipping space was reserved for
war transport needs and not for machinery imports. As a result capacity
production was quickly reached in many lines, and thereafter the
monetary stimulus resulted in price inflation. Actually India came
out of the war poorer in industrial equipment in her major industries
and her railways because they were used to the hilt during the war and
their annual replacement needs had not been filled.

The structure of India's small modern industry sector, with its over-
emphasis on textiles and its lack of a well-rounded industrial complex
of many industries, each supplying the raw materials and markets for
the other, has contributed to the periodic underutilization of her
equipment as well as to considerable wastage of industrial by-
products. In Table 12.9 is provided a breakdown of the employ-

[20] Jathar and Beri, *op. cit.*, Vol. II, p. 44.

[21] *The Monetary Policy of the Reserve Bank of India: A Study of Central
Banking in an Underdeveloped Economy* (Bombay: National Information and
Publications, 1948). Raj discusses the techniques and effects of deficit financing
1939–1945, pp. 136–162.

ment structure within the modern industrial sector. The figures reveal that the textile industry still dominates Indian industry in point of numbers employed and that, in the field of engineering, employment is concentrated in the railway workshops. Basic industry consists of the small beginnings made in iron and steel, with almost no heavy chemicals and no machine tool industry. Though the cotton textile industry has been in operation since 1850, and by 1931 contained 8.8 million spindles, there was still no textile machinery industry to supply India's textile mills either with new machinery or with spare parts. Despite the size of India's railway network, there was no production in India of locomotives or freight or passenger cars. Each World War, with its shipping crisis and the contingent long delays in obtaining even simple tools and elementary parts needed for Indian industry and the railways, has dramatized India's lack of industrial integration.

TABLE 12.9

LARGE INDUSTRIAL ESTABLISHMENTS IN INDIA
(average number of employees, 20 or more)
(1935)

Kind of Establishment	Number	Persons employed	Percentage
Textiles, primarily cotton and jute	753	827,441	44.95
Food, drink, and tobacco	2,957	257,584	13.99
Engineering, primarily railway work shops	888	220,587	11.98
Gins and presses	2,729	216,233	11.74
Tile, brick, glass factories and saw mills	532	87,066	4.72
Chemicals	514	64,539	3.50
Minerals and metals, primarily iron and steel mills	144	58,159	3.05
Paper and printing	454	48,622	2.64
Tanneries and shoe and leather manufacture	68	10,276	.55
Miscellaneous	222	52,285	2.84
Total	9,261*	1,840,792	100.00

Source: Jathar and Beri, op. cit., Vol. II, pp. 24–25.
* 4,082 were seasonal employing 364,703 persons; 5,179 were perennial employing 1,477,089 persons.

Another striking characteristic of India's industrial structure is its concentration around Calcutta and Bombay, thus rendering those areas in some respects overdeveloped. The two provinces of Bengal and Bombay, although containing approximately one-quarter of the population of British India, had 66.8 per cent of all workers engaged in large-scale industrial establishments (1938–1939).[22]

Manpower use. The occupational structure of India's population demonstrates a lack of development and considerable concealed underemployment of her human resources. This occupational structure has remained remarkably constant over the past fifty years. In 1901, 61 per cent of India's working population was engaged in the production of raw materials (agriculture, forestry, fishery, cattle, and mining); this percentage rose to 67 per cent during the next thirty years.[23] Japan offers a striking contrast, the proportion of male workers engaged in agriculture diminishing as a result of development from over 64 per cent in 1887 to under 50 per cent in 1925. To provide a wide basis for comparison, the following chart shows India's occupational distri-

TABLE 12.10

OCCUPATIONAL DISTRIBUTION OF GAINFULLY EMPLOYED POPULATION
(in percentages)

Country	Date of census	Agriculture	Mining	Manufacturing: Industrial and handicraft	Transport, trade and communications	Services, professions, administration, domestic service, etc.
Siam	1937	88.6	0.2	1.9	6.2	3.1
India	1931*	67.1	0.2	10.0	6.7	16.0
Japan	1947	52.3†	2.0	21.5	11.7	12.5
Germany	1933	32.0	4.0	36.0	19.0	12.0
Canada	1931	31.0	2.0	25.0	23.0	19.0
United States	1930	22.0	2.0	30.0	27.0	19.0
United Kingdom	1930	7.0	5.0	32.0	23.0	33.0

Source: Adapted from charts appearing in the United Nations, *Economic Survey of Asia and the Far East* (1948), pp. 109–110, and League of Nations, *Industrialization and Foreign Trade* (1945), pp. 26–27.

* The 1941 India census gives no occupational breakdown.

† In Japan the gainfully occupied population in agriculture, including forestry and fishery, rose from the prewar (1930) proportion of 48 per cent to 52.3 per cent as a result of changes in the economy arising from military defeat and allied occupation.

[22] R. Balakrishna, *Regional Planning in India* (Bangalore City, Bangalore Printing and Publishing Co., 1948), p. 92.

[23] H. Venkatasubbiah, *The Structural Basis of Indian Economy* (London: G. Allen & Unwin, Ltd., 1940), p. 41. Table based on census reports. Domestics, 4.5 per cent of the total, have been excluded from the 1901 figure by the author to put it on a basis comparable to that of 1931.

bution and that of other countries in different stages of development.

Most of India's workers engaged in manufacturing were in the handicraft industries (13 million), while less than 2 million worked in factories in 1931. The following figures for British India alone show the approximate size of the modern sector of the Indian economy in 1939:

Factory workers, seasonal and perennial	1,749,000
Workers on the Assam tea plantations	925,000
Employees of Class 1 railways	641,000
Miners	305,000
Total	3,620,000

Thus out of a working population in British India of about 117,000,000, only 3,620,000 workers were engaged in the modern sector of the economy, leaving some 113,000,000 engaged in the traditional sector. In actual practice, considerably more people have been brought under the influence of modern industry because there is a high turnover of employment. For this same reason, however, the influence of this modern impact has been weak, since the workers' roots are still in the villages. This is, no doubt, inevitable in the light of the slow increase in urbanization in India; only 12.2 per cent of the population lived in communities of 5,000 and more in 1941 (see Figure 12.2), as compared with the New Zealand figure of 52.5 per cent and the Japanese figure of 64.5 per cent (1935).

While it is clear that the modern sector grew between 1901 and 1931, it came nowhere near absorbing the increase of 15 million in working population which occurred in India (British India and the states) during this thirty-year period. As a consequence there was an actual increase of employment in agriculture, traditional handicrafts, and trade.

India's work force suffers from lack of general education, lack of training, lack of health—due largely to poor working and living conditions and inadequate diet, lack of incentives and the pressure of many barriers to mobility, and lack of equipment and of efficient organization of production.[24] All of these result in shocking inefficiency and a vicious circle of low wages and low output. Except in certain skilled

[24] R. K. Das, *Industrial Efficiency in India* (London: P. S. King & Sons, Ltd., 1930).

categories, there are usually more people available for work than there are jobs. In the backing up of population on the land and in the way agriculture is conducted, there is considerable concealed underemployment; in the total time expended, the average farmer who does not double-crop his land works perhaps no more than four full months out of the year.

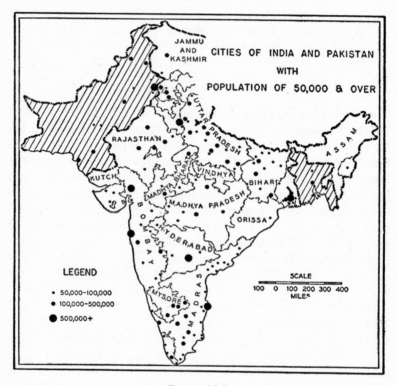

FIGURE 12.2

The picture of resource use presented in outline above disturbs the familiar stereotype of population pressing on resources—as if the resources were meager and used to the hilt, but inadequate to meet the needs of the oncoming torrent of babies. It is an oversimplification to fix on potential resource-population ratios or on lack of capital or lack of know-how as the principal bottlenecks. Rather it is a question of something broader than any of these, involving social organization and orientation.[25] People are idle or ineffectively used—so are re-sources. As the *Bengal Census Report* for 1931 summed up the agricultural situation, "Like the rest of India Bengal is notable for its undeveloped resources and the inefficiency with which such resources as it has are exploited." [26]

Table 12.11, which shows 1948–1949 national output for the Indian Union, gives precision to facts which are widely known—the low productivity of all sectors of the economy and the low proportion of industry to total output—and translates these into per capita income figures (255 rupees, or $53.55 at the current rate of exchange). Certain goals clearly emerge which are quite generally acknowledged: the need for greater over-all productivity, relatively higher proportion of industry to the total, domestic processing of raw materials, and so on.

India's situation has some (potential) similarity to Japan's. In an "ideal" world of peace and mutually beneficial international trade, India could profitably use her abundant labor resources by making the products of light industry for export and by processing raw materials from overseas in return for food and raw materials from abroad to supplement her own food resources and provide any missing components needed to build a base of heavy industry for her own industrialization. India needs industrialization for the sake of her agriculture as well as for industrial output itself, since typically a more intensified land use and greater output per acre accompany industrialization.[27] India's resource complex, as well as the distribution of her resources, suggests the need for carefully co-ordinated planning and conservation. Very important to India is the development of a technology aimed not at saving labor but more in the interests of creating new resources and more fully utilizing those she has.

The case for rapid economic development has often been put in terms of population pressure, since the benefits of a slow rate of economic growth tend to be eaten up by population increases. Some experts have envisaged the transition via industrialization from a pattern

[25] Kingsley Davis discusses these broader aspects of social and economic organization in a paper, "Social and Demographic Aspects of Economic Development in India," Social Science Research Council, *Conference on Economic Growth in Selected Countries*, April 1952, proceedings to be published.

[26] Bengal Census, *Report* (1931), Vol. I, p. 63.

[27] In densely populated areas there appears to be an inverse correlation between percentage of the population engaged in agriculture and the productivity of the land. See chart in League of Nations, *op. cit.*, p. 38.

of high birth and death rates to one of low birth and death rates as taking many generations. The prospect that Indian population will in the meantime fatally multiply several fold has understandably caused some to recoil from the very thought of Indian industrialization.

TABLE 12.11

NATIONAL INCOME OF THE INDIAN UNION BY INDUSTRIAL ORIGIN, 1948–1949

	Net output (millions of rupees)		Percentage	
Agriculture				
Agriculture, animal husbandry, and ancillary activities*	40,700		46.7	
Forestry	600		0.7	
Fishery	200		0.2	
Total		41,500		47.6
Mining, manufacturing and hand-trades				
Mining	600		0.7	
Factory establishments	5,800		6.6	
Small enterprises	8,600		9.9	
Total		15,000		17.2
Commerce, transport, and communications				
Communications (post, telegraph, and telephone)	300		0.3	
Railways	2,000		2.3	
Organized banking and insurance	500		0.6	
Other commerce and transport†	14,200		16.3	
Total		17,000		19.5
Other Services				
Professions and liberal arts	3,200		3.7	
Government services (administration)	4,600		5.3	
Domestic service	1,500		1.7	
House property	4,500		5.2	
Total		13,800		15.9
Net domestic product at factor cost		87,300		100.2
Net earned income from abroad		−200		−.2
Net national output at factor cost		87,100		100.0

Source: Government of India, Ministry of Finance, *First Report of the National Income Committee* (1951), p. 29.

* These include processing, marketing and ancillary activities performed by the cultivator in respect to his own produce.

† These include services of indigenous money lenders.

Actually, with the world's aroused conscience and the greatly improved techniques for handling epidemics, the population of underdeveloped areas will probably increase with or without industrialization. Considerable debate has centered around the prime necessity—or the total impossibility—of "solving" the Indian population problem by a direct attack through widespread introduction of birth control. Perhaps even more fundamentally, in more long-run terms, India needs the new outlook and scale of values, stressing the individual instead of the family, which accompany industrialization, and which ultimately help to bring down the birth rate.[28]

AGRICULTURE AND CAPITAL FORMATION IN INDIAN CULTURAL COMPLEX

The Indian economy has long been oriented around consumption rather than around saving and investment. The point is frequently made that this is inevitable in a poor country: people must consume what they produce in order to keep alive. But there is more to it than this, as indicated by India's extreme inequality of income and wealth.[29]

In the distant past India had a highly "developed" economy based on an intensive agriculture, first in the Indus, and later in the Ganges Valley, due to a combination of favorable soil, climate, and the skill of Indian cultivators. This intensive agriculture meant a sufficient concentration of people to make possible a relatively urban culture—the

---

[28] Speaking of the colonial world, the demographer, Frank Notestein, points out: ". . . the technologically advanced nations have disseminated and imposed that part of their culture which reduces mortality, while withholding, or at least failing to foster the transfer of, that part of their culture out of which the rational control of fertility and the small family pattern develop. . . . In fact, the only societies in which low birth rates have appeared are those dominated by the values developed in modern urban life. Such societies set great store by the individual, his health, welfare, initiative, and advancement. They develop a rational and materialistic outlook on life, view man as the master of his own destiny, and come to hold the deliberate control of fertility to be as reasonable and desirable as that of mortality." "Problems of Policy in Relation to Areas of Heavy Population Pressure," *Demographic Studies of Selected Areas of Rapid Growth* (New York: Milbank Memorial Fund, 1944), pp. 146–147. Note also Joseph Spengler's comments on the possible effect of higher "aspirations" on population growth in Chapter III.

[29] According to the very broad estimates of V. K. R. V. Rao as to the national income of British India and its distribution, less than 2 per cent of the population (income receivers and their dependents) received 18 per cent of the national income. *An Essay on India's National Income, 1925–1929* (London: G. Allen & Unwin, Ltd., 1939), p. 156.

size of India's cities having been frequently commented on by travelers since 300 B.C.—and considerable division of functions, with numerous full-time artisans engaged in producing a wide range of manufactured products. The production of a "surplus" above mere subsistence may be inferred from public works and temples, irrigation works, considerable numbers of people engaged in nonagricultural pursuits, the production of fine luxury goods, and the export of manufactured products in return for bullion.

For centuries India has been described as a "sink" for precious metals; the Romans complained of this drain two thousand years ago. This bullion flow into India plus the presence of extensive luxury industries in India catering to the princes and their entourages suggest that there has always been a high degree of income inequality. India's historic "surplus," a function of productive techniques and the control exercised over the production and distribution of goods, while no doubt small in industrial terms, was quite impressive in preindustrial terms.

More important for development than the size of the surplus is the question of what is done with it. India's potential surplus was not invested to create bigger surpluses in the future, once a certain level of living had been attained. Instead, it was dissipated in conspicuous consumption by the wealthy and accumulated in the form of gold and silver hoards. Though outwardly pre-1600 India had many of the characteristics associated with medieval Europe, some essential ingredient for precipitating the transformation from commercial capitalism on the fringes of an agrarian society into industrial capitalism was apparently lacking. After the British came to India and after modern industrial techniques had already been evolved in the West (so that the problem was only one of adapting existing techniques), the old pattern of income distribution and conspicuous consumption continued with only slight modification. Some Indians have invested some money in productive enterprises during the last hundred years, but the general tendency toward display and the building up of idle hoards of precious metals has persisted. In the 1920's, the net increase of precious metals in India equaled more than 40 per cent of the total net increase in *visible* savings (that is, bank deposits, government debt, paid-up capital and reserve of joint stock companies, premium income of insurance companies, and precious metals).[30]

[30] S. K. Muranjan, *From Hyper-Inflation to Devaluation* (Bombay: Hind Kitabs, 1949), p. 27.

Is it possible that the very inequality of wealth which theoretically made a surplus of production over consumption easier to attain somehow stood in the way of the effective utilization of this surplus for productive purposes? Perhaps a low ratio of resources in use to population, with its attendant poverty, has an important bearing on development, not in the sense that absolute limits are set, but in the sense that a country is positively inhibited from exploiting its potential when all its social and economic institutions are geared to adjusting society to this inequality and concomitant poverty. Certainly it would be hard to find a complex society more irretrievably committed to the doctrine of status than India's.

In India the rich live well and consume what they receive, while the poor live badly and go into debt. The well-to-do group consists of:

(1) Princes. The main sources of their wealth have been state revenues and rents from their privately owned estates.

(2) Landlords. The main source of their wealth is land rents along with mining royalties, if minerals have been found on their land.

(3) The British community in India. Their wealth is derived from wholesale trade, export and import trade, plantations, mines, banking, shipping, insurance, and some industry.

(4) Highly paid Indian professional people. These are in the upper echelons of government administration or serve the other well-to-do groups in India as lawyers and doctors.

(5) Bankers and moneylenders. Their wealth comes from banking, rents and trade, and speculation in goods and bullion. Some indigenous bankers have branched out and become the nucleus of the relatively new and still small Indian industrialist group and derive their wealth from modern industry, banking, etc., as well as from trade and speculation. The bulk of the moneylenders' wealth comes from agriculture.

Indian agriculture presents an anomaly: though some 67 per cent of the Indian population has been engaged in agriculture and 80 per cent of the total cultivated area has been devoted to food crops, India has been unable to maintain even a low standard of diet. Since 1937, when Burma was separated from India, grain has been imported. This is partly due to the small size of plot cultivated by the typical Indian family. There are no over-all statistics, but in Bombay, where the soil is less fertile, the average number of cultivated acres per cultivator and his family was 12.2; in the Punjab, 9.2; and in Bengal, 3.1 (1921 figures). But it is also due to the fact that, despite the growing pressure of population on the soil, there has not been an appreciable shift from extensive to intensive cultivation. There has been, to be sure, some increase in agricultural output, but this has resulted from bringing new land under cultivation through clearing and irrigation, rather than from changes in the techniques of production. The following table gives some idea of the low productivity of Indian agriculture, as compared with that of other countries in 1922. These figures indicate that India was far behind countries where intensive cultivation prevailed, and not even up to the extensive cultivation standards of the United States. During the period 1919–1939, while productivity per acre increased somewhat in the case of commercial crops, there was an actual decline in the productivity of India's principal food crop, rice, which is grown on 30 per cent of the total sown area in India.[31]

The village moneylender, both an expression and partial cause of the stagnant character of Indian agriculture, dominates the village economy, making money out of money not by productive investment but by capitalizing on the perpetual poverty of the peasant, especially in dire emergencies, such as when the rains fail or the bottom drops out of the world markets for agricultural commodities.[32] These moneylenders—a separate caste, or rather several separate castes—are vitally depended on and heartily disliked.[33] They are a group apart which violates the general mores in that their goal is to save and get ahead. Since the funds are not generally borrowed for productive purposes and there is considerable likelihood that they will never be paid in full, interest rates are exorbitant. In a situation of this kind, moneylenders do not amass wealth primarily through the snowballing of compound interest charges. Rather do they derive innumerable pecuniary benefits from having acquired control over the peasants' lives; control over the marketing of his crops by tied sales in advance of harvest time at the moneylender's price; control over which

[31] Subramanian, op. cit., pp. 7–10.

[32] A great deal has been made of the Indian peasant's willingness to go into debt to meet the heavy expenses required by the full traditional observance of weddings and funerals. (See Chapter IX.) In the Indian peasant culture these ceremonies—a nonessential "extravagance," to use the term of some outside critics—are, in fact, the expression of a deep-seated necessity, and the display and social generosity which accompany the rites are an integral and significant fulfillment in the life of the individual, the family, and the community. It is not difficult to think of parallel practices in Western urban culture which to the participants are a true necessity, while frowned on as an extravagance by other segments of the society.

[33] For a discussion of the Indian moneylender castes, see L. C. Jain, Indigenous Banking in India (London: Macmillan & Co., 1929).

crops are produced; control over the land itself (the peasant usually stays on and works the land but under less advantageous terms, the moneylender having insinuated himself and his claim into the hierarchy of intermediaries between the ultimate owner and the actual cultivator); control over the movement of the peasant; and even control over the peasant's children (only in 1933 was a law passed against the practice of a parent's pledging his child's labor for the payment of a debt).

TABLE 12.12

INDICES OF COMPARATIVE YIELDS IN SIX CROPS, VARIOUS COUNTRIES
(British India=100)

Country	Rice	Wheat	Barley	Maize	Potatoes	Cotton
British India	100	100	100	100	100	100
Siam	116†	112†	...	...	...	...
Egypt	241‡	...	...	...	...	500‡
China	293‡	152†	...	...	...	...
Japan	256†	180†	...	...	...	...
	277‡					
Italy	337†	154†	...	...	...	...
United Kingdom	...	313*	257*	...	276*	...
Australia	292*	116*	106*	189*	134*	...
		109‡				
Canada	...	141*	153*	241*	142*	...
		150‡				
United States	155*	140*				
	161†	133†	131*	230*	146*	167‡
	181‡	131‡				

Source: Davis, op. cit., p. 209.

* Figures so marked indicate percentages calculated on the basis of data given in Baljit Singh, Population and Food Planning in India (Bombay: Hind Kitabs, 1947), p. 59. The data were computed from the Statistical Yearbook of the League of Nations, 1942–44, and refer to the year 1943–44.

† Figures so marked indicate percentages calculated from D. Ghosh, Pressure of Population and Economic Efficiency in India (New Delhi: Indian Council of World Affairs, 1946), p. 44. The data on rice production refer to an average for the years 1931–32 to 1935–36, and those for wheat production to an average for the years 1924 to 1933.

‡ Figures so marked indicate percentages calculated on the basis of data given in P. C. Malhotra, "Agricultural Possibilities in India," Indian Journal of Economics, Vol. 25 (April, 1945), p. 559. Malhotra took his data from a report of the Post-War Reconstruction Committee of the Government of India, entitled "The Technological Possibilities of Agricultural Development," by W. Burns.

Under these circumstances debt naturally becomes identified with misery or catastrophe; it is not viewed as the converse side of enhanced productivity and income-earning capacity. In the Punjab where agriculture is, in Indian terms, relatively productive, only 5 per cent of rural indebtedness was contracted to improve the land.[34]

A second major obstacle to rising incomes is the fact that Indian agriculture is starved for capital. This starvation is due to many factors: tenancy; high rents because of the pressure of population on the land; high interest rates; the speculative character of agriculture in many parts of India because of the uncertainties of the monsoon; the reduced size of family holdings because of the growth of population without a comparable growth of nonagricultural employment opportunities; and the fragmentation of this holding. The last two factors retard the emergence of enterprise in Indian agriculture. For example, it is not economic for a landowner to invest in a tube well if his land area is very small or consists of scattered land strips. Similarly it does not pay to alter the pattern of crop rotation, if the cattle grazing on your neighbor's fallow land would trample down your crops. The individual becomes tied to the group and to group practices which have little to recommend them but the aura of immemorial custom. Thus Indian agriculture suffers many of the disadvantages of collectivism with no compensating advantages.[35]

If a peasant by some good fortune is able to increase the size of his holding, he is more likely than not to rent out his land to sharecroppers. The most ambitious dream of many cultivators is to get enough land so that they can live by renting it out instead of cultivating it. Renting land to others is economically profitable, has no risks,

---

[34] M. L. Darling, *The Punjab Peasant in Prosperity and Debt* (Bombay, London: Oxford University Press, 1925), quoted in Jathar and Beri, *op. cit.*, Vol. I, p. 286.

[35] There are many studies of Indian agriculture: land-ownership relations, size of unit of land cultivated, productivity per acre, agricultural practices, form of village organization, peasant income and outgo, rural debt, etc. In general, these are studies of individual districts or, at most, of provinces based on samples rather than on a study of India as a whole. This literature is summarized in Jathar and Beri, *Indian Economics* (1939), Vol. I, pp. 163–240. One study, Tarlok Singh's *Poverty and Social Change* (London, Bombay, and New York: Longmans, Green & Co., Ltd., 1945), which does not attempt a statistical presentation but rather an evaluation of the broad social causes and implications of Indian agricultural organization, should be mentioned. The discussion of India's agricultural problems has usually focused on the poverty of the peasant, the low productivity of the soil and the causes thereof. It would be interesting to see an economic and sociological study of those atypical areas and tracts in India where high productivity per acre prevails, to ascertain what factors or combination of factors are responsible.

and possesses the kudos of giving the peasant a higher social status.[36]

According to various highly tentative estimates, agricultural debt in British India alone increased from some 3 billion rupees in 1911 to 12 billion rupees in 1937.[37] This increase in agricultural debt reflected a serious depression of the agricultural population; owners became tenants, and permanent tenants with occupancy rights became tenants at will, who finally sank down to being sharecroppers and in the end agricultural laborers. And these agricultural laborers constitute the major famine sufferers since in bad times they can find no employment whatever and thus have no money with which to buy food.

BRITISH IMPACT ON INDIAN SOCIAL AND ECONOMIC STRUCTURE

Indirectly, British activity in India did much to undermine the old society of rigid status and caste. The opening up of the interior to trade, the building of the railroads, the weakening of village autonomy by the introduction of British legal concepts and British courts, the growing of new commercial crops and the beginnings of modern industry—all contributed to the disintegration of the old order. But the British did very little *directly* to hasten this disintegration or to effect a new integration of society around new goals.

With a few exceptions the British attitude was one of *laissez faire* with respect to the Indian social order. A representative of the untouchables asserted at the 1930 Round Table Conference: ". . . there certainly is no fundamental change in our position. Indeed, so far as we are concerned, the British Government has accepted the social arrangements as it found them. . . . Our wrongs have remained as open sores and have not been righted, although 150 years of British rule has rolled away." [38] Some analysts, both British and Indian, feel that Queen Victoria's promise in 1858 to "respect" religion did more than anything else to hinder the improvement of social conditions in India. Prime Minister Nehru has pointed out that much as he dislikes compulsion it may be needed in order to *free* India from the rigidities of its ancient social caste system.[39]

[36] S. G. Madiman, "Need for Institutional Changes and Regional Planning for Optimum Development of Agricultural Resources of India," University of Wisconsin Ph.D. Thesis (1949), unpublished.

[37] Jathar and Beri, *op. cit.*, Vol. I, p. 286.

[38] Quoted in D. H. Buchanan, *The Development of Capitalist Enterprise in India* (New York: The Macmillan Co., 1934), p. 456.

[39] *New York Times* (October 24, 1951), p. 4.

In numerous other ways the British did little to prepare the ground for the development of India along bona fide private enterprise lines. They did not disturb the traditional legal code of the Hindu joint family system, which has elements of great strength in a static society but does not lend itself to rapid change. The individual is submerged in the group; the young are subordinated to the old; each is responsible for the maintenance of all and must share the fruits of his labor with the whole family; and when the head of the family dies, property can be divided equally between all male descendants. In this process, property was both inconveniently tied up—making borrowing on real property difficult—and broken into small bits. Joint family property control might have worked out quite differently in a situation where hard work and "getting ahead" were important values in the culture. As it was, it resulted in a high degree of nepotism in Indian business and caused the more energetic members of the family to carry idle brothers and uncles and innumerable female relatives.

Land in many areas was not completely freed from the customary restraints of precapitalist India. The Industrial Commission *Report* pointed out that one reason why more land had not been consolidated for the efficient cultivation of sugar cane was because of the tenant's customary rights of occupancy.[40] This in-between stage, in which land is bought and sold but the actual cultivators cannot be ousted nor the occupancy rights of holders disturbed so long as they meet their obligations, suggests one reason why Indian agriculture has been so static. It also helps to explain the proliferation of modern-style intermediaries between the top landlord and the actual cultivator.

Individual freedom and mobility are essential to development based on private enterprise lines. They derive from a combination of economic opportunity, legal codes, and cultural indoctrination and, in the West, have gone hand in hand with the rise of a merchant-business-industrialist class to a position of pre-eminence and leadership in society, in which the values of business enterprise become the values of the whole society. Indian culture, like that of medieval Europe, tends to stress man's duties rather than his rights, and the legal statutes have not established individual freedom even on paper with any marked success. The Indian record throughout the nineteenth and even the twentieth centuries is full of examples of restraints on

[40] Indian Industrial Commission, *op. cit.*, p. 350.

freedom of a type which Westerners are accustomed to think of as "feudal"—indentured labor on the plantations and in the mines, debt slavery in handicraft industry, and cases of virtual agricultural serfdom.

Furthermore, the maintenance of political control was conceived primarily in terms of strengthening certain rich and powerful elements in the old order (we have already spoken of the British policy after 1858 of freezing the status quo in princely India). The Permanent Settlement (1793), which turned tax collectors in certain parts of India into proprietors of vast estates, was designed partly to win over a key group in Indian society. Taxes were so set that any future increase in income from the land, whether due to agricultural improvements, population growth, access to markets, or inflation, would accrue solely to the landlord and remain beyond the reach of the land tax assessors. Even in the areas where the Permanent Settlement was not applied, the landlord's position in India was strengthened by British law, which decreed that land be forfeited and tenants be evicted if debts and rents were not paid. British law, which in the West has symbolized the protection of property, paradoxically spelled insecurity to the illiterate Indian peasant as he became more and more caught up in the meshes of a market economy. The British policy of building irrigation works and railroads to open up the interior also strengthened the landlord's position by causing land prices to rise. Finally, when income taxes were introduced in India, agricultural income was exempted, with the result that landlords continued to be a privileged group.

For foreign investment to have set the ball rolling toward an all-round development of India it would have been necessary for native investment in modern industry to develop on a significant scale, since the profits of native investment are less likely to be expatriated than are the profits from the investments of foreigners. One reason why native investment on a decisive scale did not take place was that the surplus of production over consumption, admittedly small in a populous, underdeveloped country like India, was largely controlled by privileged groups whose wealth, as we have seen, flowed largely into nonproductive channels—conspicuous consumption, precious stones, and precious metals—and into bidding up the price of land.

It is impossible to introduce Western values of individual initiative and personal achievement into a non-Western culture unless there is also introduced a reasonable prospect of social and pecuniary rewards

from the observance of these values. The British policy, in effect, rewarded those least likely to develop the spirit of productive enterprise
and initiative—people who, rather than becoming directly and actively engaged in business, would at best be passive participants, as
rentiers, in Indian industrialization. With no effective mechanisms,
such as industrial banks or government finance corporations, to organize the flow of funds into industry and minimize the risks thereof,
some of India's wealth gravitated toward Wall Street in the 1920's.
The *Economist* estimated Indian investments in foreign securities in
1928 at 500 million rupees but added, "This figure is quoted with
some hesitancy, as the vast investments of the Ruling Princes—who
have personal connections in the world's money markets—are not altogether included." [41]

A small group of Indian industrialists did develop in response to
economic changes instituted by the British, but this class did not affect the values of the rest of society. Instead, the psychology of the
nonbusiness caste society has tended to permeate Indian business,
which has not been able to unify itself and remains divided into separate communities, such as the Parsis, the Gujaratis, the Marwaris, and
so on.

One result of British rule was to superimpose an added "caste"—
that of the British themselves. The long-run effect of this was, of
course, to unite the non-British into the Indian nationalist movement. But the short-run effect was to give India more of what she already had, rather than a new outlook. The general outlines of British
"caste" in India are well known: the establishment, on a basis of
white supremacy, of social segregation and special legal and political
privileges. In both military and civilian administration the top jobs
were reserved for British personnel. But perhaps of equal importance
was the constant easy association among the members of a small ruling group engaged in governing and doing business in India. For British businessmen not only had greater knowledge of Western technology and organization and better access to capital through modern
banking institutions, above all they had easier access to the government itself.[42]

---

[41] "Indian Investments in Foreign Securities," *Economist,* Vol. 107, 1928,
p. 599.
[42] One interesting instance of how British "caste" operated in India was brought
out in testimony before the Acworth Committee in 1919–1920. Indian subordi-

We are particularly interested in the implications of British "caste" in the business world: its effect on British enterprise as well as on Indian enterprise. The Indian economy has long had two fairly distinct sectors. There is the modern sector composed of the export business in food and raw materials and the importation of manufactured goods; a modern banking system and a modern transportation system to finance the movement of, and to haul, these goods; mines and plantations to produce raw materials and foods; and a small amount of "modern industry"—mostly textiles and jute.

Then there is the traditional sector of the Indian economy. This includes the organization and finance of the handicrafts industries, very much larger than modern industry in terms of employment; the finance of agricultural production at the local level other than plantations (plantations employ a very small percentage of the total population engaged in agriculture in India); and the handling of food crops consumed at home. This traditional sector has been financed by the so-called indigenous banks and moneylenders and lies outside the purview of modern Indian banking legislation and control. The traditional sector has been controlled, in the main, by Indians, while the small modern sector has been dominated by the British. Wedged in between these two elements was the new group of enterprising Indian businessmen emerging from the traditional sector and attempting to challenge British domination of the modern sector.

British domination was achieved through British preponderance in the modern banking field and control of modern transport, railways, and shipping, reinforced by British control of public governmental contracting. In the case of mining and plantations, the British were the pioneers and obtained the best concessions from the Indian government and from those *zamindars* whose land contained the richest ore deposits. In general, British mines and plantations were larger, more mechanized, and more profitable than Indian. British trade associations and chambers of commerce were better organized than their younger Indian counterparts. British shipping interests in particular followed monopolistic practices which obstructed the emergence of Indian shipping.

---

nate railway officials were able to capitalize on the chronic shortage of cars by exacting payments from Indian businessmen in return for prompt service, whereas British business expected and received prompt service on the Indian railways without paying bribes to petty officials. The same practice was virtually conceded by the Wedgwood Committee in 1937.

The enterprise which had built modern Britain became something quite different when combined with "caste" privileges and superimposed on a semi-inert society. Actually, British enterprise in India was not very enterprising. Railways, for example, were built by a private enterprise which handled operation and profits, but with a public underwriting of any possible losses. This combination pushed railway development but not the concept of risk-taking enterprise.

But why, when British capital had the guarantee of British control, the protection of British interests, and the use of the Indian treasury to finance development schemes, was so little invested in India and in such limited lines of endeavor? On the whole, the British followed a cautious policy of making high profits on a small volume of business in a limited number of sure lines. Thus British business tended to adopt the outlook of the old East India Company with its emphasis on British-controlled foreign trade, rather than industrial production. The *lack* of British enterprise has been especially noteworthy in three fields: basic industry—iron and steel, chemicals, and the manufacture of machinery of all kinds; production of consumer goods for local consumption other than cotton textiles; and development of industries for processing India's agricultural output.

On the other hand, industrialists in England were eager to sell the products of British industry to India on government and on private trading account. These interests were largely responsible for imposing free trade in India. Thus, in a curious way, the British in India appear to have acted out British imperial interests as popularly conceived rather than individual self-interest as described in most economics textbooks. One possible explanation may be that the British business groups in India, in guarding against government encroachment on private enterprise, were giving expression to a preference for playing a dominant role in an underdeveloped country, rather than contenting themselves with a necessarily minor role in an extensive industrialization program undertaken largely by Indians, which might have been the response to a policy of vigorous state aid to industry. And it should perhaps be added that, in the years after World War I, British industry ceased to be very enterprising even at home.

It is hard to estimate total British investment in India; estimates for the late 1920's and early 1930's range from 354 million pounds to a billion pounds, according to the methods used and the bias of the estimators.[43] Total British investment in India was composed of two parts: India's public debt held in sterling, which was £385,000,000 in 1931,[44] and private investments, mostly in plantations, trade, shipping, insurance, and banks, but with some money invested in mines and factories. In the late nineteenth century and early twentieth, considerable British profits in India were reinvested there, while by the late twenties it would appear that the British were repatriating a good part of the profits of their Indian operations.[45]

What has been the impact of British domination on the evolution of Indian enterprise? This is a fascinating and complex subject which has not been adequately treated.[46] For one thing, the increases in agricultural production and the revolution in transport, generated by British needs and financed by British capital, greatly expanded the opportunities of the moneylenders in their traditional activities. Modern industrial techniques which the British brought were taken up by a small group of Indians, initially the Parsis (a tiny, noncaste, well-educated, and prosperous group on whom the British early relied as

[43] For a discussion of the difficulties and complexities of arriving at an estimate of British investment in India, see Reserve Bank of India, *Census of India's Foreign Liabilities and Assets* (Bombay: Examiner Press, 1950), Appendix I, "Foreign Investments in India, An Analysis of Past Estimates," pp. 151–160.

[44] Indians held some of India's sterling debt at this time, as sterling issues were more attractive than rupee issues.

[45] If one compares capital formation in India with capital formation in a much less developed colony such as Northern Rhodesia, one is impressed by how much the British invested in India rather than how little. The National Institute of Economic and Social Research has made a study of Northern Rhodesia: net output and its composition; income and its division (Europeans, Africans, Asians, and government); and expenditure (consumption by the different groups, government expenditure, investment, and remittances abroad). According to this study, Europeans (individuals and companies, foreign and resident) absorbed 72 per cent of the total income in 1938. Europeans spent in Northern Rhodesia almost as much as the Africans and Asians combined; the rest of their income, by far the larger part, was drained out of the country, some of it for personal expenditure but mostly to foreign companies. The Africans and Asians tended to consume their small share (having, no doubt, a high propensity to consume). Under these circumstances, no capital formation could take place. Phyllis Deane, "The Measurement of Colonial National Incomes," *Occasional Papers XII* (London: National Institute of Economic and Social Research, 1948), pp. 64–65.

[46] A study of this subject is being undertaken by members of the Gokale Institute of Politics and Economics, sponsored by this institute and the Institute of Pacific Relations. The preliminary outline, "Notes on the Rise of the Indian Business Communities in India," with an introduction by D. R. Gadgil, has already appeared (1951).

intermediaries between themselves and the Indian population), and later by certain Indian moneylender castes, notably the Marwari. But this small group felt hedged in and cramped by the British domination of the modern sector. British "caste" meant that Indian businessmen generally had the psychology of a minority business group, usually filling the interstices of the economy which the British ignored, and driven to seeking a quick rupee by trade and speculation. With relatively few exceptions, they did not have the psychology or resources of principals engaged in long-term investments for sizable returns.

British domination was exerted beyond the range of British investment by the managing agency system. For example, by the 1920's, majority ownership of the jute mills had passed to Indian hands, but the mills were still controlled by British managing agents. (Those Indian industrialists who did emerge from the traditional sector of the Indian economy followed the British example and set up their own managing agency firms.) The managing agency system, in which each agency controls a vast agglomeration of miscellaneous and unrelated enterprises—mines, plantations, mills, public utilities, banks, shipping interests, exclusive sales agencies, and investment trusts—is both an expression and partial cause of the lack of drive toward greater efficiency and rationalization of Indian industry, and of the traditional "shyness" of the Indian investor. While managing agents have supplied industry with capital, they have exacted a high price in various charges and commissions which have had to be paid whether the operating company made a profit or not.

Several government commissions have dealt with India's capital needs and how to meet them: the Fiscal Commission in 1922, the External Capital Committee in 1925, and the various banking inquiry commissions in the 1930's. There seems to be a general consensus of opinion that there are funds in India, if only they could be tapped and brought into the organized money market. The UN Report, *Methods of Increasing Domestic Savings and of Ensuring Their Most Advantageous Use for the Purpose of Economic Development: Domestic Financing of Economic Development* (1950), contains a section on India by B. K. Madan dealing with the mechanisms needed to increase saving and investment. While industrial banks and government industrial finance corporations will no doubt be helpful, it would seem to be more a question of basic organization and leadership in Indian industry. Perhaps if the drive to industrialization had been present in greater degree, spearheaded by either private enterprise or by government action, the necessary mechansims would already have been evolved to meet the need.

There has been no over-all study of India's productive wealth, and no statistics on the amount of investment necessary to maintain this aggregate capital. These figures will have to be known before it is possible to estimate what net increment to capital has been added in a given unit of time. To obtain the ratio of net saving and investment to national income, it will also be necessary to have total national net output figures, for which no very reliable estimate exists before 1948–1949. Furthermore, since most of the investment in India is direct investment in agriculture or house building, spheres in which investment takes place outside the purview of insurance companies, banks, and large-scale industry, there is no record of it. In reality no one knows how much is saved in India, who does the saving, or what they put their savings into.

An ingenious attempt was made during the thirties by H. M. Trivedi and M. V. Divatia to calculate the reproduction value of plant and equipment in India's modern industry (plants employing twenty or more and using power).[47] They spell out their assumptions and methods of calculation in clear detail. It would appear that their methods tend, if anything, to overestimate the value of plant and equipment. According to their estimate, the value of plant and equipment in 1938–1939 was 6,748 million rupees. This figure is somewhat less than the value of India's railways, which were carried on the books at 7,319 million rupees (1930). It is interesting to compare this estimated total value of both British and Indian plant and equipment with one source of Indian nonproductive investment, namely gold and silver hoards. The net increment of these hoards for the fourteen years 1914–1928 came to 5,651.7 million rupees.[48]

WAS THE INDIAN ECONOMY OF 1914–1947 IN EQUILIBRIUM?

The Indian case affords a dramatic example of the impact of a revolution in transport unaccompanied by a similar revolution in the means and methods of production either in agriculture or in in-

[47] *Industrial Capital in India 1938–1939* (Bombay: N. M. Tripathi, 1947).
[48] D. L. Dubey, *The Indian Public Debt* (Bombay: D. B. Taraporevala Sons & Co., 1930), p. 298.

dustry. Exposure to the West through this revolution in transport and the breaking down of trade barriers tended to perpetuate the complementary nature of the British-Indian economy and to leave intact its traditional methods of organization and production. In this respect, India offers a striking contrast to Japan, where a revolution in transport was accompanied by deliberate and concerted attempts to transform Japan's production techniques as well. Sovereign Japan's exposure to the West was highly selective, the choice being made by Japan. India's exposure to the West was also selective, but the choice was made by the British.

The type of economic expansionism which fits into the framework of a complementary economy seems to have reached its peak and played itself out by World War I. The next phase, requiring a basic transformation of the economy in industry, in agriculture, and in the interplay between the two, ran counter to British interest as narrowly conceived and appears to have required the kind of financial support (putting on balance more funds into India than were drained out) which Britain after 1920 would have found it difficult to provide, even had she conceived her economic interests in less narrow terms.[49]

The period 1920–1940 is a puzzling one. Ostensibly, British policy in India shifted considerably. Certain industries were protected by tariffs. The government stores policy underwent a change to permit Indian business to compete on equal terms with British, industrial departments were set up in the provinces to aid industry in a number of ways, and so on. But the results were not impressive. Was it a case of too little and too late—too late in the sense that the Indian economy had already lost momentum and was settling down at a new equilibrium? The stores policy shift came after India's major railway construction had been completed, and thus it could not stimulate the new steel industry as it might have earlier. State aid may have been too little for a variety of reasons. Not only is there considerable evidence that many of the British administrators were still basically unsympathetic,[50] but British officials in India were in effect paralyzed,

[49] For a more detailed discussion of British-Indian economic and political relations, see the writer's "The 'State' and Economic Development in India," a paper prepared for the Social Science Research Council Conference on *Economic Growth in Selected Countries*, held April 25–27, 1952, proceedings to be published.

[50] Buchanan, *op. cit.*, p. 460.

being caught in the cross fire between the rising pressures in India for a vigorous policy of state aid to industry and the same old pressures in Great Britain for the complementary type of economy. It was these British pressures which forced imperial preference on India, though on every possible occasion the Indian legislature voted against it. The shift may have been too little for another reason, somewhat less tangible. It was inevitable that the British should think in terms of their own experience; and British experience, as the pioneer industrial country to emerge from commercial capitalism to industrialism, unfitted them for tackling the quite different task of precipitating the industrial transformation of a backward country.

Take for example central banking. As K. N. Raj has pointed out, central banking in India was long overdue.[51] When it was finally established in 1935, it was set up on the British model to perform the functions of British central banking: co-ordination of the banking system and control of the money supply. As Raj points out, the central bank in an underdeveloped country has to assume new functions: to expand banking, rather than merely to co-ordinate and control it; to set up special institutions to supply investment capital to industry; and to reverse the inherent bias of commercial banking against the less credit-conscious rural areas, i.e., to see that the banking system by building multipurpose co-operatives pours money into the countryside instead of syphoning it out. These new and greatly expanded functions may require a nationalized banking system, rather than the traditional policy of a central bank operating indirectly via other banks as a so-called bankers' bank.

Actually, for the Indian Reserve Bank to perform even the usual central banking functions, new and different mechanisms would be required, since the usual central banking devices, such as changing the rediscount rate and conducting open market operations to stimulate or retard investment, are not very effective in India. Operations at the banking apex do not ramify out to the periphery of the economy, for various reasons: because the different money markets are heterogeneous, because most business is done on a strictly cash basis rather than by check, because Indian banks do not maintain a con-

[51] *Monetary Policy of the Reserve Bank of India: A Study of Central Banking in an Underdeveloped Economy* (Bombay: National Information and Publications, 1948).

sistent ratio of cash to credit, because Indian investment is insensitive to changes in the interest rate, and because there is no established bill market.

Was the underlying agricultural situation India's Achilles' heel? Here, too, during this period there was much agitation and some legislation and increased governmental activity to aid the peasant and improve agriculture, but the fundamental land ownership relations remained intact. Even the most well-meaning British bureaucrats had to move a mountain of local Indian tradition, made higher by the entrenched power of landlords and princes, the result of deliberate British policy in the past. The British strategy of divide and rule had not only perpetuated but intensified antagonism between Hindus and Moslems, making social reintegration around new goals that much more difficult. The 1935 Indian Federation proposals, had they been accepted, would have installed the princes—still autocrats in their own domains—as integral parts of the newly federated India, with voting power in the new organs of government out of all proportion to the numbers of their voteless subjects and able, in effect, to hold the balance of power between Hindus and Moslems. Yet the princes resisted even these proposals, apparently confident of their power to exact still more favorable terms.[52]

The political struggle for independence brought to the surface the deep-rooted and endemic crisis of colonialism, between the dominant culture, policy, and economy of Great Britain and its subordinate instrument, India. The combination of colonial status and lack of economic development produced an attitude of ambivalence toward the state. The state became the key to economic development, but this particular state was suspect, both because of the British pressures impinging on it and because of British-Indian public finance, the handling of the public debt, the uses to which it was put, and the expenditure of the annual revenue for British Empire purposes as well as for Indian purposes.[53]

In one respect the political transition had a direct bearing on the stalemate. Limited self-government was introduced at the provincial

[52] A. B. Keith, A *Constitutional History of India 1600–1935* (London: Methuen & Co., 1936), pp. 473–474.

[53] See especially L. H. Jenks, *The Migration of British Capital* (New York, London: A. A. Knopf, 1927), pp. 223–224; D. L. Dubey, *op. cit.*; and Z. A. Ahmad, *Public Revenue and Expenditure in India* (Allahabad: Congress Political and Economic Studies—No. 8, 1938).

level after 1919; limited self-government at the central level was not recommended by the British until the constitutional proposals of 1935. In general, therefore, Indians wanted more and more functions transferred to the provincial government level where Indians had more say. Almost all the so-called nation-building activities were so transferred: the development of agriculture and the encouragement of industry, education, roads, and the like.

But though the provinces were assigned the functions of development, they received inadequate funds with which to implement them. The central government controlled the more expansive sources of revenue funds, such as customs duties, and the growing income taxes, of which a certain proportion, determined centrally, was returned to the provinces. Quite aside from the question of revenue allocation, however, this central abrogation of responsibility in the field of development meant a lack of co-ordination[54] and precluded any concerted attack on Indian economic development, since the provinces were not appropriate units for regional economic planning but rather congeries of districts, their boundaries due to the vagaries of conquest without even cultural or linguistic unity. The provinces were so unlike in resources, degree of development, and liquid wealth at their command that only co-ordinated central planning could have integrated and fundamentally advanced the Indian economy. This delegation of powers to the provinces also ruled out any prospects of a new and more vigorous fiscal policy calculated to advance Indian economic development. (Such a policy was perhaps already ruled out by British fiscal precepts and the steady pressure for the appreciation of the rupee in order to meet the ever-mounting Home Charges and other bills which had to be paid in pounds sterling.)

The foregoing account indicates that the development function may have a tendency to be discontinuous. Several aspects of Indian experience reinforce this view. An integrated heavy industry, in which a group of related and co-ordinated industries provide each other with both the supply and the demand for their products, seems to require a herculean effort in backward countries, both on the side of acquiring training and skills and in mobilizing the necessary capital. The development of India's power and irrigation potential suggests the necessity for a similar effort in this field. Real economic development in India requires the building of new indus-

[54] Buchanan, *op. cit.*, pp. 463–464.

trial communities in the backward provinces, which possess unused mineral and power resources. But the building of new communities from scratch again requires the mobilization of considerable resources to provide the public utilities, transportation facilities, and services of all kinds which supply industry with the external economies of production.

Likewise a transport system which has been geared to meet the needs of one type of economy does not evolve naturally and easily in the right direction for meeting the needs of a different type of economy. The layout of India's railways, their different gauges, and particularly their rate structure, all were oriented toward the syphoning of raw materials out of India and the importation of manufactured goods and thus militated against an internal integration of trade and industry. The same was true of the banking structure and shipping rates, all of which are special cases of the overriding circumstance that a colonial regime is that of a satellite, oriented around its host rather than around its own development needs.

Even Indian agriculture, so unrewarding to the Indian cultivator, had important elements of equilibrium and balance for the Indian economy as a whole. It performed several functions within the context of a nonexpanding economy, and it provided Indian industry with raw materials, possible because Indian industry was growing so slowly. The host of intermediaries preying on the cultivator were able to extract a limited surplus adequate to meet the needs of Indian cities, because these too were growing so slowly. Indian agriculture even provided foreign exchange by the sale of food and raw materials, though this was tending to break down before the war. Curiously enough, the very inefficiency of Indian agriculture was a safeguard to the stability of the system, since it kept millions of Indians underemployed, rather than completely unemployed, which was the only alternative since other avenues of employment were not expanding.

We have spoken earlier of India's "need for organization" as embracing much more than just capital. It would be more correct to speak of India's need for *reorganization*, because every branch of the Indian economy is already highly organized: agricultural production and marketing, the production and marketing of handicrafts, indigenous banking and moneylending, and trade associations in industry, tea plantations, and different branches of trade. In India the problem is not one of filling a vacuum, but of replacing one form of organization with a new form capable of generating momentum and economic growth. The existing organizational structure tends to form a static equilibrium rather than a dynamic equilibrium moving toward development. Many Indians regard a "mixed" economy as the solution, but the precise formula has yet to be spelled out and implemented.

There are two basic factors upsetting this equilibrium—the mounting aspirations of the Indian people and the increasing pressure of population. The situation in India can more adequately be described, not as an equilibrium, but as a deteriorating situation. Partition has been an important contributing factor, but it has only dramatized and accelerated the crisis in the production of India's food and raw materials in relation to her growing population. This crisis had been long in the making. This deteriorating situation can perhaps maintain a shaky "equilibrium," but not for long. It must move either closer to disintegration or toward a new social and economic reintegration through economic development. The choice of the latter goal has already been made by India's more farsighted leaders. It represents the conscious wish of many millions of India's citizens, the unconscious striving of even greater millions. It will require an immense effort on the part of the Indian people and all the understanding and support they can obtain from abroad.

CHAPTER XIII

Mexico: Rapid Growth

HENRY G. AUBREY* [1]

THE PURPOSE OF THIS CASE STUDY IS TO DEMONSTRATE THE EMPIRICAL operation in economic development of certain strategic factors which were discussed in the preceding general chapters. The usefulness of the selection of a specific country for this purpose must rest on two considerations: (1) The selected country must have important characteristics in common with other underdeveloped countries, and (2) the course of its development must give promise of setting precedents for other countries. Our sample country qualifies in both respects.

Insofar as characteristics are concerned, Mexico is typical of our general pattern. Like most underdeveloped countries, it is still predominantly agricultural. Mining, once so important in its economy, has declined recently in relative importance but still ranked second to agricultural exports during the last decade. This overwhelming dependence on primary exports for the import of necessities and development goods is typical for most underdeveloped areas. Another

* Research Associate, Institute of World Affairs; Visiting Lecturer in Graduate Faculty of Political and Social Sciences of the New School for Social Research. Author: "Small Industry in Economic Development," *Social Research* (September, 1951); "The Role of the State in Economic Development," *American Economic Review, Papers and Proceedings* (May, 1951); "The National Income of Mexico," *Estadistica*, Journal of the Inter-American Statistical Institute (June, 1950).

[1] The scarcity of comprehensive source material in English makes the use of identifying notes inadvisable in this chapter. Special mention should be made, however, of a thorough revision of Mexican statistics which took place so recently that practically all figures published in English before 1953 and the greater part of Spanish material are now obsolete. This revision was brought about by a combined working party of the International Bank for Reconstruction and Development and the Mexican Government. The author is greatly indebted to the International Bank for making an advance copy of the report available to him. See *The Economic Development of Mexico* (Baltimore: John Hopkins Press), 1953.

characteristic common to many of these countries is the recent acceleration and present high rate of population growth, a condition aggravated by the fact that an expansion of agricultural land is possible only with the help of sizable capital expenditure. Still another characteristic is the general primitive level of techniques, excepting only the most recent ventures. This condition must be attributed both to scarcity of capital and to scarcity of skills. This brief inventory of symptoms of backwardness constitutes, as it were, the lowest common denominator of characteristics which Mexico shares with other underdeveloped countries; the list could be greatly expanded and refined, but this is left to the text of this chapter, in which the reader will doubtless find more aspects worthy of generalization.

Turning to our second consideration, the course of development, we find that Mexico has a long, though spotty, history of growth. Soon after achieving independence in 1821, a deliberate, though pathetically shortlived, attempt to catch up with the industrial revolution going on in other parts of the world was begun. Though repeatedly thrown back by external wars and internal unrest, by 1910 Mexico achieved first place in industrial rank among Latin American countries. But this development was not balanced by progress in agriculture, whose semifeudal condition was largely responsible for the long period of revolution and reconstruction which followed. Recently another era of deliberate advance, on many fronts and in better balance, has produced one of the fastest rates of progress observed in modern times.

This desire for rapid development is shared by many underdeveloped countries. Mexico's experience in this field, the conditions of such advance, and the strains and stresses connected with it are the basis for our belief that a concise, though necessarily incomplete, account of Mexico's course will be of interest to students of economic development; moreover, there does not as yet exist any comprehensive economic history of the country which would enable interested persons to become systematically acquainted with all the facts to be presented here.

After a brief historical outline we shall make the problem of economic growth the center of our presentation. Sectional growth problems will be discussed first, viz., food and population and the many aspects of industrialization; the next section will deal with capital formation and the problems of financing economic development;

while the final portion will discuss the process of economic growth in its two chief aspects: rates of growth and balanced growth. In this last section, the reader with more general interests will find the most relevant growth aggregates of the economy brought together in concentrated form.

HISTORICAL ANTECEDENTS

The colonial period. It is not easy to trace the course of Mexico's modern economic development to its origins. Few historians would be inclined to credit the Spanish rule with speedy economic progress. Yet the major changes which took place during the three hundred years from conquest to independence bore the seed of future growth.

Gold and silver were what the Spanish conquerors expected to find in Mexico. Although their hopes for ready stores of wealth were disappointed, large deposits of precious metals were eventually discovered and New Spain became the empire's richest source of silver. Since the substance of the mining product was considered the property of the crown and withdrawn from the colonial economy, little gain was directly derived by that economy beyond the merest subsistence for the Indians who worked the mines, processed, and transported the silver in near servitude. It would be erroneous to believe, however, that no indirect benefits were retained for the future. To speak in modern terms, "external economies" were created: the remote and inhospitable north was explored; urban centers, agricultural supply areas, and regional and interregional transport resulted. However spotty such development might be, its incidental effects remained.

The history of manufacturing in colonial days resembles socially certain early phases preceding the Industrial Revolution in Europe. Workshops [*obrajes*], mostly for textiles, sprang up in which the workers were held in various degrees of debt-servitude, often under physical coercion. There were some short periods of prosperity in high-quality production (e.g., silk manufacture, before Far Eastern competition and the jealousies of metropolitan interests destroyed it), but such manufacture served largely local needs for plain merchandise.

In this respect, we must bear in mind that the center of Mexican economic activity was—and in some respects still is—a high plateau, separated by precipitous mountains from the routes of world commerce. Long after the colonial period this fact of physical environment provided both an element of stimulation and one of retardation to Mexican economic development: a natural protection by high freight cost, but also a barrier against progress, ranging from the importation of machinery to the accumulation of trading capital which elsewhere so often provided a reservoir of industrial finance.

In agriculture the pattern left by the colonial period was very different from the traditional communal pattern of preconquest time, but it was nonprogressive—practically stagnant. Large estates, at first nominally only "entrusted" to persons of merit [encomienda], were held in factual, later in legal, ownership, with the Indians who lived on the land as an involuntary labor force. Vast areas were owned by the Church or acquired by gifts, legacy, or foreclosure of mortgage. The hacienda remained well into the nineteenth century a semifeudal, nearly self-sufficient economic unit, trading its surplus in local or regional, rather than national, markets with very few exceptions in the case of export commodities, such as sugar. Absentee ownership, the peasant's gradual displacement from better land, and peonage instead of free labor markets—these were the agrarian patterns formed during the colonial period and intensified throughout the nineteenth century.

From independence to Díaz (1822–1876). Historically, Mexican independence came about as a successful bid for home rule by local interests, wrested from a monarchy weakened by the Napoleonic Wars. Economically and socially it hardly changed an already established pattern: a large, inarticulate, and illiterate mass of impoverished Indians and mestizos led by a landed aristocracy, a powerful bureaucracy, and some traders and manufacturers of Spanish descent, all allied with the politically influential and immensely wealthy Church organization. The groping steps of a new nation, traditionally torn by factionalism and political revolts, were not conducive to economic progress; yet, during short periods of centralized control, the federal government undertook the first fumbling promotion of industrialization. A government agency, of the type we would today call a development bank, was established in 1830 to encourage the formation of enterprises, give loans, import machinery, etc. The first modern cotton mill opened with the help of the bank in 1835. Other equipment was imported; however, renewed civil war drove the promoters of the "new era" out of power and the experiment collapsed. Yet its gestational effects were considerable in textile and paper manufacture. By 1866, more than 60 mills operated over 150,000 spindles, notwithstanding two external wars and much civil strife in the preceding 30 years.[2]

The long range continuity, financial and political, which the building of railroads requires was not present in these restless times. The first railroad line of consequence between Mexico City, the capital, and Veracruz, the traditional port of entry, was opened in 1873. Until then all trade, including bulky equipment, proceeded on muleback; thus, aside from other factors, it was not astonishing that industry did not develop faster. The same was true of metal mining, which languished as the result of remote location, provincial unrest, and shortages of labor and such vital equipment as pumps to remove the water which swamped the deep shafts of the mines during repeated periods of politically induced idleness.

The Díaz period (1876–1910). Like other dictatorships, the Díaz regime can lay claim to continuity and the outward appearances of law and order, achieved only by severe political and social repression. While limited space does not permit an appraisal of this period in political terms, certain important economic achievements were completed: railroad mileage increased from about 400 miles in 1876 to about 12,500 miles in 1911; introduction of modern power helped create preconditions for large-scale industrialization. The mines were mechanized, first by steam, then by electricity, and the use of electricity spread simultaneously to traditional industries, like paper, milling, and spinning and weaving, and newer ones, such as jute, brewing, etc. Between 1887 and 1911 more than 100 light and power companies were established. The mining of coal for fuel and power began about 1884 and reached a peak of 2.7 million tons in 1910 —a peak never since approached. The oil industry started at the turn of the century, at first as a source of fuel for the railroads, and in 1911 Mexico had reached third place among oil producers.

Industry grew rapidly; taking again the textile industry as a yardstick, more than 700,000 spindles and 22,000 mechanical looms were in operation by 1910. Modern paper manufacturing, the beginnings of cement and chemical industries, and the start of modern iron and

---

[2] For more details see Henry G. Aubrey, "Deliberate Industrialization." *Social Research*, Vol. 16, No. 2 (June 1949).

steel manufacturing also date from this period, giving Mexico at the time of the revolution the largest industrial potential of any Latin American nation. Nonetheless, only a small part of a basically agrarian nation was affected, and the growth was bought at a heavy price. While the cost of living increased, wages lagged; unions were suppressed; agrarian discontent rose as the estates grew larger; and the destruction of village agriculture was accelerated.

By 1910, it is estimated that less than 3 per cent of the agrarian population owned any land, and some *haciendas* covered much more than 100,000 acres each. This was due, in large part, to the regime's policy regarding the public land, much of which was acquired during the nationalization of church land beginning around 1860. Public land included so-called "idle" land, i.e., any for which the occupant could not show legal title. This deprived innumerable Indian villages of their holdings because they had no proof of ownership except traditional possession. The search for idle land was entrusted to corporations which were rewarded with one third of the land they surveyed and which could buy even more at bargain rates. By the end of the Díaz regime seventeen of the largest corporations had acquired 95 million acres, much of it in foreign hands. While the traditional *hacienda* remained feudal and unprogressive, some industrial and exports crops developed rapidly; cotton, henequen, rubber, sugar, and coffee increased in importance and finally outranked even the rapidly growing share of minerals in value of exports.

Thus, economic progress was fast in some sectors of the economy, but the social and political cost was too heavy. Thirty years of revolution and consolidation followed, essentially devoted to correcting the social unbalance created during the preceding four hundred years.

Revolution, stabilization, and reform (1911–1940). This short survey cannot even begin to outline the sequence of events which followed the overthrow of the Díaz regime. Political intrigues and violence were not eliminated for more than twenty years. The constitution of 1917 was, in the economic and social field, a remarkable statement of principles rather than of practicable realities. In our field of interest, its most important articles are No. 27, dealing with land, and No. 123, dealing with labor; the latter had also very important effects by providing the legal basis for a strong labor movement, the backbone of the *Partido Nacional Revolucionario*, which has held political power for the last two decades.

The period to 1934 may fairly, though crudely, be described as one of political and economic stabilization after a time of violent civil strife. Large scale land reforms did not get under way until the presidency of Lázaro Cárdenas, beginning in 1934. Because of background and inclination, Cárdenas felt that this was the greatest and most needed task. While under his successors, Avila Camacho and Alemán, the emphasis has apparently shifted to industry, this might not have been possible without attacking first the problem of land in a country with a predominantly agrarian structure.

We shall now turn to the present phase of accelerated growth which began around 1939–1940; for the purpose of a case study, this period and the problems it illustrates will be of particular interest. But as we reach this most significant period of Mexican development, we propose to shift our presentation from historical sequence to the contemplation of problems specific to economic development in general.

Sectional Growth Problems

Food and population. Mexico is an agrarian nation. According to the census of 1940, 65 per cent of the gainfully employed population were engaged in agriculture (including cattle-breeding, forestry, hunting and fishing). In 1921, the share of agriculture had been 71.4 per cent, and best available estimates for 1950 are around 62 per cent. While a significant shift is undoubtedly taking place, land and its problems still hold an important place, both objectively and in the minds of the people. Since the condition of peasant and peon provided the greatest impetus during the revolution and for a long time after, it is not surprising that land reform and its success are mentioned first in discussions of Mexican agrarian problems.

If we view the agrarian problem from a long range, as a sector of an entire economy in the process of development, other problems emerge. Structural shifts take place over time from subsistence farming to commercial agriculture and from food to commercial and export crops. Since Mexico has one of the highest rates of population increase in the world, growth of agricultural output is a matter of great concern, not only in the sense of producing more food, but of providing more raw materials for a growing industry and more exports with which to finance greater imports of necessities and development goods. The methods employed to change agriculture in Mexico, their successes and future prospects, will be set out in our survey of agricultural problems.

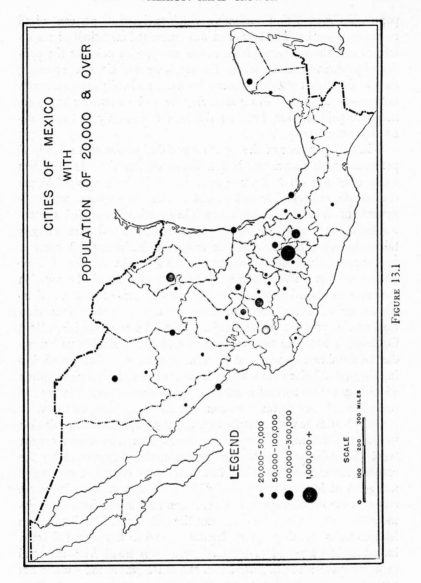

CITIES OF MEXICO WITH POPULATION OF 20,000 & OVER

LEGEND

20,000–50,000

50,000–100,000

100,000–300,000

1,000,000 +

SCALE

0   100   200   300 MILES

FIGURE 13.1

For four hundred years the landholding village fought a losing battle against the *hacienda*, or large estate.[3] By 1910, half of the rural

[3] In precolonial days, land was not held in individual ownership but by tribes
or family groups. In Spain, too, communal landholdings existed alongside private
estates, and continuing such a system in the new colony was not surprising.

population lived within *haciendas,* which enclosed 82 per cent of all rural communities. The best land was cultivated on behalf of the estate owner; the rest was left to the peasants, who paid for the privilege by unremunerated work. To supplement their meager crops, they worked also for wages whose nominal rates hardly increased however much the cost of living rose. As a rule, these small wages were not even paid in cash, but in scrip, redeemable only at the estate-owned stores.

While 97 per cent of the agrarian population owned no land, 59 per cent of all proprietors had holdings of less than 12 1/2 acres each; in 1923 less than 2 per cent of the h*aciendas* comprised 58 per cent of the cultivated area, and just 110 of them owned nearly 19 per cent of all land in private hands. The constitution of 1917 stressed restitution of land to the villages from which it had been illegally taken; however, the pace was at first slow, because the burden of providing evidence for the courts was too great for the poor and ignorant villagers. The concept of complete reform of the agrarian structure developed only gradually, taking the form of presidential initiative and of judicial reinterpretation of the constitution. Identification of the progress in land reform with the person of President Cárdenas is based on the greatly increased speed of distribution under his administration. About 20 million acres were distributed during the period before 1935, while in the six years of his regime, nearly 45 million acres changed hands. Compensation was paid in government bonds based on tax assessment values—admittedly very low.

Chief beneficiary of redistribution was the *ejido,* a village unit akin to traditional forms of communal holdings. In the most frequent type, the individual *ejido,* the land is inalienably owned by the community, each family tilling its allotted plot; collective cultivation was adopted for certain irrigated districts, usually growing industrial crops, where sizable capital was also taken over in the form of equipment, etc. The *ejido* is, however, not the only type of landholding in Mexico today. Small property, legally defined as less than 500 acres, including 250 acres of arable land, and even small *haciendas* still exist and have some importance in the north where the *ejido* is not typical.

By 1940, members of *ejidos* comprised 51 per cent of the rural population and owned about 47 per cent of the crop land, and more land has been redistributed since. The 30-year total prior to 1945 exceeded 75 million acres, given to over 20,000 villages with more than 1.8 million peasants and their dependents, thus benefiting at least a third of the population.

The preceding, oversimplified survey of Mexico's agrarian reform fails to convey the significance of the changes in tenure for economic development in general. The *hacienda* system was, without any doubt, a stationary, inefficient system. It offered no incentives to the peasant who saw only an unending, hopeless prospect of debt-servitude. In addition, the landowner's interest was not in long-range improvements, but in the highest current income he could wrest from the land to maintain his standard of living in the big cities. Not only was he unwilling to invest any capital in the land, but he usually spent more than he earned, thus incurring unproductive debts. Over the centuries, this neglectful attitude doubtlessly increased the steady exhaustion and erosion of the country's climatically vulnerable soil.

Quite apart from the social need for reform, what are its results for long-range agrarian efficiency in Mexico? It is probably still not possible to pass final, noncontroversial judgment at this time. The process of transformation, though far advanced, is not yet complete; moreover, the human element has not yet had time to adapt itself to its new conditions. The pride and the self-respect of ownership are not automatically matched by the responsibility and know-how which lead to progress. Despite great efforts towards education, in 1940 about half of those over ten years old were still illiterate. Elements of conservatism are strong in a country where 94 per cent of the population live in places of less than 500 inhabitants, many of them in cultural, as well as physical, isolation from the main stream of modernization.

It has also been said that Mexican land reform is basically nonprogressive, not only because it harks back to traditional forms, but because the grants of land were initially too small to encourage improvement. It is quite true that at first the *ejido* was devised to supplement labor income rather than to provide the chief livelihood for its members. In recognition of the fact that its allotments are generally considered insufficient for even minimum living, the allotment of crop land per unit was increased from an average of fifteen acres in the late thirties to over twenty acres ten years later and the irrigated portion from thirteen per cent to twenty per cent. As a result, about a third of *ejidatarios* worked also as laborers in 1935; only eleven per cent in 1940. Even more important from a developmental angle was the fact that they consumed a smaller, and sold on the market a larger, proportion of their output—an important aspect of a widening market and a changing economic structure.

Mexican agricultural problems must be viewed against an alarming demographic background. During the decade 1940–1950, the population increased 30.8 per cent, compared with 18.7 per cent and 15.5 per cent, respectively, during the two preceding decades; this is the result of a very high birth rate and a steadily falling death rate.[4] As a result, the average annual increase, which was only 69,000 between 1910 and 1930, has reached 600,000 for the decade 1940–1950, during which time the total population increased from 19.7 to 25.6 million.

On the other hand, the country's resources for growing food are anything but generous. Between precipitous mountains, tropical coasts, and arid plains, only 37 million acres, or 15 per cent of the total area, are considered arable. Of this potentially usable land, 87 per cent in 1940 was nonirrigated and therefore dependent on mostly insufficient rainfall. It is estimated that half of the land does not have enough moisture throughout the year; another third has insufficient rainfall during the winter, while being harassed by tropical downpours in summer. Hence, erosion is an age-old problem, increased by century-long deforestation (for lack of other fuel) and by exhaustion of the soil through primitive and wasteful cultivation.

Practically all land which can be cultivated without major investment in irrigation, drainage, and clearance is already being used. As a result of population pressure, even the most unsuitable soil serves to grow corn and beans, the two staples of Mexican popular diet. Crop rotation is nearly unknown, and change is impeded by the absence of a safe margin for transition to a more generally remunerative system of market agriculture; primitive methods of agriculture are perpetuated in an endeavor to grow the commodity most immediately needed for subsistence.

The extension of crop land is, therefore, one of the most urgent problems. Yet, in 1940, only 13 per cent of the land was irrigated. Between 1926 and 1950, over 3 million acres were brought under irrigation—nearly twice as much as were irrigated before the govern-

[4] Between 1935 and 1950 the birth rate rose from 42.3 to 45.1 per cent, while the mortality rate dropped from 22.6 to 16.2. In the first decade of the century, it was 32.7 per cent.

ment took the initiative. A large part of this land was previously cultivated and partially irrigated; but the tempo of reclaiming untilled land is being stepped up, and in 1948–1950 alone the area harvested increased by 17 per cent. Thus governmental efforts reversed, at least temporarily the historic trend of population to outgrow the increase of area; also, the ratio of cultivated land to population and to the number of persons gainfully employed in agriculture has no longer fallen recently.

From 1946 through 1950, the Mexican government invested about 1.3 billion pesos in irrigation works, and expenditure for 1951 was slated at 500 million; [5] however, some of the largest projects have hardly begun to bear fruit. One of the most interesting, in the Papaloapán Valley, will make possible the irrigation of 500,000 acres, in addition to large power production and other benefits.[6] In addition to two multipurpose river developments, thirty-seven large irrigation projects were in progress in 1950.

The shortage of cultivable area cannot be divorced from the problem of low yields; less land would be required for the same or even higher outputs if yields were increased. On the other hand, the use of unsuitable land, induced by population pressure, and with unfavorable geographical, climatic, and soil conditions, results in low yields. Primitive methods—both the cause and effect of low productivity—combine with other factors to produce some of the lowest yields in world agriculture. A great deal of effort is, however, being applied to the problem, and the results are quite encouraging.

As an example of what can be done, an average increase of about 10 per cent in 1945–1948, as compared with 1925–1929, was achieved in the yield per acre of corn—all the more impressive in view of the fact that corn is the most important single crop.[7] This increase was in part due to an extension of the main corn-growing area outward from the nonirrigated central zone to more humid land. The greatest promise, however, lies in seed improvements through government action. Greatly aided by Rockefeller assistance, the introduction of selected

[5] The Mexican peso was worth about twelve cents in 1953, after repeated devaluations. Changes of exchange rates make it inadvisable to convert peso aggregates into dollar equivalents.

[6] Including flood control, the importance of which was again illustrated by devastating damage caused after heavy rainfalls in June, 1952.

[7] It has increased faster since then, but the significance of short period changes is reduced by the influence of random factors on variations from year to year.

hybrids has increased the yield threefold in a few instances, and an average increase of 20 to 25 per cent from hybrid seed appears possible. An increasing acreage of corn is being planted with varieties developed during only the last five years. Intensification of this campaign, combined with greater use of fertilizer and other improvements of technique, should in time yield important results.

In like fashion an increase of wheat yields by about 30 per cent was achieved over the same period, and another 20 per cent rise seems to have been achieved since; a spectacular rise of over 100 per cent took place in tomatoes, which have developed into an important export crop. Among industrial crops, the yield of cotton did not increase perceptibly, but sugar cane improved by 10 per cent. Henequen, very sensitive to great fluctuations in export demand, declined considerably, however, due in part to the first effects of delayed agrarian reform in Yucatán.

It should be recalled that such long-range comparisons of yield obscure somewhat the acceleration in the tempo of improvements which has been taking place during the last decade. Actually, still greater effects may be expected in the future. The consumption of fertilizers, important on humid or irrigated land, can be stepped up with the help of demonstration and financial assistance. Domestic production of fertilizers, under government auspices, is increasing rapidly. It reached a yearly rate of over 90,000 tons by the middle of 1952, twice the output of the preceding year, in addition to sizable imports. Some estimates place the increases achievable by proper use of fertilizer from 80 per cent for corn and rice to over 100 per cent for wheat, beans, and sugar. Even if evaluated more modestly, the scope for further improvement is certainly considerable if we consider that large tracts of soil are now so exhausted that they can be planted only every other year.

The mechanization of agriculture, especially in flat, irrigated land, is only beginning to leave a mark on Mexican agriculture. In 1940, there were only 4,600 tractors in use, but from 1941 through 1949 nearly 30,000 were imported. The import of more modest equipment —improved plows, harrows, cultivators, etc.—increases also from year to year, along with expanded domestic production of such implements. The use of pesticides has multiplied several times during the last decade, though much remains to be done.

Improvement of skills by education, demonstration, and the like, a slow process at best, has made progress since the agrarian reform, but where soil, climate, and backward conditions kept the peasant in poverty, backwardness itself is due in large part to inability to improve his lot by greater investment in improvements—a vicious circle hard to break.

Agricultural credit secured by mortgage was, before the agrarian reform, a privilege of property owners of good standing who had a clear title to the land; they rarely used it for improvements, however. Smaller owners had to pledge their crops against an advance and submit to extortionate rates of interest.

In many ways, this situation still prevails because the *ejido* system has increased the need for credit. The former laborer who now tills his allotted land lacks working capital of the most elementary sort, but the individual cannot pledge the communal land for mortgage since he does not own it. A special system, the *Ejidal Agricultural Banks*, had been created in addition to the institutions for smallholders and stock farmers who depend on the National Agricultural Credit Bank. Most loans granted are crop loans, with improvement loans running a poor second. The problem of how to last through the next harvest still takes precedence over the opportunity to improve land or technique. The need to pay back the loans and cover deferred requirements of clothing and other essentials compels many farmers to sell their crops as soon as possible, usually when prices are low. However, the amount of loans granted by the *Banco Nacional de Crédito Ejidal* has been increased from year to year, reaching 245 million pesos in 1949; other public credit institutions also extended credits for various agricultural ventures, totaling in 1949 a further 195 million pesos. To this should be added 142 million granted by commercial banks for agricultural purposes, about 9 per cent of their total lending.[8]

It is fair to say that credit could make a larger contribution to the promotion of agriculture in all its important aspects of total volume, terms, and distribution. Most loans to small farmers are of an emergency nature, while improvement loans go chiefly to larger enterprises with greater resources. As a result, the bulk of agriculture has not grown as fast as it might, though great strides have been made, as we shall now proceed to show.

[8] Statistics on agricultural credit in Mexico are controversial and incomplete. A definite upward trend, especially in medium-term improvement credit, is noticeable.

If we want to evaluate the role of agriculture in a country's economic development, we have to select our indicators carefully. Value figures will, as a rule, not help much because price fluctuations in agricultural commodities are great, not only absolutely, but in relation to each other. While quantum indexes avoid the price problem, they also obscure shifts in the structure of output. Nevertheless, a decisive rise in the volume index demonstrates the agricultural sector's ability to expand relatively to the growth of population and thus to provide food and raw materials, either directly, or through imports in exchange for increased exports.

Mexico's agricultural output suffered a grave setback during the depression of the thirties, when the reduction of domestic and foreign demand and lower prices discouraged planting. Recovery started around 1936; however, the great advance began after 1939. In the following twelve years, the volume of output nearly doubled. This growth was not quite uniform, however, and the production of foodstuffs lagged slightly behind the average, while industrial crops increased more; among the latter, sugar cane and cotton took the lead, while henequen seems to have fallen behind permanently.

It is advisable to survey some of the most important crops because of their structural significance within the economy. Corn, the staple diet of the population, is grown everywhere; it is estimated that the area sown to corn increased by over one-third, to about 16 million acres, between 1925 and 1950. In the same period, production seems to have nearly doubled, increasing from about 2.9 to 4.7 million tons between 1939 and 1950 alone.[9]

Wheat bulks less large in the Mexican diet, and its area takes up only about one-tenth of that of corn. Output nearly doubled between 1925 and 1950—to 587,000 tons—the largest relative rise again taking place within the last few years. Production of beans fluctuates a great deal but also shows a rising trend.

Turning to agricultural commodities which are important for export, production of rice more than doubled between 1925 and 1950, owing to both greater area and yield, and increased another 10 per cent in 1951. Production of tomatoes, of which the United States is

[9] This revised estimate of corn output is far higher than previously available figures of 2 million tons in 1939 and 3½ million in 1950. These new figures imply not only a much larger absolute output than previously estimated (probably due to a higher estimate of subsistence agriculture) but also a faster rate of increase of output.

the largest customer, more than trebled between 1925 and 1947, chiefly due to improved methods which more than doubled yields. Even more spectacular are output increases of such relatively newly developed crops as citrus fruits and pineapples. Production of coffee rose by about 40 per cent, and its export value increased many fold as the result of price rises and diversion from domestic consumption.

The output of sugar cane increased from about 3 million tons in 1929 to nearly 9 1/2 million in 1949, thus meeting industry's increasing needs for alcohol. Production of cotton, equally important industrially, and even more so for export, increased from 53,000 tons in 1929 to 253,000 in 1950. Some economists fear, however, that such great efforts to increase a crop which is so greatly dependent on fluctuating export markets may be dangerous in the long run.

Summing up, the development of agriculture in Mexico has made great strides in the last decade and, by and large, output has kept well ahead of the increase of population. The prospects of further growth in the agrarian sector will depend on increase of area and improved methods. It has been estimated that the country's water resources could provide irrigation for about twelve million acres. Good progress has been made towards that goal, and the tempo of irrigation work is still being stepped up.

To raise the low productivity of agriculture is, however, another, and a very complex, problem. Little can be done in the short run about progressive erosion of the soil, though the importance of reforestation and the advantages of flood control are well appreciated. The use of submarginal land for corn and beans is hard to remedy when land is scarce. The introduction of crop rotation in arid soil is very difficult; thus, the greatest hope of yield improvement, including the most appropriate use of fertilizer, is in irrigated areas. Mechanization of agriculture is restricted to flat land or gentle slopes and is naturally limited in a country where 64 per cent of the territory has slopes in excess of 10 per cent.

Moreover, in spite of agrarian reform, the distribution of the population is very uneven and so is the pressure of population on the land. High concentration in certain areas, especially on the central plateau, causes a predominance of very small plots there. According to the census of 1940, 41 per cent of 1,219,000 plots in all of Mexico were smaller than 2 1/2 acres, while 35 per cent were only 2 1/2 to 12 1/2 acres. This factor, coupled with resistance to change, makes for slow transformation from subsistence to market agriculture. Statistics on this point mostly fail us; however, the *ejidos*, who sold only 44 per cent of their output in 1935 had, by 1940, increased this to 56 per cent.

We have already noted that certain crops—mostly industrial or export crops—increased much faster than the typical subsistence items. Some point to this fact as if it slowed the progress towards sufficiency in food which they consider desirable. It is well to point out, however, that a greater interchange of commodities may be more favorable to economic development. If irrigated lands are more productive in growing exportable commercial crops than in growing food, the total supply of food may be increased by exporting such crops and by importing food in return.

The problem of low agricultural productivity of labor is one of the most intractable encountered in Mexico's economic development. While some progress has undoubtedly been made, the inadequate statistical evidence is circumstantial, rather than direct: for instance, from 1929 to 1948 the number of persons gainfully employed in agriculture increased by 21 per cent, while the volume of production approximately doubled in the same period. Thus it is fair to estimate that average productivity per worker did probably increase by at least 1 to 2 per cent per annum. Since so far most improvements have been restricted to the relatively small sector of "progressive" agriculture, it becomes evident that a widening of this area is even more important than the naturally limited method of expanding the area of fertile land through irrigation and similar projects.

Industrialization. The dreams and hopes of underdeveloped countries focus on industrialization, and the examples of advanced countries point in this direction. Industrialization holds out the promise of economic independence and reduced reliance on fluctuating exports and correspondingly uncertain imports. These arguments are reinforced by deep-seated feelings of national and political pride in a country like Mexico, where the foreigner has long been regarded with mistrust as a holder of property, employer, or investor. This is not the place to trace the historical origins of such attitudes; it is enough to point out that, right or wrong, they have powerful repercussions for economic development.

Industrialization cannot be successfully discussed in mere terms of its material base; the human and the institutional elements are equally important. We shall, therefore, begin by sketching briefly the human factors involved in the Mexican situation.

Economic development proceeds slowly and is not diffused simultaneously and evenly throughout the economy. As a result, the old and the new exist side by side for generations or centuries, in a kind of dualism which manifests itself in economic, social, and political institutions, and in the minds and attitudes of the people. In Mexico, the terrain and the difficulties of transportation have slowed the process of fusion. Ethnological factors are equally important; after being Hispanized for 400 years, about 15 per cent of the Mexican population over five years of age still speak one or another of the many Indian languages, and about half of these speak no Spanish at all. The overlarge rural element in the population is the center of backward and static subsistence agriculture, complemented by primitive, though very artistic, home industry, and oriented toward self-sufficiency or local markets, in which the use of money has not entirely supplanted the spirit of barter.

Industrialism is a way of life which presupposes a value system altogether different from this type of subsistence production. Not only does industrial work-discipline require adherence to strict time schedules which clash with traditional unconcern with time, but it also demands the widespread use of money as a medium of exchange, a store of value, and a work incentive.

The provision of a mobile and market-oriented labor supply is, indeed, a very serious problem, even in those developing countries which suffer from apparent overpopulation. Mexico is no exception, though the difficulty often manifests itself in large labor turnover and low productivity—both the cause and effect of low wages in the unskilled category, rather than in actual shortages. A recent field study [10] has thrown some light on the great complexity of motivations which control the industrial labor supply in a certain Mexican district. Shortage of land and absence of rural employment, rather than positive incentives (although these are not universally absent), appear to drive the farmer to the factory. So great is the peasant's reluctance to leave the land permanently that factory workers are sometimes more easily secured from nonagricultural pursuits.

[10] Wilbert E. Moore, *Industrialization and Labor, Studies of the Institute of World Affairs* (Ithaca, New York: Cornell University Press, 1951).

The supply of skills required for progressive industrialization needs to be built up by carefully planned programs of education and training. While Mexico has tackled this task energetically, the very rapidity of its industrialization presents difficulties. Although the scope of this chapter excludes presentation of details, one point should not remain unreported: the active role of many Mexican unions in increasing and improving the labor supply. Many *sindicatos* have extended into the villages and promoted schooling, adult education, and other programs. While many unions control and promote recruitment for the factory, perhaps primarily to protect the closed shop and seniority, resistance to change and overprotection are not infrequent tendencies.

Skills of management are also an important problem in underdeveloped countries, though they usually receive less attention than those of labor. The spirit of enterprise and innovation is one aspect of the issue; experience and managerial ability, another. By tradition, the ambition of the wealthy Mexican has not been directed toward industry; landed estates and high living in the cities gave more prestige and social standing than the acquisition and the expansion of productive plant. A semifeudal system of social values thus impeded both the thrifty accumulation of capital and its investment in industry. This statement, like most generalizations, is not universally valid in Mexico, where, as we saw, the beginnings of domestically financed industry date back more than a century. But in terms of relative importance to economic development, this tendency forms the basis of two institutionally important phenomena: the roles of foreign investment and of the government.

Evidence of hostility to foreign investment has diminished considerably during the tenure of the last two Mexican presidents, Avila Camacho and Miguel Alemán; nevertheless, its presence cannot be denied, and its historical origins should be understood. During the Díaz regime, a great deal of land was acquired by foreign corporations under conditions which were later characterized as improper alienation. Díaz not only welcomed foreign capital into industry under generous and profitable terms, but he saw to it that labor unions did not get a foothold. This enforcement of "law and order" was as bitterly resented by the workers as the *de facto* expulsion of the farmer from his land was resented by the peasant. It did not matter that Díaz seemed to believe progress had to be attracted from abroad, no matter what the cost. Those who paid the price by their one-sided sacrifice acquired a grudge which has almost become a traditional attitude.

The constitution of 1917 was designed to recover land from large corporations and to make it difficult for foreigners to acquire land. But foreign investment was engaged in many other activities and almost completely controlled mining and oil. Indeed, during the first third of the twentieth century, foreign capital was the largest employer of Mexican labor in most of the important and conspicuous enterprises. No wonder then that even "normal" grudges of workers against their employers were superimposed upon nationalistic sentiments, doubtless fostered by management's lack of tact and consideration in a delicate relationship whose potential dangers are probably better understood today.

The conflict with the oil companies which led to the nationalization of 1938 proved to be the climax, as well as the turning point. Neglect of workers' welfare and flouting of laws and decisions were stated as the immediate reasons for the action. Basically, however, it was a clash of property concepts. The concessions granted by Díaz included subsoil title, but the constitution of 1917 declared the subsoil right the inalienable property of the nation. In this it seemed to have the support of traditional Spanish concepts, thus leading to the argument that Díaz had no right to grant the concessions which the companies, on their part, insisted were a matter of contract.

Whatever the merits of the case, all oil properties were taken over, and hotly disputed compensation claims were then finally settled. Bitter feelings abated, and the next two administrations took a positive attitude towards foreign capital, the importance of which for rapid development is now fully recognized.

The importance of government action is also related to the range of entrepreneurial initiative. Indeed, it may be surmised that the extent of state intervention is determined (apart from political motivation) by the intended speed of development and by the strength of private initiative.[11] In Mexico, stimulation by government has been frequent in the history of industrialization, and in the last twenty years it has become quite resolute and systematic. Outright ownership and operation by the government has not been frequent—excepting the cases of the nationalized oil industry, the railroads, and a

[11] See Henry G. Aubrey, "The Role of the State in Economic Development," *American Economic Review*, May, 1951.

few industrial enterprises. The influence of government has been mostly exercised indirectly: by government finance or credit through *Nacional Financiera*, the official development bank; by monetary and fiscal regulation; and by protection and encouragement for industries deemed desirable for continued development.

Tariff protection is traditionally strong in Mexico and is sporadically reinforced by import restrictions, which are usually justified by balance of payments pressure; two devaluations of the exchange rate also contributed to protection by abruptly raising the cost of imported goods. In 1941 the government initiated a deliberate system of direct encouragement in its Law of Manufacturing Industries which, in the 1946 revision, exempts "new and necessary" industries from most taxes and from duties on imported equipment for a period of from five to ten years. Between 1940 and 1950, 570 enterprises with capital of nearly 700 million pesos,[12] and employing about 50,000 workers, availed themselves of the privileges of the law. These made up about 14 per cent of the number, and 65 per cent of the capital, of firms newly established from 1940 to 1949.

Such *prima facie* evidence notwithstanding, the efficacy of tax incentives is not easy to assess in practice. Offhand, it might be expected that the effects would be great where taxation is high, entrepreneurial initiative potentially great, enough capital available, and markets for the new product secure. Under such conditions, mere accelerated amortization can become a powerful incentive as United States policies after the beginning of the Korean War have shown. In an underveloped country, the first two conditions are not always present, even if the government supplements its tax exemption by liberal capital assistance, as Mexico did through *Nacional Financiera*.

Hence it is not astonishing to find a lack of agreement concerning the promotional efficiency of Mexico's tax exemptions. Some believe that most enterprises would have been started without concessions while others hold that the effect of tax relief was substantial. Complex chains of reasoning do not permit a cause-effect relationship to be unambiguously established from empirical observation alone. The Mexican example will therefore be interpreted differently according to the observer's own a priori beliefs regarding the material and psychological efficiency of tax relief.

---

[12] These are nominal registration figures, not to be identified with new investment; they include old firms which expanded their operations or otherwise used the benefits of the law.

Direct economic intervention by the government has been progressively limited to large public works in the fields of irrigation and power, transportation, and similar activities, while private initiative and domestic capital developed industry, with and without foreign participation. In fact, an increasing number of entirely Mexican enterprises have sprung up during the last decades. Supported by a vigorous philosophy of national initiative, these are based on the theory that Mexico's future lies in industrialization and that private interests and national aims thus merge in its progress.

Though we first presented the human and institutional conditions of industrialization, the availability of raw materials, especially fuel and power, remains an important factor to be considered. Mexico's endowment with these resources is fairly good, but their location is not always favorable (see Figure 13.2). According to the census of 1940, manufacturing industries obtained about three-quarters of their raw materials from domestic sources. Textiles and food, the oldest industries, are using an even higher domestic percentage, which is in line with the general belief that early industry tends to depend on locally available supplies. The newer and heavier industries use a much greater percentage of imported materials.

The unfavorable location of coal in the extreme north has been an important factor in the choice of fuel for power. The railroads, previously the largest user of coal, have since resorted to oil, because this industry did not lack early investment capital in view of its export potentialities. Discounting fuel wood (for lack of statistics, though, in the form of charcoal, this is an important item), the consumption of various sources of energy, figured on the basis of kilowatt-hours electricity equivalent, has undergone a remarkable shift between 1925 and 1946.

The modest gain of electricity's share conceals a sizable absolute growth, from 445,000 kilowatts of installed capacity in 1930, to 680,-

TABLE 13.1

	Coal and coal gas	Oil and similar fuels	Natural gas	Electricity
1925	38.7%	45.6%	—	15.7%
1946	9.1%	64.5%	6.3%	20.1%

000 in 1943, and 1,400,000 in 1951, thus doubling capacity in eight years. Roughly 56 per cent of the 4.4 billion kilowatt hours generated in 1950 were of thermal origin and the rest hydroelectric. It is inter-

esting to note that until 1948 the output of hydroelectric energy exceeded the amount of energy of thermal origin. Since then, thermoelectric installations have grown more numerous because they can be brought into production faster and are less capital consuming than large hydroelectric projects. Several very large water power installations are, however, under construction and will increase the power potential considerably during future years. Preliminary figures for 1951 show an 11 per cent increase of output over 1950, to 4.9 billion kilowatt hours.

A great part of this growth occurred in the public utility sector, which increased its output between 1933 and 1950 from 1.3 to 3.5 billion kilowatt hours, with the assistance of the Federal Electricity Commission; production in private industrial plants grew from 200 million to 900 million kilowatt hours in the same period, and imports of electricity from 23 to 125 million kilowatt hours. Consumption of electricity is still largely restricted to the larger cities and commercial use; in 1950 the residential category amounted to only 14 per cent. In 1948 the Federal Electricity Commission estimated that only about 20 per cent of the population used electricity, and industry is by far the largest user, consuming over 50 per cent of the total. Agriculture, reflecting the low incomes and backward methods which we have previously illustrated, took only a little more than 5 per cent.

Mining (see Figure 13.2) has lately contributed around one-thirtieth of Mexico's national income, and a large part of its mineral exports is still in the primary form of ores and concentrates. This is, in part, due to greater stress on other economic activities but also, in absolute terms, mining has declined over the past quarter of a century: the aggregate volume index of mining (1929=100) was 72.5 in 1951. Precious metals are chiefly responsible for this drop; the index for gold and silver was 48.4 in 1950, while that of other metals went to 97.0.

Reasons for this decline are varied; exhaustion of good deposits is chiefly responsible in the case of copper, and lack of adequate transport and power, in that of lead and zinc; recurrent labor troubles have also plagued the industry. It must be added that under the stimulus of good prices the country has tried to raise its output during the last few years, but the importance of mining within the entire economic structure is clearly declining.

Mining of coal has, of course, a special role to play in contributing a fuel for power and a raw material for iron and steel. As aforemen′

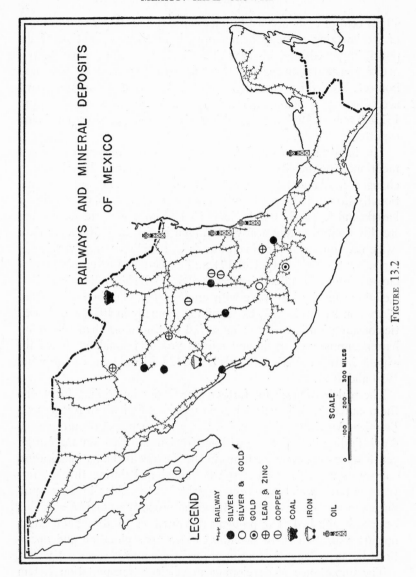

RAILWAYS AND MINERAL DEPOSITS OF MEXICO

SCALE

0   100   200   300 MILES

LEGEND

RAILWAY
SILVER
SILVER & GOLD
GOLD
LEAD & ZINC
COPPER
COAL
IRON
OIL

FIGURE 13.2

tioned, coal has been largely replaced as a fuel by oil and hydro-electric energy; most of its output is now used for low-quality coke. In spite of efforts made, coal output rose only 25 per cent since 1940 to 1,028,000 tons in 1951. For that reason, coke has still to be imported, but its insufficient supply from all sources has resulted, at times, in

40 per cent or more of blast furnace capacity and 25 per cent or more of steel-making capacity being unused. Further exploration of deposits, improved methods (washing), increased coking capacity, and better transportation may, in time, improve the outlook. Regarding iron ore, Mexico has large deposits of high grades, but only the most accessible ore is being exploited. Production of iron ore rose from 132,000 tons in 1941 to 313,000 in 1951, the unneeded surplus being exported.

The importance of oil as fuel and as a source of power has been mentioned before; its role as an export commodity has, however, changed fundamentally. During the depression, and until the nationalization in 1938, yearly output of crude oil was around 39 million barrels and fell to 35 million in 1942-43. Since then, the output has steadily risen, reaching nearly 80 million barrels in 1951—more than twice the volume at the time of crisis in 1938. This, however, is still far below the 1921 output of 194 million barrels. Proven reserves increased from 835 million barrels in 1938 to 1,424 million in 1951.[13] Refining capacity kept pace with crude production, increasing from 37 million barrels in 1938 to 72 million annually in 1951, and domestic consumption has been rising so fast that no more than 14 million barrels annually of crude and refined products could be spared for export between 1947 and 1949 and 22-23 million each during 1950 and 1951.

The real bottleneck for further growth lies in drilling, for which the resources in skill, material, and capital are limited. In this respect, *Petroleos Mexicanos* ("Pemex"), the government petroleum monopoly, is finding it hard to do without foreign participation and harder yet to agree on acceptable terms in the shadow of the nationalization controversy. Drilling contracts were concluded during the last few years on terms which vary from straight fees to a share in the oil produced; in no case have the controversial property or marketing rights been re-established. The problem remains how to attract the larger operators on such terms in order to step up exploration and operations because domestic consumption is rising 10-13 per cent yearly.

The importance of developing an efficient transportation system can hardly be overrated in a country with such adverse geography.

---

[13] By including gas and distillates, total hydrocarbon reserves seem to come close to 1,800 million barrels. Some producing fields were discovered in the last five years, and a new gas gusher raised great hopes for an extension of the traditionally richest region.

Basically, the network of railroads was completed before the revolution; indeed, less than 3,000 miles have been added since 1910 for a total of 15,150 miles in 1950, including the recent links with Yucatán in the extreme southeast and Lower California in the northwest. (See Figure 13.2.) Government control over the railroads, already in existence under Díaz, was extended by the formal nationalization of National Railways of Mexico in 1937. More recently, the few important lines remaining in foreign ownership were also purchased by the government.

The poor condition and low efficiency of the rail system reflect the lag of repairs and improvements during the revolution, the depression years, and, again, during World War II. Very determined efforts at modernization have since been made with the help of substantial loans by the Export-Import Bank. Thus growing requirements for rail transportation were met by more intensive use. While mileage increased only 25 per cent between 1910 and 1950, the volume of freight carried grew from 5.7 to 15.5 million tons in the same period, with more than half of this increase coming between 1939 and 1950.

The network of roads grew more rapidly, from about 5,000 miles in 1939 to 13,000 in 1950, plus over 2,000 miles of new rural roads. It has become a powerful competitor of the rail system, while supplementing it in other respects. Capacity or utilization cannot be estimated, but it is noteworthy that the use of gasoline quadrupled and the number of cars doubled in the ten years following 1939. Aviation developed faster still; the airlines carried 900,000 passengers in 1949, eleven times as many as in 1940, and the volume of air freight increased eight times in the same period. Communications kept pace with development in quantity, if not in quality, of service; telegraph lines increased by more than 5,000 miles from 1939 through 1948; the number of telephones, from 175,000 to 254,000. The number of items mailed grew from 340 million in 1939 to 610 million in 1949.

During the last two decades, a spectacular rise of industrial output took place in Mexico. The volume of manufacturing production increased about 60 per cent between 1929 and 1939 and nearly doubled again in the next decade. This rapid progress was accompanied by a widening of the industrial base, expansion of manufacturing activities in new directions, and diversification of products.

The textile industry is Mexico's oldest and still one of the largest. In the census of 1940, it held second place, by value of output, behind the food industry, in line with the order of wants—a typical sequence in underdeveloped countries. In the past half century the cotton textile industry has grown from about 600,000 spindles and 18,000 looms to 936,000 spindles and 34,000 looms. It illustrates the difficulties of position of an old industry in a well-protected, but not very rapidly growing, market: obsolescence, high costs and prices, and painful problems of readjustment. Most of Mexico's textile equipment dates from the turn of the century; it has been estimated that only about 15 per cent of the spindles and about 7 per cent of the looms can be called modern. Productivity is accordingly low, though it has been shown that poor layout and operational deficiencies are also responsible. Prices are high under sizable tariff protection (the wholesale price index of textiles, base 1939, was 412.5 in 1950 compared with the general index of 296.0). A short-lived export boom during the war and high profits during most of the last decade helped obscure for a time the basic efficiency problems of the industry. The fear of unavoidable unemployment in the wake of re-equipment and reorganization has caused strong resistance to change on the part of labor which is only slowly being overcome in delicate negotiations with government assistance. The example of the Mexican textile industry shows that an early start in development does not necessarily result in long-run efficiency.

While the volume index of cotton production (base, 1939=100) rose to 186, both wool and rayon goods lagged at 109 and 106 respectively. In the case of rayon, the present status follows a substantial drop during the war, owing to lack of yarn; this situation has been overcome by the creation of a substantial number of plants for making both acetate and viscose types which will supplant the larger part of previous imports. Domestic manufacturing of hard fibers, hitherto mostly exported, has quadrupled since 1939, giving the hope of partial relief to the ailing fiber industry.

The iron and steel industry dates back to the turn of the century, but it had only one modern blast furnace in operation before World War II. Two more were added during the war, quadrupling the capacity. As pointed out before, a chronic shortage of metallurgical coke, as well as transport difficulties, restricted the output of iron in 1951 to 282,000 tons, only about two-thirds of capacity. The utilization of steel-making facilities was recently improved to 71 per cent of capacity in 1951 with a production of 456,000 tons of ingots and castings, compared with 141,000 tons in 1939. Yet, rising domestic steel production has not reduced over-all imports; on the contrary, in 1951 they were at an all-time high of 364,000 tons. Thus Mexico illustrates the place of a domestic steel industry in a rapidly growing economy, even though the per capita consumption of iron and steel is only three-quarters that of such countries as Austria or Italy and less than one-twelfth that of the United States. Expansion of existing mills and the construction of a new mill on the Pacific coast, near newly discovered ore deposits, are under active consideration.

Among the major industrial groups, the construction industry has grown even faster than iron and steel—another indication of rapid growth. The cement industry may serve as an example: from eight factories in 1940, it grew to nineteen in 1951, and in this industry, capacity has also grown faster than consumption requirements. Output increased in the same period from 485,000 to 1,535,000 tons. The increase of demand reflects the construction of power facilities, industry, and commercial and residential urban buildings; some of the latter are doubtless of a speculative nature, which is very common in underdeveloped countries under inflationary conditions.

The chemical industry is a touchstone for genuine economic development, for it requires sizable investment and a measure of fairly advanced skills in the manufacture of many products increasingly needed in a growing industrial economy.

In Mexico, this industry, though still young, has made rapid progress during the last decade. Employment increased from 7,800 in the census of 1930 to over 20,000 in 1945 and has doubtless grown since because several large plants have been completed. The output of caustic soda, for example, was only 700 tons in 1940, but twenty times that much in 1949, when the total productive capacity for alkalis was estimated at around 45,000 tons; yet the demand caused ever increasing imports, which rose from about 54,000 tons in 1941 to 121,000 tons in 1951. Sulphuric acid, required by many industries, is produced in growing quantities: 33,000 tons in 1947, 44,000 in 1950, and estimated at a surprising 85,000 tons in 1951; manufacturing capacity, however, chiefly from smelter and natural gas, keeps ahead and is rarely used at more than 60 per cent. The pharmaceutical industry multiplied its output, from a value of 23 million pesos in 1940 to 200 million in 1950, and it has developed a growing export market, rising in worth from 500,000 pesos in 1939 to 30 million in 1950; yet needs grew so fast that the value of imports also rose in the same period from

20 to 165 million. Production of fertilizer, so important for progressive agriculture, increased enormously by the establishment, with government aid and foreign loans, of a plant which raised the manufacture of ammonium sulphate from about 3,000 tons yearly until 1950 to 56,000 tons in 1951. Many other types of chemical production were expanded, and it may be said that Mexico is on the way towards a well-rounded chemical industry with considerable growth possibilities.

Other industries can be mentioned only in passing. Assembly plants increasingly displace imported vehicles. The number of domestically assembled automobiles, buses, and trucks increased from 13,900 in 1941 to 45,500 in 1951; production of tires and inner tubes, from 426,000 in 1939 to 1,350,000 in 1951. Manufacture of appliances, radios, and other electrical equipment, beginning nearly from scratch a decade ago, has displaced a large part of imports, though not without the help of import controls; however, deferred wartime demand and progressive electrification have brought about large imports of motors, generators, and transformers. Manufacture of agricultural equipment is restricted to the less complicated types of implements, and most transport equipment is still largely imported, though rails and parts of rolling stock are increasingly manufactured locally.

The output of paper and board nearly tripled, from 64,000 tons in 1939 to 183,000 in 1951, and the range of products increased also. The glass industry also progressed: 99 per cent of glass containers are now made on automatic machines, and their output has nearly trebled since 1939; however, imports have also increased in the same period. Processed food production kept ahead of population growth, and certain items, such as canned food, increased greatly.

Capital formation. We have surveyed the rapid progress of production in Mexico; the question now arises as to how this development was financed. Investment is the strategic factor determining the growth of output and income. Hence, we want to determine the sources of investment capital—voluntary private savings and the involuntary types imposed by taxation and other fiscal measures. Next, we have to trace the channels through which the stream of investment flows, and the monetary and fiscal policy by which the government influences the direction and extent of credit and finance. Finally, the foreign element should be considered in its dual aspect: as a source of supplementary development finance and of foreign exchange for the importation of indispensable capital goods. Clearly these many aspects can only be treated in the most summary fashion.

Ability and inclination to save suffer from serious handicaps in Mexico, as in other underdeveloped countries. Very large numbers who live at the subsistence level cannot save regularly, or they may be compelled to consume again whatever they put by for emergencies. Moreover, the memory of civil unrest, recurrent fears of political instability, and inflationary tendencies lead to hoarding of silver and gold coins among lower income groups and to recurrent capital flight to other countries among those more wealthy. The extent of such hoards is difficult to appraise; estimates vary from 500 million to 2 billion pesos. But even such a large accumulation is only a fraction of current yearly total investment and hence less important for the course of development than is frequently believed.

Saving a large fraction of the increments of national income is more important for economic development, and more practical, than the presence of an initially high average ratio of savings to income. In that respect, we note a fairly encouraging tendency among individuals. The number of savings accounts grew rapidly, from 164,000 in 1945 to 452,000 in 1951, even though only about 18 per cent of the economically active population are believed to save, while the amount of savings deposits increased from 35 million pesos in 1940 to 450 million in 1950. To this may be added 193 million in time deposits in other banks. The Mexican Bankers' Association estimated recently that private savings in banking institutions have reached an annual level of 230 million pesos. Other types of saving also increased greatly; for example, life insurance premiums have more than quadrupled the figure of 28 million of 1940, and certificates of "capitalization banks" held by individuals have increased almost eightfold to 365 million in the years since 1940. In addition there were some 1 billion pesos worth of fixed income securities held by individuals in 1950.

While it is difficult to estimate business saving directly, circumstantial evidence makes it likely that total private saving exceeded 4 billion pesos in 1950, amounting to about 9 per cent of gross national product. It seems safe to say that both individual saving and total private saving increased somewhat faster than national income in monetary terms during the last decade.

Channeling of saving into productive investment is an even greater problem in underdeveloped countries than mere ability to save. Historically, the acquisition of land ranked with conspicuous consumption as the traditional pattern of acquiring social prestige. While urban real estate has taken the place of *haciendas*, it also offers both a hedge against inflation and an object for speculation, made safe and promising by the spectacular growth of the principal cities. (See Figure 13.1.) Actually, speculation is a common phenomenon in underdeveloped areas and applies to inventories as well as real estate. It continues in Mexico to be a vastly more popular alternative to long-term investment and is abetted by the credit system of commercial banks. The traditional preference for commerce over industry, the expectation of high, quick returns, and a traditionally speculative attitude caused Mexico to have a strong money market and a rather underdeveloped capital market. Government policy had to be adapted to this situation, as we shall see.

This simplified picture of traditional patterns should not obscure the substantial growth of private industrial and agricultural investment which has recently taken place at an accelerating pace. Despite the great amount of public works and capital assistance to agriculture and industry, the share of private investment in the total has remained near 60 per cent during the period since 1939, even though gross investment increased eightfold. A vigorous atmosphere of entrepreneurial initiative, without, and in partnership with, foreign capital, is much in evidence, though much traditional and nonprogressive activity survives. The rapid growth of industry—nearly all in private hands—bears witness to this development. Individual initiative alone could not, however, produce fast development in the absence of institutional conditions favoring capital formation.

Security exchanges in Mexico have only recently acquired sizable importance. Private marketing of securities among a small circle of individuals and banks is the traditional pattern for well-accredited entrepreneurs while others depend on financial institutions. Corporate stocks tend to be closely held, which contributes to the narrowness of capital markets, and further capital needs are usually financed by marketing bonds—again usually through private channels, including institutional investors. Many securities quoted on the stock exchange are rarely offered for sale, and around 70 per cent of the transactions are carried out over-the-counter.

Seen in the light of these limitations, the recent growth of business in the stock exchange of Mexico City[14] is noteworthy. The volume of transactions increased sixfold during the last five years and amounted to 74 billion pesos in 1951. Between 1947 and 1951, the share of stocks in the total turnover increased from 12 per cent to 22 per cent, that of industrial stocks from 7 per cent to over 17 per cent, and the price index of industrial stocks grew nearly sixfold since 1939 compared with a rise of commodity prices of three and a half times.

The limited, though increasing, facilities for security sales still leave a large share of financing to institutions. Insurance companies are growing rapidly, but their investments are heavily weighted in favor of real estate and mortgage bonds. More important for development are security investments of specialized institutions. We have already mentioned the certificates of "capitalization banks" or trust companies which combine aspects of mutual funds with lottery features. General bonds of industrial credit banks (*financieras*) were issued on the theory that they would be more acceptable than the industrial securities which back them. By far the most important instruments, however, are the participation certificates of *Nacional Financiera*, the official development bank of the Mexican government. These certificates bear fixed interest, but they are also redeemable at par and practically at sight, thus combining liquidity with the security of a guaranteed rate of return. The circulation of these participation certificates reached 914 million pesos at the end of 1951, of which 32 per cent were held by individuals, 35 per cent by commercial and industrial investors, 9 per cent by insurance companies, and the rest by banks (none, however, by the central bank). In addition, *Nacional Financiera* issues financing bonds whose circulation amounted to 198 million in 1951.

The size of operations of *Nacional Financiera* is illustrated by the growth of its assets from 45 million pesos in 1941 to 1,606 million in 1951. This institution also obtains foreign loans which are used for the promotion of new enterprises and expansion of existing ones, for the government's financing of public works, and for accommodating other banking institutions in connection with economic development. In the case of private firms, such promotional assistance consists of the purchase of securities or the issuance of credits. The

[14] There is only one other; it is in the industrial center of Monterrey and is much smaller than the one in the capital.

beneficiaries include the most important branches of industrial activities, power, and transport. Yet investment amounts to much less than credits; in 1951, the investment portfolio of *Nacional Financiera* amounted to 395.5 million pesos, and credits outstanding, to 1,003.6 million. The combined total at the end of 1951 includes transport and communications at 494.3 million, power at 294.2 million, the sugar and steel industries at 115.7 and 113.2 million respectively, construction and materials industry at 107.2 million, and most other national industries in declining order.

Assistance to the government consists in the purchase of equipment for public works against acceptance of government bonds. Thus, *Nacional Financiera* fills a serious gap in the narrow market for government securities, which is plagued by a heritage of defaults and mistrust; in fact, the bank substitutes its own popular participation certificates for less acceptable government paper. Finally, *Nacional Financiera* assists other banks, notably the public banks for agricultural credit, in the import of equipment and material, by discounting the paper of these institutions.

Commercial banks assisted the trend towards high-yielding speculative investment by their traditional credit policy. Real estate or inventories are favored security and a higher interest rate can be obtained for quick turnover. Savings banks, agricultural banks, industrial-financing banks, and even some governmental institutions are not free from those tendencies. Industrial credit goes to selected old firms; long-term credit for new ventures, undertaken by new industrialists, is hard to obtain at terms commensurate with long-range development. Thus, the rapid growth of the banking system is not fully supplemented by a purposeful credit policy.

Capital and reserves of private banks have increased greatly since 1940, and the "national credit institutions" grew even faster; the resources of the entire Mexican banking system rose from 1,471 million in 1940 to 13,040 million in 1950. Its investments and credits taken together increased from 973 million to 9,821 million. Nonetheless, the preference for commercial credit is a grave problem, as illustrated by a comparison of the distribution of credit granted by deposit banks. Between December, 1944, and 1950, the share of production credits (to industry, agriculture, stock raising, and mining) declined from 58.5 per cent to 40.8 per cent (even though the amount rose from

482 to 1,532 million), while the share of commercial credit rose from 41.5 per cent to 59.2 per cent.

The government influenced the direction of bank credits and investment by permissive measures, inducements, and central bank directives. Rediscount facilities were eased for transactions considered desirable; reserve requirements were used as the key instrument, especially in connection with increased liquidity following devaluation of the peso in 1948 and the post-Korean export boom. Vastly increased reserves were sterilized and their use permitted only for desirable categories of investment or long-term loans to industry or agriculture.[15]

Public investment averages about 40 per cent of gross investment—a substantial contribution to development. Between 1946 and 1949, federal, state, and local governments allocated about one-third of their expenditures directly or indirectly to capital formation. Since 1946, the federal government alone has spent 5 billion pesos directly on public works and 700 million through official credit agencies, in addition to 750 million for the National Railways and 1,200 million for the National Petroleum Corporation—a total of 7.6 billion pesos. Most public works are large-scale projects of irrigation, power, transport, and communication, to which we referred previously. Their importance for economic development is inadequately expressed by investment figures, for they are the nucleus of further progress in which private investment can participate more prominently.

It is not surprising to find that the spurt of development activities since 1939, which were thus paced by the government, should have led to sizable budget deficits; "involuntary" saving by means of taxes did not keep up with spending. Every year from 1940 through 1948 (with the exception of 1946, due to extraordinary revenue in that year) ended with a budget deficit of the federal government, those of 1947 and 1948 being particularly heavy. During that period, a large

[15] Partly as a result of such measures, investments and credits of deposit and savings banks of six months or longer increased from 29.3 per cent of their resources in 1945 to 43 per cent in 1950, and credits of one year or longer, from 3.9 per cent to 6.9 per cent. Taking all private credit institutions together, investments and credits of six months or longer rose from 41.8 per cent to 51.9 per cent, and credit of one year or longer, from 8.8 per cent to 10.7 per cent. It must be noted, however, that the respective figures were more favorable during 1949 and slipped somewhat during 1950.

part of public investment was financed by injections of money into the income stream through the issue of bonds and the expansion of central bank credit. Since 1949, however, this trend has been reversed, and growing investment of autonomous public agencies has gone hand in hand with sizable budget surpluses of the federal government; moreover, foreign funds have recently been financing an increasing part of the public investment.

The change of fiscal policy was influenced by a reversal of the foreign balance. During the war, increased exports and the shortage of goods available for imports were responsible for large export balances, with monetary liquidity as their domestic counterpart. After the war, large deferred imports drained the reserve of foreign exchange, and the government did not mind counteracting the consequent deflationary effects by deficit spending. Later, reduced imports and increased exports changed the position again and, coupled with the export boom after Korea, made a strict anti-inflation policy imperative. Moreover, increased customs receipts (including a compensatory export tax to siphon off a part of devaluation profits) and other major tax reforms boosted government revenue on all levels considerably, even though it still appears relatively low (at about 11 per cent of national income in 1949).

Besides the imposition of a surtax on exports in 1948, previously mentioned, and an excess profit tax in 1949, major improvements in collection methods were introduced, with interesting effects on the tax structure. Between 1939 and 1950, the share of direct taxes in total federal receipts increased from 8.7 per cent to 23.2 per cent, while that of indirect taxes dropped from 71.9 per cent to 60.7 per cent.[16] Since direct taxation, notably income taxes, is considered a touchstone of fiscal progressiveness in underdeveloped countries, it is worth noting that the share of income taxes in total federal revenue in Mexico increased from 7.2 per cent in 1939 to about 23 per cent in 1950.

Having discussed the various types of domestic capital formation, it yet remains to state the position of foreign investment. After the oil nationalization of 1938 and during the war, foreign investment lagged in Mexico; however, after 1946, it increased again, and the total of direct foreign investment was reported by the Bank of Mexico as

[16] For the purpose of this paragraph only income and capital taxes are considered direct types, although other definitions are sometimes also found.

about 4.9 billion pesos in 1950. It is interesting to note concomitant changes in composition. Foreign investment in oil, once predominant, has dwindled to insignificance; mining, which is chiefly in foreign hands, amounts to less than 20 per cent of the total, compared with 28 per cent in 1945. Electric power and other public utilities are nearly unchanged at 24 per cent, while transport and communications at 13.5 per cent are barely more than half their share of five years earlier. The most interesting change occurred in manufacturing, which lists three times the investment of 1945—a change from 14 per cent to 26 per cent. We find, therefore, a highly significant shift from the traditional pattern of raw material investment to activities better related to the progress of the domestic economy of the host country.

Mexico's foreign public debt, historically a source of repeated trouble, is no longer an unmanageable burden. The floating debt and the former railroad debt have been scaled down by agreement with the bondholders and by punctilious payments, which include compensation for oil and other property nationalized in the thirties. Sizeable loans have been obtained from the Export-Import Bank, the International Bank for Reconstruction and Development, and also from some private United States banks. During the last twelve years, amounts drawn against these loans amounted to 194 million dollars, of which 83 million have already been repaid; an additional 37 million were obtained by independent public agencies and private firms with the assistance of *Nacional Financiera*, and 7 million of these were amortized. These loans were of far greater economic importance than the amounts imply, for they were used to finance the import of equipment indispensable for basic projects of power, irrigation, transportation, and essential industries. This source of hard currency for the import of capital goods (which amount to about 40 per cent of total imports) is not without importance for Mexico's balance of payments position. Her trade balance is traditionally adverse; frequently, the production of precious metals, substantial receipts from tourists, and foreign earnings by migrant workers are not sufficient to cover the negative trade balance, in addition to foreign debt and investment service. Thus, a flow of foreign investment is an important offset to the adverse balance on current account.

Another way to assess the place of foreign investment would be to determine its share in total investment. Such calculation for the period from 1939 to 1950—admittedly most approximate—indicates that foreign investment amounted to 10 to 11 per cent of total gross investment.[17] However, economic growth is a cumulative process, and the marginal importance of such addition probably far exceeds its percentage share, especially if a large part is concentrated in basic projects and industries with great "gestation" potential for further development.

PROBLEMS OF OVER-ALL GROWTH

The rate of growth. The speed of economic development in Mexico presents a great many problems. In our attempt to grasp the process of growth, especially in its recent period of acceleration, we shall first point to certain rates of growth of output and income. Within the limitations of space, we want then to go beyond aggregative indicators and discuss problems which rank equal in importance to mere speed in economic development: the problem of balanced growth, the relationships between sectors of the economy, the growth of the market, and the distribution of income.

The only long-term indicator presently available for Mexico measures the volume of manufacturing production for the last half century, using 1929 as the base year.[18] This index increased from 35.5 in 1899 to 366 in 1950—over tenfold. It is, however, advisable to observe certain stages: by 1910 the index had reached 69.1; then, during the revolutionary period, it declined sharply and did not exceed the figure of 1910 until 1922, reaching the next peak with 125 in 1931. After several years of recession, the rise resumed around 1936, reaching 160.5 in 1939. Then came the recent period of accelerated industrialization, nearly doubling the annual average of the preceding decade's rate of growth.

Between 1939 and 1950, net domestic product at factor cost rose from 5,824 to 38,077 million pesos. This nearly sevenfold increase reflects also the effects of sizable price rises. Real net product is estimated to have increased by about 115 per cent, or 7.2 per cent an-

---

[17] Based on an increase of about 2.4 billion pesos in the value of direct foreign investment and about 850 million inflow of development loans, minus amortization of this new debt. We do not believe that amortization of prewar debt should be offset against capital inflow for the purpose of appraising properly the developmental effects of recent investment.

[18] In 1939, the old index is linked with new figures of the Bank of Mexico for the last twelve years. Judging by the trend of recent revisions, it may be assumed that the old index erred in the direction of understatement.

nually on a compound basis. This is very fast growth by any standards and probably one of the highest sustained rates ever observed. While the rapid growth of population damped, of course, the rate of progress, real net product per capita still grew by 62 per cent, or 4.5 per cent annually. If we accept per capita income as a criterion of progress, then Mexico has certainly advanced rapidly during this period.

On the other hand, if we want to know which strata of income earners benefited from the over-all growth, we must observe the relative share of factor incomes. We find that wages and salaries declined from 30.5 per cent to 23.8 per cent between 1939 and 1950, while the share of profits increased from 26.2 per cent to 41.4 per cent.[19] This shift in income distribution certainly affected consumption and savings. However great the tendency of higher income earners towards luxury consumption, over-all consumption declined from 87.7 per cent to 84.9 per cent of gross national product. Greater saving accrued to the economy, a large part of it, no doubt, through the unequal income distribution brought about by progressive inflation. Public saving—the involuntary type imposed by taxation—also increased. Gross domestic investment increased from 649 million in 1939 to 5,937 million in 1950, about threefold in real terms; its ratio to gross national product grew from 9.7 per cent to 13.8 per cent (the highest ratio was 14.4 per cent in 1949), a remarkable acceleration of investment to a ratio which compares favorably with some countries enjoying higher incomes.

While a substantial increase of real output could not be achieved without such over-all growth of investment, the impact of investment differs in various sectors, as does the rate of development. Total investment of nearly 34 billion pesos from 1939 to 1950 was unevenly distributed between the sectors. Transportation received the largest share, 28 per cent, gradually declining in relative importance throughout the period. Industrial investment ranks next with an average of 23 per cent. This average conceals a sharp decline to only 12 per cent in 1942 and a subsequent rise to a peak of nearly 30 per cent in 1947. Construction comes next, with an average of 18 per cent.

---

[19] The balance going to mixed incomes, imputed earnings of self-employed, rent, and interest—all of which shares also declined over the period. In 1946 the ratio even stood at 21.5 per cent to 45.1 per cent. These and the following estimates are in current prices.

Agriculture, on the other hand, has shown a rising trend from 10 per cent in 1946 to nearly 20 per cent in 1950. Investments in oil have been rising slowly, and those in electric power much faster—from around 1 per cent in 1940–1941 to over 5 per cent in 1949–1950.

In an attempt to appraise the effectiveness of investment in securing an increase of output, the following table may be helpful:

TABLE 13.2

	Gross investment 1939–1949 (million pesos)*	Increase of net domestic product 1939–1950 (million pesos)*	Investment— product ratio
Agriculture	3,851	4,612	.83
Mining	140	835	.17
Oil	781	494	1.58
Building and	4,910	589	8.34
Manufacturing	6,230	6,051	1.03
Power	744	139	5.35
Transport and communications	7,121	1,282	5.56
Subtotal	23,777	14,002	1.69
Proportion of total	92%	43%	
Total economy	25,714	32,253	.80

* A one-year lag has been introduced on the (admittedly arbitrary) assumption that the bulk of the output-raising effect will, on the average, be concentrated in the year after investment takes place. It can be argued that longer maturation delays in power, transport, and communications would cause a higher ratio than shown here; this may be true also for irrigation, but prompt effectiveness of investment in implements may cancel out this delay in agriculture. In any case statistical difficulties will not permit such calculation to be considered as more than a rough approximation of a very important relationship.

No estimates of depreciation being available, estimates of gross investment had to be used. Whenever a large share of gross investment went for maintenance (as in mining and, partly, in transportation), the gross investment ratio is less meaningful. On the other hand, accelerating investment carries a smaller over-all share of depreciation than would be required in a more stabilized mature economy.

The estimate is made in current prices; while a comparison in constant prices would be desirable, the lack of reliable deflators would make such an attempt at present too controversial. An inflationary trend between the valuation of investment in one year and that of product in the next would cause a systematic downward bias in our ratio. A threefold price rise over the period may have had some such effect.

Attention should be drawn to the great divergency of ratios between various industries[20]—an important factor in development pol-

[20] Peculiar conditions discouraging new investment in mining prevent generalizing conclusions from this particular low ratio in a customarily capital-intensive industry.

icy. Similar amounts of investment yield[21] greatly different increments of output. This means that to maintain any desired degree of long-term balance between the sectors may thus require quite disproportionate shares in total investment expenditure.

Balanced growth. While we may not have any precise definition of balance in economic development, it does refer to the manifest interdependence of the parts of the economy in at least two respects: (1) in production, where imbalance may lead to bottlenecks and to less than optimal output in the short or the long run; and (2) in the market, where a lag of income in one sector may cause deficiency of demand for the products of others. In the process of growth, investment opportunities are less obvious in some sections than in others, and shifting needs require adjustments without overshooting in any one direction; moreover, short-term balance and long-term aims conflict at times.

Industry tends to be favored because it is most progressive in terms of productivity, while some economists point to the necessity of developing agriculture apace. In Mexico, this controversy is not absent, and in 1948–1949, the belief was voiced that the country was developing a serious imbalance in the direction of industrialization.[22] Actually, beginning around that time, agriculture was already forging ahead more rapidly. Over the entire period from 1939 to 1950, the volume of manufacturing production increased by 128 per cent, and that of agriculture, by 84 per cent; the latter constitutes a remarkable advance, considering the large share of unprogressive subsistence farming.

It is interesting to note that, therefore, the inverse movement of relative shares of agriculture and industry in total product, considered typical for economic development, was not very prominent in a period where real output more than doubled; in fact, the share of agriculture in total net product actually increased slightly from 13.3 per cent in 1939 to 14.1 per cent in 1950, after a temporary low of 11.4 per cent in 1946. Manufacturing, on the other hand, increased its share only from

[21] The "yield" of investment is the inverse of our investment product ratio. It should not be confused with the meaning of the term "yield" in financial analysis, where it refers to a ratio of profit, variously defined, to capital, or to its market value.

[22] Sanford A. Mosk, *Industrial Revolution in Mexico* (Berkeley: Univ. of California Press, 1950).

15.7 per cent to 18.3 per cent after a temporary peak of 19.1 per cent in 1946.[23]

The share of mining declined from 4.8 per cent to 2.9 per cent in twelve years, reflecting the stagnation of this once so important branch of activity. The share of oil and its derivatives remained fairly stable at 1.6 per cent after a temporary decline. While the total of primary industries declined from 26.9 per cent to 24.1 per cent, the combined share of manufacturing, construction, and power increased from 18.1 per cent to 20.6 per cent. These changes, while significant, are also less spectacular than may have been expected in an instance of accelerated development. In fact, the total share of these "productive" activities barely changed at all.

The preceding fact seems out of line with the widely held belief that tertiary activities will increase relatively to real income. Furthermore, analysis discloses that the total share of services would have actually declined if that of commerce had not increased phenomenally in these twelve years from 23.7 per cent to 30.9 per cent. Although this growth is sometimes attributed to speculative activities, traditionally abetted by inflationary opportunities, it may be fairly surmised that a widening of the market system may also be responsible. Certainly this is characteristic of development in a geographically and culturally disunited area. Banking, insurance, and other financial services increased their share but little. Neither transportation and communications, private and professional services, nor government services, notwithstanding their actual importance, kept pace with total growth. It seems reasonable to assume that this relative decline and the failure of service industries as a whole to grow as much, or more than, other activities cannot be disassociated from the effects of inflation on the income distribution.

We have already referred to the shift in distribution which reduced the share of wages and salaries from 30.5 per cent of national income in 1939 to 23.8 per cent in 1950. This relative drop does not, however, imply an absolute decline of the wage bill, for in terms of 1939 prices, the reduced share still constitutes a two-thirds increase.[24] However, an increased number of wage earners received this share of in-

[23] This relatively insignificant movement of shares of product in current prices is paralleled in 1939 prices; in these terms, agriculture dropped to 11.4 per cent, but manufacturing only increased to 16.7 per cent.

[24] On the assumption that the share in constant prices is the same as in current prices.

come.[25] Deficient wage statistics do not permit a full appraisal but indications are that average real wages per capita did decline under the impact of inflation, at least in important categories. As a measure of inflation it should be noted that the general cost of living index in Mexico City increased from 100 in 1939 to 368 in December 1950 and to 433 a year later.[26] It would be somewhat rash to conclude from these symptoms, as is often done, that the fruits of economic development have been exclusively appropriated by a very small number of income earners. While the gulf between income extremes has doubtlessly widened, there are some indications of a broader improvement in the statistically deficient field of consumption estimates. It seems fairly certain, for instance, that the consumption of corn and beans increased somewhat faster than did population. Per capita consumption of common textiles also increased. These are mass staples the greater consumption of which cannot be explained in terms of larger incomes of the wealthy, whose extra consumption tends to go for imports. These straws in the wind permit the conclusion that the standard of living of large sections of the population must have increased somewhat, though certainly to a far smaller extent than that of the upper income strata.

EVALUATION AND CONCLUSION

In evaluating the results of economic development, the observer enters an area of potential conflict between the short and the long view—between economic expediency and demands for social justice. In Mexico, all indicators point to rapid progress, in the aggregate, and per head of population; on the other hand, it appears that the distribution of the social gains has been very unequal—a matter of concern in a country which prides itself on its continuous social "revolution."

From the angle of economic development, this problem cannot be divorced from its relation with capital formation. The bulk of a country's saving is achieved within the upper income groups because the people at or near the subsistence level cannot save on a significant

[25] The results of the census of 1950 are not yet fully available.

[26] Space does not permit discussion of the causes of inflation in detail. Apart from external factors, deliberate policies of monetary expansion were largely responsible in the early phases of accelerated development. We may also surmise that pressure of rising money incomes, always somewhat ahead of consumable output in the wake of development spending, imposes a quasi-permanent inflationary tendency on a rapidly growing economy.

scale. Moreover, notwithstanding all socio-psychological obstacles, a larger portion of the predominantly urban, upper-income saving can be drawn into productive investment than diminutive individual amounts that are widely scattered. Such differences in the propensity to save are even more pronounced in the use of additional income resulting from economic development. The best chance of increasing investment would seem to lie in saving a large part of added income. Yet the propensity to consume the entire income increment is almost universal among low-income groups, who are naturally intent on feeding or clothing themselves a little better.

It would appear, therefore, that an egalitarian distribution of gains from progress, however desirable socially and politically, is not necessarily the best procedure from a long-term, developmental point of view. Historically, of course, periods of rapid growth invariably display great contrasts of income and wealth. Our social concepts have come a long way since the industrial revolution, and the less privileged part of the population expects to share in the fruits of progress. Yet any increase of consumption cuts into the formation of capital for future development.

The realization of this conflict, with its philosophical, social, and political undertones, is not altogether absent in Mexico. It is true that part of the sacrifices which rapid development impose is concealed by the "money illusion" connected with creeping inflation. In fact, inflation may be considered as a form of "enforced saving" which, however, shifts the burden of sacrifice to the shoulders of those least able to bear it: paid workers and fixed income earners. The self-sufficient farmer is least affected, whereas the holder of real estate or inventories benefits from the speculative opportunities that accompany an inflationary situation. Seen in this manner, inflation is an evasive and often wasteful way of accomplishing saving which is not forthcoming in other, socially more desirable, ways. On the other hand, inflationary tendencies arise without intent from production lags; some are perhaps inevitable and others a symptom of the strains and stresses of a growing economy.

In this respect, Mexico seems to have steered a middle course. Gradual inflation has become a permanent feature of the economy but sufficiently well controlled to prevent its becoming a major deterrent to productive investment. Related symptoms of "growing pains" have, however, not been absent. Shortages, aggravated by the war, have occurred repeatedly in various sectors; they demonstrate the economy's inability to keep up with the growing demand from increasing incomes, additionally inflated by unusual export receipts during war and rearmament. The direction of demand was an additional source of friction. The rapid growth of incomes in the upper brackets caused an even greater rise in demand for high-class, imported consumer goods; measures were repeatedly taken to curb such imports by tariffs or by quantitative controls.

What makes such continuous expansion of demand so troublesome is the rigidity of supply from domestic output. Lags of supply result from delayed, often erratic, and sometimes misdirected, efforts at expansion, long construction periods, bottlenecks, and other forms of imbalance between industries, and between sectors of the economy. To blame these on lack of foresight or planning would be gross oversimplification. Many of these rigidities are technologically determined; others are due to the fact that economic development is a discontinuous, rather than an organic, process, however wishfully we may talk of "balanced growth." The intricate interdependence of links in an economy which is widening and deepening at the same time are probably too numerous to be successfully "controlled" by deliberate action at all times. The "growing pains" endured by centrally directed economies seem to substantiate this.

The problem of balanced growth is ultimately connected with the structural changes within a growing economy; various sectors cannot— and probably should not—grow at the same rate at all times. In fact, a kind of "acceleration principle" requires a lead on the part of some sectors before others can work up to full efficiency. This applies to physical factors, like basic services of transportation, power, etc., and to social services of education and health. It also applies to human factors, affecting skill in production, distribution, and administration. Finally, balanced growth cannot occur without mobility of labor and capital, implying both ability and willingness to recognize and heed the changing needs of a developing economy.

These prerequisites for balanced growth imply a measure of purposeful direction of resources which is hard to achieve in free economies. No wonder, then, that the direction of policy had to be adapted to varying situations in Mexico. We have seen that the government furthered irrigation and took overdue measures to improve and extend transportation and communications. At the same time, advances in agricultural development prevented an overstrong bias in the direction of industrialization—always a danger in development which is achieved under forced draft.

On the other hand, Mexico did not escape the temptations that arose from the sectional boom conditions which accompanied rapid urbanization. Construction absorbed a part of capital resources which could have better served development in other fields. Inflation must share the blame for this distortion and for the attractions of inventory speculation and other short-term opportunities in preference to long-term investment. We have seen how this fits in with traditional attitudes and how institutional factors, like banking practices, favor it. While this picture is characteristic of many underdeveloped countries, Mexico provides an illustration of attempts to curb such tendencies by monetary and credit policies.

The concept of balanced growth, discussed largely in economic terms, must also be extended into the socio-political field. Economic growth which outruns its supply of skills and administrative efficiency is apt to waste part of its efforts and lose some of its impetus. It is perhaps no accident that Ruíz Cortines, now president of Mexico, inaugurated his regime with an attack on the inefficiency and petty graft that have become time-honored attributes of public administration in many underdeveloped countries. Vision, intelligence, and energetic leadership cannot alone carry development forward when a broader social and cultural base is needed for further advance. The requisite change of attitudes and institutions is slowly beginning to assert itself in Mexico.

Selected Bibliography*

GENERAL

Adler, J. H. *The Underdeveloped Areas and Their Industrialization.* New Haven: Yale University Press, 1949.

Abramovitz, M. "Economics of Growth," in A *Survey of Contemporary Economics,* Vol. II, ed. B. Haley. Chicago: R. Irwin, Inc., 1952.

Aubrey, H. G. "Small Industry in Economic Development," *Social Research,* Vol. 18 (September, 1951), pp. 269–312.

———. "Deliberate Industrialization," *ibid.,* Vol. 16 (June, 1949), pp. 158–82.

Balogh, Thomas. "Note on the Deliberate Industrialization for Higher Incomes," *Economic Journal,* Vol. 57 (June, 1947), pp. 238–41.

Baumol, W. J. *Economic Dynamics.* New York: Macmillan Co., 1951.

Belshaw, H. "Observations on Industrialization for Higher Incomes," *Economic Journal,* Vol. 57 (September, 1947), pp. 379–87.

Bronfenbrenner, M. "The High Cost of Economic Development," *Land Economics,* Vol. 29 (May and August, 1953), pp. 93–104, 209–18.

Buchanan, N. S. "Deliberate Industrialization for Higher Incomes," *Economic Journal,* Vol. 56 (December, 1946), pp. 533–53.

Chang, Pei-kang. *Agriculture and Industrialization.* Cambridge, Mass.: Harvard University Press, 1949.

Clark, Colin. *The Conditions of Economic Progress.* (Rev. ed.) London: Macmillan Co., 1951.

Clough, S. B. *The Rise and Fall of Civilization.* New York: McGraw-Hill Book Co., 1951.

Datta, B. *The Economics of Industrialization.* Calcutta: The World Press, 1952.

Duesenberry, J. S. "Some Aspects of the Theory of Economic Development," *Explorations in Entrepreneurial History,* Vol. 3 (December, 1950), pp. 63–102.

Economic Development and Cultural Change. (A quarterly journal published at the University of Chicago.) Current issues.

* The editors wish to express their gratitude to Richard Wohl of the Center for Cultural Change and Economic Development of the University of Chicago for letting them use the bibliography on economic development prepared by the Center during 1950–51.

551

Fossum, P. R. *Principles of Economic Development*. Tacoma, Wash.: The College Press, 1952.

Formulation and Economic Appraisal of Development Projects. (2 vols.) Lahore: Technical Assistance Training Institute, 1951.

Frankel, H. "The Industrialization of Agricultural Countries," *Economic Journal*, Vol. 53 (June-September, 1943), pp. 188–201.

Gadgil, D. R. "Preconditions of Economic Development," *Indian Economic Review*, February, 1952.

Greaves, I. C. *Modern Production among Backward Peoples*. London: Allen & Unwin, 1935.

Hancock, W. K. *Wealth of Colonies*. London: Cambridge University Press, 1950.

Higgins, B. H. "Duesenberry on Economic Development (with rejoinder by J. S. Duesenberry), *Explorations in Entrepreneurial History*, Vol. 3 (April, 1951), pp. 248–53.

Holton, R. H. "Marketing Structure and Economic Development," *Quarterly Journal of Economics*, Vol. 67 (August, 1953), pp. 344–361.

Hoselitz, Bert F. (ed.). *The Progress of Underdeveloped Areas*. Chicago: University of Chicago Press, 1952.

———. "Some Limitations of Induced Economic Growth," *Explorations in Entrepreneurial History*, Vol. 3 (May, 1950).

International Approaches to Problems of Underdeveloped Areas. New York: Milbank Memorial Fund, 1948.

Kierstead, B. F. *The Theory of Economic Change*. Toronto: Macmillan Co., 1948.

Kuznets, Simon. *Economic Change*. New York: W. W. Norton, 1953.

———. "The State as a Unit in Study of Economic Growth," *Journal of Economic History*, Vol. 11 (Winter, 1951), pp. 25–41.

Mandelbaum, K. *The Industrialization of Backward Areas*. Oxford: Basil Blackwell & Mott, 1945.

McLeod, A. N. "Trade and Investment in Underdeveloped Areas—Comment" (with reply by H. W. Singer), *American Economic Review*, Vol. 41 (June, 1951), pp. 411–21.

"Measures for the Economic Development of Underdeveloped Countries," *International Labor Review*, Vol. 64 (November-December, 1951), pp. 473–503.

Moulton, H. G. *Controlling Factors in Economic Development*. Washington, D. C.: Brookings Institution, 1949.

Niebyl, K. H. "Criteria for the Formulation of an Adequate Approach in Aiding the Development of Underdeveloped Areas," *Canadian Journal of Economics and Political Science*, Vol. 18 (August, 1952), pp. 365–71.

Papers and Proceedings, *American Economic Review*, Vol. 41 (May, 1951). (Sessions on "Factors in Modern Industrial Development," "Economic Progress," "Differential Economic Progress," and "Point Four.")

——, Vol. 42 (May, 1952). (Sessions on "Growth in Underdeveloped Countries" and "The Theoretical Analysis of Economic Growth.")

——, Vol. 43 (May, 1953). (Session on "Underdeveloped Countries.")

Pim, Sir Alan. *Colonial Agricultural Production*. New York: Oxford University Press, 1946.

Problems in the Study of Economic Growth. New York: National Bureau of Economic Research (mimeographed), 1949.

"The Role of Leading Nations in the Economic Development of Other Areas," (Collected Papers), *Journal of Economic History*, Vol. 11 (Fall, 1951).

Rostow, W. W. *The Process of Economic Growth*. New York: W. W. Norton, 1952.

Schumpeter, J. A. *The Theory of Economic Development*. Cambridge, Mass.: Harvard University Press, 1934.

Seers, Dudley. "The Role of National Income Statistics in the Statistical Policy of an Underdeveloped Area," *Review of Economic Studies*, Vol. 20, No. 53 (1952–53), pp. 159–68.

Singer, H. W. "Economic Progress in Underdeveloped Countries," *Social Research*, Vol. 16 (March, 1949), pp. 1–11.

——. "Obstacles to Economic Development," *ibid.*, Vol. 20 (Spring, 1953), pp. 19–31.

Solomon, M. R. "The Structure of the Market in Underdeveloped Economies," *Quarterly Journal of Economics*, Vol. 62 (August, 1948), pp. 519–41.

Staley, Eugene. *World Economic Development*. Montreal: International Labor Organization, 1944.

Sweezy, P. M. "Duesenberry on Economic Development," (with rejoinder by J. S. Duesenberry), *Explorations in Entrepreneurial History*, Vol. 3 (February, 1951), pp. 182–86.

"The Tasks of Economic History" (collected papers on economic growth), *Journal of Economic History*, Supplement VII, 1947.

United Nations. Department of Economic Affairs. *Domestic Financing of Economic Development*, New York, 1951.

——. ——. *Measures for the Economic Development of Underdeveloped Countries* (report by a group of experts), New York, 1951.

——. Economic and Social Council. *Industrial Development and Planning: Programs and Priorities*. Report by the Economic Commission for Asia and the Far East, and a series of annexes relating to specific countries.

———. ———. *Methods of Financing Economic Development of Underdeveloped Countries*, New York, 1949.

———. Economic Commission for Latin America. *Theoretical and Practical Problems of Economic Growth*, New York, 1950.

———. Food and Agriculture Organization. *Report of International Investment and Financing Facilities*, Washington, D. C., 1949.

———. Statistical Office. *National Income and Its Distribution in Underdeveloped Countries*, New York, 1951.

United States. Department of State. *Point Four: Cooperative Program for Aid in the Development of Economically Underdeveloped Countries.* Washington, D. C.: Government Printing Office, 1950.

———. International Development Advisory Board. *Partners in Progress: A Report to the President.* Washington, D. C.: Government Printing Office, 1951.

Van Til, W. *The Economic Background of Social Policy, Including Problems of Industrialization.* New Delhi: International Labor Organization, 1947.

Wu, Yuan-Li. "A Note of the Post-War Industrialization of 'Backward' Countries and Centralist Planning," *Economica*, Vol. 12, No. 3 (August, 1945), pp. 172–178.

Young, A. A. "Increasing Returns and Economic Progress," *Economic Journal*, Vol. 38 (December, 1928), pp. 527–42.

Natural Resources

Barlowe, R. "Land Reform and Economic Development," *Journal of Farm Economics*, Vol. 35 (May, 1953), pp. 173–187.

Belshaw, Horace. *Agricultural Reconstruction in the Far East.* New York: Institute of Pacific Relations, 1947.

———. "Industry and Agrarian Reform," *Far Eastern Survey*, Vol. 16 (July 2, 1947), pp. 153–56.

Fledderus, Mary L. and van Fleeck, Mary. *The Technological Basis for National Development and Its Implications for International Cooperation.* International Industrial Relations Institute, 1948.

Frankel, S. H. "United Nations Primer for Development," *Quarterly Journal of Economics*, Vol. 66 (August, 1952), pp. 301–326.

Mason, E. S. "Raw Materials, Rearmament and Economic Development," *Quarterly Journal of Economics*, Vol. 66 (August, 1952), pp. 327–341.

Straus, M. W. *Natural Resources Development: Administration and Execution.* U. S. Bureau of Reclamation. Washington, D. C.: Government Printing Office, 1951.

United Nations. Economic and Employment Commission. *Forest Resources and Their Utilization*, New York, 1950.

———. Economic and Social Council. *Defects in Agrarian Structures as Obstacles to Economic Development*, New York, 1951.

———. ———. *Post-war Development of Mineral Resources in Asia and the Far East*, New York, 1951.

———. Department of Economic Affairs. *Proceedings of the UN Scientific Conference on the Conservation and Utilization of Resources*, New York, 1950–52.

———. ———. *World Iron Ore Resources and Their Utilization with Special Reference to the Use of Iron Ore in Underdeveloped Areas*, New York, 1950.

United States. Department of State. *Energy Resources of the World*. Washington, D. C.: Government Printing Office, 1949.

Zimmerman, Erich W. *World Resources and Industries*. (Rev. ed.) New work: Harper & Brothers, 1951.

POPULATION AND LABOR

Bauer, P. T. and Yamey, B. S. "Economic Progress and Occupational Distribution," *Economic Journal*, Vol. LXI (December, 1951).

Butler, H. B. *Problems of Industry in the East*. Geneva: International Labor Organization, 1938.

Condliffe, J. B. "The Pressure of Population in the Far East," *Economic Journal*, Vol. 42 (June, 1932), pp. 196–210.

Corbett, D. C. "Immigration and Economic Development," *Canadian Journal of Economics and Political Science*, Vol. 17 (August, 1951), pp. 360–68.

Davis, J. Merle (ed.). *Modern Industry and the African*. London: Macmillan Co., 1953.

Davis, Kingsley. "Population and the Further Spread of Industrial Society," *Proceedings of the American Philosophical Society*, Vol. 95 (February, 1951), pp. 8–19.

Hankins, F. H. "Under-developed Areas with Special Reference to Population Problems," *International Social Science Bulletin*, Vol. 2 (Autumn, 1950), pp. 307–16.

Hansen, A. H. "Economic Progress and Declining Population," *American Economic Review*, Vol. 29 (March, 1939), pp. 1–15.

International Labor Organization. Committee of Experts on Indigenous Labor. *Indigenous Workers in Independent Countries*, Geneva, 1950.

———. Committee on Work on Plantations. *Basic Problems of Plantation Labor*, Geneva, 1950.

Isaac, Julius. *Economics of Migration*. London: Kegan Paul, 1947.

Jaffe, A. J. and C. D. Stewart. *Manpower Resources and Utilization*. New York: John Wiley & Sons, 1951.

"Migration and Economic Development," *International Labor Review*, Vol. 62 (August, 1950), pp. 91–115.

Moore, W. E. *Industrialization and Labor*. Ithaca, N. Y.: Cornell University Press, 1951 (includes a bibliography).

————. "Primitives and Peasants in Industry," *Social Research*, Vol. 15 (March, 1948), pp. 44–81.

————. "Theoretical Aspects of Industrialization," *ibid.* (September, 1948), pp. 277–303.

Natal University. Department of Economics. *The African Factory Worker*. New York: Oxford University Press, 1950.

Orchard, John E. "Contrasts in the Progress of Industrialization in China and Japan," *Political Science Quarterly*, Vol. 52 (March, 1937), pp. 18–50.

————. "Social Background of Oriental Industrialization," in *Explorations in Economics: Notes and Essays Contributed in Honor of F. W. Taussig*. New York: McGraw-Hill Book Co., 1936.

Penrose, E. F. *Population Theories and Their Application*. Stanford, Calif.: Stanford University Food Research Institute, 1934.

Rottenberg, S. "Income and Leisure in an Underdeveloped Economy," *Journal of Political Economy*, Vol. 60 (April, 1952), pp. 95–101.

Spengler, J. J. "Economic Factors in the Development of Densely Settled Areas," *Proceedings of the American Philosophical Society*, Vol. 95 (February, 1951), pp. 20–53.

————. "Some Economic Aspects of the Subsidization by the State of the Formation of 'Human Capital'," *Kyklos*, Vol. IV (1950), pp. 316–43.

Thomas, B. "Migration and the Rhythm of Economic Growth, 1830–1913," *Manchester School*, Vol. 19 (September, 1951), pp. 215–71.

United Nations. Economic and Social Council. *Findings of Studies on the Relationship between Population Trends and Economic and Social Factors*, New York, 1950–51.

INVESTMENT, CONSUMPTION, AND TECHNOLOGY

Brozen, Yale. *Social Implications of Technological Change* (mimeographed). New York: Social Science Research Council, 1950.

————. "Technological Change in Underdeveloped Areas," *Explorations in Entrepreneurial History*, Vol. 3 (February, 1951), pp. 142–160.

Chenery, H. B. "The Application of Investment Criteria," *Quarterly Journal of Economics*, Vol. 67 (February, 1953), pp. 76–96.

Condliffe, J. B. *Technological Progress of Economic Development*. New Delhi: New Delhi School of Economics, 1951.

Fellner, W. "The Capital Output Ratio in Dynamic Economics," in

Money, Trade and Economic Growth. New York: Macmillan Co., 1951.

Gourvitch, Alexander. *Survey of Economic Theory on Technological Change and Employment.* Philadelphia: Works Progress Administration (National Research Project), 1940.

Heller, W. W., et al. *Savings in the Modern Economy.* Minneapolis: University of Minnesota Press, 1953 (see Part III).

Hoyt, E. E. "Want Development in Underdeveloped Areas," *Journal of Political Economy,* Vol. 59 (June, 1951), pp. 194–202.

Kahn, A. E. "Investment Criteria in Development Programs," *Quarterly Journal of Economics,* Vol. 65 (February, 1951), pp. 38–61.

Maclaurin, W. R. "The Sequence from Invention to Innovation and Its Relation to Economic Growth," *Quarterly Journal of Economics,* Vol. 67 (February, 1953), pp. 97–111.

Nurske, R. *Problems of Capital Formation in Underdeveloped Countries.* New York: Oxford University Press, 1953.

Ogburn, W. F. "Population, Private Ownership, Technology, and the Standard of Living," *American Journal of Sociology,* Vol. 56 (January, 1951), pp. 314–19.

———— (ed.). *Technology and International Relations.* Chicago: University of Chicago Press, 1949.

Rao, V. K. R. V. "Investment, Income, and the Multiplier in an Underdeveloped Economy," *Indian Economic Review,* February, 1952.

Salin, E. "European Entrepreneurship: Origin of Modern Business Enterprise," *Journal of Economic History,* Vol. 12 (Fall, 1952), pp 366–77.

Sawyer, J. E. "Entrepreneurial Error and Economic Growth," *Explorations in Entrepreneurial History,* Vol. 4 (May, 1952), pp. 199–204.

United Nations. Economic Commission for Asia and the Far East. *Mobilization of Domestic Capital,* Bangkok, 1952.

————. Food and Agricultural Organization. *Technical Assistance for Economic Development* (mimeographed), Washington, D. C., 1949.

————. Secretariat. *The Expanded Program of Technical Assistance for Economic Development of Underdeveloped Countries,* New York, 1951.

United States. Department of Commerce. *Factors Limiting U. S. Investment Abroad,* Part I. Washington, D. C.: Government Printing Office, 1953.

INTERNATIONAL ASPECTS

Brown, A. J. *Industrialization and Trade.* London: Oxford University Press, 1943.

Frankel, S. H. *Some Conceptual Aspects of International Economic Development of Underdeveloped Territories.* Princeton, N. J.: Princeton University International Finance Section, 1952.

Ganguli, B. N. "Principles of Protection in the Context of Underdeveloped Countries," *Indian Economic Review,* February, 1952.

Hunter, J. M. "Long-Term Foreign Investment and Underdeveloped Countries," *Journal of Political Economy,* Vol. 61 (February, 1953), pp. 15–24.

Lakdawala, D. E. *International Aspects of Indian Economic Development.* New York: Oxford University Press, 1952.

League of Nations. Secretariat. *Industrialization and Foreign Trade,* Geneva, 1940.

"Problems of Long Term International Balance" (collected papers), *International Social Science Bulletin,* Vol. 3 (Spring, 1951).

Schlesinger, E. R. *Multiple Exchange Rates and Economic Development.* Princeton, N. J.: Princeton University International Finance Section, 1952.

Singer, H. V. "Distribution of Gains between Investment and Borrowing Countries," Papers and Proceedings, *American Economic Review,* Vol. 40 (May, 1950), pp. 473–85.

United Nations. Department of Economic Affairs. *Instability in Export Markets of Underdeveloped Countries,* New York, 1953.

Viner, Jacob. *International Trade and Economic Development.* Glencoe, Ill.: The Free Press, 1952.

Wallich, H. C. "Underdeveloped Countries and the International Monetary Mechanism," in *Money, Trade, and Economic Growth.* New York: Macmillan Co., 1951.

CULTURAL AND POLITICAL ASPECTS

Baran, P. A. "On the Political Economy of Backwardness," *Manchester School,* Vol. 20 (January, 1952), pp. 66–84.

Barnett, H. G. "Invention and Cultural Change," *American Anthropologist,* Vol. 44 (January-March, 1942), pp. 14–30.

Boulding, K. E. "Religious Foundations of Economic Progress," *Harvard Business Review,* Vol. 30 (May-June, 1952), pp. 33–40.

Heimann, E. "Marxism and Underdeveloped Countries," *Social Research,* Vol. 19 (September, 1952), pp. 322–45.

Helleiner, K. F. "Moral Conditions for Economic Growth," *Journal of Economic History,* Vol. 11 (Spring, 1951), pp. 97–116.

Herskovitz, Melville J. *Acculturation: The Study of Culture Contact.* New York: Augustin, 1938.

———. *Man and His Works.* New York: Knopf, 1949 (Part VI).

Hertzler, J. O. "Culture Contact and Institutional Change," in E. B. Reuter (ed.), *Race and Culture Contacts.* New York: McGraw-Hill Book Co., 1934.

Hoselitz, B. F. "The Role of Cities in the Economic Growth of Underdeveloped Areas," *Journal of Political Economy,* Vol. 61 (June, 1953), pp. 195–208.

Hoover, C. B. "Foreign Economic Aid and Communism," *Journal of Political Economy,* Vol. 49 (February, 1951), pp. 1–13.

Kardiner, A. *Psychological Frontiers of Society.* New York: Columbia University Press, 1945, Chapter XIV.

Kirby, E. S. *Some Political Aspects of Far Eastern Economic Development* (mimeographed). New York: Institute of Pacific Relations, 1949.

Linton, Ralph (ed.). *The Science of Man in the World Crisis.* New York: Columbia University Press, 1945.

————. *Most of the World.* New York: Columbia University Press, 1949.

Malinowski, B. *The Dynamics of Culture Change.* New Haven: Yale University Press, 1945.

"Point Four: A Re-examination of Ends and Means," *Yale Law Journal,* June, 1950.

Salter, Sir Arthur. *Modern Mechanization and Its Effects on the Structure of Society.* London: Oxford University Press, 1953.

"Social Implications of Technical Change" (collected papers), *International Social Science Bulletin,* Vol. 4 (Summer, 1952).

United Nations. Secretariat. *Technical Assistance for Economic Development: A Plan for an Expanded Co-operative Program through the United Nations and the Specialized Agencies,* New York, 1949.

————. ————. *Radio in Fundamental Education in Underdeveloped Areas,* New York, 1950.

DEVELOPMENT IN PARTICULAR AREAS

Adler, J. H., Schlesinger, E. R., and Olson, E. C. *Public Finance and Economic Development in Guatemala.* Stanford, Calif.: Stanford University Press, 1952.

Allbaugh, L. G. *Crete, A Case Study of an Underdeveloped Area.* Princeton, N. J.: Princeton University Press, 1953.

"Area Studies" (collected papers), *International Social Science Bulletin,* Vol. 4 (Winter, 1952).

Bergson, A. (ed.). *Soviet Economic Growth.* Evanston, Ill.: Row, Patterson, 1953.

Bonne, Alfred. *The Economic Development of the Middle East.* New York: Oxford University Press, 1945.

———. "Economic Progress in Underdeveloped Countries, with Particular Reference to the Middle East," *Journal of the Middle East Society*, Autumn, 1947.

———. *State and Economics in the Middle East: A Society in Transition.* London: Kegan Paul, 1948.

Britnell, G. E. "Some Problems of Economic and Social Change in Guatemala," *Canadian Journal of Economics and Political Science*, Vol. 17 (November, 1951), pp. 468–81.

Buchanan, D. H. *The Development of Capitalist Enterprise in India.* New York: Macmillan Co., 1934.

The Colombo Plan for Co-operative Economic Development in South and South-East Asia. London: Commonwealth Consultative Committee, 1950.

Cooke, H. V. *Challenge and Response in the Middle East—the Quest for Prosperity.* New York: Harper & Brothers, 1952.

Costa Rica: A Study in Economic Development. New York: Twentieth Century Fund, 1952.

Cressey, G. B. *Asia's Lands and Peoples.* (2d. ed.) New York: McGraw-Hill Book Co., 1951.

Dobby, E. H. G. *Southeast Asia.* London: University of London Press, 1950.

Economic Development of Puerto Rico. San Juan: Puerto Rico Planning Board, 1951.

Fitzgerald, Walter. *Africa: A Social, Economic, and Political Geography of Its Major Regions.* (7th ed.) New York: E. P. Dutton, 1950.

Frankel, Herbert. *Capital Investment in Africa: Its Course and Effects.* New York: Oxford University Press, 1938.

Furnivall, J. S. *Educational Progress in Southeast Asia.* New York: Institute of Pacific Relations, 1943.

Gouru, Pierre, et al. *Development of Upland Areas in the Far East* (mimeographed; 2 vols.). New York: Institute of Pacific Relations, 1951.

Hughlett, L. J. (ed.). *Industrialization of Latin America.* New York: McGraw-Hill Book Co., 1946.

Hulse, F. S. "Technological Development and Personal Incentive in Japan," *Southwestern Journal of Anthropology*, Vol. 3 (Summer, 1947), pp. 124–29.

India Quarterly, published by the Indian Council of World Affairs, New Delhi, regularly contains articles on the development of various areas as well as other articles of interest.

Johnston, B. F. "Agricultural Productivity and Economic Development in Japan," *Journal of Political Economy*, Vol. 59 (December, 1951), pp. 498–513.

Jennings, Sir. I. *The Economy of Ceylon.* New York: Oxford University Press, 1952.

Kion, B. A. *Agricultural Development of the Middle East.* London: Her Majesty's Stationery Office, 1946.

Levy, M. J. *Some Problems of Modernization in China.* New York: Institute of Pacific Relations, 1949.

Lokshin, E. "The Soviet Method of Industrialization," *Planovoye Khozyaistvo,* July-August, 1946.

The Middle East: A Political and Economic Survey. London: Royal Institute of International Affairs, 1950.

Mitchell, Kate (ed.). *Industrialization of the Western Pacific.* New York: Institute of Pacific Relations, 1949.

Nicholls, W. H. "Domestic Trade in an Underdeveloped Country—Turkey," *Journal of Political Economy,* Vol. 59 (December, 1951), pp. 463–80.

Organization for European Economic Cooperation. *Investments in Overseas Territories, in Africa, South of the Sahara,* Paris, 1951.

Peruvian Economy. Washington, D. C.: Pan American Union, 1950.

"Puerto Rico," *The Annals* (collected papers), Vol. 285, January, 1953.

Rosen, George. *Patterns of Far Eastern Industrial Development* (mimeographed). New York. Institute of Pacific Relations, 1950.

Rosenstein-Rodan, P. N. "Problems of Industrialization of Eastern and South-Eastern Europe," *Economic Journal,* Vol. 53 (June-September, 1943), pp. 202–11.

Royal Institute of International Affairs has published studies on countries in Latin America and the Middle East.

Spiegel, H. W. *The Brazilian Economy.* Philadelphia: Blakiston, 1949.

Stamp, L. D. *Africa: A Study in Tropical Development.* New York: John Wiley & Sons, 1953.

Talbot, Phillips (ed.). *South Asia in the World Today.* Chicago: University of Chicago Press, 1950 (Part IV).

Taylor, J. *Economic Development of Poland, 1919–1950.* Ithaca, N. Y.: Cornell University Press, 1952.

United Nations. Economic and Social Council. *Economic Development of Latin America and Its Principal Problems,* New York, 1950.

———. ———. *Economic and Legal Status of Foreign Investments in Selected Countries of Latin America,* New York, 1951.

———. Economic Survey Mission for the Middle East. *Final Report: An Approach to Economic Development in the Middle East.* (2 parts), New York, 1949.

———. ———. *India* (Public Finance Survey), New York, 1952.

———. International Bank for Reconstruction and Development. A series of studies of the development of various countries has been issued under the auspices of the Bank in the past few years. These include: Ceylon, Colombia, Cuba, Guatemala, Iraq, Jamaica, Mexico, Nicaragua, Surinam, and Turkey.

————. Secretariat. *Economic Development in Selected Countries.* (2 parts) New York: 1947, 1950.

————. ————. *Special Study on Economic Conditions and Development in Non-Self Governing Territories,* New York, 1952.

United States. Department of State. *Economic Studies of Underdeveloped Countries: Latin America and Caribbean Area,* Washington, D. C.: Government Printing Office, 1950.

————. ————. *Point Four, Far East: A Selected Bibliography of Studies on Economically Underdeveloped Countries,* New York, 1951.

Wallich, H. C., and Adler, J. H. *Public Finance in a Developing Country: El Salvador.* Cambridge, Mass.: Harvard University Press, 1951.

Wilhelm, Warren. "Soviet Central Asia: Development of a Backward Area," *Foreign Policy Reports,* Vol. 2, No. 18 (February, 1950), pp. 218–29.

Wilson, Godfrey, and Wilson, Monica. *The Analysis of Social Change, Based on Observations in Central Africa.* London: Cambridge University Press, 1945.

Indexes

Indexes

Author Index[*]

* Excluding those listed in Selected Bibliography.

Subject Index